THEATRE
FOR
YOUNG
AUDIENCES
20 Great Plays for Children

THEATRE
FOR
YOUNG
AUDIENCES

20 Great Plays for Children

Edited by

Coleman A. Jennings

Foreword by Maurice Sendak

 St. Martin's Griffin ⋈ New York

Dedicated to the memory of Aurand Harris
1915–1996
playwright, teacher, humanitarian, colleague, and dear friend.

THEATRE FOR YOUNG AUDIENCES: 20 GREAT PLAYS FOR CHILDREN. Copyright © 1998 by Coleman A. Jennings. All rights reserved. Printed in the United States of America. For information, address St. Martin's Press, 175 Fifth Avenue, New York, N.Y. 10010.

www.stmartins.com

Library of Congress Cataloging-in-Publication Data

Theatre for young audiences : 20 great plays for children / edited by Coleman A. Jennings : foreword by Maurice Sendak.
     p. cm.
  Summary: A collection of plays, many of which are based on favorite children's tales, including such titles as: "Charlotte's Web," "Really Rosie," "Wiley and the Hairy Man," "Wise Men of Chelm," and "The Crane Wife."
  ISBN 0-312-18194-9 (hc)
  ISBN 0-312-33714-0 (pbk)
  EAN 978-0312-33714-8
  1. Children's plays, American. [1. Plays—Collections.]
  I. Jennings, Coleman A., 1933–
PS625.5.T44 1998
812.008'09282—dc21

                 97-36542
                 CIP

D 20 19 18 17 16

The Houston Endowment, Inc. for support from the Jesse H. Jones Professorship in Fine Arts, Department of Theatre and Dance, The University of Texas at Austin.

June Moll for editing, proofreading and inspiration.

Lola H. Jennings, my wife.

Contents

Foreword

A Conversation between Maurice Sendak and James Still

For this foreword Maurice Sendak and James Still, who have worked together on the *Little Bear* television series, were asked to have a conversation about children, about the theatre, about being an artist, about whatever they wanted to discuss. In November, 1997, with Sendak in Connecticut and Still in California, they had a one-hour telephone conversation, much of which is reproduced here.

STILL: I'm curious about your first or most vivid experience as a child seeing a live performance.

SENDAK: A live performance? It was an opera that my sister took me to. I was quite young. It was at Lewisohn Stadium—an open arena, in New York. It was very famous for concerts, and my sister took me there to see my first opera and hear a famous singer named Gladys Swarthout sing *Carmen.* I remember it only because it began to rain. Carmen came out in her Spanish dress with a very ordinary umbrella and explained to all of us that we couldn't continue . . . I burst into tears. And my sister shook me for being such a crybaby.

STILL: Was it the idea that an actor who you were enthralled with suddenly came out and talked to you as a real person?

SENDAK: It was a confusion to me, because she was this sexy, Spanish gypsy—and the next minute she was standing here with a grubby umbrella like anybody else.

STILL: The betrayal and thrill of that kind of moment is the kind of experience an artist might track down their whole careers, just trying to capture that mystery—

SENDAK: Maybe in some form or other I have. But this is a complement—there is the hateful collision—of the "fantasticalness" of an opera with lavish sets and artists acting and singing, and the next moment obliterated by nature who is blind to anything and everything and doesn't care. Opera shmopera. Whatever. If it rains, it rains. And then the sudden shift to the mundane, where this woman in the rain, with her wig flattened on her cheeks, explaining pitifully that "I'm sorry folks, I can't continue." And our having to leave, in that grubby way. It was all of those things: fixed reality, the unreality, the indifference of nature, the indifference of my sister to my suffering. All those things.

STILL: How old were you?

SENDAK: Ten years old.

STILL: I was in New York recently for the filming of my movie, *The Velocity of Gary,* when I saw your Wild Things on billboards all over the city [scenes from Sendak's book *Where the Wild Things Are* as part of a Bell Atlantic advertising campaign]. It was exciting to see the Wild Things in a different context, part of the cityscape, part of the architecture of New York. Seeing your creations larger than life with people walking around them, in front of them, reminded me that one of the things I admire about *Wild Things* is that there's both a sense of danger about them and a kind of whimsy at the same time. There's something both comforting and frightening. That dual experience captures the essence of my own childhood which was both of those things. The *Wild Things* seem to convey what it feels like to be a child. Do people tell you that? Do you believe that?

SENDAK: Yes, I believe that because I know it's true; because I was, as a child, and I am, as a grown person, very easily frightened. I mean that I can't see most modern movies. I'm always amazed that children and young adults go and laugh and see "shoot outs" where brains go splattering everywhere. I can't stand that; it frightens me so much. I was very frightened as a child by movies which were not nearly so sophisticated or mindless as contemporary movies. They were faintly silly, but I never knew that they were silly. I was just scared. I have a dread of being frightened, so there is no way in the world that I could or would frighten others—I'm not Quentin Tarantino, I don't know how to do that. I don't like to scare people because I don't like to scare myself. So the Wild Things are, of course, imbued with the qualities of appearing to be frightening, but not being frightening. I think if I had done anything less, they would never have been successful. If Max couldn't subdue the Wild Things with that inane business of staring into all their yellow eyes without blinking once, which I think is so sweetly silly . . . somewhat like Clara [from *The Nutcracker* ballet] throwing her slipper at the seven-headed Mouse King and instantly subduing him. It's something children understand—that a child with a child's puny power can overcome the most frightening thing. So it was essential to me that they're "subdueable." For my own sake, not for anybody else's sake.

STILL: I find this essential in my own work. You seem to be saying there's something different about creating something that is fearful, and creating something that is dark. Do you think that is true?

SENDAK: Yes, although I have an aversion to the word "dark" since it's a word that has now lost its meaning. So when I get a review of *Hansel and Gretel* [a recent Houston Grand Opera production designed by Sendak], and they say "It's a dark version," it irritates me. All I'm trying to do is to be extremely faithful to whatever work I'm doing, and then it is interpreted as dark. There is an element of truth, or truth as I see truth, which is somber perhaps, which maybe has a certain melancholia to it, but which, in fact, is an essence of life, whether you're a child, an adolescent or an adult. That element is reduced to the word "dark," meaning opposite of cheery and good natured, something happy to go home with.

You would never accuse Shakespeare of being dark—even though he hardly ever gives you something happy to go home with. But as John Keats says in a letter after rereading *King Lear*: that he's overwhelmed with joy at being an artist, even though he's just read the most terrible, "tragically," horrifying final scene (Not Keats's words). King Lear has his daughter only for a moment, then she's strangled and he doesn't have her, and he dies. I'm hardly comparing myself to Shakespeare, but this is not a new idea.

STILL: And you think children are obviously capable of that same experience?

SENDAK: Of course, they are because they suffer as we do. They have fun as we do, they're happy as we are, but they have their moments when they're not. Not to acknowledge that simple truth is just mind-boggling to me.

STILL: Did creating *Where the Wild Things Are*—and the body of work that followed—provide you as a person and as an artist with some sort of catharsis?

SENDAK: Of course. But since *Wild Things* ran into so much trouble after its publication . . . without my editor Ursula Nordstrom, without question the most profound influence on my life, the best guide . . . I could not have gone on so bravely as I did. I was just immensely lucky to be in her life and to be important to her. It was a very rocky time for me. I was very ambitious. I was a very normal person in my early thirties—*Wild Things* seemed to just rock the boat so dangerously that I wasn't sure I could go and do the kind of work that she had revealed to me I was capable of doing. I mean that she opened me up—I didn't have the insight or wit to do that—so I could go on to *In The Night Kitchen* and *Outside Over There*. It was certainly *Where the Wild Things Are* that was the key to everything.

STILL: It's interesting what you're saying about Ursula Nordstrom, because a lot of us are in search of mentors. Is that what she was to you, a mentor?

SENDAK: Mentor, mother, best friend.

STILL: When you say you couldn't have done it without her—what does a mentor, a person like Ursula, give an artist?

SENDAK: Total strength and confidence. Ursula very carefully determined what books I was to do, sometimes very much against my will. She insisted that I grow and not stick to any one style. I learned to draw, think and feel in a variety of ways. That's true mentoring.

And at the same time I was being published, I was earning money, and I could move into an apartment. Then, when it came to the hard times, like *Wild Things* and the rest, her strength—when bad reviews came in . . . I couldn't have dealt with it without her strength. I was afraid. I was afraid I'd gone too far out on a limb. I'd been a "good boy" until then. I'd done books that the librarians applauded. I was young and promising, and everybody adored me, it seemed, and everyone saw me as very, very gifted. But I was in line, I was following a progression.

Where the Wild Things Are was way out of line, and the establishment— and I'm speaking generally, many librarians and colleagues applauded my effort but many did not—they felt that they had been betrayed by me; that they'd let me in, to the prizes, to the sanctuaries of the New York Public Library, and I had betrayed them with this ugly book. I needed Ursula to fight with and for me, to stand up for me and be there to comfort me . . . that's what a mentor is.

STILL: And yet, as an experience from the inside, didn't *Wild Things* make total artistic sense to you? Wasn't it connected to everything you'd done before?

SENDAK: Absolutely. You see I was out on a limb to *them*. To me—

STILL: It was your next step.

SENDAK: It was my next step! Following my first book, *Kenny's Window*, which alluded already to "wild things," and my second book *Very Far Away,* both sketchy and not strong enough, but damn good, and those books were praised—more cautiously. I was already showing signs of something else. And then, on to *Rosie (The Sign on Rosie's Door)* which was more kosher, funny, but still vaguely about ordinary children in Brooklyn. Next was the very acceptable *Nutshell Library,* where I seem to have come back, but to me I was just putting one foot in front of the other, growing up like I was supposed to grow and fulfill whatever my gift was. Ursula knew better what my gift was than I did. I would love to have been that kind of mentor for somebody.

STILL: You must know in some way that that's what your books have done.

SENDAK: I hope so. I don't know that for sure. I can only hope.

STILL: Surely people have told you that.

SENDAK: Yes, they have.

STILL: But you don't know, you can't really feel that because you're not there for that experience?

SENDAK: Exactly. I meet these people briefly at an occasion, and they say that and it's very nice, but I haven't had that experience. I was always looking for it, and I'm desperate for it. Even now speaking to you, I'm studying a photograph of Ursula looking very much like Myrna Loy, very beautiful, and she's staring at me. She is still very much in my life. Every step I take is examined. I'm never sure if it's the right or the wrong step, but I always catch her voice in my head, and she says something like "What the hell do you care? If you want to do it, do it. Just do it WELL."

STILL: I want to talk about your collaborations. This conversation is for an anthology of children's plays, and the theatre is so collaborative. I'm thinking about you and Else Minarik [author of children's books] and your collaboration on the *Little Bear* books. One of the things that has continued to inspire me, writing for the television series based on *Little Bear,* are images of the times when we were in New York together. When you and Else were both there, I got to witness what was obviously a really generous collaboration between the two of you.

SENDAK: It was grand.

STILL: The thing I noticed about the two of you was your ability to listen to each other, but also your ability to play with each other.

SENDAK: Well . . . also our love for each other. And don't forget, our *duenna* was Ursula.

STILL: She was the one who arranged for you to work together?

SENDAK: Of course! She knitted us together. Ursula brought Else and me together and taught us both. And yes, what you saw there were the fruits of what happened decades ago which we learned well. We were very good apprentices.

STILL: Those times in your life when you've had other collaborations in the theatre or in opera, or in creating some of your books: is there a common denominator to a successful collaboration for you?

SENDAK: Yes, because they're not always successful. They're not successful when there isn't a genuine, totally open, frank give-and-take. If the evil shadow of ego is raised, then it's done for. And I've worked with writers who came out of left field, entirely, they turned out to be brilliant collaborators, loving people. I have the most remarkable memories of sensational, *complex* relationships with artists, and then I have very dreary and sad ones with people who held me off, or who were jealous, or who didn't acknowledge the collaboration. All those books failed as far as I'm concerned. The very necessary seeds that are transported from one to the other were not there. And it meant a lowering of ego in everyone. To me that's always the test of every collaboration, whether it be an opera production, a theatre production, a book production. Everybody must put their ego outside the door and simply listen and not pretend to have the one and only answer. You must be ready to change your point of view. That sounds obvious and banal, but it's very hard.

I was very sheltered in the publishing business, because Ursula picked people for me. Sometimes she made a mistake. I can remember a few horrible mistakes, but they were minor compared to the successes. I learned how to sniff out people to work with in the theatre, like director Frank Corsaro. We recently worked together on a new *Hansel and Gretel* for the Houston Grand Opera. In every opera I've done with Frank he didn't treat me as though I were just the set designer or the costume designer. I'm his colleague! I mean that dramatic questions are solved *between* us. He asks my advice; I ask his. Then, you make the same connection with the maestro who's conducting.

The maestro is the most important man in the opera. If he isn't on your side, he's conducting one thing and you're *doing* something else. We were fortunate to have a maestro from Germany, Sebastian Lang-Lessing. It was his first trip to America. Although he had done *Hansel and Gretel* in his German way, he became enamored with our view of the opera and changed his performance. What came out of the orchestra pit broke your heart. It was wonderful, wonderful in that he left his ego in Germany.

STILL: You must have been successful in conveying to him what your personal vision was.

SENDAK: Because I liked him, because I admired him. Because I could see immediately the "germ" of someone who was curious, a little anxious. After a couple of dinners and talks, I saw him come under the spell of another kind of *Hansel and Gretel*, and so it became an intense artistic relationship. He's a friend although I may never have the chance to see him again. I miss him. The communication was intense. And when we stood together on stage and got our applause on opening night—the way I clutched his fingers and he clutched mine was so moving to me. It was proof positive that what we had done was the best we could do. It is wonderful when that happens.

STILL: And probably more rare than people think.

SENDAK: Yes, but you have to put a lot of energy into it. It isn't just doing the book together or the play together. It's getting to know the person.

STILL: One of the things we have talked about in the past is our love for the Grimm Fairy Tales. What's the connection, what do they have to say to us today, why are we still interested in them?

SENDAK: I'm not sure I'm smart enough to answer that.

STILL: Well, why are *you* still interested in them?

SENDAK: I always answer that question with the tiny history of how those stories were collected. They were not for children. They were collected during the Napoleonic wars during the beginning of the Industrial Revolution when peasants were leaving farms and moving into the cities. The Grimm Brothers were smart enough or frightened enough to know that a whole culture—oral culture or storytelling—was coming to an end. These two brothers, who are much more famous for creating a dictionary because they were trying to preserve the language, incidentally, saved the stories. It was done simply to preserve what had never been written down, what peasants told their children around a campfire. The tales were French, they were English, they were Scandinavian—with different versions in every country—they were great stories. Although the brothers were German, the stories were never just German.

Previous to Grimm, for the most part, children read nothing but hideous religious tracts and morality tales; how to be good, so that you didn't go to hell; and if you were bad, the kind of intense punishment inflicted upon you. Being pushed into a room where your little dead sister lay showed you that if you played with fire, this was the result. Horrible things that had nothing to do with their own lives. If the stories weren't horrible, they were tedious and banal. Then, came the Grimm stories, and the children loved them. Sex. Murder. Fear. Transformation. I mean, everything that had been kept from them. The brothers were horrified—and that's not an exaggeration—when word came back to them that children were reading their stories.

STILL: That children were drawn to tales that were initially not thought of as appropriate for them by adults is an obvious connection with artists writing for young people today. We're faced with that criticism all the time. Do we—should we—consider our audience while we're creating—do we think about the audience while we're creating? Do you think about your audience in the initial—

SENDAK: I can't. I don't know how.

STILL: I can't either. But I don't think people believe us when we say that.

SENDAK: The simple fact is: I can't think of the audience. I don't know how to do that. My inspiration comes from a purely gut thing that happily bypasses my creaky brain. It is an internal thing which I feel blessed with, but it has nothing to do with a conscious need to address children. It just doesn't. I know it's the most crazy contradiction, but there it is. There is nothing you can do about it.

STILL: What does it contradict?

SENDAK: I haven't been a parent so people ask: "What do you know about children?" "If you don't rear children, how do you KNOW about children?" "Where does this information come from?" "How dare you put yourself up as a person who champions children when you know nothing about them?" Even Beatrix Potter came under that assault, but she was stronger than I was. She was contemptuous of the whole matter.

STILL: Have you ever written something, and after completing it, looked at it and thought, "Huh! Maybe this isn't for children?"

SENDAK: No. I am congenitally doomed to do things that are always for children. And I don't know why. Philip Roth and Norman Mailer and I are roughly the same generation, working at the same time, and yet I could no more write a "regular" story like Philip does, than he could do what I do.

It's just some kind of nervous system connection. I can't explain it. I never could.

STILL: How did your writing for children evolve?

SENDAK: I was writing books for children when I was a child.

STILL: Essentially you were writing something for yourself, right?

SENDAK: Yes, and that's who I am. What that means may be something to be taken care of in a psychiatrist's office.

STILL: Are you saying it's up to other people to determine that? It's not up to the artist?

SENDAK: It isn't! And take it or reject it! It's not my problem. It's what I do. I've designed operas that were absolutely not for children, such as *Love for Three Oranges* by Prokofiev. Happily there's a kind of Edward "Learian" nonsense, a kind of silly, foolish sweetness about it that fell into my lap, and there was enough in it for me. If somebody came to me and said, "We'd love for you to do the sets for *La Traviata*"—and I adore Verdi—I would say no, because I know my limits. There are lots of great stage designers who could create a boudoir in mid-nineteenth century France where a girl coughs up her life. I couldn't do that. There is nothing in it that I could offer. I don't know why I know that, but I do. I know the line in the sand beyond which I cannot go. And I've learned that through experience. Early on, there were certain books I did in my ambition to prove I could push myself. Almost always they failed. That's how I figured out the geography of my talent.

STILL: But what determines failure?

SENDAK: Me. Me. How I feel about the work afterwards. I was passionate about—I still am—three early stories by Tolstoy: *Childhood, Boyhood* and *Youth.* I finally got a publisher who would do *Childhood.* For me to illustrate a Tolstoy was . . . well, you have a good imagination. I don't have to tell you what that must have felt like. And I failed. The drawings are all right. The drawings are nice. It was praised as a book and beautifully published. Yet all I learned from it was, "Does Tolstoy NOT need pictures! Does this man NOT need me!" What I loved about the story was that I wish I'd written it! I only found that out after I had drawn these weak echoes of his imagery. Thirty or more years later, when I finally did *Pierre* by Herman Melville, I did not try to compete with him. I did my own interpretation of the book. No echoes, just me. I learned a hard lesson from *Childhood.* But I learned the right lesson, which is that I fell in love with his story, and I wanted to have written it. The book was a mistake, a waste of my time. Yet it wasn't a waste of my time . . .

STILL: As it turned out . . .

SENDAK: As it turned out, it was a very important little book.

STILL: Do you ever look back over your work and touch the pictures and writing and think, "I'm proud I did that?"

SENDAK: I must tell you something, which is probably an unsafe admission: I really like the work I've done. What fails *fails:* I have regrets. But in the most general sense I'm very proud of what I've done from the very beginning with those rough, clumsy, klutzy, untrained drawings. Ursula saw through to a little heart beating in them, and she didn't care about their graphic ineptitude. She said that with time, I would draw better. I wasn't born with a gift for drawing. Sometimes when I'm teaching, I meet people who take my breath away! It's got to be in the wiring. They draw miraculously! With me it has always been rough, hard work drawing well, drawing better, drawing better, *drawing better*. And there are still weaknesses in my drawing—that was not my gift. My gift was that I have an intuitive connection to the work. I immediately grasped it and understood it. With time the drawing began to complement the images. If I hadn't had Ursula, who had the instinct to see what my true gift was; if I'd been judged by my graphic prowess; I would have been kicked out! I couldn't draw! It's true. I used to see students who drew beautifully, and they scared me, because they had no intuition.

STILL: That was their gift that they drew beautifully.

SENDAK: It's like a necklace. You have to have every one of the beads to make a necklace. You have to be able to draw well enough, but you must also have the intuition and the sensibility. You have to know where your ambition is, and you have to know where your ego is. You have to know how to devote your life to it. You have to know how to sacrifice. Any number of beads make a necklace. If you're missing one, you'd better know which one it is and work on it. If you're missing two, you're in trouble.

STILL: I'm going to ask you something that's impossible to answer. But I'm going to ask it, because you're a good sport. As we move nearer to the year 2000, what are your impressions of art that's been created over the last century, and what do you think might lie ahead?

SENDAK: You're right, it's a hard question. I'll try to be a good sport, but I'm only one person with my own prejudices and my own narrowness. I'm disappointed. We had such a wonderful breakthrough in the 1950s and '60s, you know, the great blooming after World War II. I came on the scene in 1950. There was this glorious free play which I think has become numb and institutionalized and is no longer of any interest to me. I know people will say, "Oh, like all older people he's looking back at an earlier time," but I'm not prejudiced in that way. Today, I do see a kind of numbing. Frankly, I see it in all the art forms. The pendulum will swing back. I think it's already beginning: the big conglomerate publishing houses are toppling like Babel, and little ones are sprouting up again. Young people are dissatisfied. I would say that within ten years, I hope while I'm still living, there will be a renaissance, a kind of breaking out of this numbing. Even as we've had this conversation, any number of babies have been born who will turn out to be enormously gifted. They will have to triumph! They'll break through the gate! They will have to exist.

STILL: And create a revolution.

SENDAK: It'll all happen again. It's happened too many times in history. We have to go from high to low, and then, we go back to high again.

STILL: And what are the marks of that high time? For those of us who are trying to live through this time, what do we have to look forward to?

SENDAK: Our own ability to be inspired and punch a hole in the wall of numbness and dumbness. And now is the time to do it. It's going to take a very strong person to punch that hole. But that person or persons will lead the way to the next place. One just sits and waits for the rumpus to begin.

Acting Edition Scripts and Royalty Fees

Any group that produces a play for an audience, whether for paid admission or not, is required by copyright law to purchase from the publisher enough copies of the script for the entire production company and to pay a prescribed royalty fee for each performance in advance. Information for purchasing scripts and for paying the royalty fee precedes each play in the anthology.

Introduction

To write successful plays for children's theatre, an author must appreciate and understand the youthful audience with the same depth and thoroughness that he or she knows the technique of playwriting. An audience comprised of children of various ages, representing many stages of maturity with widely differing interests, backgrounds, life experiences, and abilities to concentrate, presents an extra dimension of challenge to the playwright. Children are sensitive and quick to react overtly and honestly to whatever they see and hear on stage. The authors represented in this collection clearly demonstrate their sensitivity to the child audiences, their practical knowledge of theatre, and their desire to create plays of high quality that adults perform for young people.

Much of the existing children's dramatic literature, including the works in this anthology, has been created for students in the late elementary grades, ages ten and eleven, with the assumption that many younger and older students would also be interested in the material. Obviously, some plays are more appropriate for younger children and others best suited for the older students. A good play imaginatively staged, however, will interest a wide age range of both children and adults.

Thirty years ago, selecting twenty great plays for children would have been impossible because so few scripts of high quality had been written for the child audience. Today when one looks at the body of work of children's dramatic literature from the 1930s through the 1990s, there are many more excellent plays written by especially perceptive and talented playwrights from which to choose. It is from this group of plays that this anthology was created, with examples that represent twenty very different playwrights.

The purpose of this collection is to demonstrate the increasing diversity in dramatic literature for children from American playwrights. The choices that comprise this anthology were dictated by subject matter, treatment, style, and language. Each playwright is represented by only one script although many have written numerable, exemplary ones. The choice of which play to use from a playwright was determined in part by the content of the whole collection. More recent plays and those never before anthologized were given preference.

Hundreds of plays were read and considered in an effort to achieve a balance among the types of plays now available for young audiences. The original plan was to include twenty-five plays, but due to the constraints of book length and costs, the collection was eventually limited to twenty.

Many plays for children are adaptations of well-known story books, hence there are often several plays based on the same classic. If that story was to be included, it was then necessary to select the one that had been most effectively transformed into a dramatic work and simultaneously retained the sense and purpose of the original book.

Another issue that influenced the final choice was the desire to have plays that reflect a variety of ethnic groups and cultures. Some of the plays from specific cultures are written by playwrights of that culture; others are created by writers who have researched and studied the culture.

The plays herein are testimony to the wide variety of scripts that now exist for young audiences. Some are historical; some current; some are set in an imaginary time and place. Some have people as characters, and some have animals or mythical beings; some have both. Some have large casts, one is a solo performance. Some experiment with language in verse, rhyme, or dialect; others are created with realistic dialogue; still others combine conversational speech with very theatrical and repetitive lines. Each has messages for the children, themes relevant to contemporary life.

Most of the works are serious, but many use humor to leaven the heaviness. One is a farce. A few include situations and words that only recently have been considered acceptable as children's theatre fare. For some these still remain unacceptable.

The plays are arranged not chronologically or alphabetically but in an order that presents a counterpoise of subject matter, style, and ideas. Each brought to life on stage in an imaginative production becomes a world of its own created to appeal to its young audience. Several will challenge even the most experienced producers.

Unlike children's literature, children's *dramatic* literature is for both the reading public and an audience in the theatre. The absolute test of any script for children, however, is to be found in production, on stage before an audience of young people. Children are honest in their evaluations of the theatrical experience. Instinctively, they know what is sincere, what is interesting and challenging, what is worth their attention. In contrast to adult audience members, the children's overt responses often reveal their opinions of the production during the performance. Their verbal and written comments after a production are equally thoughtful.

. . . The part that needs improvement is the way the scorpion dies. Yours truly, Debra K.

. . . Please thank the townfolk even though they did very little. Sincerely, Holly W.

. . . I thought your play was very good and I think it was the best play I have ever seen. "You hear me? ever seen!" Sincerely, Steven.

Obviously, the production and the script are interdependent. It is true that an inferior script can be presented in a successful manner that disguises some of its weaknesses, and a superior script can suffer in a poorly conceived and directed production. Ultimately, however, the greatest success in theatre and the most rewarding experiences for the reader are from plays of real literary merit.

As each reader or director draws his or her own conclusions about the merits of the plays presented in this collection, it is essential to remember that in theatre for young audiences:

- Selecting the best plays for any particular situation is usually one of the most difficult tasks facing directors and producers. Achieving a balance of types and styles of plays, both classic and modern, while also balancing the well-known titles with the lesser-known ones and accommodating the wide age range of the audience members, presents a special challenge in creating a commercially viable season of plays for children's theatre producers.
- There must be a lively and credible development and integration of characters, dialogue, plot, setting, and theme.
- The story should be shown in dramatic action, *not told*. The plot must tell a compelling story with unexpected consequences always impending. The various dramatic questions to be answered must develop naturally and constantly from the characters and their situations. For children the most important part of any play is the story.
- The characters must be believable, be they human beings, animals, inanimate objects, or fantasy characters. They must be consistent, interesting, and involved in the action of the plot rather than simply telling about themselves or their situation. Children want to see them in action.
- The language should stretch imaginations and create a background appropriate for the plot, characters, and theme.
- The underlying message or theme must be an integral part of the character development, not a superimposed "lesson to be learned."
- The children should be challenged to think, encouraged to become emotionally involved, and provided with a worthwhile experience.
- Patronizing, trite, and meaningless scripts have no place in theatre for young people.
- Never underestimate children by simply amusing them. Set out to entertain as well as enlighten them. A script that uses puns, sophisticated jokes, or innuendo to amuse the grown-ups while going over the heads of the main audience is unacceptable in children's theatre.
- The child audience behaves quite differently from an adult audience. As a group, children are uninhibited and will react spontaneously to what is happening on stage. Children will readily join in the action of the play by either impulsively calling out to the characters to give advice and warn them of dangers or by actually moving about or standing up to see better.
- Children see the actors not as performers but as characters in a real situation.
- The spectators' responses vary depending upon the particular mix of children and whether or not the audience is one of all children with a few adults. When the children outnumber the adults, such as during an in-school performance, the children tend to be more overt in their reactions; the more adults present, the more restraint there will be in children's reactions.
- When they are involved in the story, children are an attentive, appreciative audience for whom performing is exceedingly satisfying.
- In most children's theatres, all the characters are portrayed by adult actors or advanced high school students.
- The playing time for the majority of scripts for children is sixty to seventy-five minutes. A number of outstanding plays, however, last longer, some even with a planned intermission. Normally an intermis-

sion is unnecessary and undesirable due to the chaos that can ensue as an audience of four hundred children chooses to go to the restroom. Reestablishing the story line and mood after extended scene shifts or an intermission can be difficult. A well-written and thoughtfully staged script should capture the attention of most of the audience throughout the performance without an intermission.

• A variety of audience-actor relationships, from the traditional proscenium arch auditorium to theatre-in-the-round, can draw the audience into the play. When children are in a small theatre and close to the action, their attention and involvement increase considerably. A larger house will demand an expanded style of production to reach the entire audience With any production in any theatre, however, it is the script and the creative abilities of the director, cast, and production team that determine the success of the production.

• The main goal of any adult theatre company performing for children is to create a superior production—one that is exciting, meaningful, and excellently staged.

• Ideally, children should have the opportunity to see professional productions, whether performed in their schools by visiting troupes or in a traditional theatre where the support of complete scenery, lighting, and sound effects are possible. Although not essential, unusual stage effects can be quite a treat for children, but only if the effects truly enhance the plot and the characters.

• In directing for children, there should be enhancing, *motivated* movement. Stationary characters, seated or otherwise, are uninteresting to children. The physical action must, however, develop from the situation and the characters' behavior. Having characters move about for no reason except for the purpose of adding activity is insulting to the audience.

• In any type of production the actors must portray their characters truthfully and sincerely. Exaggerated, dishonest acting has no place in children's theatre. The actors should not "play at" being the characters, but should become the characters and devote their full creative energies to realizing the dramatic action of the story.

• The directing must dynamically enhance the script. The most effective telling of a story is through a variety of stage compositions. Whenever possible the actors should illustrate the meaning of the scene through their physical arrangement and movement on the stage.

• In order to have interesting variety in the stage compositions and to intensify the meaning of the play, the stage floor may have different levels created by steps, platforms, and ramps.

• Literal presentations of costumes are unnecessary. Children willingly accept a costume suggested by designs that convey the essence of the script requirements. Animal characters, for example, can be effectively communicated by using only a few essential elements to suggest the creature: ears and a tail will convey a mouse, and a white scarf around the head, flowing down the back, will establish the character of a skunk. Actors need not be clothed in realistic animal suits to appear "correctly" costumed in the eyes of the audience. Because they are by nature so imaginative, children will see the animal in the characterization that is merely suggested by the actor's movement and sounds, regardless of the costuming.

• In scenic design also, suggestion is preferable. Spectacular and complicated settings, although often effective, are seldom necessary in productions for children. To show each locale in detail will hinder the flow of the play. It is the actors who must establish the setting, through interaction and their own belief that these settings are real places. If the actors believe in what they are doing, so will the children.

From acting to directing to design, all the staging elements in an impressive production together create the playwright's vision on the stage.

Each of the twenty playwrights represented in this collection respects the intelligence, imagination, and judgment of the child audience. This attention to the needs of children by the playwrights is obvious in each of their scripts, in their comments at the end of each biographical sketch, and from the evaluations of such students as Amiel and Rae.

. . . I think the play was the greatest play I have seen in my whole life and I have seen a lot in that time. Your Friend, Amiel W.

[fifth grade, age ten]

. . . And the way twelve people could be so many people and with very few clothes. It was very creative, I mean when I sit for hours I usually fall asleep but I didn't, it was funny, sad and I had millions of feelings during it. Sincerely, Rae L.

[fifth grade, age ten]

CHARLOTTE'S WEB

by
Joseph Robinette

Adapted from the book by E. B. White

JOSEPH ROBINETTE, professor of theatre at Rowan University, Glassboro, New Jersey, has an M.A. and Ph.D. from Southern Illinois University in Carbondale. He is the author or coauthor of thirty-nine published plays and musicals. In 1976, he received the Charlotte B. Chorpenning Playwriting Award given annually by the American Association of Theatre and Education (AATE) to "an outstanding writer of children's plays who has received national recognition."

Robinette collaborated with E. B. White on the authorized stage version of *Charlotte's Web*, and he recently completed the musical version with composer Charles Strouse. He has also dramatized *The Paper Chase, Anne of Green Gables, A Rose for Emily*, and *The Lion, The Witch and the Wardrobe*. His plays have been presented by the Kennedy Center, Washington, D.C.; the Goodman Theatre of Chicago; Stage One of Louisville, Kentucky; the Alliance Theatre of Atlanta, and the Honolulu Theatre for Youth. In 1995, he had works produced in all fifty states and in several foreign countries, including Germany, Australia, and England.

A regular contributor to several children's theatre publications, Robinette has also served as textbook consultant for Harper & Row, and he wrote the introduction to *Fairy Tales for Theatre* by Lev Ustinov, an anthology of plays originally published in the former Soviet Union.

Robinette is a member of the American Society of Composers, Authors and Publishers (ASCAP), the American Alliance for Theatre and Education, and a founding member of the national Opera for Youth organization. He has guest-lectured at several universities including the University of Oregon, University of Maryland, and the University of Tennessee. He has also taught playwriting at the Cape Cod Writers' Conference, the Ohio State Writers' Series, and the Philadelphia Writers' Workshop.

To me the most rewarding aspect of writing plays for children is that it reconnects me with my own childhood, and in so doing, puts me in the middle of that lovely audience I am writing for. I write because I have to, and fortunately for me, most of the time I also want to.

—JOSEPH ROBINETTE

CHARLOTTE'S WEB

A Full-Length Play
for Four to Nine Men, Five to Ten Women,
Flexible Ensemble Group

CHARACTERS

Fern Arable: a young girl
John Arable: her father
Martha Arable: her mother
Avery Arable: her brother
Homer Zuckerman: her uncle
Edith Zuckerman: her aunt
Lurvy: a hired hand
Wilbur: a pig
Templeton: a rat
Charlotte: a spider
Goose, Gander, Sheep, Lamb: farm animals
Chorus
Reporter, Photographer, Spectators, Judges, Fairgoers, Announcer, Uncle
(a pig), Spiders: extras

TIME:

The Present and The Past

SETTING:

The Arables' Farm; the Zuckerman Barn; the County Fair

ACT ONE

SCENE: *An open space in a farmyard.*

AT RISE OF CURTAIN: *In darkness, the sounds of a farm just before daybreak are heard: crickets, hoot-owls, whippoorwills, etc. The sounds may be on tape or produced "live" offstage by the actors. The lights come up faintly as the* CHORUS *enters or is revealed onstage.*

FIRST MEMBER: *(To the audience.)* Shhh! Listen to the sounds of the morning. Very, very early morning. So early, in fact, the sun isn't even up yet.

SECOND MEMBER: Listen to the crickets . . . the hoot-owls . . . a frog down by the pond . . . a dog up at the next farm.

THIRD MEMBER: And today there's another sound. It tells that something exciting happened during the night. Some brand-new pigs were born. *(The squealing of young pigs is heard.)*

FIRST MEMBER: Here's one of them right now—exploring his new home.

(WILBUR, a pig, enters in wide-eyed amazement.)

FIRST MEMBER: His name is—well, actually, he doesn't have a name, yet. For the moment, he's still just a little pig. But as you'll see, he isn't just any ordinary pig.

WILBUR: Who am I? Where am I? I've never been here before. *(A beat.)* I've never been *anywhere* before. Everything seems so strange. But I like it . . . I think.

SECOND MEMBER: The new pig has been born here at the Arables' farm. Before long, you'll meet the Arables. You'll also meet the others—the people *and* the animals—who will play an important part in the little pig's life.

THIRD MEMBER: Now, where should we start? Wait a minute. We've already started. It's early morning. We're at the Arables' farm. Some pigs were born during the night. For now, that's all you need to know. *(The* CHORUS MEMBERS *exit as the lights come up full. A rooster crows. Delighted,* WILBUR *looks off in the direction of the sound. He excitedly explores his new environment until he hears offstage voices.)*

FERN: *(Offstage.)* Where's Papa going with that ax?

MRS. ARABLE: *(Offstage.)* Out to the hoghouse. Some pigs were born last night.

FERN: *(Offstage.)* I don't see why he needs an ax.

MRS. ARABLE: *(Offstage.)* Well, one of the pigs is a runt. It's very small and weak. *(WILBUR looks about in alarm, then points to himself and mouths "me?")* So your father has decided to do away with it. *(WILBUR runs to a downstage corner in fear.)*

FERN: *(Offstage.)* I've got to stop him.

(FERN, a young girl, enters hurriedly.)

FERN: Papa can't kill it just because it's smaller than the others.

(MARTHA ARABLE, Fern's mother, enters.)

MRS. ARABLE: Stop, Fern! Don't yell. Your father is right. The pig would probably die anyway. (FERN *spots* WILBUR. *She looks at him lovingly for a moment, then starts toward him.*)

(JOHN ARABLE, FERN'*s father, enters from another direction, carrying an ax.*)

FERN: (*Shielding* WILBUR *who cringes behind her.*) Papa, please don't kill it. It's unfair. (WILBUR *nods vigorously.*)

ARABLE: Fern, I know more about raising a litter of pigs than you do. A weakling makes trouble. Now run along!

FERN: But it's unfair. The pig couldn't help being born small, could it? (WILBUR *shakes his head.*) This is the most terrible case of injustice I ever heard of. (WILBUR *nods.*)

MRS. ARABLE: Fern! (*Hopelessly, to* ARABLE.) John? (FERN *and* WILBUR *fold their hands pleadingly.*)

ARABLE: (*After a pause.*) Oh . . . all right. I'll let you take care of it for a little while. (WILBUR *collapses in relief.*)

FERN: (*Hugging* ARABLE.) Thank you, Papa. (*She runs to* WILBUR *and pets him.*)

MRS. ARABLE: You can start him on a bottle, like a baby. I'll go look for one. (*She exits.*)

(AVERY, FERN'*s older brother, enters. He carries an air rifle in one hand and a wooden dagger in the other.*)

AVERY: What's going on? What's Fern doing over there?

ARABLE: Your sister has a guest for breakfast, Avery. In fact, for a little while, she's going to be raising that pig.

AVERY: (*Taking a closer look at* WILBUR.) You call that miserable thing a pig? (WILBUR *turns his nose up at the remark.*) He's nothing but a runt. (WILBUR *tries to draw himself up in a "he-man" pose, but is not very successful.* AVERY *laughs.*)

ARABLE: Come in the house and eat your breakfast, Avery. The school bus will be along in half an hour.

FERN: (*Playing with* WILBUR.) I'm going to have such a good time with this little pig.

AVERY: Can I have a pig, too, Pop?

ARABLE: No. I only distribute pigs to early risers who are trying to rid the world of injustice. Let's eat. (*He and* AVERY *exit.*)

(MRS. ARABLE *enters.*)

MRS. ARABLE: Fern, honey, I found a baby's nursing bottle and a rubber nipple. I'll pour some warm milk in it. Bring your pig in, and give him some breakfast. Say, what's his name, anyway?

FERN: Why, I don't know.

MRS. ARABLE: Hurry along now. (*She exits.*)

FERN: My very own pig. (WILBUR *smiles.*) Now, I have to name you. A perfect name for a perfect pig. (*She thinks for a moment.*) Fred. That's a good name . . . but not for you. Clarence . . . no, you don't look like a

Clarence . . . Maximilian. Because you're worth a million to me. *(A pause.* BOTH *laugh and shake their heads.)* Maybe I'm trying too hard. Let's see . . . Barney, Herman, Lawrence, Newton, Morris, Warren, Willie, Wilbur, William . . . (WILBUR *nudges her.)* Wait a minute. Wilbur. (WILBUR *nods.* FERN *tries out the name.)* Willll-bur. (WILBUR *smiles and nods vigorously.)* Wilbur! What a beautiful name!

MRS. ARABLE: *(Offstage.)* Breakfast, Fern!

FERN: I'm coming! I mean *we're* coming. Fern and *Wilbur!* *(She takes* WILBUR's *hand, then they exit.)*

*(*CHORUS MEMBERS *enter from various locales.)*

FIRST MEMBER: Wilbur.

SECOND MEMBER: Wilbur.

THIRD MEMBER: Wilbur.

FIRST MEMBER: Fern loved Wilbur more than anything.

SECOND MEMBER: Every morning, as soon as she got up, she warmed his milk, tied his bib on, and warmed his bottle for him.

*(*WILBUR *enters wearing a bib and sucking a bottle. A moment later,* FERN *enters carrying her school books. She pats* WILBUR *on the head.)*

THIRD MEMBER: After breakfast, Wilbur always walked out to the road with Fern and waited till her bus came. *(*FERN *and* WILBUR *cross to the side of the stage.)*

FERN: Now you be a good boy until I get home. *(A bus horn sounds. This may be done offstage or the sound may be made by a* CHORUS MEMBER.*)* There's the bus. 'Bye, 'bye, Wilbur. I'll see you this afternoon. *(She hugs* WILBUR *as the horn sounds again.)* Coming! *(They wave to each other as she exits.* WILBUR *slowly crosses to C and resumes sucking his bottle.)*

FIRST MEMBER: Every day was a happy day for Wilbur.

SECOND MEMBER: And every night was peaceful.

THIRD MEMBER: He was very contented living with Fern and the Arable family.

WILBUR: I *love* it here.

*(*MRS. ARABLE *enters carrying a bowl.)*

MRS. ARABLE: Wilbur, you're getting big enough to have something besides just milk. Try this bowl of cornmeal mush and honey. *(She hands the bowl to* WILBUR, *who eagerly sips from it.* MRS. ARABLE *removes his bib, takes his bottle, and exits.)*

FIRST MEMBER: No longer was Wilbur a runt. (WILBUR *pulls himself up.)*

SECOND MEMBER: He was growing each day. *(Somewhat cockily,* WILBUR *strikes a pose.)*

THIRD MEMBER: He was becoming quite a specimen of a pig.

WILBUR: *(Flexing a muscle.)* I chalk it up to good, clean living.

ARABLE: *(Offstage.)* Suppertime, Wilbur.

WILBUR: And to good, fattening food.

(ARABLE *enters carrying a bucket.*)

ARABLE: Okay, pig, it's time you graduated to slops. Skim milk, potato skins, leftover sandwiches, and marmalade drippings. (WILBUR *repeats each item after* ARABLE *with growing enthusiasm. He fairly swoons as* ARABLE *hands him the bucket, takes the bowl, and exits.* WILBUR *quickly drinks from the bucket, stopping occasionally to chew.*)

FIRST MEMBER: Before long, Wilbur was five weeks old.

WILBUR: I'd say it's about time for a birthday party.

SECOND MEMBER: He was big.

WILBUR: *Now* let them call me a runt.

THIRD MEMBER: And strong.

WILBUR: Anyone for arm-wrestling?

FIRST MEMBER: And healthy.

WILBUR: Check out the pink in the cheeks.

ENTIRE CHORUS: *And* he was ready to be sold.

WILBUR: For a pretty fair price, I'm willing to . . . (*A beat, then with panic.*) Sold! Oh, no! (*The* CHORUS *exits as* WILBUR *drops his bucket and collapses.*)

FERN: (*Offstage.*) No, Papa, you can't sell him. You just can't.

(ARABLE *enters, followed by* FERN *and* MRS. ARABLE.)

ARABLE: He's eating too much. I can't provide for him any longer. I've already sold Wilbur's ten brothers and sisters. (FERN *runs to the trembling* WILBUR. *She sobs and embraces him.*)

FERN: Oh, Wilbur. Wilbur!

MRS. ARABLE: (*After a beat.*) Listen, everybody. I have a suggestion. Why don't we call the Zuckermans? Your Uncle Homer sometimes raises a pig. And if Wilbur goes there to live, you can walk down the road and visit him anytime you like.

FERN: Oh, yes. *Please*, Papa.

ARABLE: (*After a pause.*) That's not a bad idea, Martha. Come along. We'll call Uncle Homer. (*He picks up the bucket.* FERN *and* WILBUR *embrace in great relief, then shake hands.*)

FERN: Can Wilbur come, too?

ARABLE: Why not? Maybe we'll let him make the call himself. (*He and* MRS. ARABLE *laugh as they start to exit.*)

FERN: It's not funny. He *can* talk, you know.

MRS. ARABLE: Oh, Fern. What an imagination! (ALL *exit.*)

(*The scene shifts to the Zuckerman barn. A moment later* HOMER ZUCKERMAN *enters with his wife,* EDITH, *and* LURVY, *a hired hand.* HOMER *carries a pig trough and* LURVY *holds an armload of straw.*)

EDITH: Homer Zuckerman, I want to know where you plan to keep that pig.

HOMER: (*Setting the trough down.*) Right over here in the barn, Edith. Lurvy, go out there and patch up that piece of fence that's coming down.

LURVY: (*Setting the straw down.*) Sure thing, Mr. Zuckerman. (*He exits.*)

ZUCKERMAN: I'll slide this door back so he can't get in there where the cows are. (*He slides a sizeable door at R across an opening. A large spider web is re-vealed behind the door as it is moved.*)

EDITH: Well, I just hope this pig's not going to be more trouble than it's worth.

HOMER: (*Completing the moving of the door.*) Now, I couldn't turn down Fern, could I? She seemed so desperate. (LURVY *is heard hammering offstage.*) Any-way, she only asked six dollars for it. When the pig gets big enough to slaughter, he'll be worth a lot more than six dollars.

EDITH: (*Cleaning up.*) Ugh. Dirt, spider webs . . .

HOMER: Perfect for a pig.

FERN: (*Offstage.*) Uncle Homer! Aunt Edith!

EDITH: Here they are.

(FERN *enters with* WILBUR.)

FERN: Hi. This is Wilbur.

HOMER: (*Laughing.*) Oh, he has a name, does he?

(LURVY *enters.*)

LURVY: All finished, Mr. Zuckerman. (*He spots* WILBUR.) Well, here's our new boarder.

EDITH: Fern, honey, I just opened a big can of peaches. You come in and have a dish with us.

FERN: Okay, thanks. But let me stay with Wilbur just for a minute . . . till he gets used to his surroundings. (EDITH, HOMER, *and* LURVY *exit. For a moment* FERN *and* WILBUR *look about.*) It's very nice here, Wilbur. (WILBUR *smiles.*) And I can come down and visit you almost every day. (WILBUR *nods.*) Now I'd better go. I'll see you tomorrow. (*They wave to each other as* FERN *exits.*)

WILBUR: (*After a beat, looking about.*) It's a very large barn. And old, I'll bet. I like the smell. Hay and manure. Horses and cows. It has a peaceful smell . . . as though nothing bad could happen ever again in the world. (*A beat.*) Fern was right. It *is* very nice here. (*He yawns, lies down, and closes his eyes.*)

(*A moment later, a* GOOSE *enters, followed by a* GANDER. *They circle* WILBUR, *studying him carefully.*)

GOOSE: Hello, hello, hello.

WILBUR: (*A bit startled.*) Who . . . who are you?

GOOSE: The Goose.

WILBUR: Oh. Hi, Goose.

GOOSE: And this is my friend, the Gander, Gander, Gander.

WILBUR: But I only see one Gander. You introduced me to three.

GOOSE: No, no, no.

GANDER: We tend to repeat, repeat, repeat ourselves.

GOOSE: Do you have a name . . . besides "pig"?

WILBUR: Yes. They call me Wilbur.

TEMPLETON: (*Offstage.*) Wilbur? That's a pretty tacky name, if you ask me.

GOOSE: Well, nobody, nobody, nobody asked you.

WILBUR: Who was that?

GANDER: Templeton, the rat.

(TEMPLETON, *a rat, enters. He carries string, a tin can, and an orange.*)

TEMPLETON: In person. (*He stares at* WILBUR.) Well, I will admit it's nice to have a pig around the place again. I haven't had delicious, leftover slops in an age.

WILBUR: But the slops will be for me.

TEMPLETON: I'm sure you'll find it in your charitable little heart to share your food with dear old Templeton. Especially if I make a nest right here beside your trough. (*He arranges the straw at one side of the trough and buries the string, can, and orange.*)

SHEEP: (*Offstage.*) What's all the commotion in here?

GANDER: It's the old, old Sheep.

GOOSE: And the little, little Lamb.

(*The* SHEEP *and* LAMB *enter.*)

GANDER: We have a new resident.

GOOSE: His name is Wilbur.

LAMB: (*Unenthused.*) Oh, yeah. The pig.

WILBUR: You know about me?

SHEEP: We overheard the Zuckermans discussing you. They plan to keep you nice and comfortable.

LAMB: And fatten you up with delicious slops.

WILBUR: (*Delighted.*) Oh, I *am* going to like it here.

SHEEP: Just the same, we don't envy you. You know why they want to make you fat and tender, don't you?

WILBUR: No, I don't.

GOOSE: Now, now, now, old Sheep. He'll learn soon enough.

WILBUR: Learn what?

SHEEP: (*After a beat.*) Oh, nothing. Nothing at all. Nice to meet you . . . Wilbur. Lamb, mind your manners.

LAMB: (*Not meaning it.*) Nice . . . to . . . meet . . . you . . . Wilbur.

WILBUR: (*A bit concerned.*) My pleasure, I'm sure.

GOOSE: Well, I have eggs to hatch.

TEMPLETON: And I have trash piles to raid.

GANDER: Good, good, good night, Wilbur. Better get some rest after such a long day.

WILBUR: Yes, thank you, I will. (GOOSE, GANDER, SHEEP, LAMB, *and* TEMPLETON *exit.*) The animals seem nice . . . I think. But I'm not sure about Templeton. (*A beat.*) And I'm a trifle concerned about the old Sheep's remark. (*Slightly imitating the Sheep's voice.*) "You know why they want to make you fat and tender, don't you?" . . . Well, I don't know. And old Sheep didn't tell me.

Well, I'm not going to worry about it just now. I'm much too tired. *(He yawns, lies down, and closes his eyes. The lights slowly dim.)*

(CHARLOTTE, a spider, comes out from behind the web. She is attached to it by a long drag line. She carefully creeps over to WILBUR and smiles.)

CHARLOTTE: *(Quietly.)* Go to sleep, Wilbur. Go to sleep, little pig. *(She crosses back upstage and disappears behind the web. WILBUR continues to sleep in the dim light.)*

(The CHORUS enters. There are noises of thunder, lightning, and rain. These may be done offstage or by the CHORUS. The lights come up slowly as WILBUR stirs.)

WILBUR: Oh, no. Morning already. And it's raining. In my dreams, I had made such grand plans for today. Let's see.

FIRST MEMBER: Six-thirty.

WILBUR: Breakfast.

SECOND MEMBER: Seven o'clock.

WILBUR: A nap indoors.

THIRD MEMBER: Eight o'clock.

WILBUR: A nap outdoors. *(He is dejected.)* In the sun.

FIRST MEMBER: Nine o'clock.

WILBUR: Dig a hole.

SECOND MEMBER: Ten o'clock.

WILBUR: Fill up the hole.

THIRD MEMBER: Eleven o'clock.

WILBUR: Just stand still and watch the flies. And the bees and the swallows.

FIRST MEMBER: Twelve noon.

WILBUR: Lunch.

SECOND MEMBER: One o'clock.

WILBUR: Sleep.

THIRD MEMBER: Two o'clock.

WILBUR: Scratch itchy places by rubbing against the fence.

FIRST MEMBER: Three o'clock.

WILBUR: A visit from Fern.

SECOND MEMBER: Four o'clock.

WILBUR: Supper. And four-thirty on . . .

ENTIRE CHORUS: Free time!

WILBUR: *(Moaning.)* Right. I get everything all beautifully planned out, and it has to go and rain. *(There is one final outburst of thunder and lightning, then the CHORUS exits.)* I'm lonesome. And I know Fern won't come in such bad weather. Oh, *honestly.* I'm less than two months old, and already I'm tired of living.

(LURVY, in hat and raincoat, enters with a bucket.)

LURVY: Morning, pig. Breakfast time. Lots of good leftovers today. *(He pours the slops into the trough.)* A meal fit for a pig! *(WILBUR sniffs it, then turns away.)* What's wrong with you? *(A beat.)* We must have a sick pig here. *(He calls offstage.)* Mr. Zuckerman! Come out to the barn. *(He exits.)*

WILBUR: It does look delicious. But I don't want food. I want love. I want a friend. Someone who will play with me.

CHARLOTTE: *(Offstage.)* Do you want a friend, Wilbur? I'll be a friend to you. I watched you all night, and I like you.

WILBUR: Where are you? And *who* are you?

HOMER: *(Offstage.)* I think this will do the trick, Lurvy.

(HOMER, *with a container and spoon, and* LURVY *enter.)*

HOMER: Now, he won't like this medicine, so you hold him and I'll feed it to him. (LURVY *grabs* WILBUR *who protests.)* Come on, boy. This is sulphur and molasses. It'll cure what ails you.

LURVY: Okay, dose him up, Mr. Zuckerman. (HOMER *gives* WILBUR *a spoonful.* WILBUR *gags.)* There, that wasn't so bad, was it? (WILBUR *makes a face and nods vigorously.)*

HOMER: I think I'll give you a second dose, just for good measure. *(He forces another spoonful down* WILBUR *who gags again.)* Good work, Lurvy. That pig will be well in no time. *(He and* LURVY *exit.* WILBUR *catches his breath and clears his throat.)*

WILBUR: Attention, please! Will the party who just spoke to me make himself or herself known? *(A pause.)* Please tell me where you are if you are my friend.

(CHARLOTTE *enters.)*

CHARLOTTE: Salutations.

WILBUR: *(Excitedly.)* Oh, hello. What are salutations?

CHARLOTTE: It's a fancy way of saying "hello."

WILBUR: Oh. And salutations to you, too. Very pleased to meet you. What is your name, please? May I have your name?

CHARLOTTE: My name is Charlotte.

WILBUR: Charlotte what?

CHARLOTTE: Charlotte A. Cavatica. I'm a spider.

WILBUR: I think you're beautiful.

CHARLOTTE: Thank you.

WILBUR: And your web is beautiful, too.

CHARLOTTE: It's my home. I know it looks fragile. But it's really very strong. It protects me. And I trap my food in it.

WILBUR: I'm so happy you'll be my friend. In fact, it restores my appetite. *(He begins to eat.)* Will you join me?

CHARLOTTE: No, thank you. My breakfast is waiting for me on the other side of my web.

WILBUR: Oh. What are you having?

CHARLOTTE: A fly. I caught it this morning.

WILBUR: *(Choking.)* You eat . . . flies?

CHARLOTTE: And bugs. Actually, I drink their blood.

WILBUR: Ugh!

CHARLOTTE: That's the way I'm made. I can't help it. Anyway, if I didn't catch insects and eat them, there would soon be so many they'd destroy the earth, wipe out everything.

WILBUR: Really? I wouldn't want *that* to happen.

CHARLOTTE: Now, if you'll excuse me, I'm going to have my breakfast. *(She exits behind the web.)*

WILBUR: *(With uncertainty.)* Well, I've got a new friend, all right. But Charlotte is . . . brutal, I think. And bloodthirsty. How can I learn to like her, even though she is pretty and very clever, it seems. *(He glances back at the web, then slowly lies down.)*

(The CHORUS *enters.)*

FIRST MEMBER: Wilbur was suffering the doubts and fears that often go with finding a new friend.

SECOND MEMBER: But as the days passed by, he slowly discovered that Charlotte had a kind heart and that she was loyal and true.

THIRD MEMBER: Spring soon became summer.

FIRST MEMBER: The early summer days are a jubilee for birds. From the woods, the white-throated sparrow.

SECOND MEMBER: Oh, peabody, peabody, peabody, peabody, peabody, peabody. *(*WILBUR *listens with delight.)*

FIRST MEMBER: From the apple trees, the phoebe bird.

THIRD MEMBER: Phoebe, phoe-bee; phoebe, phoe-bee; phoebe, phoe-bee.

FIRST MEMBER: The song sparrows in the birches.

SECOND MEMBER: Sweet, sweet, sweet interlude; sweet, sweet, sweet interlude; sweet, sweet, sweet interlude. *(The* SECOND *and* THIRD MEMBERS *softly continue the sounds of the birds.)*

FIRST MEMBER: The early summer days on a farm are the happiest and fairest of the year. Lilacs and apple blossoms bloom. The days grow warm and soft. And now that school was over, Fern could visit the barn almost every day.

*(*FERN *enters as the* ANIMALS, *except the* GOOSE, *enter and greet her with animal sounds which soon give way to clear voices.)*

FERN: Hi, everybody! *(She sits on the stool. The* CHORUS *exits, and the bird sounds fade.)* Wilbur, here's a little piece of pineapple-upside-down cake for you. *(*WILBUR *applauds, takes the cake, and begins to eat.)* May I stay and visit for a little while? *(*WILBUR *nods vigorously, and the other* ANIMALS *agree.)*

CHARLOTTE: *(On a perch near her web, looking offstage.)* Attention, everyone. I have an announcement. After four weeks of unremitting effort on the part of our friend, the Goose, the Goslings have arrived. *(*ALL *act excited as the Goslings chirp offstage.)* And here comes the proud mother right now.

(The GOOSE *flutters in as* ALL *applaud.)*

GOOSE: Thank you, thank you, thank you. *(She bows, then embraces the* GANDER.)

CHARLOTTE: And the father is also to be congratulated. *(There is lighter applause.)*

GANDER: We're pleased as we can be, be, be.

WILBUR: *(Looking offstage.)* How many Goslings are there?

GOOSE: Seven.

TEMPLETON: I thought there were eight eggs. What happened to the other egg?

GOOSE: It didn't hatch. It was a dud, I guess.

TEMPLETON: Can I have it?

GANDER: Certainly, -ertainly, -ertainly. Add it to your nasty collection. *(TEMPLETON exits.)*

WILBUR: Imagine wanting a junky old rotten egg.

CHARLOTTE: *(Laughing lightly.)* A rat is a rat. But, my friends, let's hope that egg never breaks. A rotten egg is a regular stink bomb.

(TEMPLETON enters with the egg.)

TEMPLETON: Don't worry. I won't break it. I handle stuff like this all the time. I'll put it right here under the trough with my other things. *(He oes so.)*

FERN: Oh, Wilbur, I have some good news. Uncle Homer and Aunt Edith seem to be glad that you're putting on weight. *(WILBUR beams.)*

LAMB: Sure they are.

SHEEP: And you know why, don't you?

WILBUR: You asked me that once before, but you didn't tell me why.

GOOSE: Now, now, now, old Sheep.

SHEEP: He has to know sometime.

WILBUR: Know what?

SHEEP: Wilbur, I don't like to spread bad news. But they're fattening you up because they're going to kill you.

WILBUR: *(Dismayed.)* They're going to *what?* *(FERN is rigid on her stool.)*

SHEEP: Kill you. Turn you into smoked bacon and ham. It'll happen when the weather turns cold. It's a regular conspiracy.

WILBUR: Stop! I don't want to die. I want to stay with all my friends. I want to breathe the beautiful air and lie in the beautiful sun.

LAMB: You're certainly making a beautiful noise.

WILBUR: But I don't want to die.

CHARLOTTE: Wilbur, quiet down. *(A beat as WILBUR tries to control himself.)* You shall not die.

WILBUR: What? Who's going to save me?

CHARLOTTE: I am.

WILBUR: How?

CHARLOTTE: I'm afraid that remains to be seen.

AVERY: *(Offstage.)* Fern!

FERN: In here, Avery.

(AVERY *enters.*)

AVERY: Mother sent me to get you. You're going to miss supper.

FERN: Coming. 'Bye, everybody. And thank you, Charlotte, for whatever it is you're going to do to save Wilbur.

AVERY: Who's Charlotte?

FERN: The spider over there.

AVERY: It's tremenjus! (*He picks up a stick.*)

FERN: Leave it alone.

AVERY: That's a fine spider, and I'm going to capture it. (*He advances toward* CHARLOTTE.)

FERN: You stop it, Avery.

AVERY: I want that spider. (FERN *grabs the stick, and they fight over it.*) Let go of my stick, Fern!

FERN: Stop it! Stop it, I say! (WILBUR *waves to* FERN *that he has an idea. He rushes behind* AVERY *and kneels, then makes a "pushing" motion with his hands.* FERN *pushes* AVERY *over* WILBUR. AVERY *falls into the trough. The* ANIMALS *react.*)

AVERY: Help!

FERN: I warned you, Avery.

AVERY: That's not fair. You and Wilbur ganged up on me.

FERN: (*Wrinkling her nose.*) What's that smell?

AVERY: I think we broke a rotten egg. Good night, what a stink! Let's get out of here. (*He and* FERN *exit hurriedly. The* SHEEP, LAMB, GOOSE, *and* GANDER *flee in different directions, protesting violently.*)

TEMPLETON: My beloved egg! (*He gathers up the egg and the rest of his belongings and exits.*)

CHARLOTTE: I'm glad that's over. I'm sure the smell will go away soon. (*A pause.*)

WILBUR: Charlotte?

CHARLOTTE: Yes.

WILBUR: Were you serious when you promised you would keep them from killing me?

CHARLOTTE: I've never been more serious in my life.

WILBUR: How are you going to save me?

CHARLOTTE: Well, I really don't know. But I want you to get plenty of sleep and stop worrying. (WILBUR *stretches out on the straw as the lights begin to dim.*)

WILBUR: Okay. Good night, Charlotte.

CHARLOTTE: Good night, Wilbur. (*A pause.*)

WILBUR: Thank you, Charlotte.

CHARLOTTE: Good night. (*The barn is now in shadows.* WILBUR *falls asleep.*) What to do. What to do. I promised to save his life, and I am determined to keep that promise. But how? (*A pause.*) Wait a minute. The way to save Wilbur is to play a trick on Zuckerman. If I can fool a bug, I can surely fool a man. People are not as smart as bugs. (*A beat.*) Of course. That's it. This will not be easy, but it must be done. *(She turns her back on the audience.)* First, I tear a section out of the web and leave an open space in the middle. Now, I shall weave new threads to take the place of the ones I removed. *(She chants slightly.)* Swing spinnerets. Let out the thread. The longer it gets, the better it's read. *(She begins to "write" with elaborate movements, though her actions are deliberately indistinguishable.)* Atta girl. Attach. Pay out line. Descend. Complete the curve. Easy now. That's it. Back up. Take your time. Now tie it off. Good. *(She chants.)* The message is spun. I've come to the end. The job that I've done is all for my friend. *(She steps aside as a special light reveals the words "Some Pig" written in the web. The center part of the web may be affixed with Velcro to the rest of the web. It can then be pulled off and discreetly discarded by Charlotte. Underneath would be the now-exposed writing which should be similarly velcroed over the next writing and so on. She reads aloud.)* Some pig. *(She smiles.)* Not bad, old girl, for the first time around. But it *was* quite exhausting. I'd better catch a little nap before daybreak. *(She exits behind the web. The lights begin to brighten, and a rooster crows.* WILBUR *stirs. He is having a bad dream.)*

WILBUR: No, no. Please don't. Stop! *(He wakes up.)* Oh, my goodness. That was a terrible dream. There were men with guns and knives coming out here to take me away.

*(*LURVY *enters with a bucket.* WILBUR *retreats slightly.)*

LURVY: Here you go, pig. Breakfast. Leftover pancakes, half a doughnut, stale toast. *(He sets the bucket down.)* Absolutely de . . . de . . . *(He sees the writing in the web.)* What's that? I'm seeing things. *(He calls offstage.)* Mr. Zuckerman! Mr. Zuckerman! I think you'd better come out to the pigpen quick! *(He exits hurriedly.)*

WILBUR: *(Unaware of the writing in the web.)* What did he see? There's nothing here but me. *(He feels himself.)* That's it! He saw me! He saw that I'm big and healthy and . . . and ready to be made into . . . ham. They're coming out here right now with guns and knives. I just know it. What can I do? *(A beat.)* Wait! The fence that Lurvy patched up. Maybe it's loose again. I have to get out. I have no choice. It's either freedom . . . or the frying pan. *(He spots the bucket.)* But, first, a little sustenance. *(He drinks from the bucket.)* Now, I'm ready. I'm breaking out of this prison. They'll never take me alive! *(A beat.)* What am I saying? I've got to get out of here. *(He starts to rush offstage.)* Chaaarrrge! *(He runs off. A crash is heard offstage.)*

*(*CHARLOTTE *enters, yawning.)*

CHARLOTTE: What was that? Wilbur, where are you?

WILBUR: *(From offstage.)* I'm free!

HOMER: *(From offstage.)* Now, Lurvy, what could be so important that you had to drag me out here before I've finished—

LURVY: *(From offstage.)* You'll see, Mr. Zuckerman. You'll see.

*(*HOMER *and* LURVY *enter.)*

HOMER: All I can see is . . . the pig's not here!

LURVY: What?

HOMER: Look out there in the chicken yard. (*He points offstage.*) He's escaped. Edith's out there gathering eggs. Maybe she can head him off. Let's go!

LURVY: But . . . look at the spider web, Mr. Zuckerman.

HOMER: No time right now. Gotta catch that pig. (*He and* LURVY *exit. From offstage.*) Edith! The pig's out! Run him back this way! Pig's out!

CHARLOTTE: Oh, no.

(SHEEP *and* LAMB *enter.*)

SHEEP: What's all the fuss?

LAMB: This racket is killing my ears.

(GOOSE *and* GANDER *enter.*)

GOOSE: There's so much noise, noise, noise.

GANDER: The Goslings can't sleep. (*Offstage noises are heard.*)

(WILBUR *enters, chased by* EDITH, HOMER, *and* LURVY. *The* ANIMALS *cheer* WILBUR.)

ANIMALS: Go, Wilbur, go! Don't let them catch you! Run, run, run! (WILBUR *does a U-turn and exits, eluding the* OTHERS. *They exit behind* WILBUR. *The chase is heard offstage.*)

CHARLOTTE: Now, stop this! Don't encourage him. If Wilbur does escape, he'll never stand a chance in the outside world. So, if he runs through here again, we've got to stop him. (*The chase is heard coming closer.*) Get set! Here he comes.

(WILBUR *runs in.*)

WILBUR: I'll make it this time! I saw an open gate that leads to the woods. Thank you, everybody, for all your—(*The* ANIMALS *tackle him and hold him down.*) What is this? Even my friends have turned against me! (*The* OTHERS *are heard offstage.* WILBUR *squirms as he is held down.*) I'll not go down without a fight! I'll struggle all the way to the butcher block! I won't be bacon for anybody!

(HOMER, LURVY, *and* EDITH *enters breathlessly. The* ANIMALS *quickly let go of* WILBUR *whose bravado disappears quickly as he cowers.*)

HOMER: Well, you certainly gave us a run for our—

LURVY: Mr. Zuckerman. Mrs. Zuckerman. Look! This is what I wanted to show you. (*He points to the web.* ALL *stare at it for a moment.* WILBUR *and the* ANIMALS *look, too.*)

HOMER: (*Amazed.*) A miracle has happened on this farm.

LURVY: A miracle.

EDITH: I don't believe it! "Some Pig." (WILBUR *begins to regain his confidence.*)

HOMER: It is clear we have no ordinary pig.

EDITH: It seems to me we have no ordinary *spider*.

HOMER: Oh, no, it's the pig that's unusual. Edith, call the minister and tell him about the miracle. Then call the Arables. Hurry. (EDITH *exits as* WILBUR *rises and sits happily on a barrel or box near the web.)* You know, Lurvy, I've thought all along that pig of ours was an extra good one.

LURVY: He's quite a pig.

HOMER: I'd say he's . . . *some pig. (He and* LURVY *laugh.)* Well, let's hurry and get the chores done. I'm sure we'll have lots of visitors when word of this leaks out. *(He and* LURVY *exit. The* ANIMALS *cheer, applaud, and congratulate* CHARLOTTE.*)*

WILBUR: *(Himself again.)* Oh, Charlotte. Thank you. Thank you. Thank you.

CHARLOTTE: It seems to have worked. At least for the present. But if we are to save Wilbur's life, I will have to write more words in the web. And I need new ideas. Any suggestions?

LAMB: How about "Pig Supreme?"

CHARLOTTE: No good. It sounds like a rich dessert.

GOOSE: How about "terrific, terrific, terrific?"

CHARLOTTE: Cut that down to one "terrific" and it will do very nicely. I think it might impress Zuckerman. Does anybody here know how to spell "terrific?"

GANDER: I think it's tee, double ee, double rr, double rr, double eye, double ff, double eye, double see, see, see, see, see.

CHARLOTTE: What kind of acrobat do you think I am?

GANDER: Sorry. Sorry. Sorry.

CHARLOTTE: I'll spell the word the best way I can.

SHEEP: *(Glancing offstage R.)* Look, here comes Templeton. Maybe he can help with this project.

*(*TEMPLETON *enters R.)*

TEMPLETON: Templeton only helps himself. What's up?

SHEEP: Did you see the message in the web?

TEMPLETON: It was there when I went out this morning. It's no big deal.

SHEEP: It was a big deal to Zuckerman. And now Charlotte needs new ideas. When you go to the dump, bring back a clipping from a magazine. Charlotte can copy the words. It will help save Wilbur's life.

TEMPLETON: Let him die. I should worry.

SHEEP: You'll worry next winter when Wilbur is dead, and nobody comes down here with a nice pail of slops.

TEMPLETON: *(After a pause.)* I'll bring back a magazine clipping.

CHARLOTTE: Thanks. The meeting is adjourned. *(The* ANIMALS *begin to exit, bidding each other farewell as they go.)* Tonight, I will tear my web apart and write "terrific." Now, go out into the yard and lie in the sun, Wilbur. I need a little rest. I was up all night.

WILBUR: *(As he exits.)* Thank you, Charlotte. You're the best friend a pig ever had. *(He exits.)*

CHARLOTTE: *(Smiling to herself.)* Some pig. *Some pig. (The lights fade.)*

(The CHORUS *enters.)*

FIRST MEMBER: As the day went on, the news about the words in Charlotte's web began to spread throughout the county.

SECOND MEMBER: People came from miles around to see the words on Charlotte's web.

THIRD MEMBER: News of the wonderful pig spread clear up into the hills where the farmers talked about the miraculous animal on Zuckerman's farm.

FIRST MEMBER: Charlotte knew there would be even more visitors the next day.

SECOND MEMBER: So that night, while the other creatures slept, she began to work on her web.

CHARLOTTE: Swing spinnerets. Let out the thread. The longer it gets, the better it's read. (*She begins to "write."*)

THIRD MEMBER: Spinning and weaving, she began to form the new letters.

FIRST MEMBER: Again, she talked to herself as though to cheer herself on.

CHARLOTTE: Descend. Pay out line. Whoa, girl. Steady. Now for the R.

SECOND MEMBER: On through the night the spider worked at her difficult task. It was nearly morning when she finally finished.

CHARLOTTE: The message is spun. I've come to the end. The job that I've done is all for my friend.

THIRD MEMBER: She then ate a small bug she was saving. And, after that . . .

CHORUS: (*Softly.*) She fell asleep. (*They exit. A light comes up on the web to reveal the word "Terrific."*)

(*A moment later,* WILBUR *enters yawning.*)

WILBUR: I can't believe I spent the entire day *and* night outside sleeping. Oh, well. It's very refreshing. Especially in the summer.

(LURVY *enters with a bucket.*)

LURVY: I'm afraid to look. I know it can't happen again. (*He looks over at the web.*) I don't believe my eyes. "Terrific." It did! It did happen again! "Terrific." Another miracle! Mr. Zuckerman! Come quick! It's another miracle! (*He exits.*)

WILBUR: (*Looking at the web.*) It's beautiful.

(FERN *enters.*)

FERN: Good morning, Wilbur. (WILBUR *motions toward the web.*) "Terrific." Hooray for Charlotte! She did it again! (WILBUR *shushes her.*) Oh, she's still sleeping. It must have been a long night for her. (WILBUR *nods.*)

HOMER: (*Offstage.*) Edith, phone the reporter on the *Weekly Chronicle* and tell him what happened!

(HOMER *enters, followed by* LURVY.)

HOMER: He may want to bring a photographer. (*He looks at the web.*) Well, what do you know. There it is as plain as day. "Terrific." What do you know!

(ARABLE, MRS. ARABLE, *and* AVERY *enter.*)

MRS. ARABLE: Did it happen again?

LURVY: (*Pointing to the web.*) Another miracle!

ARABLE: Homer, you're going to have visitors all over the place today.

HOMER: I don't know where we'll put them. Yesterday, the driveway was practically full of cars and trucks.

ARABLE: We can park the vehicles in the open field. Avery and I will direct traffic.

AVERY: Hooray. I'll be the captain of the Zuckerman police force. (ALL *laugh* as ARABLE *and* AVERY *exit.*)

FERN: Does this mean you're not going to kill Wilbur, Uncle Homer?

HOMER: Who said anything about killing him?

FERN: But that's what happens to pigs. In the cold weather. You know . . . the conspiracy.

MRS. ARABLE: Conspiracy? Where did you get a word like that?

FERN: The old sheep . . . I mean, I guess I picked it up somewhere.

HOMER: Wilbur's safe for now, Fern. As long as he's attracting all this attention. Come on Lurvy. Work to do.

LURVY: Terrific pig. (*He and* HOMER *exit.*)

MRS. ARABLE: Fern, your Aunt Edith is doing lots of baking for the visitors today. Let's go help her.

FERN: Can't I stay?

MRS. ARABLE: I think you spend too much time with these animals. You should play with children your own age. Like Tommy Watson.

FERN: Oh, Mother.

MRS. ARABLE: Or Freddy Johnson.

FERN: Yuk.

MRS. ARABLE: Or Henry Fussy.

FERN: Henry Fussy? (*She emits a Bronx cheer.*)

MRS. ARABLE: Let's go.

FERN: Oh, all right. 'Bye, Wilbur. 'Bye, Charlotte. (*She and* MRS. ARABLE *exit.*)

(CHARLOTTE *enters, stretching and yawning.*)

CHARLOTTE: Good morning, Wilbur.

WILBUR: Oh, Charlotte. Everybody's so excited about the new word. And they're expecting more visitors today. (CHARLOTTE *smiles.*)

(*The* GOOSE *and* GANDER *enter.*)

GOOSE and GANDER: Morning, morning, morning.

WILBUR: Did you see Charlotte's new word?

GOOSE: Of course, of course, of course. "Terrific" was my idea. Remember?

(*The* LAMB *enters, followed by the* SHEEP.*)

LAMB: Wilbur, is all this attention going to go to your head and make you stuck up?

WILBUR: Of course not. Fame will never spoil me.

SHEEP: Anyway, he still has to worry about the future. His life is not secure yet.

WILBUR: I know. But I can face anything with friends like you. Friendship is one of the most satisfying things in the world.

(TEMPLETON *enters holding the lid of a soapflakes box.*)

TEMPLETON: You'd better believe it, buster. And you'd better not forget the friendship of old Templeton who just happened to be at the dump all night looking for words to save you. (*He hands the box lid to* CHARLOTTE.) Try this one. It's from an empty package of soapflakes.

CHARLOTTE: (*Reading.*) "With new, radiant action." (*The* OTHERS *repeat the words approvingly.*) Wilbur, run around. I want to see you in action to see if you are radiant. (WILBUR *runs about.*) Now, back again. Faster. (WILBUR *obeys.*) Jump into the air. (WILBUR *jumps as the* OTHERS *applaud and cheer with increasing intensity as he completes each task.*) Do a front flip . . . a back flip . . . and roll over into a split! (*In the split,* WILBUR *smiles and poses.*) It may not be radiant, but it's interesting.

WILBUR: Actually, I feel radiant. I really do.

CHARLOTTE: Then radiant you shall be. (ALL *cheer.* TEMPLETON *looks offstage, quiets them, then hides.*)

(LURVY *enters with the bucket.*)

LURVY: Sorry, pig, but I got so excited, I forgot to leave your slops this morning. (*He pours the food into the trough as* WILBUR *begins to eat.*) Mrs. Zuckerman even threw in a whole fresh piece of apple strudel she's baking for the visitors. That's what you get for being a terrific pig. Oh, yes. And Mr. Zuckerman's even talking about taking you to the County Fair if all this excitement continues. (*He exits.* TEMPLETON *comes out of hiding.*)

WILBUR: Did you hear that, everybody? The County Fair. That means I would get to live for at least another month.

GOOSE: And maybe, maybe, maybe longer.

GANDER: If you win a blue, blue, blue ribbon.

WILBUR: You'll go to the Fair with me, won't you, Charlotte?

CHARLOTTE: I don't know. The Fair comes at a bad time for me. That's when I'll be making my egg sac and filling it with eggs.

WILBUR: You could lay your eggs at the Fair.

LAMB: Nobody's going to the Fair yet. Lurvy said they were just *thinking* about taking you *if* the excitement continues.

CHARLOTTE: Well, that means more new words. So I'd better start another one right away. Now, everybody stand in front of me so the others won't notice that I'm writing if they come back before I finish. (ALL *make a line in front of her, standing on boxes, bales of hay, etc. She is now partially hidden.*) Swing spinnerets. Let out the thread. The longer it gets, the better it's read. (*She begins to write.*)

GOOSE: Templeton would need to go to the Fair, too. Somebody, somebody, somebody has to run errands and do general work.

TEMPLETON: I'm staying right here. I haven't the slightest interest in Fairs.

SHEEP: That's because you've never been to one. A Fair is a rat's paradise. Everybody spills food at a Fair. Popcorn, frozen custard, candy apples.

TEMPLETON: Stop! That's enough! You've twisted my whiskers. I'll go. (ALL *applaud.*)

CHARLOTTE: Attach, ascend, repeat.

GOOSE: (*Glancing behind herself at* CHARLOTTE.) Charlotte's working fast, fast, fast.

CHARLOTTE: I've pretty well got the hang of it now.

LAMB: (*Looking off R.*) Look, here come some visitors.

SHEEP: (*Looking off R.*) It looks like a reporter and a photographer.

GANDER: Hurry, hurry, hurry, Charlotte.

CHARLOTTE: I'm almost finished. Just have to cross the final "T." Over to the right, pay out line, attach.

LAMB: They're almost here. (ALL *are very nervous.*)

CHARLOTTE: Repeat, attach . . . and finished. (ALL *quickly disassemble their "coverage" of* CHARLOTTE *and assume natural positions.* TEMPLETON *partially hides himself. In the web is the word "Radiant.")*

HOMER: (*Offstage.*) Right this way, everybody. Here we are.

(HOMER *enters. He is followed by a* REPORTER, *a* PHOTOGRAPHER, *the* ARABLES, LURVY, FERN, EDITH, *and a* CROWD.)

HOMER: Make room for the photographer and the reporter from the *Weekly Chronicle.*

FERN: May I have my picture taken with Wilbur?

REPORTER: Sure, young lady. (FERN *poses with* WILBUR.)

PHOTOGRAPHER: Say "cheese." (TEMPLETON *emerges from his hiding spot, unseen by the* PEOPLE.)

TEMPLETON: (*Licking his lips.*) Cheese? (*The* LAMB *and* SHEEP *shove him back into hiding.*)

FERN: Cheese. (*The* PHOTOGRAPHER *snaps the picture.*)

REPORTER: Now you, Mr. Zuckerman.

HOMER: Let me get my wife and my hired hand in here, too. Edith . . . Lurvy. (EDITH *and* LURVY *join* HOMER *and* WILBUR. *The* PHOTOGRAPHER *takes their picture.* ALL *applaud.*)

MRS. ARABLE: Look how big Wilbur's gotten.

ARABLE: You'll get some extra good ham and bacon, Homer, when it comes time to kill *that* pig. (WILBUR *sways back and forth, then faints.*)

FERN: Somebody help him!

AVERY: I'll be the pig! Hey, watch me! (*He kneels next to* WILBUR *and tosses straw into the air.*) Oink, oink, oink! (ALL *except* FERN *and* MRS. ARABLE *laugh.*)

FERN: Oh, keep quiet. Keep *qui*-ut!

MRS. ARABLE: Avery, what do you think you are?

AVERY: A pig! I'm a pig! Oink, oink, oink. (MRS. ARABLE *pulls him away from* WILBUR.)

FERN: (*Patting* WILBUR's *cheeks.*) Wake up, Wilbur! Wake up! (WILBUR *comes to and slowly rises as* ALL *cheer.*)

HOMER: Well, that pig *is* terrific, just like it says in the web.

REPORTER: But Mr. Zuckerman, that's not what it says in the web.

HOMER: (*Looking at the web.*) Glory be!

EDITH: We were so busy chattering, we didn't even notice there's yet another word in the web.

FERN: Radiant.

LURVY: Radiant.

EDITH: Radiant.

HOMER: Well, sir. That does it. I have an announcement that you can print in the newspaper. I'm going to enter this pig in the County Fair. (ALL *cheer.*) If he can win a blue ribbon, I guarantee we'll never make bacon and ham out of him. (*More applause.*)

EDITH: Come on, everybody. Let's go to the kitchen and celebrate with some fresh apple strudel and iced tea.

ARABLE: Sounds good, Edith. (*The* PEOPLE *exit. The* ANIMALS *cheer.*)

WILBUR: Charlotte, you did it. Thank you. Thank you.

CHARLOTTE: Well, we got you *to* the Fair. But that's only half the battle.

WILBUR: Will you come with me, Charlotte? *Please.*

CHARLOTTE: I'm not sure. I'm just not sure. (*A beat.*) Now, may I ask everyone to kindly leave? This day has been particularly exhausting, and I must have some rest.

SHEEP: Of course, Charlotte. Come on, Lamb.

TEMPLETON: I'll admit she's earned a little peace and quiet.

GOOSE: Me, me, me, too.

GANDER: Ditto, ditto, ditto.

WILBUR: I'll be out in the sun taking a nap, Charlotte. (ALL, *except* CHARLOTTE, *exit.*)

CHARLOTTE: I'm suddenly very tired. I know I won't be able to help Wilbur much longer. I'll have to lay my eggs soon, and I do want them to hatch right here in the barn where it's warm and safe. (*A beat.*) But I'll take the chance. I *will* go to the Fair with Wilbur. People will be expecting to see a word in the web. It may help him win that blue ribbon, and his whole future—if he's to have a future at all—totally depends on what happens at the Fair. (*She goes behind the web and, for a moment, the stage if empty. An optional intermission may be used at this point.*)

ACT TWO

SCENE: *The stage is empty. After a moment, the* CHORUS *enters. As they speak, they rearrange the "furnishings" from the barn to suggest an area in the livestock locale at the Fair, specifically* WILBUR's *pen and ample passage room around it. The UR web is removed and another hung UL.*

FIRST MEMBER: The days of summer drifted on.

SECOND MEMBER: Before long, summer was almost gone.

THIRD MEMBER: The end of summer brings many things. Late harvesting. Thoughts of school. *And* the County Fair. (*Carnival music is heard.*)

FIRST MEMBER: Step right up, ladies and gentlemen. Ride the giant Ferris wheel. Only ten cents. One thin dime. You can see the whole county from the top of the giant Ferris wheel.

SECOND MEMBER: Right over here, fellows. Win a genuine Navaho blanket. Knock down three cloth cats with three regulation baseballs, and you're a winner every time.

THIRD MEMBER: Come one, come all! Foot-long hot dogs, giant hamburgers, french fried potatoes. It's all here, and more, at the Lion's Club Barbecue Pavillion.

CHORUS: At the Fair. At the Fair. At the Fair. *(They begin to leave.)*

FIRST MEMBER: Harness racing.

SECOND MEMBER: Livestock judging.

THIRD MEMBER: 4-H exhibits.

CHORUS: At the Fair. At the Fair. At the Fair. *(They exit.)*

(HOMER enters. He is followed by WILBUR who is tied to a rope held by FERN.)

HOMER: *(Yelling offstage.)* We're back! *(FERN unties WILBUR, and he rolls in the straw.)*

(LURVY enters with a pitchfork filled with more straw.)

LURVY: They're mighty generous with their straw around here, Mr. Zuckerman. Thought I'd get a little more to make Wilbur comfortable. *(He dumps the straw, then exits.)*

(ARABLE enters with a trough. AVERY follows him with a bucket.)

HOMER: Right over here, John. *(ARABLE sets the trough down. AVERY pours in the slops.)*

AVERY: Pop, can I eat some of Wilbur's slops someday? *(WILBUR eats.)*

ARABLE: In a way, you already do. What he eats is leftovers from what we eat.

AVERY: Yeah, but it looks better in the bucket than it does on the table.

(MRS. ARABLE enters, holding a washcloth.)

MRS. ARABLE: Well, thank you very much. *(She scrubs Avery's face while he squirms.)* Hold still, Avery. There's something behind your ears.

(EDITH enters with a sponge and a large jar of buttermilk.)

VOICE ON LOUDSPEAKER: *(Offstage.)* Attention, please! Will the owner of a Pontiac car, license number H-two, four, three, nine, please move your car away from the fireworks shed!

HOMER: *(To EDITH, who has begun to bathe WILBUR.)* What are you doing, Edith?

EDITH: Giving the pig a buttermilk sponge bath. He worked up a sweat when you and Fern took him for that walk just now.

FERN: Can I have some money?

AVERY: Can I, too?

FERN: I'm going to win a doll.

AVERY: I'm going to crash a jet plane into another one. *(He demonstrates and almost upsets EDITH.)*

MRS. ARABLE: Avery!

AVERY: Sorry, Aunt Edith.

EDITH: It's okay. They're just excited.

FERN: Can I have a balloon?

AVERY: Can I have a cheeseburger?

MRS. ARABLE: You'll have to wait until we can go with you.

MR. ARABLE: Oh, now, Martha. Let's let the children go off by themselves. The Fair only comes once a year. (FERN and AVERY cheer.)

ARABLE: (Giving change to FERN and AVERY.) Now, run along. But, don't be gone long.

FERN: Okay, 'bye. Scrub Wilbur up real good, Aunt Edith. He's got to win that blue ribbon tomorrow.

AVERY: Come on, Fern.

ARABLE: Now hurry back. We'll be leaving in a little while. Tomorrow's the big day.

FERN: Okay, Papa. (FERN and AVERY exit as the OTHERS call after them.)

ARABLE: Don't eat lots of stuff that's going to make you sick to your stomachs.

MRS. ARABLE: And if you go on those swings, you hang on tight. Hear me?

EDITH: And don't get lost!

MRS. ARABLE: Don't get dirty!

HOMER: Don't get overheated!

ARABLE: Watch out for pickpockets!

EDITH: And don't cross the racetrack when the horses are coming! (A beat.)

MRS. ARABLE: Do you think it's all right, John?

ARABLE: Well, they've got to grow up sometime. And a Fair is a good place to start, I guess. (MRS. ARABLE sighs and blows her nose into the washrag.)

(LURVY enters with a wooden sign reading: "Zuckerman's Famous Pig.")

LURVY: Here's the sign from Wilbur's crate, Mr. Zuckerman.

HOMER: Good, Lurvy. We'll set it right here so everybody will know this is the pig they've been hearing about. (He and LURVY prop the sign up next to Wilbur's pen.) "Zuckerman's Famous Pig."

LURVY: If we're finished for the time being, Mr. Zuckerman, I think I'll go down to the midway and meet some of my friends.

HOMER: Sure thing, Lurvy.

LURVY: Maybe I'll even win one of those Navaho blankets I've been hearing about. (He exits.)

HOMER: It's great to be at the Fair, isn't it? I'm nearly as excited as the kids. Let's go look at the new tractors, Edith.

EDITH: (Drying WILBUR, who is asleep, with a towel.) Let me just dry him off. Look, he's asleep.

ARABLE: Martha, let's you and me wander over to the cattlebarn and see the Holsteins and the Guernseys.

MRS. ARABLE: Okay. But let's try to keep an occasional eye out for Fern and Avery.

EDITH: All finished. *(She sets the towel down.)*

HOMER: Let's go then.

ARABLE: We'll meet you back here in a little while. *(The two* COUPLES *exit in opposite directions.)*

*(*TEMPLETON *appears from behind a crate or box.* CHARLOTTE *enters from behind the web.)*

TEMPLETON: I thought they'd never leave. It's easier for a rat to hide in a barn than out in the open like this. Well, I think I'll do a little exploring.

CHARLOTTE: Please bring me back a word, Templeton.

TEMPLETON: I'll do what I can. *(He exits.)*

CHARLOTTE: If I don't write something, I'm sure Wilbur will have a difficult time winning that blue ribbon. *(She looks at the sleeping* WILBUR.*)* He's a cute little pig, and smart. But I'm sure there will be bigger pigs here. And even better-looking ones.

*(*UNCLE, *a large pig, enters sniffing around. A moment later, he sees* CHARLOTTE.*)*

UNCLE: Hi, there.

CHARLOTTE: May I have your name?

UNCLE: No name. Just call me Uncle.

CHARLOTTE: Very well . . . Uncle. You're rather large. Are you a spring pig?

UNCLE: Sure, I'm a spring pig. What did you think I was, a spring chicken? Haw, haw, that was a good one. Eh, sister?

CHARLOTTE: Mildly funny. I've heard funnier ones, though. What are you doing over here?

UNCLE: They're still working on my pen. I just walked away. They'll come after me when they see I'm gone. But I thought I'd wander around and look at the competition. *(He looks down at* WILBUR.*)* Well, no problem here. From what I've seen so far, I've got that blue ribbon all sewed up. But I won't *needle* you about it. Get it? Haw, haw.

VOICE: *(Offstage.)* Uncle! Where are you, Uncle?

UNCLE: Well, better be getting back. I've got to get spiffy for the crowds that will be coming to admire me. So long, sister. *(As he exits,* WILBUR *wakes up.)*

WILBUR: *(Drowsily.)* Oh, hi, Charlotte. Where is everybody?

CHARLOTTE: Off to see the Fair.

WILBUR: Did I hear you talking to someone?

CHARLOTTE: A pig that's staying next door.

WILBUR: Is he better than me? I mean . . . bigger?

CHARLOTTE: I'm afraid he is much bigger.

WILBUR: Oh, no.

CHARLOTTE: But he has a most unattractive personality. Oh, he's going to be a hard pig to beat on account of his size and weight. But with me helping you, it can be done.

WILBUR: When will you be writing the new word?

CHARLOTTE: Later on, if I'm not too tired. Just spinning this new web earlier today took a lot of my strength.

(Two SPECTATORS *enter.* CHARLOTTE *eases into the background.)*

FIRST SPECTATOR: Well, here's a good-looking fellow. *(He reads the sign.)* "Zuckerman's Famous Pig." (WILBUR *smiles.)*

SECOND SPECTATOR: Look at his silky white coat. And his nice, curly tail.

FIRST SPECTATOR: I think he's the finest pig we've seen today.

SECOND SPECTATOR: *(Looking offstage.)* Let's go look at that pig over there. *(He exits.)*

FIRST SPECTATOR: *(To* WILBUR.*)* I think I've heard of you. Aren't you that "radiant" pig who's supposed to be "terrific?" (WILBUR *smiles and nods.)*

SECOND SPECTATOR: *(Offstage.)* Look over here at *this* pig. *(The* FIRST SPECTATOR *exits.)* He's gigantic.

FIRST SPECTATOR: *(Offstage.)* And he seems to be *very* confident.

SECOND SPECTATOR: *(Offstage.)* He may get the blue ribbon after all.

FIRST SPECTATOR: *(Offstage.)* Well, let's go look at the horses and see if we can pick the winner over there.

WILBUR: Oh, dear. Did you hear that, Charlotte?

CHARLOTTE: Chin up, young friend. Those weren't the judges. They were merely the spectators. The judges are the ones who count.

*(*TEMPLETON *enters carrying an article torn from a newspaper.)*

TEMPLETON: *(Handing it to* CHARLOTTE.*)* Well, here's your order.

CHARLOTTE: I hope you brought a good one. It is the last word I shall ever write.

WILBUR: *(Alarmed.)* Charlotte, what do you mean?

CHARLOTTE: *(Studying the article.)* Templeton, my eyes seem to be going. I'm having trouble reading this. What's the word?

TEMPLETON: "Humble." *(He spells it out.)* H-u-m-b-l-e.

CHARLOTTE: Humble has two meanings. It means "not proud," and it means "close to the ground." That's Wilbur all over.

TEMPLETON: Well, I hope you're satisfied. I'm not going to spend all my time delivering papers. I came to this Fair to enjoy myself.

CHARLOTTE: You've been very helpful, Templeton. You may run along now.

TEMPLETON: I'm going to make a night of it. The old sheep was right. This Fair is a rat's paradise. What eating! What drinking! 'Bye, 'bye, my humble Wilbur. Fare thee well, Charlotte, you old schemer! This will be a night to remember in a rat's life. *(He exits.)*

WILBUR: Charlotte, what did you mean when you said this would be your last word?

CHARLOTTE: Shhh!

WILBUR: But, Charlotte . . .

(HOMER *enters with his arm around* LURVY *who holds a blanket.* EDITH *follows them in.*)

HOMER: That's terrific! Good for you, Lurvy.

LURVY: Just lucky, that's all.

(HOMER *motions to* ARABLE, MRS. ARABLE, *and* AVERY, *who is eating a candy apple and has a balloon tied to his ear, as they enter from the other side of the stage.*)

HOMER: Hey, everybody. Look what Lurvy won.

AVERY: What is it, Lurvy?

LURVY: A genuine Navaho blanket.

ARABLE: (*Inspecting the blanket.*) Well, congratulations.

MRS. ARABLE: (*Looking about.*) I do wonder where Fern is.

ARABLE: She'll be along.

HOMER: Well, I suppose we ought to think about getting home.

AVERY: Will the pig be okay?

HOMER: Sure, Avery. They have night watchmen to look after the animals after the people leave.

EDITH: (*Petting* WILBUR.) He'll be fine.

HOMER: Get lots of sleep, Wilbur. The judges come around first thing in the morning.

ARABLE: They may even get here before we do.

(FERN *enters with a doll and carrying Cracker Jacks.*)

FERN: Look at the doll I won, everybody.

AVERY: Well, it's a lucky day today.

HOMER: Let's just hope it's as lucky for Wilbur tomorrow.

MRS. ARABLE: Fern, I've been worried. Where were you?

FERN: I met Henry Fussy, and he invited me to ride with him on the Ferris wheel.

MRS. ARABLE: (*Brightening.*) Henry Fussy?

FERN: He even bought a ticket for me.

MRS. ARABLE: My, my.

HOMER: Let's load up, everybody. (ALL *begin to exit.* FERN *and* MRS. ARABLE *are the last to go.*)

FERN: I hope you weren't *too* worried about me.

MRS. ARABLE: Not really. Now that I know where you were.

FERN: I'll be thinking about you tonight, Wilbur. (*She crosses to* WILBUR.) Good luck, tomorrow. Sleep well. (*She pats* WILBUR. WILBUR *smiles at* FERN *as she and* MRS. ARABLE *start to exit.*) Mother, let me tell you about my Ferris wheel ride with Henry. One time we stopped at the very top, and you really could see the whole county. Or at least I guess it was the whole county. (*They exit. The lights fade slightly as a truck is heard to start up and then drive away.* WILBUR *waves wistfully.*)

WILBUR: It's nice that Fern found a friend here at the Fair.

CHARLOTTE: Well, I'd better be getting to work.

WILBUR: Is this really going to be your last word, Charlotte?

CHARLOTTE: I think so. I don't have much strength left. And tonight I have *another* job to do.

WILBUR: Is it something for me?

CHARLOTTE: No. It's something for *me* for a change.

WILBUR: Please tell me what it is.

CHARLOTTE: *(As the lights fade further.)* I'll show you in the morning. *(Fireworks are heard in the background. Special lighting effects may accompany the sounds.)*

WILBUR: Listen. It's the fireworks.

CHARLOTTE: Fireworks are an important part of the Fair. *(She and WILBUR listen for a moment. The sounds begin to fade. If used, the special lighting effects also fade.)*

WILBUR: This is the first night I've ever spent away from home. *(A pause.)* I'm glad you're with me, Charlotte. I never feel lonely when you're near.

CHARLOTTE: Thank you.

WILBUR: Even if I don't win the blue ribbon . . . and the worst happens . . . I will never forget you.

CHARLOTTE: That's very nice of you to say. Now, go to sleep.

WILBUR: Good night. *(WILBUR stretches out and goes to sleep.)*

(The CHORUS enters.)

FIRST MEMBER: Before long, Wilbur was asleep.

SECOND MEMBER: Charlotte could tell by the sound of his breathing that he was sleeping peacefully in the straw. *(CHARLOTTE goes to her web and, with her back turned, begins to work.)*

THIRD MEMBER: By now, the Fair was quiet, and the people were gone. It was a good time for Charlotte to work.

FIRST MEMBER: Though she was very tired, she worked quickly, for she had yet another job to do.

SECOND MEMBER: Before long, she finished writing in the web.

CHARLOTTE: *(Slowly.)* The message is spun. I've come to the end. *(A beat as she catches her breath.)* The job that I've done is all for my friend.

THIRD MEMBER: After she had written the new word in the web, she moved on to another project. *(CHARLOTTE moves away from the web slightly. Though she is largely obscured by the dim lights, her movements are now very elaborate and mysterious.)*

FIRST MEMBER: It carried her far into the night. *(CHARLOTTE climbs up and sticks an egg sac high up on the wall, then collapses.)*

SECOND MEMBER: When she was finally finished, she was exhausted, and she fell into a deep, deep sleep.

THIRD MEMBER: The first light of the next morning revealed the word in Charlotte's web. *(A light illuminates the word "Humble." The other lights come up slowly.)*

SECOND MEMBER: It was very early when the judges came around to determine the winners of the blue ribbons.

(Three JUDGES *enter silently. They observe the sleeping* WILBUR, *write on a score-sheet, then exit in the direction of Uncle's pen.)*

THIRD MEMBER: The blazing orange sun slowly began to rise on the most important day of Wilbur's life. *(The* CHORUS *exits.* WILBUR *wakes up and sees the web.)*

WILBUR: Oh, look! There's the new word. Charlotte, Charlotte! You've done it again!

CHARLOTTE: *(Waking up.)* "Humble." It fits you perfectly.

WILBUR: *(Looking at the egg sac.)* And what's that object up there? It looks like cotton candy. Did you make it?

CHARLOTTE: I did, indeed. It's my egg sac.

WILBUR: What's inside it? Eggs?

CHARLOTTE: Five hundred and fourteen of them.

WILBUR: You're kidding. Are you really going to have five hundred and fourteen children?

CHARLOTTE: *(With a touch of sadness.)* If nothing happens, yes. Of course, they won't show up till next spring.

WILBUR: You don't seem very happy about this.

CHARLOTTE: I guess I feel sad because . . . I won't ever see my children.

WILBUR: Of *course* you will. We'll *all* see them.

CHARLOTTE: Wilbur, I don't feel good at all. My eggs and I may not make it back to the barn.

WILBUR: Charlotte, don't say that.

CHARLOTTE: Now, stop worrying about me. This is your big day today. I'm sure you'll win.

TEMPLETON: *(Offstage.)* What a night!

*(*TEMPLETON *enters. His stomach is bloated.)*

TEMPLETON: What a night! What feasting and carousing. A real gorge. I must have eaten the remains of thirty lunches. Oh, it was rich, my friends, rich! *(He emits a loud, satisfied sigh.)*

CHARLOTTE: You ought to be ashamed of yourself. You'll probably have an attack of acute indigestion.

TEMPLETON: Don't worry about me. Wilbur's the one you should be worrying about.

CHARLOTTE: What do you mean?

TEMPLETON: I've got some bad news for you. As I came past that pig next door—the one that calls himself Uncle—I noticed a blue ribbon on the front of his pen. That means he won first prize. *(A pause.)*

CHARLOTTE: *(Softly.)* Oh, no. (WILBUR *sits down slowly.* CHARLOTTE *goes to him and puts her arm around him.)*

TEMPLETON: Wait till Zuckerman gets hankering for some fresh pork and smoked ham. He'll take the knife to you, my boy. (WILBUR *stares straight ahead.)*

CHARLOTTE: Be still, Templeton! Don't pay any attention to him, Wilbur.

TEMPLETON: I'll bet he's so scared he's going to faint again.

WILBUR: *(After a beat, still looking ahead.)* No, I'm not. *(Another beat.)* Whatever will happen, will happen. *(He gains courage.)* I may not live as long as I'd like, but I've lived very well. A good life is much more important than just having a *long* life. So starting now, I'm going to stop worrying about myself. There are more important things than just thinking about yourself all the time. Like *you*, Templeton. You didn't even notice that Charlotte has made an egg sac.

TEMPLETON: Egg sac?

WILBUR: *(Pointing to the egg sac.)* Up there. She is going to become a mother. For your information, there are five hundred and fourteen eggs in that peachy little sac.

TEMPLETON: Well, congratulations! This *has* been a night! *(He finds an out-of-the-way spot, covers himself with some straw or an old blanket, and goes to sleep.)*

CHARLOTTE: I'm sorry about the blue ribbon, Wilbur. But, you're being very brave about it.

WILBUR: Bravery is just one of the many things I've learned from you, Charlotte . . . my friend.

FERN: *(Offstage.)* Look! Look, everybody!

(FERN runs in.)

FERN: Look at what it says in Charlotte's web! "Humble."

(EDITH, carrying a jar of buttermilk and a towel, enters. MRS. ARABLE, ARABLE, LURVY, carrying a bucket, and HOMER enter.)

MRS. ARABLE: My goodness! "Humble."

EDITH: *Another* miracle!

HOMER: He's sure to win that blue ribbon now! *(ALL cheer.)*

AVERY: *(Offstage.)* Oh, no! I can't believe it!

ARABLE: What is it, Avery?

(AVERY enters.)

AVERY: That pig over there has already won first prize. *(ALL are in shock.)*

ALL: *(Ad-libbing.)* What? Have the judges been here already? Oh, no. I can't believe Wilbur didn't win. This is terrible. *(EDITH sobs. LURVY blows his nose into a handkerchief.)*

AVERY: It's not fair. He won just because he's fat. I'll bet the judges are fat, too. *(ALL are quiet for a moment. MRS. ARABLE, EDITH, and LURVY blow their noses.)*

HOMER: Hold on, here. What's everybody crying about? Edith, give the pig his buttermilk bath.

EDITH: But . . . he didn't win.

HOMER: People are still going to come by and see him . . . *and* what's written in the web. Now, let's get busy. *(ALL try to be a bit cheerier, though it's difficult.)*

ARABLE: That's the spirit, Homer.

LURVY: I'll give him his breakfast. *(He pours the slops. WILBUR tries to eat.)*

MRS. ARABLE: I'll help with the bath, Edith. *(She does so.)*

ARABLE: Fern, you and Avery tidy up the area. *(FERN and AVERY smooth out straw and generally straighten up.)* Homer, I think our sign needs to be a little more prominent.

AVERY: What's prominent mean?

ARABLE: *(As he and HOMER move the sign.)* It means easy to see. More noticeable.

MRS. ARABLE: You're often very prominent yourself, Avery.

VOICE ON LOUDSPEAKER: *(Offstage.)* Attention, please! Attention, please! We would like to ask as many of you as can to assemble in the livestock area where we are about to present a special award.

EDITH: Special award?

HOMER: It must be for the cows . . . or the horses.

VOICE ON LOUDSPEAKER: *(Offstage.)* When you arrive at the livestock area, please go to the section where the pigs are located.

ARABLE: It sounds like somebody around here's going to get another award.

AVERY: That fat pig over there.

VOICE ON LOUDSPEAKER: *(Offstage.)* We will ask you to report directly to the pig owned by Mr. Homer Zuckerman. *(ALL are dumbfounded.)*

AVERY: *(Slowly comprehending.)* The pig owned by Mr. Homer . . . *(He throws straw into the air.)* Ya-hoo! *(There are cheers, hugs, kisses, and general congratulations. WILBUR is ecstatic. CHARLOTTE, unseen by the OTHERS, inches out and gives WILBUR the okay sign with her fingers.)*

HOMER: We've got no time to lose. Finish bathing him, Edith. *(EDITH and MRS. ARABLE redouble their efforts.)*

LURVY: I'll get a little more straw. *(He exits hurriedly.)*

ARABLE: I'll get rid of the slop bucket. *(He takes it and exits.)*

EDITH: Homer, does my hair look all right?

HOMER: *(Busy, straightening things up.)* Looks fine.

EDITH: You didn't even look at my hair.

MRS. ARABLE: You're all right, Edith. Just keep calm.

(LURVY enters with more straw.)

EDITH: Okay, Wilbur's finished. I'll put these things back in the truck.

(EDITH exits, colliding with ARABLE who enters. BOTH laugh.)

ARABLE: Sorry, Edith.

(Three, or more, FAIRGOERS enter at various points as they gather for the award presentation.)

FIRST FAIRGOER: Good morning.

HOMER: Hello, there.

FIRST FAIRGOER: Is this the Zuckerman pig?

HOMER: Yes, indeed.

SECOND FAIRGOER: There he is. That's the pig we've been hearing about.

MRS. ARABLE: Zuckerman's famous pig. That's him.

SECOND FAIRGOER: He looks like a prize winner to me.

THIRD FAIRGOER: He isn't as big as that pig next door, but he's cleaner. That's what I like.

FIRST FAIRGOER: So do I.

SECOND FAIRGOER: And he's humble, too. Just like it says in the spider web.

THIRD FAIRGOER: Yes, sir. Mighty fine pig you got there, folks.

HOMER: Thank you.

(EDITH *enters, and* HOMER *puts his arm around her. A* REPORTER *and* PHOTOGRAPHER *are among the* CROWD *that enters with* EDITH.)

CROWD: (*Ad-libbing.*) Is this where the ceremony is? I saw that pig last month at the Zuckerman farm. I read about him in the *Weekly Chronicle*. There was a nice picture of him, too.

(*An* ANNOUNCER, *carrying a portable public address system, enters. He elbows his way through the* CROWD.)

ANNOUNCER: Coming through! Coming through! Let's open it up a little, please. Thank you very much. (*He looks at* ARABLE.) Zuckerman?

HOMER: (*Going to the* ANNOUNCER.) Right here.

ANNOUNCER: Pleased to meet you. (*He and* HOMER *shake hands. The* ANNOUNCER *climbs atop a crate or box and yells to the unseen audience in the wings.*) Those of you who can't get in close, don't worry. You'll hear everything you need to hear. (*He tests the public address system again.*) Testing, testing. Can everybody hear me? (*He doesn't wait for an answer.*) Good. (*He clears his throat.*) Ladeez and gentlemen, we now present Mr. Homer L. Zuckerman's distinguished pig. (*Applause.*) Many of you will recall when the writing first appeared mysteriously on the spider's web in Mr. Zuckerman's barn, calling the attention of all to the fact that this was some pig. (ALL *verbally agree.*) Then came the word "terrific." And he *is*. Look at him.

EDITH: (*Aside to* MRS. ARABLE.) It's the buttermilk.

ANNOUNCER: Then came the word "radiant." And finally today, the word "humble." Whence came this mysterious writing? (WILBUR *glances in the general direction of* CHARLOTTE.) This miracle has never been fully explained. We simply know that we are dealing with supernatural forces here, and we should all feel proud and grateful. (ALL *agree.*) Now, ladeez and gentlemen, I must not take anymore of your valuable time. On behalf of the governors of the Fair, I take the honor of awarding a special prize of twenty-five dollars to Mr. Zuckerman. *And* this handsome bronze medal, which far outshines any blue ribbon, to this radiant, this terrific, this humble pig! (*He produces the medal which is attached to a long ribbon.* ALL *cheer and applaud.* WILBUR *starts to bow, then faints.* ALL *gasp.*) What's wrong? What's going on, Zuckerman? What's the trouble with your pig?

HOMER: (*Trying to revive* WILBUR.) He's all right. He gets these spells. He's modest and can't stand praise.

ANNOUNCER: Well, we can't give a prize to a *dead* pig. It's never been done.

HOMER: He isn't dead. He fainted. Run for some water, Lurvy! (LURVY *exits. The* PEOPLE *turn to each other and discuss the incident. While no one is looking at* WILBUR, CHARLOTTE *steps out and looks on with great alarm.* TEMPLETON, *who has been asleep and unseen, awakens. He quickly sizes up the situation, runs to* WILBUR, *and bites his tail.*)

WILBUR: *(Stirring.)* Ouch! *(Before anyone realizes where the sound came from,* TEMPLETON *and* CHARLOTTE *quickly crawl back out of sight. Shaken,* WILBUR *gets up.)*

ALL: *(Ad-libbing.)* Hooray! He's up! The pig's up! Good work, Zuckerman! That's some pig!

ANNOUNCER: And now, ladeez and gentlemen, may I have your attention for the official awarding of the prizes. Here is twenty-five dollars for Mr. Zuckerman . . . *(He hands the money to* HOMER.*)* . . . and the bronze medal—for the star attraction of our County Fair! *(He ties the medal around Wilbur's neck as* ALL *cheer and applaud. The* PHOTOGRAPHER *takes pictures and the* ANNOUNCER *shakes hands with* HOMER. AVERY *begins to shake hands all around.)*

*(*LURVY *enters with a bucket of water. He tosses the water toward* WILBUR, *but it splashes onto* HOMER *and* AVERY. ALL *laugh.)*

HOMER: What ails you, Lurvy? Can't you see the pig is all right?

LURVY: You asked for water.

HOMER: I didn't ask for a shower bath. *(*ALL, *including* HOMER, *laugh.* AVERY *pretends to be taking a shower. He rubs imaginary soap under his armpits and dries with an imaginary towel.)*

MRS. ARABLE: *(As* ALL *continue to laugh.)* Avery, stop it!

FERN: Stop showing off, Avery. *(He continues to clown around until* MRS. ARABLE *leads him away from the center of attention. The laughter subsides.)*

ANNOUNCER: Now, folks, if you'll proceed on to the grandstand, you'll be just in time for the first heat of today's harness races. Thank you one and all for your presence at this historic awards ceremony. *(The* CROWD *cheers and begins to exit.)* Excuse me. Coming through. I've got to go call the first race. *(He exits.)*

FERN: Look at Wilbur and his new medal. *(*WILBUR *beams.)*

HOMER: We're mighty pleased with you, boy. *(He pats* WILBUR.*)* Well, now that the excitement's died down, I guess it's time to be loading up.

ARABLE: Homer, let's all celebrate the occasion by taking one last look around the midway.

HOMER: Sounds good to me.

FERN: Mother, may I have forty cents? It's my turn to take Henry on the Ferris wheel. *(*MRS. ARABLE *gives her the money.)* Thanks. *(She exits.)*

MRS. ARABLE: *(Smiling.)* Henry Fussy. Imagine that.

ARABLE: Well, let's go.

EDITH: We'll be back in a jiffy, Wilbur.

LURVY: Wear that medal with pride, boy! *(*ALL, *except* WILBUR, *exit.)*

(A moment later, FERN *returns.)*

FERN: I'm sorry, Wilbur, I was in such a hurry to meet Henry, I forgot to tell you how proud I am of you. I knew from the very first day that you were some pig. *(After a beat, she hugs* WILBUR, *then looks offstage.)* Henry! Wait for me. Let's go for a ride on the Ferris wheel. *(She exits hurriedly.)*

WILBUR: Charlotte. Charlotte? *(A beat.)* Are you all right?

CHARLOTTE: *(Coming out of hiding.)* Yes. A little tired, perhaps. But I feel peaceful now that I know you will live, Wilbur, secure and safe.

WILBUR: Oh, Charlotte. Why did you do all this for me? I've never done anything for you.

CHARLOTTE: You have been my friend. That in itself is a tremendous thing. After all, what's a life, anyway? We're born, we live a little, we die. By helping you, perhaps I was lifting up my life a trifle. Heaven knows, anyone's life can stand a little of that.

WILBUR: You have saved me, Charlotte, and I would gladly give my life for you . . . I really would.

CHARLOTTE: I'm sure you would.

WILBUR: Charlotte, we're all going home today. Won't it be wonderful to be back in the barn again?

CHARLOTTE: I will not be going back to the barn.

WILBUR: *(Alarmed.)* Not going back? What are you talking about?

CHARLOTTE: I'm done for. In a day or two, I'll be dead.

WILBUR: Charlotte!

CHARLOTTE: I'm so tired, I can't even crawl up to my egg sac.

WILBUR: Charlotte! My true friend.

CHARLOTTE: Come now, Wilbur, let's not make a scene.

WILBUR: I won't leave you alone to die. I shall stay, too.

CHARLOTTE: You can't. They won't let you. Besides, even if you did stay, there would be no one to feed you. The Fair Grounds will soon be empty and deserted. *(WILBUR goes to the side of the pen and looks offstage.)*

WILBUR: I have an idea. *(He rushes to* TEMPLETON *and awakens him.)* Templeton, Templeton! Wake up! Pay attention!

TEMPLETON: Can't a rat catch a wink of sleep?

WILBUR: Listen to me! Charlotte is very ill. She won't be coming home with us. I must take her egg sac with me. I can't reach it, and I can't climb. Please, *please*, Templeton, climb up and get the egg sac.

TEMPLETON: What do you think I am, anyway, a rat-of-all-work?

WILBUR: *(Glancing offstage.)* Hurry! They'll be back soon. Templeton, I will make you a promise. Get Charlotte's egg sac for me, and from now on I will let you eat first when Lurvy slops me. You get first choice of everything in the trough.

TEMPLETON: You mean that?

WILBUR: I promise. I cross my heart.

TEMPLETON: *(After a beat.)* All right, it's a deal. *(He climbs up to get the egg sac.)*

WILBUR: Use extreme care. I don't want a single one of those eggs harmed. *(TEMPLETON brings the egg sac to* WILBUR.*)* Charlotte, I will protect it with all my might. Thank you, Templeton. Now you'd better run to the truck and hide under the straw if you want a ride back home.

TEMPLETON: You bet I'm going back home, now that I get first choice of everything in the trough. (*He exits.*)

HOMER: (*Offstage.*) We'll take care of Wilbur, Edith. You drop the tailgate of the pickup and get his crate ready.

WILBUR: Oh, Charlotte! (*He crosses quickly to* CHARLOTTE *and embraces her.*)

(HOMER *enters, followed by* ARABLE *and* LURVY. CHARLOTTE *hides in the shadows.*)

ARABLE: (*Calling offstage.*) Martha, you and Fern and Avery get in the truck. We'll be there in a minute. (HOMER *ties a rope around* WILBUR.)

LURVY: We'd better straighten things up a little. We don't want those governors of the Fair to think the prize-winning pig left a mess behind. (ALL *laugh and begin to rearrange the setting to resemble Homer's barn.*)

HOMER: Well, sir, it turned out to be a mighty fine Fair.

ARABLE: Mighty fine.

LURVY: Best one I've ever been to. The very best one. (*He and* ARABLE *pick up the sign and any other belongings and exit.*)

HOMER: Let's go, Wilbur. This will be a day you can tell your grandchildren about. (WILBUR *looks back and sees* CHARLOTTE, *who has come out of hiding again.*)

WILBUR: (*Sotto voce.*) Goodbye, Charlotte. Goodbye. (*He waves to* CHARLOTTE, *then he and* HOMER *exit.*)

CHARLOTTE: Goodbye, Wilbur. Thank you for saving my egg sac. (*She speaks faintly.*) Thank you . . . and goodbye . . . my friend. (*The lights fade, leaving a special on* CHARLOTTE, *who slowly waves.*)

(*The* CHORUS *enters.*)

FIRST MEMBER: Charlotte summoned all her strength and waved to Wilbur.

SECOND MEMBER: She went back to her web.

THIRD MEMBER: And never moved again. (*As the* FIRST MEMBER *speaks, the* SECOND *and* THIRD MEMBERS *slowly detach the web and roll* CHARLOTTE *up in it. They carry her offstage and the special fades. If only one or two* MEMBERS *are used, or if the* CHORUS *is on tape,* CHARLOTTE *will detach the web, wrap it around herself, and slowly exit as the final* CHORUS *speech begins.*)

FIRST MEMBER: Next day, as the Ferris wheel was being taken apart and the race horses were being loaded into their vans and the entertainers were packing up their belongings and driving away in their trailers, Charlotte died. (*A pause.*) The Fair Grounds were soon deserted. The sheds and buildings were empty and forlorn. The fields were littered with bottles and trash. Of the hundreds of people that had visited the Fair, nobody knew that a gray spider had played the most important part of all. (*A beat.*) No one was with her when she died. (*A pause.*)

(*The* SECOND MEMBER *enters.*)

SECOND MEMBER: Wilbur returned to his beloved barn. The animals were delighted with his success at the Fair. But everyone missed Charlotte very much.

(The THIRD MEMBER *enters.)*

THIRD MEMBER: For the rest of the fall and all through the winter, Wilbur watched over Charlotte's egg sac as though he were guarding his own children.

FIRST MEMBER: Patiently he awaited the end of winter and the coming of the little spiders. *(The* CHORUS *exits.)*

(A moment later, TEMPLETON *enters and goes to the trough.)*

TEMPLETON: Oh, good. Wilbur hasn't eaten his breakfast yet. *(He begins to eat.)*

(The LAMB *and* SHEEP *enter.)*

LAMB: Wilbur hasn't eaten anything these past few days. He keeps waiting out in the yard for the eggs to hatch.

SHEEP: Templeton, you would live longer if you ate less.

TEMPLETON: Who wants to live forever?

(The GOOSE *and* GANDER *enter.)*

GANDER: You, you, you tell them.

GOOSE: No, no, no. You do the honors.

GANDER: Very, -ery, -ery well. I am pleased to announce that the Goose and I are expecting goslings.

LAMB: Again?

TEMPLETON: It must be spring. Everything's sprouting.

SHEEP: Including your stomach.

*(*WILBUR *enters hurriedly. He carries the open egg sac.)*

WILBUR: They're here! They're here!

LAMB: Who's here?

WILBUR: The spiders. They hatched. All five hundred and fourteen. Look! *(He points upward.)*

GOOSE: They seem to be climbing up, up, up the rafters.

WILBUR: Yes. They're going up to where the breezes are blowing. Oh, look. They're floating away on little clouds of silk. Wait! Don't go! Won't you please stay? *(He is dejected.)* They're all leaving.

SHEEP: Happens every time.

WILBUR: Wait . . . please! *(He waves, sadly.)* Goodbye. *(A beat.)* I'm glad they hatched. But I wish they would stay. Some of them anyway. *(To himself.)* I'm being deserted by Charlotte's children.

GANDER: There, there, there, Wilbur. They have to live their own lives, you know.

WILBUR: Yes, I know. But I was just hoping . . . oh, never mind.

FIRST SPIDER: *(Offstage.)* Salutations!

WILBUR: Salutations? *(He is excited.)* Who said that?

(The FIRST SPIDER *enters.)*

FIRST SPIDER: Me. I'm over here.

(The SECOND SPIDER *enters.)*

SECOND SPIDER: I'm over here.

(The THIRD SPIDER *enters.)*

THIRD SPIDER: And I'm over here. *(If the three* SPIDERS *do not actually appear, their voices should come from different places offstage.* WILBUR *and the* ANIMALS *will look in the direction of each* SPIDER *as she speaks.)*

FIRST SPIDER: Three of us are staying.

SECOND SPIDER: We like this place.

THIRD SPIDER: And we like you.

WILBUR: Oh, my goodness! Well . . . salutations to you, too. *(He is ecstatic.)* This is wonderful! Wonderful! What are your names, please?

FIRST SPIDER: Excuse me. Are you trembling?

WILBUR: Yes. Trembling with joy.

FIRST SPIDER: Then, my name is Joy.

SECOND SPIDER: What was my mother's middle initial?

WILBUR: A.

SECOND SPIDER: Then, my name is Aranea.

THIRD SPIDER: I need a name, too. Pick one out for me. Not too fancy and not too dumb.

WILBUR: How about . . . Nellie?

THIRD SPIDER: Fine. I like that very much.

WILBUR: Joy, Aranea, Nellie. Welcome to your new home.

THREE SPIDERS: Thank you. Thank you very much.

FIRST SPIDER: Where did you get that handsome medal you're wearing?

WILBUR: Well, it's a long story. And I'll tell you all about it. But right now, I'm going to take the medal off. *(He takes it off.)*

SPIDERS and ANIMALS: *(Ad-libbing.)* What? Did you hear that? What does he mean?

WILBUR: To celebrate this very special day, I'm putting the medal where it rightfully belongs. Templeton, please hang it on that nail where Charlotte's web used to be.

TEMPLETON: Another favor?

WILBUR: This is the last one, I promise.

TEMPLETON: *(Taking the medal from* WILBUR.*)* I know—till the next one. *(He climbs up and hangs the medal on the nail.)* Like this?

WILBUR: Perfect. *(*TEMPLETON *climbs down.)* I hereby dedicate my medal to the memory of dear Charlotte whom I will never forget. *(*ALL *nod in agreement.)*

SHEEP: Very thoughtful, Wilbur.

GANDER: *None* of us will ever, ever, ever forget her.

WILBUR: I will love her children and her grandchildren dearly, but none of them will ever take her place in my heart. She was in a class by herself. (*A beat.*) It is not often that someone comes along who is a true friend and a good writer. Charlotte was both. (ALL *turn and look at the medal which is now lit by a special. All of the other lights dim out. After a moment, the medal special dims to a blackout.*)

CURTAIN

THE ARKANSAW BEAR

by
Aurand Harris

AURAND HARRIS, the nation's most-published and for years the most-performed playwright for children, died in New York City, in 1996, at the age of eighty. At that time his publishers estimated that his plays had received more than thirty thousand performances.

Originally from Jamesport, Missouri, Harris received his master's degree from Northwestern University in Evanston, Illinois, working with the children's theatre pioneer Winifred Ward. He was also influenced by Charlotte Chorpenning of the Goodman Children's Theatre of Chicago.

Harris began his teaching career in 1939 in the Gary, Indiana, public schools. Two years later he became the head of the drama program at William Woods College, a junior college for girls in Fulton, Missouri. After three years he moved to New York City to study playwriting. At the same time he accepted a teaching position at Grace Episcopal Church School in Manhattan, where he remained for thirty-three years. After his retirement Harris began his college teaching career in the Department of Theatre & Dance at the University of Texas at Austin. Later he taught at a number of other universities, the last being New York University until the semester before his death.

His various teaching positions afforded Harris the security and freedom to constantly develop his skill as a playwright. Although at the beginning of his career he had written several plays for young people, Harris was originally interested in writing for adult theatre. After a number of theatrical disappointments, however, he vowed to devote his full attention to the child audience, and by 1964, he created *Androcles and the Lion*, which became his most celebrated play.

Androcles and the Lion, translated into ten languages, was for many years the single most-produced play of any American children's playwright. Almost as popular is *The Arkansaw Bear*, an original story that directly confronts the subject of death, which in 1980, was thought by some to be too controversial for young audiences.

Other outstanding titles from his thirty-six plays for children are *The Brave Little Tailor*, *Rags to Riches*, *Steal Away Home*, *A Toby Show*, *The Magician's Nephew*, *Young Black Beauty*, and his last work, *The Orphan Train*, which premiered at Northwestern University in 1996.

In 1976 Aurand Harris became the first playwright for children to receive a Creative Writing Fellowship from the National Endowment for the Arts. In 1988 he directed one of his scripts at the Shanghai Children's Art Theatre, the first production of a western children's play for Chinese children. He was inducted into the College of Fellows of the American Theatre in a ceremony at the Kennedy Center in Washington, D.C., in 1985.

Besides his playwriting Harris edited and coedited several anthologies of plays for young people. *The Theatre of Aurand Harris: His Career, His Theories, His Plays*, edited by Lowell Swortzell and containing fifteen of his plays, was published in 1997. Both the Swortzell anthology and an earlier collection, *Six Plays for Children by Aurand Harris* (1977), edited by Coleman A. Jennings, detail his philosophy and methods of teaching and writing. Also noted in these anthologies are the multitude of awards and honors Harris received over the years as a public-school teacher, university professor, and children's theatre playwright. The honors include such citations as the Charlotte B. Chorpenning Playwriting Award; two American Alliance for Theatre and Education Distinguished Play Award(s); Sara Spencer Artistic Achievement Award from the American Alliance for Theatre and Education; and a Medallion Award of the Children's Theatre Foundation of America.

Teaching has kept my focus on children and has helped me with my writing. I have learned the way a child thinks; how they react to various situations; what their interests are; how long you can hold their attention; what things they think are funny that are not amusing to adults; what behavior-reactions to anticipate in the classroom and auditorium; how to open their imaginations.

Too much philosophizing can lead to static, lifeless plays. I'd rather be doing—writing—than philosophizing . . . I consider children young adults, it is my job as a playwright to lead them into this world of make-believe on a slightly higher level.

Often I'm told, "How wonderful that you don't write down to children." This never occurs to me, as I don't know how to "write down" to a child. I never try to be "childlike." I write to please myself as an adult. . . . I like what children like in the theatre, that is, a good story, interesting characters, excitement, suspense, fantasy, beauty and fun. I am opposed to a patronizing attitude toward children. . . . It is unfortunate that children are often exposed to "cute," "camp," condescending plays. It never occurs to me to be "cute" with children in the classroom or the theatre. I write for children who are at the theatre to be entertained, pleased, excited on an honest, emotionally mature level—yet not so far above them that they cannot comprehend the meaning of the experience.

> The real test of the script naturally comes in performance on stage. The question is not "How well does it read?" but "How well does it play?"

> —AURAND HARRIS

from *Six Plays for Children by Aurand Harris, Biography and Play Analyses* by Coleman A. Jennings, University of Texas Press,1977

THE ARKANSAW BEAR

CHARACTERS

Tish
Star Bright
Mime
World's Greatest Dancing Bear
Great Ringmaster
Little Bear
Voices: Mother
Aunt Ellen
Announcer

SETTING

The present. Somewhere in Arkansas

(As the houselights dim, there is a glow of light on the front curtain. Over a loud speaker a man's whistling of "O Susannah" is heard. The curtains open. TISH walks into a large spot of warm light at L. The whistling dims out. TISH is a little girl and carries some hand-picked flowers. She listens to the voices, heard over a loud speaker, and reacts to them as if MOTHER and AUNT ELLEN were on each side of her, downstage.)

TISH: But Mother—

MOTHER'S VOICE: No, Tish! You can't see Grandpa now.

TISH: I picked him some flowers. These are Grandpa's favorites.

AUNT ELLEN'S VOICE: *(She is TISH's great aunt, elderly, gentle and emotional.)* Quiet, child.

TISH: But Aunt Ellen—

AUNT ELLEN'S VOICE: —The doctor is here.

TISH: The doctor?

MOTHER'S VOICE: Tish, dear.

TISH: Yes, mother?

MOTHER'S VOICE: Grandpa had a turn for the worse. His heart—

AUNT ELLEN'S VOICE: Oh, it's the end. *(Cries quietly.)*

TISH: The end?

AUNT ELLEN'S VOICE: The doctor said . . . no hope.

(TISH reacts.)

MOTHER'S VOICE: Don't cry, Aunt Ellen.

TISH: Is Grandpa going . . . to die?

AUNT ELLEN'S VOICE: Yes.

TISH: No! He can't.

MOTHER'S VOICE: We all have to die, dear.

TISH: I know. But not Grandpa. *(Starts to move.)*

MOTHER'S VOICE: Stop. You can't go in.

TISH: Why can't he live forever!

AUNT ELLEN'S VOICE: You're too young to understand. Too full of life.

TISH: I have to tell him there's a circus coming. I saw a poster with a bear.

MOTHER'S VOICE: It doesn't matter now.

TISH: Yes, it does! Do something!

MOTHER'S VOICE: *(Firmly.)* We've done all we can.

TISH: But not enough! I . . . I didn't do enough!

AUNT ELLEN'S VOICE: Quiet. Quiet.

TISH: *(Softly.)* Yes, if I'd been quiet so he could sleep, and—Oh! Once when I was mad, I said . . . I wish he was dead. Oh, I didn't mean it, Grandpa. I didn't mean it.

MOTHER'S VOICE: Hush, dear. It's not your fault. Grandpa loved you.

TISH: Then why is he . . . leaving me? *(Pulls away as if being held.)* Oh, let me go!

MOTHER'S VOICE: *(Sharply, becoming edgy with emotion.)* Yes. Go put the flowers in some water.

TISH: He liked the pink ones. Now . . . he'll never see them. Oh, why . . . why does Grandpa have to die?

MOTHER'S VOICE: *(Sternly, trying to control and cover her grief.)* Run along, dear. Run along.

AUNT ELLEN'S VOICE: Keep away. Away from his door. Away . . . away.

(The voices of MOTHER *and* AUNT ELLEN *overlap and mix together, as they keep repeating, "Run along," "Run . . . run," "Away . . . away," "Run," "Away," "Run . . . away; run . . . away." They build to a climax in a choral chant, "Run . . . a-way.")*

TISH: I will. I'll run away. Up the hill . . . to my tree . . . my tree.

(She runs, circling to the tree which is at R, and on which the lights come up. The circle of light on the first scene dims out, and the chanting of the voices stops. TISH *stands alone by her tree in the soft light of evening. She brushes back a tear, shakes her head, and throws the flowers on the ground. She sinks to the ground by the tree, hugs her knees, and looks up. She sees the first star, which is out of sight. Quickly she gets up, points to the star and chants.)*

TISH: *Star light, star bright,*
    First star I see tonight,
    I wish I may, I wish I might,
    Have the wish I wish tonight.
    I wish . . . I wish . . . Oh, Grandpa . . . why? *(Goes back to tree.)* Why do you have to die?

(There is star music, tinkling with bells. From above, a small swing starts descending. Magic star light spots on it. STAR BRIGHT *stands on the swing, which stops in mid-air. Music dims out.)*

STAR BRIGHT: Repeat, please.

TISH: I wish . . . I wish . . .

STAR BRIGHT: I know you are wishing. That's why I'm here. But WHAT? Repeat, please.

TISH: *(Sees and goes near him.)* Who are you?

STAR BRIGHT: *(Slowly and proudly.)* I am the first star out tonight! *(Happily)* I did it! I did it! I did it again! *(Excitedly.)* First star . . . first star . . . first star out tonight! *(To* TISH.*)* It's the early star, you know, who gets the wish. What is yours? Repeat, please.

TISH: Can you make a wish come true?

STAR BRIGHT: I've been making wishes come true for a thousand years.

TISH: A thousand years! You're older than Grandpa.

STAR BRIGHT: *(Sits on swing.)* Old? Oh, no. I'll twinkle for another thousand years.

TISH: And then?

STAR BRIGHT: *(Cheerfully.)* Then my light will go out.

TISH: Like Grandpa.

STAR BRIGHT: But there will be a new star. It's the great pattern . . .

TISH: I'll never have another Grandpa.

STAR BRIGHT: . . . the great circle of life. In every ending there is a new beginning.

TISH: (*Fully realizing it.*) I'll never see Grandpa again. I'll never hear him whistle. (*Begins to whistle "O Susannah."*)

STAR BRIGHT: Your wish? What is your wish?

TISH: I wish . . . I wish Grandpa could live a thousand years!

STAR BRIGHT: (*Startled.*) What? Repeat, please!

TISH: (*Excited.*) I wish he'd never die. Nobody would ever die! Everyone live forever!

STAR BRIGHT: Oh, no, no, no! Think what a mixed-up world it would be!

TISH: (*Speaks intently.*) I wish . . . I wish I knew why . . . why Grandpa has to die.

STAR BRIGHT: That is not a quick one-two-buckle-my-shoe wish. No. That is a think-and-show-it, then you-know-it, come-true wish.

TISH: Please.

STAR BRIGHT: (*With anticipated excitement.*) Close your eyes. Whisper the words again. Open your eyes. And your wish will begin.

(TISH *closes her eyes.* STAR BRIGHT *claps his hands, then motions. There is music and beautiful lights.* STAR BRIGHT *is delighted with the effect.*)

STAR BRIGHT: Very good! Repeat, please. (*He claps and waves his hand. Again there is music and beautiful lights.*)

STAR BRIGHT: Excellent! Thank you!

(*The swing with* STAR BRIGHT *is pulled up and out of sight. The full stage is seen, lighted in soft colors. [Never is the stage dark, eerie, or frightening.] It is* TISH's *fantasy. There are the large trees at R, and open space with beautiful sky.*

MIME *appears at R. He is a showman, a magician, and an accomplished mime who never speaks. He wears a long coat with many colorful patch pockets. He is not in white face, but his face is natural, friendly, and expressive. He enters cautiously, carrying a traveling box, which he sets down at C. On the side the audience sees the painted word, BEAR. On the other side is painted the word, DANCING. He beckons off R. The* WORLD'S GREATEST DANCING BEAR *enters R. He is a star performer, amusing, vain, and lovable like a teddy bear. He does not wear an animal mask, nor is the actor's face painted, frightening, or grotesque, with animal makeup. He wears his traveling hat. He hurries in, worried, and out of breath.*)

BEAR: I must stop and get my breath. (*Pants heavily.*) Are we safe? (*Frightened.*) I don't see him. I don't hear him. Yes, we have outrun him. (*Motions and* MIME *places box for* BEAR *to sit.*)

BEAR: Where . . . where in this wide, whirling, wonderful world . . . do you think we are? Switzerland? (MIME *makes pointed mountain with his wrist, runs his fingers up and down the "mountain," then shakes his head.*)

BEAR: You are right. No mountains. England? (MIME *opens and holds up imaginary umbrella, holds hand out to feel the rain, shakes his head.*)

BEAR: You are right. No rain. India? (MIME *leans over, swings one arm for a trunk, then other for his tail and walks.*)

BEAR: No elephants.

TISH: Excuse me.

(They freeze. She comes to them.)

TISH: I can tell you where you are. You are in Arkansas.

BEAR: Quick! Disguise. Hide.

(He and MIME *hurry to R.* MIME *quickly takes from one of his pockets a pair of dark glasses and gives them to* BEAR *who puts them on; then stands beside* BEAR *to hide him.)*

TISH: *(Recites with pride.)* Arkansas was the 25th state to be admitted to the union. It is the 27th in size, and the state flower is apple blossom.

BEAR: Who is it? *(*MIME *pantomimes a girl.)*

BEAR: A girl? *(*MIME *pantomimes a small girl.)*

BEAR: A little girl? Tell her to go away. To run away. *(*MIME *pantomimes to* TISH. BEAR *hides behind tree.)*

TISH: I have. I have run away. Have you run away, too? *(*MIME *nods.)*

TISH: Why? *(*MIME *looks frightened off R, then puts finger to lips.)*

TISH: Who are you? *(*MIME *takes a card from a pocket and presents it to her. She reads.)*

TISH: "A Mime." You never speak. *(*MIME *shakes his head, and "walks" in one spot and tips his hat.)*

TISH: "A Magician." You do tricks! *(*MIME *pulls handkerchief from sleeve.)*

TISH: "Friend." You give help. *(*MIME *touches handkerchief under her eyes.)*

TISH: Thank you. I was crying because my Grandpa . . . he's going to . . .

*(*BEAR, *without glasses, steps out from behind the tree, does a loud tap dance step and poses.* MIME *turns the traveling box around and with a flourish points to the word painted on that side of the box.* TISH *reads it with amazement.)*

TISH: Dancing. *(*MIME *turns box around again. She reads.)*

TISH: Bear. *(*MIME *motions to* BEAR *who steps forward.)*

TISH: I've never met a bear. I've never seen a DANCING bear.

BEAR: *(To* MIME.*)* Should I? *(*MIME *nods.)*

BEAR: Shall I? *(*MIME *nods.)*

BEAR: I will! My Spanish hat.

*(*MIME *jumps with joy and gets hat from box.* BEAR *motions to* TISH *who sits on the ground.)*

BEAR: Be seated, please. *(*MIME *holds up handmirror, which he takes from a pocket, holds it up for* BEAR *to look at himself, and fixes the hat.)*

BEAR: To the right . . . to the right . . . . Ah, just right!

*(*MIME *motions, and a spotlight comes on. An* ANNOUNCER'S VOICE *is heard over a loud speaker.)*

ANNOUNCER'S VOICE: Ladies and Gentlemen: Presenting in his spectacular, special, Spanish dance, the World's famous, the World's favorite, the World's Greatest Dancing Bear!

(MIME *motions, and Spanish music is heard.* BEAR *steps into the spotlight. He dances with professional perfection a Spanish dance, but he does not finish. At a climactic moment, he stops, holds his hand against his heart and speaks with short breaths.*)

BEAR: Stop the music. (MIME *motions. Music stops.*)

BEAR: Dim the lights. (MIME *motions. Spot dims out.*)

TISH: What is it?

BEAR: (*Breathing heavily.*) He is near. He is coming.

TISH: Who?

BEAR: He is almost here. Hide, I must hide. He must not find me. (MIME *points to tree.*)

BEAR: Yes, the tree. Hurry! (MIME *helps* BEAR *to tree.*)

TISH: Who? Who is coming?

BEAR: The box. Cover the box.

(*He disappears behind the tree.* MIME *sits on traveling box.* BEAR'*s head appears.*)

BEAR: Talk. (MIME *mime-talks with hands and face.*)

BEAR: Louder!

(BEAR'*s head disappears.* MIME *motions for* TISH *to talk.*)

TISH: Talk? What about?

BEAR: (*Head appears.*) Arkansas. (*Head disappears.*)

TISH: (*Recites nervously.*) Arkansas has mineral springs, natural caves, and . . . and . . . diamond mines. (*Looks off R and whispers, frightened.*) I don't hear anyone. I don't see anyone. (MIME *motions for her to talk.*)

TISH: Arkansas was first known as the state of many bears. (*Looks and whispers mysteriously.*) There isn't anyone. Nothing. Just quiet, nothing. Who is he running away from? (MIME *motions "Sh," then runs L to R and looks, then motions for* BEAR *to come out.*)

BEAR: (*Comes from behind tree.*) He didn't find me. I escaped . . . this time. (*Pleased, but short of breath.*) My traveling hat, we must go on. (MIME *takes Spanish hat and gives* BEAR *traveling hat.*)

TISH: Where? Where will you go?

BEAR: (*Looks off R, afraid.*) I must keep ahead of him.

TISH: Ahead of who? Who!

BEAR: (*Cautiously.*) Never speak his name aloud. (*Looks around.*) He may be listening, and come at once. (MIME *gives him hat.*)

BEAR: Oh, my poor hat. You and I have traveled together for many a mile and many a year. We are both beginning to look a little weary. (*Puts hat on.*)

TISH: Grandpa has an old hat.

BEAR: Perhaps, if it had a new feather. Yes! A bright new feather!

TISH: I think your hat is very stylish.

BEAR: (*Pleased.*) You do?

TISH: And very becoming.

BEAR: *(Flattered.)* Thank you. You are a very charming little girl. What is your name?

TISH: Tish.

BEAR: Tish-sh-sh? That is not a name. That is a whistle. Ti-sh-sh-sh!

TISH: It's short for Leticia. It was my Grandmother's name.

BEAR: Leticia. Ah, that is a name with beauty.

TISH: Grandpa calls me "Little Leticia."

BEAR: I shall call you . . . *(Rolling the "R.")* Princess Leticia.

TISH: Princess?

BEAR: All my friends are important people. Kings and Queens . . . Command performances for Ambassadors and Presidents . . . *(To MIME.)* The velvet box, please. *(MIME takes from a pocket a small box.)*

BEAR: I will show you my medals, my honors.

TISH: My Grandpa won a medal.

BEAR: Ah?

TISH: He was the best turkey caller in Arkansas.

BEAR: Turkey caller?

TISH: He won first prize!

BEAR: *(To MIME.)* Pin them on me so she can see. And so that I can remember . . . once again . . . all my glories.

(Royal music begins and continues during the scene. MIME puts ribbons and jeweled medals on BEAR as VOICE announces each decoration. Two are pinned on. One is on a ribbon which is fastened around BEAR's neck.)

ANNOUNCER'S VOICE: The Queen's highest honor, the Royal Medallion.

BEAR: I danced in the Great Hall. It was the Queen's birthday party.

ANNOUNCER'S VOICE: The Diamond Crescent of the East.

BEAR: Fifteen encores. Fifteen encores and they still applauded.

ANNOUNCER'S VOICE: The Royal Ribbon of Honor for Distinguished Service.

BEAR: It was during the war. I danced for the soldiers.

ANNOUNCER'S VOICE: And today, a new decoration. Her Royal Highness, Princess Leticia presents, in honor of her Grandfather, the highest award in the State of Arkansas—the Turkey Feather.

(MIME takes a bright feather from a pocket and gives it to TISH. BEAR parades to her, with a few dance steps, and she puts the feather in his hat. Royal music stops.)

BEAR: Thank you. A party! We will celebrate my new honor! *(To MIME.)* Food and festivities! Honey bread! *(MIME nods.)*

BEAR: Thick with honey spread!

(MIME nods twice, then makes magic motions toward BEAR. Suddenly MIME turns and points to LETICIA. She puts out her hand which, magically, holds a honey bun.)

TISH: *(Delighted.)* O-o-oh! It looks delicious.

(MIME *turns and points to* BEAR *who puts out his hand which, magically, holds a honey bun.*)

BEAR: A-a-ah! It IS delicious. (BEAR *puts finger in it, then licks finger.* MIME *raises his hand.*)

BEAR: Yes, give us a toast.

(BEAR *and* TISH *hold honey buns up.* MIME *pantomimes "A toast . . ." holds up his hand; "to the winner . . ." clasps his hands and shakes them high in the air; "of the turkey feather," walks like a turkey, bobbing his head, then* MIME *pulls out an imaginary feather from his hip.*)

BEAR: Thank you.

TISH: What did he say?

BEAR: You didn't listen.

TISH: How can I hear when he doesn't speak?

BEAR: You listen with your eyes, and then YOU say the words. Listen. He will repeat the toast.

TISH: (MIME *pantomimes the toast again. She watches and speaks aloud.*) "A toast . . . to the winner . . . of the turkey feather!"

BEAR: Thank you. Now entertainment! (*To* MIME.) You tell us a story. (*To* TISH.) You listen and say the words.

TISH: Me?

BEAR: And I will eat! (*Wiggles with excitement and sits on box.*)

(MIME *pantomimes a story which* TISH, *watching him, repeats in words.*)

TISH: "Once there was . . . a princess . . . a beautiful princess!"

BEAR: Named (*Sings it.*) Leticia. (*Takes a bite.*)

TISH: "One day . . . in the woods . . . she met . . . (*Doubtful.*) . . . a cat?" (MIME *shakes his head. Mimes again.*)

TISH: A . . . goosey-gander? (MIME *shakes his head. Mimes again.*)

TISH: A . . . bear!

BEAR: The World's Greatest Dancing Bear! (*Seated, he makes his own vocal music and dances with his feet.*)

TISH: "Under a spreading tree . . . they had a party . . . with honey bread, thick with honey spread."

BEAR: (*Licks his five fingers, one on each word.*) Yum . . . yum . . . TO . . . the . . . last . . . crumb. (*Licks his hand and picks and eats crumbs from his lap.*)

TISH: "Now honey bread, thick with honey spread . . . made the bear . . . very . . . sleepy. He yawned." (BEAR *follows action of the story and goes to sleep.*)

TISH: ". . . gave a little sigh . . . and took a little nap." (BEAR *snores.*)

TISH: He's asleep. Who . . . who is he running away from? (MIME *goes to sleeping* BEAR, *puts his finger to his lips then mimes.*)

TISH: "The World's Greatest Dancing Bear . . . is old and tired . . . and his heart is tired." (*To herself.*) Like Grandpa. (*Speaking for* MIME.) "He is running away from . . ." Who? "Someone is coming to take him away . . . forever." Does that mean if he's caught, he will die? (MIME *nods.*)

TISH: Is he running away . . . from death? (MIME *nods.*)

TISH: Oh! I'll help him. Yes, I'll help him. (*Faint music of a calliope is heard;* BEAR *stirs.*)

TISH: He's waking up

BEAR: (*Slowly wakes up.*) Music . . . the calliope . . . circus music . . . of the Great Center ring! (*Rises.*) The Ringmaster is coming!

TISH: (*To* MIME.) Death? (MIME *nods.*)

BEAR: He is near. I hear the music.

TISH: I don't hear it. (*To* MIME.) Do you? (MIME *shakes his head.*)

BEAR: Only I can hear him. Only I can see him. He is coming for me. Quick! We must go.

TISH: Yes, I'll help you.

BEAR: This way. Hurry! (MIME *carries box. Led by* BEAR *they start L, but stop when the music becomes louder.*)

BEAR: No! The music is coming from here. It is all around us! Here! There! Look! (*He points off R.*)

TISH: What?

BEAR: The Great Ringmaster. He is there! He is coming . . . for me!

(RINGMASTER *enters slowly from R. He wears an ornate ringmaster's jacket, boots, and a tall hat. He has a friendly face, a pleasant voice, but walks and speaks with authority. He stops. Music stops.*)

BEAR: Quick! Hide me! Hide me!

(BEAR *runs to L.* TISH *and* MIME *follow. He quickly hides behind them when they stop.* BEAR *peeks over* TISH's *shoulder.*)

BEAR: Tell him to go away.

TISH: I can't see him. Where is he?

BEAR: There. (*Hides.*)

TISH: (*Bravely speaks, facing front talking into space.*) Excuse me . . . sir. This is my secret place . . . by the big tree. You must leave at once. Go away. Now. (*Whispers to* BEAR.) Did he go?

BEAR: (*Peeks.*) No. (*Hides.*)

RINGMASTER: (*Distinctly and with authority.*) I have come for the Dancing Bear. I have come to take him to the Great Center Ring.

BEAR: Tell him he has made a mistake.

TISH: Excuse me . . . sir. You have made a mistake.

RINGMASTER: (*Opens book.*) No. It is written plainly in the book. The date is today. The name is . . . the Dancing Bear.

BEAR: (*Who was hidden by* MIME *at the side, now steps into view, wearing boxing gloves and a sport cap.*) You HAVE made a mistake. I am a BOXING bear.

(MIME *blows a whistle and continues to blow it, as* BEAR *shadowboxes, comically, with a few dance steps and kicks thrown in. He ends in a heroic pose.*)

BEAR: Goodbye.

RINGMASTER: A boxing bear? (*Looks in book.*) There has never been a mistake.

TISH: *(Whispers.)* Have you tricked him? Outwitted him?

BEAR: *(Nods, then calls loudly.)* Yes. Training time. On your mark; get set; ready—tallyho! *(Starts jogging off R.)*

RINGMASTER: *(Reads.)* The book says: His father, born in Russia, a dancing bear.

BEAR: *(Stops, indignant.)* Correct that. He was Russia's most honored dancing bear.

RINGMASTER: His mother, born in Spain, also a dancing bear.

BEAR: She was the prima ballerina bear of all Spain!

RINGMASTER: His, only son—

BEAR: Is the World's Greatest Dancing Bear!

RINGMASTER: Then you are the one I have come for!

BEAR: Yes!

RINGMASTER: Then we will have no more tricks or games. *(BEAR realizes he has revealed himself.)*

RINGMASTER: Come. Take my hand. *(BEAR always reacts with fear to the RING-MASTER's white gloved hand.)*

RINGMASTER: I will show you the way to the Great Center Ring.

BEAR: No! No!

TISH: What is he saying?

BEAR: He is going to take me away.

RINGMASTER: Come. You must. And it is easier if you go quietly.

BEAR: No! I will not go with you. I will fight! *(Holds up boxing gloves.)*

TISH: Fight him! I'll help you!

BEAR: I have fought all my life. Battled my way to the top. Look at my medals. I will fight to the end.

RINGMASTER: This, my friend, is the end.

BEAR: No! No! Not for me. Not yet! Stay away! I have new dances to do.

RINGMASTER: Today you will take your last bow.

BEAR: No! No. *(Savagely.)* I will claw! I will eat! I will crush! I will kill! Kill to live! *(Violently throws boxing gloves away.)* To live! To live!

RINGMASTER: Everyone shouts when he is frightened of the dark.

BEAR: I WILL NOT DIE!

RINGMASTER: You have no choice.

BEAR: But . . . why? Why me? ME!

RINGMASTER: You are like all the others. Everyone thinks HE will live forever. Come.

BEAR: No! What did I do wrong? What can I do now? To stop it!

RINGMASTER: Death comes to all. It has never been IF you will die. The only question has been WHEN you will die. Now you know.

BEAR: *(Runs.)* I will run. I will hide.

RINGMASTER: *(With authority.)* You cannot escape from death.

BEAR: *(Bargaining desperately.)* More time. Give me more time. I have so much to do.

RINGMASTER: *(Slightly annoyed.)* There is always that which is left undone.

BEAR: I don't know how . . . to die. I need to rehearse.

RINGMASTER: No one has to rehearse. It is very simple . . . very easy. *(Holds out hand.)* Come. It is growing late.

BEAR: No! *(Desperate for any excuse.)* I must write my memories! Tell the world the glories of my life. My life . . . *(Pause. TISH and MIME rush to him as he falters, place box, and help him sit.)*

BEAR: It is almost over. And what was it? A few medals that will be lost. No. There must be more to life. Give me time. Time to find the answer.

TISH: *(Kneeling by him, pleads into space.)* Please . . . let him live.

RINGMASTER: Your life is over. Today is the day.

BEAR: But my day is not over. *(To TISH.)* The day is not ended, is it?

TISH: Give him to the END of the day!

BEAR: Yes! To the end. Oh, you are a very smart little girl!

RINGMASTER: Well . . . *(Looks in his book.)*

TISH: What did he say?

BEAR: He's looking in his book.

RINGMASTER: The day you are to die is written plainly. But not the hour.

BEAR: Then give me the full day.

TISH: Please.

RINGMASTER: *(Pause.)* I will give you until midnight. Until the last hour of your last day.

BEAR: YES!

TISH: Can you live?

BEAR: YES! Oh, let me shout to the world! I AM ALIVE! *(To MIME.)* Give me my brightest, my happiest hat! *(To RINGMASTER, who has gone)* Oh, thank you . . . thank you . . . He is gone . . . for a while. *(To TISH.)* Oh, let me touch you. Let me feel the warmth . . . the life in you. There is so much yet to do! And so little time. My life . . . it went too fast. I didn't stop to listen . . . I didn't stop to see. *(MIME waves clown hat in front of BEAR.)*

BEAR: Oh, yes! I will be the clown! *(Puts hat on. To TISH.)* Come. Dance with me! And we will make the world spin round and round with joy!

TISH: Grandpa taught me how to whistle and how to dance a jig. *(Quickly she whistles "O Susannah," and does a little jig, looking at her feet.)*

BEAR: No, no, no. To dance is a great honor. Hold your head high. *(He follows his own instructions.)* And first you smile to the right . . . then you smile to the left . . . and you bow to the center . . . and then . . . begin.

(MIME motions. A spotlight comes on BEAR. Music is heard. BEAR does a short, charming soft-shoe dance. Spotlight and music dim out. TISH applauds. BEAR sits on box which MIME places for him. BEAR is happy, but breathless.)

TISH: Oh, how wonderful!

BEAR: Thank you.

TISH: You're better than Grandpa! He can only do a little jig.

BEAR: But he taught you?

TISH: Yes.

BEAR: And he taught you how to whistle?

TISH: Yes.

BEAR: *(Rises.)* If I could teach my dances to someone . . . if someone could carry on the fame of my family . . . All my hats . . . there will be no one to wear my hats. They, too, will be put in a box and forgotten. Tell me, are you like your Grandfather?

TISH: Daddy says I'm a chip off the old block.

BEAR: You are a part of him. And you will carry on for him in life. *(Excited.)* Yes! Yes, that is the answer to the riddle.

TISH: What riddle?

BEAR: The riddle of life. I must leave my dances! They will be a part of me that will live on! But who? Where! How!

TISH: Make a wish!

BEAR: A wish?

TISH: On the first star you see. And it will come true. It will. It will!

BEAR: *(Wanting to believe.)* You are sure it will? (TISH *nods. To* MIME.) Do you believe it will? (MIME *nods.*)

BEAR: I could try.

TISH: Quick!

BEAR: Of course, I don't believe in superstitions. But I did get up on the right side of the bed. (MIME *nods.*)

BEAR: I did find a four-leaf clover. (MIME *nods.*)

BEAR: And I haven't sneezed once. (MIME *shakes his head.*)

BEAR: Yes, luck is with me today! So . . . let me knock on wood—three times—and I will do it! (MIME *takes off hat.* BEAR *knocks on* MIME's *head three times, with sound effects.*)

BEAR: What do I say?

TISH: Point to the first star you see.

BEAR: *(Looks about, then points.)* There! I see a bright twinkling one.

TISH: Say, "Star light, star bright . . ."

BEAR: *(To* MIME.) The rabbit's foot! This wish must come true. *(Looks up.)* "Star light, star bright."

TISH: "First star I see tonight."

BEAR: "First star I see tonight." *(Takes rabbit's foot from* MIME *and rubs it vigorously.)* Oh, bring me luck. Make my wish come true.

TISH: "I wish I may, I wish I might."

BEAR: "I wish I may, I wish I might." Oh, it won't work. It's nothing but a nursery rhyme.

TISH: "Have the wish I wish tonight." Say it. Say it!

BEAR: "Have the wish I wish tonight." *(Pause.)* Nothing. Nothing. I told you so.

TISH: Look. Look! It's beginning to happen.

STAR BRIGHT: *(Star music and lights begin as* STAR BRIGHT *enters on swing. He is joyously happy.)* Tonight I'm blinking. Tonight I'm winking. Wishes are flying past. Wishes are coming quick and fast! I'm twinkling bright and RIGHT tonight! *(Laughs.)* Your wish, please.

BEAR: *(Lost in happy memories.)* Look. It is like a circus. The trapeze high in a tent of blue . . . the music of the band . . .

(MIME motions. Soft band music of the circus is heard. Colorful lights play on the backdrop.)

BEAR: The delicious smell of popcorn . . . the dance on the high wire . . .

(TISH holds up an imaginary umbrella and walks on an imaginary tight rope.)

BEAR: The sweet taste of pink lemonade . . . Oh, the beauty, the wonder of life. Let me look at it. The happiness of living . . . Oh, let me feel it. The joy of being alive! Let me keep it. Let me hold it forever. *(Holds out his arms to embrace it all.)*

STAR BRIGHT: *(Claps his hands. Music and circus scene stop.)* Your wish. Your wish. Repeat, please.

TISH: The answer to the riddle.

BEAR: *(Intently.)* I wish to leave with someone my dances so that I . . . so that they . . . will be remembered.

STAR BRIGHT: That is a wish I hear every night . . . every night. A wish to shine on earth . . . and leave behind a trace . . . to learn, to earn the grace . . . of immortality. Of your wish, half I can do. The other half is left for you. But quick! You must start. Because all wishes on a star must be done before the star is overshadowed by the sun. *(He claps his hands. Magic music and lights begin.)*

STAR BRIGHT:

> One, two;
> Sunset red;
> Midnight blue;
> The wish you wish
> I give to you.

(Magic lights and music end as STAR BRIGHT exits up and out of sight. From off L, LITTLE BEAR is heard singing. All look to L. LITTLE BEAR enters finishing his song to the tune of "Turkey in the Straw." He is a small cub, wearing country overalls and a little turned-up straw hat. Over his shoulder he carries a small fishing pole.)

LITTLE BEAR: *(Sings.)*

> Turkey in the straw, haw, haw, haw;
> Turkey in the hay, hay, hay, hay;
> Bait the hook, give the line a swish;
> Jumpin' jiggers, I caught a fish.

TISH: A little bear.

BEAR: *(LITTLE BEAR does a few dance steps of joy, and continues walking and singing.)* A little dancing bear. *(To MIME.)* Meet him. Greet him. Make him welcome. *(To TISH.)* Quick, the handmirror.

(TISH holds mirror which MIME gives her and BEAR preens. MIME hurries to LITTLE BEAR and pantomimes a big and friendly greeting. LITTLE BEAR, as if it

were a game, happily imitates every movement of the MIME. *It ends with both shaking hands. Then* LITTLE BEAR *gives a friendly good-bye wave and starts off R, singing.)*

BEAR: Stop him! (MIME *rushes in front of* LITTLE BEAR *and turns him around.)*

BEAR: I am ready to be presented. (MIME, *with a flourish, presents* BEAR.)

BEAR: How do you do.

LITTLE BEAR: Howdy-do to you.

BEAR: You have come from my WISHING on a star.

LITTLE BEAR: Uh-uh. I've come from my FISHING in the river.

BEAR: Oh, my little one, I am going to give you the treasure of my life. Bestow on you all my gifts.

LITTLE BEAR: I could use a new fishing pole.

BEAR: I am going to teach you all my dances. You will wear all my hats. Oh-ho! I have never felt so alive in my life!

(He gives a joyous whoop and jumps and clicks his heels. LITTLE BEAR *is bewildered.* BEAR, *with the eyes of a dancing master, looks* LITTLE BEAR *over.)*

BEAR: Yes, you have a good build. Good stance. Relaxed torso. (*Taps* LITTLE BEAR's *waist.* LITTLE BEAR *wiggles and giggles from the tickling.)*

BEAR: Legs sturdy, Up! Leg up! Up! (LITTLE BEAR *cautiously lifts leg.)*

BEAR: Up! Up! (BEAR *raises* LITTLE BEAR's *leg high.)*

LITTLE BEAR: Whoa!

BEAR: Point. Point!

LITTLE BEAR: (*Points with finger*) Point where?

BEAR: (*Holding* LITTLE BEAR's *foot high*) Point your foot. Ah, feet too stiff . . . too stiff. (*Lets leg down.* LITTLE BEAR *stands in profile, stomach pushed out.)*

BEAR: Stomach flat! (*Taps stomach.* LITTLE BEAR *pulls stomach in, but pushes hips out.)*

BEAR: Rear push in! (*Smacks* LITTLE BEAR *on the bottom.* LITTLE BEAR *pulls hips in, and turns facing audience.)*

BEAR: Stretch . . . up . . . up! (*Pulls* LITTLE BEAR *up who tries to stretch. His face is tense.)*

BEAR: Relax. (*Pats* LITTLE BEAR *on forehead.* LITTLE BEAR *slowly sinks to the ground.* BEAR *lifts him up.)*

BEAR: Smile. (LITTLE BEAR *forces a tortured smile.)*

BEAR: Walk! Walk! (LITTLE BEAR *starts walking stiffly.)*

TISH: Will he be a good dancer?

BEAR: He will be magnificent! (*Puts arm out and stops* LITTLE BEAR's *escape.)*

BEAR: He will be—ME! My rehearsal hat. My father's Russian dancing hat! (*He dances a few steps of a Russian dance, and shouts a few Russian words.)*

BEAR: To the dressing room. (*He continues the dance steps and shouting as he exits at R.* MIME, *with traveling box follows him, imitating the dance steps.)*

LITTLE BEAR: Who . . . who is he?

TISH: He is the greatest dancing bear in the world.

LITTLE BEAR: Oh!

TISH: And . . . he's going to die.

LITTLE BEAR: Oh.

TISH: My Grandpa is going to die and I don't know what to do.

LITTLE BEAR: Up in the hills, I've seen a lot of them die.

TISH: You have?

LITTLE BEAR: Old ones, little ones, and big ones, too. And there ain't nothing you can do about it. 'Cause as sure as you're born, you're as sure of dying.

TISH: It's sad.

LITTLE BEAR: Course it's sad.

TISH: It's frightening.

LITTLE BEAR: *(Thinking it out.)* No. It ain't dyin' that you're afraid of. It's the not knowin' what comes AFTER you die. That's what scares you.

TISH: *(Tearful.)* I'll never see Grandpa again.

LITTLE BEAR: *(With gentle understanding.)* You go on. You have yourself a good cry. It'll help you to give him up. And you got to. *(With emphasis.)* You got to let him go.

TISH: No.

LITTLE BEAR: You have to! 'Cause he gone . . . forever.

TISH: You don't know what it's like to have your Grandpa die.

LITTLE BEAR: Yes, I do. My Grandpa died last winter. And my Papa . . . I saw a hunter shoot my Papa.

TISH: *(Shocked.)* Shoot your Papa! Oh, what did you do?

LITTLE BEAR: First, I cried. Yes, I cried, and then I started hatin' and I kicked and I clawed 'cause I felt all alone.

TISH: *(Nods.)* All by yourself.

LITTLE BEAR: Then my Mama said, "You have to go on living, so . . . do your best. Give yourself to the livin'. 'Cause that's the best way to say goodbye to your Pa." So I made my peace.

TISH: Your peace?

LITTLE BEAR: Inside myself. Oh, it don't mean I understand about dyin'. I don't. But you do go on living. The next day. The next year. So if you love your Grandpa like I loved my Papa . . .

TISH: Oh, I do.

LITTLE BEAR: Then show him you do.

TISH: How?

LITTLE BEAR: Tell him goodbye . . . by giving your most to the living. I'm wanting to do something . . . something big . . . just for Papa.

BEAR: *(Off.)* All is ready!

TISH: Please, dance with him. He needs you.

LITTLE BEAR: Well, I like to help folks.

TISH: You said, "Give to the living."

LITTLE BEAR: And I do like the dance!

TISH: *(Excited with a new idea.)* This is the big thing you can do for your Papa.

LITTLE BEAR: For Papa?

TISH: *(Points with her hand as she visualizes it.)* Your name will be in lights. You will be the NEW World's Greatest Dancing Bear!

BEAR: *(BEAR and MIME enter, BEAR wearing his Russian Cossack hat.)* Let the flags fly! Let the band play! *(To LITTLE BEAR.)* We will start with a simple waltz. My mother's famous skating waltz. One, two, three; One, two, three . . . *(He dances, continuing during the next speeches.)*

LITTLE BEAR: *(Tries to do the step, then stops.)* No. I'm just a country bear, with no schoolin'.

TISH: You will be the famous . . . "Arkansaw Bear!" *(Urges him on.)*

LITTLE BEAR: Arkansaw. I ain't right sure how to spell Arkansaw. *(He moves in one spot to the beat of the music, wanting to dance, but afraid.)*

TISH: Like it sounds. A-R-K-A-N-

LITTLE BEAR: *(Shouts, eager to dance.)* S-A-W! *(With a burst of energy, he follows BEAR and dances with joy, counting loudly and happily.)* One! Two! Three! One! Two! Three! I'm doing it!

(The first chime of midnight is heard, loud and distinct. The other chimes follow slowly. MIME runs to BEAR, motions for him to listen.)

TISH: What is it?

BEAR: The chimes are striking twelve.

LITTLE BEAR: It's the end of the day. Midnight.

BEAR: No! No! Not yet! I have not taught you my dances. Stop the clock!

TISH: Run! Hide! Before he comes back!

BEAR: Where?

LITTLE BEAR: In the caves! In the hills!

TISH: Hurry!

(TISH and LITTLE BEAR help BEAR. MIME carries box. All start toward back. Soft calliope music is heard. RINGMASTER enters R.)

RINGMASTER: Twelve. *(They stop.)*

RINGMASTER: Your day is ended. Your time is up. Come. I will take you to the Great Center Ring.

BEAR: No. No!

TISH: Is he here?

BEAR: Yes, he has come for me. *(Comes down stage. Backs off toward L.)* Stop him.

RINGMASTER: There is no way to stop death.

TISH: I know a way. *(Grabs MIME and points up toward star.)*

TISH: Make a wish on the first star you see. Say, *(Shouts.)*
        Star light, star bright,
        First star I see tonight . . .

(MIME *quickly points and looks up, rapidly miming the rhyme.*)

STAR BRIGHT: (*Off.*) Louder, please.

RINGMASTER: Come. (*Holds out his hand and slowly crosses toward* BEAR *at far L.*)

TISH: (MIME *pantomimes, repeating with larger gestures, while* TISH *says the word.*)
> I wish I may, I wish I might,
> Have the wish I wish tonight.

STAR BRIGHT: (*Quickly descends into view.*) Wish quickly chanted. Wish quickly granted.

TISH: (MIME *pantomimes her words.*) Stop death!

(*With a sound effect of a roll on a cymbal,* STAR BRIGHT *points at* RINGMASTER, *who has advanced almost to* BEAR. RINGMASTER *stops in a walking position.*)

TISH: Make him go away!

(*A roll on a cymbal is heard, as* STAR BRIGHT *makes a circle with his hand.* RINGMASTER *slowly turns around.*)

TISH: LOCK HIM UP IN THE TREE! (*Another roll on the cymbal.*)

STAR BRIGHT: Walk to the tree. (RINGMASTER *slowly walks to a tree.*)

STAR BRIGHT: Your home it will be . . . for a time.

(RINGMASTER *stops.* STAR BRIGHT *points to tree again. There is a roll on a cymbal as the trunk slowly opens.*)

STAR BRIGHT: It is open wide . . . to welcome you. Step inside.

(RINGMASTER *faces tree and slowly steps inside. The tree trunk slowly closes shut.*)

STAR BRIGHT: Locked, blocked, and enclosed! (*He laughs.*)

BEAR: (*To* TISH.) You did it! You stopped death!

TISH: (*She and* BEAR *shout together, while* MIME *jumps with joy and blows whistle.*) We did it!

BEAR: We did it.

STAR BRIGHT: (*Claps his hands.*) Remember . . . soon will come the morning sun, and then . . . Remember that is when . . . all wishes become . . . undone. (*Star music and light begin as he ascends out of sight, and then stop.*)

BEAR: (*Their joy changes to concern.*) It is true! Time is short! Quick. I must teach the little one—

(*Looks about.* LITTLE BEAR *has, unnoticed, slipped away when* RINGMASTER *appeared.*)

BEAR: Where is he?

TISH: Little Bear! (*Pause. There is no answer.*)

BEAR: Little Bear, come back!

TISH: (*She and* MIME *run looking for him.*) Little Bear?

BEAR: He was frightened . . . (*Looks at tree.*) of death. He is gone. And with him all my hopes are gone. (*He slumps, wearily.*)

TISH: *(Concerned, rushes to him.)* You must rest, like Grandpa.

BEAR: Your Grandfather has had you. *(Amused.)* A chip off the old block, eh? *(She nods.)*

BEAR: You gave him happiness in life . . . peace in death.

TISH: Are you all right?

BEAR: I am old, and weary and tired. And I am going to die.

TISH: No. We stopped death.

BEAR: But only for a brief time. Death, they say is a clock. Every minute our lives are ticking away. Now . . . soon . . . my clock will stop.

TISH: No.

BEAR: When I was young like you, I wondered, "Where did I come from?" And now when I am old, I wonder, "Where am I going?"

*(*MIME *looks and listens off R, then runs to them and excitedly mimes that* LITTLE BEAR *is coming.)*

BEAR: What is it? *(*MIME *pantomimes more.)*

BEAR: Who? Where? *(*MIME *points to R. All watch as* LITTLE BEAR *enters.)*

BEAR: You have come back.

LITTLE BEAR: I left my fishing pole.

BEAR: Have no fear. Death is locked in the tree. *(*LITTLE BEAR *reacts with fright at tree.)*

TISH: You have come back to help.

LITTLE BEAR: I come back to learn all your fancy dancin'.

TISH: *(Runs to* LITTLE BEAR *and hugs him.)* Oh, you are the best, the sweetest, the most wonderful little bear in the world! *(*LITTLE BEAR *is embarrassed.)*

BEAR: Yes! Quick! We must begin the lesson. There is so little time and so much to learn. *(Looks frightened off R. To* MIME.*)* Stand watch. Yes, watch for the first rays of the sun!

*(*MIME *stands at R, anxiously looking off.* TISH *sits on box.* BEAR *motions to* LITTLE BEAR.*)* Come! Come! Attention! I will teach you all I know. *(Takes position.)* First, you smile to the right. *(*BEAR *does the action with the words.* LITTLE BEAR *watches and tries to do the action.)*

BEAR: You smile to the left. You bow to the center. And then . . . begin . . . to dance. We will start with my father's famous Russian dance. Master this and all else will be easy. *(To* MIME.*)* How many more minutes? *(*MIME *holds up ten fingers.)*

BEAR: Ten! Position. Position! *(*LITTLE BEAR *imitates him.)*

BEAR: Listen to the beat . . . the beat . . . *(Taps foot.)*

LITTLE BEAR: Beat what?

BEAR: Your feet! Your feet! The beat . . . the beat . . . *(Taps foot.* LITTLE BEAR *slowly and timidly taps beat.)*

BEAR: Too slow. Too slow. *(*LITTLE BEAR *pivots in a circle, weight on one foot while tapping fast with the other foot.)*

BEAR: Too fast. Too fast. *(*LITTLE BEAR *does it right.)*

BEAR: Ah! Ah! Ah! Good! Good!

LITTLE BEAR: I'm doing it right!

BEAR: *(Shows him next Russian step.)* The first step. Hop, hop, hop, switch, hop. *(LITTLE BEAR tries, awkward at first, then better.)*

BEAR: Hop, hop, hop, switch, hop. Yes, hop, hop, hop, switch, hop. Yes! Yes! *(Shows him next step.)* Deep knee, hop. *(LITTLE BEAR shakes his head.)*

BEAR: Try. Try. *(LITTLE BEAR tries deep knee bends with a hop.)*

BEAR: Deep knee, hop. Lower. Lower. *(LITTLE BEAR puts hands on floor in front of him and does step. He smiles at the audience at the easiness of it.)*

BEAR: No, no, no! No hands! *(Lifts LITTLE BEAR up. LITTLE BEAR continues to kick his feet.)*

BEAR: The next step. The finale. *(Shows step.)* Turn, two, up, two. Turn, two, up, two.

LITTLE BEAR: Oh, my!

BEAR: Turn, two, up, two. *(LITTLE BEAR tries.)*

BEAR: Turn, two, up, two. Faster. Faster.

LITTLE BEAR: *(Falls.)* I can't do it. I can't do it.

BEAR: You will. You must do it. I must leave my dances with you.

TISH: Try, please. Please, try.

LITTLE BEAR: Well . . . *(Gets up.)*

BEAR: Again, Again. Ready. Turn, two, up, two. *(BEAR keeps repeating the count, and LITTLE BEAR does the step better and better, until he is perfect—and happy.)*

BEAR: He did it! He did it!

TISH: He did it!

LITTLE BEAR: I did it!

BEAR: *(To MIME.)* How many minutes are left? *(MIME holds up eight fingers.)*

BEAR: Eight minutes. Time is running out. Quick. The polka. The dance of the people. Music!

(MIME motions. Music is heard. BEAR dances a few steps. LITTLE BEAR quickly follows him and masters them. Music stops. BEAR breathes heavily.)

BEAR: How many more minutes? *(MIME holds up seven fingers.)*

BEAR: Only seven minutes left! Hurry. My famous tarantella.

(MIME motions and music is heard. BEAR does a few steps. LITTLE BEAR again quickly does them and they dance together. Music stops. BEAR pants for breath. MIME runs to him and holds up six fingers.)

BEAR: Six minutes. And at the end take your bow. The first bow. *(BEAR bows, short of breath.)* The second bow. *(BEAR bows, pauses, then with trembling voice he speaks with emotion, knowing it is his last bow.)* And the last and final bow.

TISH: More, more! Encore! Encore! *(BEAR slumps to the floor. She rushes to him.)*

TISH: He's fallen. *(She and MIME cradle BEAR on either side.)*

TISH: Are you all right?

BEAR: (Stirs, weakly.) How . . . many more minutes . . . do I have left? (MIME holds up five fingers.)

BEAR: My little one, you will do my dances, you will carry on for me?

LITTLE BEAR: Yes. Yes.

BEAR: Take my father's hat . . . and it was HIS father's hat . . .

LITTLE BEAR: No, you must wear it.

BEAR: I will not need it where I am going. I have taken my last bow.

TISH: No. (Buries her head on his shoulder.)

BEAR: Ah, tears can be beautiful. But there is no need to cry. I am content. I was a part of what went before, and I will be a part of what is yet to come. That is the answer to the riddle of life. (Weakly.) How many more minutes? (MIME holds up two fingers.)

BEAR: Two. Bring me my traveling hat. I will wear it on my last journey.

(LITTLE BEAR gets traveling hat from box, as MIME and TISH help BEAR to stand.)

BEAR: I must look my best when I enter the Great Center Ring. (MIME puts hat on BEAR, who smiles at TISH.)

BEAR: Does it look stylish?

TISH: Yes.

BEAR: Is it becoming? (She nods.)

BEAR: Then I am ready. (Gently pushes TISH and MIME away.) No. This journey I must go alone. (Extends hand to MIME.) Goodbye, good friend. Thank you for everything. And sometimes when the band plays . . . think of an old bear.

(MIME motions for BEAR to wait. MIME quickly gets a pink balloon on a string from the side and holds it out to BEAR.)

BEAR: Yes, I remember when once we said, "Life is like a bright balloon." Hold it tight. Hold it tight. Because . . . once you let it go . . . it floats away forever. (Breathless.) How many more minutes? (MIME holds up one finger. BEAR turns to TISH.)

BEAR: I have one last request. When the end comes . . . when I enter the Great Center Ring . . . I want music. I want you to whistle the tune your Grandfather taught you.

TISH: "O Susannah."

BEAR: (Nods and smiles.) You will find that when you whistle you cannot cry at the same time. (A rooster is heard crowing.)

BEAR: Listen.

LITTLE BEAR: It's a rooster crowin'. It's almost mornin'.

TISH: The sun is up. The stars are fading away.

STAR BRIGHT: (Star music is heard as STAR BRIGHT descends into view. He speaks softly.) Announcing: the first ray of sun is peeping out. Warning: all wishes end as the sun begins. The new day is starting, the old departing. That is the great pattern . . . the circle of life. Tomorrow is today. (He points at the tree and claps his hands. The tree trunk slowly opens.)

STAR BRIGHT: And the night and the stars fade away . . . fade away.

(There is star music as STAR BRIGHT *disappears. Soft calliope music is heard which continues during the scene.)*

RINGMASTER: *(Steps out from tree trunk. He speaks with authority.)* There is no more time. The book is closed.

BEAR: Poets tell us death is but a sleep, but who can tell me what I will dream?

RINGMASTER: *(Walks slowly to* BEAR.) Take my hand.

BEAR: Tell me, tell me what is death?

RINGMASTER: When there is no answer, you do not ask the question. Come.

BEAR: Yes, I am ready. *(To* LITTLE BEAR.) My little one . . . I give you my feather . . . and you . . . give joy . . . to the world. *(Gives turkey feather to* LITTLE BEAR. *He whispers.)* Let the balloon go.

*(*RINGMASTER *holds out his hand, which* BEAR *takes. Together they walk off L slowly.* MIME *lets the balloon go. He,* TISH *and* LITTLE BEAR *watch as it floats up and out of sight. At the same time the calliope music builds in volume. There is a second of silence. Then the* ANNOUNCER'S VOICE *is heard, loud and distinctly.)*

ANNOUNCER'S VOICE: Ladies and gentlemen: presenting for your pleasure and entertainment, the new dancing bear, the world's famous, the world's favorite, the world's greatest—The Arkansaw Bear!

(During the announcement, MIME *points to* LITTLE BEAR. LITTLE BEAR *looks frightened, amazed, and pleased.* MIME *holds up mirror, and* LITTLE BEAR *puts feather in his hat.* MIME *motions for* LITTLE BEAR *to step forward, then motions a circle of light on the floor. Spotlight comes on, and* LITTLE BEAR *steps into the light.)*

BEAR'S VOICE: *(Over the loud speaker,* BEAR's *voice is heard. He speaks softly and with emotion.* LITTLE BEAR *follows his instructions.)* You smile to the right . . . smile to the left . . . bow to the center . . . and then begin to dance!

(Music begins, lively "Turkey in the Straw." LITTLE BEAR *begins his dance.)*

BEAR'S VOICE: My dances . . . your dances . . . and make the world spin round and round with joy.

*(*LITTLE BEAR *dances with fun, excitement, and joy, a wonderful short dance. During this* TISH *exits, and* MIME *exits with box. At the end of the dance,* LITTLE BEAR *bows as the audience applauds and exits at L, peeks out and waves again. Spotlight goes out. Fantasy music is heard, and a soft night-light illuminates the tree.* TISH *is leaning against it. She looks up, sighs, picks up the flowers, and slowly circles back to the downstage area of the first scene, which becomes light as the tree area dims out. Fantasy music also fades out.* MOTHER's *and* AUNT ELLEN's *VOICES are heard, and* TISH *answers as if they were standing on each side of her downstage.)*

MOTHER'S VOICE: *(Worried.)* Tish? Tish, is that you?

TISH: Yes, mother.

MOTHER'S VOICE: Where have you been?

TISH: I went up the hill to my tree. I want to see Grandpa.

AUNT ELLEN'S VOICE: He's dead . . . dead. *(Cries.)*

TISH: *(Trying to be brave.)* Dead. Tears can be beautiful, Aunt Ellen. But you have to give him up. Let the balloon go.

AUNT ELLEN'S VOICE: What?

TISH: *(Trying to keep back her tears.)* I know everyone . . . everything has a time to die . . . and it's sad. But Grandpa knew the answer to the riddle.

AUNT ELLEN'S VOICE: The riddle?

TISH: He left his footprint. He left a chip off the old block.

MOTHER'S VOICE: What, dear? What did he leave?

TISH: Me! And I want to do something . . . something big for Grandpa. Because that's the best way to say goodbye. *(Softly.)* Let me give him his flowers . . . the pink ones.

MOTHER'S VOICE: *(Positive, and with a mother's love and authority.)* All right, dear. Come along. We'll go together and see Grandpa. (TISH *starts L, and begins to whistle.)*

MOTHER'S VOICE: What are you doing?

TISH: Whistling . . . for the bear . . . and for Grandpa. Because it helps . . . when you are afraid and in the dark. And . . . when you whistle, you can't cry. *(Whispers.)* Goodbye, Grandpa, I . . . I love you.

(TISH *exits L, bravely trying to control her crying. At the same time lights slowly come up so the full stage is seen. The light on* TISH's *area dims out. The stage is bright with soft beautiful colors. The lone whistling of "O Susannah," the same as at the beginning of the play, is heard. There is a moment of a final picture—the living tree standing, as it has through the years, against a beautiful, endless sky. The whistling continues as the curtains close.)*

CURTAIN

REALLY ROSIE
by
Maurice Sendak
Music by Carole King

MAURICE SENDAK, a native New Yorker, was educated at the Art Students'
League, New York City, and in 1977, received an L.H.D. from Boston University. He was awarded a number of honorary degrees, including ones
from Princeton University, Vassar College, and most recently Yale University,
in 1997. He has taught at Yale and the Parson's School of Design, New York
City.

Sendak is generally acknowledged as the leading visionary in children's
literature today. For more than forty years, the books he has written and illustrated have nurtured children and adults alike and challenged established ideas about what children's literature is and should be. His
eighty-plus books have sold more than 7 million copies worldwide and are
available in a dozen languages.

Winner of the 1964 Caldecott Medal for most distinguished picture book
of the year for *Where the Wild Things Are*, Sendak, in 1970, became the first
American illustrator to receive the Hans Christian Andersen Award, given
"in recognition for an author or illustrator's entire body of work." In addi-
tion he has received the American Book Award and the Laura Ingalls Wilder
Medal. In 1990, he became the first recipient of the Empire State Award for
Excellence in Literature for Children, and he received the National Medal of
Arts award from President Clinton in January, 1997.

His career began in 1951, at age twenty-three, when he was introduced to
children's book editor Ursula Nordstrom. In the two decades following the
success of his illustrations for Ruth Krauss's *A Hole Is to Dig* in 1952, Sendak
illustrated more than fifty books, including Else Minarik's *Little Bear* books
and a two-volume edition of Grimms' fairy tales, *The Juniper Tree and Other
Tales from Grimm*.

Sendak's distinctive cross-hatched drawings and elegant painting enhanced many other authors' works and gave him the experience that enabled him to produce his masterpiece, *Where the Wild Things Are*, a book that is included in the top-ten children's book best-sellers of all time. His most recent picture book after *Dear Mili*, in 1988, is *We Are All in the Dumps with Jack and Guy*, which was published in 1993.

Recently Sendak has simultaneously focused his attention on the performing arts, designing highly acclaimed opera productions of Mozart's *The Magic Flute* and *Idomeneo*, Janáček's *The Cunning Little Vixen*, and Prokofiev's *The Love of Three Oranges*. His stage designs for both costumes and scenery of Tchaikovsky's *The Nutcracker* ballet later became the basis of a successful feature film. In addition he has written the libretti for operas based on two of his own books, *Where the Wild Things Are* and *Higglety Pigglety Pop!* In 1975, an animated television special based on his books, *The Sign on Rosie's Door* and *The Nutshell Library*, aired on CBS, and in 1980, *Really Rosie* became an Off-Broadway musical for which he wrote book and lyrics. Currently for "Nick Jr." of the Nickelodeon television channel he is designing *Maurice Sendak's Little Bear* series.

In 1990, during the twentieth anniversary year of the publication of his book *In the Night Kitchen*, Sendak cofounded with Arthur Yorinks, the children's theatre producing company, *The Night Kitchen*, a theatre company devoted entirely to the development of high quality performing arts productions for children. The plan for the nonprofit organization is to commission new works—plays, musical, ballets, and operas—or develop new productions of existing works, and then collaborate with theatres in presenting them.

As artistic director Sendak has said, "We would like *The Night Kitchen* to create and produce material that expands the range of performing arts that reach children. We both share the conviction that children deserve much more in the area of cultural enrichment. *The Night Kitchen* is an extraordinary opportunity to explore many mediums and to extend the boundaries of what is considered suitable for children. We hope to reinvigorate all forms of live theatre for children with the same energy and passion we bring to our books."

REALLY ROSIE

CHARACTERS

Rosie
Rosie's Mother
Kathy
Chicken Soup
Alligator
Pierre
Johnny
Second Mother
Johnny's Mother

Setting: A Brooklyn street with typical attached brick houses. The action takes place on the front steps—the stoop—of ROSIE's *house. And later in the cellar. The time is now, from morning to early evening of a hot July day. [Music Cue 1—Overture]*

ROSIE: Yes. My name is Rosie. I am famous and wonderful and everyone loves me and wants to be me. Who can blame them? *(She sings "Really Rosie" [Music Cue 2].)*

> I'm really Rosie
> And I'm Rosie really
> You'd better believe me
> I'm a great deal
> Believe me. Believe me.
> I'm a star from afar
> Off the golden coast
> Beat that drum. Make that toast.
> To Rosie the most.
> Believe me. Believe me.
> I can sing
> "Tea for two and two for tea"
> I can act
> "To be or not to be"
> I can tap across the Tappan Zee
> Hey, can't you see
> I'm terrific at everything.
> No star shines so bright as me.
> Rosie. Believe me.
> Kids. Believe me.
> Believe me.
> Kids. Believe me.

(Half aloud.) Clap Clap Thank you—Thank you. *(She knocks on step.)* Come in, Mr. Reporter. You're too too kind. How? It's Pond's Italian Face Cream Balm. Makes me look thirty years younger. *[Music Cue 2A—Underscore.]* Why am I here? To make the movie of my life. This is my town. This is my street. A star was born here. Me! It was a long pull, but I definitely made it. Was it hard? Oh, was it hard. The suffering—the hardships, the pain—the laughter *(Music out.)*—the tears. Oh weary, weary. And all that dancing and singing on the coast. What does it all mean? Well, I'm here to find out. To find the real me.

ROSIE'S MOTHER: Rosie! *[Music Cue 3] (Set change.)*

ROSIE: You think it's weird someone as classy as me comes from here? You can say that again. But you have to make peace with your crummy past. My town. My street. My little humble street. Ah, yes. Avenue P—the crossroads of millions of stars. *[Music Cue 4.]* You mean you've never heard of Kathy, Alligator, Johnny, Pierre? Well sweetheart, after they appear in my movie life,—WATCH OUT!—, they'll be the best-known bit players around. Wait and see! My family? Have I forgiven them? I've tried my best. Dad's an old sweety, and my stupid brother, Chicken Soup, he couldn't help being born a loser and a burden to everybody. However, I've never gotten over his loss—such a horrible tragedy. And Mom . . . Well, Mom just . . .

ROSIE'S MOTHER: (Off.) Rosie!!

ROSIE: Drives me bananas. [Music Cue 5.]

KATHY: Hey Rosie, where are you already?

MOTHER: You're not going anywhere without your brother, Chicken Soup, and that's that.

ROSIE: He's ruining my life!

MOTHER: Rosie!

ROSIE: No!

CHICKEN SOUP: Hey Rosie, you're gonna get it. (ROSIE pushes him.) Ma-Ma! Rosie's killing me!

MOTHER: Just let me get my hands . . .

ALLIGATOR: Hey Kathy, did you hear who died?

KATHY: (Pointing towards window.) Yeah. It's Rosie or maybe Chicken Soup.

ALLIGATOR: Hey, Pierre, did you hear who died?

PIERRE: Yeah, a dumb alligator.

ALLIGATOR: No, Kathy says . . .

PIERRE: I don't care.

CHICKEN SOUP: Rosie, you better take me or else!

ROSIE: I'll take you and throw you in the garbage!

CHICKEN SOUP: (Crying.) Ma-Ma! Rosie said . . .

(Crash. All the kids point to window, giggle, and hold their forefingers up to their lips, making shushing noises.)

JOHNNY: Poor Rosie, she should have stayed an only child.

KATHY: Yeah, she forgot to tell her mother, I guess.

JOHNNY: It's not too late. I just read about this new book called Sibling Robbery. It tells you ten quick ways to lose your kid brother.

KATHY: (Sarcastically.) Who wrote it? Dracula?

PIERRE: He did—Johnny, the creep.

JOHNNY: No—I mean it—I can't remember . . .

ALL THREE: Creep!

(Silhouettes appear at window.)

MOTHER: (Conciliatory.) Rosie, why do you make trouble? Why can't you be like Chicken Soup? He makes no trouble.

ROSIE: Yeah, he only makes me sick!

MOTHER: Don't be smart!

ROSIE: I can't help it!

MOTHER: When your father comes home . . .

ROSIE: He'll go straight to sleep like always.

MOTHER: That's enough, big mouth! Take your brother downstairs like I told you—right now!

ROSIE: No!

MOTHER: Now!

(Crash.)

CHICKEN SOUP: Ma-Ma!

ALLIGATOR: Is Chicken Soup dead now?

JOHNNY: Maybe Rosie shoved him into the oven and turned it up to one million degrees.

PIERRE: And maybe they'll shove you into the nut house, creep. *[Music Cue 6]* (JOHNNY, *insulted, sits away from the others and reads his book.* ROSIE *peers out the window and overhears.)*

ALLIGATOR: If Rosie's such a big shot, how come she's gotta kid brother?

KATHY: Dumb Alligator, who says she's a big shot?

PIERRE: Rosie's a big nothing!

ALLIGATOR: Yeah—let's make believe she's dead!

KATHY: Yeah—let's make believe we can't even see her.

PIERRE: Yeah—like she's invisible!

JOHNNY: Creeps!

ROSIE: Oh, excuse me, Mr. Reporter—that was just a temporary indisposition in my private life. You know . . . the pain part. Even your best friends can give you a big pain.

MOTHER: Rosie, are you listening? Chicken Soup is coming. Hold his hand tight and don't let him wander away again. He's the only brother you've got.

ROSIE: *(Sings.)*

> Oh! such sufferin'
> My days are full of sufferin'
> and . . .

MOTHER: Play nice!

KATHY: Hey, Rosie, what are we going to do today? Can we play something?

PIERRE: Why don't you play dead?

KATHY: Oh, shut up, stupid. And anyway, nobody wants to play with you.

PIERRE: I don't care.

ALLIGATOR: Did you hear who died?

KATHY: Your boring father turned into a real alligator and ate your boring mother.

ROSIE: No, he ate a boring little kid brother.

KATHY: Hey, killer, if you're a real alligator, let's see you eat up Chicken Soup. *(Kids yell.)*

SECOND MOTHER: Listen everybody, if you can't talk nice, go park on your own property.

ROSIE'S MOTHER: Isn't it something, the mouthpieces on these kids today?

SECOND MOTHER: It's no use being nice. They don't appreciate nice.

ROSIE'S MOTHER: Rosie, are you holding on to your brother? Are you looking to get crippled? *[Music Cue 7]*

(During this song CHICKEN SOUP *climbs into a large cardboard box that* ROSIE *uses for an assortment of costumes.)*

ROSIE: *(Sings "Simple Humble Neighborhood.")*

        Here's where it all began,
        Here's where I heard that beat,
        Here's where I tapped that tap
        With my natural rhythm feet.
        In my simple humble neighborhood
        On my simple humble street.
        Here's where the dreams I had
        Were crowed on a stoop,
        Were pecked and pushed and hustled
        Just like chickens in a coop.
        Life wasn't always neat.
        In my simple humble neighborhood
        On my simple humble street.

        Here's where I made up folks,
        Who came to visit me.
        Not just ordinary folks
        Coming unexpectedly,
        Talent scouts, producers, directors,
        Glamour boys.
        In other words, the hoy-poloys,
        The grand elite.
        To make them green with envy.
        (In my simple humble neighborhood
        On my simple humble street.)
        Everybody sing with me! repeat ( )
        Louder! repeat ( )

*(*ROSIE *watches* CHICKEN SOUP *crawling off under the box; she runs to box and shouts between phrases of the other kids' singing.)*

    Don't go too far!

    Now by myself! *REPEAT ( )*

PIERRE: Boring!

JOHNNY: Hey, Rosie, I read this wierd story how this kid wandered away, and nobody ever knew what happened to him. And two weeks later when everybody forgot already, and the parents even got a new kid, the cops found him crazy in the forest, stinking and wild, and they shot him dead for his own good. I read about it in this interesting book.

OTHERS: Who cares! *[Music Cue 7A—Bell Tone.]*

ROSIE: I think we got a movie here.

ALLIGATOR: Did you hear who died?

KATHY: This conversation is making me nauseous.

JOHNNY: My father says we aren't here to enjoy ourselves.

PIERRE: I don't care.

KATHY: Remember Rita—when she caught sleeping sickness on Rosie's roof . . . That was fun.

ALLIGATOR: We can go watch my father in the bathtub eating flies.

KATHY: Oh sure, I just bet.

PIERRE: Boring, boring, boring. . . .

JOHNNY: I read this article that when people are too leisurely, they go nuts on the spot, because if anything is good at all, it's gotta get terrible fast. It even says when you retire, you're supposed to be enjoying yourself, that's the kiss of death. Because you relax in the pool too much, and you drown. You know, when you retire. . . .

OTHERS: Who cares! *[Music Cue 7B—Underscore.]*

ROSIE: Now let me tell you why I've asked you all to come here today. I'm going to make a movie of my life. It'll be a very classy movie, mostly about me and those beloved few who helped me up the ladder of success: Johnny, Alligator, Kathy, Pierre, and my darling Chicken Soup.

ALLIGATOR: Where's your brother? What happened to Chicken Soup?

ROSIE: That's the name of my movie. *Did You Hear What Happened to Chicken Soup?* And it's all true.

KATHY: Oh, come on, Rosie, we did your true life movie a hundred times already.

ROSIE: Kathy, we did not.

KATHY: What about yesterday when you got that incurable disease and your boyfriend, the blind doctor, operates on the wrong patient, and then you find out you're really brother and sister, so you both jump out of the fourteenth floor of the Brooklyn Jewish Hospital.

PIERRE: That was called: *We Are Inseparable.*

ROSIE: That was a great movie. But this new one is even more inside. It's the story of my struggle to find joy at the top by overcoming the untimely and mostly ghastly disappearance of my stupid, crippled brother.

JOHNNY: Hey, Rosie, there's this much better movie where the kidnappers cut up this kid and bury him in a shoe box. Is that what happened to Chicken Soup?

ROSIE: You'll find out OK if I let you act in my picture. *(The kids are hopelessly hooked; they lean forward eagerly, waiting for ROSIE to "haul" them in. She smells success and is triumphant.)* OK, my movie is about to start! Screen tests, everybody!

ALLIGATOR: Now me, Rosie?

ROSIE: Now me what?

ALLIGATOR: You know, my screen test.

ROSIE: What do you do?

ALLIGATOR: Oh, you know, Rosie.

ROSIE: Yeah. The alphabet. Boring.

ALLIGATOR: I'm terrific.

ROSIE: Uhh, huh.

ALLIGATOR: Oh, please, Rosie?

ROSIE: OK. OK. Take one.

ALLIGATOR: *(Sings "Alligators All Around" [Music Cue 8].)*

A *Alligators all around*
B *Bursting balloons*
C *Catching colds*
D *Doing dishes*
E *Entertaining elephants*
F *Forever fooling*
G *Getting giggles*
H *Having headaches*
I *Imitating Indians*
J *Juggling jellybeans*
K *Keeping kangaroos*
L *Looking like lions*
M *Making macaroni*
N *Never napping*
O *Ordering oatmeal*
P *Pushing people*
Q *Quite quarrelsome*
R *Riding reindeer*
S *Shockingly spoiled*
T *Throwing tantrums*
U *Usually upside down*
V *Very vain*
W *Wearing wigs*
X *X-ing x's*
Y *Yackety yacking*
Z *Zippity zounds*
A *Alligators all around*

JOHNNY: Alphabets are for morons.

KATHY: Like you.

PIERRE: Who cares?

ALLIGATOR: Did you hear who died?

JOHNNY: I read in my book . . .

ALLIGATOR: Oh, shut up!

KATHY: Can I be in your real life movie story, Rosie?

ROSIE: Any experience?

KATHY: I can dance Cha Charoo, the Arabian slave girl begging for her life.

ROSIE: Seeing is believing. (KATHY *does a bit of her clumsy dance. Aside.*) I don't believe it. Everybody say ah and ooh. (*Everybody says ah and ooh.* KATHY *dances, spurred on.*) OK, everybody clap and shout hooray. (*Everybody claps and shouts hooray.* KATHY, *breathless, stares eagerly at* ROSIE.) You're hired, Sweetie. You'll be my secretary. (ROSIE *stares at* JOHNNY.) Well, who's next?

JOHNNY: Not me!

ROSIE: How come?

JOHNNY: Just because, that's how come. And anyway I looked up screen tests once in *The Reader's Digest Encyclopedia,* and it said most famous actors kill themselves because they don't pass their first screen test.

ALLIGATOR: How did they get famous then?

JOHNNY: It didn't say.

KATHY: You don't have to worry about getting famous. There's no Academy Award for creeps.

JOHNNY: I could be famous all I want, Miss Doo Doo Head, but it doesn't pay because the world loves a star too much, and nobody ever leaves him alone, and he can't call his life his own anymore.

ROSIE: Let's think up a screen test for Johnny where he's famous and nobody wants him.

PIERRE: Maybe he can play the leading man in *Did You Hear What Happened to Chicken Soup?*

KATHY: Yeah, and he's married to Rosie, and she dies right away. (ROSIE *stares hard at* KATHY.)

ALLIGATOR: Can he die, too?

ROSIE: No. It's a romantic horror movie—the leading man loves me a lot, but likes to eat by himself.

KATHY: And be by himself.

PIERRE: And everything by himself—the creep.

ALLIGATOR: Because that's the way he likes it!

JOHNNY: I like it—I like it!

ROSIE: OK. Roll 'em.

JOHNNY: (*Sings "One Was Johnny" [Music Cue 9].*)
    1 Was Johnny who lived by himself
    2 Was a rat who jumped on his shelf
    3 Was a cat who chased the rat
    4 Was a dog who came in and sat
    5 Was a turtle who bit the dog's tail
    6 Was a monkey who brought in the mail
    7 A blackbird pecked poor Johnny's nose
    8 Was a tiger out selling old clothes
    9 Was a robber who took an old shoe
    10 Was a puzzle, what should Johnny do?
    He stood on a chair and said:
    "Here's what I'll do. I'll start to count backwards
    And when I'm through,
    If this house isn't empty, I'll eat all of you!"
    9 Was the robber who left looking pale
    8 Was the tiger who chased him to jail
    7 The blackbird flew off to Havana
    6 Was the monkey who stole a banana
    5 Was the turtle who crawled off to bed
    4 Was the dog who slid home on a sled
    3 Was the cat who pounced on the rat
    2 Was the rat who left with the cat
    1 Was Johnny who lived by himself
    And liked it like that.

KATHY: OK, everybody—shout and go boo.

ROSIE: You'll boo yourself right out of a job, honey. Secretaries are a dime a dozen. (*Turns to* JOHNNY.) Very touching. You're in, darling. (*Turns to* PIERRE.) Now, the star of my movie is this raving maniac. Will you do it, sweetheart?

PIERRE: *(Gives the Bronx Cheer.)* That's what I'm gonna do!

ROSIE: You're terrific, that's real cute. Just leave your number with my secretary.

PIERRE: Don't start with me, Rosie. I don't care what happened to Chicken Soup.

ROSIE: It's a pity you won't be in my life story.

PIERRE: I don't care about your life story, and I don't care what happened to Chicken Soup, and anyway, nothing happened.

ROSIE: Hey, you guys, come on, come on, let's roll 'em. The producer will be here any minute.

PIERRE: Producer? What producer? There's no producer!

ROSIE: No producer! Are you nuts? I have a fantastic producer, and he's coming all the way from Los Angeles to good old Ave. P, now, today, and I need a cast, baby, a cast, or he'll take the whole show away from me.

PIERRE: Dumb!

ROSIE: Oh, what's the use! We could all of us have expense accounts, and free trips back and forth to the Coast.

ALLIGATOR: Could we visit the alligator swamp in Disneyland?

ROSIE: Honey, you could live in Disneyland.

JOHNNY: Why would a producer come all the way to Brooklyn in the middle of the summer?

ROSIE: Because I am a star, sweetheart, and I told him how fantastic you all are, especially Pierre.

PIERRE: I don't care, and anyway, nothing happened to Chicken Soup!

ROSIE: Nothing happened? You gotta be kidding. Agh, it was so horrible, if only he hadn't been ea . . .

PIERRE: He was eaten? Who ate 'im?

ROSIE: Such sufferin'! I'm not lyin' . . .

PIERRE: A lion? A lion ate 'im? Hey, wait a minute. That's the story of my life!

ROSIE: Lights! Camera! Action! *[Music Cue 10.]*

PIERRE: *(Sings "Pierre.")*
> There once was a boy named Pierre
> Who only would say, "I don't care."
> Hear his story, my friends, for you'll find
> at the end that a suitable
> moral lies there.
> One day his mother said
> When Pierre climbed out of bed,
> "Good Morning, darling boy, you are my only joy."
> Pierre said, "I don't care."
>
> "What would you like to eat?"
> "I don't care."
> "Some lovely Cream of Wheat?"
> "I don't care."
> "Don't sit backwards on your chair"

"I don't care."
"Or pour syrup on your hair."
"I don't care."
"You are acting like a clown."
"I don't care."
"And we have to go to town."
"I don't care."
"Don't you want to come my dear?"
"I don't care."
"Would you rather stay right here?"
"I don't care."
So his mother left him there.

His father said, "Get off your head
Or I will march you up to bed."
Pierre said, "I don't care."
"I would think that you could see."
"I don't care."
"Your head is where your feet should be."
"I don't care."
"If you keep standing upside down."
"I don't care."
"We'll never ever get to town."
"I don't care."
"If you would only say I care."
"I don't care."
"I'd let you fold the folding chair."
"I don't care."
So his parents left him there.
They didn't take him anywhere.

Now as the night began to fall
A hungry lion paid a call
He looked Pierre right in the eye
And asked him if he'd like to die
Pierre said, "I don't care."
"I can eat you, don't you see."
"I don't care."
"And you will be inside of me."
"I don't care."
"Then you won't have to bother."
"I don't care."
"With a mother and a father."
"I don't care."
"Is that all you have to say?"
"I don't care."
"Then I'll eat you if I may."
"I don't care."
So the lion ate Pierre.

Arriving at home at six o'clock
His parents had a dreadful shock.

They found the lion sick in bed
And cried, "Pierre is surely dead."
They pulled the lion by the hair
And hit him with a folding chair.
His mother asked, "Where is Pierre?"
And the lion answered, "I don't care."
His father said, "Pierre's in there."

They rushed the lion into town.
The doctor shook him up and down
And when the lion gave a roar
Pierre fell out upon the floor.

He rubbed his eyes and scratched his head
And laughed because he wasn't dead.
His mother cried and held him tight.
His father asked, "Are you alright?"
Pierre said, "I am feeling fine.
Please take me home. It's half past nine."
The lion said, "If you would care
To climb on me I'll take you there."
Then everyone looked at Pierre
Who shouted, "Yes indeed I care."
The lion took them home to rest
And stayed on as a weekend guest.
The moral of Pierre is: care!

JOHNNY: Hey, Rosie, I think I'm going to like being a star.

KATHY: Don't let him, Rosie. He was the worst Pierre's father we ever had.

ALLIGATOR: Johnny just hasn't got it.

PIERRE: Stunk!!

JOHNNY: Boy, look who's talking. That's not fair. That was the stupidest Pierre's mother anyone ever saw.

PIERRE: Stunk!

KATHY: That's how much you know. Pierre's mother is supposed to be stupid.

PIERRE: Stunk!

JOHNNY and KATHY: Oh, shut up, crazy head.

ALLIGATOR: Johnny, don't feel bad just because you haven't got it.

JOHNNY: You want all those alligator teeth knocked out of your head?

KATHY: Get lost, loser! *[Music Cue 11.]* *(They all begin to argue, scream and push.)*

ROSIE: Knock it off! Knock it off! You're a pack of animals! We have a movie to get ready and just look at you—look at you! If there were time, I'd hire a whole new company, but I'm stuck with you maniacs, hear me, stuck! What would you do without me? *(Music stops.)*

KATHY: Listen, Rosie, what would you do without us?

PIERRE: Yeah, who would act in all your dopey movies?

JOHNNY: My mother says we shouldn't play with you because you over-stimulate us.

ALLIGATOR: Yeah—and that's very bad for our stomachs.

ROSIE: *(Sings "Screaming and Yelling.")*

> *When everybody screams and yells,*
> *Who calms them down?*
> *Who rings their bells?*
> *When everybody screams and yells,*
> *The enchanted one—that's me.*
>
> *When everybody screams and yells,*
> *There's nothing to do*
> *There's nothing to see*
> *Who dreams up a place they'd like to be?*
> *The enchanted one—that's me.*
>
> *It takes personality*
> *A lot of personality*
> *To make them see it my way.*
> *It takes personality*
> *More personality*
> *To turn twelve boring hours*
> *Into a fascinating day.*
>
> *I can do it*
> *That's a fact.*
> *I can do it*
> *Don't you see*
> *And I'll do it all for free.*
> *Do you know*
> *Can you guess?*
> *Who I simply have to be?*
>
> *Stop screaming and yelling*
> *I'll tell you already*
> *Stop screaming and yelling*
> *And screaming and yelling*
> *And screaming and yelling*
> *The enchanted one*
> *That's me!*

(At the end of the song, all kids are on stoop. ROSIE *slowly wheels around, absolutely full of herself and ready to deliver. Her arms are raised and voice hushed.)* OK, OK, everybody. It's time ladies and gentlemen. It's time to tell you about the best movie ever—Did You Hear What Happened to Chicken Soup? [Music Cue 12—Cellar Change.]*

(Loud thunder, crash and lightning. Everyone clusters around ROSIE *and looks up.)*

ROSIE: I don't believe it.

ALLIGATOR: I'm getting all wet.

ROSIE: Quick, everybody, follow me.

KATHY: Where?

ROSIE: To the cellar.

ALLIGATOR: I'm getting wet.

KATHY: Big deal.

JOHNNY: Oh, go soak your head.

PIERRE: (Gives the Bronx Cheer.)

ALLIGATOR: Stop shoving.

KATHY: I think I'm getting pneumonia.

JOHNNY: Good.

PIERRE: I don't care.

ALLIGATOR: Stop pulling me.

KATHY: You dumb alligator.

JOHNNY: This is just like a horror book I read. This is spooky.

PIERRE: So are you.

ALLIGATOR: (Crawling into the cellar. There is general screaming and mêlée.) Anybody here? Anybody dead here?

KATHY: Ech. I hate it here. You could catch cold and drop dead here, and no one would find you ever.

PIERRE: So who cares?

ROSIE: Isn't it terrific down here? The light is perfect.

ALLIGATOR: Where's Chicken Soup?

KATHY: Poor kid, lost in all that rain.

ALLIGATOR: Will he be OK? Won't somebody find him?

PIERRE: Yeah, kidnappers.

JOHNNY: I read in this book how if strangers offer you a bowl of chicken soup from a car you should say no.

KATHY: You shouldn't go with them.

JOHNNY: I know.

PIERRE: I don't care.

KATHY: I betcha he did.

ALLIGATOR: What? What?

KATHY: Chicken Soup went with them and got kidnapped.

JOHNNY: He just couldn't turn it down.

KATHY: Oh my God, I'm sure they got him, and they're holding him for ransom. Oh my God, they'll bury him somewhere.

PIERRE: Alive, I hope.

ALLIGATOR: Maybe something worse even happened. This is a true story. A kid I know got caught in a storm, and the rain was like a river, and it sucked him down the sewer where the alligators from Florida ate him up. And his parents never even found a piece of his hair. (Beginning to cry.) Where's Chicken Soup? Why doesn't he come down here?

PIERRE: Maybe he is here. Hey, Rosie, your brother isn't buried alive here . . . ?

ROSIE: Nope. That's not what happened.

PIERRE: You know everything, I suppose.

ROSIE: I was there, dummy, I reported it to the police.

OTHERS: What Ro, what?

ROSIE: (*Preens before unseen cameras.*) OK, guys, roll 'em. [*Music Cue 13—"The Ballad of Chicken Soup."*] It was in the dawn, and the mist was hanging over the city. It was horrible. I tried everything, but it was too late. They wrapped him in a garbage bag and took him to the mayor's house and put him in the freezer.

PIERRE: I suppose they're gonna make chicken soup out of him.

ROSIE: They hung a ticket on his toe, and it says how he died.

ALLIGATOR: Please Ro, please tell us what the ticket says.

ROSIE: OK, my pretties, you asked for it. Lights, camera, action. (*She sings "The Ballad of Chicken Soup."*)

> *Today our dear friend Chicken Soup*
> *This very ordinary day*
> *Boiled up a pot of chicken soup*
> *And swallowed it away.*
> *A-lack, a-day.*
> *O-woe, oye-vay*
> *He swallowed it away.*
> *Now listen to what I'm gonna say.*
> *A little bone, a bitty thing*
> *No bigger than my pinky*
> *He swallowed hot*
> *From out that pot*
> *In quicker than a winky.*
> *He gulped that soup*
> *And let out a whoop*
> *And fell down croaking on the stoop*
> *And he choked*
> *And he sagged*
> *And he smothered*
> *And he gagged*
> *And he let out a scream*
> *And he let out a moan*
> *And he cried*
> *'Cause he died*
> *From choking on a bone*
> *On such an ordinary day like today.*

KATHY: I can't believe it.

ALLIGATOR: Isn't it awful?

JOHNNY: I can't believe it. Tell us again.

OTHERS: Again. Again. Do it again, Rosie.

ROSIE: Sure. (*She sings.*)

> *And he choked*
> *And he sagged*
> *And he smothered*
> *And he gagged*
> *And he let out a scream*

> *And he let out a moan*
> *And he cried*
> *'Cause he died*
> *From choking on a bone*
> *On such an ordinary day like today.*

ALL:

> *A-lack, a-day*
> *O-woe, oye-vay*
> *On an ordinary day*
> *Chicken Soup passed away.*

ALLIGATOR: Are we really dead?

PIERRE: Boring.

JOHNNY: Big deal.

KATHY: I'm all wet. I have to go home.

ROSIE: Wait a minute. We haven't even shot coming attractions yet.

ALLIGATOR: Who's she?

PIERRE: Who cares?

JOHNNY: Who needs it?

ROSIE: Who needs it! Are you kidding? Everybody knows coming attractions is how stars are born.

ALLIGATOR: Do alligators get born out of coming attractions?

PIERRE: Nobody gets born by becoming attractions.

ROSIE: Stars do! It's better than being in a real movie even. Yes, coming attractions is a big advertisement just for yourself.

ALLIGATOR: And you get richer and richer. And the bucks are bigger.

PIERRE: And everybody loves you to tiny little pieces.

JOHNNY: They don't let you alone until you are kissed all to death.

KATHY: I want to be coming attractions.

ROSIE: Well . . .

KATHY: I'm sick of secretary.

ROSIE: I don't know.

KATHY: Look, Rosie, if you don't let me be coming attractions, I'll tell your mother you lost Chicken Soup, and you'll get crippled. I will, Rosie, I swear, I really will.

ROSIE: You'd love that wouldn't you, you rotten snitch.

PIERRE: She's a great klutz too.

ALLIGATOR: And a terrific biter. She bites till she gets blood. I know from experience.

ROSIE: *(Thinking aloud.)* Hmm, a biter, a klutz, and a vicious blood-sucking snitcher. We just might have something here.

PIERRE: Yeah, something disgusting.

ROSIE: Right! A vampire coming attraction.

JOHNNY: Just like that TV movie where that gorgeous dame bites all the men in her life, and she gets blood all over herself, and she lives in a swell castle, rent-free, where she wears that dress that shows everything, and dies with all those candles burning around her, with the wood in her chest, screaming her head off?

KATHY: I'm a swell biter, Rosie, and rotten through and through; I'm perfect for the job.

ROSIE: OK kids, let's give it a shot. *[Music Cue 14.]*

KATHY: *(Sings THE AWFUL TRUTH.)*

> *The awful truth concerning me*
> *The creature-feature mystery*
> *Is simply this:*
> *In the worst way*
> *I wanna play*
> *Mrs. Dracula.*
> *The challenge is tough*
> *But I know I got the stuff*
> *To be just spectacular.*
> *Can't you see it in the lights?*
> *Kathy Grossman meets Dracula.*
> *So close your eyes and visualize:*
> *Me in a cape*
> *And fangs in my head*
> *Loving a guy who's mostly dead.*
> *I don't see him often*
> *'Cause he sleeps in a coffin.*
> *Nothing could be zanier*
> *Than our lives in Translyvania*
> *At six in the morning*
> *When my sweety is yawning*
> *I feed all the bats*
> *A mush made of rats.*
> *Then I tidy the tomb*
> *Cover all the trapdoors*
> *And wash any old blood stains*
> *Offa the floors.*
> *Don't you see?*
> *This juicy part was*
> *Meant for me.*
> *I got the looks*
> *I got the style*
> *I got bloodshot eyes*
> *And a ghastly smile.*
> *It's the dream of my life*
> *To play Dracula's wife.*
> *The reviews will all rave:*
> *This movie's a whopper,*
> *A super show-stopper*
> *And no one can top her,*
> *Not Kathy!*
> *Dear Academy, take note,*
> *I should get the Oscar vote.*
> *If I don't, I'll bite your throat.*

Signing off now
Quote, unquote.

Rosie, I was pretty good, wasn't I? What do you think, Rosie?

ROSIE: It'll never work, kid.

(We hear the voices of the mothers from offstage.)

JOHNNY'S MOTHER: Johnny, where are you?

ROSIE'S MOTHER: Rosie, is your brother with you? Did you ever see anything like these kids? It's pouring, and they could catch pneumonia, but they don't come home.

JOHNNY'S MOTHER: Of course not. And Johnny has an appointment with his orthodontist at 2:00, and I have to go through this baloney with him every time.

KATHY'S MOTHER: Kathy! Where the hell are you?

JOHNNY'S MOTHER: It's just no use.

KATHY'S MOTHER: I'll cripple her.

ROSIE'S MOTHER: If you find mine, cripple them too.

KATHY'S MOTHER: With pleasure.

JOHNNY'S MOTHER: Johnny!

ALLIGATOR: Maybe we should hide in the trunk.

JOHNNY: You should never hide in a trunk in the cellar because you could get locked inside forever and die the world's worst death.

[*Music Cue 15—Very Far Away.*]

KATHY:

> *Play nice, Kathy, Mama said,*
> *Or I'll punch your arm and bust your head.*
> *Play nice, Kathy, with your brother*
> *Or I'll break one leg and then the other.*
> *Play nice, darling, play nice, dear,*
> *But quiet, outside, over there.*
> *If I could wish one wish today*
> *I'd wish me very far away.*

ALLIGATOR:

> *I hear that very far away*
> *Wild alligators like to play*
> *In jungle swamps—in Tarzan land*
> *They'll bite my dopey sister's hand*
> *For punching me the other day.*
> *I'll meet another alligator*
> *Who is another sister hater*
> *And we'll hitch to very far away.*

JOHNNY:

> *I read in my book that desert isles*
> *Are very far away.*
> *You can only go by private ship*

> And pay for just a one-way trip.
> There's just one house up in a tree,
> A tiny place the size of me.
> I'll pack my books by Labor Day
> And sail to quiet far away.

PIERRE:

> If Mama and Papa would let me play
> Inside my lion friend all day
> I'd learn to roar, I'd learn to bite
> I'd run through Brooklyn streets all night.
> I'd hide inside my lion lair
> And think up good ideas in there,
> Like a jungle safari to Sheepshead Bay
> Just me and my lion so far away.

ROSIE:

> I dreamed the sound of rushing hoof,
> A clattering clop on the top of my roof
> The producer has come on his horse silver gray.
> To take me away to the land of L.A.
> To make me a star in the film of my life.
> Me, Rosie, in very far away.

PIERRE and JOHNNY: To Hollywood, my darling! (*[Music Cue 16—Movie Sequence.] Musical Interlude—The kids enact the fantasy of* ROSIE'S *movie. Silent Movie Interlude—* ALLIGATOR *is cameraman.* ROSIE *is Western heroine.* KATHY *is "other woman."* PIERRE *is macho cowboy who throws* ROSIE *over for* KATHY. JOHNNY *is typical Western bartender.* ROSIE *catches* PIERRE *and* KATHY *kissing. She kills* KATHY, *then herself.* PIERRE *flees. The end. [Music Cue 16A—Movie Bows].*)

MOTHER: Those kids, where are they? *[Music Cue 17—Very Far Away.]*

ALL:

> Mama's in the window
> And Papa's in the shop.
> Let's live inside a movie
> And never, ever stop.
> Our theatre's twice around the block
> Two cellar windows from the right.
> Our movie runs all through the day
> And even through the night.
> Saturday's a matinee
> Just look for very far away.

ALLIGATOR: Gee, it stopped raining.

KATHY: We gotta go now.

ROSIE: What are you telling me, we all gotta go? Don't I know we gotta go? But not just this second. Didn't I tell you the producer's coming? These big shots don't have time for a lot of chitchat. They think fast, they move fast, they decide fast, and if you guys aren't here, that's it, you're out.

OTHERS: What do we have to do, Rosie?

ROSIE: We have to put a fantastic finale number together for my life movie, something that will knock 'em dead.

KATHY: You mean like . . .

ROSIE: Yeah. A gigantic extravaganza—the big finish—with a cast of thousands—with diving and swimming and flying and eating, and it's about everything—just everything—the whole year, and everybody gets to be a month, and probably even a month and a half.

ALLIGATOR: Can I . . . ?

ROSIE: Yes, sweetheart, you're gonna be March and part of July and November, and all of September. September is a special treat just for you. Wait till you see.

ALLIGATOR: Hooray for me.

ROSIE: And Kathy—you're gonna love this—you're May and October. Don't you just love it?

KATHY: Oh, I love it, I love it!

PIERRE: I don't.

ROSIE: And you, honey, you're perfect for August and half of November. You have to be hot and cold, and that's the hardest part of all.

PIERRE: Well . . .

ROSIE: Great! And good old Johnny is all of April and a piece of July. And *(She sighs.)* I'm just gonna have to be all the rest.

PIERRE: How come you . . . ?

ROSIE: And the costumes, wait till you see the costumes. This is a super spectacular, we can have anything. There will be rivers and storms, and we'll skate on a teacup and sing and . . .

ALLIGATOR: Hey, look! The sun's out, let's play something! *[Music Cue 18— Scene Change.]*

ROSIE: Hey, we haven't finished my movie. We haven't even started it. How can I make a big extravaganza. I can't stand it. The pain part is killing me. Oh, the sufferin', the pain, the sufferin', the pain. . . .

KATHY: Hey, Rosie's gotta big pain!

JOHNNY: Looks like the last stages of coo-cooitis.

KATHY: Oh, I got such a pain—I'm going insane.

ALLIGATOR: Are you Rosie or something?

KATHY: Yeah—I'm Really Rosie and I'm rottin' away . . .
> *Oh, such sufferin',*
> *My days are full of sufferin',*
> *Gimme a Bufferin.*

ROSIE: *(Puts baby blanket over her head and sits on step.)* Oh, Mr. Producer, it's so good to see you. You really look terrific. Me? Ah, you're a doll. Thank you.

KATHY: Who're you talking to, Rosie?

ROSIE: The producer's here.

PIERRE: Producer? What producer? There's no producer.

ROSIE: Quick, everybody, sit down and shut your eyes.

PIERRE: Why?

ROSIE: 'Cause he won't come otherwise.

JOHNNY: I think I hear the leaves moving.

KATHY: I heard a gate shut.

ALLIGATOR: I think I heard a helicopter land.

PIERRE: I think I'm hearing lots of crazies.

OTHERS: Shhh.

KATHY: This is fun.

ROSIE: I know how busy you are. Really? Well, we're ready to fly to the coast whenever you want us. That soon? Well, I think we can do it. Will they let us??? Just let them try and stop us. Do you want me to tell Kathy that? Oh my, she'll love that. Pierre and Johnny and Alligator too? You're a warm and wonderful human being. Do you really have to go? Well, have a safe trip, and please give all my love to your devastating wife. Wave good-bye, everybody. Bon voyage.

OTHERS: Bon voyage!

KATHY: Can we open our eyes now, Rosie?

ROSIE: Yes.

ALLIGATOR: I didn't see him.

JOHNNY: You're eyes were shut, stupid.

ALLIGATOR: He sure was quiet.

KATHY: I saw him a little bit—I couldn't help it. Oh, he was stunning in those white pants and everything, wasn't he, Rosie?

ROSIE: Didn't you hear me tell him he looked terrific?

JOHNNY: I wish I was like that.

KATHY: Did you see those teeth? Wow, were they big and white. I betcha he bites you when he doesn't like your work.

ALLIGATOR: Yeah, but when he likes your work, he loves you a lot, and he makes you very, very rich.

PIERRE: I wonder how much he makes after taxes.

ROSIE: You can't imagine. Can you figure how much that leisure suit cost? A lot, and you better believe it.

KATHY: I think I could love a man like that.

ALLIGATOR and PIERRE: Who couldn't?

ROSIE: OK, gang, he didn't leave us much time. Let's start rehearsing right now.

ALLIGATOR: Oh God, it's five o'clock. I'll get killed. (*He leaves.*)

PIERRE: Me, too. So long, Ro.

JOHNNY: 'Bye, Ro. (JOHNNY *and* PIERRE *leave.*)

KATHY: It's getting late, Ro. I have to go in. (*She starts to leave, stops and looks back.*) Are you mad at me, Rosie?

ROSIE: Didn't we have a swell time? [*Music Cue 19.*]

KATHY: (*Nodding.*) I liked waiting for the producer best.

ROSIE: (*Dreamily.*) Wasn't he beautiful?

KATHY: (*Eagerly.*) Maybe he'll come again tomorrow?

ROSIE: *(Shrugging.)* Maybe and maybe not.

KATHY: Can I come and wait with you again tomorrow?

ROSIE: Sure.

KATHY: *(Hesitantly.)* I'll come earlier so I can wait longer. So long, Rosie.

ROSIE: So long . . . Mrs. Dracula. Ladies and gentlemen, Really Rosie will now
 sing her big number. *(She sings "Avenue P.")*

> *In dreams*
> *It seems*
> *I always see*
> *Avenue P*
> *As it ought to be*
> *In a four-star movie*
> *Directed by me*
> *And starring, of course,*
> *Yours truly,*
> *Rosie.*
> *In this fabulous movie*
> *You're all gonna see*
> *An entirely different Avenue P.*
> *Imagine me in a jungle gown*
> *And Avenue P a jungle town*
> *With King Kong swinging out of a tree*
> *And carrying me over that junglely Avenue P.*
> *Right!*
> *You don't have to sit*
> *With your face in a droop on the stoop*
> *Cause your mama the boss*
> *Says you better not cross that old Avenue P*
> *In a jungle you are free!*
> *The tom-tom beats, the tiger carouses,*
> *The jungle creeps over the red brick houses.*
> *And for chillers and thrillers,*
> *I train giant gorillas*
> *To chase mamas and papas,*
> *Clippety-cloppety,*
> *Thumping their breasts and roaring:*
> *Get offa my property.*
> *No-one's allowed to say maybe or no.*
> *They gotta get out, they just gotta go.*
> *Right!*

ROSIE'S MOTHER: *(Offstage.)* Rosie!

ROSIE:

> *In dreams*
> *It seems*
> *I always see*
> *Avenue P as it ought to be—*
> *A terrific place for people like me.*
> *You'll see,*
> *I'll make it that way.*
> *Someday.*

(CHICKEN SOUP *has entered in his carton.* ROSIE *lifts the box and finds him there.*)

CHICKEN SOUP: Are you going to kill me now, Rosie?

ROSIE: No, not now. [*Music Cue 20A—Underscore.*] Where have you been? The producer's been waiting and waiting. He even skipped cocktails with his mother uptown just to wait.

CHICKEN SOUP: Why, Rosie?

ROSIE: Because of you, dummy. He wanted you to try out for the big Chicken Soup Finale number in my movie. But he's so mad from waiting I don't think he cares anymore.

CHICKEN SOUP: Chicken Soup is me, Rosie, so I gotta be in the finale. Please, beg him Rosie. Please Ro—let me be in your big finale number with all the costumes and the months and teacups and everything.

ROSIE: OK, I'll ask him. (*Looks up at the "producer."*) How about it Mr. P.? Give the kid a break. (*Momentary pause as she waits for an answer.*) He says OK.

CHICKEN SOUP: Thanks, Rosie.

ROSIE: Now, you listen carefully. This is the chance of a lifetime. I'm sending you out a stupid, boring kid, and I want you to come back a fantastic, bit-player star. [*Music Cue 21.*]

CHICKEN SOUP: Yes, Rosie, I will. I will.

ROSIE: OK. You start out the whole year. Chicken Soup is January!

CHICKEN SOUP: Hooray for me. (*He sings "Chicken Soup with Rice."*)

> In January it's so nice
> While slipping on the sliding ice
> To sip hot chicken soup with rice.
> Sipping once, sipping twice.
> Sipping chicken soup with rice.
>
> In February it will be
> My snowman's anniversary
> With cake for him and soup for me.
> Happy once, happy twice
> Happy chicken soup with rice.
>
> In March the wind blows down the door
> And spills my soup upon the floor.
> It laps it up and roars for more.
> Blowing once, blowing twice
> Blowing chicken soup with rice.
>
> In April I will go away
> To far off Spain or Old Bombay
> And dream about hot soup all day.
> Oh my once, Oh my twice
> Oh my chicken soup with rice.
>
> In May I truly think it best
> To be a robin lightly dressed

Concocting soup inside my nest.
Mix it once, mix it twice
Mix that chicken soup with rice.

In June I saw a charming group
Of roses all begin to droop
I pepped them up with chicken soup.
Sprinkle once, sprinkle twice.
Sprinkle chicken soup with rice.

In July I'll take a peep
Into the cool and fishy deep
Where chicken soup is selling cheap.
Selling once, selling twice
Selling chicken soup with rice.

In August it will be so hot
I will become a cooking pot
Cooking soup, of course, why not?
Cooking once, cooking twice
Cooking chicken soup with rice.

In September for a while
I will ride a crocodile
Down the chicken soupy Nile
Paddle once, paddle twice
Paddle chicken soup with rice.

In October I'll be host
To witches, goblins, and a ghost
I'll serve them chicken soup on toast.
Whoopee once, whoopee twice
Whoopee chicken soup with rice.

In November's gusty gale
I will flop my flippy tail
And spout hot soup, I'll be a whale.
Spouting once, spouting twice,
Spouting chicken soup with rice.

ROSIE: Oh, Mr. Producer, now the big finish!
CHICKEN SOUP:

In December I will be
A baubled bangled Christmas tree
With soup bowls draped all over me.
Merry once, merry twice
Merry chicken soup with rice.

I told you once, I told you twice,
All seasons of the year are nice
For eating chicken soup with rice.

[Music Cue 22—Finale Ultimo (bows).]

[Music Cue 23—Exit Music.]

CURTAIN

SET DESIGN

During the Overture, Show Curtain portrays a triumphant Rosie zooming through a starry sky in an airplane, with the title of the show streaming behind. Curtain opens to a Proscenium Arch that is a replica of typical two-story Brooklyn apartment buildings. Stage Left Proscenium shows the ground floor and the upstairs window where all action related to Rosie, her brother, and her mother takes place. Stage Right Proscenium shows the ground-floor window where Pierre lives—the upstairs window has its shade permanently drawn. There are four step units: one is placed at foot of Stage Left Proscenium and one at foot of Stage Right Proscenium to suggest staircases leading up into (or out of) the apartments; two are mid-stage, representing "stoops" for the children to act out on. Clothesline poles are attached to both mid-stage units, and laundry hanging from the connecting clothesline acts as a curtain for Rosie's various roles. Behind this "set" is a flat backdrop representing a typical middle-class Brooklyn scene. The step units are hollowed out behind and painted an interior color for the cellar scene. The steps are swung around and the poles removed for that scene, and a backdrop depicting a cellar wall with scary shadows drops behind the units. At the end of "Very Far Away: Reprise," the step units are turned around again and the Brooklyn street drop comes in again. There is a complete change for "Chicken Soup with Rice": a fantasy backdrop with cutout fantasy pieces stage right and left. The step units remain. The original Show Curtain closes the show.

THE SECRET GARDEN

Adapted for the stage by
Pamela Sterling

*Based upon the book
by Frances Hodgson Burnett*

Original music by Chris Limber

PAMELA STERLING is the author of *The Secret Garden*, *The Adventures of Nate the Great*, and *Friday's Child*. *The Secret Garden* received Distinguished New Play Award of the American Alliance for Theatre and Education in 1991, and is also listed in *ASSITEJ/USA's International Bibliography of Outstanding Plays for Young Audiences*. Her unpublished scripts, *The Ugly Duckling* and *Scrapbooks*, have received the highest rating in the Unpublished Plays Reading Project of AATE.

As a professional actress, director, and playwright, Sterling has worked for such institutions as Metro Theater Company of St. Louis, Dallas Children's Theatre, Seattle Children's Theatre, Stage One: The Louisville Children's Theatre, Theatre Project Company in St. Louis, the University of Washington, Boston University, and the University of Wisconsin-Madison.

She has served as artistic director of The Muny/Student Theatre Project, The Coterie in Kansas City, and Honolulu Theatre for Youth. She has been the Artistic Director of the Idaho Theatre for Youth in Boise, since March 1996.

Sterling has two degrees from the University of Washington. Her B.F.A. is from the Professional Actor Training Program, and for her M.F.A. degree, in child drama, she studied playwriting with Suzan Zeder and was a recipient of the national Winifred Ward Scholarship.

Pamela Sterling is currently working on an adaptation of Laura Ingalls Wilder's *Little House on the Prairie*, commissioned and produced by Oregon Children's Theatre and recently selected for Stage One's Critics' Circle staged reading series.

What I find most rewarding about writing for young audiences is that they are still open to new experiences. They do not come to the theatre with preconceived ideas of what a play should or should not be. A play can be magical, realistic, sad and funny all at the same time. Worlds can happily collide! In adapting children's literature to the stage I also enjoy revisiting my own childhood and some of my all-time favorite stories.

—PAMELA STERLING

THE SECRET GARDEN

A Play in Three Acts with Music for Five Men and Three Women and One
Man or Woman*

CHARACTERS

Mary Lennox: 10 years old
Mrs. Medlock: middle-aged housekeeper at Misselthwaite Manor
Martha Sowerby: 20 years old, housemaid at Misselthwaite
Dickon Sowerby: 12–16 years old, Martha's brother
Archibald Craven: 40–50 years old, the master of Misselthwaite and
Mary's guardian
Colin Craven: 10 years old, Mary's cousin
Ben Weatherstaff: 60–70 years old, gardener of Misselthwaite
Doctor Craven: 30–40 years old, Mr. Craven's cousin and Colin's doctor
The Robin*: a puppet which may be manipulated by an actor costumed in
period dress and seen by the audience

PLACE:

An unspecified British colony of East India and on the grounds and interior of Misselthwaite Manor in Yorkshire, England.

TIME

1911

ACT ONE

SCENE: MUSIC IN [I, #1], *an eerie East Indian melody plays as the house lights fade, and the stage lights slowly come up. The* COMPANY *enters,* EACH *member taking a line of narration in story theatre style. They surround* MARY *who is by herself center stage.*

NARRATION: When Mary Lennox was sent to Misselthwaite Manor to live with her uncle, everybody said she was the most disagreeable-looking child ever seen.

It was true, too.

She had a little thin face and a little thin body, thin light hair and a sour expression.

Her hair was yellow, and her face was yellow because she had been born in India and had always been ill in one way or another.

(Lights up on MARY.)

NARRATION: One frightfully hot morning when she was about nine years old, Mary awakened feeling very cross, and she became crosser still when she saw that the servant who stood by her bedside was not her Ayah.

MARY: Why did you come? I will not let you stay. Send my Ayah to me.

WOMAN: It is not possible for the Ayah to come to Missy Sahib.

MARY: Send my Ayah to me, or I will beat you! *(*MUSIC OUT. *Sounds of whispering underscore the next lines.* FIGURES *cross and swirl around* MARY, *but no one speaks directly to her.)* Where is my Ayah? *(More whispers.)* Send my Ayah to me! *(Whispers continue, fading out as* COMPANY *exits. A* MAN *and a* WOMAN *remain.)*

MAN: She wandered out into the garden and began to play by herself under a tree near the veranda.

WOMAN: She pretended she was making a flower bed, and she muttered to herself the names she would call her Ayah when she returned. *(*MUSIC IN.*)*

MARY: Pig! Pig! Daughter of pigs! *(Lights up on* MAN *and* WOMAN *who turn to each other . . . Lights should not be up full, and* MAN *and* WOMAN *should be in profile and partly in shadow.)*

WOMAN: Is it so very bad?

MAN: Awfully, Mrs. Lennox. You ought to have gone to the hills two weeks ago.

WOMAN: Oh, I know I ought! I only stayed to go to that silly dinner party. What a fool I was! *(Voices start an eerie wailing.* MAN, WOMAN, *and* MARY *look up.)* What is it?

MAN: Someone has died. You did not tell me the cholera had broken out among your servants.

WOMAN: I did not know! Come with me. Come with me! *(*MAN *and* WOMAN *exit. The wailings grow, underscored by* MUSIC. *Shadowy* FIGURES *cross the stage, ignoring* MARY *who wanders and finally ends in her bedroom, crawling under the covers to shut out the sounds. The wailings and* MUSIC *eventually die down, leaving an even more eerie quiet. Muffled voices are heard which cause* MARY *to lift her head. Two* FIGURES *in white are seen.)*

A MAN: Barney! There is a child here! A child alone! In a place like this. Mercy on us, who is she?

MARY: I am Mary Lennox. I fell asleep when everyone had the cholera, and I have only just wakened up. Why does nobody come?

BARNEY: It is the child no one ever saw. She has actually been forgotten.

MARY: Why was I forgotten? (*Stamps her foot.*) Why does nobody come?

BARNEY: Poor little kid. There is nobody left to come. (MUSIC IN *as* MARY *is taken from her bed and given a black cape and hat with a veil during the following narration.*)

NARRATION: It was in that strange and sudden way that Mary found out she had neither father nor mother left; that they had died and been carried away in the night, and that the few native servants who had not died also had left the house as quickly as they could get out of it, none of them even remembering that there was a Missie Sahib. (MARY *is brought forward, and* COMPANY *surrounds her in a semi-circle.*)

A MAN: Mary knew that she was not going to stay at the English clergyman's house where she was taken at first.

A WOMAN: She did not want to stay. (MARY *sits and begins to pantomime playing in the earth as* COMPANY *chants in rhythm to* MUSIC.*)

COMPANY:

> *Mistress Mary, quite contrary,*
> *How does your garden grow?*
> *With silver bells and cockle shells*
> *And marigolds all in a row!*

MARY: I don't want boys. Go away!

A BOY: You are going to be sent home at the end of the week. And we're glad of it.

MARY: I'm glad of it, too. (*Pause.*) Where is home?

BOY: She doesn't know where home is! It's England, of course. You are going to your uncle. His name is Archibald Craven.

MARY: I don't know anything about him.

BOY: He lives in a great big old house in the country, called Misselthwaite Manor, and no one goes near him. He's a hunchback and he's horrid!

MARY: I don't believe you!

BOY: It doesn't matter whether you believe me or not. It's true!

MARY: It is not!

BOY: Is! (MUSIC IN.)

MARY: Isn't!

BOY: (*Lines overlapping with* MARY'S.) Mistress Mary, quite contrary . . .

MARY: You stop that.

BOY: How does your garden grow.

MARY: Stop it!

BOY: With silver bells and cockle shells and sour maids all in a row! (*He laughs and runs off.* MUSIC *with the sound of a train fading in under as* MARY *is once more brought forward by* MRS. MEDLOCK *and another* WOMAN.)

WOMAN: Mary made the long voyage to England under the care of an officer's wife who was glad to hand the child over to the woman Mr. Archibald Craven sent to meet her in London.

MRS. MEDLOCK: The woman was his housekeeper at Misselthwaite Manor, and her name was Mrs. Medlock. (MUSIC OUT, *train sounds continue.*)

WOMAN: Mary sat in her corner of the railway carriage and looked plain and fretful. (WOMAN *exits.*)

MRS. MEDLOCK: I suppose I may as well tell you something about where you are going to. Do you know anything about your uncle?

MARY: No.

MRS. MEDLOCK: Never heard your father and mother talk about him?

MARY: No.

MRS. MEDLOCK: Hmph . . . I suppose you might as well be told something—to prepare you. You are going to a strange place . . . (*She looks at* MARY *who does not respond.*) What do you think of that?

MARY: Nothing. I know nothing of such things.

MRS. MEDLOCK: Eh! But you are like an old woman . . . Well, it's a grand big place in a gloomy way, and Mr. Craven's proud of it in his way—and that's gloomy enough too. (*Her voice begins to fade as* MUSIC *resumes. She continues to pantomime talking, and* MARY *continues to look out the train window.* MUSIC *continues under the train sounds which also eventually fade, leaving just* MUSIC *under the narration.*) The house is six hundred years old, and it's on the edge of a moor, and there's near a hundred . . .

(COMPANY *enters and set up Misselthwaite during the narration.*)

NARRATION: It sounded like something in a book and it did not make Mary feel cheerful.

A house on the edge of a moor—

Whatsoever a moor was . . .
Sounded dreary.
A man with a crooked back who shut himself up also!
On and on they drove through the darkness. The trees which nearly met overhead made it seem as if they were driving through a long vault.
They drove out of the vault into a clear space and stopped before an immense stone house.
The entrance opened into an enormous hall . . .
Which was so dimly lighted that the faces in the portraits on the walls . . .
And the figures in the suits of armor . . .
Made Mary feel that she did not want to look at them.
Mary Lennox was led up a broad staircase . . .
And down a long corridor . . .
And up a short flight of steps and through another corridor . . .
And another . . .
Until a door opened in a wall and she found herself in a room with a fire in it and supper on a table.

MRS. MEDLOCK: Well, here you are! This room and the next are where you'll live—and you must keep to them. Don't you forget that! *(She exits.)*

NARRATION: It was in this way that Mistress Mary arrived at Misselthwaite Manor. (MUSIC OUT *as* MARY *takes off her cape and hat.)*

And she perhaps had never felt quite so contrary in all her life. (MARY *throws her clothes and herself onto the bed.* MUSIC TAG. *Lights out. End of Scene.)*

SCENE TWO

SCENE: (MUSIC *[I, #2]). The following morning.* MARY *awakens to find* MARTHA, *a cheerful young woman, bustling about the room. She is dusting, polishing the grate on the fireplace, humming a snatch of a song.* MUSIC *fades as* MARTHA *continues to sing. She turns to* MARY *and greets her.*

MARTHA: Eh! Tha's awake at last. I'll wager tha' was fair faintin' from thy trip. Tha's slept a good long time but Mrs. Medlock said . . .

MARY: *(Interrupts her impatiently.)* Who are you?

MARTHA: I'm Martha. Martha Sowerby. An' tha'rt Mistress Mary . . .

MARY: I know who I am and you will call me *Miss* Mary. *(She points out the window.)* What is that?

MARTHA: *(Looking out the window.)* That's the moor. Does tha' like it?

MARY: No, I hate it.

MARTHA: That's because tha'rt not used to it. Tha' thinks it's too big an' bare now, but tha' will like it.

MARY: Do you?

MARTHA: Aye, that I do. It's fair lovely in spring an' summer when th' gorse an' broom an' heather's in flower. It smells o' honey, an' there's such a lot o' fresh air, an' th' sky looks so high, an' th' bees an' skylarks make such a nice noise hummin' an' singin'. Eh! I wouldn't live away from the moor for anythin'.

MARY: Are you going to be my servant?

MARTHA: *(Goes back to her work.)* I'm Mrs. Medlock's servant. An' she's Mr. Craven's. I'm to do the housemaid's work up here an' wait on you a bit. But you won't need much waitin' on.

MARY: Who is going to dress me?

MARTHA: *(Stops a minute to look at* MARY *in amazement.)* Canna' thy dress thysel'?

MARY: What do you mean? I don't understand your language.

MARTHA: Eh! I forgot. Mrs. Medlock told me I'd have to be careful, or you wouldn't understand my Yorkshire. I mean, can't you put on your own clothes?

MARY: No. I never did in my life. My Ayah dressed me, of course.

MARTHA: Well, it's time tha' should learn. My mother always said she couldn't see why grand people's children didn't turn out fair fools, what with nurses an' bein' washed an' dressed an' bein' took out to walk as if they was puppies.

MARY: It is different in India.

MARTHA: I dare say it's because there's such a lot of heathens there instead o' respectable English people. When I heard you was comin' from India, I thought you was a heathen, too.

MARY: (*Spluttering in anger.*) What! What! You thought I was a native!

MARTHA: (*Continuing unruffled.*) Aye. An' I was fair disappointed to see tha' was no different from me, for all tha's so yeller.

MARY: (*Overriding, her anger mounting.*) You—You—Daughter of a pig!

MARTHA: (*Putting her hands on her hips.*) Who are you callin' names? That's no way for a young lady to talk. Why if you was one of my brothers or sisters, I'd give you a good hidin'!

MARY: (*Losing control and working herself into a tantrum.*) You thought I was a native! You dared! You don't know anything about natives. They are not people—they're servants who must salaam to you. (*Throwing herself on the ground and beating the floor.*) You know nothing about India. You know nothing about anything! (*She sobs uncontrollably.*)

MARTHA: (*Alarmed.*) Eh! You mustn't cry like that there! I didn't know you'd be vexed. I don't know anythin' about anythin'—just like you said. I beg your pardon, Miss. Do stop cryin'. (MARY *gradually calms down.*) There, that's a good girl. I'll wager tha'll feel better when tha's had thy breakfast. It's time for thee to get up now. I'll help thee on with thy clothes if tha'll get up off the floor. (*She picks up a dress from the chair and holds it up.* MARY *looks at it with cool approval, then sits on the bed and sticks her feet out.*) What is tha' doin'? Canna' tha' put on thy own shoes?

MARY: My Ayah always did it. It was the custom.

MARTHA: (*Plops the shoes in* MARY'S *lap.*) Hasn't tha' got good sense? Our Susan Ann is twice as sharp as thee, an' she's only four year old. (MUSIC IN [I, #3]). MARY *is stung by this remark. She grabs the shoes and puts them on, getting them on the wrong feet and struggling with the buttons.* MARTHA *watches in amusement for a moment and then begins to help her, speaking as she does so.*) Eh! None of my brothers or sisters would ever get dressed if they waited for someone to do it for 'em. Nor eat, neither. You should see 'em all. There's twelve of us, an' my father only gets sixteen shillin's a week. I can tell you, my mother's put to it to get porridge for 'em all. They tumble about on th' moor an' play there all day, an' Mother says th' air of th' moor fattens 'em. She says she believes they eat th' grass same as th' wild ponies do. (MUSIC OUT.) Our Dickon, he's fourteen years old, and he's got a pony he calls his own.

MARY: I've never had a pet. There were mostly snakes and elephants in India.

MARTHA: Eh! I'll warrant our Dickon could make friends with 'em. He's a kind lad, an' animals likes him. If tha's ready for thy breakfast now, the porridge is still hot.

MARY: I don't want it.

MARTHA: (*Looking at her, speculatively.*) If our children was at this table, they'd clean it bare in five minutes.

MARY: Why?

MARTHA: Why? Because they scarce ever had their stomachs full in their lives.

MARY: Why don't you take it to them?

MARTHA: *(With a touch of pride.)* It's not mine. An' this isn't my day out. I get my day out once a month. Same as the rest. Then I go home an' clean up for Mother an' give her a day's rest.

MARY: I'll have some tea and toast.

MARTHA: *(Removes the porridge and hands MARY the toast.)* When you're finished, you can wrap up warm an' run out an' play. It'll do you good an' give you some stomach for your meat.

MARY: Out? Why should I go out on a day like this?

MARTHA: Well, if tha' doesn't go out, tha'll have to stay in, an' what has tha' got to do?

MARY: Who will go with me?

MARTHA: You'll go by yourself. Our Dickon goes off on the moor by himself an' plays for hours. That's how he made friends with th' pony. He's got sheep on th' moors as knows him, an' birds as comes an' eats out of his hands.

MARY: I guess I'll go out.

MARTHA: Here's thy hat an' coat. Now, if tha' goes round that way, tha'll come to th' gardens. *(She points the way.)* One of th' gardens is locked up. No one has been in it for ten years.

MARY: Why?

MARTHA: *(Pauses for a split second.)* Mr. Craven had it shut up when his wife died. He won't let no one go inside. It was her garden. He locked th' door an' dug a hole and buried th' key.

MARY: I didn't know he had a wife . . . *(Sound of a bell offstage.)*

MARTHA: There's Mrs. Medlock's bell. I must run. Tha'll have to button th' front of thy coat thysel'. *(MARTHA grins at MARY.)* I'm certain tha' can do it. *(MUSIC IN [I, #4]. She leaves, and MARY struggles to put on her coat. She finishes, rather proud of her accomplishment. MUSIC changes to a slightly melancholy theme as she wanders outside and stands looking about, rather lost. A refrain is heard . . . "I know something you don't know . . ." and MARY looks up to see the ROBIN perched on a tree branch. The flute, which is his voice, continues alone, warbling cheerfully. MARY stands still, listening in delight, and as ROBIN finishes, she almost smiles and steps forward, raising her hand.)*

(ROBIN flies away, and MARY drops her hand as BEN WEATHERSTAFF enters, carrying gardening tools. He is surprised by her presence but says nothing, touches his cap and begins to work.)

MARY: What is this place?

BEN: One o' th' kitchen gardens.

MARY: *(Pointing over the wall.)* What is that?

BEN: Another of 'em. There's another on t'other side o' th' wall, and there's th' orchard t'other side of that.

MARY: Can I go in them?

BEN: There's no dog to bite thee. But there's nowt to see.

MARY: What about the other garden?

BEN: What garden?

MARY: The one on the farthest side of the wall. There are trees there. I can see them. A bird with a red breast was sitting on one of them, and he sang.

(MUSIC IN [I, #5]. BEN *stops his work, breaks into an uncharacteristic grin and whistles.* ROBIN *appears.*)

BEN: Where has tha' been, tha' cheeky little beggar? Has tha' begun thy courtin' this early in th' season? Tha'rt too forrard. (ROBIN *chirps . . . Early bird gets the worm . . .*)

MARY: Will he always come when you call him?

BEN: Aye, that he will. He come out of th' nest in th' other garden, an' when first he flew over th' wall, he was too weak to fly back for a few days, an' we got friendly. When he went over th' wall again, th' rest of th' brood was gone, an' he was lonely, an' he come back to me.

MARY: What kind of bird is he?

BEN: Doesn't tha' know? He's a robin redbreast, an' they're the curiousest birds alive. Watch him peckin' about there an' lookin' round at us now an' ag'in. He's a conceited one. (BEN *whispers.*) He likes to hear folks talk about him. (ROBIN *chirps.*) Aye, I'm talkin' about you. (*Chirp.*) He's always comin' to see what I'm plantin'. He knows all the things Mester Craven never troubles hisself to find out. (*Chirp.*) Aye, you're the head gardener, you are.

MARY: Where did the rest of the brood fly to?

BEN: There's no knowin'. The old ones turn 'em out o' their nest an' make 'em fly, an' they're scattered before you know it. This one was a knowin' one, an' he knew he was lonely.

MARY: I'm lonely.

BEN: Art tha' th' little wench from India? (MARY *nods.*) Then no wonder tha'rt lonely. Tha'll be lonelier before tha's done. (*He goes back to work.*)

MARY: What's your name?

BEN: Ben Weatherstaff. I'm lonely mysel' except when he's with me. He's th' only friend I've got.

MARY: I have no friends at all. I never had. My Ayah didn't like me, and I never played with anyone.

BEN: Tha' an' me are a good bit alike. We're neither of us good lookin', an' we're both of us as sour as we look.

MARY: How dare you . . .

BEN: Aye, we've got the same nasty tempers, I'll warrant.

MARY: You . . . you . . .

BEN: Aye?

MARY: Nothing. (BEN *goes back to work.* MARY *stands kicking the ground when suddenly* ROBIN *bursts into a short scrap of song.*) What did he do that for?

BEN: Dang me, if he hasn't took a fancy to thee.

MARY: To me? (ROBIN *chirps.*) Would you make friends with me? (*Chirp.*) Would you? (*Chirp, chirp . . .* ROBIN *continues softly under dialogue.*)

BEN: Why, tha' said that as nice an' human as if tha' was a real child instead of a sharp old woman. Tha' said it almost like Dickon talks to his wild things on th' moor.

MARY: (*Turning to him sharply.*) Do you know Dickon?

BEN: Everybody knows him. Dickon's wanderin' about everywhere. Th' very blackberries and heather bells knows him.

MARY: Does Dickon ever come . . . (ROBIN *finishes his song and flies away.*) He has flown over the wall! (MUSIC IN *[I, #6].*) He has flown into the orchard—he has flown across the other wall—into the garden where there is no door!

BEN: He came out o' th' egg there. If he's courtin', he's makin' up to some young madam of a robin that lives among th' old rose trees there.

MARY: Rose trees? Are there rose trees?

BEN: There was ten year ago.

MARY: I should like to see them. Where is the door? There must be a door somewhere.

BEN: There was ten year ago, but there isn't now.

MARY: There must be.

BEN: None as anyone can find, an' none as is anyone's business. Don't you be a meddlesome wench an' poke your nose where it's no cause to go. Here, I must go on with my work. Get you gone an' play you. (*He leaves.* MUSIC OUT.)

MARY: How can there be no door? There must have been one ten years ago, because Mr. Craven buried the key.

(MUSIC IN *[I, #7]*). ROBIN *appears again, chirping mysteriously.*)

MARY: You know where the door is. I'm sure of it. (ROBIN *chirps again, a little taunting.*) Show me! (ROBIN *chirps indignantly.*) Will you show me? (*Chirp . . . that's better.*) Please? (*Even better.*) Where is the door? (*I have to go now.*) No, don't leave . . . (ROBIN *flies away.*) He's gone. I hope I see him again.

(MUSIC IN *[I, #8] for scene change and underscoring* MARTHA *who delivers the narration as* MARY *returns to her room.*)

MARTHA: At first, each day which passed by for Mary Lennox was exactly like the others. After each breakfast she gazed out of the window across to the huge moor which seemed to spread out on all sides and climb up to the sky, and after she had stared for a while, she realized that if she did not go out she would have to stay in and do nothing—and so she went out. And after a few days spent entirely out of doors, she wakened one morning knowing what it was to be hungry. (MUSIC OUT.)

SCENE THREE

SCENE: *The sound of wind and rain.* MARTHA *looks at* MARY'S *empty plate with satisfaction.*

MARTHA: Tha' got on well enough with that this mornin', didn't tha'?

MARY: It tastes nice today.

MARTHA: You go on playin' out o' doors every day, an' you'll get some flesh on your bones, an' you won't be so yeller.

MARY: (*Wanders to the window.*) I can't go out today.

MARTHA: Aye, listen to th' wind wutherin' round th' house.

MARY: It sounds as if a giant were trying to get inside.

MARTHA: You could bare stand up on th' moor if you was out on it today.

MARY: Where is the library? I think I'll go there.

MARTHA: No, tha' mustn't. If Mrs. Medlock found thee wanderin' about th' house, she'd be very angry.

MARY: I don't care.

MARTHA: Please, Miss Mary. If tha' doesn't care for thysel', think of me. I could lose my place, an' then what would Mother an' the little ones do?

MARY: Oh, very well. But you must stay and talk to me.

MARTHA: I have my work to do.

MARY: Please? Just for a little while? I . . . I'd like you to.

MARTHA: Well, p'raps Mrs. Medlock won't miss me if I stay with thee a while. (MARY sits on her bed. MARTHA sits beside her.)

MARY: Martha, why did Mr. Craven hate the garden?

MARTHA: Art tha' thinkin' about th' garden yet? I knew tha' would. That was just th' same with me when I first heard about it.

MARY: Why did he hate it?

MARTHA: Mind, Mrs. Medlock said it's not to be talked about. That's Mr. Craven's orders. His troubles are none servants' business, he says. But for the garden he wouldn't be like he is. (MUSIC IN [I, #9].) It was Mrs. Craven's garden that she had made when first they were married, an' she just loved it, an' they used to tend the flowers themselves. Him an' her used to go in an' shut th' door an' stay there hours an' hours. An' she was just a bit of a girl, an' there was an old tree branch bent like a seat on it. An' she made roses grow over it, an' she used to sit there. But one day when she was sittin' there, th' branch broke, an' she fell on th' ground an' was hurt so bad that next day she died. Th' doctors thought he'd go out o' his mind an' die too. That's why he hates it. No one's gone in since, an' he won't let anyone talk about it.

MARY: I see. (MUSIC OUT. *The wind wuthers some more. Underneath the sound is heard a faint whimpering.*) Do you hear anyone crying?

MARTHA: It's th' wind. Sometimes it sounds like as if someone was lost on th' moor an' wailin'. It's got all sorts o' sounds.

MARY: But, listen—It's in the house—down one of those long corridors. It sounds like a child.

MARTHA: (*Stubbornly.*) It's th' wind. An' if it isn't, it's little Betty Butterworth, th' scullery maid. She's had th' toothache all day. There's Mrs. Medlock's bell. I must be goin'.

MARY: Martha . . . (MARY *tries to stop her, but* MARTHA *is gone.* MARY *wanders her room, goes to the window and looks out. The wind rises, and suddenly a draft blows open her door. The wind dies down, and* MARY *hears a cry again.*) There! It is someone crying! And it isn't a grown-up person. (*She goes to the door.*) I wonder if there really are a hundred rooms in this house. (*She steps outside of the room into the hallway. She wanders through the corridors . . . pools of lights or panels which turn. She continues to wander. Stops, confused.*) I don't know which way to go. How still everything is. (*The cry is heard once more.*) The crying! It's nearer than it was. And it is crying!

(MARY *puts her hand near a panel with a tapestry, pulls back the curtain and discovers a door behind the tapestry.* MRS. MEDLOCK *appears behind her.*)

MRS. MEDLOCK: What are you doing here? What did I tell you?

MARY: I turned round the wrong corner, and I heard someone crying.

MRS. MEDLOCK: You didn't hear anything of the sort. You come along back to your own room, or I'll box your ears! *(She takes* MARY *roughly by the arm and hustles her back to her room; the accompanying* MUSIC *becomes faster and rougher, stopping abruptly with* MRS. MEDLOCK's *line.)* Now you stay where you're told to stay, or you'll find yourself locked up. The master had better get you a governess, same as he said he would. You're one that needs someone to look sharp after you. I've got enough to do. *(She slams the door behind her, leaving* MARY *grinding her teeth in rage.)*

MARY: There was someone crying—there was—there was! *(*MUSICAL BUT-TON *to emphasize the end of the scene, [I, #10].)*

SCENE FOUR

SCENE: MUSIC *[I, #11] underscores scene change and narration. Scene Four may be done outside.*

MARTHA: Two days later when Mary looked out her window, she could scarce believe her eyes . . .

MARY: Look at the moor! Martha, come and look!

MARTHA: Aye. Th' storm's over for a bit. It does that at this time o' year. Eh! It was pretty this mornin' when I come across th' moor.

MARY: Did you enjoy your day at home?

MARTHA: That I did. An' Mother was that glad to see me, too. We had all the bakin' an' washin' done early in th' day, an' then we made each of the children a dough cake with a bit of brown sugar in it. An' in th' evenin' we sat around th' fire, and I told 'em all about you.

MARY: About me?

MARTHA: Aye. They wanted to know all about the Indians an' about th' ship you came in. I couldn't tell 'em enough.

MARY: Did Dickon and your mother like to hear you talk about me?

MARTHA: Why, our Dickon's eyes nearly started out o' his head, they got that round. But Mother, she was put out about your seemin' to be all by your-self like. She said, "Hasn't Mr. Craven got no governess for her, nor no nurse?"

MARY: I don't want a governess.

MARTHA: Mother said to me, she said, "Martha, you just think how'd you feel yourself, wanderin' about a big place like that alone, an' no mother. You do your best to cheer her up." An' I said I would. *(Pause.)*

MARY: You do cheer me up. I like to hear you talk. *(Another pause as* MARY *and* MARTHA *look at each other shyly.)*

MARTHA: What does tha' think? I've brought thee a present.

MARY: A present?

MARTHA: *(Going to her carpetbag and rummaging through.)* A man was drivin' across th' moor peddlin', and I was sendin' him away because we had no money to buy anythin', when Mother sees th' skippin' ropes with red an' blue handles. She says to me, "Martha," she says, "tha's brought me tha' wages like a good lass, an' I've got four places to put every penny, but I'm just goin' to take tuppence out of it to buy that child a skippin' rope," an' she bought one, an' here it is! *(She displays it proudly.)*

MARY: What is it for?

MARTHA: For! Does tha' mean that they've not got skippin' ropes in India for all they've got elephants and tigers an' camels? This is what it's for, just you watch me. *(Skipping* MUSIC IN *[I, #12] as she expertly displays her prowess, only getting a little out of breath.)* I've skipped as much as five hundred when I was twelve, but I wasn't as fat then as I am now, an' I was in practice.

MARY: Do you think I could ever skip like that?

MARTHA: You just try it. *(She hands* MARY *the rope, and* MARY *gives it a try, only stumbling a few times.)* A skippin' rope's the sensiblest toy a child can have, that's what Mother says.

MARY: I think I like your mother.

MARTHA: I should think tha' would . . . Go on now.

MARY: *(Starts out the door, then stops and turns to* MARTHA.*)* Martha, they were your wages. It was your two pence really . . . Thank you. *(She holds out her hand.* MARTHA *shakes it awkwardly.)*

MARTHA: Eh! Tha'rt a queer old womanish thing. If tha'd been our 'Lizabeth Ellen, tha'd have given me a kiss.

MARY: *(With a touch of alarm.)* Do you want me to kiss you?

MARTHA: *(Laughs and puts her hands on* MARY's *shoulders.)* Nay, not me. If tha' was different, p'raps tha'd want to thysel'. But tha' isn't. Run off an' play with thy rope now. *(As* MARTHA *watches,* MARY *begins to skip.* MARTHA *exits, and* MARY *skips to the garden path.)*

(BEN enters, and he and MARY *almost collide.)*

BEN: Well, upon my word! P'raps tha'rt a young one after all, an' p'raps tha's got child's blood in thy veins instead of sour buttermilk. Tha's skipped red into thy cheeks as sure as my name's Ben Weatherstaff. I wouldn't ha' believed tha' could do it.

MARY: I've never skipped before. I can only go up to twenty.

BEN: Tha' keep on. Tha' shapes well enough for a young'un that's lived with heathen. (MUSIC *[I, #13].* ROBIN *appears and chirps curiously.)* Just see how he's watchin' thee.

MARY: Do you think he remembers me?

BEN: He knows every cabbage stump in th' gardens, let alone the people. *(ROBIN chirps in agreement.)* Eh! Tha' curiosity will be the death of thee sometime if tha' doesn't look sharp. *(MARY tries a few skips.* ROBIN *chirps encouragement as* BEN *begins to work. He sniffs the air appreciatively.)* Springtime's comin'. Cannot tha' smell it?

MARY: *(Stops her skipping and also sniffs in imitation of* BEN.*)* I smell something nice and fresh and damp.

BEN: *(Reaching down and picking up a bit of earth.)* That's th' good rich earth. It's in a good humor makin' ready to grow things. In th' flower gardens things will be stirrin' down below in the dark. You'll see bits o' green spikes stickin' out o' th' black earth after a bit.

MARY: *(Also picking up some earth.)* What will they be?

BEN: Crocuses an' snowdrops an' daffydowndillies. Has tha' never seen them?

MARY: No. Everything is hot and wet and green after the rains in India. And I think things grow up in a night.

BEN: These won't grow up in a night. Tha'll have to wait for 'em. (ROBIN *chirps in agreement.)*

MARY: Are things stirring down below in the dark in that garden where the robin lives?

BEN: *(Surly again.)* What garden?

MARY: The one where the old rose trees are. Are all the flowers dead, or do some of them come again in the summer? Are there ever any roses?

BEN: *(Nods his head at* ROBIN.*)* Ask him. He's th' only one as knows. No one else has seen inside it for ten year. *(He leaves in a gruff.* ROBIN *whistles . . . "What a grouch.")*

MARY: *(Answers* ROBIN.*)* Yes, I think so, too. (ROBIN *chirps brightly.)* You do remember me! You do! *(Chirp.)* Oh, I like you. You are prettier than anything else in the whole world. (MUSIC [I, #14]. ROBIN *chirps in agreement.* MARY *tries to whistle as he does.* ROBIN *corrects her. She tries again, a little closer this time.* ROBIN *encourages her and adds a phrase.* MARY *can't get it right, starts to stamp her foot, stops herself, then tries a third time. She gets it right or sings the correct notes, and* ROBIN *congratulates her.* MARY *laughs and begins to skip.)* I'm going to try and skip all around the garden. (ROBIN *chirps a question.)* Yes, of course you may come. (MARY *skips,* ROBIN *following, then he flies ahead.)* Not that way—Where are you going—Oh, very well. *(She follows him, skipping up to thirty.)* Maybe next time I can skip up to fifty. (MUSIC [I, #15] ROBIN *chirps a command.)* Well, after all, it is my first day! *(Chirp.)* What are you trying to tell me? (ROBIN *chirps impatiently.)* You needn't be vexed, that's no way for a young gentleman to . . . *(Chirps again. Flies down closer to* MARY. *She looks down at him and notices something at her feet.)* There's something buried here in the soil. (ROBIN *chirps in excitement.)* Is that what you were . . . ("I know something . . .") It's a key! It looks like it's been buried for a long time. (". . . you don't know . . .") Perhaps it's been buried for ten years. Perhaps it is the key to the garden! ("I know something you don't know.") Well, if it is the key to the garden, then you ought to show me the door; but I don't believe you know! (ROBIN *chirps a command and flies to the top of the wall, moving along it as* MARY *follows him. He is chirping all the while, encouraging* MARY *as she searches.)* Is it here? *(Warm.)* Here? *(Warmer.)* Here? *(Hot, very hot! "I know something . . ." a gust of wind, a magical trill,* MARY *pushes aside the ivy boughs, and the door is revealed. She tremblingly puts the key in the lock, turns it, opens the door, and steps inside the secret garden.* MUSIC OUT. *In breathless wonder:)* How still it is. How still. (MUSIC IN [I, #16]. *Lights slowly fade.)*

END OF ACT ONE

(or if done in two acts, the next scene may continue without MUSIC [I, #16] AND [II, OPENING].)

ACT TWO

SCENE: MUSIC IN [II, opening]. MARY is discovered in the same place as at the end of Act One. She continues with her line.

MARY: No wonder it is still. I am the first one who has spoken in here for ten years. (MUSIC [II, #1]. ROBIN alights on a tree branch and gives a trill.) Well, perhaps not the first one. (ROBIN chirps approvingly.) That must be Mrs. Craven's tree! (ROBIN chirps, a little sadly. MARY examines the tree.) I wonder if it's all a quite dead garden. I wish it wasn't. (ROBIN chirps in agreement. MARY moves on. She bends down.) Yes, there are tiny growing things, and they might be crocuses or snowdrops or daffodils. (She finds a stick and begins to dig.) It isn't quite a dead garden. Even if the roses are dead, there are other things alive. (She digs some more, throwing off her coat.) Now, they look as if they could breathe. (The dinner bell rings. MUSIC fades slowly.) It's time for dinner already. (Chirp.) I shall come back this afternoon. (She stands and picks up her coat.) I shall come back. (MUSIC [II, #2]. ROBIN chirps approvingly as MARY leaves the garden, carefully closing the door behind her and making sure no one is about.)

(MARY runs to her room where MARTHA is setting out her dinner.)

MARTHA: Eh! Tha' has some roses in thy cheeks. Tha'rt ready for thy dinner, I'll warrant.

MARY: Yes, please, Martha. It all looks so good. (She begins eating hungrily.)

MARTHA: Mother will be pleased when I tell her what th' skippin' ropes' done for thee.

MARY: Martha, what are those white roots that look like onions?

MARTHA: They're bulbs. Lots o' spring flowers grow from 'em. Dickon's got a whole lot of 'em planted in our bit of garden at home.

MARY: Does Dickon know all about them?

MARTHA: Our Dickon can make a flower grow out of a brick walk.

MARY: Do bulbs live a long time? Even if no one helped them?

MARTHA: They're things as helps themselves.

MARY: I wish . . . I wish . . . I had a little spade.

MARTHA: Whatever does tha' want a spade for? Art tha' goin' to take to diggin'?

MARY: This is such a big lonely place, and I have nothing to do. I thought if I had a little spade I could dig somewhere as Ben Weatherstaff does, and I might make a little garden if he would give me some seeds. Would a spade cost very much . . . a little one?

MARTHA: Well, at Thwaite village there's a shop, an' I saw a little garden set there with a spade an' a rake an' a fork all tied together for two shillin's.

MARY: (Hurriedly wipes her mouth and goes to her purse.) I believe I've got more than that in my purse. Mrs. Medlock gave me some money from Mr. Craven.

MARTHA: Did he remember thee that much?

MARY: Mrs. Medlock gives me a shilling every Saturday from him. (She shakes the purse, and the money falls into her hand.) I didn't know what to spend it on.

MARTHA: My word! That's riches! Now, I've just thought o' somethin'.

MARY: What?

MARTHA: In th' shop at Thwaite they sell packages o' flower seeds for a penny each, and our Dickon, he knows which is th' prettiest ones an' how to make 'em grow. He walks over to Thwaite many a day just for th' fun of it. We could write a letter to him an' ask him to go an' buy th' tools an' th' seeds at th' same time.

MARY: (*Hugs* MARTHA *unabashedly.*) Oh, you're a good girl! I didn't know you were so nice!

MARTHA: (*Makes no comment on the hug, but it is obvious she is pleased.*) Eh! I'll get thee some pen an' ink an' paper. (*She leaves.*)

MARY: (*Paces in excitement.*) If I have a spade, I can make the earth nice and soft, and if I have seeds, I can make the garden come alive. (*From far off there is a faint whimpering cry.* MARY *looks up and starts toward the door.*)

(MARTHA *enters.*)

MARY: Martha! I heard the cry again! That's the third time, and there is no wind today.

MARTHA: (*Agitated.*) Eh! Tha' mustn't go walkin' about the corridors listenin'. Mr. Craven would be that angry there's no knowin' what he'd do.

MARY: (*Indignantly.*) I wasn't listening. I was just waiting for you, and I heard it.

MARTHA: Here's thy pen an' ink. When tha's finished with th' letter, I'll put it with th' money in th' envelope, an' I'll get the butcher boy to take it in his cart.

MARY: But Martha . . .

MARTHA: I must run now. (*She exits, leaving* MARY *to her writing. As she sits and begins to write,* MARY *shakes her head.*)

MARY: This is the strangest house anyone has ever lived in.

(MUSIC IN [II, #3] *as lights fade on* MARY *and come up on* BEN *in the garden.*)

SCENE TWO

SCENE: MUSIC OUT. BEN *is talking to* ROBIN.

BEN: Aye, there tha'rt. Tha' can put up with me a bit sometimes when tha's got no one better. Tha's been reddin' up thy waistcoat an' polishin' thy feathers this two weeks. I know what tha's up to. Tha's courtin' some bold young madam somewhere, tellin' thy lies to her about bein' the finest cock robin on Missel Moor an' ready to fight all th' rest of 'em! (*With a shake of his feather,* ROBIN *is gone.*)

(MARY *enters and surprises* BEN.)

MARY: Hello, Ben Weatherstaff.

BEN: (*Whirls around, a little embarrassed.*) Now, if tha'rt just like the robin. I never knows when I shall see thee or which side tha'll come from.

MARY: He's friends with me now. (BEN *goes back to work, and* MARY *watches him a minute.*) Have you a garden of your own?

BEN: No. I'm a bachelder and lodge with Martin at the gate.

MARY: If you had one, what would you plant?

BEN: Cabbages an' 'taters an' onions.

MARY: If you had a *flower* garden, what would you plant?

BEN: Bulbs and sweet smellin' things. But mostly roses.

MARY: Do you like roses?

BEN: Well, yes I do. I was learned that by a young lady I was gardener to. She had a lot in a place she was fond of, an' she loved 'em like they was children—or robins. That were as much as ten year ago.

MARY: Where is she now?

BEN: Heaven, 'cording to what parson says.

MARY: What happened to the roses?

BEN: They was left to themselves.

MARY: Do roses quite die when they are left to themselves?

BEN: Well, I'd got to like 'em—an' I liked her—an' she liked 'em. Once or twice a year I'd go and work at 'em a bit. They run wild, but they was in rich soil, so some of 'em lived.

MARY: When they have no leaves and look grey and brown and dry, how can you tell whether they are dead or alive?

BEN: Why does tha' care so much about roses an' such, all of a sudden?

MARY: I—I want to play that—that I have a garden of my own. I have nothing—and no one.

BEN: Well, that's true. Tha' hasn't.

MARY: Do you go and see those other roses now?

BEN: Tha'rt the worst wench for askin' questions I've ever come across. Get thee gone and play thee. I've done talkin' for today.

(MUSIC [II, #4]. ROBIN *enters as* BEN *leaves and whistles a comment.*)

MARY: Yes, I know. But I think I like him just the same. And I believe he knows everything there is to know about flowers. (*She skips down the path,* ROBIN *accompanying her. Suddenly,* ROBIN's *song is answered by another pipe.* MARY *and* ROBIN *stop.*)

(*A soft, gentle voice comes from behind a tree. It is* DICKON.)

DICKON: Don't tha' move. It'd flight 'em. (MARY *stands very still as* DICKON *slowly stands and comes from behind the tree. He watches the creatures leave and then speaks to* MARY.) I'm Dickon. I know tha'rt Miss Mary.

MARY: You—you came.

DICKON: (*Grins.*) That I did. I got up slow, because if tha' makes a quick move, it startles 'em. A body 'as to move gentle an' speak low when wild things is about.

MARY: Did you get my letter?

DICKON: That's why I come. (*Picks up a parcel from the ground.*) I've got th' garden tools. Eh! They are good 'uns.

MARY: (*Addresses him stiffly, out of shyness.*) Where are the seeds?

DICKON: (*Taking an envelope from his pocket.*) Th' woman in th' shop threw in a packet o' white poppy an' one o' blue larkspur when I bought th' other seeds. Oh, there's a trowel, too. *(He grins again.* MARY *relaxes and smiles back.* ROBIN *is heard, and* DICKON *looks up alertly.)* Where's that robin as is callin' us?

MARY: Is it really calling us?

DICKON: Aye, he's callin' someone he's friends with. There he is in th' bush. Whose is he?

MARY: He's Ben Weatherstaff's, but I think he knows me a little.

DICKON: Aye, he knows thee. He'll tell me all about thee in a minute. *(*DICKON *whistles a question, and* ROBIN *responds.* MUSIC *[II, #5].)* Aye, he's a friend o' yours. *(He laughs, and* MARY *smiles in delight.)* Does tha' know how to plant these seeds? *(*MARY *shakes her head no.)* Then I'll show thee how. Would you like that? *(*MARY *nods her head yes.)* Where is tha' garden?

MARY: I—I—

DICKON: Tha's got a bit o' garden, hasn't tha'?

MARY: Yes, I mean no, I mean I don't . . .

DICKON: Wouldn't they give thee a bit? Hasn't tha' got any yet?

MARY: I don't know anything about boys. Could you keep a secret if I told you one? I don't know what I should do if anyone found out. *(Fiercely.)* I believe I should die!

DICKON: If I couldn't keep secrets from th' other lads, about wild things' homes an' such, there'd be naught safe on th' moor. Aye, I can keep a secret.

MARY: *(Takes a deep breath and begins to speak in a rush.)* I've stolen a garden. Nobody wants it, nobody cares for it, nobody goes into it. Perhaps everything is dead in it already. I don't know. *(She begins to pace.)* I don't care. I don't care! Nobody has any right to take it from me when I care about it, and they don't. They're letting it die, all shut in by itself! *(She begins to cry.)*

DICKON: Ehhhh!

MARY: I found it myself, and I got into it myself. I was only just like the robin and they wouldn't take it from the robin.

DICKON: *(Gently.)* Where is it?

MARY: *(Gets control of herself and stands.)* Come with me, and I'll show you. *(*MUSIC IN *[II, #6]. As if she were a wild creature,* DICKON *slowly stands and follows* MARY. *She leads him to the secret garden and throws open the door.)* It's this. It's a secret garden, and I'm the only one in the world who wants it to be alive.

DICKON: *(Looking about him in wonder.)* Eh! It is a strange, pretty place. It's like as if a body was in a dream. *(He begins to examine the flowers.)*

MARY: Will there be roses?

DICKON: Shhh. *(*MUSIC OUT. *He nods his head toward the door to remind her that people might be about.)*

MARY: *(Whispering as well.)* I forgot . . . Can you tell if there will be roses? I thought perhaps they were all dead.

DICKON: Eh! No! Not them, not all of 'em.

MARY: *(Pointing.)* That one? Is that one quite alive?

DICKON: It's as wick as you an' me.

MARY: That means alive, doesn't it?

DICKON: Aye.

MARY: I'm glad it's wick! I want them all to be wick! Let us go round the garden and count how many wick ones there are. (MUSIC IN [II, #7]. *They begin to examine the garden.*)

DICKON: They've run wild. But the strongest ones has fair thrived on it. (*A* ROBIN *trill.*) See here . . . A body might think this was dead wood, but I don't believe it is down to the root. (*Another trill as* MARY *looks.* DICKON *notices something else.*) Why, who did that there?

MARY: I did it.

DICKON: I thought tha' didn't know nothin' about gardenin'.

MARY: I don't. But they looked as if they had no room to breathe, so I made a place for them.

DICKON: A gardener couldn't have told thee better. They'll grow now like Jack's beanstalk. (MUSIC *begins to fade.*)

MARY: Will you come again and help me work here, Dickon?

DICKON: I'll come every day if tha' wants me to, rain or shine. (*Pausing and scratching his head.* MUSIC OUT.) Seems as if there'd been some prunin' done here an' there, later than ten year ago.

MARY: But the door was locked, and the key was buried. No one could get in.

DICKON: Aye, that's true. (*He shrugs and goes back to work.*)

MARY: (*Pauses and looks at* DICKON.) Dickon, I like you, and you make the fifth person. I never thought I should like five people.

DICKON: Only five folk as tha' likes? Who is the other four?

MARY: Your mother and Martha and the robin and Ben Weatherstaff.

DICKON: (*Lets out a hearty laugh and stifles it with his sleeve.*) I know tha' thinks I'm a strange lad, but I think tha'rt the strangest little lass I ever saw.

MARY: (*Very serious.*) Does tha' like me?

DICKON: Eh! That I does. I likes thee wonderful. (MUSIC [II, #8]. ROBIN *chirps.*) An' so does th' robin, I do believe! (*Chirp.*)

MARY: That's two then! (*Chirp.*) That's two for me. (*Chirp. She goes back to work.* DICKON *watches her in amusement. The dinner bell rings, and* MARY *looks up in disappointment.*) I have to go . . .

DICKON: Run along and eat thy victuals. I'll eat my dinner here an' stay an' work a bit.

MARY: (*Stands and takes a step. Turns back.*) Whatever happens, you—you would never tell?

DICKON: If tha' was a missel thrush an' showed me where thy nest was, does tha' think I'd tell anyone? Not me. Tha'rt as safe as a missel thrush. (MUSIC IN [II, #9]. DICKON *goes back to work.* MARY *watches him a moment, then leaves as the lights fade.*)

SCENE THREE

SCENE: *Lights come up on* MARTHA *in* MARY'S *room as* MARY *enters at a run.*

MARTHA: Tha's late. Where has tha' been?

MARY: I've seen Dickon!

MARTHA: I knew he'd come. How does tha' like him?

MARY: I think—I think he's beautiful!

MARTHA: Well, he's th' best lad as ever was born, but us never thought he was handsome.

MARY: He's going to show me how to plant the seeds, Martha.

MARTHA: Who did tha' ask about a place for thy flowers?

MARY: I—I haven't asked anyone yet.

MARTHA: If I was you, I'd ask Ben Weatherstaff. P'raps he'd find you a corner somewhere out o' th' way. (MRS. MEDLOCK *calls for* MARY *offstage.*) I clean forgot to tell you. Mr. Craven came back this mornin', an' I think he wants to see you.

MARY: Oh! Why? He didn't want to see me when I came. Mrs. Medlock said he didn't. (MRS. MEDLOCK *calls again.* MARTHA *continues in a hurried whisper.*)

MARTHA: Well, Mrs. Medlock says it's because o' Mother. She was walkin' to Thwaite village, an' she met him. I don't know what she said to him, but it put him in th' mind to see you before he goes away again, tomorrow.

(MRS. MEDLOCK *enters in a self-important bustle.*)

MRS. MEDLOCK: Your hair's rough. (MUSIC IN *[II, #10].*) Go and brush it. And Martha, help her put on her best pinafore. Mr. Craven sent me to bring her to him in his study.

MARY: (*As* MARTHA *helps her to get dressed.*) What does Mr. Craven want to see me about, did he say?

MRS. MEDLOCK: It's not for the likes of you or me to question Mr. Craven's wishes. Now come along, he doesn't like to be kept waiting. (MUSIC *continues as she hurries* MARY *along the corridor.*)

(*Lights come up on* MR. CRAVEN *sitting in an armchair, reading a book. He looks up as they enter.*)

MRS. MEDLOCK: This is Miss Mary, sir. (MUSIC OUT.)

MR. CRAVEN: You can go and leave her here. I will ring for you when I want you to take her away. (MRS. MEDLOCK *leaves.*) Come here. (MARY *takes a tentative step forward. They stare at each other a moment.*) Are you well?

MARY: Yes.

MR. CRAVEN: Do they take good care of you?

MARY: Yes.

MR. CRAVEN: You are very thin.

MARY: (*Stiffly.*) I am getting fatter.

MR. CRAVEN: I forgot you. I intended to send you a governess or a nurse, but I forgot.

MARY: Please . . . Please . . . (*She chokes.*)

MR. CRAVEN: What do you want to say?

MARY: I—I am too big for a nurse. And please—please, don't make me have a governess yet.

MR. CRAVEN: That was what the Sowerby woman said.

MARY: Martha's mother?

MR. CRAVEN: Yes, I believe so.

MARY: She knows about children, sir. She has twelve. She knows.

MR. CRAVEN: What do you want to do?

MARY: I want to play out of doors.

MR. CRAVEN: Mrs. Sowerby said it would do you good. Where do you play?

MARY: Everywhere. I skip and run about, and I look to see if things are beginning to stick up out of the earth. I don't do any harm.

MR. CRAVEN: Don't look so frightened. You could not do any harm, a child
like you! You may do what you like.

MARY: May I?

MR. CRAVEN: Please don't look so frightened. Of course, you may. I am your
guardian, though I am a poor one for any child. I cannot give you time or
attention. I am too ill and wretched and distracted, but I wish you to be
happy and comfortable. I sent for you today, because Susan Sowerby said
her daughter Martha had talked about you. I thought her rather bold to
stop me on the moor, but she said—Mrs. Craven had been kind to her . . .
Is there anything you want? Toys, books, dolls?

MARY: Might I . . . might I have a bit of earth? (MUSIC IN [II, #11].)

MR. CRAVEN: Earth! What do you mean?

MARY: To plant seeds in—to make things grow—to make them come alive.

MR. CRAVEN: Do you care about gardens so much?

MARY: I didn't know about them in India. I was always ill and tired, and it
was too hot. But here it is different.

MR. CRAVEN: A bit of earth . . . You remind me of someone else who loved the
earth and things that grow. When you see a bit of earth you want, take it
child, and make it come alive. (MUSIC fades.)

MARY: May I take it from anywhere? If it's not wanted?

MR. CRAVEN: Anywhere. (He rings the bell.) There! You must go now. I am
tired.

(MRS. MEDLOCK enters. MR. CRAVEN speaks to MARY.)

MR. CRAVEN: Goodbye, I shall be away all summer.

MRS. MEDLOCK: Sir?

MR. CRAVEN: Mrs. Medlock, now I have seen the child I understand what
Mrs. Sowerby meant. She must be less delicate before she begins lessons.
Give her simple, healthy food. Don't look after her too much. She needs
liberty and fresh air and romping about.

MRS. MEDLOCK: Thank you, sir. I'd always take Susan Sowerby's advice
about children, myself. She's what you might call healthy-minded, if you
understand me.

MR. CRAVEN: I understand. Take Miss Mary away now and send my manser-
vant to me. (MRS. MEDLOCK and MARY leave. Lights out on MR. CRAVEN.)

MRS. MEDLOCK: Well, I'm glad he's listened to Susan's advice. Susan Sowerby
an' me went to school together, an' she's a sensible soul . . . Here you are.
Mind now, just because Mr. Craven said you were to be allowed to roam

out of doors, you're not to go poking about the house. (MARY *and* MARTHA *watch* MRS. MEDLOCK *leave.* MARY *turns to* MARTHA, *joyously.*)

MARY: I can have my garden! I may have it where I like! I am not going to have a governess for a long time. I may do what I like—anywhere!

MARTHA: Eh! That was nice of him, wasn't it?

MARY: (*Getting ready for bed.*) Martha, he is really a nice man, only his face is so miserable, and his forehead is all drawn together.

MARTHA: I've heard tell he was different when his Missus was alive. People say she married him for his money, but I don't think she did.

MARY: I don't think so either.

MARTHA: Oh! I've somethin' for thee from Dickon. (MUSIC IN [*II, #12*].) He had to go, but he said to give this to thee. (*She hands* MARY *a piece of paper.*)

MARY: But he said he'd stay in the . . . What is it?

MARTHA: (*Looking over her shoulder.*) Eh! I never knew our Dickon was as clever as that. That there's a picture of a missel thrush on her nest, as large as life an' twice as natural.

MARY: A missel thrush? . . . Oh . . .

MARTHA: An' there's some words there, too. What does it say?

MARY: I will (*Spelling it out.*) c-u-m b-a-k . . . I will come back! (*Lights fade as* MARY *looks at* MARTHA *happily.* MUSIC *continues into scene change.*)

Scene Four

SCENE: *Lights come up with wind and rain sounds as* MARY *is discovered tossing and turning in her bed.*

MARY: (*Sitting up and punching her pillow.*) The wind is as contrary as ever I was. It came because I did not want it. (*The wind dies down, and the sound of heartbroken sobbing is heard.*) It isn't the wind now. It is different. (*More sobbing.*) I am going to find out what it is. (MUSIC IN [*II, #13*]. *She puts on her wrapper.*) I don't care about Mrs. Medlock. I don't care! (MARY *gets out of bed. She goes to her door and carefully opens it. The crying continues, getting louder as* MARY *wanders through the corridors of the house.* MUSIC *plays as she comes to the panel with the tapestry. She pushes back the tapestry, opens the door and enters a bedroom. A young* BOY *is discovered crying in his bed. He looks up at her with large eyes and speaks.*)

COLIN: Who are you? Are you a ghost?

MARY: No. Are you one?

COLIN: No. I am Colin.

MARY: Who is Colin?

COLIN: I am Colin Craven. Who are you?

MARY: I am Mary Lennox. I heard someone crying, and I wanted to find out who it was. Mr. Craven is my uncle.

COLIN: He is my father.

MARY: Your father! No one ever told me he had a boy.

COLIN: You are real, aren't you? I have such real dreams very often. You might be one of them. (MARY *goes to* COLIN *and pinches him.*) Ouch!

MARY: You see, I am real. Did no one tell you I had come here to live?

COLIN: They daren't.

MARY: Why?

COLIN: Because I hate for people to look at me.

MARY: Why?

COLIN: Because I am like this, always ill and always having to lie down. If I live I may be a hunchback. My father hates to think I may be like him. He hates to see me.

MARY: Why?

COLIN: My mother died when I was born, and it makes him wretched to look at me.

MARY: (To herself.) He hates the garden because she died.

COLIN: What garden?

MARY: Oh—just a garden she used to like . . . If you don't like people to see you, do you want me to go away?

COLIN: (Giving a tug on her wrapper.) No. I should be sure you were a dream if you went. Sit there. (He pats his bed.) I want to hear about you. How old are you?

MARY: I am ten. And so are you.

COLIN: How do you know that?

MARY: Because when you were born, the garden door was locked, and the key was buried. And it's been locked for ten years.

COLIN: What garden door was locked?

MARY: The . . . garden Mr. Craven hates.

COLIN: Who locked it?

MARY: He did.

COLIN: Where is the key?

MARY: No one knows.

COLIN: Why?

MARY: No one will talk about it.

COLIN: Why?

MARY: I think . . . I think they have been told not to answer questions.

COLIN: I would make them. (There is a pause as MARY digests this information.)

MARY: Could you?

COLIN: Everyone is obliged to please me. If I were to live, this place would sometime belong to me. I would make them tell me.

MARY: (Trying to change the subject.) Do you think you won't live?

COLIN: Ever since I can remember anything, I have heard people say I shan't. At first, they thought I was too little to understand, and now they think I don't hear. But I do. My doctor is my father's cousin. He is quite poor, and if I die, he will have all Misselthwaite when my father is dead. I should think he wouldn't want me to live.

MARY: Do you want to live?

COLIN: No. But I don't want to die either. Let us talk about something else. Talk about that garden. Don't you want to see it?

MARY: Yes.

COLIN: I do. I don't think I ever really wanted to see anything before. They have to please me. I will make them take me there, and I will let you go too.

MARY: Oh don't—don't—don't—don't do that!

COLIN: Why? You said you wanted to see it.

MARY: I do, but if you make them open the door and take you in like that, it will never be a secret again.

COLIN: A secret? What do you mean? Tell me.

MARY: You see—if no one knows but ourselves—if there was a door—hidden somewhere—and we could find it—and dig in the garden and play and bring it back to life, so the pale green points push up through the green earth because the spring is coming—if the garden was a secret, and we could get into it, we could see how many roses were alive—Oh, don't you see how much nicer it would be if it was a secret?

COLIN: I never had a secret, except that one about not living to grow up. I like this kind better . . . I am going to let you look at something . . . Do you see that curtain?

MARY: Yes.

COLIN: There is a chord, hanging from it. Go and pull it. (MUSIC *[II, #14]*. MARY *pulls the cord, and the curtain pulls back to reveal a picture of a lovely young woman. The "garden theme" plays softly.*) That is my mother. I don't see why she died. Sometimes I hate her for doing it. Draw the curtain again. (MARY *does so, and the* MUSIC *fades out.*) I don't like to see her looking at me.

MARY: Why?

COLIN: She smiles too much when I am ill and miserable. Besides, she's a kind of secret—and I think you shall be a secret, too . . . Do you know Martha?

MARY: Yes.

COLIN: She is the one who is asleep in the other room. Martha shall tell you when I want you to come here.

MARY: Martha knew about you all the time?

COLIN: Yes, she often attends to me.

MARY: Shall I go away now? Your eyes look sleepy.

COLIN: I wish I could go to sleep before you leave me.

MARY: Shut your eyes, and I will do what my Ayah used to do in India. I will pat your hand and stroke it and sing something quite low.

COLIN: I should like that, perhaps. (MARY *begins to sing.* MUSIC *[II, #15].*)

MARY:

> *Khum pada ne mashe peshe*
> *Khum mere bah dyijo*
> *Bata bhore pan debo;*
> *Gale bore kheo.*

COLIN: *(Dreamily.)* That is nice. (MARY *continues to sing as* COLIN *falls asleep, and tiptoes out of his room.*)

MARY:

> Ehsho mashi ehsho pishi
> Khocare khate ehsho
> Khatane; palong enai,
> Choka pate bosho . . .

(Lights fade and ACT II playout, "Raja Theme" plays MUSIC *[II, #16].)*

END OF ACT TWO
(. . . OR ACT ONE)

ACT THREE (OR TWO)

SCENE: PRELUDE MUSIC *begins [III, #1] and segues to a solo piano playing "Mary's Theme." Lights up on* MARTHA *and* MARY *in tableau.* MARTHA *has some knitting in her hand.*

MARTHA: The moor was hidden in mist when the morning came. There could be no going out of doors. Martha was so busy that Mary had no opportunity of talking to her, but in the afternoon she asked her to come and sit with her. (MUSIC *fades as* MARTHA *sits and begins knitting.* MARY *paces.)* Tha' looks as if tha' had somethin' to say.

MARY: *(Stops her pacing and confronts* MARTHA.*)* I have found out what the crying was.

MARTHA: Tha' hasn't!

MARY: It was Colin. I found him.

MARTHA: Eh! Miss Mary! If Mrs. Medlock finds out, she'll think I broke orders and told thee. I shall lose my place, and then what'll Mother do! *(A bell rings.)* That's him ringin' now. I hope he's in a good temper. *(She leaves.)*

MARY: *(Paces.)* I think he sounds like a very spoiled boy, even if he has been ill a good bit. Well, if he ever gets angry at me, I'll never go and see him again.

(MARTHA *returns.)*

MARTHA: Well, tha' has bewitched him. "I want Mary Lennox to come and talk to me, and remember you're not to tell anyone," he said. You'd better go as quick as you can. (MARTHA *accompanies* MARY *to* COLIN's *room.)*

(Lights up on COLIN *who is sitting in bed, a large book in his hands.)*

COLIN: Come in. I've been thinking about you all morning.

MARY: I've been thinking about you, too. You don't know how frightened Martha is.

MARTHA: Please, Miss . . .

COLIN: *(Interrupting her.)* Martha, have you to do what I please or have you not?

MARTHA: I have to do what you please, sir.

COLIN: Has Medlock to do what I please?

MARTHA: Everybody has, sir.

COLIN: Well, then, if I order you to bring Miss Mary to me, how can Medlock send you away if she finds out?

MARTHA: Please don't let her, sir.

COLIN: I'll send her away if she dares to say a word about such a thing.

MARTHA: Thank you, sir. I want to do my duty, sir.

COLIN: What I want is your duty. I'll take care of you. Now, go away. (MARTHA *bobs a curtsey and leaves.* COLIN *turns to* MARY *who is staring at him.*) Why are you looking at me like that? What are you thinking about?

MARY: I am thinking about two things.

COLIN: Sit down and tell me.

MARY: This is the first one. Once when I was in India, I saw a boy who was a Rajah. He had rubies and emeralds and diamonds stuck all over him. He spoke to his people just as you spoke to Martha.

COLIN: I shall make you tell me about Rajahs presently, but first, tell me what the second thing was.

MARY: I was thinking how different you are from Dickon.

COLIN: Who is Dickon? What a funny name!

MARY: He is Martha's brother. He is not like anyone else in the world. He can charm foxes and squirrels and birds just as the natives in India charm snakes.

COLIN: Tell me some more about him.

MARY: He knows about everything that grows on the moor.

COLIN: How can he like the moor when it's such a big, bare, ugly place?

MARY: When Dickon talks about it, it's beautiful.

COLIN: I couldn't go on the moor.

MARY: Why?

COLIN: It's cold, and the flowers make me sneeze. And the gardeners are always looking at me. I hate for people to look at me.

MARY: Why?

COLIN: Because I know they are looking for my hunchback lump. And people are always patting my cheeks and saying, "Poor thing." Once when a lady did that to me, I screamed and bit her hand. She looked quite frightened and ran away.

MARY: She thought you had gone mad, like a dog.

COLIN: I don't care what she thought.

MARY: Would you hate it—if a boy looked at you?

COLIN: There's one boy . . . there's one boy I believe I shouldn't mind. It's that boy you were talking about—Dickon.

MARY: I'm sure you wouldn't mind him.

COLIN: The animals don't, and perhaps that is why I shouldn't. He's a sort of animal charmer, and I am a boy animal.

MARY: You are! (COLIN *barks a little, and* MARY *laughs. She barks back, and he laughs. And they start to laugh together.* COLIN *pauses a moment and looks at* MARY.)

COLIN: I just thought of something.

MARY: What?

COLIN: You and I—are cousins!

MARY: We are!

COLIN: And we never thought of it before . . .

MARY: . . . talking all this time . . .

COLIN: . . . last night . . .

MARY: . . . and this morning . . .

COLIN: . . . and we never realized we were cousins!

MARY: Oh, that's funny!

COLIN: It's not that funny!

MARY: Yes, it is!

COLIN: You're right. It is! *(They giggle hysterically.)*

(DR. CRAVEN *and* MRS. MEDLOCK *enter in a hurry and stop abruptly, amazed at the sight of* MARY *and* COLIN *laughing so hard they are almost crying.)*

MRS. MEDLOCK: Good Lord!

DR. CRAVEN: What is this? What does this mean?

COLIN: *(Wiping the tears of laughter from his eyes.)* This is Mary Lennox. She is my c . . . c . . . cousin! *(He bursts into more laughter.)*

DR. CRAVEN: *(Threatening.)* Mrs. Medlock . . .

MRS. MEDLOCK: Oh, sir, I don't know how it's happened. There's not a servant on the place that'd dare to talk. They all have their orders.

COLIN: *(Gaining control, once more the Rajah.)* Nobody told her anything. She heard me crying and found me herself. I am glad she came. Don't be silly, Medlock.

DR. CRAVEN: *(Rubbing his hands together in a nervous gesture.)* Well, well, well . . . Hello, Mary. I am Doctor Craven.

MARY: I know.

DR. CRAVEN: *(Sitting by* COLIN *and taking his pulse.)* I am afraid Miss Mary's visit has excited you, my boy. Excitement is not good for you, you know.

COLIN: I should be excited if she kept away. I am better. She makes me better.

MRS. MEDLOCK: He does look rather better, sir. (DR. CRAVEN *raises an eyebrow.* MRS. MEDLOCK *amends her statement.)* But, he looked better this morning before she came into the room.

COLIN: She came into the room last night. She stayed with me a long time. I was better when I wakened up. I want my breakfast. Tell them, Medlock.

MRS. MEDLOCK: Yes sir. *(She exits.)*

DR. CRAVEN: Well, my boy, you do seem to be a little bit better, but you must not forget how very ill you are. You must not talk too much, you must not forget that you are easily tired, and you must not forget that . . .

COLIN: *(Interrupting.)* I want to forget. Mary makes me forget. That is why I want her to come and talk to me.

DR. CRAVEN: Very well, Master Colin, if that is what you wish.

COLIN: It is. And there is something else I wish.

DR. CRAVEN: What is that?

COLIN: I wish you would go away and leave me alone with my cousin. (DR. CRAVEN *stands and sighs. He goes out the door, shaking his head.* COLIN *turns to* MARY.) Now, Mary Lennox, sit here. I want you to tell me more about Dickon and the moor, but first, I want you to tell me about Rajahs. (MUSIC IN [III, #2].)

(Lights fade on COLIN *and* MARY *and come up on* MARTHA *in the nursery.)*

SCENE TWO

MARTHA: After another week of rain the high arch of blue sky appeared again, and the sun which poured down was quite hot. Though there had been no chance to see Dickon, Mistress Mary had enjoyed herself very much, spending hours with Colin in his room. But on that first day when the sky was blue again, Mary could not wait to be outside. (MUSIC OUT.)

MARY: Isn't it a beautiful morning, Martha? Smell that good fresh air!

MARTHA: Aye, the air from th' moor has done thee good already. Even tha' hair doesn't slamp down on thy head so flat. *(She fluffs* MARY's *hair.)* Tha'rt not half so ugly when it's fluffed up a bit, an' there's red in thy cheeks.

MARY: My hair is getting stronger just like me. Maybe if we can get Colin to go outside, he'll get stronger, too.

MARTHA: P'raps. He's not had a tantrum or a whining fit since tha's made friends with him. He wants to see thee right away.

MARY: *(Starting out the door.)* I'll see him later. I'm going to be very busy in the garden.

MARTHA: *(Alarmed.)* Eh! Miss Mary, it may put him all out of humor when I tell him that.

MARY: I can't stay. Dickon's waiting for me.

MARTHA: Oh, Miss Mary, please don't make me tell him.

MARY: Very well, I shall tell him myself.

MARTHA: Oh, Miss . . .

*(*MARY *marches to* COLIN's *room, followed nervously by* MARTHA.)*

COLIN: Oh, there you are. Come and sit by me, but don't talk too loudly. My back aches, and my head aches, I want you to sing to me again.

MARY: *(Remains standing.)* I can't.

COLIN: Why not?

MARY: I have to go.

COLIN: Where?

MARY: Outside. Dickon is waiting for me.

COLIN: I won't let that boy come here if you go and stay with him instead of coming to talk with me.

MARY: If you send Dickon away, I'll never come to this room again.

COLIN: You'll have to if I want you.

MARY: I won't.

COLIN: I'll make you. They shall drag you in.

MARY: Shall they, Mr. Rajah? They may drag me in, but they can't make me talk when they get me here. I'll sit and clench my teeth and never tell you one thing!

COLIN: You are a selfish beast!

MARY: What are you? Selfish people always say that. You're the most selfish boy I ever saw.

COLIN: I'm not as selfish as you, because I'm always ill, and I'm sure there is a lump coming on my back. And I'm going to die besides.

MARY: You're not!

COLIN: I am! You know I am! Everybody says so.

MARY: I don't believe it! You just say that to make people sorry. I believe you're proud of it. If you were a nice boy, it might be true—but you're too nasty!

COLIN: Get out of my room! Get out! Get out!! GET OUT! (*He throws a pillow at her.* MARY *catches the pillow and throws it back at him.*)

MARY: I will! And I'm not coming back! (*She starts out as* COLIN *begins to scream and cry hysterically.* MARTHA *looks on helplessly as* MARY *stops and turns back to* COLIN. MARY *stamps her foot.*) You stop it! (*She stamps again.*) I hate you! (*She stamps back into the room on the next lines until she is face to face with* COLIN, *topping his tantrum with her own.*) Everybody hates you! I wish everybody would run out of the house and let you scream yourself to death. You will scream yourself to death in a minute, and I wish you would! (COLIN *pauses a moment, open-mouthed.*) If you scream another scream, I'll scream too—and I can scream louder than you! (*She opens her mouth to scream.*)

COLIN: I can't stop! I can't!

MARY: (*Closes her mouth.*) You can. Mrs. Medlock says that half that ails you is hysterics and temper—just hysterics—(*She stamps her foot on each word.*) hysterics—(*Stamp.*) hysterics! (*Stamp.*)

COLIN: I felt the lump—I felt it.

MARY: You didn't feel a lump! If you did, it was only a hysterical lump. There's nothing wrong with your horrid back. Turn over and let me look at it. Martha, come here and show me his back this minute!

MARTHA: (*Hesitates.*) What if he won't let me . . .

COLIN: Show her! Sh-she'll see then! (MARTHA *unbuttons the back of his nightshirt.* MARY *examines his back.*)

MARY: There's not a single lump there! Except backbone lumps, and you can only feel them because you're so thin. There's not a lump as big as a pin! If you ever say there is again, I shall laugh!

MARTHA: I didn't know he thought he had a lump on his back. I could ha' told him there wasna' lump there.

COLIN: (*Calming down, but hiccupping a little.*) C-could you?

MARTHA: Yes, sir.

MARY: There!

COLIN: Do you think—I could—live to grow up?

MARTHA: I think so, sir, if you do what you are told to do and not give way to your temper and stay out a great deal in th' fresh air.

COLIN: I'll—I'll go out with you, Mary. I shan't hate fresh air if we can find the—(MARY *gives a warning cough.* COLIN *shuts up.*) I should like to go outside with you.

MARTHA: Tha' must try an' rest now, Mester Colin.

MARY: I will put him to sleep. You may go if you like, Martha.

MARTHA: Well, if he doesn't go to sleep in half an hour, tha' must call me.

MARY: I will. (MARTHA *leaves.*)

COLIN: I almost told, but I stopped myself in time. Do you—do you think you will find out anything at all about the way into the secret garden?

MARY: Yes. I think I already have in fact. And if you will go to sleep, I will tell you tomorrow.

COLIN: Oh, Mary! If I could get into it, I think I should live to grow up! Do you suppose—would you tell me softly as you did that first night— what you imagine it looks like inside? I am sure it will make me go to sleep.

MARY: Yes. Shut your eyes.

(COLIN *shuts his eyes, and* MARY *begins to describe the secret garden. As she does so, the "garden theme" plays and lights slowly come up on* DICKON *as he begins to unfold more of the secret garden.*)

MARY: I think it has been left alone so long—that it has grown all into a lovely tangle. I think the roses have climbed and climbed and climbed until they hang from the branches and walls and creep over the ground— almost like a strange, grey mist. Some of them have died but many—are alive (MUSIC IN *[III, #3].*) and when the summer comes, there will be curtains and fountains of roses. Perhaps the leaves are beginning to break out and uncurl—and perhaps—the grey is changing, and a green gauze veil is creeping over—everything. And the birds are coming to look at it—because it is—so safe and still. And perhaps—perhaps—perhaps—

(ROBIN *enters and joins* DICKON.)

MARY: The robin has found a mate—and is building a nest.

(MUSIC *continues as* COLIN *falls asleep, and* MARY *runs to join* DICKON *in the garden.* ROBIN *joins them, serenading.* MUSIC *continues under* DICKON's *lines.*)

DICKON: Eh! Just listen to them birds—th' world seems full of 'em—all whistlin' an' pipin'. Look at 'em dartin' about an' hearken at 'em callin' to each other. Come springtime seems like as if all th' world's callin'.

MARY: Oh, Dickon, Dickon, I'm so happy, I can scarcely breathe! (*She whirls around in ecstasy.* ROBIN *chirps.*) Look, Dickon! (*Another chirp.*) It's the robin, and he has something in his beak!

DICKON: Aye, we munnot stir. He'll stay here if we don't flight him. (*They carefully sit.*) He's settin' up housekeepin'. Us must keep still a bit an' try an' look as if us was grass an' trees an' bushes.

MARY: If we talk about him, I can't help looking at him. We must talk of something else. There is something I must tell you.

DICKON: What is it?

MARY: Well—do you know about Colin?

DICKON: I've heard Martha speak of him.

MARY: I've seen him. I have been to talk to him every day. We argued, but we've made it up. He likes to hear me talk about the garden. He says it makes him forget about being ill and dying.

DICKON: If he was out here, he wouldn't be thinkin' of dyin', he'd be watchin' for buds to break on bushes, an' likely he'd be healthier.

MARY: I've thought of that almost every time I've talked to him. I've wondered if he could keep a secret, and I've wondered if we could bring him here without anyone seeing us. I have a plan, but I don't know if it will work.

DICKON: Eh! My! We mun get him out here—we mun get him watchin' an' listenin' an' sniffin' up th' air an' get him just soaked with sunshine. An' we munnot lose no time about it.

MARY: (Carefully and proudly trying out her Yorkshire.) Aye, that we mun. I'll tell thee what us'll do first. He's took a graidely fancy to thee. When I go back to th' house to talk to him, I'll ax him if tha' canna' come and see him an' bring thy creatures with thee . . . an' then—in a bit, we'll get him to come here an' show him everything.

DICKON: (Amused.) Tha' mun talk a bit o' Yorkshire like that to Mester Colin. Tha'll make him laugh, an' Mother says there's nowt as good for ill folks as laughin' is.

MARY: I'm going to talk Yorkshire to him this very day. (MUSIC IN [III, #4]. MARY leaves, and DICKON closes the door of the secret garden.)

(Lights up on COLIN's room as MARY enters.)

COLIN: You smell like flowers and fresh things! What is it you smell of? It's cool and warm and sweet all at the same time!

MARY: It's th' wind from the moor. It comes o' sittin' on th' grass under a tree wi' Dickon an' his creatures. It's th' springtime as smells so graidely.

COLIN: What are you doing? I've never heard you talk like that before.

MARY: I'm givin' thee a bit o' Yorkshire.

COLIN: How funny it sounds!

MARY: Doesn't tha' understand a bit o' Yorkshire, an' tha' a Yorkshire lad thysel'?

COLIN: Do it some more!

MARY: Eh! I wonder tha'rt not ashamed o' thy face!

COLIN: (Laughing in delight.) That's wonderful!

MARY: It has come, Colin, the springtime has come. Dickon says so.

COLIN: Well, open the window. Perhaps we shall hear golden trumpets!

MARY: (Goes to the window and throws it open.) That's the fresh air you smell, now, Colin. Take long breaths of it, like Dickon does. He says it makes him feel as if he could live forever and ever!

COLIN: Forever and ever! Does it make him feel like that? (And he takes some deep breaths.) Mary . . . I'm sorry for saying what I did about sending Dickon away.

MARY: I'm glad.

COLIN: I should like to see him.

MARY: Really?

COLIN: Really.

MARY: Can I trust you? I trusted Dickon because birds trusted him. Can I trust you—for sure—for sure?

COLIN: Yes. Yes!

MARY: Well, Dickon will come to see you this afternoon, and he'll bring his creatures with him.

COLIN: Oh!

MARY: But that's not all. The rest is better. There is a door into the garden. It is under the ivy on the wall.

COLIN: Oh! Mary! Shall I see it? Shall I get into it? Shall I live to get into it?

MARY: Of course, you'll live to get into it. Don't be silly.

COLIN: I dreamt about it all night long. I dreamt of the roses and the robin— just as you described it. It sounded just as if you'd seen it. *(There is a pause as* MARY *considers him.)*

MARY: I had seen it—and I had been in. I found the key and got in weeks ago. But I daren't tell you—I daren't because I was so afraid I couldn't trust you for sure!

COLIN: *(Gasps in delight.)* Tell me, Mary. Tell me all about it!

(Lights up on MRS. MEDLOCK *as* DR. CRAVEN *enters.)*

MRS. MEDLOCK: Oh, Doctor, I'm so glad you've come. The boy . . .

DR. CRAVEN: How is he? I heard he had another tantrum last night. The boy will break a blood vessel in one of his fits someday.

MRS. MEDLOCK: Well, sir, you'll scarcely believe it. That plain, sourfaced child, that's almost as bad as himself, has bewitched him. How she's done it, there's no telling. Come and look, sir, it's past crediting.

*(*MRS. MEDLOCK *leads* DR. CRAVEN *to* COLIN's *room where he and* MARY *are deep in conversation.)*

COLIN: Those long spires of blue ones—we'll have a lot of those. They're called Del-phin-i-ums . . .

MARY: Dickon says . . . *(She coughs as she sees* DR. CRAVEN *and* MRS. MEDLOCK.)*

DR. CRAVEN: I'm sorry to hear you were ill last night, my boy.

COLIN: I'm better now—much better. I am going out in my chair in a day or two. I want some fresh air.

DR. CRAVEN: I thought you did not like fresh air.

COLIN: I don't when I am by myself, but my cousin is going out with me. A very strong boy I know will push my carriage.

DR. CRAVEN: He must be a strong boy and a steady boy. And I must know something about him. Who is he?

MARY: It's Dickon.

DR. CRAVEN: Oh, Dickon.

MRS. MEDLOCK: If it is Dickon, he'll be safe enough.

DR. CRAVEN: Well, if it amuses you, perhaps it won't do any harm. But you must remember . . .

COLIN: I don't want to remember. If there was a doctor anywhere who could make you forget you were ill instead of remembering, it I would have him brought here.

DR. CRAVEN: Well, well, well . . .

COLIN: And Medlock . . .

MRS. MEDLOCK: Yes, sir?

COLIN: Dickon is going to visit me today. He is bringing a fox, a crow, two squirrels, and a newborn lamb. You can tell Martha to bring them here.

MRS. MEDLOCK: I hope the animals won't bite, sir.

COLIN: Dickon is an animal charmer. Charmer's animals never bite.

MARY: There are snake charmers in India that can put their snakes' heads in their mouths.

MRS. MEDLOCK: Goodness!

COLIN: That is all. (MRS. MEDLOCK and DR. CRAVEN leave, discussing COLIN when out of earshot.)

MRS. MEDLOCK: Well, sir, could you have believed it?

DR. CRAVEN: It is certainly a new state of affairs. And there's no denying it is better than the old one. (COLIN and MARY are heard laughing in delight as the lights fade, and the scene changes. MUSIC IN [III, #5].)

SCENE THREE

MARTHA: They were obliged to wait more than a week because first, there came some very windy days, and then, Colin was threatened with a cold, which two things happening one after the other would no doubt have thrown him into a rage but that there was so much careful planning to do. The most absorbing thing, however, was the preparations to be made before Colin could be transported with sufficient secrecy to the garden.

(DICKON pushes COLIN onstage, accompanied by MARY, DR. CRAVEN and MRS. MEDLOCK.)

COLIN: Now, if the fresh air agrees with me, I may go out every day. Remember, none of the gardeners are to be anywhere near the long walk by the garden walls. No one is to be there. Everyone must keep away until I send word that they may go back to their work.

MRS. MEDLOCK: Very good, sir.

DR. CRAVEN: I'll call later, after you have come in. I must see how the going out agrees with you. I do wish you would let Mrs. Medlock or myself accompany you.

COLIN: Are you suggesting that my cousin and Dickon are not to be trusted? I don't like that suggestion.

DR. CRAVEN: No, no, I wasn't suggesting anything of the sort. We'll try this experiment.

COLIN: Very well . . . Mary, what is that thing you say in India when you have finished talking and want people to go?

MARY: You say, "You have my permission to go."

COLIN: Medlock, Doctor, you have my permission to go.

MRS. MEDLOCK and DR. CRAVEN: Yes, sir. *(They leave. MARY, COLIN and DICKON giggle.)*

COLIN: We're safe now. *(MUSIC [III, #6] accompanies MARY, DICKON and COLIN as DICKON pushes COLIN's chair along the garden walk.)* There are so many sounds of singing and humming and calling out . . . What is that scent the puffs of wind bring?

DICKON: It's the gorse on th' moor that's openin' out. Eh! Th' bees are at it wonderful today.

MARY: This is where the robin flew over the wall. And that is where he perched on the little heap of earth and showed me the key . . . And this is the ivy the wind pushed back . . . And here is the handle, and here is the door . . . *(She opens it slowly.)* Dickon, push him in, push him in quickly! *(MUSIC OUT. With a strong, sturdy push DICKON does so as MARY opens the door, and the garden is revealed.)*

COLIN: It's beautiful! Mary! Dickon! I shall get well! I shall get well! And I shall live forever and ever! *(MUSIC [III, #7] underscores the narration as COLIN, MARY and DICKON make the garden grow.)*

(BEN enters from another side of the stage.)

BEN: One of the strange things about living in the world is that it is only now and then that one is quite sure one is going to live forever and ever. One knows it sometimes when one gets up at the tender, solemn dawn time, and goes out and stands alone, and throws one's head far back and looks up and up, and watches the pale sky slowly changing and flushing and marvelous things happening, until the east almost makes one cry out and one's heart stands still at the strange unchanging majesty of the sun . . . Then sometimes the immense quiet of the dark blue at night with millions of stars waiting and watching makes one sure; and sometimes a sound of far-off music makes it true; and sometimes a look in someone's eyes . . . *(Exits as DICKON speaks.)*

DICKON: Seems to me like I never see'd an afternoon as graidely as this 'ere.

MARY: I'll warrant it's the graidliest one as ever was in this world.

COLIN: Does tha' think as happen it was made loike this 'ere all o' purpose for me?

DICKON: My word! That there is a bit o' good Yorkshire. Tha'rt shapin' first-rate, that tha'rt.

COLIN: *(Noticing his mother's tree.)* That's a very old tree over there, isn't it?

DICKON: *(Exchanging a look with MARY.)* Yes.

COLIN: It looks as if a big branch had been broken off. I wonder how it was done.

DICKON: It's been done many a year.

(ROBIN appears and softly lands on the old tree.)

DICKON: Eh! Look at that robin! *(COLIN wheels away to look at ROBIN. DICKON takes MARY aside.)* We could never tell him how the tree was broken, poor lad. If he says anything about it, we mun try to look cheerful.

MARY: Aye, that we mun.

DICKON: Mrs. Craven was a very lovely young lady. An' Mother says she thinks she's about Misselthwaite still, lookin' after Mester Colin, same as all mothers do.

COLIN: *(Turning back to them.)* I don't want this afternoon to go. But I'm going to come back here every day. I'm going to see everything grow. I'm going to grow here myself. (MUSIC *fades.*)

DICKON: That tha' will. Us'll have thee walkin' about here an' diggin' same as other folk afore long.

COLIN: Walk! Dig! Shall I?

DICKON: For sure tha' will. Tha's got legs o' thine own, same as other folks.

MARY: *(Warningly.)* Dickon . . .

COLIN: *(Unperturbed.)* Nothing really ails them, but they are so thin and weak. I'm afraid to try and stand on them.

DICKON: When tha' stops bein' afraid, tha'll stand on 'em.

(COLIN *looks up and sees* BEN *peering at them from over the wall.* BEN *is speechless with anger.)*

COLIN: Who is that man?

BEN: *(To* MARY.) If I wasn't a bachelder an' tha' was a wench o' mine, I'd give thee a hidin'. I never knowed how tha' got so thick wi' me. If it hadna' been for the robin . . .

MARY: Ben Weatherstaff, it was the robin who showed me the way.

BEN: Tha' bad young'un, layin' thy badness on a robin. *(Unable to contain his curiosity.)* Eh! Tha' young nowt—however in th' world did tha' get in!?

MARY: I can't tell you from here while you're shakin' your fist at me.

COLIN: Dickon, wheel me over there! (DICKON *does so.*) Do you know who I am? Answer me!

BEN: *(Staring in amazement.)* Aye, that I do—wi' thy mother's eyes starin' at me out o' tha' face. Tha'rt th' poor cripple.

COLIN: I'm not a cripple.

MARY: He's not! He's not got a lump as big as a pin!

BEN: Tha' hasn't got a crooked back?

COLIN: No!

BEN: Tha' hasn't got crooked legs?

COLIN and MARY: NO!

COLIN: Dickon! Come here! Come here this minute! (MUSIC IN [III, #8]. DICKON *runs to* COLIN. MARY *begins to gabble in excitement as she realizes what* COLIN *means to do.)*

MARY: He can do it, he can do it, he can do it, he can, he can!

COLIN: *(Leaning on* DICKON's *shoulders, he stands.)* Look at me—you! Just look!

DICKON: He's as straight as I am! He's as straight as any lad in Yorkshire!

BEN: Eh! Th' lies folks tells. There's not a knob on thee. Tha'lt make a mon yet. God bless thee!

COLIN: Get down from that ladder and come in here. We did not want you, but now you will have to be in the secret. Be quick!

BEN: *(Scrambling down from the ladder.)* Eh! Lad. Eh! My lad! Yes, sir! Yes, sir!

COLIN: *(To MARY.)* Go and meet him.

MARY: *(Goes, still muttering to herself.)* You can do it! You can do it! I told you you could! You can do it. You can! *(She is out.)*

COLIN: *(To DICKON.)* I can stand.

DICKON: I told thee tha' could as soon as tha's stopped bein' afraid.

COLIN: *(Suspiciously.)* Are you making magic?

DICKON: Tha's doin' magic thysel'. It's same magic as made these 'ere work out o' th' earth.

COLIN: Aye, there couldna' be bigger magic than that there . . . I'm going to walk to that tree. Bring the rug from the chair.

(BEN enters.)

COLIN: *(To BEN.)* Look at me! Am I a hunchback?

BEN: Nowt o' th' sort! But what did tha' shut thysel' up for?

COLIN: Everyone thought I was going to die. I'm not!

BEN: Tha' die! Tha's got too much pluck in thee. Sit thee down on th' rug, young Mester, an' give me my orders.

COLIN: What work do you do in the gardens, Weatherstaff?

BEN: Anythin' I'm told to. I'm kep' on by favor because tha' mother liked me.

COLIN: My mother? This was her garden, wasn't it?

BEN: Aye, it was that. She were main fond of it.

COLIN: I am fond of it, too. I am going to work here every day. I shall send for you to help sometimes . . . but only when no one can see you.

BEN: I've come here before when no one saw me.

MARY: But there was no door!

BEN: I come over th' wall. But th' rheumatics held me back th' last two year.

DICKON: Th' come an' did a bit o' prunin'!

BEN: "Ben," she said to me once, "if ever I go away, you must take care of my roses." When she did go away, th' orders was no one was ever to come nigh. But I come. She'd gave her orders first.

COLIN: I'm glad you did it, Weatherstaff. You'll know how to keep a secret.

BEN: I'll know, sir. An' it'll be easier for a man wi' rheumatics to come in at th' door. *(COLIN has been absently digging in the earth. He picks up the trowel and looks at it.)*

COLIN: *(To DICKON.)* Tha' said tha'd have me walkin' about an' diggin'—I thought tha' was just leein' to please me. This is th' first day an' I've walked—an' here I am diggin'.

BEN: How'd tha' like to plant a bit o' somethin'? I can get thee a rose in a pot.

COLIN: Go and get it! Quick! Quick! *(BEN leaves.)* Mary, Dickon, help me deepen the hole. *(MARY, DICKON and COLIN dig.)* I want to do it before the sun goes quite—quite down.

(BEN enters.)

BEN: Here, lad. Set it in th' earth thysel', same as a king does when he goes to a new place. (MUSIC IN [III, #9]. ROBIN sings as BEN helps them plant the rose. As the MUSIC softens, the dialogue resumes, underscored.)

DICKON: It's planted!

MARY: And the sun is only slipping over the edge.

COLIN: Help me up, Dickon. I want to be standing when it goes. That's part of the magic.

(Lights come down on the garden and come up on MRS. MEDLOCK and DR. CRAVEN in the house as MUSIC fades.)

DR. CRAVEN: He stays out in the garden a great deal. Where do you think he goes?

MRS. MEDLOCK: Lord knows. He won't let anyone follow him, excepting Miss Mary and Dickon.

DR. CRAVEN: His appetite is still good?

MRS. MEDLOCK: Enormous. Him an' Miss Mary both. But it's very strange . . .

DR. CRAVEN: What?

MRS. MEDLOCK: Well, when I complimented him on it, he suggested it was . . . unnatural. It's almost as if he didn't want anyone thinking he was well.

DR. CRAVEN: Yes. And when I mentioned writing to his father, he grew quite irritated.

SCENE FOUR

SCENE: MUSIC [III, #10]. Lights up on BEN.

BEN: While the secret garden was coming alive and two children were coming alive with it, there was a man wandering around certain faraway places in the Norwegian fjords and mountains of Switzerland, and he was a man who for ten years had kept his mind filled with dark and heartbroken thinking.

(MR. CRAVEN enters.)

BEN: He was a tall man with a drawn face and crooked shoulders, and the name he always entered on hotel registers was . . . (MUSIC OUT.)

MR. CRAVEN: Archibald Craven, Misselthwaite Manor, Yorkshire, England . . . I've come so far, yet I can't escape . . . The valley is so still . . . except this little stream, which almost seems alive . . . And the light . . . I never noticed—touching the mountains—it looks as if the world is just being born. What is happening? I almost feel . . . I don't understand . . . I almost feel as if I were alive!

(MUSIC IN [III, #11]. Lights up on COLIN's room. MARY, COLIN and DICKON are joyfully stuffing their mouths with currant buns. MARTHA's voice is heard.)

MARTHA: (Off.) Art tha' in, Mester Colin? I have thy tea! (With much giggling, MARY and DICKON get COLIN into bed. COLIN makes an attempt at sounding weak, as they ALL hurriedly try to finish eating the last of their food.)

COLIN: Come in . . .

(MARTHA enters.)

MARTHA: Here, Mester Colin. See what wonderful things Cook's sent up to thee.

COLIN: I don't want it.

MARTHA: Not want it? But tha's eaten nothing in two days. And tha' was doin' so well before.

COLIN: I told you it was an unnatural appetite. (MARY *starts to laugh and tries to stifle it, almost choking in the process.*)

MARTHA: What's the matter?

MARY: It was something between a sneeze and a cough, and it got into my throat.

MARTHA: (*Looks at* DICKON *who only shrugs.*) Well, I'm fair mothered to death wi' th' both of ye! And Dickon, tha'rt just as bad! (*She slams the tray down and stalks out.*)

MARY: Martha, we didn't mean . . .

DICKON: I'll make it right with her.

COLIN: Please do, Dickon. I don't want Martha to be angry. (DICKON *goes outside the room and approaches* MARTHA.)

DICKON: 'Ere, Martha, us weren't laughin' at you.

MARTHA: Eh! I know that, Dickon. But there's somethin' mysterious happenin' in this house, an' I'm worried about Mester Colin.

DICKON: Don't tha' be worryin' about him. He's as healthy as a young hawk.

MARTHA: Then why won't he eat?

DICKON: Martha, I've got a secret to keep. It's not a bad 'un, tha' knows that.

MARTHA: Is it about Mester Colin?

DICKON: Aye, but it's no worse than hidin' where a bird's nest is. Tha' doesn't mind it, does tha'?

MARTHA: If tha'rt in it, then it must be a good secret.

DICKON: There's a good girl!

MARTHA: An' Mester Colin is really gettin' better?

DICKON: He's so better that when his father comes home he won't be recognizin' him.

MARTHA: Eh! Mester Craven mun come home soon!

DICKON: Aye. Th' lad doesn't say so, but he misses him, I can tell.

MARTHA: Then someone mun send word to him. An' I know just th' person!

DICKON: Who?

MARTHA: If tha' can have thy secrets, I can have mine. (MUSIC, *lights up on house.* MARTHA *exits.*)

(*Lights up on* COLIN *and* MARY *as* DICKON *shrugs. He pops into the room, gives a thumbs-up sign and leaves.* COLIN *and* MARY *shout for joy.*)

COLIN: Hooray!

MARY: Shhh!

COLIN: (*Sighs.*) I wish my father would come home. I can't go on pretending like this much longer. Now that I am a real boy my legs and body are so full of magic that I can't keep them still . . . I wish it wasn't raining today. (MUSIC IN [III, #12].)

MARY: Colin, do you know how many rooms there are in this house?

COLIN: About a thousand, I suppose.

MARY: There's about a hundred, all locked up.

COLIN: It sounds like a secret garden. Suppose we go and look at them. You could wheel me in my chair when we got into the hall.

MARY: That's what I was thinking. (They start out. MARY notices Mrs. Craven's picture.) Colin . . .

COLIN: I know what you want me to tell you . . . I'm going to keep the curtain drawn back.

MARY: Why?

COLIN: Because it doesn't make me angry anymore to see her. I want to see her laughing all the time. I think she must have been a magic sort of person, perhaps.

MARY: You are so like her now that sometimes I think you are her ghost made into a boy.

COLIN: If I were her ghost—my father would be fond of me.

(They exit as lights come up on MR. CRAVEN. MARTHA enters above MR. CRAVEN. MUSIC changes.)

MARTHA: As the golden summer changed into the deep golden autumn, Mr. Craven went to the Lake of Como. There he found the loveliness of a dream. And it was there that a certain letter found its way to him. (MR. CRAVEN takes a letter from his vest pocket and begins to read it aloud.)

MR. CRAVEN: "Dear Sir, I am Susan Sowerby that made bold to speak to you once on the moor . . ." Susan Sowerby? Ah, yes. Martha and Dickon's mother . . . "It was about Miss Mary, I spoke" . . . (MUSIC OUT.) That's right. Miss Mary and her bit of earth . . . (Reads again.) "Please, sir, I would come home if I were you . . ." Home . . . Perhaps I should. But, Colin . . . No, I don't think I could bear to look at Colin just yet.

(MR. CRAVEN freezes as lights come up on COLIN, MARY, DICKON and BEN in the garden.)

COLIN: Mary! Dickon! Just look at me. I'm well!

MARY: Aye, that tha'rt.

COLIN: I feel as if I want to shout out something—something thankful, joyful! Something magic!

BEN: (Gruffly.) Tha' might sing th' Doxology.

COLIN: What is that?

BEN: Dickon can sing it for thee, I'll warrant.

DICKON: They sing it in church. Mother says she believes th' skylarks sing it when they get up in th' mornin'.

COLIN: Then it must be a nice song. Sing it, Dickon. I want to hear it.

DICKON: Tha' must take off tha' cap, an' so mun tha', Ben, an' tha' mun stand up, tha' knows . . . (As they prepare to sing, MR. CRAVEN sits. He continues to read the letter.)

MR. CRAVEN: "Please sir, I would come home if I was you. I think you would be glad to come, and if you will excuse me, sir—I think your lady would ask you to come if she was here. Your obedient servant, Susan Sowerby." My lady . . . Lilias . . . Ten years . . . *(His head nods as he begins to fall asleep.)* Too late . . . too late . . .

DICKON: *(Using his pipe to get a note, he begins to sing, his voice floating angelically.* MUSIC *[III, #13]).* Praise God from whom all blessings flow . . . *(A* WOMAN's *voice is heard, softly calling above the music.)*

WOMAN'S VOICE: Archie . . . Archie . . .

MR. CRAVEN: *(Lifting his head.)* Lilias? Lilias, where are you?

DICKON: Praise him all creatures here below . . .

WOMAN'S VOICE: In the garden . . .

MR. CRAVEN: In the garden? But the door is locked, and the key is buried deep.

DICKON: Praise him above ye heavenly host . . .

WOMAN'S VOICE: In the garden, Archie . . .

DICKON: Praise father, son and holy ghost . . . *(MR.* CRAVEN *wakes up on the word "ghost," looks at the letter in his hand, folds it.)*

MR. CRAVEN: I will go back to Misselthwaite. I'll go at once.

(The lights fade on MR. CRAVEN *as he exits to return home and come up full on* MARY, COLIN *and* DICKON *in the secret garden as they continue their celebration. The door is shut on the garden as* MR. CRAVEN *reenters.* MUSIC *underscores to the end of the play.)*

MR. CRAVEN: I will try to find the key. I will try to open the door. I must—though I don't know why.

(MRS. MEDLOCK *enters.)*

MRS. MEDLOCK: Mr. Craven! We did not expect . . .

MR. CRAVEN: How is Master Colin, Medlock?

MRS. MEDLOCK: Master Colin, sir? Well, sir, he's different in a manner of speaking.

MR. CRAVEN: Worse?

MRS. MEDLOCK: To tell the truth, sir, Master Colin might be better and he might be changing for the worse. His appetite, sir, is past understanding and his ways . . .

MR. CRAVEN: Where is Master Colin now?

MRS. MEDLOCK: He's in the garden, sir. He's always . . .

MR. CRAVEN: In the garden!

(MR. CRAVEN *leaves* MRS. MEDLOCK *and enters the garden path. As he approaches the door of the secret garden, he almost collides with* COLIN *who is triumphantly finishing a race with* DICKON *and* MARY *close behind.)*

MR. CRAVEN: What—Who—

COLIN: *(Breathlessly.)* Father!! I'm Colin. You can't believe it. I scarcely can believe it myself. I'm Colin!

MR. CRAVEN: (*Connecting his dream and reality in joyous discovery.*) In the garden . . .

COLIN: Yes. It was the garden that did it—and Mary and Dickon and the creatures. Aren't you glad, Father? Aren't you glad? I'm going to live forever and ever!

(*They exit as* MUSIC *fades, and lights come up on* MRS. MEDLOCK *and* BEN.)

MRS. MEDLOCK: Did you see either of them, Weatherstaff?

BEN: Aye, that I did.

MRS. MEDLOCK: Both of them?

BEN: Both of 'em.

MRS. MEDLOCK: Together?

BEN: Together, ma'am.

MRS. MEDLOCK: Where was Master Colin? How did he look? What did they say to each other?

BEN: I didna' hear that, along o' only bein' on th' stepladder lookin' over the wall. But I'll tell thee this . . . (MUSIC *resumes.*) . . . there's things goin' on outside as you house people knows nowt about. An' what tha'll find out tha'll find out soon . . . Look there, if tha's curious. Look what's comin' across the grass.

(MUSIC *swells triumphantly as the door of the secret garden is flung open by* MARY *and* DICKON. COLIN *and* MR. CRAVEN *walk through.* MARTHA *and* DR. CRAVEN *enter from opposite sides.*)

MARTHA: Across the lawn came the master of Misselthwaite.

DR. CRAVEN: And he looked as many of them had never seen him.

MRS. MEDLOCK: And by his side with his head up in the air . . .

BEN: And his eyes full of laughter . . .

DICKON: Walked as strongly and steadily as any boy in Yorkshire . . .

MARY: Master Colin! (MUSIC *swells as* COLIN *and* MR. CRAVEN, *flanked by* MARY *and* DICKON, *walk to center, and the lights fade.*)

CURTAIN

WILEY AND THE HAIRY MAN

by
Suzan Zeder

Suzan Zeder, who holds a master's degree in theatre from Southern Methodist University in Dallas, Texas, and a doctorate from Florida State University, has been recognized nationally and internationally as one of the nation's leading playwrights for family audiences. Her plays have been performed in all fifty states, Canada, Great Britain, Japan, Australia, Germany, Israel, and New Zealand, and have been published in Great Britain, Germany, and Japan. *Step on a Crack, Wiley and the Hairy Man, In a Room Somewhere,* and *The Death and Life of Sherlock Holmes* are performed regularly by professional and university theatres throughout the country. *Doors* and *Mother Hicks* were produced at the Kennedy Center in Washington, D.C., which also cocommissioned *Do Not Go Gentle.* In 1990 Anchorage Press published *Wish in One Hand and Spit in the Other,* an anthology of Zeder's nine published plays edited by Susan Pearson Davis. *The Taste of Sunrise: Tuc's Story,* the prequel to *Mother Hicks,* premiered at Seattle Children's Theatre in 1996.

Zeder is a three-time winner of the Distinguished Play Award given by the American Alliance for Theatre and Education. From 1989 to 1991 she chaired the Playwrights' Fellowship Panel and served on the Professional Companies' Panel for the National Endowment for the Arts. In 1996 Zeder was inducted into the College of Fellows of the American Theatre.

In 1991 Professor Zeder became the first holder of the newly created Endowed Chair in Theatre for Youth/Playwriting at The University of Texas at Austin, the first endowed chair in this area of study in the United States. The endowment funds made it possible for Zeder to be instrumental in the development of new works such as *The Yellow Boat, Wolf Child, Ellen Foster,* and her own, *The Taste of Sunrise.*

In addition to playwriting, teaching, and collaboration with other playwrights on the new play-development projects, Zeder is immersed in the writing of her first novel, *The Milk Dragon,* which has to do with creativity, censorship, and the impact of fear upon society and upon children.

The most rewarding aspect of writing plays *about* young people is the possibility of dealing with dynamic young characters of enormous emotional velocity at a time when their lives change forever. The dignity and depth of children are sources of constant inspiration and challenge me to render their world as faithfully as I can.

—SUZAN ZEDER

WILEY AND THE HAIRY MAN

CHARACTERS

Wiley
Mammy
The Hairy Man
Dog
Chorus
(Four suggested but more may be used)

SETTING

Mammy's House
The Swamp

TIME

Any Time

(*As the audience enters, they find themselves in the gloomy, mysterious atmosphere of the swamp. The set suggests a rough lattice-work of boards which reach out at angles forming odd tree-like structures. One section of the set suggests Mammy's house which is merely an extension of the environment. Several sharply raked platforms are covered with vines and moss. The theatre is filled with strange swamp sounds: moans and creaks and rattles and wind sounds are made by the* CHORUS. *The lights are dim and cast strange shadows.*)

WILEY *lies sleeping in a single shaft of light. Around him the* CHORUS *lie in various positions on the set. They are formless creatures, part of the swamp made up of moss, vines, and odd bits of swamp grass.*

The swamp sounds grow louder, and the CHORUS *begins to move in an eerie, rhythmic nightmare.* WILEY *tosses and turns, caught in his dream. The sounds, strange and abstract at first, slowly form themselves into words.*)

CHORUS I: Wiiiiiiley . . . Wiiiiiiley. . . .

CHORUS II: Haaaaaairy Man! Haaaaaairy Man!

CHORUS III: Look out, Wiley! Wake up, Wiley!

CHORUS IV: He done got your Pappy, and he's gonna get you!

CHORUS III: He done got your Pappy . . .

CHORUS I: . . . And he's gonna get you!

CHORUS II: Haaaaaairy Man! Haaaaaairy Man!

CHORUS IV: He done got your Pappy, and he's gonna get you!

CHORUS I: Wiiiiiiley . . . Wiiiiiiley . . .

CHORUS IV: He done got your Pappy . . .

CHORUS I: . . . And he's gonna get you! (*A shrouded* FIGURE *with a candle enters and slowly walks toward* WILEY.)

CHORUS III: Look out, Wiley. Wake up, Wiley.

CHORUS II: Haaaaaairy Man! Haaaaaairy Man!

CHORUS IV: He done got your Pappy, and he's gonna get you!

CHORUS I: He done got your Pappy . . .

CHORUS III: . . . And he's gonna get you! (FIGURE *reaches out toward* WILEY.)

FIGURE: Wiley!

CHORUS I: (*Echo.*) Wiiiiiiley. . . .

CHORUS IV: He done got your Pappy, and he's gonna get you!

CHORUS II: He done got your Pappy . . .

ALL CHORUS: . . . AND HE'S GONNA GET . . .

FIGURE: WILEY! Wake up, Wiley! (WILEY *wakes up with a bolt, sees the* FIGURE *and dives beneath the covers with his bottom in the air.*)

WILEY: Go 'way, Hairy Man. Leave me alone, Hairy Man. Don't touch me, Hairy Man!

MAMMY: (*Taking off the hood.*) I ain't no Hairy Man. I is your Mammy! (MAMMY *punctuates her sentence with a swat on* WILEY's *rear.*)

WILEY: (*Up and rubbing his bottom.*) Owwweeeee. That sure is my Mammy. No Hairy Man kin hit that hard.

MAMMY: Wiley, you was just havin' a bad dream.

WILEY: I saw him. I saw the Hairy Man, and he was comin' for me. I was trying to run, but I couldn't, and there I was starin' right into the Hairy Man's hairy eyeball.

MAMMY: You ain't got no cause to fear. There ain't no Hairy Man not nowheres near.

WILEY: But I saw Him! I saw his hairy hands, and his hairy teeth and his horrible hairy breath.

MAMMY: You know your Mammy's got more magic than any old Hairy Man.

WILEY: But he done got my Pappy and . . .

MAMMY: Looks like I gots to do a magic spell to get that Hairy Man outta your head. (MAMMY *assumes the conjure position and holds* WILEY's *head between her hands.* CHORUS *makes "conjure sounds.")*

MAMMY: (*Conjuring.*) Hairy Man, Hairy Man, git outta his head. Go scare yourself a tree toad instead. Hairy Man, Hairy Man, git outta his eyes. Listen to me while I conjurize. Hairy Man, Hairy Man, git outta his mouth. Git away from here. Go way down south! (*Pause.*)

MAMMY: Well, is he gone? (CHORUS IV *waves his arms.*)

WILEY: What's that?

MAMMY: Just a shadow on the wall. Sun's comin up, that's all.

WILEY: It's the Hairy Man.

MAMMY: I better hurry up the day and get some light in here. (MAMMY *assumes the conjure position and throws a quick spell.*) Rumble, bumble, snider, rup. Sun, sun, hurry it up!

(CHORUS I *hoists a colored sun up one of the structures, and* CHORUS II *crows like a rooster.*)

WILEY: What's that?

MAMMY: Jest some old rooster.

WILEY: It's the Hairy Man!

MAMMY: (*Conjuring.*) Beetle, tweedle, sneedle, sneak. Rooster, Rooster, shut your beak! (CHORUS II *stops mid-crow.*)

WILEY: I'm gonna get my dog and bring him right here in bed with me!

MAMMY: You are gonna do no such thing.

WILEY: But the Hairy Man cain't stand no dogs, everybody knows that.

MAMMY: Wiley, I am the best conjure woman in the whole southwest county. I kin make the sun come up and the moon go down. I kin do spells an' conjures, an' charms, an' chants; I kin cure a cold or heal a wart fifty miles away. But there are two things I cannot do; I cannot get that fear outta your head, and I cannot stand that Dog slobbering up my house!

WILEY: Mammy, how did the Hairy Man git my Pappy?

MAMMY: He just did, Wiley.

WILEY: People say my Pappy was a bad man and a no count.

MAMMY: People say.

WILEY: People say he slept while the weeds grew higher than the cotton, that he used to git himself hog drunk and chicken wild, and that he never even spit lessen someone else did it for him.

MAMMY: People say.

WILEY: Was my Pappy a bad man?

MAMMY: *(With respect.)* Wiley, he was your Pappy!

WILEY: But people say he'd never cross the Jordan, cause when he died, the Hairy Man'd be there waitin' for him. When he fell into the river near Tombigbee, they never did find him. They jest heard a big man laughin' across the river.

MAMMY: He done got your Pappy.

CHORUS I and II: Said Mammy, said she . . .

MAMMY: And you better be keerful.

WILEY: Or he's gonna get me.

MAMMY: Now, git yourself up and dressed, it is time for breakfast.

WILEY: Do I gotta go to the swamp today?

MAMMY: You have got to build a hound house for that dog of yours.

WILEY: I'm jest gonna sit here and do nothin' jest like my Pappy.

MAMMY: *(Angry.)* Wiley, don't you ever say that! Now, get yourself up and wash. (MAMMY *crosses into the kitchen area.* WILEY *dives back under the covers.)*

WILEY: I'm tired. That Hairy Man scared all the restin' outta me.

MAMMY: Breakfast . . . *(She conjures a quick off-handed spell.)*

MAMMY: Ashes, embers, soot on my face. Make me right there a fireplace.

(CHORUS *form a fireplace with a cauldron.)*

MAMMY: Wiley, I want to hear feet on that floor and washin' in those ears right now!

WILEY: *(In a gruff voice.)* There ain't no Wiley here. He's been ete all up by the Hairy Man.

MAMMY: I ain't foolin.

WILEY: *(Lumping about.)* I tol' you Mammy there ain't no Wiley here. Jest an old ugly Hairy Man with fourteen toes and a bone in his nose.

MAMMY: You get up and put on your clothes!

WILEY: Hairy Man, Hairy Man, comin' through the trees; stampin' and a-squishin' everything he sees. *(Realizing what he has just said.)* Hairy Man? (WILEY *dives under the covers.)*

MAMMY: What are you doing?

WILEY: *(In a small voice.)* I jest skeered myself all over again.

MAMMY: There is only one way to get you outta that bed, and boy, you asked for it! (MAMMY *storms into* WILEY's *room and douses him with a wash-basin full of water.)* Now, git up!

WILEY: I am up, I'm up, I'm up!!! (MAMMY *scrubs him with the cloth.)*

MAMMY: I swear you are the dirtiest boy I ever laid eyes on. Open up them ears. Hold still. Now, come eat! (MAMMY *returns to the kitchen.)*

MAMMY: Now, where was I? Breakfast. *(She conjures.)*

MAMMY: Tables and chairs . . . Right over theres . . .

(CHORUS *become table and chairs.*)

MAMMY: *(Conjuring.)* Pot, pot, get yourself hot!

(CHORUS *with cauldron make bubbling sounds,* WILEY *enters kitchen.*)

MAMMY: What do you want to eat this morning?

WILEY: Not much. Jest some flap jacks an' lasses, and taters an' lasses, and biscuits an' lasses, and eggs an' lasses, and catfish an' grits, an' lasses. *(As he says each one* MAMMY *scoops some out of the cauldron into a bowl.)*

MAMMY: *(Concerned.)* What's the matter, Wiley? Ain't you hongry? I never knew you to eat so skimpy.

WILEY: The Hairy Man musta skeered the hongries outta me. *(WILEY gobbles his food.)*

MAMMY: Don't forget to drink your milk.

WILEY: *(Turning the glass upside down.)* There ain't no milk in here.

MAMMY: I forgot. *(MAMMY wordlessly snaps her fingers and points to WILEY's glass.)*

WILEY: There still ain't . . . ooops. *(WILEY turns the glass again, this time there is milk which spills.)**

MAMMY: Dumbhead! When I say there's milk, there's milk!

WILEY: Yasum. *(Pause.)* Mammy, I think tomorrow's a better day for goin' to the swamp for wood for my hound house. . . .

MAMMY: No! Today is the day. I told you that. But maybe I ought to teach you a conjure or two to keep you safe from the Hairy Man.

WILEY: You know I ain't no good at conjurin' no way no how.

MAMMY: Wiley, you hesh and come here now. *(WILEY crosses to MAMMY.)* Wiley, you knows I's the best, the best conjure woman in the whole south-west county.

CHORUS II: The best conjure woman in the whole southwest. *(MAMMY shoots a look at WILEY.)*

WILEY: I didn't say nothin'.

MAMMY: You are my son and my only child, and you are gonna learn. This here's a spell for changin' stickers and prickers and bonkers and briars into rubber so's they cain't hurt you.

WILEY: I cain't learn it.

MAMMY: Yes, you can. It jest goes . . . "Chip chop, chum, blubber. Turn this tree trunk into rubber."

WILEY: *(Carelessly.)* Chip, champ, chomp, grubber. Blubber, drubber scrubber, flubber . . .

---

*A trick glass is used for this; one with a wide lip inside one half the glass. When you pour this glass on one side, nothing comes out; when you pour it from the other, the contents spill out. These are available at Magic stores.

MAMMY: *(Furious.)* Wiley! You gotta listen to the conjure words, cause when they are outta your mouth there is no takin' them back!

WILEY: But I cain't keep it all in my head. Powders, 'n potions, 'n magic, 'n charms. An' raising' the spirits, 'n wavin' my arms. An' screechin' an' stampin', an' mutterin' low! I jest cain't do it, the answer is no!

MAMMY: Well, someday you gotta learn.

WILEY: Well, someday ain't today!

MAMMY: You better get yourself goin', ya hear? If'n you take your hound Dog, you got nothin' to fear.

WILEY: 'Cause the Hairy Man sure cain't stand no Dogs . . .

MAMMY: Everybody knows that. *(WILEY turns to go, and MAMMY stops him.)*

MAMMY: Take this here bag. It's got some magic on it. It'll catch up the wind and hold it for you till you let it go.

WILEY: *(Taking the bag.)* Thanks. Mammy. *(WILEY turns to go.)*

MAMMY: And Wiley, take some of this here powder. Jest a pinch will make every livin' creature your friend . . . except the Hairy Man.

WILEY: *(Taking the powder.)* Thanks, Mammy. *(WILEY turns to go.)*

MAMMY: And Wiley? You be sure to take your hound Dog.

WILEY: Yasum . . . YASUM! *(WILEY crosses out of the house, and MAMMY watches.)*

MAMMY: *(Muttering to herself.)* He done got his Pappy.

CHORUS I and II: Said Mammy, said she . . .

MAMMY: . . . And he better be keerful . . .

WILEY: Or he's gonna get me.

(As WILEY crosses down, the house disappears. MAMMY exits and CHORUS comes to life.)

CHORUS IV: So Wiley . . .

CHORUS II and III: Wherever he goes . . .

CHORUS I: Takes his Dog.

WILEY: *(Calling.)* Dog!

CHORUS IV: Cause the Hairy Man sure cain't stand no dogs . . .

CHORUS I: Everybody knows that. Everybody knows that.

(WILEY whistles, and DOG enters in a bound. He is extremely fierce looking, but he moves with the lumbering playfullness of an overgrown puppy. He looks about ready to spring and then flops over asleep. WILEY laughs.)

WILEY: Hey there, Dog, what'cha doing there sleeping in the sun? Come on, boy, let's have some fun. *(DOG opens one eye and rolls over.)* I know what'll get you. *(WILEY creeps up beside DOG and meows, DOG leaps up wide awake and growls, then he licks WILEY's face.)* Good Dog, O.K. Boy, fetch . . .

(WILEY throws a stick, DOG watches it go and sprawls out asleep.)

WILEY: DOG? Hey, Boy, I know what let's do. I gotta game for you. Now, I'm going to hold my breath for a full minute and hold real, real still; and you gotta come over here and try to make me move. You gotta make me flinch, or move, or blink, or somethin'. If you do, I'll give you something to eat.

(At this promise DOG *is interested.* WILEY *takes a deep breath and strikes a pose.* DOG *sniffs him, tugs at his pants, barks at him, and finally climbs up and stands balancing his paws on* WILEY's *shoulders and slobbers in his face.* WILEY *surpresses a smile and finally exhales. They laugh and play.)*

WILEY: I won! You didn't make me flinch, or move, or blink, or nothin'. Now, Dog, Mammy says we gotta go to the swamp and cut down a tree. 'Cause I'm gonna make you a hound house. But we gotta be careful of the Hairy Man, see! 'Cause he done got my Pappy, and he's tryin' to get me! Come on, you old hound dog! (DOG *barks twice, and they set off.)*

CHORUS IV: So Wiley . . .

CHORUS ALL: He takes up his axe. And he goes to the swamp, but he don't leave tracks. 'Cause the Hairy Man's hiding somewhere, you see. And he done got his Pappy . . .

WILEY: . . . and he's tryin' to get me.

CHORUS: But the Hairy Man sure cain't stand no Dogs . . . Everybody knows that. Everybody knows that. Everybody knows that.

(On this line the CHORUS *become the swamp;* WILEY *and* DOG *make their way cautiously.* CHORUS *make swamp sounds.)*

WILEY: Here we are, Dog, the deepest part of the swamp. Now, this here's a mightly dangerous place 'cause the Hairy Man lives somewhere near and everything's magic . . . Hairy Man magic. You stay close . . . Come on, Boy . . . *(Swamp sounds are louder and become words.)*

CHORUS I: Oh, the sun never shines . . .

CHORUS II: . . . And the wind never blows,

CHORUS III: And the mud turns to slime,

CHORUS IV: The deeper you goes. (CHORUS *becomes mud which oozes around* WILEY's *feet and makes a slurping sound as he moves through it.)*

WILEY: Gulp.

DOG: Gulp.

CHORUS I and III: And the branches reach, And the vines twine around (CHORUS *become reaching branches and vines.)*

CHORUS IV: And the stumps and the stickers stick up through the ground. (CHORUS *becomes a huge sticker bush.)*

WILEY: Lookee there, DOG! I never seen that sticker bush there before. It must be Hairy Man magic. Maybe it's a trap! We gotta be keerful and jest kinda wiggle in and squiggle out. Now, look here, Dog, and I'll show you, 'cause I am the best at wigglin' and squigglin' in the whole southwest county. (DOG *zips right through the bush.)*

WILEY: Hey, that's not the right way! You gotta kinda squinch yourself down and . . . (DOG *zips through again as* WILEY *tries to squeeze through the sticker bush.* CHORUS *pinch him and stick him with the briars.)*

WILEY: Owwwww oweeeeee Owwwwweee Ouch, Ouch, Ouch! (DOG *bounds in and pulls* WILEY *through.*) I made it. Hairy Man didn't get me, no siree. But Dog, I gotta bottom full of briars. Oww, ow, ow, Ouch. (DOG *helps* WILEY *pull out the stickers.* CHORUS *dissolves sticker bush.*)

CHORUS: Shhhh, shhh, shhh, shhh, The Hairy Man listens and the Hairy Man sees; He's got eyes in the bushes and ears in the trees . . . (WILEY *and* DOG *move on.*)

CHORUS: 'Cause the skeeters and the flies is all his spies. And they's setting up a trap for sure, for sure. So's you better watch your step for sure.

(CHORUS *becomes a bubbling pool of quicksand.*)

WILEY: Dog! Don't move. Lookee there! That's a pool of quicksand. That's Hairy Man magic for sure, and we gotta be keerful elsewise it'll swaller us up for sure. (DOG *growls at the quick sand.*)

WILEY: We got to leapfrog ourselves right over it. Now, git down and . . . (DOG *crouches, and* WILEY *leapfrogs; they do it several times, and* DOG *finally leapfrogs over the quicksand.* WILEY *is still on the other side.*)

WILEY: Dog, that ain't no good. Now, you gotta come back so's I kin leapfrog over you. (DOG *leaps over the pool, and he and* WILEY *repeat the leapfrogging until* WILEY *leapfrogs over the quicksand.* WILEY *looks puzzled because* DOG *is on the other side.*)

WILEY: Now, I gotta come back so's you kin leapfrog over me. (WILEY *tries to leap over the quicksand but falls a bit short and lands in it.*)

WILEY: Ooooops. (*He starts to sink.*)

WILEY: Dog, Dog! I'm sinkin'! Help! The Hairy Man's got me. Help! (DOG *bounds over the pool and leans forward.* WILEY *takes hold of his collar, and* CHORUS *slowly rolls away as if* WILEY *is being pulled out.* CHORUS *moves off and forms the tree.*)

WILEY: Good Dog! Good Boy! That stuff almost swallered me up. Now, let's go and find ourselves a tree.

(CHORUS *makes "Hairy Man" sounds heard in the nightmare.*)

CHORUS I and IV: There's some mighty scarey sounds, When the Hairy Man's around.

WILEY: Gulp!

DOG: Gulp!

WILEY: (*Coming upon the tree.*) Hey Dog, what do you see? Ain't that there the finest tree you ever laid eyes on? Now, you stay right there and don't move; 'cause when I start swinging them chips is gonna fly. ("*Hairy Man*" *sounds are louder.* WILEY *sizes up the tree.*)

WILEY: This here's a good tree. Jest look at that trunk.

(*From offstage a huge bone tied to a string is thrown directly in front of* DOG. DOG *watches as the bone is slowly pulled offstage.* WILEY *sees none of this, he has his back to* DOG.)

WILEY: Now, Dog, you stay right here; 'cause as long as you do, we ain't gonna have no trouble with the Hairy Man. (*Bone is thrown on again.* DOG *sniffs it but does not move.*)

WILEY: 'Cause the Hairy Man sure cain't stand no dogs. Everybody knows that. (*Bone is thrown on a third time, this time bonking* DOG *on the head.* DOG *barks loudly and bone zips off.* DOG *bounds off after it.*)

WILEY: (*Turning.*) Hey, come back . . . Hound Dog don't chase no bones. CHASE NO BONES? Oh me, oh my, I never did see no bone in the sky. The Hairy Man must be nearby. (WILEY *goes back to the tree.*)

CHORUS I: Keerful, Wiley . . . (WILEY *chops.*)

CHORUS: Whack. (WILEY *lifts axe.*)

CHORUS II: Look out, Wiley. (WILEY *chops.*)

CHORUS: Whack. (WILEY *lifts axe.*)

CHORUS III and IV: Lookee there, Wiley. (WILEY *turns slowly.*)

CHORUS: (*Starting at a whisper and building.*) Stampin', stompin', coming through the trees. Shufflin' through the swamp grass, blowin' in the breeze. Bounding, pounding, fast as he can, What did Wiley see? . . . He saw the HAIRY MAN!

(*The* HAIRY MAN *enters slowly stalking* WILEY. WILEY *yelps and climbs the tree.*)

WILEY: (*Terrified.*) THE HAIRY MAN?

CHORUS: The Hairy Man! (*Echoing.*) Hairy Man . . . Hairy Man . . . Hairy Man . . . Hairy Man. (CHORUS *makes "Hairy Man" sounds.*)

(HAIRY MAN *slowly approaches the tree where* WILEY *tries to hide.*)

CHORUS I: (*Wailing.*) Wiiiiiiley . . .

HAIRY MAN: (*Echoing.*) Wiiiiiiley.

WILEY: You get away from me, Hairy Man. You go on. I'll sic my hound Dog on you.

HAIRY MAN: Wiley.

WILEY: Hairy Man, I tol' you . . . Hound DOG!!! Here, DOG!

HAIRY MAN: There ain't no hound Dog not nowhere's here.

WILEY: Says you, Hairy Man, I know he's near.

HAIRY MAN: He's chasin' my magic miles from here.

WILEY: (*Desperate.*) HOUND DOG!

HAIRY MAN: What'cha doin' up in that tree?

WILEY: Climbin'.

HAIRY MAN: But it's only me.

WILEY: I know, that's why I'm climbin'.

HAIRY MAN: Why don't'cha come home with me for supper?

WILEY: I ain't even had lunch yet.

HAIRY MAN: Neither have I, Wiley . . .

WILEY: My Mammy, she tol me don't you never have no conversation with no Hairy Man. So you get away from here.

HAIRY MAN: If you come on down, I'll give you a nice piece of sugar cane.

WILEY: If'n you is so hongry, you eat it yourself.

HAIRY MAN: I am tryin' to be nice, Wiley, but you is gonna get me riled. If'n you don't come down, I is comin' up.

WILEY: You cain't, cause you got the ugliest, slimiest, no tree climbinest feet in the whole county.

HAIRY MAN: *(Wiggling his feet in the air.)* Why don't you come down for a closer look?

WILEY: I don't need no closer look. I kin smell 'em all the way up here. P.U.! Hairy Man, you got smelly feet.

HAIRY MAN: *(Angry.)* WILEY! I'm gonna cast a spell on this tree, boy, gonna be your end.

WILEY: No, siree, this tree's my friend.

HAIRY MAN: Look out, Wiley! There are snakes in that tree.

WILEY: No, there ain't.

HAIRY MAN: There is now. (HAIRY MAN *shakes all over and throws a wild conjure at the tree.)* I shakes, I shakes, That tree's full of snakes.

*(*CHORUS *become snakes and wind all over* WILEY.)*

WILEY: Oh No, OOOOOOOH NOOOOOO! Oh snakes, nice snakes, Hey, Mammy's powder! (WILEY *takes the powder and blows it on the snakes.)*

WILEY: Snakes, snakes be my friend. Sic HIM. (WILEY *pats the snakes on the head, points to the* HAIRY MAN. *They turn and hiss at the* HAIRY MAN.)

WILEY: Dumb ole Hairy Man, even snakes like me better'n you.

HAIRY MAN: GO WAY, snakes! Now, I'll show you not to fool with the Hairy Man. (HAIRY MAN *throws himself into another wild conjure.)* Branches, Branches, Brittle as ice. Snap in two when I clap twice. (HAIRY MAN *claps twice. Branches snap under* WILEY; *but he manages to catch himself.)*

HAIRY MAN: I got you, WILEY!

WILEY: Oh, no, you don't.

HAIRY MAN: Then I'll blow you out. *(He conjures.)*

HAIRY MAN: Wind, wind, rise and howl. Make those branches creak and growl.

(A huge wind blows the tree. CHORUS *make the branches bend,* WILEY *grabs up the bag.)*

WILEY: Mammy's WIND BAG!! Bag, bag, do your charm. Keep me. Keep me safe from harm. (WILEY *opens the bag. It inflates as the wind sound dies down.)*

WILEY: Hairy Man, I always knew you were a wind bag. How do you like this here? (WILEY *opens the bag. It deflates.* CHORUS *makes a rushing sound. The* HAIRY MAN *is blown over.)*

WILEY: Hairy Man, I am as safe as I kin be; sitting here in this old tree.

HAIRY MAN: *(Recovering.)* Wiley! Now, I am gonna do something terrible.

WILEY: You ain't so scarey now. (HAIRY MAN *spies the axe, and picks it up, brandishing it.)*

HAIRY MAN: I AIN'T?

WILEY: OH, you is, you is, you is, you is!

HAIRY MAN: *(Advancing.)* Lookee here what I found.

WILEY: Gulp.

HAIRY MAN: Now, I am gonna chop you to the ground. (HAIRY MAN *starts chopping slowly. As he does, the tree shakes.*)

WILEY: Ohhhhh, Nooooo!

CHORUS: Chop.

WILEY: Ohhh! Mammy tried to teach me a conjure for this.

CHORUS: Chop.

WILEY: What are the words, the words, the words?

CHORUS: Chop.

WILEY: Chip, yes . . . chip, chip chop. Chip chop, chip chop.

CHORUS: Chop.

WILEY: Chip chop chump, that's it . . . Chip chop chump . . .

CHORUS: Chop.

WILEY: Chip, chop, chump, blubber. Turn this tree trunk into rubber.

CHORUS: BOINK.

WILEY: Chip, chop, chump, blubber. Turn this tree trunk into rubber.

CHORUS: BOINK. (*On the "Boink," the* HAIRY MAN's *axe bounces off the tree.* HAIRY MAN *speeds up chopping.* WILEY *speeds up chanting.*)

WILEY: Chip, chop, chump, blubber. Turn this tree trunk into rubber. Chip, chop, chump, blubber. Turn this tree trunk into rubber. Chip, chop, chump, blubber. Turn this tree trunk into rubber. Chip, chop, chump, blubber. Turn this tree trunk into rubber.

CHORUS: Boink, Boink, Boink, Boink, Boink. (HAIRY MAN *falls exhausted, but still chopping.* DOG *is heard barking in the distance.*)

WILEY: HOUND DOG!!!

HAIRY MAN: (*Gasping.*) W . . . W . . . Wiley, don't you call no . . .

WILEY: DOG. (DOG's *barking gets closer.*)

WILEY: Run, Hairy Man. My Dog's gonna bite you like you never been bit before.

HAIRY MAN: I cain't stand no DOGS.

WILEY: (*Delighted.*) Everybody knows that . . . DOG.

(DOG *enters in a bound.* HAIRY MAN *grabs the axe. There is a moment of face-to-face confrontation.* HAIRY MAN *advances.*)

WILEY: Git him, DOG. Git him. (*They circle each other.* CHORUS III *slowly rolls out of the tree and lies down in back of the* HAIRY MAN.)

WILEY: Hairy Man. Look out for that old LOG behind you. You is about to fall over it.

HAIRY MAN: Hesh up, Wiley, I ain't fallin' for no dumb tricks.

WILEY: You is about to, Hairy Man.

HAIRY MAN: Yeeeeeowwwww. (HAIRY MAN *falls over the log, drops the axe, and exits at a run chased by* DOG. WILEY *comes down.*)

WILEY: Git him, Dog. Git him.

HAIRY MAN: (*Offstage.*) Yeeeeeooowwwww. (DOG *returns with tuft of hair.*)

WILEY: You all right, DOG? Good Boy. Thank you, Boy. We got him that time, but he'll be back. Let's go see Mammy, she'll know what to do. Oh, Dog, Oh, Boy, she's jest got to.

CHORUS: Cause when the Hairy Man gets mad . . . THAT'S BAD.

(MAMMY's *house*)

(WILEY *and* DOG *run back through the swamp to the house.* CHORUS *sets up house as before.* MAMMY *enters with cauldron and gazes into it intently.*)

WILEY: (*Outside the house.*) Dog, you go down to the hen house and you make sure that Hairy Man ain't nowheres near here. (DOG *exits, barking.* WILEY *enters house.*) Mammy? Mammy! Come here! You gotta help me, Mammy!

MAMMY: Don't hurry me boy, I'm comin'.

WILEY: (*Excited.*) He tried! He tried! He got me up a tree. He done got my Pappy, and he's gonna . . .

MAMMY: No, he ain't, Wiley!

WILEY: He came for me. I saw his hairy eyes, and his hairy teeth, and his horrible hairy feet. So I climbed a tree, and there he was lookin' up at me.

MAMMY: (*Quietly.*) I know, Wiley.

WILEY: (*Acting it out.*) And HE said . . . "Wiley!" And I said . . . "Hairy Man, you better leave me alone." And HE said . . . "Wiley!"

MAMMY: I know, Wiley.

WILEY: Oh, it was terrible, terrible. But I remembered the conjure and . . .

MAMMY: I know, Wiley.

WILEY: How do you know lessen I tell you?

MAMMY: I looked in my conjure pot and saw the whole thing. Wiley, we got trouble.

CHORUS I: 'Cause when the Hairy Man gets mad . . .

CHORUS IV: That's Bad!

WILEY: Mammy! Why don't you do a conjure to turn the Hairy Man into a mosquito, and I'll . . . (CHORUS *makes a buzzing sound, and* WILEY *slaps an imaginary insect.*) No more Hairy Man!

MAMMY: You think the Hairy Man would be dumb enough to let you squish him like that?

WILEY: (*Flicking it off his hand.*) Nope.

MAMMY: We gotta be smart to fool the Hairy Man.

WILEY: We are in a mess of trouble . . . I know, why don't you conjure up a big pit filled with slimey grimies, and the Hairy Man'll fall in and . . .

MAMMY: Wiley, I cain't conjure up a way to protect you from the Hairy Man.

WILEY: But my Dog! I'll get my Dog, and he'll . . . Dog! Dog!

MAMMY: Wiley! There ain't no magic, nor no dog strong enough to keep you safe every every minute. You gotta learn how to do it yourself.

WILEY: But that ain't fair. He's bigger than me.

MAMMY: Yep.

WILEY: What are we gonna do?

MAMMY: I am gonna try just once more to teach you how to conjure. Boy, you gotta fight magic with magic!

WILEY: I cain't.

MAMMY: Hesh up and pay attention. You gotta listen to what I tell you, and you gotta say just what I say, 'cause once the conjure words is spoke they's spoke forever. Now, stand here like this and put your feet apart . . .

WILEY: Apart from what?

MAMMY: From each other! Now, concentrate! Hard! (WILEY *closes his eyes and squinches up his face.*)

MAMMY: (*Exasperated.*) Open your eyes.

WILEY: I'm concentrating, Mammy. I'm concentrating.

MAMMY: How are you gonna see what I'm doin' lessen you got your eyes open? (WILEY *opens his eyes and stares.*)

MAMMY: Now, this is jest to practice . . . say . . . Snagle Blume . . . (MAMMY *makes small controlled circles with her hands as she says the magic words.*)

WILEY: (*Jumping up and down and making wild circles.*) SNAGLE BLOOOO.

MAMMY: What you jumpin' around like a tree toad for? Anyone would hear you conjuring fifty miles away! Now, a conjure is a QUIET thing! Snagle Blume.

WILEY: (*Whispering and making microscopic circles.*) Sngl Blm.

MAMMY: You couldn't conjure up a hiccup with that. Now, start small and grow gradual.

WILEY: (*Following her, but mixing up the words.*) Snnoooooooble gluuuume . . . snubble Blooooooom . . . Snooooo gleeeeee Blooooooom. . . . Snooooooo Gooooo Blooooooo. Snooooooow Gooooooo Blooooooow. Snow go Blooooooooow.

(*At the first mention of the words "Snow go blow,"* CHORUS *makes wind sounds and begin building a snow storm. As* WILEY *chants the storm grows, and snow starts falling and blowing.*)

WILEY: Snooooooow Gooooo Blooooooow . . . Snooooow Gooooooo Blooow. Mammy it's getting cold in here. Snoooo Gooooo Blooooooow. (MAMMY *looks up and sees what is going on.*)

MAMMY: Wiley! It's snowing in here!

WILEY: Snoooooooowwww Gooooo Blooooooow.

MAMMY: You got the words all mixed up!

WILEY: Snooooooww Goooo Bloooow.

MAMMY: (*Clapping her hand over his mouth.*) Stop it!

WILEY: (*Delighted.*) Look what I did!

MAMMY: I know, Dumbhead, now I gotta get rid of it!

WILEY: But I did it all by myself!

MAMMY: (*Conjuring.*) Snow Gooo Way! Snow Gooo Way! And don't come back no other day! (*Storm stops instantly.*)

WILEY: That was fun. I want to do it again.

MAMMY: Oh, no you don't!

WILEY: Maybe we could freeze the Hairy Man.

MAMMY: Ain't we got trouble enough without having snowstorms in the house? My Son, my son! The son of the best conjure woman in the whole southwest county can't even do a simple conjure. What can you do?

WILEY: Well . . . I kin wiggle in and squiggle out of all sorts of places. I kin leapfrog better'n the tree toads, AND I kin hold my breath for a full minute and not even flinch, or move, or blink, or nothing!

MAMMY: That ain't gonna help you with the Hairy Man. That's a conjure man, and when you face to face with him, you better have magic working for you.

WILEY: What are we gonna do?

MAMMY: *(Seriously.)* There is only one thing we can do. We've tried everything else.

WILEY: *(Stunned.)* You mean?

MAMMY: Yes, Wiley, Git . . .

CHORUS: *(Whispering.)* The BOOK!

WILEY: *(In awe.)* The book? (MAMMY *nods, and they ceremoniously move to a trap in the floor.)*

CHORUS: Oh, the screech owl howled . . .

CHORUS II: The sun went beneath a cloud.

CHORUS III: And the breeze in the trees . . .

CHORUS IV: . . . Whispered low.

CHORUS: 'Cause when Mammy takes a look, In the magic book, Then there's trouble up ahead for sure, for sure. Wiley better stay in bed for sure.

(MAMMY *and* WILEY *remove the Book from the trap and carry it to the center of the room.)*

MAMMY: The last thing my Mammy ever said to me was "Mammy, don't you never use this book lessen you got big trouble." And Wiley, we got big trouble. (CHORUS *makes magic sounds.)*

MAMMY: *(Turning pages carefully.)* Let's see now . . . B . . . Boogy Men, no we ain't got no Boogy Men here. . . . YET! Devils . . . no not Devils . . . E . . . Ear wax. (MAMMY *looks in* WILEY's *ears.)*

MAMMY: I'll get to that later . . . Hmmmmm Ghosts . . . Werewolf. . . . Whoops, I went too far . . . H . . . Here we are . . . Hellfire . . . Hairy Man!

WILEY: That sure is HIM!

MAMMY: Hairy Man . . .

WILEY: *(Sneezing all over the page.)* Achoooooooooo!

MAMMY: *(Furious.)* Dumbhead! You spit all over Hunchback! You cain't hardly read it no more. (MAMMY *wipes the book with her sleeve and continues reading.)* "You cain't outmagic the Hairy Man when he's mad . . . too bad."

WILEY: Gulp.

MAMMY: "You cain't outfight him."

CHORUS: Nope.

MAMMY: "You cain't outlick him."

CHORUS: Nope.

MAMMY: "You cain't outbite him."

CHORUS: Nope.

MAMMY: "You cain't outkick him."

CHORUS: Nope.

MAMMY: "You cain't outrun him,"

CHORUS: Nope.

MAMMY: "And you cain't outfun him."

CHORUS: Nope.

MAMMY: But you CAN . . .

CHORUS: Ahhhhhhhh!

MAMMY: Outfox him.

WILEY: I'll go and get a fox.

MAMMY: That ain't what it is talking about. Sit down, there's more. "If you can trick the Hairy Man three times in a row, he'll go away and never bother you no more . . . Good Luck" . . . Now, I know just what to do! (MAMMY *puts the book away.*) Wiley, what'cha going to do the next time you see the Hairy Man?

WILEY: I'm gonna run and climb the biggest tree I can find.

MAMMY: Oh, no, you ain't.

WILEY: Oh, yes, I am!

MAMMY: You are gonna stay right there on the ground and say "Hello, Hairy Man."

WILEY: Oh, no, I ain't.

MAMMY: Oh, yes, you are. And then you are gonna look him right in the eye and say, "What you got in that croaker sack?"

WILEY: And then I'm gonna run.

MAMMY: Oh, no, you ain't! Wiley, you gotta trick him three times, and you cain't do that if'n you keep running away!

WILEY: I cain't trick him if'n I'm dead!

MAMMY: That ain't gonna happen, Wiley. Not if'n you face to face with him and trick him.

WILEY: But how?

MAMMY: Listen . . . (MAMMY *whispers to* WILEY, *and* CHORUS *makes whispering sounds.*)

MAMMY: You understand?

WILEY: Yasum. I think so.

MAMMY: Remember you gotta trick him three times. Now, let me hear you say "Hello, Hairy Man."

WILEY: (*Weakly.*) Hello, Hairy Man.

MAMMY: STRONGER! You gotta be fierce! You gotta show no fear.

WILEY: (*Stronger.*) Hello, Hairy Man.

MAMMY: Come on, boy, Stronger! Louder!

WILEY: (*Flexing his muscles.*) Hello, Hairy Man!

MAMMY: GOOD! Now, I'll pretend to be the Hairy Man, and you come say "Hello."

WILEY: Hello, Hairy Man. HELLO, HAIRY MAN. HELLO, HAIRY MAN!

MAMMY: *(Sneaking up behind.)* Hello, Wiley!

WILEY: *(Crumbling in terror.)* Ahhhhhhhhhhh!

MAMMY: I sure do hope that Hairy Man is dumber than you are.

WILEY: I cain't do it.

MAMMY: Yes, you can, and I don't want to hear no never mind! Now, go get a rope.

WILEY: A rope? Do I gotta tie up the Hairy Man?

MAMMY: No, your Dog.

WILEY: Oh, my Dog . . . *(Dawns on him.)*

WILEY: MY DOG?

MAMMY: Yep.

WILEY: But Mammy, cain't I take him with me? The Hairy Man cain't stand no dogs. Everybody knows that!

MAMMY: That Hairy Man won't come anywhere near you if you got that Dog. Wiley you gotta seek out the Hairy Man. You are hunting him now, boy! You gotta face to face and trick him three times just like I told you.

WILEY: But my Dog . . .

MAMMY: Tie him up good and tight.

WILEY: Yasum.

MAMMY: And Wiley, be keerful.

WILEY: Yasum.

MAMMY: You can do it, Wiley . . .

WILEY: *(Not so sure.)* Yasum. (WILEY *takes a piece of rope, shivers, looks back, and crosses down.)*

MAMMY: *(Looking after him.)* Leastwise I hope you can.

WILEY: Hello, Hairy Man. Hello, Hairy Man. Hello, Hairy Man . . . Hello, Hairy Man . . . Hello . . .

(MAMMY *exits and the scene shifts to the swamp.* CHORUS *moves to swamp positions and makes swamp sounds. As* WILEY *passes through the swamp they reach for him menacingly.)*

(The swamp.)

CHORUS I: Oh, the Hairy Man listens . . .

CHORUS II: . . . And the Hairy Man sees.

CHORUS III: He's got eyes in the bushes . . .

CHORUS IV: And ears in the trees . . .

CHORUS ALL: There's some mighty scarey sounds, 'cause the Hairy Man's around. (CHORUS *form themselves into the tree.)*

WILEY: Hello, Hairy Man . . . Hello . . . Gulp.

CHORUS I: Keerful, Wiley.

WILEY: Gulp.

CHORUS II: Look out, Wiley.

WILEY: Gulp.

CHORUS III and IV: Lookee there, Wiley . . .

(CHORUS *point to a spot where the* HAIRY MAN *enters slowly with his croaker sack.*)

CHORUS: Stampin', Stompin', Comin' through the trees. Shufflin' through the swamp grass, Blowin' in the breeze; Bounding, Pounding fast as he can, What did Wiley see?

CHORUS IV: He saw the Hairy Man!

WILEY: The Hairy Man?

HAIRY MAN: The Hairy Man!

CHORUS: Hairy Man, Hairy Man, Hairy Man, Hairy Man. (WILEY *tries to climb the tree, but* CHORUS *pushes him back to the ground.*)

WILEY: (*High and squeaky.*) H . . . h . . . hello, Hairy Man.

HAIRY MAN: (*Grinning.*) Well, Hello, Wiley.

WILEY: Hello, Hairy Man.

HAIRY MAN: I said, Hello, Wiley.

WILEY: Uhhhhh, Hello, Hairy Man.

HAIRY MAN: Cain't you say nothin' but "Hello, Hairy Man"?

WILEY: What you got in that croaker sack?

HAIRY MAN: I ain't got nothin' . . . yet! I aims to carry home my supper in it.

WILEY and CHORUS: Gulp!

WILEY: Hairy Man, my Mammy says she is the best at castin' spells in the whole southwest county.

HAIRY MAN: Your Mammy is a gabby woman.

WILEY: My Mammy says you's a gabby Hairy Man.

HAIRY MAN: I is the best at conjuring in the whole southwest.

WILEY: P . . . P . . . Prove it! My Mammy she can turn herself into something she ain't.

HAIRY MAN: Shoot, that ain't nothin'.

WILEY: I reckon you cain't.

HAIRY MAN: I reckon I can.

WILEY: You cain't!

HAIRY MAN: I can!

WILEY: Cain't!

HAIRY MAN: CAN! I bet your Mammy cain't change herself into no Alligator! Ahhhhhhhhhhhhhliiiiiiigaaaaaator.

(HAIRY MAN *makes a dreadful hissing roar and throws himself into a conjure.* CHORUS *join him in wild gesticulations and finally throw themselves to the ground and form themselves into a gigantic alligator with huge crude snapping jaws. They advance on* WILEY.)

WILEY: (*Bravado.*) Ohhh. That ain't much. (*The jaws snap at him.*) My . . . mmmmm . . . My Mammy does that all the time. That's how she chops kindlin'. (WILEY *tosses a stick into the alligator's mouth and snaps the stick.*)

(CHORUS *and* HAIRY MAN *come out of the conjure and return to their own forms.*)

HAIRY MAN: What do you mean that ain't no good?

WILEY: My Mammy kin do that easy.

HAIRY MAN: You jest tell me something your Mammy cain't do, and by durn, I'll do it!

WILEY: There is jest one thing, Hairy Man, try as she will my Mammy ain't never changed herself into something smaller than she is.

HAIRY MAN: She ain't?

WILEY: No, she ain't, and I reckon you cain't neither. I reckon you cain't change yourself into no . . . Bat.

HAIRY MAN: Jest you watch. Baaaaaaaaaaatttttt. Baaaaaaaaaaattttttt.

(HAIRY MAN *assumes conjure position and bellows.* CHORUS *form a tight circle around him, and all sink down as small as possible. There is a puff of smoke and the* CHORUS *fall away, and a Bat, held by one* CHORUS *member on a pole and string flies out of the group.* WILEY *reaches and catches the Bat in his hat and stuffs the Bat into the* HAIRY MAN's *croaker sack.*)

WILEY: I got you, Hairy Man! I'm gonna throw you in the river! (WILEY *runs down stage and tosses the sack off, and there is a splash.*) I fooled you, Hairy Man! I fooled you one time! Two more times and you'll leave me alone. Good-bye, Hairy Man. So long, Hairy Man!

(CHORUS *makes "Hairy Man" sounds.*)

CHORUS I: Keerful, Wiley.

WILEY: Good-bye, Hairy Man.

CHORUS II: Look Out, Wiley.

WILEY: So long, Hairy Man.

CHORUS III *and* IV: Lookee there, Wiley. (WILEY *turns in disbelief.*)

CHORUS: (*Whispering.*) Stampin', Stompin', Comin' through the trees. Shufflin' through the swamp grass. Blowin' in the breeze. Bounding, Pounding fast as he can, What did Wiley see? (HAIRY MAN *enters swinging from a vine.*)

HAIRY MAN: He saw the Hairy Man!

WILEY: The Hairy Man?????

HAIRY MAN: (*On the backswing.*) The Hairy Man. (WILEY *climbs the tree frantically.*)

WILEY: HOW did you get outta that croaker sack?

HAIRY MAN: I turned myself into a cyclone and blewed myself out!

WILEY: What are you gonna do now, Hairy Man?

HAIRY MAN: Why, Wiley, I am plumb tuckered out. So I am gonna sit right down here till your belly gets the hongry grombles, and you fall outta that tree. Wiley, there ain't nothin' that can save you now, not your Mammy and not your Dog.

WILEY: *(Gets an idea.)* I still says that my Mammy is better at conjurin' than you.

HAIRY MAN: No, she ain't.

WILEY: After all, you did fail the test.

HAIRY MAN: I turned myself into a bat jest like you said.

WILEY: Did not. That bat was much too pretty to be you.

HAIRY MAN: Were, not.

WILEY: Were, too.

HAIRY MAN: Not!

WILEY: Too!

HAIRY MAN: Wiley, you gonna get me riled.

WILEY: I bet you cain't take a thing that's really here and make that thing plumb disappear.

HAIRY MAN: I can! *(Tree toad starts croaking.)*

HAIRY MAN: You see that tree toad? GONE! *(Sound stops mid-croak.)*

WILEY: I didn't see no tree toad! You is cheatin'.

HAIRY MAN: Well, take a look at your hat! . . . GONE! (CHORUS *snatches* WILEY's *hat.)*

WILEY: *(Lamely.)* What hat? I wasn't wearin' no hat. Hairy Man, you cain't do it.

HAIRY MAN: *(Throwing a tantrum.)* I can! I can! I can! I can!

WILEY: You see this rope 'round my pants? I know it's here! Make this rope disappear!

HAIRY MAN: I kin make all the rope in the whole county disappear; 'cause this is my county and what I say goes! (HAIRY MAN *conjures.)* Rope, rope, Wherever you are. Go away, I don't know whar. Rope disappear, git away from here!

WILEY: I reckon that means rope holdin' pants up?

HAIRY MAN: I said All rope! (WILEY's *pants fall down.)*

WILEY: I reckon that means rope danglin' buckets in wells?

HAIRY MAN: I said ALL rope! (CHORUS *drops a bucket.)*

WILEY: I reckon that includes ropes that ties DOGS up?

HAIRY MAN: I said . . .

WILEY: I said, I reckon that includes ropes that ties DOGS up?

HAIRY MAN: *(It sinks in.)* Uh-oh . . .

WILEY: *(Calling.)* Heeeeeeeahhhhh DOG! *(Offstage we hear* DOG *barking.)*

WILEY: Run, Hairy Man, or my Dog's gonna bite you again. (HAIRY MAN, *confused, runs right into* DOG *as he enters.* DOG *stands his ground and growls.)*

HAIRY MAN: I'll get you, Wiley, you see if I don't. You tell your Mammy I'm comin' for you!

WILEY: Git him, Dog. (DOG *takes off after* HAIRY MAN *who runs offstage.)*

HAIRY MAN: *(Off.)* Yeooooooowwwwwww.

(DOG *returns with another tuft of* HAIRY MAN *hair in his mouth.* WILEY *scrambles out of the tree and hugs* DOG.)

WILEY: We got him! We got him! That's the second time we tricked him Dog! One more time and he'll leave me alone. (DOG *barks happily.*) (*Thinks twice.*) One more time! Oh Dog, he's comin' for me now!! And it sure is gettin' dark here. We gotta get some help. Now, we need MAGIC! We never been in trouble like we's in now! Let's go home!

(WILEY *and* DOG *run home. Scene shifts back to* MAMMY's *house.* MAMMY *enters and sits center stage gazing intently into a candle on a small table.*)

(MAMMY's *house.*)

(WILEY *and* DOG *enter house area.* WILEY *stations* DOG *outside the house.*)

WILEY: Now, Dog, you stay right here and don't move.

(WILEY *enters the house, and* MAMMY *does not break her concentration.*)

WILEY: (*Panicked.*) Mammy! I done it! I fooled the Hairy Man twice! But I cain't fool him again. He's more than mad; he's got fire in his eyeballs, and he's spittin' sparks! (MAMMY *does not move.*)

MAMMY: (*Quietly.*) Hesh, Wiley.

WILEY: He's comin' for me!

MAMMY: I know. I kin feel it in my bones. (CHORUS *makes "magic" sounds.*)

WILEY: Do a spell! Do magic! Conjure up a storm! DO SOMETHING!

MAMMY: I am. (CHORUS *sounds increase and* MAMMY *falls into a deep trance.*)

WILEY: Mammy, Mammy? MAMMY! You gone to sleep? Mammy, help me!

MAMMY: (*In her trance.*) Wiiiiiiley.

WILEY: (*Startled.*) Oh My!!!!

MAMMY: Wiley!

CHORUS: Wiley, Wiley, Wiley, Wiley.

MAMMY: Put . . .

CHORUS I: . . . Your . . .

CHORUS II: . . . Dog . . .

CHORUS III: . . . In Your . . .

CHORUS IV: . . . Little Bed . . .

MAMMY: And Cover . . .

CHORUS I: . . . Him Up . . .

CHORUS II: . . . From . . .

CHORUS III: . . . Tail . . .

CHORUS IV: . . . To Head!

WILEY: I sure will, Mammy. (WILEY *gets* DOG *and places him in bed.*) Boy, I gotta put you in my bed. I don't know why, but Mammy's got a powerful conjure workin'. (WILEY *covers* DOG *with a sheet.*) I done it, Mammy; now, what do I do?

MAMMY: (*Still in trance.*) Get yourself under the table and make yourself as small as you are able.

WILEY: But why, Mammy?

MAMMY: *(Out of the trance.)* 'Cause I said so! *(They both duck under the table.* CHORUS *makes "*HAIRY MAN*" sounds.)*

CHORUS I: Stampin', Stompin', Comin' through the trees . . .

CHORUS II: He done got your Pappy, and he's gonna get you.

CHORUS III: . . . Shufflin' through the swamp grass . . .

CHORUS IV: He done got your Pappy . . .

CHORUS I: . . . Blowin' in the breeze . . .

CHORUS II: . . . and he's gonna get you.

CHORUS ALL: Bounding, Pounding, fast as he can. What did they see?

*(*HAIRY MAN *enters and comes to the door.)*

HAIRY MAN: They saw the Hairy Man. Mammy! I has come for your child! *(He listens.)*

HAIRY MAN: I said I has come for your child! And I is comin' IN. *(He makes a rush for the door and finds it is unlocked. He looks cautiously about.)*

HAIRY MAN: Wiiiiiiley. There ain't no way out 'ceptin' with me, now. Wiley? Mammy?

WILEY: *(Peeking out.)* Snore, Dog, Snore! *(*DOG *starts snoring, and* HAIRY MAN *notices the shape in the bed and moves toward it.)*

HAIRY MAN: SO there you are, Wiley. Sleepin' and a dreamin'. Well, boy, I is your bad dream come true. And now, I gotcha . . .

*(*HAIRY MAN *pulls the blanket away, and* DOG *leaps at him snarling.* DOG *chases him out the door where the* HAIRY MAN *throws the blanket over* DOG'S *head and throws a wild conjure.)*

HAIRY MAN: Howl, growl, moan, groan. Turn this hound Dog into stone. *(*DOG *freezes mid-attack.)*

HAIRY MAN: I gotcha Dog! That dumb trick was Mammy's idea, and it don't count. I'm comin for Wiley now, and there ain't nothing you can do about it. *(*MAMMY *and* WILEY *have not heard this. They come cautiously out of hiding.)*

WILEY: What happened, Mammy?

MAMMY: I dunno, but I think we won.

WILEY: *(Looking about.)* Dog! Dog? Mammy, where is my Dog?

HAIRY MAN: *(Shouting from outside.)* Mammy! I give up. Looks like I lost. Looks like I better go away and never come back. Looks like I gotta find myself a new territory.

MAMMY: *(Not so sure.)* Let me hear you say . . . "Mammy, you is the best at conjuring in the whole southwest county."

HAIRY MAN: *(Nearly choking.)* You is the best at conjuring in the whole southwest . . .

MAMMY: . . . County.

HAIRY MAN: County!

MAMMY: We won, Wiley.

WILEY: I dunno . . . Mammy, what about my dog? *(*WILEY *is looking frantically for* DOG *while* MAMMY *is preoccupied with her success.)*

HAIRY MAN: I know when I am licked, and just to show you, I'm gonna put all my magic right here in this croaker sack. Now, you is the best conjure person in the whole county and you is gonna need all the magic you can get. (HAIRY MAN *puts himself into the sack and chuckles.*) Good-bye, Mammy . . . Good-bye, Wiley . . . (HAIRY MAN *closes the sack.*)

MAMMY: (*After a pause.*) He's gone.

WILEY: You sure?

MAMMY: You heard him say that I'm the best conjure woman in . . .

WILEY: I don't trust him.

MAMMY: I'll show you. (*She starts for the door.*)

WILEY: Don't go out there!

MAMMY: Oh, Wiley . . . hesh.

(MAMMY *and* WILEY *slowly go outside.* MAMMY *goes right for the sack, but* WILEY *is horrified to see his* DOG *turned to stone.*)

WILEY: DOG!

MAMMY: (*Looking at the sack.*) Now, ain't that nice.

WILEY: DOG! Oh, No! MAMMY! He turned my Dog to stone.

MAMMY: What?

WILEY: Look at my Dog! Oh, No.

MAMMY: Now, Wiley, it's all right. Now that I got all his magic I kin unconjurize that dog like nothin'.

WILEY: Do it now!

MAMMY: First, help me get this inside.

WILEY: No, now!

MAMMY: It's heavy . . . He must'a left me all his magic. (*Reluctantly* WILEY *helps her push the sack into the house as they do so the* CHORUS *makes* "HAIRY MAN" *sounds.*) Now, let's just have a little look-see. I wonder what all this can be.

CHORUS: Guess what Mammy? (*She opens the sack, and* HAIRY MAN *stands up.*)

HAIRY MAN: It's the Hairy Man!

MAMMY and WILEY: The HAIRY MAN???

HAIRY MAN: The Hairy Man! I fooled you, Mammy. You ain't no kind of conjure woman. I has come for your child.

MAMMY: Well, you ain't getting him.

HAIRY MAN: Says who?

MAMMY: Says me! (MAMMY *picks up the book.*)

HAIRY MAN: Oh, yeah?

CHORUS: Think ugly things, Hairy Man.

HAIRY MAN: Well, s'posen I have a look in this here book. (HAIRY MAN *lunges for the book.*)

CHORUS: Think fast, Mammy.

(MAMMY *tosses the book to* WILEY. *They toss it several times keeping it away from the* HAIRY MAN, *who finally intercepts it.*)

MAMMY: You wouldn't do that. Why, that's plumb underhanded.

HAIRY MAN: Well, I's a plumb underhanded Hairy Man. How about a "Mammy Whammy?" (HAIRY MAN *flips open the book and throws a wild conjure.*) Fliminy, Flaminy ... Al-a-ca-zaminy ... Mammy Whammy! (MAMMY *tries to get away but is frozen in her tracks.*)

WILEY: You cain't do that!

HAIRY MAN: I jest did. Come on now, Wiley ... come with me!

WILEY: I ain't goin nowhere till you un-whammy my Mammy!

HAIRY MAN: Wiley!

WILEY: (*Too mad to be scared.*) You cheat, Hairy Man! You is one big cheater. You may be bigger'n me and stronger'n me, but you cain't do nothin' without cheating.

HAIRY MAN: Come on, Wiley.

WILEY: I'll fight you, Hairy Man. I'll fight you myself.

HAIRY MAN: You? You's just a kid.

WILEY: Come on, fight me!

HAIRY MAN: (*Toying with him.*) O.K., Wiley. I'll give you one chance, boy. If you kin git yourself out of that there sticker bush ... (HAIRY MAN *conjures the* CHORUS *into a sticker bush which surrounds* WILEY.) You kin go free.

WILEY: I can do that! 'Cause if there is one thing that I am good at it is wigglin' in and squigglin' out.

(WILEY *wiggles and squiggles and almost makes it out, but at the last minute the* HAIRY MAN *throws a sneaky conjure.*)

HAIRY MAN: Stickle him. Prickle him. (*The sticker bush closes in around* WILEY *and traps him.*)

WILEY: Owwweeeeeee.

HAIRY MAN: You lose.

WILEY: You did that! You magicked them stickers.

HAIRY MAN: (*All innocence.*) I didn't do nothin'. Why, I am all the way over here.

WILEY: You cheat, Hairy Man. That weren't no kinda chance.

HAIRY MAN: (*Knowing he has him and playing with him.*) Why, then I'll give you another chance. If'n you can leapfrog, (HAIRY MAN *conjures the* CHORUS *into a line of stumps.*) over all of these stumps ... I'll let you go.

WILEY: I know I kin do that because I kin leapfrog better'n the tree toads. (*As* WILEY *leaps over them, the* HAIRY MAN *conjures them higher and higher.*)

HAIRY MAN: Git up ... Git up ... Git up ... (WILEY *falls.*)

HAIRY MAN: Awww, shucks.

WILEY: (*Furious.*) You magicked them up. Hairy Man, that ain't fair.

HAIRY MAN: (*Grinning.*) I never said I was fair, Wiley.

WILEY: (*Desperate.*) Hairy Man, you want magic? I'll fight you with magic!

HAIRY MAN: You cain't do no magic.

WILEY: I can too, 'cause I'm the son of the best conjure woman in the whole southwest county.

HAIRY MAN: Come on, Wiley.

WILEY: I can . . . I can turn my whole self into . . . STONE, and you cain't make me flinch, or move, or blink, or nothin'.

HAIRY MAN: Come on now, Wiley . . .

WILEY: Come and get me, Hairy Man. (WILEY *throws a desperate but totally fake conjure.*) Eeny, meany, miney, moan . . . Turn my whole self into stone. (WILEY *freezes, but his expression tells us it is a fake.*)

HAIRY MAN: (*Amused, at first.*) Wiley . . . (WILEY *does not move.*) I said, Wiley . . . (WILEY *does not move.*) Now, cut that out!!! You ain't really . . .

(HAIRY MAN *does all sorts of things to make* WILEY *move, much in the same way as the game seen earlier with* DOG. *He waves his hands in front of his face, pretends to poke his fingers at his eyes, etc.*)

HAIRY MAN: Is you?

(HAIRY MAN *turns his back on* WILEY, *and we see him gasp for breath, but he resumes his pose the moment the* HAIRY MAN *turns back. Finally the* HAIRY MAN *walks right up to* WILEY *and stands with both hands on his shoulders and breathes in his face.* WILEY *trembles but does not break.*)

HAIRY MAN: (*Breaking away.*) Now, I'm through foolin' with you. There's just one thing that I can do. A conjure that will unfroze you! (WILEY's *face brightens, but he does not move.*) (*Conjuring.*) Statue, Statue, Turned to stone. Unfroze you now to flesh and bone. (WILEY *springs to life, and* DOG *slowly comes out of his spell.*)

WILEY: Wooooooooeeeeeee. Hairy Man, I'm free! I weren't no stone, no way no how. You just unfroze my hound Dog now! Hound DOG!!

HAIRY MAN: Wiley, that ain't fair.

WILEY: Oh yeah! Hound DOG!

(HOUND DOG *enters, and* HAIRY MAN *makes a final lunge for* WILEY *who dives under his legs and trips him.* DOG *chomps down on the* HAIRY MAN's *hair.*)

HAIRY MAN: Let Go. Let Go . . . Let Go . . . (HAIRY MAN *pulls away leaving his hair in* DOG's *mouth.* DOG *looks slightly astonished.*) He got my Hairy Hair!

WILEY: You ain't so scarey now. You ain't so hairy now! You is bald. Now, disappear, git away from here.

CHORUS: Well, the Hairy Man yelled. (HAIRY MAN *yells.*)

CHORUS: And the Hairy Man raged. (HAIRY MAN *rages.*)

CHORUS: And the Hairy Man stomped. (HAIRY MAN *stomps.*)

CHORUS: And the Hairy Man G-nashed his teeth. (HAIRY MAN *G-nashes his teeth.*)

WILEY: I said GIT! (HAIRY MAN *storms out followed by* DOG. MAMMY *becomes unconjurized.*)

WILEY: Mammy, we did it. We fooled the Hairy Man three times. We did it!

MAMMY: No, Wiley, we didn't do it . . . YOU did it.

WILEY: Yasum. Hey DOG . . . Come here. (DOG *enters with the blanket.*)

WILEY: Good boy. He ain't never comin' back no more.

MAMMY: No, we saw the last of him. (DOG *barks happily.*)

MAMMY: Come on, Wiley, time for bed.

WILEY: Awww, Mammy, I got too many things going on in my head.

MAMMY: The least little thing happens, and you want to stay up all night. Git to bed. *(DOG whimpers.)*

WILEY: Kin Dog sleep here with me tonight?

MAMMY: Yes.

WILEY: *(As he gets in bed.)* Dog. You and I are goin' down to the swamp tomorrow to get some wood for a hound house.

MAMMY: *(Tucking him in.)* Go to sleep now. *(MAMMY starts out.)*

WILEY: Thank you, Mammy.

MAMMY: *(Smiling.)* G'night, Wiley. *(She starts out again and then stops.)* Wiley?

WILEY: Yasum?

MAMMY: We is the best conjure people in the whole southwest county.

WILEY: I know it, Mammy. Good night. *(MAMMY exits, WILEY starts to lie back, but the "HAIRY MAN" sounds begin.)*

CHORUS I: Keerful, Wiley . . . *(WILEY looks around.)*

CHORUS II: Look out, Wiley . . .

CHORUS III: Lookee there, Wiley . . .

CHORUS: *(Starting at a whisper.)* Stampin', Stompin', Comin' through the trees, Shufflin' through the swamp grass, Blowin' in the breeze. Bounding, Pounding, Fast as he can . . . What did Wiley see? *(WILEY looks around, and CHORUS disappears.)*

WILEY: I didn't see nothin'! *(WILEY flips over and goes to sleep.)*

CURTAIN

ACCORDING TO COYOTE

by
John Kauffman

JOHN KAUFFMAN was the son of a German father and a Nez Percé Native American mother. He was raised on a reservation in Idaho and received a tribal scholarship to attend the Professional Actor's Training Program at the University of Washington. After graduating in 1970, he worked in Seattle and Los Angeles as an actor and director. For four years, he directed his own theatre group, Red Earth Performing Arts Company in Seattle, which focused on American Indian themes. He later served as associate director for the American Conservatory Theatre in San Francisco and as associate artistic director for Seattle's Empty Space Theatre, prior to being appointed artistic director of Honolulu Theatre for Youth in 1983. He was in his seventh season with HTY when he died in 1990, at the age of forty-three.

Kauffman won an Emmy Award in 1972, for the telecast of *The Indian Experience,* a one-man theatre piece that he later performed as part of the John F. Kennedy Center for the Performing Arts Imagination Celebration 1977. He earned Hawaii State Theatre Council Po'oKela Awards for his direction of *According to Coyote* and Edward Mast's *Junglbook* in the 1988 season, and was named arts educator of the year by the Hawaii Alliance for Arts Education.

According to Coyote was commissioned by the Education Program of the John F. Kennedy Center for the Performing Arts, Washington, D.C., and received its world premiere at their Imagination Celebration 1987. His signature work has been created from stories and myths of American Plains Indians that were told him by his grandmother. In the summer of 1987, he performed *Coyote* in Honolulu for the Honolulu Theatre for Youth. Subsequently he toured the piece extensively on the U.S. mainland. In Australia he played in Adelaide, Melbourne, and at the Sydney Opera House as a feature of the international arts-in-education conference, "Arts Dialogue—Australia." He was also invited to perform *According to Coyote* at an international directors' seminar in the former Soviet Union. It was enthusiastically received at the Central Children's Theatre of Moscow.

For the March, 1990, issue of *American Theatre* Jane Campbell, managing director of HTY, wrote a moving tribute to Kauffman in her article "When an Artistic Director Has AIDS: Honolulu Theatre for Youth Faced the Crisis with Care and Compassion." In the last year of his life he inaugurated and won national funding for two new long-range artistic projects.

I was in kindergarten when my grandmother told me my first Coyote story. My fascination with this incredibly foolish, wise, sneaky, brave, outrageous character has grown with me ever since then. . . . The coyote explains how things came to be, and he demonstrates how not to behave. The stories deal with such basic human issues as pride, self-esteem, vulnerability, love of family and having permission to fail. They also encourage us to think about the fact that we are all a part of something that is bigger than us. . . . In sharing *Coyote* with you, I hope also to share with you what it means to be an Indian today.

—JOHN KAUFFMAN, 1987

ACCORDING TO COYOTE

A one-person theatre piece

John Kauffman had intended to add stage directions to the script of *According to Coyote* that would have suggested how the piece looked in performance. Sadly, death intervened before he was able to carry out this plan. His program note on the play, reprinted here, gives some indication of the staging.

A review by Joseph T. Tozmiarek in *The Honolulu Advertiser* gives a brief but vivid glimpse of Kauffman on stage: "Much of the performance is literally done on the run, with Kauffman pumping out the demanding physical side of the role while keeping up a narrative with only an occasional pause for breath. He changes footwear as he goes, from running gear to cowboy boots to moccasins, subtly adding bits of costume as he goes. He applies facial paint mid-stream, and finishes up the performance resplendent in leggings, vest, and genuine coyote headdress."

PLAYWRIGHT/DIRECTOR'S NOTES

Coyote is the mythological trickster/hero of Plains and Plateau Indian tribes of the Western United States. There are hundreds of stories telling how Coyote made the world ready for human beings. He brought fire and death and the stars and the seasons and all of the natural world into order, and then slew a monster, and from the monster's body Coyote made the first human beings.

But Coyote isn't always as heroic as he might appear. Most of Coyote's supposedly great deeds were the result of mishaps or accidents as the sly Coyote was trying to manipulate someone. Therein lies the other major function of Coyote tales—they tell us how to behave, or more precisely, how not to behave.

Storytelling is an age-old tradition among Native Americans. It's a tradition that continues today. Indian stories are essentially dramatic in conception, monodramas in which an actor/narrator plays all the parts.

I am helped immeasurably in playing all the parts by a simple but dramatic set that depicts a Plains Indian–style war shield, with a Coyote motif in the center. Lighting for the production is very important in the storytelling as it emphasizes the mood changes between stories and heightens the dramatic moments. Sound may be the most important of all. The sound designer used traditional Indian rhythms and instruments to create, through a synthesizer, sounds that are timeless and fitting for the creation of human beings, when the animals still ruled the earth and spoke with one another.

—JOHN KAUFFMAN

ACCORDING TO COYOTE

CHARACTERS

Coyote

LOCATION

A Gathering Place for Storytelling

TIME

The Present and the Past

(The sound of wind.)

In the Beginning there was nothing. According to some, God said, "Let there be light," and there was. And He fashioned the Heavens and the Earth, and He placed men and animals on the earth, and after seven days He rested.

According to others, there was a gigantic explosion, a big bang—and from that explosion all life in the Universe was formed. That creative explosion formed the very substance, the laws of the Universe, our earth, our bodies.

According to Coyote, the Earth was once a human being. The Creator made her out of a woman. "You will be the Mother of all people," He said. And the Earth is still alive today. The soil is her flesh, the rocks are her bones, the wind is her breath, the trees and grass her hair. She lives all spread out, and we live on top of her. Whenever she moves, we have an earthquake.

The creator gathered some of her flesh and rolled it into balls. And these balls became the first creatures of the early world, the Ancients. The Ancients were half-people, half-animal. Some walked on two legs, some on all fours, some could fly and others could swim. They all had the gift of speech and lived together.

But there was a difficulty with this early world. The Ancients knew they had to hunt in order to live, but they sometimes got mixed up as to which creatures were food and which were themselves, and sometimes they ate their own people by mistake.

At last the creator said, "Soon there will be no more people if I let things go on like this." So he sent Coyote down to kill all the monsters and other evil beings, and to teach all of us how to live.

Song: *Ya no way ho ya a ni*
Ya no way ho ya ni
Ya no way ho ya a ni
Ya no way ho ya ni
Ya no way ho ya a ni
Ya no way ho ya ni
Ya no way ho ya a ni
Ya no way ho ya ni

One day Coyote was going along up the river, and it was really hot. Coyote was feeling pretty good. He came up to a large rock and said, "Grandfather Rock, I am going to give you my fine blanket. It's too hot, you may have it."

It was beautiful blanket covered with beads, porcupine quills and hummingbird feathers that moved in the wind. He spread the blanket over the rock and went on his way. After awhile, Coyote saw a storm approaching and thought, "Hmm. I need my blanket." So he went back to get it.

"Rock, Rock, I want my blanket back."

And the Rock said, "No." And Coyote said, "Rock, I must have my blanket." And the Rock said, "No, no. Rocks never give back presents. Once you give something to a rock, you cannot take it back." Now, Coyote was very angry. He rushed up to the Rock and snatched off the blanket.

Ya no way ho ya a ni, ya no way ho ya ni.

Coyote had only gone a little way when he heard something behind him, a rumbling noise. He turned around and saw Rock rolling after him. Coyote ran to the people for help, but no one would help him; not the Grizzly Bear nor the Mountain Lion or even the Buffalo. At last Coyote came to the Nighthawk people and asked them for help.

"Hide inside our lodge, Coyote, and we will take care of this." The Rock came rolling up and said, "Where is Coyote?" The Nighthawks flew straight up into the air, dove down and chipped the rock into little pieces. Then they told Coyote to come out and go on his way.

Well, Coyote went down through the valley and up to the next hill. He turned around and shouted to the Nighthawk people, "Hey! Hey! Hey, you big-nosed, weirdo birdbrains. I sure fooled you. I was playing a game with the Rock, and you guys wrecked it. Idiots!"

The Nighthawks pretended they didn't hear Coyote. "Hey! Hey! *(Coyote makes fart noises.)* Hey, you beady-eyed, bandy-legged bug-chewers. Your mother lays eggs."

The Nighthawks people got angry and put Rock back together again, and Rock went rolling after Coyote. Coyote jumped up and ran off as fast as he could. He jumped over a ditch, but the Rock was right behind him. The Rock fell on Coyote and crushed him flat as a pancake. And Coyote died. The Fox came up and felt very sorry for Coyote, after all they had been friends. So Fox jumped over Coyote four times. No sooner had he finished the fourth jump, than Coyote's body sprang upright and began to move. Coyote said, "Oh man, what'd you wake me up for? I dreamt I was upriver helping the chief's daughter get into her canoe." *(Coyote pants.)*

And Fox said, "Oh Coyote, you weren't dreaming. You were dead. I just brought you back to life. Come on, Coyote, we have to go. The Great Spirit has called us all together. There is going to be a change. The Great Spirit is going to give us new names. Some of us have names now, some of us don't. Tomorrow everyone will have a name. This will be your name forever, for all your descendants. The first one to arrive at the Great Spirit's lodge tomorrow morning will get to choose whatever name he wants!"

Well, Coyote walked around saying he was going to be first. Coyote didn't like his name. Everyone called him Trickster and Imitator and Old Coyote. Everybody said those names fitted him, but he wanted a new name.

"A new name! *(Howls.)* I will take one of the three powerful names. Yeah, like Grizzly Bear, king of the forest who rules all the four-legged! *(Flexes.)* Aye! Or how about Eagle, chief of the air? Aye! Or Salmon, the big fish! Aye! Yeah. Those are the best names, I'll take one of those."

So Coyote took two small sticks and wedged them between his eyelids to hold his eyes open so that he wouldn't fall asleep. And he sat down in front of the fire and thought of all the wonderful things he was going to be. Before long he was asleep with his eyes wide open.

The next day when the sun was high in the sky, Coyote woke up and ran over to the lodge of Great Spirit, Coyote saw that no one was around and thought he was the first one there. He yelled to the Great Spirit, "I want to be called Grizzly Bear, king of the forest."

The Great Spirit said, "The name of Grizzly Bear was taken at dawn." "Then my name shall be Eagle, king of the air." "Eagle flew away with that name at sunrise." "Salmon?" "That name has been taken as well, Coyote. As a matter of fact, all the names have been taken except for yours. No one wanted to be called Coyote."

Coyote looked very sad. He tucked his tail between his legs and walked away. The Great Spirit was touched.

"Coyote, Imitator, your must keep your name. Coyote is a good name for you. I wanted you to have that name, and so I made you sleep late. I have important work for you to do. The New People are coming, you will be their chief.

"The New People will not know anything when they come—not how to dress, how to sing, how to shoot an arrow. You will teach them all the ways of living.

"But you will also do foolish things, too, and for this the New People will laugh at you. You cannot help it. This will be your way. But I will give you a special power. When you die, you will always come back to life again. This will be your way, Coyote, Afraid of No One. Go and do your work well!"

Song: Hey ya-hey ya-hey e ya
    Ya hey ya hey e ya, ya hey e ya
    Hey ya hey ya ya hey yo

    Ya hey ya hey e ya
    Ya hey ya hey e ya, ye hey e ya
    Hey ya hey ya ya hey yo

In the beginning, the animal people had no fire. The only fire anywhere was on the top of a high, snow-covered mountain, where it was guarded by the skookums. The skookums were three sisters who were wrinkled and old and really, really gross. The skookums were afraid that if the animal people had any fire they might become very powerful—as powerful as the skookums themselves. So the skookums wouldn't give the fire to anyone.

Because the animal people had no fire, they were always shivering, and they had to eat their food raw. When Coyote came along, he found them cold and miserable.

"C-C-Coyote," they begged, "you must bring us fire from the mountain or we will d-d-d-die from all this c-c-c-cold." "I will see what I can do for you," promised Coyote.

Well, Coyote didn't know what to do. He thought and thought, but couldn't come up with a plan. So Coyote decided to ask his three sisters to help him. His sisters were huckleberries that lived in his stomach. They were very wise and could tell him what to do.

"Wake up sisters!" At first Coyote's sisters were reluctant to help him. "If we tell you what to do, you'll just say you knew it all along." "No, I won't do that. Now, tell me how to get fire from the skookums." (Shakes head no.) "Tell me!" (Shakes head no.) "Tell me!! All right, then. Hail, hail, fall down from the sky!"

This made the sisters very afraid. They cried, "Stop, don't bring the hail down. We'll tell you what you want to know. The skookums may be old, but they're fast. Now, Coyote, you must hide in the bushes until the one guarding the fire turns to wake up her sisters. The second she turns her back on the fire, race in and grab it."

Coyote said, "Oh well I knew that all along." His sisters walked back down into his stomach, and Coyote went to see the animal people. He picked out the fastest runners and had them stand in a long line from the village all the way up to the mountain. Coyote crept in among the bushes around the skookums' fire and waited.

It was just as the huckleberries had said. Two of the skookums were sleeping while the third guarded the fire. Just as soon as the wrinkled, old skookum got up to call her sisters, Coyote sprang from the bushes, seized a burning brand of fire and ran away as fast as he could. The three skookums were behind him in an instant. They were so close they were showering

Coyote with snow and ice churned up by their feet. Coyote ran faster than he had ever run in his life. He leaped over cracks in the ice. He rolled down the mountain like a snowball. But the skookums were right behind him, so close that their hot breath scorched his fur.

Coyote reached the tree line, and Cougar jumped out from his hiding place. So Coyote passed the fire to Cougar as Coyote fell flat on his face from exhaustion. Cougar ran through the high trees until he met the Fox, who took the fire and ran through the underbrush until he met Squirrel, who took the fire and ran up the trees, through the branches back down the trees until he came to the edge of the woods. Squirrel then gave the fire to Antelope who bounded across the plains.

By now, the fire was only a little glowing coal. Antelope passed the coal to Frog. Frog took the coal and swallowed it. He dove into the deep river. When he got to the other side, he found the skookums all around him! The Frog leapt between their legs, but he was an old frog, and the skookums caught him and tried to squeeze the coal out of him. So Frog spat the hot coal out onto Wood, and Wood swallowed the coal.

The three skookums just stood there and didn't know what to do. None of them could figure out a way to get fire out of Wood. After awhile they got discouraged and left, making their way slowly back up to their snow-covered mountaintop.

Coyote then called all the animals together, and they all gathered around the Wood. Coyote was very wise, he knew how to get fire out of Wood. He told the animals, "What you must do is take two dry sticks and rub them together. Pretty soon sparks will jump out. Then add dry moss and twigs to those sparks, and you will have a fire."

From then on the people knew how to get the fire out of Wood. They cooked their meat. Their houses were warm, and they were never cold again.
Song: Just one more kiss for the last time
Until I come back
Hold me close in the beautiful moonlight
Farewell sweetheart
Wey ya hiyah, wey ya hiyo
Coyote loved the night.
Song: Come from Oklahoma,
Got no one for my own
So I come here looking for you, hiya
I will be your sugar, you will be my honey
By and by-ya, wey ya hiya
All night long he would sit and watch the stars. There was one star in particular that was more beautiful than anything Coyote had ever seen. He was in love with that star and would talk to her night after night, and all night long. But the star wouldn't answer him; she walked across the sky, looking at him, but saying nothing.

Wey ya hiyah, wey ya hiyo.

Coyote grew more and more crazy for that star. He noticed that always, as she walked through the sky, she passed very close to a certain mountain peak, so close it would be easy to touch her. Coyote traveled as fast as he could, a long long way; until very tired, he stood on this mountain peak. And he waited.

In the evening he saw her coming; she was very beautiful. He could see now that she and the other stars were dancing; they moved through his skin, but he kept quiet. The star danced nearer and nearer; at last she was at the mountain peak. He reached up as high as he could, but he could not quite touch her. He begged her to take his hand. "Please." She reached down and took his paws into her hands.

Slowly she danced with him, up from the mountains; far up into the sky, over the earth. Coyote got dizzy; his heart was afraid. They went higher into the sky, among all the other stars. It was bitter cold and silent. None of the stars spoke. Coyote looked down and fear filled his heart. He begged the stars to take him back to earth. When they reached the very top of the sky, the stars let go of Coyote.

Wey ya hiyah, wey ya hiyo.

Coyote fell for thirty days and thirty nights, and when he finally struck the earth, he knocked a great big hole in it, which became Crater Lake.

One day Rabbit was out on a plain eating when Coyote came up. "I am very hungry, I'm going to eat you!"

"Oh no Coyote, don't eat me. They're cooking a really good meal of chicken right over there. Wait here and I'll bring it to you." And the Rabbit hopped off toward the mountain. Coyote happily waited, singing in anticipation of a fine meal. He waited a long time. At last he became angry, and he followed the tracks of Rabbit.

He found Rabbit in a gully standing by a cliff with his forepaws up against the wall. "I bet you're wondering what I'm doing here, right Coyote? I'm holding this cliff up." At that moment a little rock fell, and the Rabbit pushed even harder. "Here you hold the cliff up while I go and get the food I was talking about. It's almost ready."

And the Rabbit hopped away. Coyote put his paws up against the cliff, pushing desperately while the Rabbit ran off. At that moment another rock fell, and Coyote pushed all the harder. He waited for a long time. He was very tired and terribly hungry. Suddenly he let go of the cliff and ran as fast as he could. Nothing happened. He followed the tracks of Rabbit.

"This time I'm really going to eat you!"

"Just sit down, They're going to bring that food right here. They'll be here soon." So Coyote sat down, looking hungrily at Rabbit. Rabbit jumped up. "I'm going to hurry them. I'll be right back, I promise." So Rabbit hopped off, and Coyote waited.

Meanwhile Rabbit set fire all around the edges of the thicket. He went hopping back to Coyote. "There, You smell the smoke? Do you hear the fire, Coyote? They're bringing you a wonderful meal of fry bread, mouse and chicken!" And the Rabbit ran away as fast as he could.

Coyote happily danced and sang as he waited for his meal. The fire soon surrounded him, and he was burned up.

Poor Coyote.

So Fox had to jump over his friend again.

One day Coyote was walking up the river when he came upon a lodge. No one lived there, but inside the lodge was a box. And inside the box was a pair of white leggings. These were magic leggings, fire leggings. Whoever wore these leggings would not only be protected from fire, but they would also have the strength of fire, the strength to transform an object from one thing to another.

One winter Coyote's wife became ill. She died. In time Coyote became very lonely. He did nothing but weep for his wife. One night the Death Spirit came to him and asked if he was crying for his wife.

Coyote said, "Yes, my friend, I long for her. There is a great pain in my heart."

After awhile the Death Spirit felt sorry for Coyote and said, "I can take you to the place where your wife has gone, but if I do, you must do exactly what I say. You can't disregard a single word." He knew Coyote had trouble following directions.

"What would you expect me to do? Of course, I will do whatever you say, anything, my friend." "Well then, let's go." After they had gone a ways, the Death Spirit again cautioned Coyote to do exactly as he was told, and Coyote said he would.

By then it was morning, and Coyote was having trouble seeing the Death Spirit. It was like a shadow on an overcast day. They were going across the prairie to the east when suddenly the Ghost stopped and said, "Oh, look at all these horses over there. It must be a roundup." Coyote couldn't see any horses, but he said, "Yes, yes!"

They went on a little farther. "Oh, look at all those service berries! Let's pick some to eat." Coyote couldn't see any berries, and the Ghost said, "When you see me reach up and pull the limb down, you do the same."

Even though Coyote couldn't see anything, he imitated the Ghost, putting his hand to his mouth as though he were eating. He watched how the Ghost did everything and imitated him. "Very good, Coyote."

They walked a short distance. "Coyote, we are coming to a door now. Do in every way exactly what I do. I will take hold of the door flap, raise it up, and, bending low, will enter. Then you take hold of the door flap and do the same." In this way they went in. The Ghost said, "Sit down here by your wife."

Coyote could see nothing. He sat down in an open prairie in the middle of the afternoon with nothing in sight. "Your wife has prepared food for us! Let us eat." Coyote could only see grass and dust in front of him. They ate. And then the Ghost said, "I must go now Coyote. You stay here."

Now, it was getting dark and Coyote thought he could hear voices, very faintly, talking all around him. Then darkness set in, and Coyote began to see many small fires in the long house. He began to see people, like shadows. And then he saw his wife sitting by his side. He was overjoyed. He cried. Coyote went around and greeted all his old friends who had died long ago. This made him very happy. All night long, he went among them visiting and talking with everyone.

Toward morning, the Death Spirit said, "Coyote, the sun is coming up, and in a little while you will not see us. But you must stay here. Do not move. In the evening you will see all these people again." "Where would I go my friend? Sure, I will stay right here."

When dawn came, Coyote found himself sitting alone in the middle of the prairie. The sun got very hot, and Coyote thought he could hear meadowlarks somewhere. Finally evening came and he saw the lodge again. This went on for over a week, Coyote would sit in the hot sun in the daytime, and at night he would visit with his wife and his friends.

One night the Death Spirit came to him and said, "Coyote, tomorrow you will go home. You will take your wife with you. Listen to me. There are five mountains to the west. You will travel for five days. You must not under any circumstances touch your wife. When you have crossed the fifth mountain, then you can do whatever you want."

"That is the way it will be then," said Coyote. When dawn came, Coyote and his wife set out. They crossed over one mountain, then two mountains, then three. On the fourth mountain, Coyote built a fire. Coyote sat on one side of the fire, his wife on the other.

Coyote could see the firelight dancing on her buckskin dress, on her face and in her eyes. How he wanted to embrace his wife. But he didn't dare touch her. But as Coyote watched his wife, an overwhelming and irresistible urge came over him. He had to kiss his wife. He jumped up and ran around the fire to embrace her.

"No! Stop! Stop! Coyote do not touch me!"

But her warning had no effect. Coyote rushed to her, and just as he touched her she vanished. She disappeared and returned to Shadowland. When the Death Spirit learned what Coyote had done, he was furious. "Why are you always doing things like this, Coyote? I told you not to do anything foolish. You were about to establish the practice of returning from death. Now, that will never happen, and you have made it this way."

Coyote wept and wept. His sorrow was very deep. He decided that he would go back, find the death lodge and find his wife again. And this time he would do it right. He crossed back over the mountains, went out onto the prairie, and began to do the same things he had done on his first trip to Shadowland.

"Oh, look at all those horses. It must be round-up!" "Oh, such choice service berries. Let's pick some and eat." He came to the place where the Death Lodge had stood. "Now, I must do everything my friend told me. I will reach for the door flap and bending low will enter. And here is the spot where I sat with my wife. My wife has prepared food for us, let us eat."

Darkness fell and Coyote listened for the voices. He looked all around, but nothing happened. Coyote was just sitting in the middle of the prairie. He sat there all night long, but the lodge never appeared again. In the morning he heard the sound of meadowlarks.

"The Human Beings, the New People, my children will be coming soon. I feel it. I'll give them a start with the Monster of Kamiah!"

The Monster Coyote was talking about, was over eleven miles long. It lived in the Kamiah valley and had swallowed all the people living there.

"Oh, you horrible Monster, it is I who am here now. Inhale me! Inhale me! You have already swallowed all the other people around here, you may as well swallow me as well. I don't want to be lonely. Aye. Inhale me! Inhale Coyote, the powerful Itsiyaya! I have come here to destroy you with my strong medicine. Suck me in if you can."

(Sounds of wind—COYOTE tumbles in slow motion.)

Hello. Hello! Oh, yuck, I must be inside the Monster's stomach. Now where is the Monster's heart? Oh, this is disgusting. Hello, Moose. And Grizzly Bear? And my friend Fox! And my auntie Meadowlark. Tots maybe. Listen up, all of you. I'm going to cut the Monster's heart off. As soon as I do, all of you must run out the opening nearest you. Get yourselves ready. The heart is here."

"One. Two. Three. Four. Five. RUN!

> Hey ya hey ya hey e ya
> Ya hey ya hey e ya
> Ya hey hey e ya
> Hey ya hey ya ya hey yo

"From the Monster's legs I make the Blackfeet and the Sioux. You are the New People. You will be good runners!

"From the Monster's arms I make the Cayuse! You will be strong and brave. You are the New People!

"From the Monster's stomach I make the Blood and the Cree. You will eat well and be good hunters. You are the New People!

"From the bones I make the Flathead! You are the New People! Think and act wisely.

"From the Monster's body I make the Klickitat, the Yakima, the Colville. You are the New People!

"And from the Monster's blood I make the Nez Percé. You will live here in this valley. You may be small, but like the light you must be brilliant. You are the New People!"

Coyote's work was done. He was going through the woods up above Kamiah when he noticed a rope hanging down from the sky. Coyote thought, "What the heck is going on here? A rope has to be attached to something."

What Coyote didn't know was that the rope was attached to A-kum-kinny-koo, Heaven. And the rope was for Coyote. The Great Spirit had put it there so Coyote could climb up the rope and join the Great Spirit in Heaven. But the only way Coyote could grab hold of the rope was if he confessed to all of his tricks.

"Oh shoot! Well, once I gave a present to a Rock, and then I took it back again. And then once I called all these birds nasty names. And then I stole something once, but it was fire from the skookums! And then there was the time I had taken my eyeballs out and was juggling with them, when someone stole them and ran away! So I had to accidentally beat up an old woman, put on her clothes so I could get my eyeballs back.

"And once I stepped on this Rattlesnake's head and squished it flat. You should have seen his face! And then once I turned myself into a little bitty baby, and I got all these pretty girls to hold me and burp me and to change my diapers!

"And once I got this real dumb guy to marry me! No, he was real conceited and waiting for just the right wife. Boy, that was a good one. OH! There's the time I stole the sun and the moon, but then I put them in the sky for all of us to see. Should I go on?"

"No, Coyote, don't go on. Just grab hold of the rope and let me pull you to Heaven." So Coyote grabbed hold of the rope, and he went higher and higher, up past the clouds, up to A-kum-kinny-koo. But unfortunately, many of the people Coyote had tricked were now living in Heaven. And when they heard that Coyote was coming up to live in their world, they got mad. One of them grabbed a knife, and cut the rope.

And Coyote fell down through the air and hit the earth.

And he changed.

He turned into the timid and slinking creature that we see running through the hills and valleys today. The Great Coyote, the powerful Itsiyaya, and all of the animal kingdom was no more.

But then again I heard that Coyote is now living in L.A. I mean he's starring in movies as Wile E. Coyote.

I remember when the astronauts first landed on the moon. I was back on the reservation and talking to my grandfather, my Pelukut. And he said, "Oh, those people think they're so smart. They don't even know Coyote's already been to the moon and back."

CURTAIN

THE MISCHIEF MAKERS

by

Lowell Swortzell

LOWELL SWORTZELL saw his first play performed in Washington, D.C., when he was in a fifth-grade class studying civilization in ancient Greece. He dramatized a day in the life of an Athenian boy exactly his own age and, not surprisingly, the teacher asked him to play the leading role. On large sheets of brown wrapping paper affixed to the blackboards, the class painted a panorama of the Acropolis; the actors brought countless bed sheets from home to be draped into togas and robes. Swortzell cannot recall the plot, but the school principal was sufficiently impressed to require every grade, from kindergarten through sixth, to see a performance. The production enjoyed the longest run of any play in the history of the Benjamin Stoddard Elementary School. In the process, a playwright, if not an actor, was born.

In high school he gained more dramatic experience when his musical, *Outlaw Days*, a satire of Hollywood westerns, was presented by the Drama Club to the entire student body. In college he first began to write plays for young audiences, three of which were later produced by Tufts University and six by Rutgers University.

While at the Yale Drama School he served as assistant to John Gassner and taught beginning playwriting. His New York University doctoral dissertation on the subject of evaluating plays for children included five original scripts. Among his sixteen published plays are *Cinderella: The World's Favorite Fairy Tale*, *The Little Humpback Horse*, *Gulliver's Travels*, and *The Arabian Nights*. His three Christmas plays have been produced widely in America and Europe.

Swortzell has edited several collections of plays: *All the World's a Stage: Modern Plays for Young People*, *The Theatre of Aurand Harris*, and *Theatre for Young Audiences: Around the World in 21 Plays*. His books have won the *New York Times* Notable Book of the Year Award and the Distinguished Book of the Year Award by the American Alliance for Theatre and Education. His *International Guide to Children's Theatre and Educational Theatre* was named "Outstanding Academic Book 1990" by *Choice* magazine.

Professor of Educational Theatre at New York University, Swortzell heads the program and teaches courses in research methods, playwriting, and American theatre, among others. His interest in Eugene O'Neill has resulted in various publications and now that NYU has renovated the Provincetown Playhouse in Greenwich Village to produce plays and events for young audiences, his two major areas of specialization have merged. The plot of his recent play about O'Neill, *Young Eugene*, is actually set on the stage of the Provincetown Playhouse.

Swortzell originally planned *The Mischief Makers* as three separate works, each centering on a famous trickster drawn from folklore or mythology. But after settling on the Raven, Anansi the Spider, and Reynard the Fox as his subjects, he realized they should come together to trick one another and to determine which one could make the most mischief.

Lowell Swortzell was inducted into the College of Fellows of the American Theatre at the Kennedy Center in 1992. In 1995, he was awarded a Fulbright Scholarship to lecture and study in Australia.

What I find most gratifying in writing plays for young people is not the money (very little), not the fame (even less) and certainly not the critical approval (absolutely none—how can there be when we have no critics?). And not what you may expect me to claim: those 600 smiling faces and 1,200 clapping hands at the end of the performance. Of course, they are what we are all about, but dramatists who write primarily to please spectators, child or adult, are defeated before they begin. You write a play to please yourself. And if and when it does, you hope that someone else will recognize at least a measure of your intention and artistry. If not, you still have the satisfaction of knowing that it works for you, the creator.

Also, you know that you have corrected its problems—dramatic, theatrical, technical—and all of those other demons that plague playwrights. You then feel as if you are both a master puzzle maker and solver, a clock maker whose instruments tick precisely on time and a sorcerer or conjurer whose creations breathe as if alive. And, to be sure, you are *all* of these because, miracle of miracles, you have written a play. Should your audience like it, too, as sometimes happens, well, that's true happiness. Who needs fame and fortune? Your next play is all you'll ever need. And what could be more gratifying as you begin to write than those great expectations renewing your excitement, your enthusiasm, and your energy?

—LOWELL SWORTZELL

THE MISCHIEF MAKERS

A Comedy for Three Actors
About the World's Best-Loved Tricksters,
Rascals and Rogues

CAST

Raven *(also plays Ano and Crying Mother)*
Anansi the Spider *(also plays Daughter)*
Reynard the Fox *(also plays Chiefs One, Two, Three, Four and Father)*
The Voice of Nyame, the sky god, from the mythology of the Shanti region
now known as Ghana

The characters may be played by three women, three men, or by any combination thereof; likewise, the Voice of Nyame may be that of either a male or female performer, as long as it comes from a source of considerable power.

SCENE

A clearing deep in a forest somewhere on the Northwest Pacific Coast. A large totem pole rises in the center of the clearing, surrounded by several smaller poles, a boulder or two, logs, and rocks.

(The lights come up upon a totem pole standing center stage. While this pole is three dimensional, others rising at various heights to its left and right are silhouettes looming against a now-pale sky in the distance. Their shapes and designs are in the style and tradition of the Northwest Pacific Coast Native American cultures of Canada.

Gradually, as the lights rise, three figures carved in the face of the predominant pole become evident. They rest one on top of the other and are, in fact, three actors trying, for once in their lives, to be as wooden as possible.

They stare straight ahead but after a pause, the middle face, that of the RAVEN, *looks up, then down and instantly becomes puzzled, although still not moving anything but the eyes.)*

RAVEN: Something's wrong with this totem pole. *(No response comes from either the face above, that of* ANANSI, *or from below, that belonging to* REYNARD.) I say this is one peculiar totem pole. *(Still no response.* RAVEN *speaks louder.)* Doesn't anybody hear me?

ANANSI: I don't.

REYNARD: Neither do I.

RAVEN: But you must agree that this totem pole is mixed up—*seriously* mixed up.

ANANSI: I rather like it.

REYNARD: So do I.

RAVEN: How can you? No one ever saw a totem pole like this before.

ANANSI: Maybe it's time.

RAVEN: For what?

ANANSI: A new look in totem poles.

REYNARD: Everything's got to change sooner or later, even totem poles.

RAVEN: Why should they?

ANANSI: Why shouldn't they?

REYNARD: What don't you like about it?

RAVEN: Well, it just seems to me . . . *(Choosing words carefully.)* no offense, nothing personal, and all that, but we've got some faces here that don't belong. Who are you? Where did you come from?

ANANSI: I'm from Africa.

RAVEN: I knew it! Get down! Right this minute! Off you go! One. Two. Three. And you're out of here.

ANANSI: You have a problem with Africans?

RAVEN: Africans are great. Except on totem poles.

ANANSI: Well, this African isn't going any place. I'm Anansi, the spider. Glad to meet you. *(Lowers arm, running over the* RAVEN's *forehead.)*

RAVEN: Spiders give me the creeps, the heebie-jeebies . . .

ANANSI: It's not as if I were running up and down your back—

RAVEN: Don't say that! *(Begins to shake and shiver at the thought.)*

ANANSI: Or walking over your face.

RAVEN: Stop it, will you?

ANANSI: Or crawling up your nose.

RAVEN: I said "ENOUGH." Besides, I don't have a nose.

ANANSI: No nose? How come?

RAVEN: I'm a bird with a beak. A raven.

ANANSI: Relax. Relax. I'm not crawling around any beaks. I'm smarter than that.

RAVEN: And you down below, on whose broad shoulders we stand. Who are you?

REYNARD: I'm from Europe.

RAVEN: I knew it. They don't have totem poles in Europe.

REYNARD: We're much too civilized.

RAVEN: Then put us down and go back to Europe.

REYNARD: I've never been part of a totem pole. And I rather like it. Brings out my primitive instincts.

RAVEN: *(Clearly upset.)* You're both imposters.

ANANSI: Not at all, I'm Anansi, the spider. Haven't my hairy feet and hands convinced you? *(Rubbing them over* RAVEN's *face.)*

RAVEN: *(Twitching all over.)* Hold still. PLEASE! I take your word.

REYNARD: And if you care to look behind you and check out my big bushy tail, I think you'll agree it could only belong to a fox. Note the color, the shape, the quality. A *French* fox, of course.

RAVEN: *(Taking a quick glance around and down.)* I guess so.

REYNARD: And if the tail doesn't convince you, these large white teeth in the sharpest of shape will. *(Snaps at* RAVEN's *feet who lifts foot trying to avoid being bitten.)*

RAVEN: You're a fox all right. But you don't belong here.

REYNARD: And what makes you think *you* belong?

RAVEN: I'm a raven. I'm on practically every totem pole ever carved. I'm authentic . . . the real thing. Ask anybody!

ANANSI: I thought totem poles told stories . . .

RAVEN: They do. MY story!

ANANSI: If you keep quiet long enough, this totem pole can tell my story.

REYNARD: And mine, too, if you will listen . . .

RAVEN: But, we have nothing in common: a spider, a raven, and a fox. Why should I listen to you?

ANANSI: Maybe we can figure that out.

RAVEN: What?

REYNARD: What we have in common.

RAVEN: Look, I know who I am. I like sitting on poles, minding my own business . . .

REYNARD: Maybe we do, too!

RAVEN: *(Trying another way to get rid of them.)* Well, to be honest, I never learned to mind my own business. Not really. That's been true of us ravens for centuries and centuries . . . we're just a bunch of busybodies. You don't want to get mixed up with me. I'm a trickster. Do you know what that means?

ANANSI: *(Smiling.)* Yes, I think I've heard that word before.

REYNARD: And I've had some experience along those lines myself. *(Winks knowingly at the audience.)*

RAVEN: The fact of the matter is you can't trust me. *(Climbs down from the pole and moves about, looking at ANANSI and REYNARD, still on the pole.)*

ANANSI: That's fine with me.

REYNARD: I have no quarrel with that.

RAVEN: Why? Why would want to live near a trickster like me?

ANANSI: Another trickster might.

RAVEN: Then that leaves you out. How could a little itsy-bitsy spider trick anyone? Scare them to death, maybe, but trick them, oh, no . . . Forgive me for laughing . . . *(Convulsed.)*

ANANSI: Well, my friend, the laugh's on you. For I'm a great trickster.

RAVEN: *(Still laughing.)* Well, maybe you could trick another spider. I'll grant you that.

ANANSI: Apparently, you didn't catch my name. Anansi. Doesn't that mean anything to you?

RAVEN: It means you're an itsy-bitsy spider. *(Laughs again.)*

ANANSI: I'm known as one of the great tricksters of the world.

RAVEN: At spinning webs and that sort of thing?

ANANSI: At tricking. You know: fooling people and causing trouble.

RAVEN: A little thing like you?

ANANSI: I may be an "itsy-bitsy spider" to you, but to everybody else I'm one helluva hell-raiser. I'm the best trickster in Africa. Meet Anansi, the spider.

REYNARD: Obviously, dear Raven, you haven't a clue to my identity.

RAVEN: I saw your big bushy tail, and I have some *impression* of your teeth. *(Rubs ankle which REYNARD has snapped at.)*

REYNARD: I'm the greatest rascal in Europe. Reynard's the name. Reynard, the Fox.

RAVEN: Well, nice to meet you both. Maybe we do have something in common, after all, because I am also the greatest . . .

REYNARD: But you do nothing but sit about on totem poles. You said so yourself.

ANANSI: Who could you trick?

RAVEN: Everybody and everything! You two may have fooled Africa and Europe, but my tricks have changed the whole world! Even the sun and the stars.

ANANSI: Now it's our turn to laugh. *(They do.)*

RAYNARD: Come, come, dear Raven. I think you're trying to trick us now.

RAVEN: Not at all. It's quite simple: there are tricksters and tricksters, and no doubt both of you are good at what you do, but I am the greatest.

ANANSI: No, you're not!

REYNARD: Absolutely, not!

ANANSI: I'm the cleverest!

REYNARD: I'm the most cunning!

RAVEN: But I'm the mischief maker who *created* mischief! The original, first and foremost troublemaker of the world. That's me.

ANANSI: I have an idea. Think of a trick.

RAVEN: I have thousands.

ANANSI: Pick the one of which you're proudest. We'll act them out to see which one is best.

RAVEN: I know that already!

REYNARD: *We* don't, so let's find out right now.

RAVEN: I hate contests.

ANANSI: You're not afraid of losing, are you, Raven?

RAVEN: Definitely not!

ANANSI: Then let's begin. (*Climbs down.*)

REYNARD: A good idea, Anansi. (*Climbs down.*)

ANANSI: I told you I was clever.

RAVEN: That remains to be seen.

ANANSI: Then why don't *you* start?

RAVEN: (*Caught off guard.*) There are so many to choose from. I have to think about this for a while.

ANANSI: I'm not afraid to go first. Here's my story . . . Have you heard of Nyame?

REYNARD: You mean Nyame, the god of the skies?

RAVEN: Of course, everybody knows Nyame.

ANANSI: He's very important in my story.

RAVEN: Can I play the part?

ANANSI: We only hear him; we don't see him.

RAVEN: Then who do I play?

ANANSI: I'll tell you as we go along. This story has lots of roles. Don't worry.

RAVEN: I just want to be ready, that's all. I'm not worried.

REYNARD: Well, let Anansi begin so we can find out who we are.

RAVEN: If it's all the same to you, I don't think I'd make a very good spider. I just can't see myself in that role.

ANANSI: I'm already cast, thank you very much.

REYNARD: A good actor can play anything he puts his mind to, I always say.

ANANSI: Look, this story is about a spider. I'm a spider, right? So, if you don't mind, I think I've got the part.

REYNARD: Let's start.

ANANSI: Thank you. One day Nyame looked down from the skies and saw just how stupid everyone was. He thought someone must be wise among them and decided to give a test to find who it was.

RAVEN: (*To* REYNARD.) And guess who took it?

ANANSI: As a matter of fact, everyone was afraid to try.

RAVEN: If that's true, then your story is over right now.

ANANSI: Well, there was one who stepped forth . . .

RAVEN: I repeat, guess who?

ANANSI: You're right, for as I said to my wife, "Everyone knows I'm the wisest of all. Let me prove it to Nyame, too." So I called to him. (Looking up, shouting.) Nyame. Listen, I want to take the wisdom test. Me, down here.

NYAME: (Offstage voice.) Down where? I don't see anyone.

ANANSI: Right here.

NYAME: You're just a speck from up here—a spot.

ANANSI: (Waving arms and jumping up and down trying to be noticed.) This spot is a spider. Anansi's the name.

NYAME: And you think you're the wisest creature in my kingdom?

ANANSI: And the cleverest, too!

NYAME: A smart spider? I have to laugh. (Roaring loudly.)

ANANSI: Please give me the chance to prove myself.

NYAME: Well, I did say "all creatures in my kingdom" and, however small, you're still a creature. All right. But remember, if you fail, calamity will come to you and your family. Do you still want to try?

ANANSI: I'm willing to take the consequences.

NYAME: Good. Now listen carefully.

ANANSI: I'm ready.

NYAME: Hold out your hand. (ANANSI does so.) I'm going to drop something into it. (From above, a small object falls, as if coming from the sky. It lands in ANANSI's hand.)

ANANSI: What's this?

NYAME: What does it look like?

ANANSI: A grain of corn.

NYAME: That's exactly what it is.

ANANSI: What am I going to do with it?

NYAME: Bring all the people of my kingdom together.

ANANSI: With one grain of corn? But how?

NYAME: That's for you to figure out, clever spider.

ANANSI: Aren't you going to give me a hint?

NYAME: Use your wisdom, oh, wise one.

ANANSI: A grain of corn is a grain of corn. What more can I say?

NYAME: It's time to begin.

ANANSI: Do I plant it or cook it or eat it? (Looking at the grain.) Nothing magical about it.

NYAME: It's just an ordinary grain of corn, that's all . . . I grow impatient, little one.

ANANSI: (Bowing.) Thank you, Nyame, for the great honor of serving you. I'll do my best.

NYAME: The consequences will be severe if you fail. *(Voice trails off.)* Good-bye for now.

ANANSI: I'm really in trouble this time. My wife will kill me.

RAVEN: *(Interrupting the story.)* I've changed my mind. I can play a spider after all. That's the part I want—your wife.

ANANSI: Very well, it's yours.

RAVEN: *(Immediately jumping into the character of* ANO.) You did WHAT? *(Swats him with broom.)* You promised Nyame WHAT? *(Swats again.)* And all he gave you was a grain of WHAT? *(Hits hard this time.)*

ANANSI: I just told you, good wife.

RAVEN: Don't "good wife" me.

ANANSI: How was I to know what the test would be?

RAVEN: You could have kept your mouth shut like everybody else.

ANANSI: But I *am* the cleverest creature in the kingdom. You know that.

RAVEN: I know that if you fail, my children will suffer. You may call that smart but I call it foolish, crazy, idiotic, stupid, stupid, stupid. Do I make myself clear? *(Breaking character.)* I love this part.

ANANSI: Don't carry on, wife.

RAVEN: My family is doomed. Nyame said so. *(Sobbing and overacting.)* My poor innocent children! What's to become of them!

ANANSI: I thought you believed in me.

RAVEN: It's one thing to trick your fellow spiders. You're good at that. But now you're trying to trick a god. That's dangerous.

ANANSI: Don't shout; the neighbors will hear you.

RAVEN: I can't believe you've done this. My poor, helpless babies, my fatherless children.

ANANSI: Fatherless?

RAVEN: After this, they'll have no father. Nyame will see to that.

ANANSI: But I *am* the smartest, the cleverest, the wisest . . .

RAVEN: Then take your grain of corn and prove it . . .

ANANSI: I will.

RAVEN: Just leave this poor widow and her abandoned children to fend for themselves . . .

ANANSI: It's not that bad, at least not yet.

RAVEN: Fatherless! Homeless! Helpless! All because of you.

ANANSI: Give me a chance, will you, please?

RAVEN: Now, I'm nothing but a poor black widow spider. Woe! Woe! Woe! *(Breaking character.)* I'm really getting into this.

ANANSI: You're Ano, the wife of Anansi, and somehow, someday, I'll return.

RAVEN: Woe! Woe! Woe! *(Collapses in misery and crawls off.)*

ANANSI: *(As* STORYTELLER.) I couldn't take anymore of that. So I set out to prove myself. I just wandered down the road, not knowing what I'd find. As it grew dark, I became hungry. *(Back in character, sniffing the air.)* Something's cooking. I smell food just ahead. Must be a village. And here is the Chief. *(Breaking character again.)* Fox, you play the Chief.

REYNARD: (As CHIEF.) Who approaches my village?

ANANSI: (In character.) A messenger of the gods.

REYNARD: (Impressed.) Here? We are honored.

ANANSI: Thank you.

REYNARD: Which of the gods do you represent?

ANANSI: I work for Nyame.

REYNARD: Then, of course, you're welcome. Won't you join me for dinner?

ANANSI: Dinner! Yes, I'd like that very much. (As STORYTELLER.) And so we dined on a feast of yams and I told the Chief some wonderful stories about my work as a messenger of Nyame.

REYNARD: You certainly lead an exciting life up there in the sky, my friend.

ANANSI: And you dine very well down here. Now, if you don't mind, I'll retire, for I must set out early in the morning.

REYNARD: I'll show you your room.

ANANSI: Thank you. Oh, I almost forgot. I'm carrying this grain of corn . . . (Shows REYNARD.) . . . which requires special care. It doesn't like to sleep with people.

REYNARD: Would you like me to put it outside then?

ANANSI: Let it sleep in the chicken house.

REYNARD: Very well, if you think it will be happy. I'll take it now.

ANANSI: Be careful. It's a very special grain of corn.

REYNARD: I can see that. Fit for the gods. (Leaving.) I've never seen a grain of corn so beautiful.

ANANSI: (As STORYTELLER.) And after a good night's sleep, I was ready to be on my way.

REYNARD: (Reenters carrying a large chicken puppet.) It's been an honor to have so distinguished a guest.

ANANSI: Your hospitality shall be known far and wide, I assure you.

REYNARD: You're too kind. Safe journey to you. (ANANSI is almost out of the house.)

ANANSI: Oh, I just remembered. My grain of corn. Please, give it to me.

REYNARD: I don't know how to tell you this. I prayed you'd forgotten all about it. We've searched everywhere, but I'm sorry to report that the grain of corn is gone. Apparently, the chickens ate it. This one, I think.

ANANSI: (Staggers as if about to faint.) It belonged to Nyame himself. What will he say? What will he do when he hears you've lost it?

REYNARD: Please, protect me from his punishment.

ANANSI: I don't know if I can.

REYNARD: Think of something, I beg you.

ANANSI: Nyame will be very angry . . . but since you've been good to me, I'll do my best.

REYNARD: Thank you. Take this chicken, please. (REYNARD gives ANANSI the chicken puppet.) It's the least I can do to show my appreciation.

ANANSI: (Taking the chicken and speaking to it.) Did you eat Nyame's grain of corn? (Chicken nods.) You bad, bad chicken. (To REYNARD.) Good-bye.

REYNARD: Please, forgive me, good sir. *(Waves good-bye and leaves.)*

ANANSI: *(As* STORYTELLER.*)* And I was on my way. With a new friend. *(To chicken.)* You were not bad to eat the grain of corn. In fact, I thank you. *(Chicken is happy to hear this.)* So far, my adventure goes very well. I've received a good dinner, a good rest, and now you. *(Chicken flutters happily again.)* What do I hear ahead? *(Listens.)* Drums announcing a holiday . . . the entire town's celebrating.

*(*REYNARD, *entering as the Chief of this village, wears a different hat from the last episode and now carries a drum.)*

REYNARD: Stranger, you've come at just the right time. Welcome to our village.

ANANSI: Thank you.

REYNARD: May I ask where you come from?

ANANSI: The sky above. I'm a messenger of the god Nyame.

REYNARD: Nyame has sent you to our celebration?

ANANSI: I bring his greetings.

REYNARD: We are blessed by the gods. You must stay the night.

ANANSI: Thank you.

REYNARD: And I will beat the drums to salute you. *(Beats drum.)*

ANANSI: *(As* STORYTELLER.*)* And we had drums, dinner, and more drums. *(In character, with hands over ears.)* That is loud and lovely. I am honored. But I must retire for an early morning departure.

REYNARD: Of course, go to your room and rest.

ANANSI: One thing before I go. My chicken here does not like to sleep with people. Could she spend the night in the barn with the sheep?

REYNARD: I'll take her there myself.

ANANSI: *(Whispering to chicken.)* If you're smart, you'll escape in the night and go home to your family. *(*ANANSI *passes the chicken to* REYNARD *who carries it off.)* Good night. *(As* STORYTELLER.*)* And after a good sleep, I was ready to leave. *(*REYNARD *returns.)* I'll tell Nyame of your kindness to me.

REYNARD: I'm most grateful for that.

ANANSI: Now, may I have my chicken, please?

REYNARD: Kind Sir, it's missing. We've searched the barn high and low, and it's nowhere to be seen.

ANANSI: Don't tell me you've lost the chicken!

REYNARD: It's gone.

ANANSI: That was Nyame's chicken! His favorite! He asked me to take special care of that chicken. It laid the best eggs he's ever eaten.

REYNARD: What can I do?

ANANSI: No more omelettes for Nyame! He'll never forgive you.

REYNARD: I'll give him another.

ANANSI: That would be an insult.

REYNARD: Then a sheep. My best sheep. Wool for Nyame!

ANANSI: It does get chilly up there in the clouds. Yes, I'll take him a sheep.

REYNARD: *(Reaching off and bringing forth a sheep puppet.)* Here, take this. *(Hands it to ANANSI.)*

ANANSI: *(Taking the sheep.)* Nyame will be pleased, I'm certain. Thank you. And now good-bye. *(REYNARD exits. As STORYTELLER.)* And so my new friend and I were on our way. Oh, look, we're approaching a river and there's a fisherman sitting on the bank. *(REYNARD enters wearing a fisherman's hat.)* Fisherman, will you take me to meet the Chief of your village?

REYNARD: I'm the Chief! What can I do for you?

ANANSI: I just happen to be passing this way.

REYNARD: And who do you *happen* to be?

ANANSI: Nyame's messenger.

REYNARD: I've heard of you. They say you're some kind of god.

ANANSI: Just his servant, sort of.

REYNARD: And so I try to be myself.

ANANSI: *(Hoping to be invited for supper.)* I can see at once that you're a good man.

REYNARD: A simple man, that's me.

ANANSI: And a kind man.

REYNARD: That, too.

ANANSI: Especially to strangers!

REYNARD: Yes.

ANANSI: Like me!

REYNARD: Yes. *(Finally getting the point.)* Oh, yes. Of course. Won't you stay for supper in my humble house? And spend the night?

ANANSI: Thank you. And could my sheep sleep with the cows?

REYNARD: Of course. I'll make a bed of hay.

ANANSI: *(Handing over the sheep and whispering.)* If I were you, I'd run away the first chance you get. Go back to your master. *(REYNARD exits. As STORYTELLER.)* This was a simple man who provided a simple supper and a simple resting place. Still I felt fortunate to have survived another night. And I was ready to continue my journey the next morning. *(To REYNARD who has reentered.)* Chief, tell me the best place to cross the river.

REYNARD: It's safe right here. But you must swim.

ANANSI: But my sheep can't swim.

REYNARD: I don't know how to tell you this but your sheep has vanished.

ANANSI: What do you mean?

REYNARD: Without a trace.

ANANSI: Calamity!

REYNARD: I made it a lovely bed of hay.

ANANSI: Tragedy!

REYNARD: I did my best, really I did.

ANANSI: Catastrophe!

REYNARD: I'm ever so sorry.

ANANSI: That was Nyame's favorite sheep! He will make the river rise and flood your village.

REYNARD: No, no, we're simple people. Spare us!

ANANSI: I pity you!

REYNARD: Look, take my cow. You can ride on its back across the river.

ANANSI: Perhaps Nyame will forgive you, after all.

REYNARD: My cow is a good worker. *(Leaves as if to fetch cow.)*

ANANSI: All right, I'll take it. *(As* STORYTELLER.*)* And I climbed on and rode across the river without getting wet. Everywhere I went people were impressed by my new friend. Several wanted to buy it, but I refused all offers. Then we came upon a terrible sight. *(As* ANANSI.*)* Raven, I need you to play the role of a crying mother. We want to see real tears.

RAVEN: I can do it. I can do it. Where do you want me?

ANANSI: Kneel here, over the body of your dying baby.

RAVEN: Dying baby? I'm crying already. Really I am.

ANANSI: Pretend this bundle of rags is your baby son.

RAVEN: *(Picks up bundle and caresses it in arms.)* My poor baby. Please, don't die. Please, don't die. If only someone would help me!

ANANSI: *(In character.)* I'll be glad to, dear lady.

RAVEN: My baby is sick. I have no medicine, no money.

ANANSI: Don't worry. I'll take care of him.

RAVEN: Thank you.

ANANSI: *(Pointing off.)* See that magnificent cow there. It's yours.

RAVEN: Mine!

ANANSI: You'll never be poor again.

RAVEN: Thank you, but what about my baby?

ANANSI: Leave him with me. Someday I'll give him back to you, well and sound.

RAVEN: Bless you! Bless you! *(Withdraws.)*

ANANSI: *(As* STORYTELLER.*)* And I took the frail baby and set out, not really knowing where I was going or who I'd find next. But, as before, when evening came I approached another man who turned out to be the Chief of *his* village. *(*REYNARD *enters as yet another Chief.)* Thank you for a wonderful dinner. I shall tell Nyame of your generosity. Now, I must retire.

REYNARD: Your room is ready.

ANANSI: I'm leaving this baby here for the night. No one must touch him. Do you understand? No one. Place a guard at the door.

REYNARD: As you say, mysterious stranger. I will stand watch myself.

ANANSI: Let him sleep undisturbed. Good night. *(Goes off.)*

REYNARD: A baby wrapped in these rags. I wonder if he's telling the truth. *(Going nearer and nearer the bundle.)* Is he hiding something? Something valuable! Something I might like . . . *(Touches the rags.)* like gold or silver? *(Opening bundle.)* Or like . . . *(Seeing what is inside.)* a baby, but it's dead! *(He shakes bundle to make sure, then runs toward* ANANSI's *room.)* Sir, sir! Come quickly, your baby is dead. *(*ANANSI *enters immediately.)*

ANANSI: Dead? How do you know that?

REYNARD: I looked in the bundle.

ANANSI: Then you killed him.

REYNARD: Me?

ANANSI: I told you not to touch him. You're responsible for this tragedy.

REYNARD: I opened the bundle ever so gently.

ANANSI: You've killed the son of Nyame!

REYNARD: Oh, no! I'm doomed forever.

ANANSI: You disobeyed. Poor man. And now you must live in shame.

REYNARD: Take my life, my possessions, but do not disgrace me before my people.

ANANSI: Nyame will be revenged; you face destruction! Thunder, lightning, plagues, earthquakes.

REYNARD: Save my people, please!

ANANSI: You and your people must follow me.

REYNARD: We will go anywhere. Only spare us.

ANANSI: Come with me to the Kingdom Beyond the River and stand before Nyame. I will plead your case to him.

REYNARD: If he does not punish my people, I'll give you gold and silver.

ANANSI: Everyone must accompany us, old and young, sick and well, rich and poor.

REYNARD: I promise no one will be left behind.

ANANSI: *(As* STORYTELLER.*)* And we set off to find Nyame. At first hundreds followed, then thousands. *(We hear the hubbub of a great crowd gathering around* ANANSI *and* REYNARD.*)*

REYNARD: You see, I've kept my word. We're all here. And more. They're coming from all the villages to see what's going on.

ANANSI: Nyame will be pleased . . .

REYNARD: I hope so.

ANANSI: Until he sees his baby.

REYNARD: But you will calm his wrath. He will listen to his own messenger.

ANANSI: Let me call him. *(Calling up.)* Nyame! NYAME! Look down and see all your people gathered in the Kingdom Beyond the River, just as you requested. Here we are.

NYAME: *(Offstage voice.)* Yes, little spider, I see.

ANANSI: Are you impressed?

NYAME: A great, great sight. How did you do it, Anansi?

ANANSI: Very simple, really. With a grain of corn. The one you gave me. Remember?

NYAME: I certainly do. Then you have proven yourself to be the wisest creature in my kingdom. Everyone should sing your praises. *(Cheers are heard from the crowds surrounding them.)*

ANANSI: Thank you, Nyame. Thank you, everyone. *(More cheers.)* But there is a problem, great god of the skies.

NYAME: No, you have accomplished all my wishes, exactly. I am pleased.

ANANSI: On the way here, Sire, this baby died.

NYAME: Let me see him. *(ANANSI holds bundle up toward the sky.)*

ANANSI: Our hearts are broken.

NYAME: I take great pity upon all those who love him. And to honor this day when my people are gathered in the Kingdom Beyond the River, I will help you.

REYNARD: Thank you.

ANANSI: We praise your name, Nyame. *(Cries of a baby are heard coming from the bundle. ANANSI looks inside.)* Nyame has breathed life into the child. *(Searching for the mother, who runs to him and takes baby.)* Here, good mother, is your son, well and sound, as I promised.

REYNARD: He's alive! He's alive! I'm saved.

RAVEN: *(Crying with happiness.)* He's alive. Thank you, messenger of the gods.

ANANSI: I'm not Nyame's messenger, but only Anansi the spider.

NYAME: And the wisest creature in my kingdom.

REYNARD: I believe it.

RAVEN: *(As the Mother.)* So do I.

NYAME: Now I must give you a most appropriate gift.

ANANSI: Oh thank you, good god.

NYAME: What would the wisest creature want, I wonder?

REYNARD: Ask him for gold and silver.

ANANSI: He knows best . . .

NYAME: I have it . . . the very thing . . .

ANANSI: And what is that?

NYAME: More wisdom, of course. Knowledge!

ANANSI: How good of you, Nyame.

REYNARD: I'd have preferred gold and silver myself.

NYAME: Look about you. I am dropping some of my best thoughts. You will enjoy them. *(A stream of notes written on odd scraps of paper float down from the sky. ANANSI runs about picking them up and shoving them into pockets.)*

ANANSI: Oh, great Nyame, these are better than money.

REYNARD: I seriously doubt that.

NYAME: Read them and grow wiser. Good-bye.

ANANSI: I will, oh, great master. I will. *(Starting to leave.)*

REYNARD: I know I promised to help you as you've helped me. But seeing how clever you've become, you don't need my help. So thank you and farewell. *(Exit.)*

ANANSI: Thanks, anyway. Now, I must get back to my family and tell my wife of all the adventures I've had. Won't she be proud of me? *(As STORY-TELLER.)* And so I made my way back over the countryside and finally reached my own village. *(In character, boasting.)* And then, dear wife, as a reward Nyame gave me all this wisdom. (*Shows her notes.*) Aren't they wonderful?

RAVEN: You come back after all these days away with a story about a chicken, a sheep, and a cow and think I should be impressed?

ANANSI: Yes, I do.

RAVEN: Then you show me some scraps of paper that are supposed to make you smart.

ANANSI: Not just smart but the smartest.

RAVEN: Well, that's no evidence. (*Knocks the notes out of his hand.*)

ANANSI: What more do you want?

RAVEN: A chicken, a sheep, and a cow might be nice.

ANANSI: But I proved to everyone that I'm the cleverest creature in the kingdom.

RAVEN: To everyone except me and your hungry children. You may be the wisest creature in Nyame's kingdom, but around here you're just another fast-talking spider.

ANANSI: If that's the way you feel, I'll keep my wisdom to myself. (*Picking up notes.*) I'll put it in a clay pot and seal it up.

RAVEN: (*Handing him a tiny pot.*) Here, this should do.

ANANSI: (*Shocked.*) What do you mean? I'm much brighter than that! This one should hold it. (*Secures a very large pot—so big it can scarcely be carried.*)

RAVEN: That's a smart choice, all right. You can hardly move it.

ANANSI: (*Stuffing all the notes into the pot.*) There, everything I know is in this pot. But it's too valuable to stay here. I must hide it.

RAVEN: You're good at hiding your wisdom, all right. (*Laughs loudly at joke.*)

ANANSI: I'll place it high in the tree where no one can see it.

RAVEN: Try to remember where you put it. You may need it again. (*Laughs again.*)

ANANSI: It's a heavy burden, all this wisdom.

RAVEN: You should have thought of that. (*Laughing.*)

ANANSI: You don't have to stand there, making fun of me. How many creatures are as smart as this?

RAVEN: Not many, Anansi.

ANANSI: Well then, stop laughing, and just watch.

RAVEN: I am watching. And laughing.

ANANSI: (*Struggling, but holding the pot makes it impossible to climb.*) I can't grip the trunk. I can't get a footing.

RAVEN: Maybe one of your notes tells you how to climb a tree.

(*Ever more determined not to be defeated,* ANANSI *works harder and harder to climb but with no success.*)

ANANSI: (*Swearing.*) You stupid tree! With your dumb trunk!

RAVEN: I should have known you'd blame the tree.

ANANSI: It won't cooperate. (*Kicks tree.*)

RAVEN: Anansi, the tree is just standing here as it has for years, doing its job.

ANANSI: Are you suggesting I'm at fault?

RAVEN: Well, let's put it this way, it's not the tree. If you'd put the pot on your back, your hands would be free, and you could go right up.

ANANSI: What do you mean?

RAVEN: Try it, oh, wise one.

(ANANSI *ties rope around pot, switches pot from front to back and sees it is now possible to climb tree.*)

ANANSI: But how could you know this?

RAVEN: My wisdom's not in a pot. (*Laughs again.*)

ANANSI: (*Climbing.*) Just keep laughing. I don't mind. I've got my great gift up here safe and sound.

RAVEN: Be careful, Anansi. Drop that pot and you lose everything you know. (*More laughter, then quickly, looking off.*) You'd best get down from there. A storm's coming.

ANANSI: But I haven't tied the pot yet.

RAVEN: I'm telling you, the wind is rising, and it's getting dark.

ANANSI: In a minute.

RAVEN: Come down now if you have any sense.

ANANSI: One more second.

RAVEN: Very well, don't listen to me. The wind will blow you down.

ANANSI: I'm staying here to protect all my wisdom.

RAVEN: Go ahead and fall, it may knock some sense into you. (*Sounds of rising wind increase.*) Anansi, let go of that pot before you get hurt.

ANANSI: Never, it's mine. Mine. (*Wind is fierce.*) Oh, dear, the tree is moving. I can't hold on. (*The pot crashes to the ground and breaks open.*)

RAVEN: The pot is broken.

ANANSI: (*Coming down the tree.*) Help me pick up my wisdom.

RAVEN: It's too late. (*Pointing off.*) Your notes are sailing through the air.

ANANSI: My wisdom's blowing away.

RAVEN: With the wind.

ANANSI: Look, the notes are floating in the river.

RAVEN: And the river's carrying them to the ocean.

ANANSI: There's not one note left.

RAVEN: Well, your head should be clear for the first time in a long while. (*Laughing.*) Empty but clear.

ANANSI: This is all your fault. If you had believed me, I wouldn't have been up in that tree. Now, I've lost everything!

RAVEN: No need to worry. I still have my wisdom, safe and sound and stored where it's supposed to be.

ANANSI: But wife, wait a minute, don't you understand what's happened?

RAVEN: You dropped the pot, that's all.

ANANSI: No, this was meant to be.

RAVEN: What?

ANANSI: It's all perfectly clear. My loss will benefit everyone.

RAVEN: How?

ANANSI: The winds and the rivers are spreading my knowledge everywhere.

RAVEN: WHAT?

ANANSI: I've given them my wisdom. (*As* STORYTELLER.) And so ends the story of how Anansi the spider sent wisdom throughout the world. (*Bows as* RAVEN *and* REYNARD *applaud.*)

REYNARD: I admit that's pretty good.

RAVEN: Yes, and with two great parts for me.

ANANSI: Which you played extremely well.

RAVEN: Thanks. But there's a problem.

ANANSI: What's that?

RAVEN: The message.

ANANSI: You don't like the message?

RAVEN: I love the message.

ANANSI: That Anansi brought wisdom to the world?

RAVEN: No, that your wife is wiser than you.

ANANSI: What? Then I told it wrong.

RAVEN: No you didn't, your wife *is* wiser than you. And for this, I thank you, Anansi. Really, I do. You tricked yourself. (*They all laugh.*)

ANANSI: (*Eager to change the subject.*) Well, Raven, you've had lots of time to think about your story. What's it going to be?

RAVEN: Oh, I've wracked my head, and I still don't know. Should it be the one about me tricking the big fisherman, or about the killer whales, or the frog . . .

REYNARD: How about the one in which you say your trick changed the whole world?

RAVEN: That's a good story, all right, but I just don't know—

REYNARD: If I had been so clever, I'd want everyone to know it.

ANANSI: Maybe you think we'll see through it.

RAVEN: It *is* my favorite story. Yes, here goes . . . Anansi, you play the Daughter and, Reynard, you are the Father . . .

REYNARD: Are we ravens?

RAVEN: Heavens, no! I'll play the raven myself.

ANANSI: The best part I bet.

RAVEN: It *is* my story, after all. But don't worry, you've got good parts, too. Now, listen carefully because we must create an atmosphere.

REYNARD: What kind?

RAVEN: This play takes place in the dark.

ANANSI: Then how are we going to see it?

REYNARD: Maybe that's the trick; we don't!

RAVEN: We can't even see each other, none of us can.

ANANSI: That will be difficult.

REYNARD: Not for me, I've always known my way in the dark. *(Smiles knowingly.)* But why was there no light?

RAVEN: That's easy, Fox. Simply because the character you play, the Father, has hidden the light, so no one can see.

ANANSI: Not even his daughter?

RAVEN: She cooks, cleans, and sews—always in the dark.

ANANSI: But why?

(The lights begin to fade.)

REYNARD: *(Now playing the* FATHER, *holds up large box.)* All the light in the world is here, and I'll never give it up.

RAVEN: *(As* STORYTELLER.*)* Well, hearing this, I knew the time had come to trick the old man. *(In character.)* So I made my way to his house to steal the light. *(Carefully feeling the way.)* I waited in the corner for the right moment.

(By now, the stage is dark except for the area where this story is played. Of course, we, the audience, can see the action even though the characters themselves cannot. ANANSI, *playing the* DAUGHTER, *enters carrying a bowl of food, slowly groping in the dark.)*

ANANSI: Here's your supper, Father. I hope you're hungry.

REYNARD: Yes, famished, as usual. Thank you. *(Reaching out to take the bowl, accidently knocks it down.)* I'm sorry. I thought you were over here.

ANANSI: No, it's my fault. I thought you were there. *(Bends down and scoops up the food.)* I'll clean this up and prepare more . . . I hope you're not too hungry.

REYNARD: Take your time. And don't cut yourself.

ANANSI: I'll be careful, I promise. *(Feeling the way, goes off.)*

REYNARD: I have such a good daughter. So beautiful.

RAVEN: How do you know that?

REYNARD: *(Startled.)* Who said that?

RAVEN: A little bird.

REYNARD: Who are you? No one is allowed here.

RAVEN: Your daughter must be beautiful, caring for you, day after day . . . I agree.

REYNARD: Of course, she is.

RAVEN: You can find out for certain.

REYNARD: No! *(Pause.)* How?

RAVEN: By allowing light to come into the world.

REYNARD: Never.

RAVEN: Why not?

REYNARD: I'm afraid of what I might see. I can't take the risk.

RAVEN: But no matter what she looks like, you'd love her just the same.

REYNARD: It's better to live in the dark and not know.

RAVEN: And so you prevent everyone from seeing what we look like and how the world appears.

REYNARD: Besides, I have no light.

RAVEN: I think you do.

REYNARD: *(Louder.)* I have no light.

RAVEN: I hear you keep a ball of light hidden in a small box which you hide inside a number of other boxes.

REYNARD: There are no boxes here.

RAVEN: Well, just because I can't see them, doesn't mean they aren't here. *(Begins to move about as if searching, and suddenly falls over some boxes.)* Even this could be the very box!

REYNARD: Put it down! And leave, this very instant! At once.

RAVEN: But why should I stumble about? Indeed, why should we all be falling over ourselves, because you're afraid to open a box?

REYNARD: I don't know what you're talking about.

RAVEN: Simply this. I'm tired of looking for food in the dark. I'm tired of . . .

REYNARD: *(Drowning RAVEN out.)* I'm tired of hearing you complain. Leave!

RAVEN: How can I? I can't see the door.

REYNARD: Hold out your hands, as we all do, and feel your way.

RAVEN: I'm a bird meant to fly, but without light my wings are useless. I have no hands.

REYNARD: Then use your feet! But go! *(Thrusts arm toward the door and accidentally hits RAVEN who falls down.)*

RAVEN: *(Stunned.)* You needn't beat me!

REYNARD: I didn't mean to hurt you. Only to make you leave.

RAVEN: Very well, I'm going. *(Struggles to feet.)* But know this, old man: someday I'll return and find that box.

REYNARD: My doors will be locked.

RAVEN: I'll find a way in, you may be certain.

REYNARD: And you may be certain, I'll be waiting.

RAVEN: But you won't know me.

REYNARD: Of course, I will. I felt your feathers just now. You're a raven. I'll know you even in the dark.

RAVEN: And I'll trick you all the same!

(As REYNARD gropes his way off, the RAVEN leaves the house.)

(As STORYTELLER.) Then I faced the most difficult task of my life. I had to be cleverer than ever before. *(In character.)* I must figure out a way to steal that light. But I can't if the old man knows I'm in the house. How can I get back inside?

(ANANSI enters and calls out, as if speaking to FATHER.)

ANANSI: Father, I'm going to the river to get some water. I'll be right back.

RAVEN: Perhaps, this is my chance. Yes, of course, the daughter is the answer! I'll go with her to the river. And when she kneels down to take up the water, I'll change myself into . . . ? What can I change myself into? I know. Something small. A pine needle fallen from the tree.

(ANANSI *is now kneeling beside the river.*)

ANANSI: The water feels so good running over my hands. I think I'll have a drink.

RAVEN: (*As* STORYTELLER.) And disguised as a pine needle, I slipped into the bowl of water . . .

(ANANSI *drinks, then suddenly coughs.*)

ANANSI: Something's in the water. Whatever it is, I've swallowed it. (*Taking the bowl, rises and returns to the house.* REYNARD *returns.*)

REYNARD: I heard you coughing. Are you all right?

ANANSI: Yes, just something in the water, that's all. I'm fine now, thank you.

RAVEN: (*As* STORYTELLER.) And so was I. Fine and safe inside her stomach. Where I remained sleeping and sleeping, and growing and growing for a long time. And then, transforming myself once again, I was born as a human being . . . a big bouncing boy. (*Begins to cry like an infant.*)

REYNARD: What's that? Who's crying?

ANANSI: It's a baby.

REYNARD: What baby?

ANANSI: Father, I seem to have had a baby. Just listen!

REYNARD: Why didn't you tell me?

ANANSI: I didn't know!

REYNARD: Is it a boy or a girl?

ANANSI: I can't see!

REYNARD: Well, hand the baby to me, and I'll find out.

RAVEN: (*Ever so quickly.*) A boy. I'm a boy, Grandfather. A BOY! And very pleased to meet you, wherever you are.

REYNARD: My very own grandson! What a wonderful surprise! Tell me about yourself.

RAVEN: There's not much to tell, really. I was born just a few seconds ago. But let's see . . . (*Taking stock.*) I have a nose, yes, this is a nose.

REYNARD: Well, I'm certain you will be the perfect grandson.

RAVEN: No, as a matter of fact, I've come here to make your life miserable. (*Bursts into gales of laughter that indeed have a bit of the raven's cry about them.*)

REYNARD: You're a noisy one, aren't you?

RAVEN: Oh, I like to laugh and cry, Granddaddy! (*Bellows louder.*)

REYNARD: It certainly hurts to hear you going on like this, but I do want you to grow up healthy and happy.

RAVEN: You know what would make me really happy, Granddaddy?

REYNARD: Just tell me, my boy.

RAVEN: If we could play together.

REYNARD: Well, of course.

RAVEN: And if I could have some toys like most little boys, lots and lots of toys!

REYNARD: Whatever you want. I'll make them myself.

RAVEN: Oh, you're the best Granddaddy a baby boy could wish for. I'm so happy I have to scream again. *(Does just this.)*

5ARD: Go ahead. I'll just pretend I don't hear you. *(Putting hands over ears.)* Oh, that hurts, that really hurts.

RAVEN: You make me feel right at home.

REYNARD: Whatever you want is yours.

RAVEN: Granddaddy, do you really mean that?

REYNARD: Why, of course, I do. Why do you ask?

RAVEN: Anything?

REYNARD: That's what I said.

RAVEN: Well, there is one thing I would like . . .

REYNARD: Just name it.

RAVEN: And it's mine?

REYNARD: Forever and forever.

RAVEN: I want to open this box.

REYNARD: *(Alarmed.)* Which box?

RAVEN: Why, this one. It seems to be a box within a box within a box within a box within a box within a box within a box . . .

REYNARD: Quiet! QUIET! There are better boxes to open. You can find a nice one, I know.

RAVEN: I like this one. *(Shouting.)* AND ONLY THIS ONE.

REYNARD: No, that is not for you, dear boy.

RAVEN: You promised! *(Screams and more screams.)*

REYNARD: Please, don't do that.

ANANSI: What's wrong? Why is he crying? What have you done to him?

RAVEN: He promised I could open this box, and now, he won't let me. What kind of Granddaddy is this?

ANANSI: Well, of course, you can open it. Go ahead. Right, Father?

REYNARD: The outer box, yes, but no more.

RAVEN: *(Ripping the box open.)* Oh, this is fun! I want to do this again. Again and again.

REYNARD: I said the outer box and no more.

RAVEN: This is the most fun I've had since I was born. Whoopee!

ANANSI: Father, let him open the next box, please.

REYNARD: Very well, but only one more.

RAVEN: *(Ripping the next box open.)* Mother, guess what's inside this box.

ANANSI: I can't see anything. Tell me.

RAVEN: Another box.

ANANSI: What's inside that? Can you tell?

REYNARD: I said not to open any more. Stop!

ANANSI: But he's having such a good time, Father.

REYNARD: No! No! No!

RAVEN: I thought you loved me.

REYNARD: I do!

RAVEN: Oh, I'm the most unfortunate little boy to come into a world in which grandfathers don't love their grandchildren. (*Cries louder than before, with more sounds of the* RAVEN *coming through.*)

ANANSI: Father, you've made him miserable.

REYNARD: He's precious to me.

RAVEN: Then let me open the last box!

REYNARD: The last box? Have you gone so far?

RAVEN: I want to see what's inside.

REYNARD: Just another box, of course.

RAVEN: (*Shaking the box.*) No, it's something round that rattles.

ANANSI: If you really love him, let him see . . .

RAVEN: What do you say, Grandfather?

REYNARD: I can't deny you, my boy, even though I'm frightened at what may happen. Truly terrified. But go ahead. (*Covers eyes with hands.*)

RAVEN: (*Struggling to open the box.*) It's sealed tighter than all the others. There, the lid is coming off. Yes, I've got it. (*As the lid is lifted, a glow of light emanates from inside.*)

ANANSI: What is it, my son?

RAVEN: A ball of light!

REYNARD: Now that you've seen it, put it back and close the lid, so I may uncover my eyes.

RAVEN: No.

REYNARD: Your Grandfather begs you. Please, my boy, please.

RAVEN: (*Suddenly changing voice and appearance.*) I am not your grandson.

ANANSI: What?

REYNARD: Then who are you? (RAVEN *runs to him and brushes his wing against his face.*) RAVEN!

RAVEN: I said I'd trick you and I have. (*Laughs a pure raven laugh.*)

REYNARD: You've destroyed me, clever bird.

RAVEN: Only if you fail to make good use of the light that's yours. Now, I must fly throughout the world, bringing sunshine to the mountains, the oceans, the people . . .

REYNARD: Daughter, stop him. Don't let him leave. Grab the ball of light.

ANANSI: No, Father, I want him to steal the light. (*To* RAVEN.) Take it, please, take it!

RAVEN: No one can stop me now. You forget my powerful wings that have been waiting all these years to soar through the air. (*Begins to flap wings.*) Good-bye, old man. (*Running in a circle as if about to take off.*) Good-bye, dear lady. (ANANSI *waves farewell as* RAVEN *speeds off.*)

REYNARD: I'm ruined. (*Sinking to ground and crying, still covering eyes with hands.*) My life is finished.

ANANSI: No, Father, I will take care of you, always. (*Bending over, comforts* FATHER.) I'm here.

(From a high point, RAVEN suddenly reappears, flapping wings.)

RAVEN: Look, everywhere I go, light follows. *(Demonstrates by moving to the opposite side, and the light indeed comes up behind him wherever he moves.)* The world is more beautiful than I ever dreamed. There's so much to see . . . Look down there at that valley . . . Trees filled with fruit just waiting to be eaten. I can have it all! I'll never be hungry again! I'll just eat this. *(Gulps.)* And one of these. *(Gulps.)* And maybe one of those. *(Gulps.)* My head's swimming. My stomach's churning. *(Spins about.)* I'm just a wee bit dizzy and a wee bit sick.

(Clutching stomach, drops the ball of light which falls to the ground and crashes. Some pieces bounce up into the sky; they remain glowing wherever they land.)

Oops! Oh, no! I got carried away. *(Screams out raven call, then flies off.)*

REYNARD: What was that noise?

ANANSI: The raven dropped the ball of light. It's broken and scattered everywhere.

REYNARD: Has it become dark again?

ANANSI: No, there is more light than ever. It's spread all about.

(RAVEN flies in, circling about ANANSI and REYNARD.)

ANANSI: And some pieces have bounced back into the sky.

REYNARD: Are we in danger?

RAVEN: Not at all! The pieces are stuck in the sky.

ANANSI: They glow beautifully! Oh, Father, you must see them.

RAVEN: They are called the moon and the stars.

(The sky lights up, dazzlingly.)

ANANSI: To give us light even at night.

RAVEN: We need never be in the dark again.

ANANSI: Father, please, look out and see the wonder of it.

REYNARD: I'm afraid.

RAVEN: There's no need to be.

ANANSI: You'll be overjoyed, just open your eyes . . .

RAVEN: I'll help you. *(Brushes wings in REYNARD's face. REYNARD begins to push RAVEN away.)*

REYNARD: Leave me alone, Raven. You've done enough harm already.

RAVEN: *(Tickling REYNARD's face with feathers.)* See how splendid the world is.

(Still fighting RAVEN off, REYNARD removes hands from eyes and suddenly sees for the first time.)

RAVEN: Now, look up! And behold!

ANANSI: So beautiful!

REYNARD: Oh, yes! Oh, yes! *(REYNARD is not looking at the sky, but at ANANSI.)*

RAVEN: Old man, aren't you happy now?

REYNARD: So happy I can cry! Oh, my dear daughter, you are beautiful, truly beautiful. *(Takes ANANSI's hand.)*

ANANSI: And I'm happy to see you, Father. *(Takes* REYNARD's *hand.)*

REYNARD: And even you, my wicked grandson, look good to me.

RAVEN: *(As* STORYTELLER.*)* And that is how I brought light into the world. The end.

(The moon and stars suddenly shine brightly in the sky. ANANSI *and* REYNARD *applaud.)*

REYNARD: A good story, Raven, a very good story.

RAVEN: Thank you. Thank you very much.

ANANSI: Well, Reynard, it's time for yours.

RAVEN: I bet you're a sly old fox, all right. What's in your bag of tricks?

REYNARD: I've spread no knowledge and brought no light into the world like you two.

ANANSI: Don't be modest. Just tell us what you do.

REYNARD: I don't deal in miracles and magic—only cleverness.

RAVEN: And that's exactly what we want to see. Isn't it, Anansi? Show us a little cleverness.

ANANSI: Yes! Let us experience it.

REYNARD: Well, if you think you're up to it.

RAVEN: I live for a good trick.

ANANSI: But it must be well played—with style.

RAVEN: I think we've demonstrated we've got plenty of style, and I say that with all modesty.

REYNARD: My style is quite different from yours, less hopeful, less uplifting.

ANANSI: You're not going to depress us, I trust.

REYNARD: Well, sometimes my stories do end tragically.

RAVEN: Oh, dear, and I was having such a good time.

REYNARD: Not for me, you understand, but for others.

RAVEN: Well, I suppose we have to take the bitter with the sweet.

ANANSI: It's too bad you didn't go first, so we could end on a happy note.

REYNARD: Oh, we will end on a happy note, I promise, happy for me, at least.

ANANSI: Well, if it's happy for you, then it's happy for us.

REYNARD: Not necessarily.

RAVEN: I'm not certain I'm going to like this, but go ahead.

REYNARD: My life is often harsh and hard.

RAVEN: All the more reason for a few laughs, I would think.

REYNARD: Yes, but my sense of humor may not strike you as being very funny.

ANANSI: Well, let us decide that for ourselves.

REYNARD: It gets cold in my part of the world.

ANANSI: *(Shivering.)* I'm depressed already. Can't stand the cold.

REYNARD: Winter is worst. You have to be clever just to stay alive, just to find the next meal. Speaking of the next meal, I'm getting hungry. The chicken in Anansi's story made my mouth water.

ANANSI: So did those dinners the Chiefs gave me.

RAVEN: And the apples and grapes I ate in mine. I could use a few right now.

ANANSI: (Looking about.) There's nothing to eat around here. Just sticks and twigs. (Picks up twig and throws it down in disgust.)

RAVEN: You have to fly far away.

REYNARD: I think I see something.

ANANSI: Where?

REYNARD: Oh, fairly close.

RAVEN: What are you talking about?

REYNARD: Oh, nothing, just a passing thought.

RAVEN: You can't eat a thought.

REYNARD: Oh, I don't know. These could be delicious. (Smiles knowingly.) Of course, I'd prefer a fat chicken.

RAVEN: You're out of luck. The closest chicken lives a hundred miles away.

REYNARD: Then I'll have to settle for something closer, won't I?

RAVEN: (Beginning to get the meaning of REYNARD's remarks.) Oh, now that I think of it, some fat chickens did move into the neighborhood just last week. If you take that path (Pointing.), you'll come to the barn where they live. A big red barn. You can't miss it.

REYNARD: Good try, Raven, but as my grandmother used to say, a bird in hand is worth two in the barn.

ANANSI: But they're no birds around here.

REYNARD: You might look again, my furry friend.

RAVEN: And, furry friend, as small as you are, he can make a meal of you, too.

ANANSI: Me? Nobody eats spiders! It just isn't done! The very thought is disgusting.

RAVEN: Clearly, he's thinking of being the first to try.

ANANSI: But I'd crawl around inside you and spin webs throughout your intestines.

RAVEN: Stop making me squirm.

REYNARD: I'm willing to take my chances. After all, what choice do I have?

RAVEN: (Trying once more.) Don't forget those chickens down the path. Very plump, very tender. Not like some tough old birds I could name.

REYNARD: Forget the chickens. I'll take care of them later. After I've had my first course here. (Moves toward them.)

RAVEN: I think I'll look for food myself—up there. (Points to the top of the pole.)

ANANSI: (Sensing real danger.) And I'll come with you.

REYNARD: But, good friends, don't you want to hear my story? I'm next.

RAVEN: (Going up the pole.) I can hear from up here, thank you.

ANANSI: (Scrambling up behind RAVEN.) Me, too, just fine.

REYNARD: But I need you to act in my story. Come down.

RAVEN: Why don't you do a one-man show?

ANANSI: Yes, play all the parts yourself.

REYNARD: I'm not that talented.

ANANSI: Oh, but you are. You made each Chief in my story separate and distinct.

RAVEN: And in mine you found the heart of the character, the soul, the spine. You moved me deeply, profoundly.

REYNARD: Flattery, flattery, flattery. I hate flattery!

RAVEN: But I mean every word.

ANANSI: So do I!

REYNARD: Hypocrites. I can't stand hypocrites.

ANANSI: You go right ahead. We're ready to see you strut your stuff.

RAVEN: We've got the best seats in the house.

REYNARD: It's not in the nature of a fox to say the word "please." (*Coughs.*) It makes me gag. So let me put it this way, it would be awfully good of you to climb down *now. NOW!*

RAVEN: Awfully foolish, you mean.

ANANSI: Awfully easy for you to eat us.

RAVEN: Awfully awful for us.

REYNARD: Well, you know foxes can climb, too, if we must. We're fast of foot.

RAVEN: Not faster than I am.

ANANSI: Nor me.

REYNARD: I'll show you.

RAVEN: Let's move, Anansi.

ANANSI: I'm right behind you, Raven.

(*As* REYNARD *goes up the back side of the pole, they scramble down the front.*)

RAVEN: Run into the woods and hide deep in the brush.

ANANSI: I'm right behind you.

RAVEN: No, you go that way and I'll go this. It's safer.

ANANSI: See you later.

RAVEN: I hope so.

(REYNARD *is on top of the totem pole by this time.*)

REYNARD: Where did they go? (*Looks off left and right.*)

RAVEN and ANANSI: (*As they exit.*) Good-bye, Reynard.

REYNARD: (*To self.*) They've gone. I won't have it. But how can I get them back? I've got it. (*Jumps from the pole, lands, then jumps up and rolls over.*) Oh, I've broken my neck. (*Picks up sticks and twigs and begins to break them, making a loud snapping sound.*) Yes, it's definitely broken. They say that can be fatal. (*Snaps some more dry twigs.*) Certainly sounds fatal to me. (*Groans in pain.*) What a way to end my days, dying out here, alone, forsaken. Without a friend. Let me try to move one last time. (*Snaps twigs again.*) No use. Every bone's broken. (*Calling off.*) Farewell, friends. I'm glad I spent my final hours with you. You both brought joy into my life. I thank you, Anansi, for spreading knowledge, and you, Raven, for giving us light. That was really good of you. All I ever did was show how despite nature and man, the fox survives. Well, that is, up to now. (*Snaps another twig.*) There goes the last bone. This is it. (*Gets up, spins around several times.*) Good-bye, ole buddies. (*Throws himself down with an enormous thud.*) I'm dead.

(*There is a long pause—milked to the last drop—and then from far off, on opposite sides.*)

ANANSI: Raven!

RAVEN: I'm over here, Anansi.

ANANSI: Did you hear that?

RAVEN: Sad, wasn't it? Terribly sad.

ANANSI: I'm fighting back the tears. (*They emerge.*)

RAVEN: And to think he used his last words to thank us.

ANANSI: Truly beautiful, that's what it was.

RAVEN: Very moving.

ANANSI: Should we bury him? You could make a few remarks to wish him well.

RAVEN: And maybe you could sing something appropriate. (*They move closer to* REYNARD.)

ANANSI: Look at that poor mutilated body. The fallen tail. Those fallen ears.

RAVEN: But he's still handsome in death.

ANANSI: Oh, Raven, that's it. Exactly what we need.

RAVEN: For what?

ANANSI: His tombstone. "Still handsome in death." He couldn't ask for a better epitaph.

RAVEN: It's pretty good, I admit.

ANANSI: It would make him happy. (*They are now within arms reach of* REYNARD.)

RAVEN: Where do you think he'd like to lie?

ANANSI: We should pick a pretty spot.

RAVEN: With a great view . . .

ANANSI: . . . of something he'd especially like to see. (*They are now standing over* REYNARD.)

RAVEN: What would he most like to behold?

ANANSI: I don't know.

REYNARD: I do. YOU! (*Reaches out and grabs an ankle of each, holding them firmly.*)

RAVEN: Run, Anansi.

ANANSI: I can't. Run, Raven.

RAVEN: I can't.

REYNARD: No, you can't. Reynard the Fox survives again! Still handsome in life!

RAVEN: He's got me this time!

ANANSI: Me, too!

REYNARD: My teeth will have you, too. *(Snaps at ANANSI.)*

ANANSI: You really would eat me?

REYNARD: You're still not convinced? I'll begin with you.

ANANSI: I never thought I'd see the day anyone would eat a spider.

RAVEN: There seems to be little doubt about me, is there?

REYNARD: Your feathers are a problem. But I've dealt with that before, and being as hungry as I am, I will again.

ANANSI: Then I guess you win, Reynard. You certainly fooled me.

RAVEN: There's no doubt about it, we've been tricked all right.

REYNARD: You said you wanted a story you could experience.

ANANSI: I think you can say we're pretty involved.

RAVEN: I find it downright gripping.

REYNARD: And I did warn you it could end tragically.

ANANSI: For us, but happily for you.

RAVEN: With bodies strewn about the stage.

REYNARD: So, you acknowledge that I'm the greatest trickster in the world?

RAVEN: Do we have any choice?

REYNARD: No. You don't.

ANANSI and RAVEN: You're the greatest all right.

REYNARD: That's all I wanted to hear. There. You're free. *(Lets go, and they break away.)* And that's the story of how Reynard the Fox caught the Raven and the Spider.

RAVEN: *(Pulling back and shaking leg.)* You mean it?

ANANSI: What's going on here? *(Doing the same.)*

REYNARD: Surely you see! It was a joke.

RAVEN: You're right. I don't find your sense of humor funny.

REYNARD: A hoax, to prove I'm the cleverest.

ANANSI: First, we thought you were dead, and then we thought we were. Did you have to go that far?

REYNARD: To make my point, yes. I tricked you not once but twice.

ANANSI: You never intended to eat us?

REYNARD: My furry friend, I who have spent much of my life in France and know my *gastromique* would be the last to eat a spider, however desperate.

ANANSI: I'm certainly relieved to hear it.

REYNARD: And the same goes for an old crow.

RAVEN: I'm not a crow!

REYNARD: Pardon me, Raven.

RAVEN: And my age is none of your business!

REYNARD: Do I get a prize?

ANANSI: For what?

REYNARD: For winning our contest.

RAVEN: Who says you won?

REYNARD: You just did. Both of you.

ANANSI: We said you were the greatest to us.

RAVEN: How could we think otherwise under the circumstances?

REYNARD: Precisely. The evidence is overwhelming in my favor.

RAVEN: That's not for us to say.

ANANSI: Others may see it differently.

RAVEN: I think we should get some outside opinions.

REYNARD: But, clearly, anyone who saw the trick I pulled just now could never doubt my supremacy.

ANANSI: Easy for you to say.

RAVEN: Let's find out.

ANANSI: Let's ask.

REYNARD: Who?

RAVEN: Them. (Points to the audience.) They saw you.

ANANSI: And they saw us.

RAVEN: They've got opinions.

ANANSI: See what they think.

REYNARD: I know what you're doing. You're making a new contest out of the contest I've already won. That's not allowed.

ANANSI: You're just afraid you'll lose.

REYNARD: But I won, fair and square.

RAVEN: Perhaps, we have, too.

ANANSI: We want to be certain.

REYNARD: Very well. But they should know I'll do anything to win this contest. (To the audience.) Is that clear? (Snaps teeth at them.) Anything.

RAVEN: All right, let's hear the applause for Anansi. (They listen.) That's a lot. I don't know if I can beat it.

ANANSI: All right, let's hear the applause for the Raven. (They listen.) Wow! You really like the Raven, don't you?

REYNARD: Hold on. This doesn't look good.

RAVEN: You said you weren't worried.

REYNARD: Now, I'm not so certain.

ANANSI: There's one way to find out. Let's hear the applause for Reynard. (Applause.)

REYNARD: That wasn't bad, but I need more. Lots more.

RAVEN: Well, that's all you get.

REYNARD: No, it's not. (Looking around for something to help him, he sees two buckets at the side and scurries over and looks in.) Just what I need. Two buckets of water. (Returns carrying them.)

ANANSI: Are you going to give everyone a drink?

REYNARD: That depends on them. (To audience.) If you don't applaud louder this time, guess what? (Lifts bucket.)

ANANSI: You wouldn't!

RAVEN: You're shameless!

REYNARD: I said I'd do anything. WATCH OUT. It's April showers!

RAVEN: Reynard, this is a new low in trickery.

REYNARD: No, a new high. (*Lifts the bucket higher, aiming it at a section of the audience.*) Now, CLAP! That's good. (*Runs about the audience threateningly.*) That's good. Music to my ears! I'm winning. I'm winning. Thank you, dear friends. I really appreciate your support. (*Returns to stage.*) That does it! I've won again!

ANANSI: Anyone can win that way.

RAVEN: Threatening the voters.

ANANSI: They had to applaud or get wet.

REYNARD: Get wet? Who says so? I just held the bucket up in the air. Nothing wrong with that. I could have thrown it all over everybody . . . like this. (*Throws contents of bucket and confetti flies everywhere.*) Now, that would have been a trick. But I didn't do that, did I? And nobody's wet.

RAVEN: Some day, Reynard, you'll go too far.

REYNARD: And when I do, you can be certain it will be the best trick yet. I won!

RAVEN: No, I won!

ANANSI: No, I won!

(*They each encourage sections of the audience to call out their names by such remarks as the following.*)

REYNARD: You voted for me. I saw you!

RAVEN: Tell them how much you like me!

ANANSI: You know I'm the best. Everybody knows!

Audience is now calling out names and cheering their favorites, as the three mischief makers continue to manipulate them. Soon each of the three rascals is claiming victory, and we hear them chanting through the general melee.

REYNARD: (*Jumping up and down.*) I won! I won! I won! *etc.*

RAVEN: I won! I won! I won! *etc.*

ANANSI: I won! I won! I won! *etc.*

(*Convinced each has won, they begin to celebrate by dancing about and playing with the theatre itself. One pulls the curtain, another sends the backdrop lifting upward, another plays with the lights. Bright colors flash everywhere—on stage and in the audience. They swing on ropes. They fly on battens in the air. They climb ladders. They are all over the stage, clearly having a great time as they create theatrical pandemonium. And all through it, they loudly sing, "I won! I won! I won!"*

When this party atmosphere reaches its height, NYAME's *voice booms above the din.*)

NYAME: (*Offstage voice.*) I can't hear myself think. What's going on down there?

ANANSI: Calm down, you two. Nyame's trying to say something.

REYNARD: Wouldn't you know, just when we're having fun.

RAVEN: *(Still caught up in celebrating.)* I won! I won! I thank everyone who voted for me! I really won!

NYAME: Raven, stand still and listen to me.

RAVEN: *(Finally realizing who is calling.)* Well, it won't be easy. I want to sing! I want to dance!

By now ANANSI *has curtailed the celebration and the theatre quickly quiets, with the lights and focus returning entirely to the stage.*

NYAME: You three have given me a headache . . . a walapuluzza!

ANANSI: Sorry, Nyame, we didn't know you were listening.

NYAME: How could I not—with all that commotion.

ANANSI: Things got a little out of hand, I guess.

RAVEN: That's what happens when tricksters get together.

REYNARD: All hell breaks loose.

NYAME: I beg your pardon.

REYNARD: No offense. I mean we got carried away, can't help ourselves.

NYAME: And that's what I want to talk to you about. Raven, you're a rogue.

RAVEN: I can't deny it, I am.

NYAME: Reynard, you're a rascal.

REYNARD: And a scoundrel.

NYAME: Don't boast about it. And Anansi, we all know what you are.

ANANSI: The best trickster in the world. I won! I won! I won!

NYAME: Don't start that again. Do you hear me?

ANANSI: Yes, Sire.

NYAME: Yes, you have won. Anansi the Spider is the best.

ANANSI: Oh, thank you, master.

RAVEN: Hey, wait a minute here . . .

NYAME: *(Clearly annoyed.)* Will you please listen!

RAVEN: Sorry.

NYAME: And Raven, you are the best.

RAVEN: Well, that's more like it.

NYAME: Be quiet before I throw something. And Reynard, you are the best.

REYNARD: Merci beaucoup, mon ami. *(Bowing low.)*

NYAME: You are all three the best. *(They cheer.)* It is I who have lost.

ANANSI: You? How?

NYAME: I brought you together here and placed you on the totem pole, with the hope that when the foremost tricksters in the world met one another they would repent and reform, change their ways and give up their mischief. Instead, you've been more mischievous than ever, tricking each other and everybody else. Including me.

RAVEN: You? How have we tricked you?

NYAME: Into realizing that despite all your faults, you serve an important purpose. You make people laugh.

RAVEN: We did pretty well today, didn't we? Of course, it's a very good audience.

NYAME: Raven, I have my hand on a bolt of lightning, and if you keep . . .

RAVEN: I'll stop. I'll stop. I'll stop.

NYAME: So I'm sending you back into the world again, to make more trouble and more laughter.

ANANSI: Oh, thank you, Nyame.

REYNARD: Merci beaucoup, mon ami.

NYAME: But I'm also warning everyone to beware of clever characters like you, to beware of your trickery. So, in the future it will be harder than ever for you to succeed.

ANANSI: I'm not worried. We spiders have many more webs to spin.

RAVEN: We ravens have many more skies to fly.

REYNARD: We foxes many more lives to live.

NYAME: Then go, spread your mischief and your merriment. Anansi to the warm lands, Reynard to the cold. Raven, back to your totem pole.

ALL THREE: Thank you, Nyame.

NYAME: And remember I'm watching, for I also discovered today that it's not only people who must laugh. Every now and then, even a god needs a good giggle. *(Begins to giggle.)*

RAVEN: I should think so.

NYAME: Good-bye. *(His laughter trails off.)*

ANANSI: He's gone.

REYNARD: So long, Raven. So long, Anansi. I won't forget your stories.

ANANSI: Good-bye, Raven. Good-bye, Reynard. Thank you for yours.

RAVEN: Farewell, Anansi. I really enjoyed playing your wife. Farewell, Reynard. I enjoyed your story, too, after it was over. *(Climbs up pole.)*

When REYNARD *and* ANANSI *are at the far side of the stage or in the aisles of the theatre, they turn to* RAVEN *who, astride the top of the pole, rises tall.*

And whenever you feel like spending some time on a totem pole, telling stories, I'll be here. Good-bye, friends.

REYNARD: Au revoir!

ANANSI: Farewell!

(They wave to RAVEN *who lifts wings, proudly spreading them across the starlit sky, as if waving farewell. With this majestic silhouette before us, the lights fade.)*

CURTAIN

THE WISE MEN OF CHELM

by
Sandra Fenichel Asher

SANDRA FENICHEL ASHER's plays have been produced nationwide. Of her fifteen published scripts, a number are children's plays, such as *The Wise Men of Chelm, Dancing with Strangers,* and *Once, in the Time of Trolls.*

Best known among her plays, *A Woman Called Truth* received the American Alliance for Theatre and Education's Distinguished Play Award. The script was also named an "Outstanding Play for Young Audiences" by the International Association of Theatre for Children and Young People (AS-SITEJ) and was given the Joseph Campbell Memorial Fund Award by The Open Eye Theatre in New York City. A celebration of the life of Sojourner Truth, the play has been produced by over one hundred theatre groups in the United States, Canada, and Australia.

Across the Plain: The Journey of the Palace Wagon Family, commissioned by The Coterie Theatre of Kansas City, Missouri, had its premiere in 1996, after an initial reading at the Kennedy Center in Washington, D.C., as one of eight plays selected for the New Visions/New Voices Forum. The script was also one of two selected for the 1996 Playreading Project Awards of the American Alliance for Theatre and Education and has recently been published by Dramatic Publishing Company.

Among Asher's works in progress are *The Wolf and its Shadows,* which was commissioned by the Omaha Theatre Company for Young People and had its professional premiere there in 1995; *I Will Sing Life: Voices from the Hole-in-the-Wall Gang Camp,* which began its development with a reading by the Open Eye Theatre in Roxbury, New York; and *Where Do You Get Your*

Ideas?, a dramatized writing workshop adapted from her book by the same name.

A recipient of a National Endowment for the Arts grant in playwriting, Asher is also the author of nineteen books for young readers written under the name of Sandy Asher. Her latest published titles are *Out of Here*, a collection of interwoven short stories about teenagers and *But That's Another Story*, an anthology of twelve stories in a variety of genres by different authors, which she edited. *Stella's Dancing Days*, a picture book, is scheduled for future release by Harcourt Brace.

Sandra Fenichel Asher is writer-in-residence at Drury College in Springfield, Missouri. She is a member of the Dramatists Guild and serves on the boards of the Society of Children's Book Writers and Illustrators and the Missouri Center for the Book.

My favorite thing about writing for children is exactly the same as my favorite thing about writing for anybody: the day-to-day doing of it— playing with language, character, story, form; the incredible privilege of being able to do work I love. Sometimes the results find an audience of young people; other times, adults. The best appeals to both.

—SANDRA FENICHEL ASHER

THE WISE MEN OF CHELM

A Play in One Act
For Four Men and Two Women, Doubling*

CHARACTERS

Storyteller
Mottel: a merchant, as practical as Chelmites get, bearded
Gimpel: a younger man, unmarried, clean-shaven
Pinchas: an intellectual, by Chelm standards, bearded
Stranger: from another shtetl, bearded
Cow: brown, old and skinny, but no fool
Berel: a school boy, 11 or 12
Zalman: another school boy, same age
Rifke: Pinchas's long-suffering wife
Rooster: may be a puppet or an offstage voice
Other Chelmites, as desired

PLACE

In and around Chelm, a tiny town in Poland.

TIME

Late nineteenth century.

---

*Note on Casting: Directions in the script refer to a cast of six players—four men and two women, with doubling as follows:

Storyteller also plays stranger
Berel also plays Rifke, and ½ of COW
Zalman also plays Rooster, and ½ of COW

AT RISE: *The stage is empty, except for a wooden sign at center that points stage left and reads TO CHELM. After a moment,* ROOSTER *is heard offstage, crowing loudly.*

ROOSTER: Cockadoodle-doo! Cockadoodle-doo!

(The STORYTELLER *enters, approaches the sign, and turns it halfway around, so that it points stage right and reads TO WARSAW. He then returns it to its original position. Observing the audience, he moves downstage, pauses, and then cries—)*

STORYTELLER: Sholem aleichem!

(Immediately, MUSIC *begins.* ALL *dance on in a line from stage left. As they join* STORYTELLER *in a joyful dance,* ALL *circle the sign, spinning it round and round, then leaving it so that TO WARSAW shows. This circle motif should be carried out in as many ways as possible: the dances are circular, the action of the play is circular, and the thinking of the Chelmites is . . . well, dizzying.* ALL *dance off right, then reenter, spin the sign to read TO CHELM and then dance off left with it, toward CHELM, leaving* STORYTELLER *downstage as* MUSIC *fades.)*

STORYTELLER: *(To audience.)* When the earth was created, and the time came to fill it with people, two angels were chosen, and each was given a sack: one filled with wise souls and the other with foolish souls. The idea was to sprinkle wise and foolish souls evenly over the earth, but—oooops, whooops! The angel carrying the sack of foolish souls tripped over a mountain peak, and the entire sack of fools spilled out—

*(*MOTTEL, PINCHAS, *and* GIMPEL *twirl on from UL, as if falling.)*

STORYTELLER: Nitwits, noodlebrains, and puddingheads tumbled from the heavens—(GIMPEL *actually falls to the ground.* PINCHAS *and* MOTTEL *stop in mid-topple, arms and legs flailing. They freeze.)* Schlemiels, schlemazels, and dumkops of every kind landed in one spot—one tiny shtetl—one ridiculous speck of a town made up entirely of fools—Chelm! (STORYTELLER *indicates three frozen* FIGURES.) Mottel, the Mayor. A pious man, but practical, in a Chelmish sort of way. Pinchas, the rebbe, the teacher. An intellectual. Not so practical. And Gimpel. What can I tell you about Gimpel? He is young yet. A wise man in training. (STORYTELLER *moves away to watch as* MOTTEL *and* PINCHAS *resume movement, reacting in alarm that* GIMPEL *still lies motionless on the ground.)*

PINCHAS: Gimpel, Gimpel, what did I tell you? Did I warn you not to climb up on that roof? Did I tell you you would fall off and get yourself killed?

GIMPEL: *(Motionless.)* Enough, already, Reb Pinchas. I'm dead.

MOTTEL: What do you mean, you're dead?

GIMPEL: What do I mean I'm dead? I mean, I'm dead!

PINCHAS: Gimpel, what are you talking about? How can you be dead?

GIMPEL: Did you not say I'd fall down and get killed?

PINCHAS: I did. I warned you.

GIMPEL: And are you not an honest man?

PINCHAS: I am.

MOTTEL: He is. An honest man.

GIMPEL: Ah-hah, and did I not climb up on the roof in spite of your warning, Reb Pinchas?

PINCHAS: Yes, yes. You climbed up, and you fell down, just as I said you would.

GIMPEL: Then I must have been killed. So I'm dead.

PINCHAS: (*Convinced.*) Ah! I see. So—the matter is settled.

MOTTEL: But he's talking, Reb Pinchas.

PINCHAS: True, true, Reb Mottel. But that is not proof that he is not dead. It is written that the scholars murmur in the grave when their names are cited. We need proof that he isn't dead, or we must bury him.

MOTTEL: You would bury him?

PINCHAS: The dead must be buried. It is written.

MOTTEL: But, he's alive!

PINCHAS: Not according to him.

MOTTEL: Gimpel! Gimpel! Do you have pain?

GIMPEL: How can I have pain? I'm dead.

PINCHAS: There you have it. He feels no pain. He must be dead.

MOTTEL: Gimpel! Gimpel! Do you not feel anything at all?

GIMPEL: Well, to be perfectly honest, Reb Mottel—

MOTTEL: Yes? Yes?

GIMPEL: I feel . . . hungry.

MOTTEL: Hungry?

PINCHAS: No, thank you. I had just now a bowl of soup.

MOTTEL: Not you, Reb Pinchas. *Gimpel.*

PINCHAS: Gimpel had a bowl of soup? When? How? He's *dead.*

MOTTEL: Reb Pinchas, I ask you: Do the dead feel hunger?

PINCHAS: No. It is not possible. It is not written.

MOTTEL: Then there is your proof. Gimpel is not dead.

GIMPEL: (*Sits up.*) I'm not dead?

MOTTEL: You're alive—and hungry.

GIMPEL: (*Perplexed, but willing.*) Oh.

MOTTEL: So, come. A little bread, a little herring—it couldn't hurt. (MOTTEL *cheerfully helps* GIMPEL *up and leads him off left.*)

PINCHAS: (*To audience, as he follows them off.*) So—the matter is settled.

STORYTELLER: Of course, the people of Chelm did not know they were fools, for no one who was from there could tell them. And no one who was *not* from there could convince them. So—who are we to break such news? They simply believed that, for some peculiar reason, foolish things were always happening to them. (MUSIC *plays;* STORYTELLER *glances off right.*) Ah! But here comes a stranger. A stranger with a cow!

(COW *enters, wearing a hat, which* STORYTELLER *exchanges for his own to become the* STRANGER. STRANGER *and* COW *dance around stage,* COW *resisting and* STRANGER *urging her on.*)

COW: *(Troubled.)* Mooo!

STRANGER: There, there, Yenta. I don't want to sell you, but I am a poor man, and I don't know what else to do. *(Takes a gold coin from his pocket.)* You and this one gold coin are all I have left in the world. Together you and I will surely starve to death. Apart, we may still starve, but at least not so *soon.*

COW: *(Not comforted.)* Moooooo!

(GIMPEL enters left and notices STRANGER and COW.)

GIMPEL: Ah, sholem aleichem, stranger! Peace be with you. And also, with your cow.

STRANGER: And with you, kind sir. Aleichem sholem. With whom do I have the pleasure of exchanging greetings?

GIMPEL: My name is Gimpel, and I am off to see the world. (STRANGER *begins to circle* GIMPEL, *eyeing him for items of value worth bartering for or begging for, or, if it comes to that, stealing.* GIMPEL *is unaware of this.)*

STRANGER: Off to see the world, are you? And how much of it have you seen so far?

GIMPEL: Only the shtetl of my birth. Also, the shtetl of my childhood. And the shtetl of my youth.

STRANGER: All of those places!

GIMPEL: All? No. Only one. Chelm. I've never left it, until today.

STRANGER: Chelm? Is that where we are?

GIMPEL: Just outside. It's there, over the next hill.

STRANGER: It seems to me I've heard of Chelm.

GIMPEL: *(Proudly.)* No doubt. Its reputation travels before me wherever I go.

STRANGER: Over one hill, you mean?

GIMPEL: So far.

STRANGER: I see. And why is it that Chelm is so well known from one hill to the next valley?

GIMPEL: Why is it? Why shouldn't it be? Everyone in Chelm is wise.

STRANGER: Everyone?

GIMPEL: Everyone.

STRANGER: All wise men?

GIMPEL: All wise men.

STRANGER: And wise women?

GIMPEL: Of course, wise women.

STRANGER: Wise children, too?

GIMPEL: Certainly, wise children. Also, wise dogs, wise cats, wise chickens. Even wise cows.

COW: *(Impressed.)* Mooooo!

STRANGER: How is this possible, a town wise to the last living creature and not a single fool among them?

GIMPEL: How is it possible?

STRANGER: Yes, I ask you: how?

GIMPEL: It's possible, dear stranger, because it is . . . possible.

STRANGER: Interesting! *(To audience.)* Something tells me this Chelm is where I must go to sell my poor old Yenta.

COW: *(Wary.)* Mooooooo!

STRANGER: *(Hushing* COW.*)* Shah, Yentele. *(As* GIMPEL *sits downstage right and takes off his boots.)* What are you up to, my dear man?

GIMPEL: *(With a big yawn.)* Well, I have come a long way, and I have yet a long way to go. I believe I must take a nap.

STRANGER: *(With his eye on* GIMPEL's *boots.)* I see. *(As* GIMPEL, *after careful calculation, places his boots downstage center, toes pointing toward Warsaw.)* And what are you up to now, I wonder?

GIMPEL: I am pointing my boots toward Warsaw, my destination. That way, when I wake up, I'll know in which direction I'm headed.

STRANGER: *(Definitely interested in those boots.)* Hmmmm. Perhaps Yenta and I could use a short nap ourselves. *(He yawns mightily.* COW *does, too.* STRANGER *leads* COW *to downstage left.)*

GIMPEL: Then I suggest you point your boots toward Chelm.

STRANGER: *(A bit suspicious of* GIMPEL's *motives.)* I prefer to wear my boots, such as they are.

GIMPEL: In that case, you could point your cow toward Chelm.

STRANGER: *(Indicating* COW, *who faces Warsaw.)* My cow prefers to sleep facing this way.

GIMPEL: *(Concerned; he's going to stay awake and worry about this.)* Well, it's up to you, I suppose. As for me, I like a little travel insurance.

STRANGER: *(Humoring* GIMPEL, *as in "When in Chelm, do as the Chelmites do"— and wanting* GIMPEL *to relax and to go to sleep.)* And who am I to argue with one so wise? *(Turns* COW *with considerable difficulty.)* Come, come, Yenta. That's a good Yentele. There you go.

COW: *(Not pleased.)* Moooooo!

STRANGER: A pleasant rest to you, Reb Gimpel.

GIMPEL: *(Pleased at the* STRANGER's *respectful use of "Reb.")* And to you, stranger. And to your cow. *(*MUSIC *plays, softly.* GIMPEL *falls asleep and begins to snore.* STRANGER *and* COW *pretend to be asleep by snoring even louder. After a moment,* STRANGER *gets up, stealthily creeps over to try on* GIMPEL's *boots. While he does so,* COW *gets up, also stealthily, turns herself toward Warsaw, then goes to sleep.)*

STRANGER: *(Discovering the boots don't fit.)* Feh! Tiny feet like a cheder boy. *(Sniffs in disdain. Boots stink.)* Phew! *(A huge sneeze escapes him in spite of efforts to stifle it.)* Ahhhh-hah-hah-chooooo! *(*MUSIC *stops.* STRANGER *sits wide-eyed, waiting to be caught with the boots.)*

GIMPEL: *(Polite even in his sleep.)* Gesundheit!

STRANGER: Thank you! *(Relieved, he slaps boots down where they were, but unintentionally turned toward Chelm. He then scuttles over to settle down beside* COW, *with his own boots on. He takes out his gold coin, admires it, bites it, kisses it, and falls asleep, clutching it for comfort. Loud snores.* GIMPEL *awakens with snorting and stretching, sees* STRANGER *and* COW *asleep, puts his finger to his lips to hush himself and audience.)*

GIMPEL: *(Whispers.)* Oi-oi-oi, already the sun gallops across the sky. I must be on my way. Sholem aleichem, stranger. And cow. *(He examines his boots and the* COW, *then tiptoes off left toward Chelm, carrying the boots, which point the way, ahead of him.* STRANGER *harrumphs and changes position as* GIMPEL *exits. As he does so, the gold coin falls out of his hand and lands nearby.)*

(After a moment, MOTTEL *and* PINCHAS *enter.)*

MOTTEL: I am telling you, Reb Pinchas, it's a miracle. With the new steam lo-comotive they're talking about, you can leave Chelm in the morning and be in Warsaw by midnight.

PINCHAS: *(More puzzled than impressed.)* That's a fact, Reb Mottel?

MOTTEL: That's a fact. Chelm in the morning, Warsaw at midnight.

PINCHAS: *(With a shrug, he doesn't get it.)* I see. So tell me, Reb Mottel—what would I do in Warsaw in the middle of the night? *(*MOTTEL *shrugs back; he hasn't thought of this difficulty.)*

MOTTEL: An excellent question, Reb Pinchas. Who knows? *(Notices* STRANGER *and* COW.*)* Vas iz das? Reb Pinchas, give a look what we have here.

PINCHAS: I have never seen such a skinny cow in all my life.

MOTTEL: *(Picks up gold coin and carries it center.)* And what is this?

PINCHAS: It looks like a gold coin.

MOTTEL: *(Bites it.)* It *is* a gold coin. *(Puts it right back where he found it.)* Where do you think it came from?

PINCHAS: Where could it have come from? No one here has gold coins to toss out on the ground. We are not such wealthy people.

MOTTEL: So what are you saying? It fell from the sky?

PINCHAS: *(Considers the possibility.)* Hmmmmm . . . no. I don't think so. The sky is too far away.

MOTTEL: A tree then? You think it grew on a tree?

PINCHAS: *(Considers it.)* Not possible. *(Points offstage.)* There are trees over there. But the coin was over here.

MOTTEL: Then what are you saying, Reb Pinchas?

PINCHAS: I'm saying what is obvious to me. And what is obvious to me should be obvious to you, Reb Mottel. The coin came from the cow.

MOTTEL: You think this cow gives golden coins?

PINCHAS: What other reason would a man have to keep a cow as skinny as that? *(They look at* COW.*)*

MOTTEL: Ah! *(They look at each other.)*

MOTTEL *and* PINCHAS: At-ha! *(They pounce on* STRANGER.*)*

PINCHAS: Stranger! Stranger, wake up!

MOTTEL: Get up, stranger. We want to buy your cow!

STRANGER: *(As he and* COW *struggle to their feet.)* What? My cow? My Yenta? *(He sees the coin, snatches it up and pockets it quickly, fearing robbery.)*

COW: *(Alarmed.)* Mooooooo!

MOTTEL: I will give you my best winter coat for her.

STRANGER: *(Amazed.)* Your winter coat—? You offer me your winter coat for this cow?

MOTTEL: *(Embarrassed.)* All right, all right! It's not much, I admit—

PINCHAS: *(Pulls a watch out of his pocket.)* Mottel's coat plus my pocket watch. It was my papa's watch, and my zayda's before him. Three generations. An heirloom.

STRANGER: *(Takes watch and strokes it, in awe.)* An heirloom, you say?

PINCHAS: *(Misinterpreting* STRANGER's *reaction.)* Not enough?

MOTTEL: *(Aside, to* PINCHAS, *also taking* STRANGER's *hesitation for doubt.)* Leave this in my hands, Reb Pinchas. Matters of the marketplace are not for a man of higher learning like yourself. *(To* STRANGER.*)* I see you are insulted by our meager offers. That is understandable. By us an heirloom is not exactly by the Tsar an heirloom. Come with us to our homes, and we will trade you all we have of value for your remarkable cow.

STRANGER: Excuse me, gentlemen, but have you maybe lost your minds?

MOTTEL: *(Aside, to* PINCHAS.*)* Still not enough.

PINCHAS: *(Motioning* MOTTEL *aside.)* Pssssst! Reb Mottel! Over here.

STRANGER: *(To audience,* MOTTEL *and* PINCHAS *confer.)* I can't understand it. These people want to give me all they own for my poor old Yenta.

COW: *(Disturbed; something is not kosher here.)* Mooooo!

STRANGER: Shah!

PINCHAS: *(Quietly, to* MOTTEL.*)* We must go back to the shtetl. We must ask our neighbors to help us. With a cow like this, for the rest of our days, we will want for nothing. It is only proper we share this golden opportunity with everyone.

MOTTEL: You are absolutely right, Reb Pinchas. Like a shooting star, your wisdom dazzles me! *(To* STRANGER.*)* Stranger, wait here for us, please. We'll get you everything you want for that cow. Please wait. *(*MOTTEL *and* PINCHAS *hurry off left.)*

STRANGER: I'll wait. I'll wait. Where would I go?

COW: *(Worried.)* Mooooo!

STRANGER: You worry too much, Yenta. What could be so bad? Worse off than we are now, we're not going to get.

COW: *(Not convinced.)* Mooooooo!

STRANGER: *(Looks at watch, which he is still holding.)* Of course, an heirloom is an heirloom. I could take it and run. Who could catch me? Who would know?

COW: *(Disapproving.)* Mooooooo!

STRANGER: No. It's better we stay. Something tells me we have met up with a very unusual situation here. These Chelmites and their strange ways of thinking—it could be a sign, hah? A sign that our luck is about to improve.

*(*MOTTEL *and* PINCHAS *hurry on, each maneuvering a heavy sack. They set the sacks down in front of* STRANGER.*)*

MOTTEL: Here we are. Here we are. Just as Reb Pinchas predicted, our neighbors were extremely interested in this deal. We have gathered the entire town's valuables, and we now offer them to you in exchange for your COW.

STRANGER: *(Pokes around in sacks, pulls out a pearl necklace.)* Pearls?

PINCHAS: *(Indicates MOTTEL, who bows modestly.)* From the mayor's wife.

STRANGER: This is your final offer?

MOTTEL: This is it. This is everything.

STRANGER: *(Looks at PINCHAS, who nods in agreement.)* Done!

MOTTEL: Done? It's a bargain? The cow is ours?

STRANGER: The cow is yours.

COW: *(In protest.)* Mooooo!

STRANGER: Don't worry, Yentele. These people will take good care of you. Look how nicely they have treated me! *(Through the following dialogue, PINCHAS and MOTTEL struggle to move resisting COW off left as STRANGER struggles to maneuver unwieldy sacks off right.)*

PINCHAS: Oh, yes! The best of care. Nothing but the best!

MOTTEL: Thank you, stranger. We can never express our gratitude.

STRANGER: Nor I! My blessings upon you, upon you and your children for a thousand generations.

COW: *(Protesting.)* Mooooooooo!

STRANGER: My blessings on you, too, Yentele! Sholem aleichem. Peace be with you!

PINCHAS: Aleichem sholem, stranger!

MOTTEL: *(To audience, as he and PINCHAS finally exit with COW.)* Such a deal!

STRANGER: *(To audience.)* Such a deal! *(Straightening up, almost off right.)* So what am I schlepping for? I'm a rich man now! *(Looks offstage right, whistles.)* Here, boys! You want to earn maybe a couple kopeks? *(Exits right with sacks. Offstage:)* Boys! Yes! Here we are!

COW: *(Offstage, in despair.)* Mooooooo!

(MUSIC begins. ALL dance on with bits and pieces of scenery—a doorway, a fence, a gate—to indicate the town. ALL exit. MUSIC fades. After a moment, PINCHAS enters, followed by his students, ZALMAN and BEREL, who each carry a stool. PINCHAS paces around the stage as he thinks and talks. At ZALMAN's urging, STUDENTS play a kind of "Blind Man's Bluff" with him, attempting to get their stools placed where he's least likely to see them, and be seated and innocent-looking whenever he turns to speak to them. They are greatly amused each time he's forced to search for them.)

BEREL: What is the surprise you have for us, beloved Rebbe?

PINCHAS: First, your lesson. Then, the surprise. *(He turns to pace; they maneuver around him.)* Everything in its due time. Very well, my learned scholars of Chelm, let us review our lessons thus far. *(He turns; they sit; he searches for them.)* Hah? Berel? Zalman? Where—? *(Finds them, always assuming the confusion is his fault, not theirs.)* Ah! Yes. Tell me this, if you can—Why are summer days long and winter days short? *(ZALMAN and*

BEREL *wave their hands, eager to answer.* PINCHAS *chooses* ZALMAN.) Yes, Zalman. You may speak.

ZALMAN: (*Pleased; rises.*) Thank you, beloved Rebbe. In summer, the days are long because it is hot, and, as everyone knows, the heat causes things to expand. In winter, the days are short because the cold causes them to contract. (BEREL *registers doubt.*)

PINCHAS: (*To* BEREL'*s surprise.*) Precisely, my dear Zalman, my star pupil! (*He paces; they maneuver.*) I am very pleased, very pleased indeed. Yes, yes, yes. (*He turns; they sit; he searches.*) And now, learned scholars—What? But how—? Didn't I—? (*Finds them.*) Oh. There you are. Answer me this, if you will: If the distance from Chelm to Warsaw is four miles, what is the distance from Warsaw back to Chelm? (*Again,* BOTH *wave and* PINCHAS, *after a moment's consideration, chooses* ZALMAN, *to* BEREL'*s consternation.*) Yes, Zalman, I would like to hear from you this time.

ZALMAN: Thank you, beloved Rebbe. If the distance from Chelm to Warsaw is four miles, the distance from Warsaw back to Chelm is eight miles. (BEREL *again registers doubt.*)

PINCHAS: And why is that?

ZALMAN: For the answer to this question, we look to our calendar. There we discover that the distance from Chanukah in the winter to Pesach in the spring is four months, while the distance from Pesach back to Chanukah is eight months.

PINCHAS: Excellent reasoning, Zalman. (*To* BEREL, *who is dumbstruck.*) It would not hurt you, Berel, to pay closer attention to this brilliant thinker. I don't see that your responses come anywhere close to his! I'll give you one more chance. (*He paces; they maneuver.*) One more. Only one. Hmmmm, hmmmmm, hmmmmm. (*He turns; they sit; he searches.*) Very well, learned scholars of Chelm. Learned scholars? Learned scholars? (*Finds them.*) Ah, learned scholars. Very well. Explain to me, please, which is more important, the sun or the moon? (*Same handwaving business, followed by exasperation from* BEREL.) Zalman! What is it that you have to say on this subject?

ZALMAN: Thank you, beloved Rebbe. The moon is more important than the sun, without a doubt.

PINCHAS: Because?

ZALMAN: Because the moon shines at night, when it is needed. The sun shines only during the day, when there is already plenty of light.

PINCHAS: Splendid, Zalman! Oh, how I wish all of my students could shine as brightly as this one fine diamond of a boy. (*He pinches* ZALMAN'*s cheek in delight.* ZALMAN *struggles to keep smiling through the pain, to* BEREL'*s extreme satisfaction.*) Zalman, Zalman, Zalman, Zalman!

ZALMAN: Is it time for the surprise now, beloved Rebbe?

PINCHAS: (*Confused; lets go of* ZALMAN.) The surprise? What surprise?

BEREL: After our lessons. You said there would be a surprise.

PINCHAS: (*At a loss.*) I did? What could I have been thinking of?

COW: (*Offstage.*) Moooooooooooooo!

PINCHAS: Ah, yes! The surprise! I believe I hear it mooing now.

ZALMAN: The surprise moos? (PINCHAS *starts off left.* ZALMAN *and* BEREL *follow, with their stools.*)

PINCHAS: Come, come, my scholars. Hurry. This way.

(*As* PINCHAS, ZALMAN, *and* BEREL *exit left,* GIMPEL *enters right.*)

GIMPEL: (*To audience.*) Who would have thought it possible? It's a miracle, I tell you! Warsaw looks exactly like my own village of Chelm! Every pebble, every tree, every house, every gate. Why, even that rebbe and his students look exactly like Reb Pinchas and Zalman and Berel. I am amazed. I am stunned.

(MOTTEL *enters L.*)

MOTTEL: Gimpel! Back from seeing the world already?

GIMPEL: Back already? What are you talking "back already"?

MOTTEL: I'm talking back already because you are back already.

GIMPEL: Back where?

MOTTEL: Where? Where? In Chelm, is where.

GIMPEL: Don't be ridiculous. This is not Chelm. This is Warsaw.

MOTTEL: How can this be Warsaw? I am here, am I not?

GIMPEL: Yes, you're here. Why shouldn't you be here? (*Pause.*) Who are you?

MOTTEL: Who am I? I'm Mottel the Mayor. Who else would I be?

GIMPEL: (*Amazed.*) No!

MOTTEL: No? You don't recognize me? I'm Mottel, I tell you.

GIMPEL: I believe you. It's just that in my village of Chelm, we too have a Mottel the Mayor. And he looks exactly like you!

MOTTEL: Gimpel, what is this nonsense? Have you taken leave of your senses? (*Aside, to audience.*) Perhaps it was the fall from the roof? (*He smacks his head and shrugs, indicating* GIMPEL *may have suffered more serious injury than previously supposed.*)

GIMPEL: (*Aside, to audience.*) Gimpel! Gimpel, he calls me! (*To* MOTTEL.) How is it that you know my name?

MOTTEL: Why should I not know your name? Have I not known you since the day you were born?

GIMPEL: That's not possible. You must have me confused with another Gimpel. If there's a Mottel in Chelm who looks like you, no doubt there's a Gimpel in Warsaw who looks like me. In every town in the world, perhaps, there's a Mottel and a Gimpel, a Gimpel and a Mottel.

MOTTEL: There is no Gimpel in Warsaw who looks like you!

GIMPEL: No? Then he too is off seeing the world?

MOTTEL: (*Beside himself.*) No! He's not—He isn't—He's—not—He's—oi vay!

(PINCHAS, *carrying a bucket and stool, enters with* COW.)

COW: (*Ashamed.*) Mooooooo!

GIMPEL: Reb Mottel, look! It's the stranger's cow.

MOTTEL: You know this cow?

GIMPEL: Well, I know a cow who looks like this one.

MOTTEL: *(Proudly.)* Two cows like this there can never be in this world.

PINCHAS: *(Grimly.)* One cow like this there already isn't in this world.

MOTTEL: What are you talking about, Reb Pinchas? Why have you suddenly brought us the cow?

PINCHAS: It doesn't work.

MOTTEL: What doesn't work?

PINCHAS: The cow. She doesn't give gold.

MOTTEL: You tried?

PINCHAS: I tried. Zalman tried. Berel tried. Every person in the village not already in the grave tried. She doesn't give gold. She doesn't even give milk. She is old and skinny and useless.

MOTTEL: *(Fussing over cow.)* Impossible. You must have done something wrong.

PINCHAS: We did everything we could think to do. We gave her what to eat. We gave her what to drink. We gave her where to rest. And what did she give to us? Nothing. It doesn't work.

MOTTEL: But we saw the gold coin. With our own eyes, we saw.

PINCHAS: We saw. We saw. And now we don't see. Nu?

MOTTEL: We gave the stranger all our valuables. She *must* give gold. Here, let me try. *(He grabs bucket and stool and tries to milk* COW.) Nice Yentele, Yentele.

COW: *(In progressively more distress.)* Moo.

MOTTEL: *(With increasing anxiety.)* Good Yentele, Yentele.

COW: Mooooooooo!

MOTTEL: GOLD, YENTELE, YENTELE!

COW: MOOOOOOOOOOOO!

MOTTEL: Nothing. Not gold. Not milk. Nothing.

PINCHAS: What did I tell you? It doesn't work.

GIMPEL: You thought this cow gave gold? (OTHERS *nod, ashamed of themselves.)* Then there is a difference between Warsaw and Chelm.

MOTTEL: What are you raving about now, Gimpel?

GIMPEL: In Chelm, we have no cow that gives gold.

MOTTEL: With that I cannot argue.

GIMPEL: So—I rest my case.

PINCHAS: I don't know what the two of you are talking about, but this I do know: We must find that stranger and return his cow. We must get back our valuables.

MOTTEL: What makes you think the stranger will return our valuables? Why should he give back such treasure for a cow that gives no gold?

PINCHAS: You're right, Reb Mottel.

MOTTEL: Of course I'm right. A deal is a deal.

PINCHAS: *(As a thought strikes him.)* Except you're wrong, Reb Mottel!

MOTTEL: What do you mean I'm wrong?

PINCHAS: The cow gives no gold to *us*. That doesn't mean she wouldn't give gold to the stranger.

MOTTEL: A fine point, Reb Pinchas! A very fine point!

PINCHAS: So why shouldn't the stranger give back our valuables? Rich enough he'll be, either way. It makes no difference to him.

MOTTEL: You are a wise man, Reb Pinchas. Like the sages of old, wisdom perfumes your every breath. (*As* PINCHAS *nods, enjoying the flattery.*) But there is one thing you have not thought of.

PINCHAS: Yes?

MOTTEL: The stranger could be anywhere by now.

PINCHAS: (*Confused.*) The stranger? What stranger?

MOTTEL: Reb Pinchas—the stranger with the *cow*.

PINCHAS: I see no stranger with the cow.

MOTTEL: The stranger with our *valuables*.

PINCHAS: Ah, yes! The stranger. Where is he, I wonder?

MOTTEL: Who knows? Somewhere. Anywhere. Who has time to spend searching the world for him? (*Looks at* GIMPEL.) Ah! (*Looks back at* PINCHAS.)

MOTTEL and PINCHAS: (*As they exchange smiles.*) Ah-ha!

MOTTEL: Gimpel, my friend, you recognize this cow. Would you also recognize the stranger who sold her to us?

GIMPEL: Well, it might not be the same stranger, only one who looks like him.

MOTTEL: Close enough! You, Gimpel, are the world traveler among us. Take the cow with you. When your path crosses that of the stranger again, give the cow back and get us our valuables.

GIMPEL: (*Hesitates.*) This is a big job you are asking, Reb Mottel.

MOTTEL: Please, Gimpel. It's a mitzvah. A kindness. A blessing.

GIMPEL: All right, already. I'll go. I'll give a look.

MOTTEL: Thank you, Gimpel! (*Hands him* COW'S *rope.*)

GIMPEL: (*Takes* COW'S *lead rope and exits right.*) Come on, Yenta. That's a good Yentele. Come along.

COW: (*Eagerly, as they go off.*) Mooooo!

MOTTEL: (*Watches them go.*) So. Now, we must wait. (*He offers* PINCHAS *the stool, moving it down right.* PINCHAS *sits.* MOTTEL *sits beside him on the overturned bucket.*)

PINCHAS: Yes, yes, we'll wait.

MOTTEL: (*As* MUSIC *begins softly.*) A day or two, we'll wait.

PINCHAS: Or three or four, we'll wait.

MOTTEL: For seven days and seven nights, we'll wait.

PINCHAS: We'll wait, we'll wait.

(MUSIC *up. They hum along, absently, patiently waiting. Upstage,* OTHERS *dance on and remove village pieces, replacing them with* PINCHAS' *bedroom.* ALL *except* MOTTEL *and* PINCHAS *dance off.* MUSIC *fades.*)

PINCHAS: Reb Mottel.

MOTTEL: Yes, Reb Pinchas?

PINCHAS: Reb Mottel, I must speak to you privately for a moment. I am a deeply troubled man.

MOTTEL: What troubles you, my friend? (PINCHAS *rises, looks right and left to see that they're alone, moves into bedroom.*)

PINCHAS: A terrifying thing happened to me this morning.

MOTTEL: A terrifying thing?

PINCHAS: Yes. Terrifying. I don't want the others to hear.

MOTTEL: What is this terrifying thing that happened to you, Reb Pinchas?

PINCHAS: (*At bed.* MOTTEL *remains on bucket, right.*) You remember this morning? You remember how it began—with the cock's crow? Cockadoodle-doo! Cockadoodle-doo!

ROOSTER: (*Offstage, or as puppet behind headboard.*) COCKADOODLE-DOO! COCKADOODLE-DOO!

MOTTEL: Yes, it began just like any other morning.

ROOSTER: COCKADOODLE-DOO!

PINCHAS: No, no. It did not.

ROOSTER: (*Miffed.*) BRAAAACK! (*Exits, if puppet.*)

PINCHAS: (*Begins to act scene as he tells it.*) I heard the crowing, and I jumped out of bed, just like any other morning, except that it was entirely different.

MOTTEL: Why was it different, Reb Pinchas?

PINCHAS: Why? Why? I'm telling you why. It was different because suddenly I found myself whirling and twirling this way and that. "Oi! Oi, vay iz mer!" I cried. "A catastrophe! A disaster! What to do? What to do?" I called to my wife, "Rifke! Help me!" My poor wife rushed to my side,

(RIFKE *rushes in, up left.*)

RIFKE: My darling Pinchas—

PINCHAS: —she said—

RIFKE: What is it? What's wrong? Are you ill? Are you dying?

MOTTEL: And?

PINCHAS: (*To both* RIFKE *and* MOTTEL.) And I said, "No, no, I'm not ill. I'm not dying. Listen to me, Rifke, please. I have just awakened from a long night's sleep—and I do not remember where I put my clothes before going to bed!"

MOTTEL: And she said? (PINCHAS *speaks to* MOTTEL *as* RIFKE *speaks to* PINCHAS.)

PINCHAS and RIFKE: Dumkop!

MOTTEL: (*Offended.*) I beg your pardon?

PINCHAS and RIFKE: (*Same business.*) Dumkop!

MOTTEL: Who are you calling a dumkop?

PINCHAS: (Confused; RIFKE mimes gathering his clothes and piling them on bed.) Me? No one. Why do you ask?

MOTTEL: Did you not just scream, "dumkop" right to my face?

PINCHAS: Not me! Rifke. Rifke screamed, "Dumkop!"

MOTTEL: Your wife called me a dumkop? She thinks I'm an idiot?

PINCHAS: No, no! Not you. Me! Me, she called an idiot.

MOTTEL: Oh, well, that makes more sense.

PINCHAS: Of course. When does my Rifke not make sense?

RIFKE: Dumkop!

PINCHAS: —she said—

RIFKE: If you'll look for once with your eyes open and your mouth shut, maybe you'll see something for a change! Hah? Your clothes are right in front of your nose! (She pinches his nose a good one.)

PINCHAS: (Enduring pinch.) Oi! Oi! Vay iz mer! (RIFKE finally lets go and exits. PINCHAS staggers down to MOTTEL.) How could I forget a thing like that, Reb Mottel? Right in front of my nose! My nose is always here, and the front of it is always there, and—(Stops, perplexed.)

MOTTEL: Reb Pinchas, my friend, you know what the good people of Chelm always say.

PINCHAS: Of course, I know what they always say. (Pauses, confused.) What? What do they always say?

MOTTEL: They say your absent-mindedness only proves what a wise man you are.

PINCHAS: It does?

MOTTEL: So they say. With a head so filled with glorious thoughts, should you be bothered to remember trivial details?

PINCHAS: (Pleased.) Do they say that?

MOTTEL: Oh, yes, especially when you forget your name and where you live, and we have to help you home at the end of the day.

PINCHAS: Well, I do have matters of importance to consider.

MOTTEL: No question about it. So I suggest you make a list.

PINCHAS: A list?

MOTTEL: Yes. Tonight, as you get undressed and put your clothes away, write down where each and every item goes. Tomorrow morning, when you wake up, all you have to do is follow your list.

PINCHAS: (Delighted.) My list!

MOTTEL: (Leading him into bedroom area.) Nothing could be simpler, Reb Pinchas.

PINCHAS: A list! I'll do it! (Searches for pen and paper. MUSIC begins and continues through PINCHAS' listmaking.)

MOTTEL: (Handing PINCHAS pen and paper.) Good night, Reb Pinchas. (He exits.)

PINCHAS: Good night! Good night, Reb Mottel! A list! (PINCHAS strips down to long underwear and socks. His listmaking and undressing become a chant and *gleeful dance performed in rhythm to the music.)* What could be simpler? Let me see. My coat I hang on a peg, like so. *(Writing.)* Coat . . . on . . . peg. So!

(Alternates undressing and writing.)
> My boots I place under the bed, like so.
> Boots . . . under . . . bed. So!
> My trousers go over the chair, like so.
> Trousers . . . over . . . chair. So!
> My shirt I drape on the bedpost, like so.
> Shirt . . . on . . . bedpost. So!
> My tallis I fold up neat, like so.
> Tallis . . . neatly folded . . . so!
> My hat on the other post, like so.
> Hat . . . on . . . post. So! *(Climbs into bed, with list.)*
> And myself I put into the bed, like so.
> I . . . am . . . in . . . bed. So!
> A list! Good night. *(Falls asleep, holding list.)*

(MUSIC *up,* ALL *dance on, circle bed, remove clothes* PINCHAS *has taken off, and furniture, and eventually carry off bed as well, then dance off, leaving the stage empty.* MUSIC *fades as* GIMPEL *and* COW *enter up left.)*

COW: *(Exhausted, she refuses to go any farther.)* Mooooooo!

GIMPEL: I know, Yenta. You're tired and thirsty. So am I. *(Pointing down right.)* Look, here is a nice, fresh spring. We'll stop and have ourselves a drink. Just a few more steps. (COW *falls to her knees.)* Oi vay!

(GIMPEL *runs to spring, mimes scooping water into his hands, carries it back to* COW. *While* COW *drinks,* STRANGER *enters right. Unaware of* GIMPEL *and* COW, *he kneels at spring, drinks, dampens a handkerchief to mop his brow, etc. As* GIMPEL *returns for a second scoop of water for the* COW, *he sees* STRANGER.)

GIMPEL: Yossel! My old friend Yossel!

STRANGER: *(Mystified.)* Who—? Yossel? What—?

GIMPEL: *(Unfazed.)* It's so good to see you again, Yossel! But what has become of you? Just look at you, how you've changed—

STRANGER: But I'm not—

GIMPEL: I can't get over it. You used to be so big and strong. Like a horse you were, like an ox. And now, you're a little bird, a pipsqueak. Have you been ill?

STRANGER: No! But I'm not—

GIMPEL: And your hair! Yossel, you used to be bald! Even as a young man, I remember it distinctly, you were already going bald. How is it you now have such a nice head of hair?

STRANGER: I'm not—

GIMPEL: I tell you, Yossel, it's a miracle I even recognized you. I've never known a person to change as much as you have.

STRANGER: But, I'm not Yossel!

GIMPEL: What? You've even changed your name?

STRANGER: I *have never been Yossel!* (COW *revives at sound of* STRANGER's *voice, struggles to her feet.)*

GIMPEL: You're sure of this?

STRANGER: I'm sure! I'm sure!

GIMPEL: How is it, then, that you look so familiar to me? As familiar as my good friend Yossel, whom you claim not to be?

STRANGER: I am not—

COW: (Approaching STRANGER.) Mooooooooo!

STRANGER: Yenta. My poor old Yentele. You've missed me, haven't you? Oi, and I've missed you, too.

GIMPEL: He never had a cow, my friend Yossel. Chickens, I remember, but not—(It finally dawns on him.) Wait! You're the stranger who sold Yenta to Reb Mottel and Reb Pinchas!

STRANGER: Yes. Yes, it is I.

GIMPEL: Well, I am here to tell you the cow doesn't work.

STRANGER: Doesn't work?

GIMPEL: Doesn't give gold. Doesn't even give milk. Doesn't work.

STRANGER: (To audience.) So THAT'S why they wanted my Yenta! They thought she gave gold! What FOOLS!

GIMPEL: Obviously, the gold she gives is meant only for you. So—whether you have their valuables or whether you have her gold makes no difference by you, does it? Either way, you remain a rich man. To Reb Mottel and Reb Pinchas and their neighbors, however, it makes a big difference. So—I bring you your beloved Yentele. And I ask you please to return the price that was paid for her.

STRANGER: (To audience.) This is impossible. Their treasure has bought me a house, a wife, a seat in the synagogue by the Eastern Wall! I cannot give these things up. There must be another way. But what?

GIMPEL: So, stranger? What do you say?

STRANGER: (Stalling for time.) What do I say? What can I say? It's true that valuables were exchanged for my Yenta, so huge a treasure it took two men to carry it. But now—

GIMPEL: Two men carried it?

STRANGER: Oh, yes. Two men. And then two boys. I paid them myself.

GIMPEL: Then that presents a problem for me.

STRANGER: For you? How is this a problem for you?

GIMPEL: How can I carry such a load, one man traveling such a distance alone?

STRANGER: (Seeing a ray of hope.) That is a problem, isn't it?

GIMPEL: Yes, it's a problem. A very heavy problem.

STRANGER: (Sensing the arrival of inspiration.) Then here is my suggestion. Instead of the original valuables, which are so very heavy and impossible for one man to carry, I will give you an equal amount of . . . of something lighter.

GIMPEL: Something lighter?

STRANGER: (Inspired.) Feathers.

GIMPEL: (To STRANGER.) Feathers?

STRANGER: What could be lighter than feathers?

GIMPEL: *(To audience.)* Feathers?

STRANGER: Yes! Feathers to fluff your pillows, feathers to stuff your comforters, feathers to warm like an oven the linings of your winter coats. A delightful idea, no? It will be winter soon enough. Who needs a necklace here, a pocket watch there when the wind blows cold and hard down the neck and up the sleeves? What could be better—or lighter to carry—than feathers?

GIMPEL: Feathers! Nothing could be better! Feathers, it is!

STRANGER: Done!

COW: *(Dubious.)* Mooooooo!

STRANGER: Shah, Yentele! *(To* GIMPEL.*)* Wait here, my friend. *(Quickly exits right.)*

GIMPEL: I'll wait. I'll wait. Who wouldn't wait for a stroke of good fortune? Feathers!

*(*STRANGER *returns immediately with two sacks and sets them in front of* GIMPEL.*)*

STRANGER: Feathers! Yes! And more feathers!

GIMPEL: Done!

STRANGER: Sholem aleichem, my friend.

GIMPEL: Aleichem sholem, stranger. Peace be with you, and also, with your cow.

COW: Mooooooo!

STRANGER: *(As he hurries off right with* COW.*)* Such a deal!

GIMPEL: *(Admiring sacks.)* Such a deal! *(Tries to pick up sacks, finds they're heavier than expected.)* Now, here is an interesting thing. *(*MUSIC *begins softly as he mimes pulling out one feather and blowing it away.)* One feather is light as a feather. But a whole sack of feathers taken together? A different situation entirely. *(Takes out another feather and blows it away.)* The wind can carry one feather, or it can carry a thousand feathers. A wind is stronger than a man. *(Thinks this over, licks his finger and tests the wind.)* And this wind is blowing my way. Why should a man schlep when the wind has nothing better to do? *(Taps his head in approval of his cleverness.)* I'll let the strong wind carry the feathers for me. *(*MUSIC *comes up and a* WIND *whistles as* GIMPEL *dances around the sacks, pretending to toss away handfuls of feathers.)* Fly, little feathers. Fly away home! Whoosh! Whoosh!

(After a few moments, ALL *dance in to whirl off sacks and bring in town, including bucket and stool.* ALL *dance off, except* MOTTEL *who sits on stool, humming and waiting as before.* GIMPEL *enters up right, carrying two empty sacks.* MUSIC *fades.)*

GIMPEL: Reb Mottel!

MOTTEL: Gimpel! You're back! You found the stranger? You returned the cow?

GIMPEL: I found the stranger. I returned the cow.

MOTTEL: So—?

GIMPEL: So—?

MOTTEL: So where are our valuables?

GIMPEL: Still with the stranger.

MOTTEL: Impossible! You found the stranger, you gave him the cow. What have you done with our valuables?

GIMPEL: Nothing. I never saw your valuables. I never touched your valuables. The stranger explained to me that your valuables were given to him in two very heavy sacks. Two men, it took, to carry those sacks, did it not?

MOTTEL: Reb Pinchas and I carried them, yes.

GIMPEL: And how did you expect one man to carry them back?

MOTTEL: Well, I never gave that much thought.

GIMPEL: Ah ha! But the stranger and I did. Instead of two heavy sacks, he gave me two not-so-heavy sacks—filled with feathers.

MOTTEL: Feathers?

GIMPEL: Feathers.

MOTTEL: (To audience.) Feathers?

GIMPEL: Feathers for your pillows. Feathers for your comforters. Feathers for the linings of your coats. Feathers for the cold, north wind that is blowing our way this very moment, carrying winter in its icy teeth.

MOTTEL: Ah! Feathers! Yes! That's very good. That's very nice. But where are they, these feathers?

GIMPEL: Also, being carried by the wind. Two sacks of feathers is not so light and airy as you would suppose, Reb Mottel. But the wind can carry them with ease, so I gave them to the wind. All you have to do now is wait for the wind to blow them in, and in no time, you'll gather them up. I have here two sacks for the job. (MOTTEL *looks at sacks, looks at* GIMPEL, *looks at the audience, gives the idea some thought, decides it makes sense, takes the sacks.*)

MOTTEL: All right. So we'll wait.

GIMPEL: We'll wait. (MUSIC *plays softly as* MOTTEL *motions* GIMPEL *over to bucket and stool.*)

MOTTEL: A day or two, we'll wait.

GIMPEL: Or three or four, we'll wait.

MOTTEL: For seven days and seven nights, we'll wait.

GIMPEL: We'll wait, we'll wait. (*They sit, humming and waiting.*)

GIMPEL: (*After a moment.*) Reb Mottel. (MUSIC *fades.*)

MOTTEL: Yes?

GIMPEL: Reb Mottel, there is something I would like to discuss with you. A matter which has been gnawing at me lately.

MOTTEL: And what is that?

GIMPEL: You have noticed, perhaps, that I have no beard?

MOTTEL: What are you talking? Who could not notice?

GIMPEL: Why is that, I wonder? When I was a cheder boy, I could understand. But now I'm of an age when a man should have a beard—(*Shrugs, perplexed.*)

MOTTEL: Hmmmmm. Let us think about this, you and I. (*Eyes* GIMPEL *thoughtfully for a moment.*) Tell me, which do you resemble more, do you think, your mother's side of the family or your father's side?

GIMPEL: My mother's side. No question. I have by them the eyes. Also the hair.

MOTTEL: In other words, you look like your mother.

GIMPEL: Like my mother, yes.

MOTTEL: And does your mother have a beard?

GIMPEL: What kind of a question is that? No! Why should my mother have a beard?

MOTTEL: Then, there is your answer. You resemble your mother, so you have no beard.

GIMPEL: (*Amazed.*) Why didn't I think of that?

MOTTEL: You're young yet, my friend. Great wisdom, like wine, requires a certain aging.

GIMPEL: Ah, yes! I understand.

(MUSIC *up.* ALL *dance in, removing village and returning* PINCHAS, *his furniture, his list, and his clothes to their former places.* ALL *dance off, including* MOTTEL *and* GIMPEL, *leaving* PINCHAS *in bed as before.* MUSIC *fades slightly as* ROOSTER CROWS.*)

ROOSTER: COCKADOODLE-DOO! COCKADOODLE-DOO!

PINCHAS: (*Wakes up, groggily.*) What? What is it? I'm coming, already. I'm coming.

ROOSTER: COCKADOODLE-DOO!

PINCHAS: (*Sitting up.*) Enough, Rifke, enough. I hear you, darling.

ROOSTER: (*Insulted.*) BRAAAAACK! (*Exits.*)

PINCHAS: (*Sees list, still clutched in his hand.*) Aha! My list. Now we're in business. (*Gets out of bed, following list.* MUSIC *continues as he chants and dances as before.*) Let me see. (*Gathers each item onto bed.*)
> Coat . . . on . . . peg. So!
> My coat I hung from a peg. Like so!
> Boots . . . under . . . bed. So!
> My boots I placed under the bed. Like so!
> Trousers . . . over . . . chair. So!
> My trousers went over the chair. Like so!
> Shirt . . . on . . . bedpost. So!
> My shirt I draped on the bedpost. Like so!
> Tallis . . . neatly folded. So!
> My tallis I folded up neat. Like so!
> Hat . . . on . . . post. So!
> My hat's on the other post. Like so!
> (*He dons hat by habit.*)
> Everything right in front of my nose! (*Checks list.*)
> What's this? One more item on my list.
> I . . . am . . . in . . . bed. (*Checks bed.*)
> But I am not in bed!
> (*Begins tossing things off bed frantically.*)
> Oi vay! I'm gone! Help! Help!

(RIFKE *rushes on.*)

RIFKE: What is it, Pinchas? What's wrong? Are you hurt?

PINCHAS: No, I am not hurt. I am *gone!*

RIFKE: Gone? Gone where?

PINCHAS: How should I know where? I'm gone! I'm a missing person!

RIFKE: A missing person, now? A dumkop, you mean! (*Taps her head to indicate his craziness.*) A meshuggener. Fahrblondjet. Tsedrayt. What did I do to deserve such craziness in my house? Close the windows, the neighbors shouldn't hear.

PINCHAS: (*Truly panicked now, runs from* RIFKE *to bed to window.*) No! No! Open the windows! Rifke! Someone! Anyone! Help me! Help me . . . wherever I am! (*Checks all his pockets.*)

RIFKE: Dumkop!

(GIMPEL *rushes on.*)

GIMPEL: Reb Pinchas, what's all the shouting? What's wrong?

RIFKE: (*To* GIMPEL.) Rifke, Rifke, help me, he says. I'm a missing person, he says. I could mention what's missing by him, but what good would it do me, hah? Don't ask!

GIMPEL: (*With no malice, a mere observation.*) You know something? In Chelm, where I come from, our Reb Pinchas has a Rifke who looks exactly like you! Rifke with the Big Mouth, we call her. Of course, never to her face.

RIFKE: (*Grabs her head in both hands and exits.*) Oi, oi, oi, oi, oi, oi . . .

PINCHAS: Rifke, wait! (*Gives up; he'll have her to deal with later.*) Vay iz mer! (*Shows* GIMPEL *list.*) Look at my list, Gimpel, my list I prepared so carefully last night. It says right here: *I am in bed.* Does it not?

GIMPEL: It does.

PINCHAS: But am I in bed?

GIMPEL: No, you are not.

PINCHAS: Then, I'm gone! Where could I be?

GIMPEL: Reb Pinchas, please! Calm down for just a minute. Let us think this problem through. (*Hands* PINCHAS *clothes, which* PINCHAS *puts on as they chat.*)

PINCHAS: Yes, yes, we must think. Thinking is good. We'll think.

GIMPEL: So. Where are you usually?

PINCHAS: Where am I usually?

GIMPEL: Yes. The last time you looked, where were you?

PINCHAS: I was *here.* In *bed.* At *home.* In *Chelm.*

GIMPEL: Aha! There we spot the problem.

PINCHAS: We do?

GIMPEL: We do. Reb Pinchas, this is not Chelm.

PINCHAS: This is not Chelm?

GIMPEL: No, it is not.

PINCHAS: It looks like Chelm.

GIMPEL: I know, I know. It looks like Chelm, it sounds like Chelm . . . remarkable, isn't it? Every place you go is *like* Chelm, but *not* Chelm. We must return to our own little town, Reb Pinchas, and then you will be—exactly where you are.

PINCHAS: I see. I think I see. I think. *(They freeze.* MUSIC *begins softly.)*

*(*STORYTELLER *enters; changes from* STRANGER's *hat to* STORYTELLER's *hat.)*

STORYTELLER: *(To audience.)* To save time, Reb Pinchas and Gimpel decided to take the new train between Warsaw and Chelm. "If you want to go somewhere by train," they asked a passer-by, "what do you do?" "What do you do?" the man said. "What's to do? You want to ride the train, you go to the station. You sit down there by the waiting room, and you wait. And that's what you do." So Reb Pinchas and Gimpel went to the station. They sat down there by the waiting room, and they waited. When they felt they had waited long enough, they stood up and they left. Lo and behold, they were in Chelm. *(*MUSIC *fades as* PINCHAS *and* GIMPEL *resume action.)*

PINCHAS: Yes, yes. Here is my room, just as I left it. *(He examines bed.)* But I am not in my bed! What do you make of this, Gimpel?

STORYTELLER: Gimpel gave it some thought.

GIMPEL: *(Musing, without looking at* PINCHAS.*)* You know, Reb Pinchas, what is not *in* the bed has often fallen *under* the bed. I remember one time—

PINCHAS: *(Diving under the bed.)* Under the bed! *(*GIMPEL *turns toward* PINCHAS *to continue his story and discovers he's gone.)*

GIMPEL: Reb Pinchas? Reb Pinchas, where are you?

PINCHAS: I'm under the bed, Gimpel.

GIMPEL: *(Peering under bed.)* Ah, so here you are! Just as I suspected.

PINCHAS: So here I am! I'm under the bed! I'm found!

GIMPEL: *(As they* BOTH *stand, triumphant.)* What did I tell you, Reb Pinchas?

PINCHAS: It's a miracle!

GIMPEL: It's *Chelm.*

*(*MOTTEL *rushes on.)*

MOTTEL: Gimpel, Gimpel, here you are. Finally, I've found you.

GIMPEL: And why not? Today is a day for finding.

MOTTEL: Some things, maybe. Others, not so much. Not, for instance, feathers.

GIMPEL: Feathers?

PINCHAS: *(To audience.)* Feathers?

MOTTEL: *Feathers.* I have been watching and waiting—

GIMPEL: Here also you've been watching and waiting? I'm amazed! When I was in Warsaw—

MOTTEL: Enough Warsaw already! The entire shtetl has been watching and waiting. The wind blows and blows, and we watch and we wait. But there are no feathers.

GIMPEL: Not a single one?

MOTTEL: Not a single one.

GIMPEL: Hmmmmmm.

MOTTEL: Hmmmmmm? *(To audience.)* Hmmmmmmm, he says? *(To GIMPEL, in high agitation.)* I'll give you a "hmmmmmmmm." This problem requires serious thought. Gimpel, Reb Pinchas, help me to think. (MUSIC *plays.* MOTTEL, GIMPEL, *and* PINCHAS *freeze, thinking.)*

STORYTELLER: For seven days and seven nights, the sages of Chelm gave the problem of the missing feathers serious thought. (MUSIC *fades.* MOTTEL, GIMPEL, *and* PINCHAS *become animated again.)*

MOTTEL: *(Still agitated.)* Perhaps, if we take a walk down the road, we'll find the feathers as we go? We'll meet them and we'll wave them in?

PINCHAS: All right, we'll walk. It couldn't hurt.

(MUSIC *plays softly as they wander stage, searching for feathers.* OTHERS *dance on, remove bedroom and whirl in town set, then exit. After a bit,* MOTTEL, PINCHAS, *and* GIMPEL *reconvene at center.* MUSIC *fades.)*

MOTTEL: Gimpel?

GIMPEL: Yes, Reb Mottel?

MOTTEL: Suppose we never see them, these feathers? Suppose the wind has scattered them all over the world? It's possible, you know.

GIMPEL: Yes, it's . . . possible.

MOTTEL: And if it happens? What then?

PINCHAS: This is something we must consider very carefully. (MUSIC *plays. They freeze, rethinking.)*

STORYTELLER: Once again, for seven days and seven nights, the wise men pondered this imponderable question. At last, drawing on ancient wisdom, as it is written, Reb Pinchas decided that the scattering of the feathers was a sign. (MUSIC *stops.* MOTTEL, PINCHAS, *and* GIMPEL *become animated.)*

GIMPEL: A sign, Reb Pinchas?

PINCHAS: Yes, yes. A sign.

MOTTEL: A sign of what, Reb Pinchas?

PINCHAS: This, we don't yet know. We must think. (MUSIC *plays. They freeze.)*

STORYTELLER: Seven more days and seven more nights were given over to thinking. And this time, it was Gimpel, the world traveler, who answered the question. (MUSIC *stops.* WISE MEN *become animated.)*

GIMPEL: This sign, Reb Pinchas, of feathers in the wind. Perhaps it tells us that we, too, must be scattered. We, too, must go out, out into the world.

MOTTEL: What do you think, Reb Pinchas? Could this be the sign?

PINCHAS: It is possible. It is written.

GIMPEL: Reb Mottel, Reb Pinchas, I have often thought about this. Our fortune, it is out there—with our feathers.

MOTTEL: *(Thinking it over.)* We have waited for cows to give gold, and for the wind to return our feathers—

PINCHAS: For the train, we have waited—

GIMPEL: And for my beard to grow! *(Looks at* MOTTEL *hopefully.)*

PINCHAS: *(Also, looks at* MOTTEL, *palms up, as in "What do you make of this?")* Nu?

MOTTEL: *(Another moment's thought.)* Enough waiting, already! Tell everyone—we must go!

GIMPEL: *(Extending his hand for* MOTTEL *and* PINCHAS *to grasp.)* To the world!

MOTTEL: To the feathers!

PINCHAS: To life!

ALL: L'chayim! *(*MUSIC *up. They dance furiously.* STORYTELLER *and* OTHERS *join them.* ALL *remove town and replace* TO CHELM *sign to center.* ALL *dance off one by one in various directions, until only* STORYTELLER *is left.* MUSIC *fades.)*

STORYTELLER: And so it came to pass that the foolish souls of Chelm left their tiny shtetl and were scattered throughout the world as it was intended in the beginning. If, in your own wanderings, or even in your own town, you happen upon a foolish person, perhaps that person is a descendent of the people of Chelm. *(Begins to leave, then turns back.)* Oh, and if you ever find yourself acting foolishly, perhaps you are one, as well. It is . . . possible. *(He spins sign, which now reads* TO CHELM *any way you look at it.)*

ROOSTER: *(Offstage.)* COCKADOODLE-DOO! COCKADOODLE-DOO!

*(*STORYTELLER *refers audience to* ROOSTER *with a knowing nod, as in "Yes, we could all stand to wake up to our foolishness."* MUSIC *swells,* ALL *dance on, circle and spin sign, bow, and exit in all directions.* MUSIC *fades.)*

CURTAIN

AUTHOR'S NOTE

Some people worry about Chelm.

They worry that the stories may be anti-Semitic, casting all Jews in the roles of fools. But these tales, said to date back to the 1500s, were told *by* Jews *to* Jews *about* Jews, and have been handed down, parent to child, through generations of Jewish families. No baiting of another, supposedly inferior ethnic group is intended in their telling. They are ethnic humor only in that they belong to the folklore of a particular ethnic group.

Maybe so, the worriers say, but then they are typical of self-deprecating Jewish humor, proof that Jews internalize the anti-Semitism around them and even contribute to it.

Evidence contradicts this theory as well. First, the tales put a premium on cleverness in the telling: the Chelmites do foolish things in ingenious ways. Their silliness appeals to children, but the older one gets, the more one can appreciate their totally original thinking—and the wit of the Jewish storytellers responsible for them. Second, the Chelmites, for all their foolishness, are an endearing lot. Their antics are never meant to cause anyone pain; they result, instead, from efforts toward the common good. Because of this, the earnest bumbling is as charming as it is funny. Third, the Chelmites are unfailingly self-confident. Whatever is broken can be fixed. Whatever is lost can be regained. Where there's a question, there is always an answer. Granted their methods, solutions, and answers tend toward the bizarre, and no problem is ever fully solved—in fact, solutions seem to lead only to new problems—but no matter the odds, they survive and press on. One would be hardpressed to read self-deprecation into such optimism. And the optimism, both for the Chelmites and their creators, is justified: The Jewish people and their stories, no matter the odds, survive and press on.

The Chelmites, true to the story of the feathers included in this play, go beyond the borders of their village. In *Yiddish Folktales*, Beatrice Silverman Weinreich characterizes them as "... experts at misreading Bible verse, misinterpreting injunction, ignoring reality, and overlooking laws of nature." Sound familiar? No one people and no one century can lay sole claim to those human frailties. The good intentions, the bumbling, and the courage to go on are not limited to one people, and that, of course, gives these stories their universal appeal.

CROW & WEASEL

Adapted for the stage
by
Jim Leonard, Jr.

From a story by Barry López
Music by John Luther Adams

Based on the book by Barry López
with illustrations by Tom Pohrt

JIM LEONARD, JR., was born and raised in Indiana. He received a B.A. from Hanover College, where he began writing plays. In addition to *Crow & Weasel* his plays include *The Diviners, And They Dance Real Slow in Jackson, V & V Only*, and *Battle Hymn*. Leonard's plays have been produced at the Kennedy Center and numerous New York Off-Broadway theatres, including the Circle Repertory Theatre, as well as regional repertory theatres. His plays have also been produced internationally.

Leonard spent six years as a creative writing professor at Arizona State University in Tempe, where he headed the M.F.A. Playwriting Program before moving into television and film. He has created and cocreated pilots for the Fox, NBC, and ABC television networks and is currently coexecutive producer of the new ABC one-hour series called *Cracker*. His film, *My Own Country*, is in production at Showtime, and his film adaptation of his own play, *The Diviners*, is in pre-production with Avenue Pictures.

Leonard has received three National Endowment for the Arts playwriting fellowships and honors such as the Dramatist Guild New Play Award and the Samuel French Award.

Jim Leonard is married to Linda, his high school sweetheart. They have two children and live in Los Angeles, where he divides his time between writing for the stage, television, and film and coaching Little League.

————————————

I hope *Crow & Weasel* is a theatrical experience that is *accessible* to young people, as opposed to just "for" them. I doubt I'm much different than other playwrights in that I want older people to enjoy my plays, too.

As with all my plays the most rewarding and terrifying moment for me is sitting in the dark theatre, shrouded in nervous anonymity, experiencing the play with an audience. Will they be bored? Will they laugh in the right places? Will they pay attention? Will the play hold them? I'm grateful that when the play was produced at The Children's Theatre of Minneapolis, the answer to all these questions was "yes." I was amazed by the children's capacity to pay attention to the mysterious world that Crow and Weasel move through, by their willingness to live with the actors in inexplicable emotional moments and to feel the presence of grace emanating from the stage. I like writing plays with younger people in mind, because I want them to love the theatre as much as I do.

—JIM LEONARD, JR.

PLAYWRIGHT'S NOTES

The making of *Crow & Weasel* was a true, and in my experience, unprecedented collaboration. Barry Lõpez, the book's author, and I worked closely together for more than three years. It has not been an easy journey we've taken, but I think it's been a fruitful one.

A few things I learned along the way . . .

Casting. This story is not specific to any existing culture; it takes place in a North American myth-culture, which I see best reflected in a multi-ethnic cast—a cast that looks like our continent. In other words, don't worry too much about color—cast the best actors.

Design. John Luther Adam's music encompasses the geographies of landscape, emotion, and weather. The simplicity, passion, and elegance of John's approach to music informed most of my choices as a writer; my advice to designers is to let John's music do the same for you. The set, costume, and lighting designs should strive for the essence of the story. Nothing is more difficult to achieve than simplicity, of course, largely because being simple in the theatre means being right. Warning: if it seems "cute," it probably is cute, and cute is not what we're after. *(Side note: John and I jokingly call the style we were after "Post-modern Shaker," and I don't think that's too far off the mark.)*

Props. Property design is central to the telling of this story for two reasons: first, all the props in the play are useful (i.e., utilitarian); second, several of the props become holy. For instance, Crow's medicine bag and the pipe are both sacred, and it is essential that they are treated by the actors as such. The wooden horse figures that the boys carry when they "ride," begin as simple stylized carvings, but by the time the play is half over, it's clear that these carvings have a weight, a personality, a presence of their own.

Movement/Dance. Gary Gisselman, who directed the first production of this play at The Children's Theatre Company in Minneapolis, worked closely with a brilliant choreographer named Myron Johnson. Their answer to the often-asked question, "Are they animals or people?" was yes. Each of the actors concentrated on finding several "signature" movements or gestures for his or her character(s). Mother Crow and Crow, for instance, fluttered their wings and bent their beaks low to the ground in a gesture of farewell. Weasel and his mother sort of "nuzzled" each other. Each character, each animal person, was imbued with an essential dignity that radiated through his or her movement. And, for me, this became the key: finding the essence of the animal in the character and allowing its dignity to shine through the person of the actor. This balance is delicate: dignity without pretension, joy without slapstick. The narrative world moves sometimes in counterpoint to Crow and Weasel, oftentimes dances with them, and propels them through the story.

The Sedna story is told in dance at the end of the first act, and then told in dance/narration, given to the village, at the end of the play; so dance both frames and holds the play.

The actors' journey. Crow & Weasel is a coming-of-age story, yes; but it's more than that. At the beginning of their journey, Crow and Weasel are tempted to impose themselves upon the landscape—they want to make their mark on the world; this is only natural. What happens is the opposite: the world makes its mark upon them. They learn to listen. They learn to see. They learn to take care of each other. And they learn to tell stories. The difference between owning a story and caring for a story is subtle, but crucial.

Crow and Weasel travel from the plains of North America to the Arctic Circle, and home again. For Crow's and Weasel's journey is to grace; and grace, for them, is in community.

The theatre, for me, is community at its best.

—JIM LEONARD, JR.

AUTHOR'S NOTES

The story of Crow and Weasel unfolds at a time in North America during which all the elements of creation could understand each other's language, a time when virtue lay in listening. The discoveries that await the two of them—friendship, terrifying wonders, loss of ego, profound respect—are complicated, but achievement in their journey hinges on attentiveness to the entire surround of the landscape, to both its spiritual and physical dimensions. That world speaks to these two young men through Badger, Grizzly Bear, and the chorus of voices that comprises the Trees, the River, and the Tundra. As they travel, we see maturing within Crow and Weasel an expression of what is beautiful in the world: thoughtful, careful, and loving relationships.

The tone of voice here is elevated but not solemn, the frame of mind serious but not humorless. Crow's and Weasel's encounter is with the sacred, with the elements of myth, not the secular events of legend. The pipe they carry is as holy an object as the ciborium or monstrance in the Christian tradition or the Torah in Jewish tradition. (It should be handled as carefully as a newborn child.)

Crow & Weasel is not based on a Native American story, but the values celebrated here—the importance of gift exchange, considering the needs of the community ahead of an individual's desires, cultivating a spiritual awareness of the world—are emphasized in indigenous North American traditions and are still integral to the lives of native North American people.

As Mountain Lion makes clear, we are indebted to Crow and Weasel for the wisdom they come to possess and convey. No matter their tradition or our historical era, Crow and Weasel finally reach us as modern heroes, people on the verge of leading helpful lives in the community.

—BARRY LÓPEZ

CROW & WEASEL

CHARACTERS

Crow
Weasel
Seven actors

*These seven actors play many characters and places, including: the River of Float-
ing Ashes, Birds-with-No-Name, Trees, Yellow-shafted Flicker, Caribou, Horses,
and Narrators.*

Actor One plays:
  Mountain Lion, Narrator #1, & Inuit Elder
Actor Two plays:
  Red Fox, Narrator #2, one of the Caribou, & Inuit Man #2
Actor Three plays:
  Porcupine, Narrator #3, Grizzly Bear, & Inuit Man #3
Actor Four plays:
  Marmot, Narrator #4, one of the Caribou, & Crow's Horse
Actor Five plays:
  Racoon, Narrator #5, Inuit Woman #1, Badger, & Weasel's Horse
Actor Six plays:
  Mother Weasel, Narrator #6, Inuit Woman #2, & Lead Caribou
Actor Seven plays:
  Mother Crow, Mouse, Narrator #7, & Inuit Woman #3

Note: parts certainly can be shifted among the actors, according
to abilities and needs; but it seems important that the same man
who plays Mountain Lion, for instance, also plays the Elder he dreams of . . .
there is some design to this . . .

SETTING

North America, the earth.
  Where we are on this earth is a confluence of acting, sonic geography, and
the quality of light. CROW's and WEASEL's world is as informed by music and
movement as it is by language.
  The ground rises upstage, like a rolling hill; there is a sense that the earth
and the sky are not separate. As the play moves northward, it covers many
lands—these places are probably best realized through a combination of
sound and good acting, rather than attempting to realistically portray the
land. I think in terms of finding one or two very simple, even elegant scenic
images, for each part of the world that we travel through: i.e., tall grass, big
trees, the sun, the moon, fire and ice.

MUSIC & SOUND

We're not talking "songs" here. We're talking a "sonic geography," a sense of the essence of the landscapes we live in, and also, of course, music of the emotional terrain that we travel.

COSTUMES & PROPS

For costumes: look at the book, and also the Chandler-Pohrt Collection of North American Indian artifacts in *Art of the American Indian Frontier* by David W. Penny. The Animal People are animals. This is not an "American Indian" story, it's a Creation fable.

Prop design should also study the Chandler-Pohrt Collection and Inuit artifacts. *Absolutely nothing* should be on the stage that's not necessary and useful.

ACT ONE

(In darkness . . . rain. Drumming, like a rhythmic breath of the earth. We are in a dream . . . Lightning flashes. Lights slowly rise on the figure of MOUNTAIN LION *in the falling rain. Mist rolls across the stage. The* OLD MAN *is having a vision. In this dream-mist we see the shadows or figures of strange looking creatures—Inuit dream figures emerging from the darkness. Possibly a huge mask on a tall pole. And birds with blood on their wings. And now we see teeth, huge, tusk-like teeth, towering over* MOUNTAIN LION. CROW, WEASEL, *and the other* ANIMAL PEOPLE *begin to emerge from the mist, moving, dancing around* MOUNTAIN LION *as the* DREAM SOUNDS *build in intensity. And just at the moment when it seems the teeth are about to be plunged into* MOUNTAIN LION's *body, a bird screams, thunder crashes, fire leaps to life, and the old man awakens)*

MOUNTAIN LION: I dream of the earth! *(Music changes. Lights change. As the* ANIMAL PEOPLE *of his village gather around him,* MOUNTAIN LION *tells them of his vision.* MUSIC *of the northern plains . . . a "sonic geography" of the place, gives us a rhythmic-breath, a measured background to hold his story. The* ANIMAL PEOPLE *sigh . . . as one breath.)* Our people, the Animal People, have always lived here—on the ribs of the earth. All of our lives we have lived in the Land of Short Grasses. But my dream tells me the Circle is larger.

RED FOX: Larger . . . ?

MOUNTAIN LION: Much larger than even our stories foretell.

MARMOT: Larger . . .

ANIMAL PEOPLE: *(Not in unison.)* Yes. . . .

MOUNTAIN LION: In my dream I saw two of our people crossing the river. Up north.

RED FOX: The River of Ashes?

MOUNTAIN LION: Crossing and traveling farther and farther to the North. Traveling to a far-away place where winter is born. To the Land Where Dreaming Begins!

RACCOON: This will be a difficult journey.

MOUNTAIN LION: If I were younger and stronger I would go there myself. But I am not young, and my eyes are not as strong as they used to be.

RED FOX: It seems to me that whoever goes to the Land Where Dreams Are Born ought to be someone exceedingly wise, don't you think?

PORCUPINE: A strong and resourceful man.

MOUNTAIN LION: Yes.

RED FOX: Somebody who rides well—

MARMOT: And hides well—

PORCUPINE: Who fights when it's needed.

RACCOON: A strong man who understands his medicine.

MOUNTAIN LION: Yes.

RED FOX: But, of course, the most humble man from our village should go. Which is why I am humbly pleased to respectfully suggest to you—

MOUNTAIN LION: Weasel and Crow.

(Beat.)

RED FOX: I beg your pardon?

MOUNTAIN LION: In my dream I saw Weasel and Crow.

PORCUPINE: Weasel?

RACCOON: And Crow?

RED FOX: But these are not men—they're still boys, MountainLion . . . !

MOUNTAIN LION: This dream is a powerful vision.

MARMOT: In your dream, Crow and Weasel are clear?

MOUNTAIN LION: Tell them to prepare for a journey.

(As the ANIMAL PEOPLE *exit. . . .)*

PORCUPINE: Crow and Weasel . . . ?

RACCOON: Of all people. . . .

RED FOX: They're just children. . . .

MARMOT: Mere children. . . .

(A light rises on MOTHER CROW. *She speaks to the theatre.)*

MOTHER CROW: Now all of the Animal People knew that Mountain Lion's dream was a very strong vision, and all of us knew without question that young Crow and Weasel must go. But their families especially were worried about them.

(Lights rise on MOTHER WEASEL *with her son during the speech above.)*

MOTHER WEASEL: Weasel, Weasel, Weasel.

WEASEL: Mother, Mother, Mother.

MOTHER WEASEL: You're so young to go so far from home.

WEASEL: Mother, please. Crow and I have always wanted to go north. I can take care of myself.

*(*CROW *joins his* MOTHER. *The two conversations are separate.)*

MOTHER CROW: The whole idea of it frightens me, Crow.

CROW: Mother, this is a very great honor.

MOTHER CROW: I know it's an honor. I'm proud you've chosen to go—but that doesn't mean it's not dangerous.

MOTHER WEASEL: None of our people have ever been north of the river before.

MOTHER CROW: You will be without stories to guide you.

WEASEL: I'm a good hunter, Mother.

CROW: I think we'll do fine.

MOTHER WEASEL: Never brag, Weasel.

WEASEL: I won't.

MOTHER WEASEL: Never boast.

MOTHER CROW: You take care of each other.

CROW: We will, Mother.

MOTHER WEASEL: Worry—

MOTHER CROW: Worry—

MOTHER WEASEL: Worry—

MOTHER CROW: We can't help but worry about you.

(MOUNTAIN LION *calls to them. He holds the "pipe bag."*)

MOUNTAIN LION: Weasel and Crow!

WEASEL: Yes, Mountain Lion.

MOUNTAIN LION: You are not old enough, either one of you for this; but my dream tells me to give you the pipe, to share with those you meet.

CROW: We're grateful, Mountain Lion.

MOUNTAIN LION: I must tell you, not all of my dream is entirely clear. I saw something which frightens me deeply. There is a new creature in our world—a creature that I've never seen before.

WEASEL: What kind of animal is it?

MOUNTAIN LION: In my dream he travels upon the water. And he has no fur or feathers at all.

CROW: A creature who walks on the water?

WEASEL: With no feathers or fur?

MOUNTAIN LION: (*Touching his head.*) Except here. It only has fur on the top of its face. (WEASEL *laughs.*) And its teeth were really big.

WEASEL: How big is big, Mountain Lion?

CROW: Bigger than yours?

(MOUNTAIN LION *gestures that the teeth are a good four feet in length.*)

MOUNTAIN LION: Its teeth were this long in my dream. And very sharp. If you see it, I think I would try to avoid it.

WEASEL: We will.

MOUNTAIN LION: I know you are both prepared to die if you must. (CROW *and* WEASEL *look at each other.*) Remember: wherever you travel you carry our way of life with you for everyone to see. Listen. Be strong. When you are tempted to give up, think of your relatives. And if you must die, then die well. Remember your people. Wah-hey!

CROW & WEASEL: Wah-hey!

MOUNTAIN LION: (*Crossing off.*) It should be an interesting journey.

(*A horse whinnies. Two* NARRATORS *enter with horse effigies, large and gracefully simple necklaces that represent the horses. Others enter as* HORSES *as well, becoming/representing the "herd."*)

NARRATOR #3: Horses shivered off the night.

NARRATOR #4: Pintos and sorrels, blue roans and buckskins stood grazing near the stream.

NARRATOR #3: Each boy chose a young horse.

NARRATOR #4: Weasel selected his quickly.

(Taking the horse effigy necklace from the NARRATOR.*)*

WEASEL: I like this pale brown mare with the dark brown ears. It's a spirited horse with long, strong, tall legs.

NARRATOR #3: But the boy we called Crow walked a long time among the herd, watching the animals graze, before carefully choosing.

CROW: *(Taking the necklace.)* This pinto colt is gentle and sure-footed, I think. I like the way he watches me.

*(*MOTHER CROW *speaks to the theatre.)*

MOTHER CROW: Crow and Weasel were eager to leave. They bade good-bye to the Land of Short Grasses. At first light they saddled their horses, reined their mounts north, and rode into the face of a dream.

*(*CROW *and* WEASEL *are alone on stage.* WEASEL *is "fired,"* CROW's *a little worried as they "ride.")*

WEASEL: I can't believe we're doing this! Look at us! Riding North, Crow!

CROW: I feel uneasy about this.

WEASEL: Uneasy? What for? I'm not afraid of what's out there.

CROW: I don't know why Mountain Lion chose me to go.

WEASEL: Don't worry about it. He chose you. Enjoy it. Did you see the way everyone was watching us?

CROW: You I can understand, Weasel. You make sense for a journey like this. You trap well. You ride well. Your arrows always fly straight.

WEASEL: You're good at a lot of things, Crow.

CROW: Really? You think so?

WEASEL: Of course, you are. I just can't think of what those things are at the moment. . . .

CROW: I'm not a good hunter, like you.

WEASEL: You're a pretty good tracker.

CROW: No, I'm not, Weasel. I don't track well at all. I stumble on food if I'm lucky.

WEASEL: Well, maybe you're good at luck then.

CROW: Mountain Lion must have had reason to send me—I just wish I knew what it was.

WEASEL: Maybe he sees things in you, you don't see in yourself.

(As the sun sets, NARRATORS *enter.)*

NARRATOR #2: In the evening they made a small fire and lay themselves down on the prairie to rest.

NARRATOR #6: Birds described the air as a consciousness above them.

NARRATOR #5: They began to hear voices. New voices. New creatures were calling.

(Night sounds. A little eerie. . . . The MUSIC *gives us the sound of unfamiliar birds, of owls.)*

WEASEL: Crow?

CROW: Yes, Weasel?

WEASEL: *(Sitting up.)* How can you sleep at a time like this?

CROW: I shut my eyes, Weasel.

WEASEL: Of course, of course . . . *(Beat.)* I can't believe we're doing this.

*(The "*BIRDS*" call several times. *WEASEL *imitates their voices with a more "real-istic" owl call. He's good at it. They call back and forth to each other two times.)*

CROW: Weasel?

WEASEL: What?

CROW: What are they saying to you?

WEASEL: I don't know. They're just talking.

CROW: What kind of birds are they? I've never heard voices like that before.

WEASEL: Well, maybe they're not really birds.

CROW: What do you mean?

WEASEL: I mean we've been traveling for some time, and we've seen no signs of any *living* creatures at all. Why would that be? There's good grass here and plenty of berries. So why would no people be living here, Crow?

CROW: I don't know, Weasel.

WEASEL: Perhaps, it's the Land of the Dead.

*(The "*BIRD VOICES*" call again . . .)*

CROW: Do you mean these voices are dead people's spirits?

WEASEL: I don't know. Maybe.

CROW: Dead people's spirits are living right here? Watching us?

WEASEL: Possibly.

*(More "*BIRD*" calls . . . *WEASEL *answers them. *CROW's *wide awake.)*

CROW: I wonder what sign we will see when we've come far enough?

WEASEL: We'll worry about that after we're over the river.

*(As the moon becomes the sun . . . The *NARRATORS *bring on several large pieces of cloth—the "River." *CROW *and *WEASEL *continue their travels.)*

NARRATOR #1: The boys journeyed for many days. Up and over the ribs of the earth.

NARRATOR #3: Past the Sweet Berry Hills and onto the Land of Blue Buffalo Grass.

NARRATOR #5: Until far, far away in the distance—

NARRATOR #6: They saw a great river.

NARRATOR #5: Flowing like blood on the land.

*(The "River" is made by all the *NARRATORS, *holding three or four pieces of blue cloth. Each piece of cloth is, say, three feet wide and almost as long as the stage is wide. There are poles on each end, so the *NARRATORS *can make the river undulate, wave when they need to . . .)*

WEASEL: Look, Crow: the water.

NARRATOR #7: The river was Covered with Ashes.

NARRATORS #4 & 7: *Floating with Ashes.*

CROW: This must be the water that Mountain Lion saw in his dream.

WEASEL: Are you ready to cross?

CROW: I'll tell you the truth, Weasel: part of me wants to go home.

WEASEL: There's nothing to be afraid of.

CROW: Only death, Weasel.

WEASEL: It's only a river. I admit it's a little blacker than I expected and wider—but don't you want to know what's on the other side?

CROW: *(Truly nervous.)* I'm not feeling terribly curious just now.

WEASEL: Do you know how to swim?

CROW: No.

WEASEL: Well then, you better hold onto your horse. *(And with that, WEASEL steps into the "River"—it's colder than he expected. The cloth undulates beneath him.)* Hai! Hai! Hai! Hai!

CROW: *(Calling.)* Are you all right, Weasel?!

WEASEL: *(Calling.)* Come on, Crow! I'm fine! Stay upstream of your horse!

> *(CROW takes a big breath, and steps into the "River" as well. WEASEL's crossing is comparatively easy. CROW, on the other hand, is petrified, and seems to feel something pulling him under.)*

CROW: *(Almost a high pitched whisper.)* Upstream. Hai-hai-hai-hai-hai . . . !!!

ALL NARRATORS: The black water bubbled around them—

NARRATOR #1: The fast water carried Crow farther—

NARRATOR #3: And farther—

NARRATOR #5: And farther downstream!—

NARRATOR #4: Crow felt himself sinking!—

> *(MUSIC, of course, is rising . . .)*

WEASEL: *Hold onto your horse, Crow!*

CROW: *I'm freezing!*

WEASEL: *Keep your head up! We're almost across!* (CROW *is almost frozen with fear*—WEASEL *bursts clear of the water.* CROW's *face is tilted high, as he gasps for air . . . and the "River" wraps around and around him, tangling him in the cloth.* WEASEL *calls.)* Crow?!?

CROW: *(To himself.)* Breathe . . . ! Breathe . . . !

> *(And finally, after a harrowing moment,* CROW, *too, is "released," almost "thrust" from the "River." The* RIVER PEOPLE *exit . . . as)*

WEASEL: *(Elated.)* We made it! We made it!

CROW: We're still alive?

WEASEL: *Look at this land!* Look around you, Crow! We are the very first people to ever set foot here! Someday, I tell you, our village will sing about this!

(WEASEL is "fired," CROW is still on his knees, still struggling to regain both his breath and composure.)

CROW: I suppose they might, Weasel.

WEASEL: I told you there was nothing to worry about! Come on! Let's keep moving! I want to go North!

CROW: Just wait for a moment.

WEASEL: Why? Did you hurt yourself? What are you doing? *(Beat.* CROW *remains on his knees.)* Crow? Come on. What are you thinking about?

CROW: I'm not thinking; I'm praying.

(Beat.)

WEASEL: Of course, of course.

CROW: We should offer our prayers to the Ones Who Live Above Us.

(As the BOYS pray . . . The dark line of the forest appears in the distance, as if lowered from the sky. The trees are huge. We see only their trunks. Mottled light, forest light. TREE MUSIC . . . WIND . . .)

CROW: Weasel: listen. What is that crying sound, Weasel?

WEASEL: It's only the wind, Crow.

CROW: The air's growing cooler.

WEASEL: And moister.

CROW: Have you ever seen trees so tall?

WEASEL: This is a very strange world. *(Beat.)* If this forest is even halfway as wide as the Land of Short Grasses, I don't think we'll ever come out of it. Crow, we could go home right now, and people would still sing about us.

CROW: It'd be a short song, Weasel. *(WEASEL "looks" at him.)* Besides, I'm not too anxious to cross that black water again. A few days ago, when we were swimming our horses across, I felt something in the water come up around me.

WEASEL: What?

CROW: It took hold of my legs, and it tried to pull me under.

WEASEL: Why didn't you tell me?

CROW: Because I'm still trying to understand what it was. I don't know if it was something in the river, or something in me. Do you understand?

WEASEL: Something like that, you just get away from it! The water, that's not your place.

CROW: Whatever it was, I don't want to fight it again.

(Beat. Sounds of the forest seem to grow just a touch in intensity. A WOODPECKER hammers. A light mist or fog has slowly been settling over the forest floor as they've traveled. The NARRATORS might be "frozen" in place as if they are parts of the trees—the sense is that they blend into the forest, that this is their world.)

WEASEL: Crow? Which way is south?

CROW: I think north is that way.

WEASEL: No. No, I think you're all turned around, Crow. North is up that way—south is back here.

CROW: But we came from that direction.

WEASEL: We did not.

CROW: We did.

WEASEL: *(Looking up, turning around.)* Look: where's the sun?

CROW: Where do you think it is?

WEASEL: *(Short-tempered.)* I don't know, Crow! I can't see in these trees.

CROW: Have you lost your sense of direction? A great tracker, like you?

WEASEL: I'm not actually lost. I just don't know quite where I'm going.

CROW: That's reassuring.

WEASEL: Not that I want to turn back, of course.

(CROW takes the pipe bag out during the speech below.)

CROW: I keep thinking about who these trees are. And how long they've been here. I think if Mountain Lion was lost along with us, he'd try to speak to them.

WEASEL: I told you: we're not really lost. Only a little confused.

(As CROW holds the pipe bag in his hands, MUSIC sneaks in—a "Song of the Pipe." CROW holds the pipe bag with two hands, lifting it carefully above his head. The pipe is never taken out of the bag. Smoke rises upstage as a sort of a visual "emblem" of the pipe, but the boys don't smoke the pipe, itself. CROW speaks to the trees. This is some serious prayer.)

CROW: My relatives: hear me. My brother Weasel and I have come from the ribs of the earth. We have never seen creatures like you. We can see that you are old, and we know that you must be very wise. Please: take pity on us. Please: tell us what trail this is we are on (WEASEL *looks at the trees, looks at* CROW—*it isn't working* . . . CROW *continues—more intense* . . .) My relatives: hear me. We are young men trying to understand the world.

(And now we hear voices, voices like a wind, only stronger, fuller.)

TREES: Lissssten . . . Lissssten . . . Lissssten to the wind . . . *(Voices building to perfect unison.)* You, young men . . . You are brave to come here . . . You have traveled far, we know . . . But you have farther to go . . .

CROW: We need your wisdom.

TREES: All Things That Are Known Everywhere On The Earth Come To Us, On The Wind. We Know Of Mountain Lion's Dream, Which Came To Us Too, On The Wind. We Have Been Expecting You, Weasel. Crow.

WEASEL: *(Whispers, amazed.)* They know our names . . .

CROW: Our fathers and mothers: with your help we will travel as far as the edge of the forest.

WEASEL: How will we know when our journey is over?

TREES: Be Patient. Be Strong. Pay Attention. Yellow-Shafted Flicker Will Show You The Way.

(And with that, YELLOW-SHAFTED FLICKER appears high above them in the forest. It is an effigy—possibly a yellow feather—on a long pole, controlled by an ACTOR. FLICKER calls.)

TREES: *(Echoing, fading.)* Lissssten . . . Lissssten . . . Lissssten to the world . . .

(FLICKER calls, a beautiful sound, a benediction.)

WEASEL: *(Sees/hears the bird.)* Yellow-shafted Flicker.

CROW: Wah-hey.

(The BOYS follow FLICKER through shafts of light in the forest.)

WEASEL: Follow her.

CROW: Where is she, Weasel?

WEASEL: Right there. *(SHE calls. THEY follow.)* No, over there. Over here . . . !

CROW: Wait . . . ! *(And, as THEY follow FLICKER, a small person called MOUSE appears. MOUSE is a fierce, but friendly little person. SHE carries a small traveling bag. CROW sees MOUSE first. Everyone's on edge—a little frightened of each other.)* Weasel?

WEASEL: Yes?

CROW: *(Concerned.)* Weasel . . . !

(WEASEL sees MOUSE. WEASEL immediately draws his knife.)

MOUSE: Hello, boys.

WEASEL: *(Brandishing the knife.)* We come in peace.

MOUSE: Good! Good! I'm a peaceful person. I take it you two are traveling . . . ?

CROW: North.

MOUSE: North! North! How interesting—north? Why would you want to go north? It's cold in the north. I'm going west myself. I'm on a vision quest. West.

WEASEL: We are trying to go to the Place Where Dreams Come From.

MOUSE: Really? How interesting. North . . . ?

WEASEL: *(Boasting a bit.)* We've already come farther than anyone else has before.

MOUSE: Except for me, of course. And all those who live here.

WEASEL: Yes, but we plan to keep going.

MOUSE: Well good! That's very good, Weasel! I'm traveling a long ways myself. Among my people—the Mouse People—

CROW: Yes?

MOUSE: West is the direction we fear the most.

WEASEL: West?

MOUSE: And so, that's the direction we follow when we go on a vision quest. We travel very far, indeed: then we go to a high place and fast. And fast. And fast. And wait for a dream, you see?

CROW: Yes.

MOUSE: Fear. Follow. Fast. Dream.

CROW: Mouse, what you have set out to do is not easy.

MOUSE: Oh, no, it's quite difficult, Crow. But you need a strong vision to give your life direction. Don't you agree? Mouse People believe that we measure the world by our stories, but we measure a Mouse by his dream. It's not easy to lead a good life.

WEASEL: (*Not quite "dismissively."*) My Mother often says the same thing.

MOUSE: Well, then, your mother is wise indeed, Weasel. To have a good family. To live among friends. To be truthful instead of clever with people. I don't know about you, boys, but that's all I want. Simple, simple, simple— but easy? *Hah!!*

CROW: Are you hungry, Mouse? Would you like to camp with us?

MOUSE: I'm fasting, so no, I won't eat. But I'll rest awhile, yes.

WEASEL: I'll start a fire.

(MOUSE *sits.* WEASEL *takes a "fire drill" out of his traveling sack and attempts to start a fire.*)

MOUSE: Ah, but it's good to have company, boys. What is that stick there you're struggling with?

WEASEL: We call it a fire drill.

MOUSE: I see the drill, Weasel, but where is the fire?

WEASEL: Be patient, Mouse.

MOUSE: Be patient, he says. Oh, he's a wise one, this Weasel. Wise indeed.

CROW: He'll get it started.

MOUSE: Well, of course he will, yes—the only question is when? (WEASEL *looks at* MOUSE. MOUSE *offers a piece of flint.*) You might like to try starting a fire with this.

CROW: What is it?

WEASEL: A rock?

MOUSE: Oh, it's not just a rock—it's a fire stone, Weasel. You'll find that it's quite efficacious. If I might be so presumptuous . . .

WEASEL: (*Certain it won't work.*) Please, go ahead. Try.

MOUSE: One merely strikes the stone, so, and: (*Fire light leaps to life.* CROW *and* WEASEL *are duly amazed.*) Hah!

CROW: Fire . . . ! Mouse . . . !

MOUSE: Simple.

WEASEL: What kind of magic is in that rock?

MOUSE: (*Handing him the stone.*) Oh, it's not magic—it's flint, Weasel.

WEASEL: Flint?

MOUSE: It's amazing, efficient, and oftentimes comforting, yes—but, no, it's not magic. It's useful, that's all. Everything has its own medicine.

CROW: Yes.

(As WEASEL *starts to hand the fire stone back.*)

MOUSE: No, no. Please. Keep it. I'd like you boys to have it.

WEASEL: Thank you very much, Mouse.

MOUSE: You're quite welcome. North, of all directions . . . ? Try to stay warm, boys.

CROW: That's very kind of you.

(CROW *and* WEASEL *exchange gifts with* MOUSE *by the Fire Light, becoming shadow-like, as . . . Several* NARRATORS *enter holding what we will eventually see to be "*HORSE FIGURES*." During this section of the story, the* TREES *will slowly and silently disappear.* MOUSE *exits. Only the* NARRATORS' *faces are lit. A single "yellow-shafted" feather floats to earth during this section.*)

NARRATOR #5: At the beginning of the Red Berry Moon—and how odd this was, they thought, for the Red Berry Moon would have already come and gone if they were at home.

NARRATOR #4: But the North Moons were different. As if Time, itself, were breathing and stretching its arms.

NARRATOR #5: And *why* were the Moon and the seasons so strange here, they wondered?

NARRATOR #4: It was during what they *thought of* as the Red Berry Moon that finally Crow and Weasel began to emerge from the trees.

NARRATOR #2: The air was immediately warmer and dryer.

NARRATOR #3: The ground felt much firmer.

NARRATORS #4 & 5: It felt good to be free of the trees.

(CROW *and* WEASEL *are now on the tundra.* YELLOW-SHAFTED FLICKER *calls.* CROW *holds a yellow-shafted feather.*)

CROW: (*Looking up.*) Yellow-shafted Flicker! Wherever we go we will always remember you. Thank you for guiding us here. We wear your feathers with pride, little sister.

(YELLOW-SHAFTED FLICKER *sounds a "good-bye."* CROW *places the feather in his "hair." As the* BIRD *"exits," its sweet voice an echo . . .*)

NARRATOR #3: The landscape before them was much like the Land of Short Grasses, but different.

NARRATOR #2: They could see for many miles.

NARRATORS #4 & 5: And their horses were eager to run, to stretch out.

CROW: (*Talking to his "horse."*) Easy, boy; easy . . .

WEASEL: Crow? Do you see that mound of blue rock over there?

CROW: The close one or far?

WEASEL: The blue rock, way in the distance. A full look away.

CROW: Easy, boy . . .

WEASEL: I could be wrong, Crow, but I think that my horse might reach that blue rock before your colt is even close to it.

(NARRATORS #2 *and* #3 *wrap a piece of cloth around* CROW's *and* WEASEL's *midsection, so that the boys can lean forward, supported by the* NARRATORS—*as if leaning/riding into the wind. Lights grow brighter, sharper. The other* NARRATORS *hold their respective* HORSE FIGURES *high, strong—downstage in front of the boys.*)

NARRATOR #3: Crow looked at Weasel—

NARRATOR #2: And Weasel at Crow—

NARRATORS #4 & 5: And with that, they started to fly!

(The HORSE FIGURES/NARRATORS circle around downstage, running, racing as CROW and WEASEL lean into the wind, supported by NARRATORS #2 and #3. MUSIC gives us a race.)

NARRATORS #2 & 3: They rode across the tundra like two racing winds! Flying north—Galloping—Faster—And faster they flew! Until:

(WEASEL and CROW fall to the floor, as if they just tumbled from their HORSES, just finished their "race." They're both out of breath, both "fired" from racing.)

WEASEL: Whooooaaaa . . . ! Crow! I think your horse is more seasoned than mine. It's a very strong colt. I'm impressed with him.

CROW: But, Weasel, you *won* the race . . . !

WEASEL: Yes. I did.

CROW: Well, you stinking defecation of a sick calf.

(CROW leaps on WEASEL—they wrestle.)

WEASEL: Now, Crow.

CROW: My horse is faster, but you won the race?

WEASEL: Let me tell you something, Crow: choosing a good horse is much like selecting a wife.

CROW: A wife? Is that so?

(CROW laughs. They stop wrestling.)

WEASEL: What I mean is you have to watch for more than only good looks in a horse. I know you like the Appaloosa pattern and spots on the ears. But a man wants a horse that stays calm when you're hunting, that rides well at night—and not just a fast horse or merely good-looking.

CROW: Selecting a wife, Weasel? What do you know about women?

WEASEL: Plenty! I know plenty! I know more than you do . . . !

CROW: Well, that's not too difficult, Weasel. I don't know a thing.

WEASEL: You're more frightened of women than I am.

(Beat.)

CROW: This could be true. But I thought we were talking about horses.

(WEASEL notices a print on the ground.)

WEASEL: Crow. This is interesting. The hoof mark is something like an elk.

CROW: *(Looks.)* Look stronger. It's not an elk, Weasel. Its toes curl in further.

(During the speech below: Several NARRATORS enter—either dressed as CARIBOU, wearing an "effigistic" caribou mask. They move like the CARIBOU: graceful, strong, timid, precise. They are beautiful and otherworldly, and yet of this world completely.)

WEASEL: From the way it places its foot, I think it might be a food animal, Crow. But I've never seen anything like it.

CROW: *(Looking up.)* I've seen it.

WEASEL: You've seen this animal? Where?

CROW: There. *(And now WEASEL, too, sees the CARIBOU. He immediately, carefully reaches for his bow, and CROW hands him an arrow. THEY WHISPER.)* Move slowly. Don't scare them away.

WEASEL: They move like deer, only different.

CROW: Why don't they run from us? Why aren't they frightened?

WEASEL: I don't know, Crow.

CROW: Maybe they've never seen people like us before.

WEASEL: Maybe they've never been hunted before.

(As WEASEL notches an arrow, CROW addresses the CARIBOU with great respect.)

CROW: Animal With Antlers: we do not know your name. But my brother and I are far away from home, and we need strength such as this to help us survive.

(The LEAD CARIBOU takes a step forward.)

WEASEL: *(Addresses the animal.)* Please, tell us: Do you wish to be hunted?

(The LEAD CARIBOU seems to bow her head in their direction. The sound of the CARIBOU, a sound like the tapping of hooves on the tundra, heightens this moment. WEASEL pulls his bow taught . . .)

CROW: Release it . . . !

(A NARRATOR takes WEASEL's arrow, and arching it through the air, says . . .)

NARRATOR #3: The arrow flew strong and straight. It rose, and it fell into caribou's heart. And the animal gave them its life.

(The LEAD CARIBOU takes the arrow from the NARRATOR, as if the animal is taking it into itself. The CARIBOU slowly "folds," its knees gracefully buckle, beginning to sink towards the earth, as . . .)

CROW: What have we done . . . ?!

WEASEL: I found its heart! Perfect shot!

CROW: I hope that this animal's journey was to us. I hope it was trying to get to us.

(The CARIBOU rises from its "folded" position, and presents them with a bundle of its hide—and in that bundle is a vertebrae necklace which WEASEL will put on during the NARRATION which follows, and also a long sinew. The sense here is that the boys cut the animal "open," peering into the hide.)

NARRATOR #1: They skinned and dressed the animal carefully. They inspected the way its bones fit together. They studied the contents of its stomach. Where the heart was. The color of its lungs. For they wanted not only to nourish themselves with this creature, they wanted to learn it.

NARRATOR #3: The caribou gave them much more than knowledge and food.

NARRATOR #1: From its hide the boys made a warm robe.

NARRATOR #3: A long thread from its sinews. From the caribou's bones they formed eating utensils.

NARRATOR #1: And weapons. (As NARRATOR #3 *takes the folded hide to a high place upstage and presents it once again to the waiting* LEAD CARIBOU.) That evening they gathered its bones and placed them on a sandy ledge near the place where the caribou gave them the gift of its life.

NARRATOR #3: And in that way their journey continued.

NARRATOR #1: The caribou's spirit propelled them across the tundra. Past a country of many lakes. Over the breast of the earth and up the shallow hills. Until they had traveled so far to the North that the sun, itself, stayed in the sky all night long. They felt they had come to the eyes of the world.

(*Sounds of the Arctic . . . distant birds, and eerie emptiness about the land. And a feeling of "ice," and of "dreams." This is Skyscape we are in—all light is side light, and eerie.*)

WEASEL: This is a very strange sky we're in. I am tempted to say it's like this or like that, but, truly, it is only like itself.

CROW: The way the Sun circles beside us—it seems to be watching us all the time, Weasel.

WEASEL: I know.

CROW: I think we've come close to the Place Where Daylight Is Born.

WEASEL: Even my dreams here are strange. For three nights in a row—or at least I assume it was night—I've dreamed about a bear coming into our camp.

CROW: I dreamed of that woman at home, who sleeps in the lodge next to yours.

WEASEL: The one they call Crow Wing Girl?

CROW: I'm in a deep river, drowning. She pulls on a long rope attached to my waist. But I'm stuck, I can't move. Then I begin pulling on the line, and when I pull myself onto the shore, she is standing there with two small white buffalo calves.

WEASEL: You need to tell this dream to one of the older men at home.

CROW: But it's about women. Maybe if we understood the women's songs, we would know what to make of this dream.

WEASEL: I wish we were older.

CROW: I wish we were wiser.

WEASEL: If between us we can't understand our own dreams, then how will we know when we've come far enough? What if there's already *been* a sign, Crow? . . . ! What if the sign is right here, and we don't understand it?!

CROW: Mountain Lion said we will know.

WEASEL: (*Truly afraid.*) I can't tell day from night! I don't know north from south!

(MUSIC *changes. They are in a dream.*)

CROW: I dream of a hot, sandy country.

WEASEL: Thorn bushes. Rattlesnakes . . . !

CROW: I ride—

WEASEL: We ride—

CROW & WEASEL: —in a long narrow canyon. A strange people are attacking us! (CROW *speaks only the underlined words in the next section.*) They wear an<u>imal skins—sharp nails</u>—are <u>raking me, scratching me</u>! They're <u>biting</u> biting <u>biting the horses!</u>

WEASEL: They tear at the horses!

CROW: I see the sky through them!

CROW & WEASEL: Tearing us! Pulling our skin off!—

WEASEL: Our feet off, our—

CROW: *(Waking.)* Stop! We must stop!

WEASEL: *(Waking.)* We have dreamt the same dream!

(Behind the dream: Thunder tolls in the distance. And other sounds, too: a rising wind, and a sound like birds screeching.)

CROW: This dark breath we have taken—this dream is a sign! What lies beyond us is not light, but darkness!

WEASEL: Is this dream our vision?

(The wind is sharp. CROW's *medicine bundle flies from his hands high upstage—he catches it just before it hits the ground.)*

CROW: *Our medicine!*

WEASEL: Crow!

*(*CROW *is on his knees with his medicine bundle in his hands; all this—the confluence of the dream and the weather, and the catching of the medicine bundle—has happened in fluid motion.)*

CROW: We have come far enough! Here is the place we turn home! *(The sky opens . . . we hear* SINGING. *Inuit voices. But the voices and the songs are so foreign as to seem otherworldly. As a huge boat, a "Umiak," is paddled by the Inuit people straight downstage through the sky. As if the sky is a river. As if they are floating on air. Note: the* INUIT PEOPLE *might wear masks, "neutral" masks—blank human faces . . . The* YOUNG MEN *stand transfixed now and frightened.)* Weasel. My friend?? Are we truly awake?

WEASEL: I have never seen anything like this.

CROW: They move on the water—they walk on the water . . . !

WEASEL: No fur! They have no fur or feathers, Crow!!

CROW: What kind of animals are they?!

(And now the INUIT *see* THEM. *And the* INUIT *are afraid of* CROW *and* WEASEL.)*

INUIT WOMAN #1: *(Calling her husband's name, frightened.)* Aua!!—Aua!! *(AH-oo-ah.)*

INUIT MAN #1: *("Two-headed monsters.")* Marruunnik niaquliit tuurngait!

WEASEL: They've seen us . . . !

INUIT ELDER: *Inuit? Inuit?*

INUIT MAN #2 & WOMAN #2: *("No!")* Naaggaa!! *(Naah-GAH.)*

INUIT WOMAN #3: *("One looks like a black bird.")* Ilangat tingmiangujaaqtuq kiniqtaq.

INUIT MAN #3: *("I've never seen anything like them.")* Taimaittunik takulausi-manngitiaqtunga.

(WEASEL *holds his lance high, ready to use it. The* INUIT ELDER *raises a huge pair of walrus tusks—Teeth—above his head. They are long, and they are sharp. Everyone is petrified of everyone else.*)

WEASEL: These are the creatures that Mountain Lion dreamed of!

INUIT ELDER: *("Those aren't people!")* Inuit—naagga!!

CROW: Look at their teeth, Weasel!!

INUIT WOMAN #1: *("Is it Raven?")* Aua? Tulugauva?

INUIT ELDER: *("No")* Naagga!

INUIT MAN #1: *("Two-headed monsters.")* Marruuunik niaquliit tuurngait!

CROW: Look at those teeth!

WEASEL: If we must die, they will die along with us.

CROW: There is no need to fight them . . . ! *(Definite.)* Lower your lance, Weasel. *Lower your lance!*

(*The tone changes as* WEASEL *lowers his lance. The* INUIT *speak among themselves, then row forwards onto the stage.*)

INUIT MAN #3: *(The name of a monster.)* Tupilak? *(tuh-PI-lahk.)*

INUIT MAN #1: Tuurngait?

INUIT WOMAN #1: Tulugaaq?

INUIT WOMAN #2: *("A two-headed weasel!")* Marruunnik Niaqulik tiriaq!

(*The space between* CROW *and* WEASEL *and the* INUIT PEOPLE *is "charged." The* INUIT PEOPLE *talk frantically, taking counsel among themselves—gesturing toward* CROW *and* WEASEL. *As, over this* INUIT *talk . . .*)

CROW: What language is this? What are they saying?!

WEASEL: I want to go home, Crow.

CROW: We will.

WEASEL: If we live . . . !

INUIT ELDER: *(Defining first himself, then his people.)* Inuk! Inuk! *(EE-nuk.)* Inuit!

(*As the* ELDER *climbs out and approaches them,* CROW *makes a gesture of vulnerability—trying to communicate.*)

CROW: We come in peace.

(*The* INUIT *look at each other—"What is he saying?"*)

INUIT MAN #2: *("What are you doing?")* Kisu?

INUIT MAN #1: *("What is that thing?")* Suva?

INUIT ELDER: *(Naming them, "Raven" and "Weasel.")* Tulugaaq! Tiriaq!

INUIT WOMAN #1: (*Almost whispers, "That's no monster."*) Tupilak . . . naaggaa.

CROW: (*Formal, and clear.*) My brother Weasel and I come from a land far away to the south. Our people have dreamed about you. We mean you no harm.

INUIT ELDER: (*Tries again.*) Inuk! Inuk! Inuit!

WEASEL: What kind of creatures are you?

INUIT ELDER: (*Impatient.*) Inuit! Inuit!

CROW: My name is Crow. I am Crow.

INUIT WOMAN #2: (*"Who?"*) Kina?

INUIT ELDER: Crow?

WEASEL: And I'm Weasel.

INUIT WOMAN #1: (*What a funny name.*) Weasel?

(*The* INUIT *howl with laughter, repeating their names and pointing.*)

INUIT PEOPLE: —Weasel?!—Weasel?!—Crow!??—Weeeeeeeeeasel!??

WEASEL: These people sure have a unique odor, don't they?

CROW: Yes. So do we.

WEASEL: They stink, Crow.

(INUIT WOMAN #1 *makes a circle in the air with her hand, meaning "family."*)

INUIT WOMAN #1: Ilagiit.

(*The* ELDER *opens his arms wide. He likes these guys.*)

INUIT ELDER: (*"Welcome."*) Tunngasugit, Crow!

INUIT WOMAN #1: Tunngasugit, Wea-sell!

(*The* INUIT *have all piled out of their boat; they bring an animal skin bag of food, and offer a delicacy for* CROW *and* WEASEL *to eat. It's called "muktuk," and it is a small square of whale skin and blubber.*)

INUIT WOMAN #2: (*"Eat, eat!"*) Nirigissik! Nirigissik!

INUIT WOMAN #3: (*"Ah, you eat, yes?"*) Ah, nirigit—ii?

INUIT MAN #3: Maktaaq (*MUHK-tuk.*)! Atii!

INUIT WOMAN #2: (*"Eat, eat!"*) Nirigissik! Nirigissik!

INUIT ELDER: (*"Muktuk! Welcome to you both!"*) Maktaaq! Tunngasuktipassik!

INUIT WOMAN #1: (*"Muktuk! Good!"*) Maktaaq! Piujuq?

(*The* INUIT, *of course, make very definite "eating" gestures, leaving* CROW *and* WEASEL *with little choice.*)

INUIT MAN #3: (*"Muktak. Eat. Welcome. Yes."*) Maktaaq. Nirigissik. Tunnga-suktipassik. Atii.

CROW: This is food?

INUIT WOMAN #1: Food! Food! Nirigit! Nirigit!

(CROW *and* WEASEL *eat "muktuk." The* INUIT *pound them on their backs.*)

INUIT ELDER: (*"Friends, welcome!"*) Crow! Weasel! Piqatikka! Tunngasugitti!

INUIT PEOPLE: —Piqatikka!—Piqatikka!—Tunngasugitti!—Piujuq!—Piujuq!—Ilagiit!—Atii!—Atii, Crow!—Atii, Weasel!

WEASEL: *(Has crossed away.)* Crow? Can I speak to you for a moment? Here, please?

CROW: *(Crossing to him.)* Yes, Weasel?

(As CROW and WEASEL talk, the INUIT unload more supplies from their umiak, including some marvelous drums. As they work, we hear words like "Kina" [who?], "Sura" [what?], and "Kisu" [what are you doing?]. WEASEL tries to find a way to spit his muktuk out without drawing attention to himself.)

WEASEL: This muktuk tastes terrible!

CROW: They're friendly. They mean well.

WEASEL: It's rancid! It's awful!

CROW: Don't spit it out, Weasel . . . ! They mean it as a gift.

WEASEL: I know it. I'm sorry. It just tastes so bad.

CROW: These are the most interesting people.

WEASEL: Well, they're not very smart, Crow. They don't talk like us. They smell, and I'm sorry, but I find them ugly.

CROW: They're different, that's all. They're not bad.

INUIT ELDER: Crow? Weasel? Maktaaq?

INUIT WOMAN #1: Nirigit?

WEASEL: Crow, don't make me eat any more of that rancid meat, please.

CROW: We should offer a gift in return.

INUIT WOMAN #1: *("Friends.")* Maktaaq? Piqatikka!

(INUIT MAN #3 is trying to make a fire with a fire drill.)

WEASEL: I know what to give them.

CROW: What?

WEASEL: *(The fire stone.)* I have something useful in mind.

INUIT WOMAN #1: Maktaaq?

WEASEL: No, thank you. (WEASEL *approaches* INUIT MAN #3, *the "fire-maker."*) Excuse me.

INUIT WOMAN #1: *("What about you?")* Maktaaq?

CROW: *(Refusing, crossing to Weasel.)* We appreciate the offer.

WEASEL: Inuk? Inuk? Can I help with the fire?

INUIT MAN #3: *("No, no, it's only the wind.")* Naagga, naagga, naagga. Anuriinna.

WEASEL: I think that you'll find this quite useful. It was given to me by an efficacious Mouse. (WEASEL *makes a gesture for "mouse."*) Mouse.

INUIT ELDER: *("A lemming?")* A vingaq?

INUIT MAN #3: *("What?")* Kisu?

CROW: Watch.

WEASEL: You hold it like this—strike the stone, so, and . . .

(The Fire Light leaps to life. The INUIT *are truly amazed.)*

INUIT MAN #3: *("Lightning!")* Kalliq!

INUIT MAN #2: *("Spark.")* Auma?

WEASEL: Fire! Yes, fire—it makes sparks, you see?

INUIT ELDER: Weasel, Weasel, Weasel! *("An amazing stone.")* Kamanaqtuq ujarak.

INUIT WOMAN #1: *("Fire.")* Ikuma . . .

WEASEL: Flint.

INUIT MAN #3: *(Mispronouncing.)* Plint.

WEASEL: *(Correcting.)* Flint.

INUIT MAN #3: Flint.

(The INUIT PEOPLE *"memorize" the flint by touching its every contour, tasting it, etc., passing it among themselves.)*

INUIT PEOPLE:—Flint.—Auma.—Kamanaqtuq ujarak.

WEASEL: No, keep it. Please. Truly. Crow and I would like you to have it.

INUIT MAN #3: *("Thank you.")* Qujannamiik. Qujannamiik!

INUIT WOMAN #1: *(A pronouncement: "Friends. Family. Welcome.")* Weasel. Crow. Piqatikka! Ilagiit!

(A drum is played and the INUIT *begin to prepare for a dance. As dancing begins, bullroarers are swung above the men's heads—making an incredible sound. A bowl of fire is lit. They dance the story of Sedna. The* INUIT *dance/sing this story in their own language. It is a sacred story for them. Sedna, a child, goes to sea with her father. Her father grows angry and throws her from his boat. She clings to the boat. He cuts off her fingers, and her fingers become the seals. And so, Sedna, the child, is the Mother of Seals, the giver of food and of life.* CROW *and* WEASEL *watch with respect, and eventually might even join in the dancing. Time seems to pass, the sky is changing, growing towards a twilight. And as the song ends: We see the Northern Lights.* EVERYONE *falls silent and looks at the sky. Some of the* INUIT *open their arms to it and welcome its presence into their lives. A distant wind begins to blow . . .)*

INUIT ELDER: *("The sky, the sun, the stars.")* Qila, siqiniq, ulluriat.

CROW: Ulluriat. The sky's changing, atii.

WEASEL: The weather grows cold.

INUIT ELDER: *("The northern lights.")* Aqsarniit.

INUIT WOMAN #1: *("Winter is coming. Ice.")* Ukiuliqtuq. Siku.

INUIT ELDER: *("Yes. Ice.")* Ii. Siku.

CROW: Siku. Ice?

ALL OTHER INUIT PEOPLE: *(Not in unison.)* Ii. Ii. Siku.

CROW: Weasel: they pray to the Ones Above.

*(*INUIT MAN #3 *gives the* ELDER *a gift to present to* CROW *and* WEASEL*. A beautiful knife, carved from the tusk of a walrus—it glistens in the light. The knife carries a sound with it. We will come to see that this knife is inlaid with figures that represent an* INUIT *creation story.)*

INUIT MAN #3: *("Take this gift home.")* Taanna tunirrut angirrautiliruk.

CROW: We thank the Inuit People for all you have given us. *(A formal "Thank you.")* Qujannamiik.

WEASEL: We will take this gift home to the Animal People. Qujannamiik.

CROW: And with your permission we will tell them the stories you have told us, and the ones you have danced.

INUIT ELDER: *("We honor you.")* Niqsuqpattigit: Crow: Weasel: Niqsuqpattigit.

(A light rises on NARRATOR #5, the same woman who danced the part of SEDNA in the story-dance above. She speaks to us without a mask—the first fully human face we have seen in this story. During the speech below: the lights focus on CROW and WEASEL—leaving the INUIT in "relief," silhouetted behind them; "framed," as it were, by the sky. This NARRATOR picks up the bowl of fire.)

NARRATOR #5: And so, Crow and Weasel had come to the Place Where Winter Is Born, to the Land Where Dreaming Begins. They had traveled a dream, but they still had a long way to journey before they returned to their home.

CROW: We must tell our village of this. Our people will marvel.

WEASEL: The weather is changing.

CROW: I fear the path home will be difficult, Weasel.

NARRATOR #5: For the eyes of the world, they could see, were beginning to grow darker, colder with each passing day.

(SHE blows out the fire.)

END OF ACT ONE

ACT TWO

(Black. Music . . . In dim light, fire light, we find BADGER stirring a pot on a tripod over a fire. As lights rise we see a huge wooden ladder—made of branches—which extends clear up off into a shaft of bright light, into the sky far above. And at the top of that ladder are WEASEL and CROW. We are, of course, under the ground. WEASEL and CROW see BADGER and whisper . . .)

WEASEL: Crow . . .

CROW: Weasel . . .

(BADGER crosses to the foot of the ladder.)

BADGER: You know it's extraordinarily rude to come into somebody's home uninvited.

WEASEL: We just wanted to see what was down in this hole.

BADGER: Well, that would be me.

CROW: And you are?

BADGER: *I'm Badger.* Fortunately, I've been expecting you. Come in. Come down! I'm not going to bite. *(WEASEL starts down. He might slip on one of the rungs.)* Why don't you drop me that traveling sack? I'll catch it.

WEASEL: But—

BADGER: Drop it—I'll catch it. I love to catch things.

WEASEL: Be careful, Badger. It's heavier than it looks to be.

(HE *drops it.* SHE *catches it.*)

BADGER: *(To herself.)* So am I. *(Beat.)* There's nothing to be afraid of! I've heard you two boys coming towards me all day. I hear everything through the ground, you understand.

WEASEL: Everything?

BADGER: Just about everything, yes. Trees growing. Rocks resting. Bugs. Worms. Water. Dreams. Rumors. To tell you the truth, I hear so many things it's hard to keep track of sometimes.

CROW: You can hear *dreams* down here, Badger?

BADGER: I'm familiar with Mountain Lion's vision, if that's what you mean. I hear many dreams in the ground. As I said, I've been expecting you boys for quite some time now. I trust you boys both brought good appetites with you.

WEASEL: I know I did, Badger.

CROW: You prepared a whole meal for us?

BADGER: Oh, I do hope you like it, but if you don't like it, don't worry about it—I'll eat it myself.

CROW: It smells wonderful, Badger.

BADGER: Well what are you waiting for? Dig in and eat! Eat! Good food and a good conversation's the best combination I know.

(CROW *and* WEASEL *eat.* SHE *watches them, ready to offer seconds.*)

CROW: Good. Very good.

WEASEL: This is the best food I've tasted since I don't know when. How can we ever return such a kindness?

BADGER: If you young men can tell me the stories of where you've been, Weasel, and the things you've done and seen, then food or not, I'm the one fuller by far.

WEASEL: You want us to tell you a story?

BADGER: You boys have been North, am I right? (WEASEL *nods.*) I've always wanted to know what it's like up there.

WEASEL: Cold.

BADGER: Cold?

WEASEL: Really cold.

BADGER: Yes, cold, of course it's cold—but what is it like?

WEASEL: Well, it's sort of empty.

CROW: And full.

BADGER: I've had the most intriguing dreams about North. Peopled by creatures that I'm not familiar with.

CROW: You mean the Inuit People?

BADGER: They call themselves Inuit?

CROW: Yes.

WEASEL: We camped with them for many days, Badger.

BADGER: Tell me, please—what are they like? I've heard some interesting rumors about them, but you're the first people I know of to actually meet them.

WEASEL: When Crow and I first saw the Inuit People, we were on horseback and they were in a boat, and all of us started to panic.

BADGER: Why don't you stand up and tell this properly?

WEASEL: What?

BADGER: Stand up, young man. Stand up and express yourself fully. If a story's worth telling, then tell it well. Take a deep breath, and start again, Weasel.

(WEASEL *stands up and clears his throat.* WEASEL's *more than a little nervous, and the fact that* BADGER *continually interrupts him doesn't help things at all.*)

WEASEL: Well, when we first saw the Inuit coming, my horse began rearing and crashed into Crow's horse; and then we saw—

BADGER: Wait, wait, wait—tell me where you were when this happened.

WEASEL: I told you—up north.

BADGER: Yes, north, but where north precisely?

WEASEL: About ten sleeps away. Up by a river.

BADGER: Wait—now, you say they were in a boat?

WEASEL: Yes.

BADGER: What kind of boat was it?

WEASEL: It's made from the skin of a female walrus.

BADGER: Walrus? What is a walrus?

WEASEL: It's kind of like a very round moose with big teeth and no legs. And the Inuit hunt them, but—

BADGER: How do they hunt them?

WEASEL: Well—

BADGER: Tell me more of this. What are they like?

WEASEL: (*Overlapping from "What."*) I'm trying, but—

BADGER: What do they look like exactly?

WEASEL: Well—

BADGER: How do they survive in a place that's so cold?

WEASEL: Well—

BADGER: Traveling stories intrigue me. They always have, really. So, tell me what happens next.

(*Beat.* WEASEL *sits back down.*)

WEASEL: My tongue turns to wood.

BADGER: Then gesture more, use your whole body.

WEASEL: I'm not a good dancer.

CROW: Badger, my friend is trying very hard to tell his story. I can see what you're trying to do. Asking him to call on all the details of his memory and to put the parts together in a pattern that's pleasing.

BADGER: And?

CROW: My friend is quite smart. Let's give Weasel a chance now to finish his thoughts.

WEASEL: Why don't *you* tell her a story?

CROW: Me?

BADGER: Yes! That's a grand idea, Crow! Both of you tell me . . . !

CROW: But, I thought you wanted—

BADGER: *(Sharp, like a teacher.)* Listen! If something of value has happened to you, and you cannot find a dignified way to express it, then what do you have to bring home to your people? Both of you: Answer me that.

(Beat.)

CROW: Show her the knife.

(WEASEL takes the knife out of his traveling sack and carefully unwraps it. Music begins . . . faintly at first, and then growing. The knife carries a sound reminiscent of ice and of dreams . . .)

BADGER: The Inuit gave you a gift?

WEASEL: They're very fine craftsmen. It's made from the tusk of a walrus, you see?

CROW: They've carved many people and places into the handle.

(WEASEL holds the knife before them, glistening in the light. BADGER takes it and admires it. The sound of the dream grows more and more present.)

BADGER: *(In awe.)* Ohhhhh . . . would you look at that? This is a wondrous gift . . . ! What is this? Who are these people they've carved?

WEASEL: Polar Bear People.

CROW: Ringed Seals.

WEASEL: Muskox.

BADGER: The moon and the sea and the stars and the sun. Why, a story of creation is here . . . !

CROW: The Inuit danced for us the story of Sedna; the mother of much of their world.

BADGER: Please. Tell me everything. *(Music swells. CROW and WEASEL dance some of the story of Sedna, using gestures reminiscent of the Inuit dance. Time seems to pass as this happens.)* To care for such sacred stories as this is a great obligation. You young men have been given a task beyond measure.

WEASEL: We hope to carry this home to our people.

BADGER: I would ask you to remember one thing: The stories people tell have a way of taking care of them. If you care for them, they will care for you, too. That is why we place them in each other's memories. Sometimes a person needs a story more than food to stay alive. One day perhaps you will be good storytellers. Never forget these obligations.

(Lights rise on NARRATORS. As BADGER exits, the ladder flies gracefully, easily into the heavens. CROW and WEASEL exit during the narration below.)

NARRATOR #3: The young men found comfort and courage in what Badger taught them.

NARRATOR #2: It was good that they ate well and rested, for that was the last food that Weasel and Crow were to find in a very—

NARRATOR #3: Very—

NARRATOR #2: Very—

NARRATOR #3: Long time.

MOTHER WEASEL: They traveled across the shoulders of the world—across country that had once been mysterious to them, but now many things were familiar.

MOTHER CROW: The storm clouds of winter were chasing them now.

MOTHER WEASEL: Each day the North Wind blew deeper, blew harsher.

MOTHER CROW: Their stomachs were empty.

MOTHER WEASEL: Their clothes were worn thin.

MOTHER CROW: And in spite of the fact they'd traveled this country before, Crow and Weasel saw few signs of food.

MOTHER WEASEL: Until one cold, crisp day, as a snowstorm goose flew in the clouds high above them:

(*Sound of a snow goose as lights rise on the boys looking up at the "bird." *CROW *and *WEASEL *look more than a little bedraggled; this journey has taken its toll on them.*)

CROW: The sight of that bird makes me hungry.

WEASEL: Crow, anything that moves makes me hungry.

CROW: I wish it'd fly low enough to get a good shot at. My stomach is twisted shut.

WEASEL: I'll find something to eat, Crow—don't worry about it.

(*Thunder rumbles in the distance.*)

CROW: You can't find the animals if they don't want you to. Don't be so sure of yourself.

WEASEL: Crow, do me a favor, and don't try to correct every thought that I have.

CROW: I just said—

WEASEL: I have parents at home. I don't need another mother from you.

CROW: I just meant it's not wise to take hunting for granted.

WEASEL: You think I don't know that?

CROW: Don't be so arrogant, Weasel.

WEASEL: Arrogant? You call me arrogant? You're the most arrogant person I know.

CROW: What is that supposed to mean?

WEASEL: You think you know everything, don't you?

CROW: I didn't mean to insult you.

WEASEL: I'm not a child. I know how to hunt. I killed the caribou, didn't I?

(Snow begins falling upstage.)

CROW: Weasel: that animal gave itself to us. It *wanted* to feed us. Don't credit yourself with its life.

(WEASEL pushes CROW, hard.)

WEASEL: That's not what I'm saying.

CROW: Well, that's how it sounded to me.

WEASEL: Let me tell you something, Crow. You'd starve without me, and you know it! I'm twice the hunter you are.

(CROW pushes WEASEL to the ground.)

CROW: No, you're just two times as arrogant!

WEASEL: I can hunt anything.

CROW: How can you say that?

WEASEL: Because I can, Crow!

CROW: *(Low, worried.)* Don't talk like that.

WEASEL: I'll kill a buffalo.

(Thunder rumbles in the distance. The snow fall continues. An icy wind rises.)

CROW: Weasel . . . !

WEASEL: *I will kill buffalo. I will kill.*

(A singular drum begins to sound. Like the heart of the land growing closer. After a moment, CROW quietly says . . .)

CROW: Look, we're both tired and hungry. Let's just try to find our way home.

(The drum beat continues. The snow fall continues. Thunder describes the sky. And the wind gradually grows, as . . . NARRATORS enter.)

NARRATOR #2: The snow kept on falling—

NARRATOR #3: And falling—

NARRATOR #7: And drifting for days.

(NARRATORS #4 and #5 carry the horse figures.)

NARRATOR #4: Their horses were young and inexperienced.

NARRATOR #5: The deeper the snow fell, the more they grew weary.

NARRATOR #2: Until finally Crow and Weasel got down off their horses and attempted to lead their friends home through the high drifting weather.

(NARRATORS #4 and #5 have now "become" HORSES. CROW and WEASEL pull them by reins or by rope, attempting to coax them and lead them through the weather. The wind blows even harder. The snow is still falling.)

CROW: This wind is a knife . . . !

WEASEL: Come on, now. It's alright. Keep walking, Crow.

CROW: Easy, boy.

WEASEL: Come on, girl. Follow me.

NARRATOR #7: With each step they grow thinner. Weaker.

WEASEL: There's no sign of food animals anywhere, Crow.

(*The* NARRATORS *become like an eerie "Voice of the Weather," pounding and pelting the young men with its presence. Voices continue while* CROW *and* WEASEL *talk until otherwise noted.*)

WHISPERING VOICES: No food—No prints—No food—No tracks—No food—
No animals—No food—No fire—No warmth—No food—No animals—

WEASEL: My feet are like rocks . . . ! I feel like the weather is haunting us,
Crow . . . !

CROW: Keep moving. We don't want to freeze.

WEASEL: *This is my fault!* I should never have said what I said about killing
the animals, Crow.

CROW: (*Stopping.*) I must rest.

WEASEL: It was a horrible thing to say! I think all the animals heard me, and
now they have gone away . . . !

(*The whispering voices stop now.* CROW *has sunk down and sits in the snow.* HE
shivers against the cold. As WEASEL *crosses away.*)

CROW: Weasel?

(WEASEL *strips the robe from his body, as he crosses upstage.*)

WEASEL: I wish I could roll the sun backwards and take back the things I
have spoken. *I am not fit to be protected by this!* I know that my heart
has been wrong! (*Framed by the moon,* WEASEL *falls to his knees in the snow.
He begins to pray, taking the clothes from his body, so we see his bare back. He
raises his arms high above him. His back is to the audience. The wind is a terrible howl . . . like the sound of someone who's wounded.*) Ones Who Live Above,
hear me! My relatives, hear me! I bare myself before you to beg your for-
giveness. Please hear my prayer! I will never again act as though I expected the land to feed me. I will remind myself, always, that this is a
gift! I will never again take them for granted! Please, hear my prayer!
My relatives, help me: forgive me: and know of my sorrow . . . ! (CROW
slowly crosses to WEASEL, *puts his robe around him, and silently helps his friend
back to camp. They fall to the ground, and it seems as if they will die here. After
some time in silence . . .* WEASEL *continues in almost a whisper . . .*) There is only
one thing to do now . . . if we do not find food, then we must kill one of
the horses.

CROW: (*After a moment.*) Perhaps in the morning . . .

(*Silence. We assume they will freeze to death here. A shadow falls across the
stage . . . it is a shadow in the shape of a bear. The Moon glows behind him as* GRIZ-
ZLY BEAR *enters, as if casting his shadow before. He is huge, towering high, high
above them. He is a magnificent presence.* GRIZZLY BEAR's *voice is like the sound of
a deep cavern speaking.*)

GRIZZLY BEAR: My friends. You have come a great distance. I know that you
are hungry and cold. I will make a fire and feed you.

(GRIZZLY BEAR *raises his paw and the light of a fire springs to life.*)

WEASEL: *(Weak, whispering.)* Grizzly Bear . . .

CROW: Yes . . .

(As GRIZZLY BEAR *tells them the story that follows, the moon and the Stars become the Sun bright behind him; then they transform into the moon once again. As if days are passing and "time" itself circles and swirls in the heavens.)*

GRIZZLY BEAR: Once I was traveling all alone. And I, too, was starving. I laid myself down on the earth and prepared myself to die, when I saw a flock of geese fly across the face of the sun. *(We hear the call of geese echoing like music . . . we see their shadows fly across the sun, as:)* The moment went straight to my heart; and I found the strength to go on.

WEASEL: Sometimes it is what is beautiful that carries you.

GRIZZLY BEAR: It is not the beauty of the earth that sustains you, my friends— it is your relationship with it. Everything in the world is your relative.

CROW: Holiness . . .

GRIZZLY BEAR: Sleep, my friends. Rest now. And when you awaken, you will be strong. Remember me always.

CROW: May you travel safely, grandfather.

GRIZZLY BEAR: Remember me always, Wah-hey.

CROW & WEASEL: *(A weak whisper.)* Wah-hey . . .

(A strong special rises on a NARRATOR.*)*

NARRATOR #1: Crow and Weasel rested for three days and nights. They nourished themselves with what Grizzly Bear gave them. And on the fourth day, they headed for home.

(Lights give us a morning. Music changes as NARRATORS *enter with bolts of white plastic cloth. There are at least three bolts of this cloth. They form a line across the upstage edge of the set, as:)*

NARRATORS #1 & #7: It only remained now to cross the wide river.

ALL NARRATORS: The River of Floating Ashes.

(The NARRATORS *roll their bolts of white plastic cloth straight downstage, and the stage is transformed into a frozen white "River of Ice.")*

FEMALE NARRATORS: But this time the river was frozen.

MALE NARRATORS: This time there was—

ALL NARRATORS: *Ice* on the water.

(Half of the NARRATORS *cross downstage, taking one end of their bolts of "ice," and all counter around, so the "River" now runs right to left, across the stage.* CROW *and* WEASEL *look at the expanse of the "River.")*

CROW: I'm not anxious to test that black water again . . . I nearly drowned last time.

WEASEL: I think the ice is thick enough to hold us. Your horse is surefooted. Just climb on his back and allow him to find the way for you.

*(*WEASEL *gives* CROW *a "leg up" as* CROW *climbs onto the back of the* COLT/NAR-

RATOR #4. Note: *This is the first time we've seen a young man actually "riding" a horse—it is, of course, a delicate image to handle well, but I think it can be done with some dignity.* WEASEL *takes his horse figure from* NARRATOR #5, *and carefully steps onto the ice.)*

CROW: *(To his "horse.")* Easy now . . . that's it . . .

(All NARRATORS *gesture with both hands towards* WEASEL *as if inviting him, beckoning him onto and across the expanse of frozen ice. Their hands follow him, "guide" him across . . .)*

WEASEL: *(Stepping carefully.)* Just walk after me. Home is on the other side, Crow. We're so close to our village, our families . . . !

(As soon as WEASEL *steps off the ice, all the* NARRATORS' *hands swing towards* CROW—*beckoning him onto the frozen "river." Music rises and rises towards some kind of cacophony. As* CROW *and his "*COLT*" step onto the ice—one painstakingly careful step at a time—the* NARRATORS *rise, and with their hands they lift* CROW *from his horse, almost caressing him, seducing him with their presence and the attraction of death. And as* CROW *turns upstage, suddenly—the ice begins breaking. Everything changes . . .)*

CROW: *(Screams.) Weasel! The river!* (*The* COLT *screams, whinnies . . . sinking to his knees as the* NARRATORS *lift the white plastic in a perpendicular motion—as if the ice has cracked, and the river is now open and trying to drown him.)* Whoa!!!

*(The sound of the horse screaming punctuates everything else. The "*COLT's*" belly splits open, and red ribbons stream from it—ribbons of "blood" on the ice. The underside of the white plastic is dripping with red paint—with blood. Sounds rise in intensity.)*

WEASEL: *Crow!! Hold on!!*

CROW: *My horse—!!*

WEASEL: *Just hold onto the ice, Crow—I'll help you!*

*(*WEASEL *takes the "*COLT*" by its reins and pulls it from the "river," leading it to safety. Then he comes back to try and save* CROW. *The "river" continues to move up and down, and* CROW *is caught in the middle—freezing to death.)*

CROW: My hands! I can't move my hands!

WEASEL: Just hold on—

*(*WEASEL *tries to come onto the ice, but the river refuses him—knocking him backwards.)*

CROW: *No!! Stay off the ice! Get off the ice!*

WEASEL: Please, Crow, you have to take hold of my hand!

CROW: Let me die! Save yourself!

WEASEL: *Never! Take my hand!*

CROW: I can't!

WEASEL: *Please! Take it, Crow: Live!* (CROW *finally grabs* WEASEL's *hand. And* WEASEL, *struggling with all his might, pulls his friend out of the "river" and into his arms. Lifts him and carries him to the shore as the "*RIVER*"* PEOPLE *exit . . .)* Hold on!

CROW: I can't feel my legs!

WEASEL: It's all right. We're all right. We're going to be fine, Crow, I promise.

(HE *holds him, warming his friend. Sunset glows like a fire beyond them; the light of a small campfire appears.*)

NARRATOR #3: As the circle of sun met the long shadow of white land beyond them, Weasel carried his friend from the freezing cold water.

NARRATOR #1: He made camp by the River of Floating Ashes that night.

(NARRATOR #2 *wraps* CROW's *buffalo robe around his shoulders during the speech below.*)

NARRATOR #2: He made a small fire and melted the ice.

(*All* NARRATORS *quietly filter on, kneeling, sitting back on their haunches in a sort of ritualistic semi-circle upstage. Just listening, witnessing.*)

CROW: (*Very weak still.*) Weasel . . . ?

WEASEL: Yes, Crow?

CROW: Is my horse all right?

WEASEL: I think more of his blood got on you than him.

(WEASEL *takes a rag of some sort from his parka. We see the rag is bloody as he cleans the blood from* CROW.)

CROW: I thought I was dying.

WEASEL: You have great courage.

CROW: (*Still shaking.*) No. I don't know that that's true.

WEASEL: Your father was courageous. And you are much like him. Your father saved my father's life one time.

CROW: I remember.

WEASEL: They were hunting buffalo, when a wounded bull turned on my father and threw him from his horse. My father ran to the base of a cottonwood tree. The buffalo chased him around and around it, hooking huge pieces of bark from the tree with every single thrust of his horns . . . ! Until your father finally came in on a horse, snatched up my father and got him away.

CROW: Weasel?

WEASEL: Yes?

CROW: Thank you for saving my life.

(*There is a "moment" as* WEASEL *silently acknowledges this thanks.*)

WEASEL: Crow, I couldn't go home without you. Your mother would kill me.

CROW: I see the river much differently now. Every place we travel through has its own power; power that calls to different people in different ways.

WEASEL: Yes.

CROW: Many things hunger to consume and destroy us, my friend. Sometimes we cannot avoid them. (CROW, *downstage center, raises the sacred pipe bag high above his head and addresses the "river," as if it's before him.*) River of

Floating Ashes: I am grateful to feel the sky in my lungs—I am grateful to be alive: Now. *(To his friend.)* I will not try to cross this dark water again.

(A HORSE *whinnies offstage . . . the "*COLT*" answers that whinny, and follows the sound off as music of home makes itself known.)*
CROW: Look, Weasel: Antelope Prairie. Our village is over the rise . . . !

*(*RACCOON *enters.)*
RACCOON: Weasel! Crow!
WEASEL: Hello, Raccoon.

*(*RACCOON *runs off, announcing:)*
RACCOON: Weasel and Crow have returned!

(Their mothers are the first of their village to enter . . .)
MOTHER WEASEL: Weasel . . . ! Weasel? Is that you, my son?
WEASEL: Hello, Mother.
MOTHER WEASEL: Weasel, Weasel, Weasel . . . !
MOTHER CROW: *(Entering.)* There you are! Here they are!
CROW: Mother!
MOTHER CROW: You're home!
MOTHER WEASEL: Look at you—look at you! Look how you've grown!
WEASEL: Mother, please.
CROW: Mother, you've lost a few feathers.
MOTHER CROW: I'm molting. I've worried. I can't help it, Crow.
MOTHER WEASEL: We've been so worried about you.
WEASEL: Oh, Mother, it is good to be back.

(Other Villagers have started to filter on. The young men are glad to see them, they all greet each other.)
PORCUPINE: Crow!
CROW: Hello, Porcupine.
MARMOT: Welcome, welcome . . . !
WEASEL: Marmot—
CROW: Red Fox—
WEASEL: Raccoon.
RED FOX: Hello, boys.
MARMOT: We thought you might never return.
RED FOX: We'd just about given up on you two.

*(*MOUNTAIN LION *Enters. He seems, if anything, older and blinder—more imbued with authority than ever.)*
MOUNTAIN LION: Crow. Weasel. Is it truly you?
CROW: Mountain Lion.
WEASEL: Wah-hey.

CROW: Your dream was a hard path to follow.

WEASEL: We've been to that far-away place in the North, Mountain Lion. We met the people you saw in your vision.

MOUNTAIN LION: The ones without feathers or fur?

CROW: We have carried your pipe to the eyes of the world.

(CROW presents the pipe bag, but MOUNTAIN LION respectfully refuses it.)

MOUNTAIN LION: No. The pipe belongs with you, Crow. It is right you should keep it.

PORCUPINE: *(Privately.)* Raccoon? Did he tell him to keep the pipe?

RACCOON: Yes.

MOUNTAIN LION: In the future, our traveling bundle will hang before Weasel's lodge.

MARMOT: Oh, me, oh, my.

RACCOON: *(Under his breath.)* This is highly unusual . . . !

PORCUPINE: Keep the pipe?

RED FOX: *(Clears his throat, and:)* Mountain Lion, I feel some need to remind you that these are young men. No person this young has ever cared for the pipe.

RACCOON: Or guarded the traveling bundle.

MARMOT: No, never.

MOUNTAIN LION: Red Fox, I appreciate your concern.

RED FOX: Thank you, I thought you might.

MOUNTAIN LION: Look at Weasel and Crow. Even a blind man can see who these men are. This pipe and the bundle are in the right hands.

(RED FOX acquiesces with some grace.)

RED FOX: I see.

(MOUNTAIN LION crosses back to CROW and WEASEL.)

MOUNTAIN LION: Our village has watched the horizons for you. I have of-tentimes dreamt of your return. *(RACCOON and PORCUPINE unfold and show the village and the theatre two rather extraordinary buffalo robes—robes painted with pictographs representing the journey of WEASEL and CROW. CROW's robe has totemic pictures of the Inuit people and horses; WEASEL's has a picture of the sun and maybe the waves of the far-away sea.)* I have colored these robes with my dreams.

(As PORCUPINE and RACCOON put the robes around WEASEL and CROW:)

RACCOON: Weasel and Crow, you have made a great journey.

PORCUPINE: The wisdom you carry is our wisdom now.

CROW: *(Formally, to MOUNTAIN LION.)* My brother and I bring you a gift from the Inuit people.

MOUNTAIN LION: Inuit?

WEASEL: It is a snowknife, Grandfather.

(The blind old man feels the knife, the carvings with his hands.)

MOUNTAIN LION: *(Awed.)* I feel the creatures who lived in my vision . . . ! Please, my sons, tell us of the things that are carved here. *(As the VIL-LAGERS form a circle, reminiscent of the opening of the play.)* May the poem that is living within you place itself in order on the threshold of your tongue.

(CROW and WEASEL stand in the center of the circle. They address their village— telling them a story.)

CROW: The people that Mountain Lion saw in his dream live much of their lives on a vast body of salt water and ice.

WEASEL: The ocean—it stretches as large as the sky.

ANIMAL PEOPLE: Ocean . . . the ocean . . .

WEASEL: The ocean—for them it's like land is with us.

CROW: They danced for us the story of Sedna. Perhaps we do not understand it completely, but this is a story of how understanding begins.

(We hear a sound—a steady rhythm which begins during the speech above—a bit distant at first, and then more and more present. It is the sound of Inuit drums, the music of the Inuit people made present through the story that CROW and WEASEL tell. We hear the INUIT ELDER's voice echoing the key words of the Sedna story in his own language as WEASEL and CROW continue.)

WEASEL: Sedna is the Mother of Seals. Sedna is the giver of food, and through food, of life.

MOUNTAIN LION: Yes.

CROW: The Inuit told us that in The Beginning Time, when the One they call Sedna was still just a child, she went on a boat to the sea with her father. Sedna's father was angry because she had disobeyed him.

WEASEL: Sedna, the child, was thrown from the boat, but she clung to the gunnel with her hands.

CROW: She had no wish to die in the dark, freezing ocean. But her father determined to end Sedna's life, to kill her for disobeying him.

WEASEL: Her fingers were cut from the side of the boat.

CROW: Sedna's fingers were cut. Her blood flowed like water . . . !

CROW & WEASEL: Each of her fingers fell into the sea, and her fingers became many seals.

CROW: The seals that feed the Dream People are the fingers of Sedna, you see? Her suffering feeds them. Sedna gives her seals to the hunters, and the hunters bring them home. The Inuit strive to be worthy of Sedna.

WEASEL: Like us, they're trying to live a good life.

(The story is over. The Inuit memory sounds fade . . .)

MOUNTAIN LION: I marvel at the strangeness of the world.

CROW: The wonder and the strangeness, the terror and the beauty of the world will never be over.

MOUNTAIN LION: *(A benediction.)* You have traveled well. Both of you.

(WEASEL and CROW cross downstage in their robes of honor, isolated in light. Their village remains in a circle.)

WEASEL: Crow, my friend?

CROW: Weasel.

WEASEL: I can't believe we've done this . . . !

CROW: Yes.

WEASEL: It is good to be home.

CROW: To be among family.

WEASEL: Yes.

CROW: This is the way it should be.

(The ANIMAL PEOPLE *look at the sky, and as one they take a large Breath . . . a breath of astonishment, of awe, of a circle complete . . . as the sounds of the prairie grow in intensity for a moment and a hint of the northern lights flickers against the horizon, as the lights fade to black . . .)*

CURTAIN

THE ICE WOLF

by

Joanna Halpert Kraus

JOANNA H. KRAUS is an award-winning playwright of twelve published scripts that are widely produced throughout the United States, Canada, England, and Australia. *The Ice Wolf* and *Remember My Name* were produced Off-Off Broadway. *The Ice Wolf*, in addition to being in this anthology, has appeared in several other collections: *New Women's Theatre*, Honor Moore, editor; *Dramatic Literature: A Century in Review*, Roger L. Bedard, editor; *Around the World in 21 Plays*, Lowell Swortzell, editor. Another of her popular plays for young people is *Mean to Be Free*.

Kraus is Professor Emeritus of Theatre, State University of New York at Brockport. While there, she served from 1980 to 1995 as Coordinator of the Interdisciplinary Arts for Children Program for both undergraduate and graduate students. A specialist in child drama, playwriting and improvisation, Kraus holds a doctorate from Columbia University, a master's from the University of California, Los Angeles, and a B.A. from Sarah Lawrence College.

In 1976 she received the Charlotte B. Chorpenning Cup for Achievement in Playwriting from the American Alliance of Theatre and Education and in 1995, a Lifetime Achievement Award from the New York State Theatre Education Association. Her play *Angel in the Night* won the 1996 Distinguished Play Award from the American Alliance for Theatre and Education. She has received several play commissions, the latest being a partnership between the Raleigh Little Theatre and the North Carolina Museum of History for her script, *Sunday Gold*.

Now living in northern California, Joanna Kraus is a correspondent for the Knight-Ridder newspaper *Contra Costa Times* and the weekly *Rossmoor News*. In addition to working on a new play and a children's novel she conducts classes and workshops and does residencies in playwriting, improvisational theatre, drama and the curriculum, and drama and social issues. She writes play manuscript critiques and serves as a consultant in arts and education. Her most recent book is *Ms Courageous: Two Famous Women Scientists*.

———————

Young people are an open-minded, imaginative, curious, and honest audience. They are interactive spectators leaping into the story with energy and emotion and welcome a journey of the mind and spirit. As a writer I want to evoke tears of compassion and laughs of empathy. Ultimately I hope my plays will provoke their thoughtful questioning on issues that concern us all—issues of freedom, prejudice, and courage.

—JOANNA H. KRAUS

THE ICE WOLF

A Tale of the Eskimos

CHARACTERS

Storyteller
Anatou: a girl born to Eskimo parents. Her skin is pale and her hair blond;
a phenomenon in the village
Karvik: her father
Arnarqik: her mother
Tarto: her best friend, a village boy
Kiviog: Tarto's father
Atata: an old man of the village but a good hunter
Shikikanaq: a village girl
Motomiak: a village boy
Villager 1: a woman
Villager 2: a man
Wood God: the God of the Forest
A Beaver
A Fox
An Ermine

PLACE AND TIME

The entire action of the play takes place in a small, isolated Eskimo village,
Little Whale River, and the forest, a few days inland. It is located in the Hudson Bay area of Canada.

The time is long before the missionaries established their settlements, long
before white man had been seen, a time when the spirits and the Shaman, or
the Wise Man, ruled.

PROLOGUE

It is the end of January. In the foreground we see an expanse of white spread out. It is broken in a few places by hillocks which rise up like seal's heads from the plains. There is an atmosphere of cold beauty and awesome space.

The STORYTELLER *enters on the apron of the stage. He is dressed, as all the Eskimos, in the attire of the Hudson Bay Eskimos, but somehow there is the quality about him of excitement. He is no ordinary hunter.*

STORYTELLER:

> Far beyond the world you know—
> Of sun, rushing rivers, and trees
> Is the Northland
> Where the winter snow is gray.
> There is no sound of birds
> Nothing but the stillness of space
> Of endless snow
> And endless cold.
> There, the child Anatou was born
> In the village of Little Whale River.
> It was small, beside the sea.
> But the search for food never ended.

(Lights up on igloo, Eskimos in circle, one beating drum, chanting.)

Aja, I remember. It was one of the coldest nights of the year, so cold the dog team had buried themselves in the snow.

ATATA: And the seal-oil lamps trembled before the Great North wind.

KARVIK: Just before dawn, when the baby came, Karvik had to go out and repair their home. His fingers seemed to freeze at once. Never had there been such a storm in Little Whale River.

(Lights up on KARVIK *cutting a snow block and fitting it into dome.)*

ARNARQIK: Inside Arnarqik sewed the caribou skins she had chewed. She was making new clothes for Karvik. Only once did she dare to look at the small child beside her wrapped in skins. It was strangely still, strangely quiet. It was unlike any child Arnarqik had ever seen.

STORYTELLER: Atata was at the seal's breathing hole . . .

(Lights up on ATATA *crouched by breathing hole, poised, ready with harpoon.)*

. . . waiting . . . waiting until the seal came up for air. For days there had been no food in Little Whale River. He thought the birth of a new child might bring him luck! Then . . . he struck with his harpoon! (ATATA *harpoons seal.)*

ATATA: Aja, Nuliayuk, now, everyone will eat!

STORYTELLER: He took the choice bit of meat, the seal's liver, to return to the seal goddess, Nuliayuk. The Shaman, the wise man, had told him to do this so she would feast on it and then remember to send more seals to the hunters of Little Whale River. Atata rushed back. Now, there was something to celebrate. A new child, a fresh caught seal. There would be drum chants and dancing and stories in the long white night. (*Drum chants begin. They break off abruptly.*) But there was no singing or dancing.

KARVIK: It was long ago . . .

ARNARQIK: Just about this time.

STORYTELLER: It was a pale dawn . . .

ATATA: Like this one . . .

STORYTELLER: When Anatou was born.

ACT I

SCENE 1

The interior of KARVIK *and* ARNARQIK's *home in Little Whale River. Masses of thick, heavy caribou skins are spread about. Seal-oil lamps, made of soapstone, light the home.*

At rise, the sound of Eskimo dogs howling. A strong wind is blowing. Villagers come in from all sides, dressed in their habitual furs. They crawl through the passageway, and lights come up in the interior of the igloo. KARVIK *and* ARNARQIK *are seated. Their new child is beside* ARNARQIK *on a caribou skin not visible from the entrance.*

KARVIK: Welcome! Welcome, all of you!

VILLAGER 2: Aja! Your first child. Of course, we'd come. (*To others.*) We must sing many songs to welcome it.

KIVIOG: And if it's a man child, Karvik will already have made him a harpoon, a sled, and a whip.

VILLAGER 1: By the next moon he will be able to use them. Wait and see! (*They laugh.*)

VILLAGER 2: Good, he can hunt a seal with us this winter and the caribou next fall. If he's as good a hunter as Karvik, we'll get twice as much.

KIVIOG: And he'll be a companion for my son, Tarto, born under the same moon. (*They all laugh except* KARVIK *and* ARNARQIK, *who are strangely quiet.*)

VILLAGER 1: Karvik! Arnarqik! You are silent. Show us the man child. We've come a long way to see him. (ARNARQIK *moves slowly.*)

ARNARQIK: It is a girl-child . . . but we are glad.

KARVIK: She will be good.

ARNARQIK: It is true. There is joy in feeling new life come to the great world.

VILLAGER 1: A girl! Ah-ah. That means more care.

VILLAGER 2: And more attention.

KIVIOG: She cannot hunt.

VILLAGERS: (*Politely.*) But let us see her anyway. (ARNARQIK *moves away troubled, then points to the caribou skin.*)

ARNARQIK: There, look for yourself. (KARVIK *has turned away. Villagers crowd around the child, move back abruptly, and whirl on* KARVIK *and* ARNARQIK.)

VILLAGER 1: (*In low horror.*) Her hair is white!

VILLAGER 2: Her face is pale.

KIVIOG: She cannot be an Eskimo.

VILLAGER 1: She cannot be one of us!

KARVIK: Of course, she is. Her hair will get darker. Wait.

VILLAGER 2: But her face. Look at it. No Eskimo child was ever born as pale as that.

VILLAGER 1: She's a devil.

ARNARQIK: No!

VILLAGER 1: She will not live one moon.

ARNARQIK: She will live.

VILLAGER 1: She will bring bad luck.

ARNARQIK: She's only a baby.

KIVIOG: Put her out in the snow now, before she turns the gods against us.

VILLAGER 2: And our stomachs shrink.

VILLAGER 1: And our dishes are empty.

VILLAGER 2: It's happened before. We all know it. Get rid of the child before it's too late.

KIVIOG: She will offend Nuliayuk, the goddess of the seals. Nuliayuk will stay at the bottom of the sea and keep the seals beside her, and we will all go hungry. Put the child out into the snow, or we will die of famine!

ARNARQIK: No! She will be a good Eskimo.

VILLAGER 2: Then let her grow up in another village. We don't want her here.

KIVIOG: She doesn't look like us. She won't think like us.

VILLAGER 1: She doesn't belong here.

KARVIK: Then where does she belong? Where should she go?

VILLAGER 1: Put her out in the snow. *(Starts to grab her.)*

ARNARQIK: No! No! No, I can't. Don't you understand? She is our child.

VILLAGER 2: Then leave our village in peace. Don't anger the spirits of Little Whale River.

KARVIK: But this is our village, and you are our people. How can we leave it? Wait! She will be like the others. You'll see. She'll sew and cook just as well as any Eskimo girl. Better! Arnarqik will teach her.

KIVIOG: *(Holds up his hands.)* Very well. We will watch and wait. Perhaps you are right, and we will see her hair and cheeks grow darker. But we have no gifts or good wishes to welcome a white-faced child—a white-faced girl child!

(VILLAGERS exit. ARNARQIK tries to run after them.)

ARNARQIK: Come back! Please wait. Don't go yet. Oh, Karvik, what will we do?

KARVIK: *(Slowly.)* Her hair should be as dark as the raven's wing.

ARNARQIK: It is as white as the caribou's belly. Karvik, what if they are right? She is different. Karvik, why is her hair pale? Why doesn't she cry? Why is she so still! It's not natural.

KARVIK: She is frightened already. The Fair One will have a hard journey.

(Looks out the passageway.)

Arnarqik, the villagers spoke wisely. *(Looks for a long time at his wife.)* She would never know. It would not hurt if we put her in the snow now.

ARNARQIK: No, Karvik! You mustn't ask me to.

KARVIK: But if we leave, will the next village think she looks more like an Eskimo?

ARNARQIK: *(Shakes her head.)* No, she is Anatou, the Fair One—she will not change. But I will teach her, Karvik. She will be a good Eskimo girl!

KARVIK: But will they ever think she is like the others?

ARNARQIK: Yes. Yes. Of course, they will. Let us stay here. Who knows what is beyond the snow?

KARVIK: Then we must be strong. We must teach Anatou to be strong. Only then will our home be her home and our friends her friends. It won't be easy, Arnarqik. (ARNARQIK *is beside the baby.*)

ARNARQIK: Oh Karvik, I couldn't leave her. Not like that! *(Abruptly she changes.)*

Look, Karvik . . . she is smiling. *(Picks her up.)* Oh, Karvik, we mustn't let them hurt her. We must protect her.

KARVIK: Sing, Arnarqik, sing the morning song. Bring Anatou luck. She will have a hard journey.

ARNARQIK: *(Sits, sings or chants.)*

> I rise up from rest
> Moving swiftly as the raven's wing
> I rise up to greet the day
> Wo-wa
> My face is turned from dark of night
> My gaze toward the dawn
> Toward the whitening dawn.

(Lights fade.)

STORYTELLER: But her hair did not grow dark as the raven's wing. Instead, each day she grew fairer. They called her the "different one," and when the blinding snow swept across the North or when the hunters returned with empty sleds, the villagers whispered, "It's Anatou. She's the one."

ACT I

SCENE 2

The village. TARTO, SHIKIKANAQ, and MOTOMIAK are playing an Eskimo game, a combination of Hide-and-Seek and Touch. MOTOMIAK is just dashing for the goal pursued by SHIKIKANAQ. TARTO is at the goal, watching and laughing.

TARTO: Hurry up, Motomiak. She's right behind you. Shikikanaq is right behind you!

(MOTOMIAK turns to look, still running. ANATOU enters. She sees the race but moves out of the way too late, and they collide. MOTOMIAK falls, and SHIKIKANAQ tags him.)

SHIKIKANAQ: There! I won!

MOTOMIAK: That wasn't fair. You made me lose the game, Anatou. I've never lost before—not to a girl! See what you made me do. Clumsy!

ANATOU: I'm sorry. I tried to get out of the way. I didn't see you in time.

SHIKIKANAQ: *(Whispering.)* You better not say anything more, Motomiak, or Anatou will put a spell on you—the way she did the seals.

TARTO: What are you talking about? You know that isn't true.

ANATOU: Oh, I'm sorry I spoiled your game, Motomiak, but couldn't you start again?

SHIKIKANAQ: No. I won. Tarto saw. Didn't you, Tarto? *(He nods.)*

MOTOMIAK: Beside, we don't want to play in front of a freak. (ANATOU *gasps.)*

TARTO: Who's a freak?

MOTOMIAK: She is. The whole village says so.

ANATOU: *(Furious.)* No, I'm not! I'm an Eskimo just like you.

SHIKIKANAQ: *(Doubtfully.)* Ohh . . .

MOTOMIAK: Well, her face is different enough. (ANATOU *touches it.)*

TARTO: Why, what's wrong with it? It has two eyes, a nose, and a mouth just like everyone else's.

SHIKIKANAQ: But it's white, Tarto—like snow. I bet if you put her in the sun she'll melt, and that's why she stays inside all the time.

TARTO: You're just jealous because she's prettier than you, Shikikanaq.

ANATOU: Stop it. Stop it, all of you. *(She is crying.)* Leave me alone. *(Starts to go.)*

TARTO: *(Furious.)* Now, see what you've done. If she were made of snow, Shikikanaq, she couldn't cry. *(Crosses to her.)* Come on, Anatou. They didn't mean it. Please, come back. *(To others.)* Let's have another game—all four of us.

SHIKIKANAQ: Well . . . all right . . . if she'll tell us why she looks that way.

TARTO: *(Sharply.)* What way?

SHIKIKANAQ: I mean her eyes and her hair. They're such funny colors. There must be a reason.

ANATOU: *(Desperate.)* I don't know. Each time you've asked me, I said I didn't know.

SHIKIKANAQ: I bet if you asked your mother and father they'd know. It must be something terrible, or they'd tell you.

MOTOMIAK: Maybe the Wood God from the forest put a spell on an animal and sent it back here. No one else in Little Whale River looks like you. Maybe that's why you look so funny. They say he has the power to make an animal appear like a human.

SHIKIKANAQ: And he can make people look like animals, too . . . just by saying a spell! My father says that's why no Eskimo should go into the forest.

ANATOU: No! No! It's not true. I'm just like you are!

MOTOMIAK: Then, maybe, some devil spirit looked at you, and it took all the color away.

SHIKIKANAQ: Yes, that's it. And why do you always sit inside and sew?

ANATOU: (Lying.) There's a lot of work. It has to get done.

TARTO: (Quickly.) She can sew better than any woman in the whole village! Show them, Anatou. (He points to her dress which is carefully and beautifully stitched. SHIKIKANAQ examines it.)

SHIKIKANAQ: It is beautiful. There aren't any mistakes at all.

ANATOU: (Can't believe her praise.) My mother taught me, and she is very good and careful.

SHIKIKANAQ: Can you make anything else?

ANATOU: Two snows ago, I made warm boots for my father. Very special boots and he's worn them ever since.

MOTOMIAK: Then how come he's lost in the snow right now, if the boots you made were so special.

ANATOU: He went to look for food. Both my mother and father did. That's all I know.

MOTOMIAK: There's barely any food left in the village. For three days the hunters have returned with empty sleds.

ANATOU: Famine is everywhere. Not just here. I heard my father say so before he left. That is why he said he was going far away to look.

MOTOMIAK: You made those boots your father wore. I bet you put a charm on them. Shikikanaq and I saw you talking to them once and blowing on them.

ANATOU: That's not true. I was cleaning them.

MOTOMIAK: But you were talking, too. You were putting a charm on them, weren't you?

ANATOU: Don't you see? If I did have any magic powers, I'd bring them back. They're my parents. I love them. They're the only ones who've been good to me. (Softly.) I couldn't stay in Little Whale River if it weren't for them.

SHIKIKANAQ: (Cruelly.) Well, they're gone now. So you can go, too.

ANATOU: What do you mean? They're coming back. I know they are.

MOTOMIAK: Maybe. But my father says you killed your own parents.

ANATOU: (With a cry.) No!

TARTO: (Challenging him and pinning his arm back.) Take that back or else!

MOTOMIAK: (Stubbornly.) That's what my father said.

TARTO: (Knocking him down.) Well, he's wrong. (A fight starts. SHIKIKANAQ shrieks and ANATOU watches horrified. VILLAGERS rush in.)

SHIKIKANAQ: (Quickly.) She started it. It's all her fault. Anatou's fault!

KIVIOG: (To ANATOU.) Get away from our children. (VILLAGER 2 has separated the boys.)

TARTO: Anatou wasn't doing anything.

KIVIOG: Be still!

VILLAGER 1: She's brought nothing but trouble since the day she was born.

TARTO: (To KIVIOG.) But it's not fair, Father, she . . .

KIVIOG: Silence! For days we have searched for Kavrik and Arnarqik. They are good people. Karvik was the best hunter we had. But no man can fight off charmed boots.

VILLAGER 2: No wonder they got lost in the blizzard.

VILLAGER 1: Look at her. She doesn't care her parents are gone.

ANATOU: *(Suddenly.)* I don't understand. Do you mean they're . . . they're dead? *(KIVIOG nods.)* How can you be sure?

KIVIOG: If they haven't frozen, they have starved. We cannot find them anywhere.

VILLAGER 1: You're to blame. You and your witchcraft.

VILLAGER 2: Look, she doesn't even care.

ANATOU: Don't you think I want them here? Don't you think the fire is colder without my mother's face and lonesome without my father's singing? They went to look for food . . . for all of us. I'm hungry, too . . . just like the rest of you.

VILLAGER 1: Then, why do you anger the Seal Goddess? We used to have days of feasting.

VILLAGER 2: Pots boiling . . .

KIVIOG: But since the same day you were born, the hunters have had to work twice as hard—twice as hard for the same amount!

VILLAGER 2: We used to thank the Seal Goddess, bow down to her and give her seal liver. Now, there is none to give her, and she is angry—at the bottom of the sea. Our harpoons break in our hands.

ANATOU: It is the bitter cold.

VILLAGER 2: Why is there blizzard after blizzard if the gods aren't angry?

VILLAGER 1: Why is there a famine if the gods aren't angry?

KIVIOG: It's your fault.

VILLAGER 2: You're to blame.

KIVIOG: We have kept silent for the sake of Karvik and Arnarqik, but now they are no longer here.

VILLAGER 1: They took care of you and see what it brought them to!

ANATOU: *(Sobbing.)* But I am all alone, too.

VILLAGER 2: There is no more to eat.

VILLAGER 1: No oil to burn.

VILLAGER 2: We fear sickness.

KIVIOG: And the souls of the dead.

VILLAGER 1: The souls of animals and men.

VILLAGER 2: We know the spirits of the earth and the air are angry with us.

ANATOU: What am I to do? What do you want of me?

KIVIOG: Leave here. Leave us!

ANATOU: But I haven't done anything. Where will I go? I'll never find my way alone.

KIVIOG: If you stay, you will get no help or protection from us, Anatou. From now on, find your own food and eat with the dogs. No one else will eat with you.

VILLAGER 2: And from now on, speak to yourself. No one else will listen. *(Adults start off.)*

VILLAGER 1: Go home, children, all of you. Go home quickly.

KIVIOG: Don't talk to that one. That one is evil. Leave her alone.

(They leave. ANATOU *has turned away.* TARTO *looks back before exiting but she doesn't see it.* ANATOU *sinks down, unable to bear it.)*

ANATOU: It isn't true! I loved my parents. Even Tarto believed them. He didn't say a word—he didn't even say good-bye. Oh, Moon God, is there nothing I can do?

(She is crying. TARTO *reappears, puts his hand out to touch her hair, then in fear withdraws it.)*

TARTO: *(Gently.)* What are you going to do? Where will you go?

ANATOU: *(Jerks her head up abruptly but doesn't turn around.)* All right! All right! I'm leaving. Are you satisfied now?

TARTO: But it's me, Anatou—Tarto. I wanted to say good-bye.

ANATOU: *(Turns around.)* Tarto, you came back!

TARTO: But I can't stay. If they catch me . . . I'll . . . get into trouble. I brought you some food, Anatou. It's just a little, but I thought . . .

ANATOU: Thank you, Tarto. *(Suddenly she takes off an amulet that she is wearing.)* Tarto, you're the only friend I have now. I want you to keep this to remember me. The shaman gave it to my mother before I was born. It's to bring good luck, but it was really always meant for a boy-child, not a girl. *(He takes it.)* Tarto, I wish I had something special to give you, but it's all I have.

TARTO: Then it is special, Anatou. I'll always keep it. I won't forget you. I promise. And when I am older, Anatou, I'll harpoon my own seal. I'll be the best hunter in the village, and the men will do anything I say because I'll know all the hiding places of the seals. Then they'll listen to me and . . . *(Breaks off and slowly asks what he has always wondered.)* Anatou, why is your hair so light?

ANATOU: *(Pierced by the question.)* Tarto, why is the sky gray in the winter? I don't know. All I want is to be like the others, to play with you and sing with you, and I want to see my mother and father again. I love them. Do you believe me? *(He nods.)* I want to be friends with the villagers, but they won't let me. You're the only one who tries to understand. I used to wake up and say, "Today will be different." My mother said, "Anatou, every day is the beginning of some new wonderful thing." But it wasn't true! Each day ended the same way, and each dawn I was frightened again. And then today . . . today was the worst of all.

TARTO: I'm sorry, Anatou.

ANATOU: Tarto, you were brave to come back here. You know they'll be angry if they find you here.

TARTO: I know.

ANATOU: You will be a fine hunter, Tarto . . . the finest of the whole village one day. Tarto, why did you come back?

TARTO: I am your friend, Anatou. I always will be even if . . .

ANATOU: Even if what, Tarto?

TARTO: Anatou, listen. My father said . . . that . . . well, he said . . . (*Gulps.*) He said you put spells on the seals, so they couldn't come out of the water. Anatou, couldn't you say another spell so we could all eat? Then it would be all right again, Anatou.

ANATOU: (*Horrified.*) Do you believe that, Tarto?

TARTO: (*Miserably.*) Well, first, I said it wasn't true! But today . . .

ANATOU: Tarto, listen. There's nothing I can do. I can't make a spell like a shaman, like the wise man. I'm hungry, too, just like you. Even if I wanted to, there is nothing I can do.

TARTO: (*Slowly.*) Don't you want to? Don't you want to help us, Anatou?

ANATOU: Don't you believe me either, Tarto? Doesn't anyone? I'm not any different. I don't have any magic powers. I'm just like anyone else.

TARTO: Your skin is white. Mine is brown. Your hair is pale like the dawn. Mine is dark like the night. (*He is colder now.*) You're not like anyone I've seen. (*A long pause.*)

ANATOU: I've never heard you say that before. Everyone else, but not you! You never seemed to care. You made up for all the others.

(*Sound of Eskimo dogs.*)

TARTO: (*Uncomfortably.*) I have to go. Anatou . . . it's late. What will you do?

ANATOU: (*With a horrible realization.*) I know I can't stay here now. Tarto, when you lose everything at once, your choice has been made. You can only follow it.

TARTO: But, where will you go? What will you do?

ANATOU: (*Pauses, makes difficult decision.*) The forest, Tarto. It's only a few days from here. I've heard about it from the old men and the Shaman.

TARTO: (*Impulsively.*) But you can't. Don't you know about it? It's a place of whispers in the night, of strange whines. They say the trees are living beings, but they can't speak. It's not safe for an Eskimo to spend a night in the forest. What if the Wood God changes you into a wolf or another animal?

ANATOU: (*Slowly.*) Yes . . . what if he changes me into a wolf?

TARTO: (*Continuing without hearing her.*) It's dark and mysterious, Anatou. It's a place where Eskimos never go.

ANATOU: But, don't you see? That's just why. There is no place else! (*Pauses.*) Maybe the Wood God won't care if my hair is pale . . . like the dawn!

ACT II

SCENE 1

Outside the forest at night. Late March. The opening of this scene is mimed, and the audience only sees ANATOU's *silhouette.*

STORYTELLER: Anatou ran. It was dark and frightening. The only sound she heard was the wind whipping the snow around her. (ANATOU *drops from exhaustion. She is crying, but she must continue.*)

ANATOU: Where shall I go?

STORYTELLER: No one could hear her cry. There was no one but the wind. Anatou knew if she stopped too long, she would freeze in the fierce cold. Then suddenly she saw the place where no one had ever been.

(Part of the forest appears stage right. ANATOU *stops stage left.)*

ANATOU: The forest! I remember the old men used to tell each other tales by the fire. What did they say? No Eskimo must ever go into the forest. You must never spend the night there. But that's where the Wood God lives. *(She starts to move toward the forest.)* I must go. I must ask him.

(Rest of forest scrim appears as ANATOU *runs first to stage right, then stage left, stopping at center stage. Exhausted, she sinks to the ground. She is trembling with fear and slowly rises to her knees. Softly.)*

Wood God! *(Louder.)* Wood God! *(Looks all around her.)* Wood God . . . help me.

(The WOOD GOD *enters. He appears, as the spirits are reputed to, in the shape of an animal. He has chosen the shape of an awesome owl which is white in color.)*

WOOD GOD: Who dares to come into my forest where the wind and snow cry into the darkness?

ANATOU: *(Draws back.)* Are you the Wood God?

WOOD GOD: I am! And will be till the end of time! Who said you could enter my forest?

ANATOU: *(Terrified.)* No one.

WOOD GOD: Where do you come from?

ANATOU: I come from Little Whale River.

WOOD GOD: Are you an Eskimo? *(She nods.)* Then why did you come here? Don't you know no Eskimo comes into the middle of the forest and dares to disturb my sleep? Leave my kingdom now and be glad you still have your life.

ANATOU: *(Pleading.)* No! You don't understand. Please, don't send me away. *(Crying. The* WOOD GOD *comes closer and as he approaches, moonlight shines around them both.)*

WOOD GOD: Ah-ah. Even in the darkness your hair shines. Is it the moon, child?

ANATOU: *(Desperate.)* Wood God. Wood God, can't you see? Even hidden here it shines and glitters. If I were to crawl into a cave, it would be the same.

WOOD GOD: *(Lifts her face and peers into it.)* Your face is as pale as ice. *(Softer.)* And your eyes are red from crying. *(Shakes his head.)* That's too bad. It means you're human.

ANATOU: I am an Eskimo. But they don't believe me. Nobody does. Help me. Wood God, help me!

WOOD GOD: How can I help you? Are you hungry, child? Is that why you came here?

ANATOU: *(Nods.)* We all are . . . no one has eaten in days. But it is not my fault . . . they blame me because my hair shines, because it isn't like the raven's wing. But I am hungry, too. I can't go any farther . . . I can't.

WOOD GOD: We have no food to give you, child. You must leave. Your people will be worried. *(He starts to exit.)*

ANATOU: Wait! Wait and hear me. Wood God. It is not food I want. It is not food that made me wake the great spirit of the Wood God.

WOOD GOD: What then?

ANATOU: *(Slowly.)* I want what only your powers can grant. But first, Wood God, hear my story.

WOOD GOD: Begin. Quickly, child. You mustn't savor what tastes bitter.

ANATOU: Aja. It is true. You do see much.

WOOD GOD: Begin from the beginning; when you were born.

ANATOU: Even though I was a girl, my parents were happy, or at least they seemed to be. Even though I couldn't hunt . . . even though . . . even though I was different.

WOOD GOD: Why? You have two arms, two legs, and a face with two eyes and a mouth.

ANATOU: But a face that people were afraid of, and hair that grew lighter instead of darker. They named me Anatou, the Fair One.

WOOD GOD: So you are Anatou. Then not all the spirits of the earth and air can help you. You are as you are.

ANATOU: But you can help me, Wood God. Please. You must.

WOOD GOD: Go home, fair child. I can do nothing. I cannot turn your pale hair to the dark of the night or your fair skin brown. I cannot teach them to like you. You must do that yourself. Go home to your parents. Go home where you belong.

ANATOU: *(Blurts out.)* I can't. They'll kill me if I do.

WOOD GOD: *(Puzzled.)* Who will? Your parents, too?

ANATOU: No, they are spirits now. They were the only good people I ever knew. I did love them, Wood God. Some people say that I am a witch and that I cursed my parents, that the Seal Goddess is angry with me. They say that is why there is no food. But it isn't true, Wood God! It isn't true!

WOOD GOD: My power would only hurt you, Anatou. You are young. Go back.

ANATOU: I've heard you can make a seal seem like a man, or a girl seem like a wolf. Is that true?

WOOD GOD: I can.

ANATOU: Then, Wood God . . .

WOOD GOD: *(Interrupts.)* Think, Anatou. Is it so terrible to be an Eskimo girl, to learn to laugh and sing, or sew or cook?

ANATOU: Wood God, my father and mother taught me to sew and cook, but not to laugh and sing. I don't know what that is.

WOOD GOD: But what about the villagers?

ANATOU: They only taught me one thing—to hate. When my parents were gone, they wanted me to eat in the passageway with the dogs. They would not give me a skin to sew. Everywhere I went they turned away. *(Softly.)* Even Tarto.

WOOD GOD: Tarto?

ANATOU: My best friend.

WOOD GOD: Where is he?

ANATOU: Wood God, they all say I'm planning evil, and now even Tarto thinks so, too. Wood God, Wood God, there are more ways of killing than with a harpoon!

WOOD GOD: *(Pauses before he speaks.)* What do you wish, Anatou?

ANATOU: I don't want to be human any more. It hurts too much. I want you to turn me into a wolf. Then they'll be afraid of me. Then they'll leave me alone.

WOOD GOD: Think, Anatou, think! An animal cannot . . .

ANATOU: Is a wolf's face white like mine?

WOOD GOD: You know it is not.

ANATOU: Then quickly change me into a beast.

WOOD GOD: An animal is hungry.

ANATOU: I am used to that.

WOOD GOD: He tears with his teeth to eat. A wolf is alone.

ANATOU: I am alone now.

WOOD GOD: Anatou, there is no return. What if you miss your village?

ANATOU: Miss them! When you take a thorn out of an animal's paw, does it miss it? When you fill an empty stomach, does it miss the ache? When you cannot remember pain, do you miss the tears? What would I miss, Wood God, but all of these things?

WOOD GOD: Once it is done, you cannot change your mind.

ANATOU: I will not want to.

WOOD GOD: You will never be an Eskimo girl again, not until you are about to die. Not 'till then. Are you sure? Are you sure, Anatou?

ANATOU: Will I forget everything? I want to forget everything. Now.

WOOD GOD: No, Anatou. Not at first. As time goes by, you'll forget more and more and only remember your life here.

ANATOU: No! I want to forget everything now. Everything, Wood God. I want to forget I was ever Anatou, the Fair One.

WOOD GOD: But you can't escape pain, Anatou. Even a wolf can't escape that. *(She pauses to think; she looks up. He watches her closely.)* Are you ready?

ANATOU: Yes. *(Suddenly frightened.)* Wood God, will it hurt much?

WOOD GOD: Listen to my words. Hear them well. *(Lifts his arms so it appears as though his spirit, in the shape of a white owl, were commanding the universe. Drum beat begins.)*

> Come spirits of earth and sky.
> Rise through the snow.
> Speed over the ice.
> Encircle this child in a coat of thick fur.

(Three forest animals appear, a FOX, *a* BEAVER, *and an* ERMINE—*and form a circle around* ANATOU.)

FOX: Night protect it.

BEAVER: Forest watch it.

ERMINE: Nothing harm it.

WOOD GOD: As long as it remembers . . .

FOX: As long as it remembers . . .

BEAVER: As long as it remembers . . .

WOOD GOD: To stay in the forest far from man.

ERMINE: Far from man.

FOX: *(Echoes.)* . . . from man.

(There is more dancing. Animals close in. Their movements become more intense, then with a cry, they disappear and we see the wolf. This should not be a realistic representation, but rather done with masks in a costume, lean and sleek, that would be worn under the Eskimo dress, removed and disposed of at the end of the enchantment with a momentary darkening of the stage and more intense beating of the drum. There should be a marked difference in the movement once ANATOU has been changed into a wolf.)

FOX: It is done!

ERMINE: Now you are a wolf!

BEAVER: A Wolf!

CURTAIN

ACT II

SCENE 2

STORYTELLER: All that winter Anatou lived with the animals enjoying the forest. She made friends with the beaver, fox, and ermine. She forgot she had ever been Anatou, the Fair One—an Eskimo. Then one morning she woke up to a spring sun. It warmed the air and touched her fur.

(Spring in the forest. Early dawn. ANATOU wakes, stretches, and smells the air with curiosity.)

ANATOU: Whorlberries. That's what I smell. And sunlight! Even the forest can't shut it out. *(She puts a paw down on a patch of melting snow.)* Beaver! Fox! Wake up. The snow's melting. *(They enter.)*

FOX: Did you have to wake me up to tell me that? It happens every spring.

ANATOU: *(With growing excitement.)* But there are at least a thousand things to see and smell and hear. Come on. I'll race you through the forest, and we'll explore the other side.

BEAVER: *(Slowly.)* What do you mean by the other side? We've never gone beyond the edge.

ANATOU: Oh, that was all right in the winter time. But now it's spring. I want to leave the forest today, see what else there is.

FOX: *(Sharply.)* No, Anatou.

BEAVER: I thought you liked it here in the forest.

ANATOU: Of course, I do, but . . . (*Reluctant to speak of it.*) But last night I had a strange dream. I can't remember it now. But it was something out there. There's something I have to see.

BEAVER: Outside the forest?

FOX: Don't go there, Anatou.

ANATOU: Why not?

FOX: Don't go, or you'll be sorry.

ANATOU: I just want to look. It's a beautiful day. I want to run in the sunlight and explore.

FOX: If you leave, the Wood God will be furious.

ANATOU: The Wood God? Why? I'll be back tonight, I promise. What's there to be afraid of?

FOX: (*Quietly.*) Danger.

BEAVER: Danger.

ANATOU: Maybe there's something dangerous for little animals like you, but I'm strong. I've got sharp teeth and claws. (*Boasting.*) Nothing can hurt me.

FOX: You're a fool!

ANATOU: (*Angry.*) Wait and see. I'll be back without a scratch on me. I'm not afraid like the rest of you.

BEAVER: Listen to her! Well, let her go if she wants to.

FOX: For the last time. We're warning you. Don't go. There'll be trouble if you do.

ANATOU: I must go. I don't know why, but I must. Don't try to stop me.

FOX: Remember, we warned you!

BEAVER: You wouldn't listen.

ANATOU: I can't help it. It's something inside.

(*Lights fade, animals exit. Forest scrim rises, and* ANATOU *mimes her journey through the forest. She stops at the edge. The hilltops are brown, and there are black willow twigs with new buds.*)

Willow trees! And sunlight everywhere. Wood God, what a beautiful world outside your forest. (*Her journey continues in dance movement. The lights fade to indicate twilight. She stops, worn out.*) Loons on the water. It's so peaceful here. (*Enjoying it.*) I'm all alone in the world.

(*She prepares to settle down when lights begin to come up on a summer village tent, and we hear the sharp sound of an Eskimo dog howling.* ANATOU *peers at the tent and moves in cautiously, closer and closer. The tent should be a movable unit that glides on. As* ANATOU *gets closer, we hear the sound of Eskimo singing or chanting.* ANATOU *realizes what it is and cries out.*)

Eskimos! Wood God! Wood God! I'd forgotten. Oh, I should never have left the forest. (*As she watches,* KIVIOG *and* TARTO *cross stage to tent.*) Tarto. And he still has the charm I gave him. He still has it.

KIVIOG: Tarto, we'll never have to worry with you as a hunter. All the pots of the village will boil this spring. Aja, since Anatou left, there's been plenty to eat.

TARTO: There'd be enough for her, too, if she were here.

KIVIOG: Forget about her, Tarto. *(They go inside.)*

ANATOU: *(Creeping closer.)* Look at them eating, laughing, and singing. "Let her die in the snow." That's what they said. I'll show them. I'm strong now. I'll get even. If it's the last thing I do, I'll get even. *(She moves nearer the tent and sees a piece of meat outside.)* I'll take some back to the forest.

(But the dogs hear her, and they start howling. The singing stops, and a VILLAGER *runs out with his bow and arrow.* ANATOU *sees him and runs, but not before he shoots an arrow at her.* ANATOU *falls, and the man disappears into the tent.* ANATOU *is hurt but gets up, limping to the side of the tent.)*

That one! That one used to call me names. He hurt my mother and father. *(In pain.)* I'm remembering. His arrow cut through my heart!

*(*VILLAGER *comes out to check whether the animal is dead or not, and he carries another weapon. He looks about.)*

He'll kill me! Unless . . . *(*ANATOU *springs. There is a short struggle and the man falls without a sound.)* Who is stronger now, Eskimo? Who's stronger now?

*(*ANATOU *leaves.)*

ACT II

SCENE 3

In the forest. ANATOU *goes toward* FOX. FOX *retreats.* ANATOU *approaches* BEAVER. *He moves away in fear.*

WOOD GOD: You must leave man alone.

ANATOU: He did not leave me alone. Why should I?

WOOD GOD: Man has a bow, harpoons, knives, spears. You will see, Anatou. He will hunt you out. Stay away! Do not hurt another human.

ANATOU: But he wounded me.

FOX: You shouldn't have gone near his tent.

BEAVER: You don't deserve to stay in the forest with us.

ANATOU: But the wound hurt. *(Softly.)* And then . . . I saw his face. I remembered. I remembered everything before then!

WOOD GOD: That wound will heal, Anatou. But will this new wound heal? Your hatred is more chilling than the ice caves near the sea. It will grow, if you don't kill it now, Anatou. It will grow and freeze your heart.

FOX: You are a disgrace to the animals.

BEAVER: Animals kill because they must eat.

FOX: They must survive.

WOOD GOD: It's the law of the forest. But you, Anatou, killed out of hate. Men do that, not the animals!

ANATOU: *(With awful realization.)* Wood God . . . when I saw him, and I saw the tent, and I remembered how they made me leave the village, and the arrow pierced me . . . I felt something . . . something I had forgotten. I had to get even!

WOOD GOD: *(Sternly.)* Live in peace with man, Anatou, or leave the forest forever.

(He sweeps off with the animals.)

ACT II

SCENE 4

The interior of a snow house. Drums are beating. Three village hunters are assembled in a circle. In the distance there is the piercing cry of a wolf. They shudder.

KIVIOG: *(Rises.)* We must try again. The wolf must be stopped.

ATATA: Never was a wolf spirit so hungry for men's souls.

VILLAGER 2: Hunter after hunter has gone and not returned. What can we do?

ATATA: Aja! But what good is a bow and arrow?

VILLAGER 2: What good are knives if we live in terror in our own houses?

KIVIOG: The great North is no longer safe. We mustn't let the wolf escape this time. Since spring, he has not let us alone. At night he always disappears into the forest . . . where no Eskimo ever goes.

VILLAGER 2: Even if it does go into the forest, we must find it and put an end to this.

ATATA: But if we go into the forest, we'll be trapped.

KIVIOG: We are trapped in our own homes now!

ALL: Aja! Aja!

ATATA: Never has there been a wolf like this. Its howl makes the fire die, and the seal-oil lamp tremble.

VILLAGER 2: We must hunt till we find it.

ATATA: We have lost many good hunters.

VILLAGER 2: They have all failed.

KIVIOG: But we must find it.

TARTO: *(Has been sitting there all the time unnoticed by the others.)* I have hunted before. Let me go, Father.

KIVIOG: Tarto! This is a council for our best hunters. Go outside. You should not be here. You're too young.

VILLAGER 2: He is so small that we don't notice him. It's all right, Kiviog.

ATATA: Perhaps, he is so small that he could creep up on the wolf, and he wouldn't notice him either. *(They all laugh.)*

TARTO: Please, Father. Please, I'm strong.

KIVIOG: No. We go too far. You will be tired.

TARTO: I won't. Wait and see.

KIVIOG: The men of Little Whale River are going to the forest, Tarto. It's dangerous.

TARTO: Then I will find the wolf's hiding place.

VILLAGER 2: He is swift, Kiviog. His eyes are sharp. He is as good a hunter as the men. If he wishes, let him come. (KIVIOG *thinks, then nods to* TARTO, TARTO *beams.*)

KIVIOG: We must cover the great North and not stop till the snow is free of the wolf's tracks.

VILLAGERS: Aja! Aja!

VILLAGER 2: We must hunt toward the great plains.

KIVIOG: And hunt toward the forest.

ATATA: And by the caves along the sea.

KIVIOG: We've no time to waste. Harness the dogs! (*Drums increase. Men leave to get dog teams and begin the hunt. Interior fades.*)

ACT III

SCENE 1

The forest. There is snow on the ground, and a rock unit has been added left center. There is a group of tangled trees that have been blown down in the winter near the right center. ANATOU *sleepily comes from behind the rock. She sniffs the air casually, then her body tenses.*

ANATOU: (*Calling with increasing alarm.*) Wood God! Wood God! Wood God! I smell danger. (BEAVER *and* FOX *appear.*)

FOX: The hunters are here.

BEAVER: The hunters.

ANATOU: But the Eskimos are afraid of the forest. Why do they come here?

FOX: They hunt the wolf.

BEAVER: They hunt you.

FOX: Anatou. (WOOD GOD *enters.*)

WOOD GOD: I warned you, Anatou. You have hurt too many of them. They are angry, angry enough to enter the forest and to hunt you out.

ANATOU: I'm frightened, Wood God. Please, help me.

WOOD GOD: You hate and so you killed. You deliberately disobeyed me after I first sheltered you. I cannot protect you now.

ANATOU: Was I wrong to defend myself, Wood God, to wound when I was wounded?

WOOD GOD: You've been cruel, Anatou, and hate is like a disease spreading through your heart. If you strike an Eskimo, how does the Beaver know that you won't strike him, too, when he sleeps in the night?

ANATOU: No! I'd never do that. You know that, Wood God.

WOOD GOD: How do I know? I only see what you do. That speaks for itself.

ANATOU: (*Ashamed.*) I won't leave the forest again, Wood God. I have been wrong.

WOOD GOD: (*Angry.*) It's too late for that, Anatou. The hunters are here.

FOX: They're coming closer.

BEAVER: Closer.

ANATOU: (*Panicked.*) Wood God, what should I do?

WOOD GOD: *(Harshly.)* Replace the hunters you made them lose. Erase the terror you've caused them. Anatou, even the animals have been frightened of you.

ANATOU: But I didn't mean them. They've been good to me. I didn't want to hurt the animals.

WOOD GOD: *(Watching her intently.)* If you cannot live in peace with man, Anatou, then one day you will have to face his bow and arrow. There is no law of the forest that can protect you from that time.

ANATOU: Wood God, why didn't you warn me? Why did not you stop me? I have worn a coat of thick hate—so thick it stopped my feeling or seeing anything else.

WOOD GOD: We tried, Anatou, but before you weren't ready to hear our words.

ANATOU: I am now, Wood God. Please, please, animals.

FOX: Hurry, Anatou. They are closer.

ANATOU: What should I do?

WOOD GOD: Run, Anatou. There is no time if the hunters find you.

ANATOU: I know.

WOOD GOD: But remember this: if you are truly sorry, if you know what understanding means, if you can show me your heart is empty of all its dark hate and cruelty, no matter what happens, your spirit will not die. It will live forever and teach others. Remember that.

ANATOU: Thank you, Wood God.

WOOD GOD: Now run, Anatou.

ANIMALS: Run, Anatou, run. (ANATOU *exits across the stage. Village hunters enter. They are frightened. Suddenly a wind comes up.)*

VILLAGER 2: Aja! The wind is alive.

ATATA: Let's leave. No Eskimo should be here.

KIVIOG: No! We have promised our village.

TARTO: We cannot return 'till the wolf is found.

KIVIOG: Look! His tracks are here.

VILLAGER 2: Follow them!

KIVIOG: Sh-h-h-h. Fresh tracks. Quickly, carefully. *(There is silence as they begin the serious search.)*

ANIMALS: *(Whispering.)* Hurry, Anatou. Hurry. (ANATOU *streaks across the stage. They see her.)*

VILLAGER 1: Follow it! Follow it!

(They rush off left. TARTO, *who is behind them, gets trapped in the fallen trees; his bow and arrow fly to the side.* TARTO *tries to escape, but is caught fast.)*

TARTO: I can't get out! *(Trying to free himself.)* I'm trapped! *(There is deathly silence around him.)* Where did they go? I can't even hear them. *(Shouting.)* Father! Father, come back. Hurry! *(Sees his bow and arrow, but he can't reach it.* ANATOU *runs on right. She stumbles on bow and arrow and in so doing kicks it to other side.* TARTO *is terrified. He whispers horrified.)* The wolf. What'll I do? *(He tries to struggle out, but he can't.* ANATOU *comes closer.* TARTO *is wearing the charm she gave him. She half turns away.)*

ANATOU: It's Tarto! I've got to help him. (ANATOU *moves in.* TARTO *thinks she is going to attack him. He becomes more and more terrified.*)

TARTO: No! No! Father! Help! Help!

(*He covers his face instinctively, afraid to watch, but then forces himself to look. She pushes with all her might, and finally the pressure is released, and* TARTO *is out of the trap. He is amazed and does not understand what happened. As soon as* TARTO *is free,* ANATOU *starts to run, but it is too late. Just as she is passing the rock unit, we hear the whiz of an arrow, and* ANATOU *falls behind the rock unit.*)

No! He set me free. Don't kill him. He set me free. (KIVIOG, ATATA, *and* VIL-LAGER 2 *rush in.*)

KIVIOG: Tarto, what happened?

TARRTO: I got trapped over there in the logs . . . and then the wolf . . . he set me free.

KIVIOG: What?

TARTO: The wolf, Father, the wolf. That's the truth. He pulled the log away so I could get out. I thought he was going to kill me.

KIVIOG: Where is your bow and arrow?

TARTO: There! I couldn't reach them. But Father, he saved my life. He pushed the log away.

ATATA: Aja. The forest is alive with things we can't understand.

KIVIOG: Where is he now?

TARTO: The arrow hit him near the rock . . . but . . . (*They look. She is not there.*) He's not there. Where did he go?

ATATA: It may be a trick.

VILLAGER 2: (*Advancing cautiously.*) Here's a fresh footprint.

ATATA: Watch out. (*They move cautiously.*)

TARTO: (*With a cry.*) It's . . . (*Turns to* KIVIOG.) Anatou. It's Anatou. We've hurt her.

(*They all stare amazed by the sight of the girl.* TARTO *kneels down by the rock unit.* ANATOU's *spirit appears above. This can be done by seeing her through a scrim on a higher level so that she looks the same but paler, as though in a dream.*)

ANATOU: Tarto . . . don't cry.

TARTO: (*To himself.*) Anatou. You were my best friend. (*To her.*) I didn't mean to hurt you. Do you understand. We didn't mean . . . (*He can't say it.* TARTO *tries to hold back the anguish inside.*)

ANATOU: I do, Tarto, I do. Oh, Wood God, they can't hear me.

TARTO: She could have killed me, Father, but she didn't. She saved my life in-stead.

VILLAGER 2: Aja. She was brave.

KIVIOG: Braver than all the hunters of Little Whale River. None of us would have done what she did. (*He puts his hand on* TARTO's *shoulder, but he can't say what he'd like to.*)

VILLAGER 2: But why did she run into the forest?

TARTO: Don't you see? She had no place else to go. We chased her here. (*This is the most painful of all.*) Anatou, even I chased you away.

KIVIOG: We would not speak or smile at the different one, remember. Our silence was worse than a hundred harpoons.

TARTO: Will she forgive me, Father?

KIVIOG: The spirits of the dead know our hearts, Tarto. You cannot keep a secret from them.

TARTO: But will she forgive me.

KIVIOG: We are all to blame.

TARTO: But I want to know! I have to know! She saved me, Father, and then the hunters shot an arrow when she finished.

KIVIOG: She had a bigger heart than you or I, Tarto, but if she is angry, we'll be trapped by the snow and the wind and lose our way. No Eskimo should ever enter the realm of the forest. If she forgives us, our way will be safe.

ANATOU: Wood God! Please, let me help them.

WOOD GOD: (*Pleased.*) 'Til the end of the forest, and then I will guide them.

ANATOU: Do they understand, Wood God? How will they remember?

WOOD GOD: Tarto will tell your story tonight, the first time, and they will tell it for many nights. They will remember, for someone will always tell the story of Anatou, the Fair One.

VILLAGER 2: (*Goes over slowly and picks up the arrow, holds it thoughtfully.*) I shot it! I killed her!

KIVIOG: No, we all killed her. But when? Today or long ago?

CURTAIN

HOME ON THE MORNIN' TRAIN

by
Kim Hines

KIM HINES, a Minnesota actress, playwright, and director, first appeared on the professional stage as a child when she became a member of Children's Theatre Company of Minneapolis. She attended the theatre school and continued to perform in CTC productions for five years. She received a B.A. in Speech and Theatre and Visual Art from Macalester College in St. Paul, Minnesota.

As an actress Hines has performed at the majority of theatres in the Minneapolis/St. Paul area, including the Tyrone Guthrie. Her plays have been performed not only in the Twin Cities area but also in Philadelphia, Oakland, Chicago, and Washington, D.C.

As a director Hines has worked with many theatres in Minneapolis including Theatre Mu, Theatre in the Round, Park Square Theatre, Illusion Theatre, and Augsburg College. For the Great American History Theatre in St. Paul, she directed *Tom Boy Stone*, a play about an African-American who was the first woman to play major-league baseball. Recently, she directed Chekhov's *The Seagull* at Cornell University in New York.

Hines has received many awards for her plays that confront social issues and change in the lives of African-Americans as well as within the gay and lesbian communities. She has also been awarded numerous grants and fellowships including the prestigious Minnesota Bush Artist Fellowship Award for playwriting.

Kim Hines is a core member of the Playwrights' Center, a member of the

Screenwriter's Workshop and a member of Actor's Equity Association, as well as an Associate Artist at Illusion Theatre in Minneapolis.

—————————

For me the most rewarding aspect of writing plays for young people is their belief in the magical, the mystical, the enchanting . . . even if it is in everyday situations with everyday things and everyday people. Most young people believe (even if that belief is the size of a mustard seed) that magical and bizarre things will happen at some point and most times do . . . and the most magical moment is when they are there to witness it.

Writing for young people has, at times, not so gently, pushed me toward seeing the world in not such an adult way. It's a way of seeing, feeling, hearing, and even tasting that is not always fully appreciated for what it is . . . a gift.

—KIM HINES

The plays printed in this anthology are not to be used as acting
scripts. All inquiries regarding *Home on the Mornin' Train*
performance rights should be addressed to:

Dramatic Publishing Company
311 Washington Street
Woodstock, Illinois 60098

HOME ON THE MORNIN' TRAIN

CHARACTERS

1839	1939
Voices	Baruch Fischer
Jessie	Rifka Rubin
Brave Mary	Aaron
Kindred	Ledah Bergmann
Kati-Mae	Herr Westemeier
Sara Jane	Karl Westemeier
Lucius	David Müller
Adelaide	Young Man
Olivia	

SETTING

1839—Plantation, Talledega, Alabama
1939—Berlin, Germany

[*Home on the Mornin' Train* was originally produced by Steppingstone Theatre, Minneapolis, Minnesota.]

Scene 1

(The stage is black. A voice is heard singing in the darkness.)

VOICE: *(Singing.)*

> Steal away—
> Steal away—
> Steal away . . . to freedom.
> Steal away.
> Steal away home . . .
> I ain't got long to stay here . . .

(Singing segues into SOUND CUE: *barking dogs, men tracking a runaway female slave at night.)*

VOICE-OVER #1:

Over here! I think she's over here. . . . Hold that lantern up higher so we can see something! Damn! Damn! I don't see nothing out there. I think we lost her!

JESSIE:

(Whispers.) Lord—help me. . . .
*(*LIGHTS: *slowly fade up a pool of light.* JESSIE *is running in slow motion as she frantically looks over her shoulder, trying to outrun the men and dogs. Lights slowly fade to black.)*

VOICE-OVER #2: No—I think she went that way—I think I saw her.

VOICE-OVER #3: Well—just let the dogs loose and let *them* find her. These dogs are good at trackin' runaway slaves!

*(*SOUND CUE: *fades away and segues into the sound of wooden flute or clarinet playing a Jewish folk melody. The melody segues into sounds of "Polizei" sirens.*

A pool of light fades up on BARUCH *wearing a cloth yellow Star of David on his coat. He looks in both directions, flips up the collar of his coat, takes the star off of his coat and places it tentatively in his pocket and exits cautiously.*

LIGHTS *fade to black.)*

Scene 2

(The stage fills with fog or mist of early morning and late evening. As lights slowly fade up we see a silhouette of RIFKA *carrying a small suitcase.)*

RIFKA: Mother woke us up real early that morning. June 10th . . . 1939. I will always remember this date. It was about four or five in the morning.

BRAVE MARY: *(Enters opposite side of stage with small cloth bag slung over her shoulder.)* I didn't know the exact date . . . because I didn't know my numbers and I didn't know how to read. I just knew that it was the summer of 1839.

RIFKA: It was still dark. Just before sunrise.

BRAVE MARY: It was just after dusk . . . almost dark . . . about that time of night when skeeters don't bite as much. . . .

RIFKA: Mother told us to be very quiet . . . and to quickly pack a bag . . . we could only take *one* bag.

(JESSIE *enters on one side of the stage and* AARON *enters with bag in hand on other side of stage.*)

JESSIE: Just bring yourself.

BRAVE MARY: That's what Jessie said.

JESSIE: Don't need no bags to slow us down.

AARON: *(Puts his bag down and opens it and pulls out a small toy horse.)* Mommy said I could bring my horse . . . *(He looks through his bag and holds up a small wooden horse.)* But not my bear . . . she said it took up too much space. I packed some shirts. . . .

RIFKA: Underclothes, of course . . .

AARON: some socks. . . .

BRAVE MARY: He said . . .

JESSIE: Bring only what can never be replaced . . .

RIFKA: One dress and two skirts. . . .

AARON: Some pants and my blue sweater. But I left lots of room for—

RIFKA: My diary, some pictures of my best friends from Jewish school, Ellie and Rachel . . . and I packed my books—one from school . . . and one from America. My cousin in America sent me a book. I couldn't leave it behind. I haven't read it yet. Oh—and, of course, my prayer book.

AARON: *(Takes dreidel from his pocket and holds it up.)* And my lucky dreidel from last Channuka. I won a lot of geld with this dreidel.

JESSIE: And bring along what food that will keep on the road . . . and c'mon!

RIFKA: Mother and father took us to the edge of town.

KATIE-MAE: There was buzzing all over the plantation. But real quiet—secret-like. Couldn't have master finding out about us planning to leave, now, could we?

RIFKA: They took us to see a man named . . .

BARUCH: *(Walking out of the fog with bag in hand.)* Herr Westemeier. I never knew his first name, only his last name—Westemeier. He was tall and blonde and dressed—well—not like he lived in the city. More like a farmer. I could tell by his hands. They were rough and his nails dirty.

AARON: He didn't bring his wife with him only his son. His son named . . .

LEDAH: *(Walking out of the fog with bag in hand.)* Karl. He is young like us. Only he is a German gentile, and *we* are German Jews. We met in the woods on the edge of town. Karl said that his father had agreed to take five children this time.

KINDRED: When I heard that some younguns like me was planning to escape to freedom—I knew I had to go, too.

LEDAH: *(Turns to* RIFKA.) Rifka Rubin was there . . . and her little brother, Aaron.

RIFKA: There was Baruch Fischer . . .

DAVID: And Ledah Bergmann . . .

AARON: And the Muller's son, David.

JESSIE: I could only take about four with me, this time. (*Turning to* BRAVE MARY.) What do they call you?

BRAVE MARY: Brave Mary.

KATIE-MAE: Katie-Mae.

KINDRED: Kindred. And I know what they call you . . .

ALL/BLACK KIDS: Runaway Jessie.

JESSIE: Because I lead runaway slaves to freedom. (JESSIE *quiets the kids and motions for them to follow her. They exit.*)

BARUCH: My father said I was to listen to and obey the Westemeiers. My father said that not many gentiles were willing to help the Jews.

RIFKA: My mother said to be thankful.

LEDAH: Thankful that there were people courageous enough to help us.

DAVID: (*Walking out of the fog with bag in hand.*) Courageous enough to help us out of the city of Hamburg.

AARON: Out of Germany—

LEDAH: On to Denmark—

RIFKA: And finally to Sweden. We would be safe in Sweden.

BARUCH: It may take awhile. Because we have to hide along the way. Herr Westemeier said he has many friends that will help us get to Sweden. They will help along the way.

DAVID: But we must be very careful. He told us . . . that we might even have to lie and change our names.

RIFKA: But we can get rid of these. (*She unpins the yellow Star of David from her coat.*) I hate these yellow stars. . . . they make us wear them, so that people will know that we are different. . . .

LEDAH: So people will know that we are Jews. . . .

ALL: So people will hate us. . . .

RIFKA: I will be glad to leave this country. I want to be somewhere safe. Maybe one day I will live in America.

AARON: I asked Mommy when she and Daddy would meet up with us. She only cried and said—

LEDAH: Soon—my parents said they would join us soon. When? When is soon?

(LIGHTS *fade to black*)

SCENE 3

(*A small room in a barn on a small German farm.* AARON *plays with his dreidel,* DAVID *naps,* BARUCH *is reading a book,* LEDAH *sits playing with her doll.* RIFKA *sits with her suitcase open beside her, writing in her diary.*)

AARON: (*Tired of playing with his dreidel, moves over to his sister.*) What are you doing?

RIFKA: I'm writing in my diary.

AARON: (*Sitting next to her.*) What do you write about?

RIFKA: I write about what I experience . . . or what I'm thinking or what I'm feeling.

AARON: That sounds boring.

DAVID: It's what girls do. Girls always do boring things.

RIFKA: Girls are not the only ones who keep diaries, David. My father keeps a diary. . . .

AARON: Daddy keeps a diary? How do you know?

RIFKA: Because Mama and Daddy gave me this one. Daddy said that it's good to write down what happens in your life. Then many years from now you will look back and remember where you've been . . .

LEDAH: *(Holding up a very small doll.)* Rifka—will you tie this ribbon for me? *(RIFKA ties the ribbon in the doll's hair.)*

AARON: How long have we been here, Rifka?

RIFKA: Eleven days. . . .

BARUCH: *(Looking up from his book.)* Actually it's been twelve days. . . . I've been keeping track.

LEDAH: How long will we be here? Twelve more days?

AARON: Twelve weeks?

LEDAH: Twelve months?

BARUCH: *(Barely looking up from his book.)* Years?

RIFKA: Don't be silly.

DAVID: We're not going to stay here forever.

LEDAH: *(Crossing to DAVID.)* How long *are* we going to stay here?

DAVID: I don't know. Ask Rifka. . . .

RIFKA: Don't ask me . . . I don't know. I'm just as much in the dark as you are.

AARON: *(Looking through a small cloth bag.)* Look! You've got jewels . . . you're rich Rifka . . . *(DAVID and LEDAH move to RIFKA's suitcase and look at it's contents.)*

RIFKA: No, I'm not. Put those down, Aaron.

DAVID: *(Stroking the outside of the suitcase.)* My mother has a suitcase like this. She got it while on holiday in Great Britain.

AARON: *(Grabbing a strand of pearls.)* Do you think kings wear jewels? If I put these on, will I be a king?

RIFKA: Hardly—here give them to me. *(She takes pearls from AARON and puts them with her other jewelry. LEDAH has now pulled out a skirt from RIFKA's suitcase and stands holding it up against her body.)*

LEDAH: Oh Rifka . . . what a beautiful skirt. Can I have this when you get too big for it?

RIFKA: *(Grabbing her skirt.)* No! This is my favorite skirt. *(Holding it up and admiring it.)* I don't think I'll ever give it up . . . even if I grow out of it.

DAVID: *(paging through book)* Where did you get this book? It's not German. . . .

RIFKA: No—it's not. It's a book from America. From my cousin, Greta. She lives in a place called New Braunfels. It's in Texas.

LEDAH: Where's that?

AARON: *(Smugly.)* In the United States of America. . . .

DAVID: What's this book about?

RIFKA: I don't know. I haven't read it yet.

DAVID: When are you going to read it?

RIFKA: When I feel like it.

DAVID: Well, if you're not going to read it soon, can I read the book, now?

RIFKA: *(Taking the book and putting it back in her suitcase.)* No! I want to read it first. *(She goes back to writing in her diary.)*

DAVID: That may take centuries!

LEDAH: *(Picking up book and looking at it.)* I don't think I can read this book, it looks too hard. Will you read it to me?

RIFKA: Ledah, please I'm trying to write. . . .

AARON: Why not? It will give us something to do.

DAVID: Yeah—a good way to kill time.

RIFKA: Oh—all right. *(Sets down her pen and diary.)*

LEDAH: What's the name of the book, Rifka?

RIFKA: *(Reading the title of the book.)* "Following the Drinking Gourd: A Negro Slave Girl's Escape to Freedom." *(She sits and makes herself comfortable as she starts to read from the book.)* "Dear reader . . . I want to stress that though this journey may seem treacherous and doubtful, it did indeed happen. Every word of this story is true. My name is Mary Cunningham. I was born a slave. I am now a free woman, but while I was a slave, people called me . . .

BRAVE MARY: *(Appears in a pool of light.)* "Brave Mary—because I spoke of freedom so often. Freedom was a fearful subject to speak or even think of. But since I spoke of freedom in spite of the threat of death . . . people called me Brave Mary. I lived in . . . Tus-ca-loosa, Alabama—"

LEDAH: Where is that, Rifka?

RIFKA: It's someplace in America. I'm not sure where, but I know that it's in America. *(Reads.)* "The year is 1839.

BRAVE MARY: "Master Herbert Cole's plantation stood surrounded by a deep, thick, pine forest. The Cole plantation was known for its lumber and the making of turpentine.

RIFKA: "Master Cole was a very rich white man and owned many things.

BRAVE MARY: "He owned over one thousand acres of land,

RIFKA: "Three homes, several stables of horses, and over two hundred slaves. . . ." *(LIGHTS fade out on BRAVE MARY.)*

AARON: What are slaves, Rifka?

RIFKA: Slaves are people . . . who are owned by . . . and made to work for other people for no pay. Many times slaves are treated very badly. . . .

AARON: Oh.

DAVID: We were once slaves . . .

AARON: I've never been a slave!

DAVID: I'm talking about us . . . Jews.

LEDAH: Jews were once slaves? Is that true, Rifka?

RIFKA: Yes, Ledah . . .

AARON: When did this happen? I don't remember about us being slaves.

DAVID: It happened a long, long, long time ago, silly. What do you think Pesach is about? We were in Egypt. We were slaves to the Egyptians.

AARON: But this story . . . (Pointing to the book.) Are these slaves owned by the Egyptians, too?

RIFKA: No, Aaron. This story is about the blacks in America. They were slaves, too. But not so long ago.

LEDAH: If I were treated badly, I wouldn't stay. I don't understand. Why didn't the slaves just leave?

DAVID: They can't, Ledah. If they want to leave they have to run away . . . in secret. . . .

RIFKA: (Goes back to reading aloud.) "It is late at night. The moon sits high in the sky. Stars twinkle against the dark sky . . ."

(JESSIE, a slave in her teens, sits in the underbrush. A walking stick lays by her side. She also has a small bag slung across her body. She dozes for a moment. The sound of a birdcall breaks the silence. JESSIE awakes with a start. She quietly scrambles to her feet and makes the sound of a bird call in response to the sound she just heard. There is silence, and then the bird call in response to JESSIE.)

BRAVE MARY: (Softly calls from offstage at a distance.) Jessie, Jessie—

JESSIE: Over here—straight due north. (She strains to see if she spots anything.)

BRAVE MARY: (Off stage.) C'mon Katie-Mae, you gotta keep up now. . . . (BRAVE MARY enters. She is followed by KINDRED. KATIE-MAE brings up the rear.)

KATIE-MAE: (Entering.) I'm coming . . . I'm coming. Y'all walk so fast . . .

BRAVE MARY: We ain't got no time to waste. . . .

KATIE-MAE: (Mumbling.) It's hard to keep up . . . like you going to a house o' fire or something. . . .

JESSIE: Shhhhhhh! Y'all better keep your voices down. Y'all don't know who's all up in this forest. They would've done found you out, and next thing you know, they'd be dragging y'all back to the plantation.

KATIE-MAE: I ain't going back to that place.

BRAVE MARY: You're always fussing—

KATIE-MAE: I ain't going back there ever again in this life.

JESSIE: Keep talking out loud like that, and you ain't gonna have a choice. (To BRAVE MARY.) Is this all that's coming this time, Brave Mary?

BRAVE MARY: All that had the nerve to take a chance on freedom. This here is Sara Jane. That's Kindred . . . and you've already heard Lucius' mouth.

KATIE-MAE: Shhhhh! You're talking too loud.

BRAVE MARY: Shhhhhh—yourself!

JESSIE: I'll let you set and rest for a moment, but then we've got to be on our way. We've got to reach the first house before daylight. And we've got a lot of road to cover before then.

KINDRED: How far do we have to go? Where is this first house?

JESSIE: We've got to get to a place just on the other side of the Setterholm plantation.

BRAVE MARY: That *is* some distance. I don't know . . .

JESSIE: We'll do whatever we need to do. We've got to get there before daylight.

KATIE-MAE: What's the hurry? By the time Master Cole finds out that we're gone, we'll be long out of sight. We could take our time, and when daylight comes, we can sleep in the tall grasses, bushes . . . trees . . .

BRAVE MARY: Girl, I'm glad you ain't leading us. . . .

JESSIE: We can't be out and about in the daylight, Katie-Mae. Tomorrow morning is market day. There's gonna be all sorts folks on the road taking their wares to the market. We can't take a chance on being seen. We need to be up and out of the way long before them wagons start out on them roads. That means at dawn we have to be safely at the Sunshine house.

KINDRED: Sunshine house? I ain't never heard of such a place.

BRAVE MARY: That ain't their real name. It's best that you don't know their real name. So if we get caught . . . you won't be forced to tell whose house it really is.

KATIE-MAE: Can we trust these white people?

JESSIE: We can sure enough trust them. Not all white people believe in owning slaves. Some of these people have been helping black folks to get up north for many a year.

BRAVE MARY: And not without fearing the law themselves.

JESSIE: The Sunshine house is the first stop on the underground railroad.

KATIE-MAE: Now, I know that you're funning us, 'cause everybody knows that railroads don't run underneath the ground. . . .

DAVID: Yes, they do, Rifka. We have the Untergrundbahn. And they have trains that run underneath the ground in Britain, too.

AARON: They even have them in America . . . in a city called New York. They call them subways. I know, my uncle sent me a postcard from there, once.

RIFKA: But, this was a long time ago, before the Untergrundbahn, and subways were built. Anyhow, I don't think they're talking about real trains running under the ground.

JESSIE: *(Laughs.)* Sho', trains run underground. That's how I move my passengers on to freedom. We have stops to make all along the way . . . like the Birmingham line or the Gadsden line. You're gonna make stops, and folks will have to hide you so no one will know that you're on the run.

BRAVE MARY: Sometimes you'll get hid up in someone's old attic . . . or maybe you might get hid out in a barn . . . or down underneath in a cellar. . . .

LEDAH: That's just like us . . . they keep hiding us, too.

AARON: We're hiding in a barn right now.

JESSIE: You'll rest and get fed, and then you'll move on just like a train. People will help you along 'til you make your way to freedom.

KINDRED: Brave Mary. . . .

BRAVE MARY: Yes . . .

KINDRED: I'm hungry.

JESSIE: *(Opens her pouch.)* I've got a little pork rind here. . . . I'm willing to share.

KATIE-MAE: I'll take a little of that, myself. . . .

JESSIE: *(Breaks off pieces for everyone.)* Here—this will get your energy up . . . when you're finished eating, we'll be on our way.

(She breaks off a piece for herself. As she chews on the piece of pork rind, she moves away from the group and looks up into the sky. BRAVE MARY sees JESSIE and moves down to her.)

BRAVE MARY: Pretty sky, isn't it?

JESSIE: It's beautiful all right. And so clear. You can see the dipping gourd as plain as can be.

KINDRED: *(Moving down to them.)* Where? Where's the dipping gourd?

BRAVE MARY: You see that big shining star? If you were to take your finger . . . *(She takes KINDRED's finger and traces in the air.)* . . . start here . . . and see . . . here is the cup part, and here is the handle . . . see a drinking gourd. . . .

JESSIE: You're gonna follow the drinking gourd to get you up north . . . to get you to Canada . . .

KINDRED: But how are we gonna do that?

BRAVE MARY: The stars will guide us to our new home. The stars will guide us to freedom. . .

(Starts to sing.)

> *Follow the drink-ing gourd!*
> *Follow the drink-ing gourd.*
> *For Tom is a-waiting*
> *For to carry you to free-dom,*
> *If you follow the drink-ing gourd.*

JESSIE: C'mon gather yourselves up. You're about to board the train right now. You're about to travel on the underground railroad. Brave Mary and I are the conductors.

(Sings.)

> *The riverbank makes a very good road,*
> *The dead trees will show you the way.*
> *Left foot, right foot, traveling on,*
> *Follow the drinking gourd.*

ALL:

> *Follow the drink-ing gourd!*
> *Follow the drink-ing gourd.*
> *For Jessie is a-waiting*
> *For to carry you to free-dom,*
> *If you follow the drink-ing gourd.*

JESSIE: All aboard!

BRAVE MARY: All aboard! *(She lines the children up.)*

ALL: *(Making sound of train.)* Choo-Choo!

JESSIE: First stop on the line . . . the Sunshine house. *(All children on stage laugh.)*

Shhhhhh! Follow me.

(The black children exit as KARL *knocks on the door, startling the Jewish children. He enters with food and a bucket of water.)*

KARL: I've got a little something for you to eat.

AARON: You scared us. . . .

LEDAH: Sssssssh! *(To* KARL.*)* Rifka is reading us a story.

KARL: What are you reading?

AARON: It's about the underground railroad.

KARL: What kind of railroad?

RIFKA: A wonderful story from America. . . .

AARON: About the blacks. . . .

DAVID: And a railroad. . . .

LEDAH: Yeah—they're running away from . . . what's that place called?

AARON: Egypt.

RIFKA: No—it's called a plantation.

AARON: Ohhh yes, that's right.

DAVID: Start a new chapter, Rifka . . . I want to know what happens. *(Children ad-lib.)*

RIFKA: Baruch, do you have your time piece? What is the time?

BARUCH: *(Pulls watch out and looks at it.)* We've only got about another hour of daylight . . .

KARL: You will have to wait until tomorrow to finish reading. You must eat now. *(Passing out food.)* I won't be back anymore today.

BARUCH: *(Taking food.)* What was it like outside, today? It's hard to know. It's so hot and stuffy in here.

KARL: It was a beautiful day today, Baruch. Nice sunny day with just a hint of breeze. I spent the day working in the garden. It was a good day for that.

DAVID: I wish we could go outside. *(Turning to* KARL.*)* Your farm is so far away from town. If you let us out for a little bit each day—no one will know. And if they did know, I bet people would just turn their heads. I bet no one would even give a thought to our being here.

KARL: People travel the roads all the time, David. Suppose we let all of you out to play in the field or in the garden near the house, and you are seen? How could we explain? What would we say? People chattering throughout the town like hens . . . "Uh—yes Frau Westemeier has *six* children now! How could that be, when they just had only one son yesterday!" *(He takes out a cup from his back pocket and dips it into the bucket of water as children takes turns to sip water.)*

Once word reaches the Nazis—they will not turn their heads. They will come and take you AND my parents AND me away. We will all lose our lives. And there will be three less Germans to help the Jews to safety.

AARON: When are we leaving here?

KARL: I don't know. All I know is that my father is working on it. He doesn't always tell my mother and I where or what he's doing when he looks for places for Jews to hide.

BARUCH: *(Takes cup of water and pours it over his hands, washing them.)* Karl—if I were to write a letter ... home ... would your father be able to get it to my parents? Safely?

KARL: Nothing and no one is safe. But—you write the letter—I'll ask my father.

DAVID: What's there to write about? Nothing happens here. We can't leave this place. . . . And there's practically nothing to do.

AARON: We could write about the treats that the Westemeiers give us.

LEDAH: I haven't eaten my piece of chocolate, yet. I'm saving it.

AARON: What for?

LEDAH: For when we can go home. Then I will share it with Mama, Papa, and my little dog Sacha.

BARUCH: You should eat your piece of chocolate, Ledah. We may never get out of here.

RIFKA: *(Throws a look at BARUCH.)* The Westemeiers said that they wouldn't let the soldiers take us.

KARL: And if you're careful no one will even know that you're up here.

BARUCH: I'll write my letter. It's the only way that our parents know that I'm alive.

KARL: Well—eat, first. There will be no more food until tomorrow mid day. Eat—everyone eat.

(KARL exits. The children take their food and settle themselves and eat. LEDAH sits with RIFKA . . . they chatter away as they eat. DAVID sits near BARUCH. BARUCH sets his food in front of him and says a prayer. AARON watches him from a distance.)

BARUCH: Baruch ata, adonai eloheinu, melekh ha olam, ha-motzi lechem min ha-aretz. Blessed are You, our God, Ruler of the universe. We thank You for the bread which comes from the seeds which grow in the earth that You created.

(In the background a lone flute is softly heard playing a Jewish folk song.)

AARON: *(Approaches BARUCH.)* My father doesn't make Rifka and me say our prayers in Hebrew.

BARUCH: So, what? *(Starts to eat his food.)*

AARON: So, why do you? And why do you wear your kipah? You don't have to, you know. You don't have to wear it in here. Your father is not watching.

BARUCH: My father has nothing to do with my wearing my kipah. I wear it because I want to. I wear it out of respect to God.

AARON: My father thinks that some Jews want to stand out ... that's why we have so many problems. They should try to blend in more.

BARUCH: Aaron . . . there are many different kinds of Jews in the world. We all do not do the same things in the same way. We all do not have the same ideas. And sometimes we don't wear the same type of clothing or speak the same language ... yet we are all Jews. And—there is room for all of us. There is room for everybody . . . gentile and Jew . . . there is room for everybody.

DAVID: Tell that to the Nazis.

RIFKA: *(Laughing with LEDAH.)* Okay—do you know this song? "You Are the Plowman and You Sow?" *(LEDAH shakes her head "no.")* All right, it goes like this . . . *(Sings.)*

> You are the plowman and you sow,
> You are the farmers and you mow,
> And you toil with might and main:
> What, my people, is your gain?
>
> Kling klang, kling klang,
> The hammer beats relentlessly.
> Kling, klang, kling, klang,
> Break the bonds of slavery.
>
> Day and night you weave on the loom,
> Dig out metals in the gloom,
> Reap the harvest in due time,
> Flowing horn of bread and wine.

(All the other children join in on the chorus.)

ALL:

> Kling klang, kling klang,
> The hammer beats relentlessly.
> Kling, klang, kling, klang,
> Break the bonds of slavery.

RIFKA:

> But what feasts have you to share?
> And what festive clothes to wear?
> Where, my people, is your sharp sword?
> Where, oh, where is your reward?

ALL:

> Kling klang, kling klang,
> The hammer beats relentlessly.
> Kling, klang, kling, klang,
> Break the bonds of slavery.
>
> Kling klang, kling klang,
> The hammer beats relentlessly.
> Kling, klang, kling, klang,
> Break the bonds of slavery.

(The children are singing and dancing with abandon . . . suddenly there is a loud pounding on the door.)

VOICE: Ruhe! Ruhe! Quiet—please!

(The children suddenly are quiet and each picks a place to "settle-in" . . . they hum quietly.

LIGHTS *fade to black.)*

SCENE 4

(It is late . . . all the children are asleep, except for BARUCH. *He burns a small candle as he writes his letter to his parents . . . reading from his paper.)*

BARUCH: ". . . There isn't any need to worry about me. I am safe and sound. We are treated well . . . and we get two meals each day. Mostly bread, corn, and soup. I miss Mama's cooking . . . especially her Kartoffel mit Käse . . . I can almost smell it cooking now. *(Pause.)* I wonder who picks up *Die Zeitung* for Herr Jungmann. He likes his paper at a quarter past eight o'clock . . . to read before going to work. And I hope that Mitzie is not proving to be a problem. I'm sure she misses me . . . because I miss her so much. I'm sorry I didn't bring her with me. There are mice here, and they come out at night and feed on the crumbs we leave on the floor. I hate the sound of mice rustling through the hay."

(He stops reading.) I worry about my parents. I'm their only child. It was hard to leave them. But my father says that there are rumors about the Juden. That we aren't being sent away temporarily like the government said. We are being sent away for good. There are stories about ovens and . . . fire . . . and guns . . . death. My parents, sent me away just in case the government lied. They said that I should have a chance to live . . . to be free . . .

JESSIE: *(Holding a lantern as if talking to a group of people.)* Freedom! I've heard that word since I was this high. *(Indicates with her hand.)* Mama singing songs, Daddy talking about when we were back in Africa, free as we wanted to be . . . and how someday we would be free again. Mama died giving birth to her fourteenth child for the master to sell. Daddy got traded off up the Mississippi to someplace called Missouri. When I turned twelve, I figured I'd take my chance on freedom . . . now I come back and help others to be free. . . .

(Sings.)
                    Oh freedom—

KINDRED: *(Lights come up on him as if he is sitting by a fire.)* When I get up to Canada—

JESSIE: *(Sings.)*
                    Oh freedom—

KINDRED: First thing I'm gonna do—

JESSIE: *(Sings.)*
                    Oh freedom, over me . . .

KINDRED: . . . is thank the Lord for getting us there safe.

JESSIE: *(Sings.)*
            And before I stay a slave . . . I'll be buried in my grave . . .

KINDRED: And then I'm gonna do the buck and wing, and laugh and strut all over the place. I'm gonna shout about how I'm free and bound to no man ever again.

JESSIE: *(Sings.)*
                And go home . . . and go home and be free. . . .
                And go home . . . and go home and be free. . . .

BARUCH: *(Sings prayer.)*
> Baruch ata, adonai eloheinu, melekh ha-olam,

KINDRED: *(Sings.)*
> Oh Freedom. . . . Oh freedom. . . .

BARUCH: *(Sings.)*
> Sim shalom, tova u-v'rakha, chen va-chessed ve-rachamim . . .

JESSIE & KINDRED: *(Sings.)*
> Oh Freedom over me. . . .

BARUCH: *(Sings.)*
> Aleinu ve-al kol yisrae'el amehkha.

JESSIE & KINDRED: *(Sings.)*
> And before I be a slave, I'll be buried in my grave.
> And go home and go home and be free . . .

BARUCH: *(Speaks.)* Blessed are You, our God, Ruler of the universe, God grant us peace and goodness, blessings and grace, kindness and mercy.

JESSIE & KINDRED: *(Sings.)*
> And go home and go home and be free . . .

(Lights fade out on KINDRED and JESSIE.)

BARUCH: *(Speaks.)* Ha-rachaman hu yevarekh et avi mori ve-et immi morati. *(Quietly.)* God bless my mother and my father.

(BARUCH blows his candle out. Lights fade to black.)

SCENE 5

(ADELAIDE quickly enters with blankets and pillows followed by the black children. KATIE-MAE is the last one in as she hobbles in on a bad foot. She sits as soon as she can.)

ADELAIDE: You've come so late. We thought for a while you had changed your minds. We expected you six hours ago.

JESSIE: No, ma'am. A person never changes his mind about freedom. It's either you want it, or you don't.

ADELAIDE: You're lucky that you weren't seen. Why, any number of people would start talking to see five coloreds stealing into this house in broad daylight.

KINDRED: We had one heck of a time getting here and not being seen.

BRAVE MARY: We tried to get here before sun up. But we had to take turns helping Katie-Mae . . .

KINDRED: We had to half carry her, and she's a lot heavier than any of us thought.

JESSIE: Katie-Mae has got a bad foot. She's gonna need some attention.

ADELAIDE: *(Moves to KATIE-MAE.)* Let me take a look at your foot.

KINDRED: She's been working in the main house for so long—she ain't had a chance for her feet to toughen up . . .

KATIE-MAE: Be quiet, Kindred—you ain't got no right—

JESSIE: *(Cuts them off.)* Stop it, the both of you! *(Turning to Adelaide.)* I tried to bust open them blisters as best I could, but her foot keeps oozing and looks like she's got an infection set in already.

BRAVE MARY: If we had had a little more light and a little more time in the woods, I maybe coulda found some herbs to place on her foot.

ADELAIDE: *(To* KATIE-MAE.*)* I'll have to clean this all out and bandage your foot. It's the best I can do for you. The doctor in this town is not to be trusted.

KATIE-MAE: Whatever you can do, ma'am. I ain't complainin'.

ADELAIDE: I'll be right back. I'll help set up your bedding, and then I'll get you your food. I'm sure you travelers are hungry.

JESSIE: Thank you, ma'am . . . thank you.

(ADELAIDE exits.)

BRAVE MARY: *(Turning to* KINDRED.*)* You stop picking on Katie-Mae. You hear me, Kindred?

KINDRED: Well, it ain't my fault that she's so soft that she can't make the journey without her feet blistering up. If she had been working out in the fields like some of us, she'd be ready to travel anywhere. . . .

KATIE-MAE: I ain't had no say as to where I work on the plantation, Kindred. You know that as well as I do. Besides if you had a chance to come out of those fields and work in the house—wouldn't you do it?

KINDRED: *(Hesitant.)* I don't know—

KATIE-MAE: I bet you, you would!

JESSIE: Y'all quit fussing. Miss Adelaide's been nice enough to take us in at this point, and we're gonna act accordingly. So, y'all better stop this, all this snapping at each other—

(ADELAIDE enters with some blankets and a small box with bandages.)

ADELAIDE: *(Sorting out the blankets and giving one to each of the children.)* Here are some blankets for you. *(Beat.)* I think I should tell you that there have been some changes in plans.

BRAVE MARY: What changes?

ADELAIDE: The original plan was to have y'all staying here for a couple of days 'til a boat could be . . . "borrowed" . . . to get you part way up the Black Warrior River. I thought it would take several days to get the boat. But I got one a little sooner than I expected.

BRAVE MARY: *(Smiling.)* Well, I don't see anything wrong with that. Leaving here sooner means that we get up to Canada sooner. No, I don't see nothing wrong with that, at all.

ADELAIDE: Canada is an awful long ways from here. . . .

KINDRED: *(Sensing* ADELAIDE's *hesitancy.)* How long are we staying?

ADELAIDE: You've got about about nine hours before dusk . . . and then I'll be taking you down to the river.

BRAVE MARY: Nine hours? Why so soon?

ADELAIDE: If you miss the boat tonight . . . I can't guarantee when I will be able to get you another. You could be walled up in this room for weeks . . . maybe even months.

KINDRED: I'm hungry. When are we going to eat?

BRAVE MARY: *(To* ADELAIDE.*)* We need rest and food. We can't go back out on that road tonight.

JESSIE: To get to the river will take us five or six hours on foot . . . maybe even longer, unless you've got a wagon.

ADELAIDE: No. We'll have to go on foot. *(The children look at each other, not knowing what to say.)* Well, you do what you will. I'll be back to find out what decision you've made. I'll get your food now. *(Starts to exit.)* You know you won't be able to stay here indefinitely. The sheriff and the paddy-rollers come through every now and then looking for runaways. We've done a good job in keeping one step ahead of the law. But no one is without enemies. . . . My family has been accused of harboring slaves even when we had none in hiding with us. The Lord's been good. We've never been caught. But just the same, I don't want to try our luck anymore than is needed. *(Exits.)*

KINDRED: *(Almost to himself.)* That white girl is gonna take us down to the river, by foot?

BRAVE MARY: What are we gonna do?

JESSIE: What you asking a question like that for? You know what we have to do.

BRAVE MARY: I'm so tired now. I don't think I can make it down to the river. And Katie-Mae . . . poor Katie-Mae over there is in a lot of pain already . . . how are we gonna make it down there to meet that boat?

KATIE-MAE: Well—maybe y'all will have to go on without me. I'm not about to hold anybody back.

JESSIE: We can't leave you behind, Katie-Mae.

KATIE-MAE: And you sure enough can't wait for me to catch up with y'all, either. The pain is so bad in my feet . . . if that white woman were to come back here with the biggest butcher knife she could find, and tell me that I had to lose my feet in order not to feel the pain . . . why I'd let her cut these feet right off my legs.

BRAVE MARY: We ain't letting her take your feet, Katie-Mae.

KATIE-MAE: I wanted to see Canada so bad. I wanted to see freedom. We ain't even out of Alabama, and just my luck to have my feet give out on me. . . .

BRAVE MARY: You just get some rest . . . see how you feel later . . .

(Lights cross fade from the slave children to the Jewish children. The door opens and startles them.)

KARL: *(Out of breath, putting on his jacket.)* David, Aaron, and Ledah, get your things . . .

RIFKA: Why, what is wrong? Where are they going?

KARL: Father says that he has a chance to move some of you on by boat to Denmark. There's only room for the little ones right now.

AARON: I want to stay with my sister.

LEDAH: I want to stay with Rifka, too.

KARL: *(Urgently.)* There is no time for this. Father wants to leave within minutes. He's going to hide you in the wagon under straw and vegetables. Get your things! I'll be back to take you to the wagon. (*Exits.*)

AARON: I don't want to go! (*Crying, running to* RIFKA.)

RIFKA: (*Trying to comfort* AARON.) Aaron, it's all right. Herr Westemeier will take very good care of you. . . .

AARON: But, I want you to come, too.

RIFKA: I'll be there, it'll just be later.

LEDAH: (*Pulling* RIFKA's *arm.*) I want to go when you go . . .

RIFKA: (*Turning to* LEDAH.) You and Aaron and David are lucky. You know why? Because you'll get there before Baruch and I will get there. Won't that be fun?

AARON: But how do you know? How do you know that it will be fun?

LEDAH: How do you know that you'll get there?

AARON: What if something happens, and they come and take you away?

DAVID: What if *we* get taken away?

BARUCH: (*Breaks in and grabs* DAVID.) You won't . . . they can't take you away . . .

DAVID: Yes, they can. . . .

BARUCH: (*Sternly.*) No, they won't—because you will have something special to keep you safe.

AARON: What is that?

BARUCH: (*Stalling, as he thinks.*) Something . . . something . . . magical. You will have something magical to keep you safe. (*He moves quickly going through his bag and pulls out five marbles.*) You will each have your own magic marble.

DAVID: And what will a stupid marble do?

BARUCH: It will protect you. Here. (*He places a marble in* DAVID's *hand.*) David, I will give you rot, red for strength . . . strength to fight off all enemies. Aaron, I will give you blau, blue for peace . . . so that your journey will be a peaceful one. Ledah, gelb, yellow for joy . . . so that when you reach safety, you will encounter nothing but joy.

AARON: What about Rifka . . . what color marble are you going to give to her?

BARUCH: (*Turning to* RIFKA.) Rifka will have purpurn, purple for honor and dignity . . . so that she will be treated well.

LEDAH: What color will you have Baruch?

BARUCH: I will take the grün, green.

AARON: Let me see. (BARUCH *gives him the marble.* AARON *holds it up.*) What does yours stand for?

BARUCH: Friendship. Friends are very important. They help you when you are in need. I will always remember you . . . my friends. (*Beat.*) And when you look at your marbles or hold them in your hand . . . (*He holds his marble in his hand and the others follow suit.*) You will magically protect yourself and the others as well.

RIFKA: (*Breaking the moment.*) Come—we must get you ready. . . . Karl will be back soon. Where is your bag, Aaron?

AARON: (*Pointing.*) Over there.

RIFKA: Well, get it then. Ledah . . . bring your hat over here so that I can tie it for you. (LEDAH *brings the hat to* RIFKA *who ties it on her head.*)

BARUCH: *(To* DAVID.) Do you have everything?

DAVID: Yes.

BARUCH: *(Pats his back.)* It will be all right.

(KARL *enters*)

KARL: Father is ready with the wagon. Are you ready to go?

RIFKA: They're ready. *(Turning to the children.)* You be good . . . *(Kisses* DAVID.) . . . and listen to what Herr Westemeier has to tell you . . . *(Kisses Ledah.)* . . . and do what they say. *(Kisses and holds* AARON.)

AARON: Rifka? *(Pulls horse from his bag.)* Here . . . I think my horse wants to stay and keep you and Baruch company.

RIFKA: *(Taking the horse from* AARON *and holding it.)* Thank you, Aaron . . . Baruch and I would be very pleased to have your horse stay with us.

KARL: I'm sorry we have to go.

(RIFKA *hugs and kisses* AARON *again. As* KARL *ushers the children out, the room darkens.* BARUCH *goes and sits in his corner of the room, and* RIFKA *moves down into the pool of light, holding her brother's toy horse.*)

RIFKA: *(sings)*
> The Lord bless you and keep you.
> The Lord make his face to shine upon you, and be gracious to you.
> The Lord lift up his countenance toward you and grant you peace.
> And may it be good in Thy sight to bless the People of Israel and
> All peoples at all times and in every hour, with Thy peace.
> Amen.

(LIGHTS *fade to black.*)

SCENE 6

(KARL *stands in a pool of light.*)

KARL: When the German government made it law to treat the Jews badly, meine Eltern . . . my parents . . . felt that it was wrong. They had few Jewish friends so I did not understand at first why they felt the laws were not right. Mein Vater said . . .

VOICE-OVER #4: Today, it is Jews. Tomorrow, it may be only farmers . . . or people who walk with a cane . . . or perhaps, little boys named Karl. It is wrong to single out people like the government has done. These people have done nothing wrong. No! It is the government that is wrong!

KARL: I get a little worried when Vater takes Jews to the next site unaided. I usually ride with him in the wagon. But Vater wanted me to stay here with Mutter and watch over things. There is talk that someone has told the SS about us. Truth or not, it will not be safe to keep Baruch and Rifka here for much longer. I have gotten them both papers and new birth certificates . . . and new names. I hope that I haven't forgotten anything. We had to move so quickly this time.

KARL: *(Beat.)* Why would someone turn us in when we are helping so many people. Why?

(Lights cross-fade to ADELAIDE *who is sitting at a small desk writing.)*

ADELAIDE: There! *(Holding up the paper to admire her work.)* That looks official. *(To the audience.)* I'm getting better and better at this. I forge these papers for runaway slaves. If they are stopped they will have the "proper papers" to get them on their way . . . without incident. It warms my heart to be able to help in this manner. *(Beat.)* My father is the banker in town. We don't own slaves because my father doesn't believe in slavery. We are a family of abolitionists and we fight for the freedom of the slaves. But when you live in the land of Dixie—you don't let others know what you feel or what you're doing. You see, it's against the law to help slaves to escape. It's practically against the law to let them breathe . . . as long as they are working . . . no problem . . . but if we were to treat the Negroes as human beings . . . we could be thrown in prison or worse yet, put to death. We've got a lot of greedy, ignorant people that want Negroes to stay slaves. It's all about money. And I should know, my father's a banker. *(Beat.)* My family and I are committed to helping slaves escape to the North for as long as we can . . . for as long as it takes . . . until the Negroes are freed from slavery.

(LIGHTS fade to black.)

SCENE 7

(Black children start singing in darkness. Lights fade up on BARUCH *reading from the book. The singing continues underneath* BARUCH's *reading)*

ALL:
> Wade in the water
> Wade in the water, children . . .
> Wade in the water—
> God's gonna trouble the water.

> Wade in the water
> Wade in the water, children . . .
> Wade in the water—
> God's gonna trouble the water.

> See that man all dressed in white.
> God's gonna trouble the water.
> Must be the leader of the Israelites.
> God's gonna trouble the water.

> See that man all dressed in red.
> God's gonna trouble the water.
> Must be the band that Moses led.
> God's gonna trouble the water.

> Wade in the water
> Wade in the water, children . . .

Wade in the water—
God's gonna trouble the water.

BARUCH: *(Reading from book.)* Dear reader, we were cautious as we made our way down to the river—to the boat waiting to bring us closer to freedom. *(Pause.)* We kept clear of the road and traveled through the underbrush, just on the edge of the woods. Adelaide had us dressed in dark clothing and gave us forged papers saying that we were free to travel, just in case we were stopped along the way. *(Pause.)* When we reached the river, we were met by a young woman dressed in men's clothing. She wore a tattered hat and black boots and had a gun strapped to her waist.

(Light fades up on the black children gathered at the river. ADELAIDE *is making introductions for* OLIVIA.)

ADELAIDE: Y'all—this is Olivia. She will take you up Black Warrior River.

OLIVIA: *(Notices JESSIE.)* Jessie! *(They laugh and hug.)*

JESSIE: *(To ADELAIDE.)* You should've told me that Olivia was gonna be our conductor up this here river.

ADELAIDE: I didn't know that you knew one another.

JESSIE: Olivia helped me the first time I escaped on my own. She helped me get to a place called Ohio. She told me who to trust and what not.

OLIVIA: Well, I'm gonna get you as far as the river flows, and then Jessie you'll have to lead 'em up through Corona, and further north will get y'all into Tennessee.

ADELAIDE: Now, listen . . . when you get to Corona, you're gonna stop at a green and brown house just on the edge of town. It's the largest house in the area. You can't miss it. When you reach the house, you will ask for a Mr. Wheeler. You will ask him for the best way to get to Hamilton, Alabama, . . . and he will answer "By way of truth and honor." By those words you will know that you have the correct house and are safe.

BRAVE MARY: Thank you, Miss Adelaide.

JESSIE: My thanks to you, too.

ADELAIDE: It is with love and honor that I help you. *(Reaches into her bag, takes out a small pouch, and hands it to* KATIE-MAE.)* This is for your foot.

KATIE-MAE: Thank you, ma'am.

ADELAIDE: *(Turning to BRAVE MARY and JESSIE.)* Try to keep her warm and dry. I've packed several more bandages. If you can, see if at the next stop they can find a doctor to look at her foot.

JESSIE: We'll do that.

ADELAIDE: *(Extends her hands to them.)* Be safe . . . God speed. Send word if you can. So long.

BRAVE MARY: Thank you for everything, and God bless you, too. (ADELAIDE *exits.*)

OLIVIA: Let's get in the boat quickly, we've got several days by water . . . and we've got to get as far as we can this night. *(Children get into boat.)*

JESSIE: How were you able to get such a nice boat for traveling?

OLIVIA: Not too far from here lives a white man what owns so much, he don't even know what he's got. So, he don't know what's missing when something gets taken. And I ain't about to tell him!

(OLIVIA *and* JESSIE *get on either side of boat and push it off farther into the water. They jump into the boat, take up paddles, and start paddling.*)

JESSIE: It's so good to see you, Olivia. Glad to know you're still kicking around.

OLIVIA: I should say the same about you. I didn't see you for such a long time . . . I was beginning to think maybe you didn't make it on one of your trips outta here.

JESSIE: Bite your tongue, Olivia. The Lord protects those who further the cause of righteousness.

BRAVE MARY: I can't wait to get outta the South. My heart is bubbling over with hope and . . . joy. When I'm free for sure—there are so many things I want to do.

KATIE-MAE: What's the first thing you want to do, Brave Mary?

BRAVE MARY: The first thing? The first thing I'm gonna do is learn to read and write. Then I'm gonna write me a book about escaping to freedom . . . and y'all will be in my book. Especially you, Jessie.

JESSIE: Ohhh, don't waste no ink on me. Write about the ones that really make the sacrifice . . . like Olivia here.

KINDRED: What kind of sacrifice is she making to steal . . .

KATIE-MAE: (*Interjects.*) Borrow—

KINDRED: All right, to borrow . . . a boat that ain't even gonna be missed.

JESSIE: Ask Olivia why a *freed* slave would bother staying down here in the South when they could be living a better life up North?

KATIE-MAE: You a *freed* woman?

OLIVIA: No one is free 'til we're all free.

KATIE-MAE: I don't understand. Does that mean you're free or not?

OLIVIA: I have been blessed with a father that worked and earned the money to buy his own freedom . . . then he worked and bought my mama's freedom. Then my sister's freedom, and then mine. My family no longer lives here in the South, but in the North.

KATIE-MAE: In Canada?

OLIVIA: No—not that far north. But near Canada in Indian Territory.

KINDRED: Why are you staying down here for? If I were free . . . I'd hightail it outta here faster than you could say "jack rabbit!" I'd never look back. Once we get up north, I ain't never coming back down here.

KATIE-MAE: Miss Olivia?

OLIVIA: Yes?

KATIE-MAE: You ever get scared?

OLIVIA: You'd be foolish not to get scared of some things. But I get more scared thinking that colored folks is gonna have to be slaves for the rest of their natural lives. Now, that's a thought that makes me both scared and brave all at the same time. I keep saying over and over to myself that no one is free 'til we're all free.

(Lights fade out on this scene and come up on Jewish children, sitting in a small boat. A teenage boy is manning the boat.)

YOUNG MAN: *(Pointing off into the distance.)* You see those lights . . . those lights are Denmark. Hopefully, if things are not delayed, this time tomorrow night, you will be in Sweden. And you will be free to live as any gentile.

(Lights fade to black.)

SCENE 8

(Lonely strains of a Jewish melody are heard in the distance. RIFKA *and* BARUCH *have retired for the night.)*

BARUCH: Rifka? Rifka, are you asleep?

RIFKA: No.

BARUCH: What are you thinking about.

RIFKA: Brave Mary and the other children in the story we've been reading about.

BARUCH: It has been a good story so far. The story sounds so real.

RIFKA: It *is* real, Baruch. Don't you remember what Brave Mary said in the beginning of the book? She said it was a real story.

BARUCH: *(Chuckling.)* It's hard to believe such a story really happened when you've never had anything exciting or dangerous happen in your life.

RIFKA: Ohhh, I would say that hiding from the Nazis is pretty exciting, not to mention a little dangerous.

BARUCH: It's different when you read someone else's story.

RIFKA: When we get to safety, Baruch, you can write all about our "escape."

BARUCH: Do you think we will make it?

RIFKA: To safety?

BARUCH: Yeah.

RIFKA: I have to think that we will, Baruch. If I didn't, there would be no need to go any further. *(Silence.)*

BARUCH: What do you miss the most about not being home?

RIFKA: My parents, of course. But I really miss good food. I know Frau Westemeier works hard . . . but she's not a very good cook at all. *(They chuckle.)*

BARUCH: You know what I miss more than anything?

RIFKA: What?

BARUCH: Hearing my mother sing to me. I miss her voice . . . her songs.

RIFKA: I don't think I've heard my mother sing more than one or two songs. She doesn't think she can sing. And I think we all agree with her.

BARUCH: Ohhh, my mother is a very good singer and sings all the time. She has songs for work, songs for baking the bread, songs for holidays. . . .

RIFKA: Did she sing you lullabies, Baruch—

BARUCH: Yes, of course. There was one lullaby that my mother would sing to me all the time. It has been my favorite since I was a baby.

RIFKA: Sing it. Let me see if I know the song.

BARUCH: I didn't say that *I* could sing.

RIFKA: Ohhh—c'mon Baruch . . . try to sing the song.

BARUCH: *(Hesitantly sings.)*

> Shlof mayn kind, mayn treyst mayn sheyner,
> Shlof-she zunenyu,
> Shlof mayn lebn, mayn kadish eyner
> Shlof-zhe, lyu-lyu-lyu.

RIFKA: I never fully learned Yiddish, Baruch. I mean I'm not good at it. . . .

BARUCH: It's all right.

(Sings.)

> Sleep my child, my consolation,
> Sleep, sleep. lyu-lyu-lyu.
> Sleep, my life, my adoration,
> Sonny, sleep, lyu-lyu.
>
> Your mother standing by your cradle
> Crying, croons a lullaby.
> Some day you may understand
> Why your mother cries.

(BARUCH starts to cry. RIFKA moves to him and holds him.)

RIFKA: It's okay—Baruch. I want to cry most days myself.

BARUCH: Sometimes I get the feeling that I'm never going to see home again. That I'll never see my parents alive ever again. Or my friends . . . that I will have to live in this world alone.

RIFKA: Don't think such things!

BARUCH: You can say that because you have a brother . . . I'm an only child . . . it's different . . .

RIFKA: Baruch. . . .

BARUCH: I don't want to get caught, Rifka. . . . I don't want to die!

RIFKA: We're not going to die, Baruch . . . stop that kind of talk!

BARUCH: *(Rushing to his things, he pulls out papers.)* The Westemeiers have given us until tomorrow to memorize our new identities. I'm no longer Baruch Fischer . . . but a German boy named "Johann Schweppe" and I have to memorize a new town and new parents and—

RIFKA: *(Cuts him off.)* So do I!

BARUCH: But I don't think I can do it! If I make a mistake, we will both be found out to be Jews trying to escape. What if we are asked questions that we can't answer? What are we going to do?

RIFKA: We lie.

BARUCH: But what if we're too scared to think of a good enough lie? What will we do then? I don't think I can do this, Rifka. I don't think I can do this. . . . *(Starts to cry. RIFKA holds him and rocks him in silence.)*

RIFKA: Maybe, we should think about leaving here . . . tonight. Maybe we should run and hide in the woods.

BARUCH: How would we get to Sweden?

RIFKA: I don't know. Maybe we shouldn't go to Sweden. Maybe we should fend for ourselves here in Deutschland . . . in der wald . . . maybe some of the farmers will take pity on us and let us sleep in their barns at night . . . maybe some will share their food with us . . . maybe—

BARUCH: *(Cuts in.)*

Maybe . . . we will die and all of this won't matter. *(Sighs.)* Sometimes I wish we had a Brave Mary to "lead" us where we need to go . . . where we wouldn't have to worry about a thing. . . .

(Lights fade up on the slave children, resting in a barn.)

KINDRED: Sometimes I wish we had us Moses to led us up to freedom. I always heard that Moses could lead a person anywhere.

KATIE-MAE: He sure enough led them Israelites . . . led them clear on into the promised land. I heard tell that if you followed Moses, you didn't have to worry about a thing.

BRAVE MARY: Mr. Moses was sure enough a leader. But, Jessie here—is doing a right good job as far as I can see it. And we ain't come into no harm, yet. It's a lucky person that don't have to worry about anything.

RIFKA: Most people have to worry about something, every now and then . . . that's only normal . . . that's only human. . . .

BARUCH: Do you think it ever got easier for those black children? Do you suppose that once they got to a certain point that they no longer were scared?

BRAVE MARY: It's gonna get harder before it gets easier. How's your foot, Katie-Mae?

KATIE-MAE: I ain't thinking about my feet right now. My mind is set on freedom. . . .

BRAVE MARY: We'll rest a little while longer . . . but then we'll have to get going.

JESSIE: We've got a long road ahead before dawn.

KINDRED: Are we almost there? I'm so tired. . . .

JESSIE: We're not even half way. . . .

BRAVE MARY: We're still a long ways from freedom. . . .

BARUCH: What do you think protected them?

RIFKA: What?

BARUCH: I said, what do you think protected them all along their journey? Do you think they believed in God or angels?

RIFKA: *(Thoughtful.)* I'm sure they believed in something. I mean . . . it just seems logical that when people are in trouble . . . they start to believe in something . . . even if they didn't believe in anything before.

BARUCH: Do you think the Nazis believe?

RIFKA: No. I think they only believe in themselves. . . .

BRAVE MARY: Before we get started, I'm gonna ask that Spirit continue to stay with us . . . and guide us . . . and that our ancestors that have gone on before us continue to feed us knowledge so that we can keep one step ahead of them paddy-rollers and carpetbaggers. . . .

RIFKA: You know, I wasn't going to tell you, but I snuck ahead in the book—

BARUCH: You didn't, Rifka.

RIFKA: Yes, I did.

BARUCH: When did you do that?

RIFKA: A little bit each day . . . it gets very exciting. . . .

BARUCH: Oh, Rifka . . . tell me. Tell me what happens.

RIFKA: No—it'll be more fun to read it.

BARUCH: Well, then tell me a little bit.

RIFKA: Well—there's a part of the story where they had to hide in a snake-filled swamp. And then there's a part where they hide in the walls of an old pastor's house. And then they had to rub an herb on Katie-Mae's foot to numb the pain to keep her quiet, because she cried so much. . . .

BARUCH: No!

RIFKA: Yes. . . . It's quite a journey! But when they make it to Canada . . . it will make their getting there just that much sweeter!

BARUCH: Ohhh, get the book! Read me some more. . . . (RIFKA *gets the book and reads it to* BARUCH.)

BRAVE MARY: Amen!

ALL/BLACK KIDS: Amen!

BRAVE MARY: Well, let's get going. . . . (*They gather up their things.*)

KATIE-MAE: Can't we rest a little longer, Brave Mary? I'm so tired . . . and my foot hurts a lot . . .

BRAVE MARY: I know, Katie-Mae. But we can't stay here.

KATIE-MAE: Maybe we should just go back . . . go back to the plantation?

JESSIE: Ohhhh now, Katie-Mae . . . you don't want to go back to the plantation, do you?

KATIE-MAE: It's too hard to keep going. And I'm scared. I'm scared that we'll never see freedom. I'm afraid that we'll get hunted down by dogs . . . what if we get caught and sent back to the plantation?—

JESSIE: We're not gonna get caught—

KATIE-MAE: How do you know? How do you know that we won't get caught. It's easy for you to say that, because you're never scared.

JESSIE: (*Pause.*) Well, I'll tell you a secret. (*Quietly.*) I am scared. I'm just as scared as you are. (*Beat.*) How about you Brave Mary?

BRAVE MARY: (*Hesitantly, quietly.*) I'm sure enough scared.

JESSIE: Kindred?

KINDRED: Yeah—I guess so. . . .

JESSIE: See, we're *all* scared. Now, there ain't nothing wrong with being scared. You can do a lot of things and be scared all the while you doing it. You just can never let fear take hold of you. . . . 'Cause fear grab on to you and never let you go . . . and then you know where you'd be?

KATIE-MAE: Nowhere.

JESSIE: That's right. No-where! (*Beat.*) Now, we know what we have to do. . . . (ALL *nod their heads.*) Remember now, we're on the underground railroad. We've got our tickets ready . . . and we're gonna meet that mornin' train . . . and trust that it's gonna take us where we need to go. . . .

(Sings.)

> I'm going home on the mornin' train. . . .
> Oh, Lord, Lord, Lord!
> I'm going home on the mornin' train. . . .
> Lord, Lord, Lord!
> Mornin' train . . . mornin' train
> I'm going home on the mornin' train. . . .

(Speaks.)

> And you know if you wait too late . . . you gonna miss that train . . .
> and then you'll miss your chance for freedom. . . .

(Sings.)

> Evenin' train gonna be too late. . . .
> Oh, Lord, Lord, Lord!

KATIE-MAE: *(Sings and starts to dance.)*

> Evenin' train gonna be too late. . . .

BRAVE MARY:

> Lord, Lord, Lord . . .

ALL:

> Evenin' train. . . . evenin' train . . .
> Evenin' train gonna be too late!
> Evenin' train gonna be too late. . . .
> Oh, Lord, Lord, Lord!

BRAVE MARY:

> Get right, y'all, and let's go home. . . .
> Oh, Lord, Lord, Lord . . .

ALL:

> Get right, y'all, and let's go home. . . .

BRAVE MARY:

> Oh, Lord, Lord, Lord. . . .

ALL:

> Get right, y'all, get right, y'all . . .
> Get right, y'all, and let's go home. . . .

(Dancing comes to a stop as RIFKA *and* BARUCH *retire to their sleeping pallets. Singing continues quietly.)*

> Evenin' train. . . . evenin' train . . .
> Evenin' train gonna be too late!

BRAVE MARY: *(Sings quietly and stoically.)*
I'm going home on the mornin' train. . . .
Oh, Lord, Lord, Lord!
I'm going home on the mornin' train. . . .
Lord, Lord, Lord!
I'm going home. . . . I'm going home . . .
I'm going home on the mornin' train. . . . (BRAVE MARY *has disappeared from sight.)*

BARUCH & RIFKA: *(Quietly singing.)*
I'm going home. . . . I'm going home. . . . I'm going home . . . on the mornin'
train. . . .

(BARUCH and RIFKA fall asleep.)

(Lights fade to black.)

SCENE 9

(Lights fade up on BRAVE MARY and JESSIE.)

BRAVE MARY: We made it all the way up to Canada—

JESSIE: We made it all the way up to freedom—

BRAVE MARY: And Runaway Jessie got us there.

JESSIE: I've made that run four times now, and I've never lost a passenger.

BRAVE MARY: And we all made our own way in our new lives. . . . Kindred—
is working as an apprentice in a blacksmith shop.

JESSIE: Katie-Mae is a seamstress. The skills she picked up working in the
main house served her right nicely.

BRAVE MARY: And I got an education just like I planned—

JESSIE: And she wrote that book she said she was gonna write.

BRAVE MARY: And Jessie keeps going down into the Deep South bringing
slaves up and out. . . .

JESSIE: —Because I believe in freedom . . . freedom and justice for everyone. . . .

*(Lights fade out on them and lights come up on the barn. It is empty . . . except
for the book lying in the corner.)*

RIFKA: *(Offstage.)* I won't be long . . . I think I accidently left something behind. . . . *(She enters . . . looking about the room.)* I know it's got to be here
somewhere. . . . I can't . . . leave . . . without . . . it. . . .

*(She finds it. RIFKA takes a scarf from her pocket and starts to wrap the book in
it. She kisses and holds the book for a moment, wraps it in her scarf, and starts to
exit.)*

BRAVE MARY: *(Voice-over.)* Freedom—justice—God speed!

(RIFKA looks up, smiling . . . exits.)

(Lights fade to black.)

CURTAIN

THE FALCON

by
Greg Palmer

Adapted from the Russian Folktale
"Fenist, the Bright Falcon"

GREG PALMER has written for a wide variety of media and is now president of Palmer/Fenster, a Seattle-based broadcast writing and production company. For the theatre Palmer has written six plays that have been published and presented professionally around the world, including *The Big Bad Wolf (And How He Got That Way)* and an adaptation of *The Hunchback of Notre Dame*. Three of his plays were adapted for television, including *The Falcon*, which was broadcast to an audience of 200 million in the Soviet Union in 1990. The stage version has had extensive productions, most recently on tour and in residence at Childsplay, Tempe, Arizona.

Palmer's television productions include *Vaudeville: An American Masters Special*, a two-hour history of America's first live entertainment medium for families, part of the Public Broadcasting System 1997–98 season. Also, for the 1997–98 PBS schedule he wrote and narrated the documentary series, *The Art of Magic*. Palmer's connection with another recent international production was as the writer of a Discovery Channel documentary, *Rediscovering America: The Building of the Alaska Highway*, which won the prestigious Cine Golden Eagle award.

In 1993 Greg Palmer created and presented the PBS series *Death: The Trip of a Lifetime*, the highest rated PBS documentary special series of the 1993–94 season and winner of a National Education Association award for "the enhancement of learning through broadcasting." Palmer's companion book to *Death* was published by HarperCollins, and the educational video version was distributed to more than twenty thousand school and public libraries throughout North America.

In other broadcast writing and production, Palmer's documentaries include *Ski-to-Sea; The Seven Deadly Sins and Where to Find Them; D-day: The Last Wave*, commemorating the anniversary of the Normandy invasion; and the Emmy Award–winning *The Year (So Far) In Review*.

For thirteen years Greg Palmer was theatre/film critic and signature reporter for KING, the Seattle NBC affiliate, and a frequent contributor to national publications and broadcasts, including *NBC Overnight* and *Entertainment Weekly*. He has been a radio talk show host, National Public Radio correspondent in London and the creative director of an advertising agency.

Besides thirteen Emmy Awards, Palmer has received broadcasting's highest honor, the Peabody Award; three Ohio State Awards; two Action for Children's Television Achievement Awards, and numerous other honors.

In 1986 I was commissioned by the Seattle Children's Theatre to create a musical adaptation of *Snow White*, a project I eagerly undertook, because I've always thought the message of the original tale was exactly the wrong thing to teach children. In the Grimm/Disney tale—beside the fact that Dopey is clearly a developmentally disabled adult who is continually abused, both physically and verbally, by his brothers—the evil queen ultimately loses not because she is vain, murderous, and amoral, but because she is no longer the most beautiful. (Snow White doesn't die because the Dwarfs cannot bring themselves to bury this most beautiful girl.) And on awakening Snow White does exactly what her stepmother would have done—she rides off to marry the Prince, with whom she has never exchanged a single word, *because he is a handsome prince*, and for no other ostensible reason.

My Snow White rejects the Prince, who though handsome is a vain fool, and indicates she has fallen in love with Elliot Dwarf, the Grumpy equivalent, because he truly cares about her. There is a moment in the last scene where Snow stands center stage, with the Prince on one side, and Elliot on the other, and must decide. And day after day during the run of the production, I watched little girls on the verge of womanhood whispering up to Snow, "Elliot! Pick Elliot!" That would have been enough to make the whole project worthwhile for me—that these children facing horrendous peer pressure to be pretty—and be *with* the pretty—at least had an inkling from the play that there are more important things in life than appearance.

One day the audience included ten children from a nearby hospital. They were patients undergoing chemotherapy for cancer: bald-headed, pale, scared kids. And after the curtain their parents came up to the actress playing Snow White and thanked her. They said, sobbing, how important it was for their children to see that what you look like is not nearly as important as what you are. They got an entertainment, but the entertainment gave them so much more. And Snow started to cry, and then the place went up. That's why I write plays for young people.

—GREG PALMER

THE FALCON

CAST

Father: later Ivane (ee-VAWN-uh)
Agripina: later The Three Sisters (AW-gri-PEEN-uh)
Tevdore: later Fenist (tev-DORE-ay, fenn-EEST)
Marta: later the Tsarevna (tzar-EV-nuh)
Anna
The Storyteller

SCENE

A Georgian farmhouse and Anna's imagination.

Additional pronunciations: NOCK VAWM DEES
chedd-EE-uh
KOLE-KISS
MOGE ZAWN DEE

Although *The Falcon* is adapted from a centuries-old Russian folktale, this version places the story in the Republic of Georgia and features, not only the unique Georgian language, but aspects of Georgian culture as well. For instance, hospitality to strangers, the importance of toasts at ceremonial events, and the sense of mountains looming nearby are all very Georgian. With very little adaptation, it would be possible to present *The Falcon* in Russian style, rather than Georgian. But eventually the Georgians would get you for it.

(The main room of a Georgian farmhouse, circa 1850, with one door to the exterior and other doors to other rooms of the house. Discovered at a central table, sitting on short Georgian stools, is the family. FATHER *in the center,* MARTA *and* AGRIPINA *to one side,* TEVDORE *and* ANNA *to the other. It is late in the evening; food and drink cover the table. The family sings a Georgian wedding song; eventually* TEVDORE *and* ANNA *dance.)*

ALL: *(Singing.)*

> Ar-mo-mee pah ravs me pov-nee-ah
> Eh-hkla chem-ee ah,
> Patara go gos sik va ru-lee
> O-hka-ra dznelia
> Dznelia dznelia
> O-hka-ra dznelia
> Patara go-gos sik va ru-lee
> O-hka-ra dznelia
>
> Rim pa dau dam pee dau ree
> Dam pee tau ree ta
> Drim tam rim tam tam
> Tau ri tau ri tam!

FATHER: Agripina! More wine here! It's time for the toasts!

AGRIPINA: *(Rising.)* All right—a little patience . . . (AGRIPINA *goes to the shelf of bottles.)*

FATHER: *(Standing—*TEVDORE *alone, also stands.)* This is a great day—an historic day! My Anna and Tevdore are finally engaged to be wed!

*(*AGRIPINA *returns with a bottle.* FATHER *takes it, fills his and* TEVDORE's *cup.* FATHER *hands the bottle back to* AGRIPINA, *who fills her own and* MARTA's *cup and then sits.)*

FATHER: Let's see. A good marriage is like . . . like a good saddle. It gets softer and smoother as you rub up against it over the years.

ANNA: Oh, Papa . . .

FATHER: But a bad marriage, a bad marriage is like a bad horse. After a while you don't care what happens to it. You just want another one.

TEVDORE: Sir . . .

FATHER: Anna, Tevdore, I wish you a saddle marriage, not a horse marriage. My Anna engaged. The same age as your mother when we were wed. You look just as she did then; as she looked to me the day she died. Life is hard, even for women. (FATHER *drinks, then remembers* TEVDORE.) And Tevdore, whom we've known all our lives, from right next door. So not exactly a dream come true. More of an understanding. Tevdore, you're an understanding come true.

TEVDORE: Thank you, Sir. (FATHER *and* TEVDORE *drink and sit.)*

MARTA: NOW, can we go to bed?

TEVDORE: *(Jumping back up.)* Esteemed father-in-law to be!

MARTA and AGRIPINA: Oh, nooo . . .

TEVDORE: Now that Anna has agreed to become my bride, to share my life, to make my bed, to have my children . . . (MARTA *pounds her fist on the table;* TEVDORE *glances nervously at her and picks up the pace.*) uhhhh, I promise you from the moment of our vows she'll have a warm house to live in, all she wants to eat, perhaps a vacation in the mountains if I should sell a cow, though who has a spare cow these days, I don't know, and that we will always be as happy as we are right now. To Father! And Anna, of course. (TEVDORE *and* FATHER *drink.* TEVDORE *sits.*)

FATHER: Not too happy yet, I hope? Not till after the wedding, eh?

TEVDORE: Oh, no sir, not till then!

AGRIPINA: We haven't heard from the bride-to-be!

MARTA: Indeed!

FATHER: Certainly! Let a woman speak for once.

TEVDORE: Speech! Speech! (ANNA *rises reluctantly as the others cheer her on.*)

ANNA: Father . . . Tevdore . . . Sisters; I . . . I don't know what to say . . .

(*A loud knock at the door.* AGRIPINA, *on a wave from* FATHER, *goes to answer it, as* ANNA *watches in strange fascination.* AGRIPINA *opens the door and* STORYTELLER *enters; an old man with a beard, dusty clothes, his hat in his hand and a travelling bag over his shoulder.*)

STORYTELLER: Good evening, dear lady. I wonder if you might have a scrap of bread for a poor man on a long journey . . .

AGRIPINA: Certainly not! Be off . . .

FATHER: Of course! Come in! Nakh vom dees!

(AGRIPINA *hands* STORYTELLER *some bread, points to the corner, and rejoins the family at the table.* STORYTELLER *moves toward the indicated corner, but suddenly stops and stares with fascination at* ANNA, *who stares back.*)

AGRIPINA: Over there! (STORYTELLER's *stare is broken.*)

STORYTELLER: Thank you for your kindness. (STORYTELLER *moves to his corner and sits, still watching* ANNA.)

FATHER: Go on, Anna.

ANNA: What?

FATHER: Your toast . . .

ANNA: Oh, yes. I . . . I suppose I always knew that Tevdore and I would marry. Everyone's been expecting it since we were children. I'd have to be a fool not to be happy . . .

MARTA: Here, here! A fool!

ANNA: Tevdore, I'll try to be a good wife to you, if only, well . . . (TEVDORE *stands, waves his cup at* ANNA.)

TEVDORE: I can't ask for more! (STORYTELLER *rises, approaches* ANNA, *and bows.*)

STORYTELLER: My dear young woman. I couldn't help overhearing. Congratulations.

ANNA: Thank you.

STORYTELLER: (*To* FATHER.) Sir, may I offer a gift to the bride-to-be?

AGRIPINA: What could you possibly have that she'd want?

STORYTELLER: The most valuable thing I possess.

MARTA: What? Your hat? Hahahaha . . .

STORYTELLER: A story . . .

ANNA: You're a storyteller?

STORYTELLER: I am.

TEVDORE: Of course! Let's have your story, old man.

STORYTELLER: It is the story of . . . The Falcon. Not that long ago, not that far from here, there lived a kind, generous father, and loving husband. But his young wife was taken from him, long before her time . . .

FATHER: I think I know this story!

STORYTELLER: So the father had no wife. But he did have three daughters.

MARTA: Three?

STORYTELLER: Three. The youngest was gentle, sweet, and as fresh and beautiful as a clear mountain stream. So naturally, the father loved her quite the best. He didn't think much about the other two. They were just as beautiful, but their hearts were cold. So instead of love, he gave them everything else they wanted. And they took it.

FATHER: *(To himself.)* The only joy he had was the youngest . . .

MARTA: Hush up!

AGRIPINA: *(To STORYTELLER.)* Go on.

STORYTELLER: One day, as the father was going to town, he asked his daughters what gifts they would like when he returned.

(AGRIPINA and MARTA, with TEVDORE's help, begin clearing whatever needs clearing as they listen. ANNA continues to sit in rapt attention. FATHER listens as well, but seems to be thinking his own thoughts as much as listening to the STORYTELLER.)

The two older sisters asked for the finest silk to make beautiful dresses . . .

AGRIPINA: Silk! Very shrewd!

MARTA: Something in a nice, dark blue, probably.

STORYTELLER: But the youngest said, "I want nothing but a feather. The feather of Fenist, the Falcon."

AGRIPINA: *(As she exits.)* A feather? What's the matter with the girl?

MARTA: *(Exiting with AGRIPINA.)* She's always been strange.

(TEVDORE, MARTA, and AGRIPINA exit with table props, etc. STORYTELLER is by this time telling the story to the audience and ANNA.)

STORYTELLER: Twice the father went to town, returning with silks and then golden rings for the older sisters. But he searched in vain for the feather.

ANNA: Why did she want the feather? How did she know about it? *(FATHER quietly exits.)*

STORYTELLER: Why, Anna; she just *knew.*

ANNA: Oh.

STORYTELLER: On the way home from his third trip, walking through the great forest, the father saw a strange man, sitting on . . . on a stool by the side of the path.

(STORYTELLER *places stool next to* ANNA, *sits up on it, looks up at her quizzically.* ANNA *looks at him, looks offstage in the direction from which* FATHER *will come.*)

ANNA: Oh! (ANNA *exits the other way on a run.* STORYTELLER *takes the box from his bag.*)

STORYTELLER: And he held a small box—glowing, in his hand.

(*Box glows.* FATHER *enters, with a coat on now, walking along with a walking stick and bag over his shoulder. He stops short of the* STORYTELLER, *who ignores him.*)

FATHER: You there!

STORYTELLER: . . . said the father . . .

FATHER: What's that you have?

STORYTELLER: What? Where? Here?

FATHER: Yes.

STORYTELLER: A box. A little box, that's all.

FATHER: I can see that. What's in it?

STORYTELLER: And who are you then, the Government Box Inspector?

FATHER: Of course not!

STORYTELLER: Bring out all your boxes, girls! The Government Box Inspector is here!

FATHER: Wait!

STORYTELLER: Personal Box Inspector to the Tsarevna herself! Coming through!

FATHER: Stop shouting! I was curious, that's all!

STORYTELLER: Oh, well! That's different! NOW, I'll tell you.

FATHER: (*Starting to exit.*) NOW, I don't care any more!

STORYTELLER: (*Calling after him.*) There's nothing in the box . . . but a feather.

FATHER: (*Stopping abruptly.*) A feather?

STORYTELLER: You heard me.

FATHER: What kind of feather?

STORYTELLER: Bird. Bird feather.

FATHER: I've been looking for a feather.

STORYTELLER: They're very popular right now.

FATHER: The *right* feather.

STORYTELLER: This is it. The feather of The Falcon.

FATHER: I'll give you 500 gold pieces for that feather.

STORYTELLER: A thousand.

FATHER: That's too much!

STORYTELLER: All right, I'll throw in the box.

FATHER: Agreed.

(FATHER *gives* STORYTELLER *a bag of coins;* STORYTELLER *carefully hands* FATHER *the box, which immediately stops glowing.* FATHER *starts to open it.*)

STORYTELLER: Is the feather for you?

FATHER: No. For my daughter.

STORYTELLER: Then don't open the box.

FATHER: But what . . .

STORYTELLER: Don't open the box.

FATHER: How do I know there's really a . . .

STORYTELLER: DON'T OPEN THE BOX!

FATHER: All right! I won't open the box! Good day!

(FATHER *stomps out;* STORYTELLER *watches him go, then turns back to audience, as* MARTA *and* AGRIPINA *move into home behind, falling asleep on chairs.*)

STORYTELLER: So at last the father had what his youngest daughter most desired. He hurried home, clutching his rare prize in his hand.

(STORYTELLER *exits;* MARTA *and* AGRIPINA *asleep.* ANNA *comes sweeping in with her broom, glances at her sisters.* FATHER *enters, watching the box carefully. Then he sees* ANNA.)

FATHER: Anna! I found it! The feather!

ANNA: I knew you would, Papa. (MARTA *and* AGRIPINA *wake instantly.*)

MARTA and AGRIPINA: PAPA!!

(MARTA *and* AGRIPINA *come screaming at* FATHER, *strip him of his bag, throw it to the ground and begin madly pulling articles of clothing from it until they find two necklaces.* ANNA *and* FATHER *glance at them, but are more intent on the box.*)

FATHER: The box used to glow. I . . . I hope it's the right one. (ANNA *gently takes the box from him; in her hands it glows instantly.*)

ANNA: It's the right one, Papa.

MARTA: Yours is prettier than mine, and you know it!

AGRIPINA: Is not!

MARTA: Is so!

AGRIPINA: Is not!

MARTA: Papa! Her necklace is prettier than mine!

AGRIPINA: Hers is prettier than mine!

FATHER: If that's the way you both feel, why don't you trade?

MARTA and AGRIPINA: (*Snatching the necklaces away from each other.*) Never!

AGRIPINA: (*Seeing the box.*) Hey, what's she got?

MARTA: What's that?

FATHER: It's the feather! I was walking through the forest and I met . . .

MARTA: Let's see it!

AGRIPINA: Let's see what's so special about this feather!

ANNA: (*Nodding to* FATHER, *beginning to exit.*) No.

(ANNA *starts out slowly, passing the entering* STORYTELLER, *to whom she shows the box. He nods knowingly;* ANNA *exits.*)

FATHER: (*Calling to* ANNA.) But Anna . . . !

MARTA: What insolence! I'd keep a close eye on her, Papa!

AGRIPINA: (*Also calling to* ANNA.) So, you want to be alone with your feather?

(MARTA *and* AGRIPINA *flounce out in disgust.* FATHER *stuffs his possessions back into his bag and follows them out.*)

STORYTELLER: The truth is, Anna *did* want to be alone with her feather. (ANNA *enters her room, carrying the glowing box.*) And there was only one place in the small house: the quiet of her room.

(STORYTELLER *sits on stool throughout the following.* ANNA *sits on her bed for a moment, then stands, gently takes the feather from the box and drops the feather to the floor. A puff of smoke, and* FENIST *stands in front of her.*)

FENIST: Where am I?

ANNA: You're in our home. You're in my room.

FENIST: (*Looking around, bird-like.*) Are we inside a tree?

ANNA: No. A house. A wooden house.

FENIST: Ah. (*Looking at* ANNA *for the first time.*) I am Fenist.

ANNA: I'm called Anna.

FENIST: Anna? It's a nightingale's name.

ANNA: Oh? Thank you. Would you like something to eat?

FENIST: Yes.

ANNA: We have some bread, and cheese . . .

FENIST: No. A mouse, if you have one.

ANNA: A mouse? I . . . I'm afraid we don't have any mice.

FENIST: (*Sniffing and looking.*) Yes, you do.

ANNA: Well, none that are ready.

FENIST: Ah.

ANNA: Who are you? Where do you come from? How do you . . .

FENIST: No questions. No explanations. There is only a beginning for us, and that is now.

ANNA: Us?

FENIST: Yes. (FENIST *slowly reaches with a talon-like hand, gently touches* ANNA's *face, the talon becoming more of a hand as he does so.*) Skin. I hadn't realized it was so . . . soft. I am for you, Anna, if you want me.

ANNA: I've dreamed about you. What you'd look like . . .

FENIST: Stop. There are two people . . . there.

MARTA: (*Either behind the door, or offstage in direction* FENIST *points.*) Who are you talking to in there?

AGRIPINA: (*Ditto.*) Open up at once!

ANNA: (*Panicked.*) You have to hide!

FENIST: Hide?

ANNA: (*Pointing under the bed.*) There! Quickly! (FENIST *dives under the bed, just as the door bursts open and* MARTA *and* AGRIPINA *fall through, quickly rising.*)

MARTA: All right, where is he?

ANNA: Who?

AGRIPINA: The man! We heard a man in here!

ANNA: That's nonsense!

AGRIPINA: Oh, really!? Let's see . . . *(Looking around.)* Aha! The bed! (AGRIP-
INA *starts to look under the bed.)*

ANNA: NO!

(AGRIPINA looks under the bed. Pause.)

AGRIPINA: Well, he's not under here.

ANNA: He's not? I mean, of course, he's not. There IS no he!

MARTA: We heard him!

AGRIPINA: He sounded tall. And extremely handsome!

ANNA: And you think some strange man just . . . just flew in the window?

MARTA and AGRIPINA: The window! (MARTA *and* AGRIPINA *rush to the window.
During the following,* ANNA *looks under the bed, finds the feather, palms it.)*

AGRIPINA: Do you see anything?

MARTA: Yes. Night. There's a lot of night out here. Could he have made it to
the forest?

AGRIPINA: If he did, he was flying.

MARTA: I like a man who's fast on his feet.

AGRIPINA: I like a man who's on his feet.

MARTA: Indeed!

AGRIPINA: Let's make her think she's fooled us.

MARTA: Right. (MARTA *and* AGRIPINA *come in from the window and sit demurely
on* ANNA*'s bed.)*

ANNA: Are you satisfied?

AGRIPINA: It must have been the wind.

MARTA: Silly us!

ANNA: Then if you don't mind . . . (MARTA *and* AGRIPINA *rise slowly and head
for the door.)*

MARTA: Papa wants his dinner.

ANNA: *(Moving them out.)* I'm coming.

(MARTA *and* AGRIPINA *exit.* AGRIPINA *swings around and hides near the
window.* ANNA *takes out the feather, once again drops it to the floor, in full view of
the audience. Nothing happens. She nudges it with her toe.)* Fenist? *(Nothing;
finally . . .)*

FENIST: *(Under the bed.)* Pardon me . . .

ANNA: Ahhh! (FENIST *sticks his head out from under the bed; indicates the feather.)*

FENIST: Could I have that back, please?

ANNA: *(Fetching the feather.)* Of course.

FENIST: Thank you. (FENIST *disappears under the bed, as if inserting the feather
in some body part. As he emerges from under the bed . . .)* Ahhh, that's better!
Who are they?

ANNA: My sisters.

FENIST: They remind me of crows. In my world those are the eggs you leave out for the snakes.

ANNA: They won't give up, either. I know them too well. You must fly away, into the forest, where it's safe.

FENIST: If you wish.

MARTA: (Offstage; a very crow-like:) Anna! Dinner!

FENIST: Yes, definitely. Crows.

ANNA: You'll wait for me?

FENIST: I think we have been waiting for each other for a very long time.

ANNA: Oh, yes!

FENIST: (Moving to the window.) I wish you could fly with me.

ANNA: Oh, I'd be afraid . . .

FENIST: No, you wouldn't. When you stepped off into the sky and saw the earth turn into a little puddle below, you'd never want to walk again.

ANNA: I suppose it's that first step . . .

FENIST: Never try, never know.

ANNA: Please, Fenist, go. (FENIST comes close to kissing her good-bye; at the last moment . . .)

MARTA: (Offstage.) ANNA! Are you coming!?

(FENIST utters a bird-like awk of disgust, then leaps from the window and disappears. ANNA watches him go. AGRIPINA, also, watches in fascination, then sneaks out.)

STORYTELLER: Fenist leapt from the window as a man, but he was a falcon before he touched the sky. (FATHER enters.)

FATHER: I'm confused. Is this Fenist a man or a bird?

STORYTELLER: He's a man, AND a bird. A falcon, and therefore, a Prince.

ANNA: Oh, yes!

FATHER: (Irritably hearing her.) I don't care if he is a prince.

(MARTA and AGRIPINA enter with their wine and join the group around the STORYTELLER. During the following, ANNA gets into bed.)

What's he doing in that young woman's bedroom?? It's scandalous!

AGRIPINA: You'd prefer he sat around in the parlor with her father, listening to long, dull stories about the war?

FATHER: Of course! THAT'S courtship.

TEVDORE: I wouldn't think of entering a lady's room, Sir.

FATHER: Good boy.

MARTA: Ever? Hahaha!

TEVDORE: What does she really know about him? They're from completely different worlds!

STORYTELLER: That doesn't mean they can't be friends.

TEVDORE: But he's . . . he's a mouse eater!

STORYTELLER: Young man, in this world you'll find there are some things you see with your eyes, and some things you see with your heart.

AGRIPINA: Isn't it a little early in your story for a moral, old man?

STORYTELLER: This story has no moral. It has a question. And that's why it's a good story.

MARTA: *(Exiting with* AGRIPINA.*)* We'll see.

STORYTELLER: Anna tried to stay awake that night, waiting for Fenist to return. But she soon fell into a deep, magical sleep. (MARTA *and* AGRIPINA *enter, sneaking toward window.*) Of course, Agripina told Marta all she had seen and heard. THEY did not sleep.

(TEVDORE *and* FATHER *exit.*)

AGRIPINA: *(At the window.)* Give me the pins.

MARTA: *(Doing so.)* Are you sure she was talking to this bird?

AGRIPINA: Yes! Ouch!

MARTA: And the bird talked back?

AGRIPINA: Ouch! Yes! How many times do I have to tell you? Ouch!

MARTA: And it wasn't a parrot? Did it talk like this: "Polly want a cracker! Polly want a . . . ?"

AGRIPINA: It was a magical bird, Marta! Ouch!

MARTA: Why should she get a magical bird when all we get is jewelry?

AGRIPINA: Ouch! Ouch!

MARTA: Agripina?

AGRIPINA: Ouch! Yes?

MARTA: What are you doing?

AGRIPINA: Sticking pins in the windowsill! So help me! Ouch!

MARTA: *(Helping.)* Ouch!

AGRIPINA: Ouch!

MARTA: Ouch!

AGRIPINA: Ouch!

MARTA: Ouch! Agripina!

AGRIPINA: WHAT IS IT??!

MARTA: Why are we sticking pins in the windowsill?

AGRIPINA: When the falcon comes back, he'll get stuck on the pins. He won't be able to see them in the dark.

MARTA: Ouch! I can't see them either.

AGRIPINA: *(Rising from window.)* That's enough.

MARTA: *(Rising from window.)* I think I'm bleeding.

AGRIPINA: Let's go.

MARTA: Already I feel a little lightheaded.

AGRIPINA: Come on!

MARTA: What'll happen to the bird?

AGRIPINA: If he tries once and flies away, he'll just get a little scratched. But if he really cares about Anna and keeps trying to reach her, he will surely die.

MARTA: Oooooo! (MARTA *and* AGRIPINA *exit.*)

STORYTELLER: Fenist sat in the forest a long time that night, listening for silence—silence that meant safety. At last he heard nothing, and flew quickly, quietly, to Anna.

(FENIST *enters, carrying a small white flower, "flying" towards the window. He tries to land, cries out, tries again and again, as* ANNA *writhes in her sleep.*)

ANNA: No! No! (FENIST *drops below the window; struggles to a crouch, whispering.*)

ANNA: Fenist!

FENIST: Anna—I must go. If you ever want to see me again, look beyond the nine mountains, to the tenth kingdom. I will be there.

ANNA: Don't leave . . .

FENIST: But you won't find me until you've worn out three pairs of iron shoes, broken three iron staffs, and eaten three stone loaves. So it must be. (FENIST *sinks to the floor, gathering his strength.*) Farewell, Anna . . . (FENIST *rises to fly away, with difficulty.*) And if you need help, ask the Three Sisters . . . (FENIST *exits; then offstage*) Farewell. . . .

ANNA: Please . . . No!

STORYTELLER: And though Anna heard his voice in her sleep, she could not wake. A few hours later it was a new day—and for Anna, a new world.

(ANNA *wakes with a start; jumps from bed, runs to the window, where the bloody pins confirm her nightmare.*)

ANNA: (*Finding a feather on the pins.*) What have they done to you? (ANNA *looks at the house, and starts walking away from it. She stops, turns, stands for a moment.*) Good-bye, Papa. (ANNA *exits, with determination.*)

STORYTELLER: A quest, then; as the falcon said, beyond the nine mountains, to the tenth kingdom. Anna walked away from all she had ever known . . . for a dream. (FATHER *enters.*)

FATHER: Her poor father.

STORYTELLER: One way or another that's how it always happens.

FATHER: That doesn't make it any easier.

STORYTELLER: No.

(FATHER *exits;* STORYTELLER *watches him go.*)

From a blacksmith in the village Anna got three pairs of iron shoes, three iron staffs, and three stone loaves.

(*Clanking heard;* ANNA *enters, dressed for travel, carrying the required articles in her father's bag from the box scene.*)

Then she began walking, across the mountains. How long she walked and how far she went, no one knows. And when the first pair of shoes was gone, and the first staff broken, she saw a small house by the side of the road, and she remembered what The Falcon had said about the three sisters.

(AGRIPINA, *as Sister One, enters, dressing up the house exterior.* ANNA *comes quietly up behind her.*)

ANNA: Excuse me . . .

AGRIPINA: Ahhhhh!!! *(Whirling around.)* You gave me quite a start, you did. My heart's jumping like a frog in a fry pan!

ANNA: I'm sorry, I didn't mean to . . .

AGRIPINA: Kind of fun, actually. Who are you?

ANNA: My name is Anna. I'm looking for the Three Sisters.

AGRIPINA: Oh, that's me! I'm the first sister. Well, I'm the first sister if you're going that way, and the third sister if you're going that way. You must be going that way.

ANNA: Y . . . yes.

AGRIPINA: Thought so. *(Surreptitiously checking* ANNA's *shoes.)* Where you headed?

ANNA: To the tenth kingdom.

AGRIPINA: Uh-huh. Taking the nine mountain route?

ANNA: Yes!

AGRIPINA: That's the easiest way.

ANNA: *(Exhausted.)* It is?

AGRIPINA: Oh, you're tired, aren't you? Rest here, and I'll get you some good hot soup.

ANNA: I don't want to disturb you . . .

AGRIPINA: Nonsense! Why be a mysterious woman by the side of the road if you can't help complete strangers on their hopeless quests? (AGRIPINA *comes down to the* STORYTELLER, *who hands her a bowl of soup.*)

ANNA: Hopeless? Did you say hopeless?

AGRIPINA: *(Giving Anna the soup, sitting beside her.)* So! You're following Fenist?

ANNA: Yes. Yes! How did you know?

AGRIPINA: He flew through a while back. Everyone comes by here eventually. Beasts of all kinds, princes, maidens such as yourself . . .

ANNA: How was he? I've been so worried . . .

AGRIPINA: You did that to him?

ANNA: No!

AGRIPINA: I didn't think so.

ANNA: Tell me . . .

AGRIPINA: You should rest, child, you have a long way to go.

ANNA: Tell me about Fenist. What did he say? Did he mention me?

AGRIPINA: Falcons don't "mention" things, child. They either talk about something, or they don't. Usually don't. Very closed beak are falcons. Now, your mockingbirds, can't shut them up. But falcons . . .

ANNA: Please! Tell me everything you know about Fenist!

(AGRIPINA *places her hand gently on* ANNA's *brow.*)

AGRIPINA: No.

(ANNA *instantly falls asleep, and* AGRIPINA *lowers* ANNA's *head into her lap.*)
Nighty night.

STORYTELLER: The night passed, as Anna dreamed of flying . . .

AGRIPINA: Good morning.

ANNA: Good morning . . .

AGRIPINA: You snore a little.

ANNA: (*Finally waking.*) What? What?

AGRIPINA: Snoring. You know, snort snort? You snore a little. But don't worry,
on you it's cute. I think you should tell people when they snore—it saves
a lot of heartache later on.

ANNA: I must have fallen asleep. What were we talking about?

AGRIPINA: (*Fetching soup bowl.*) Nothing special. Finish your soup.

ANNA: No, it WAS special. (*Taking soup bowl.*) The soup is still hot!

AGRIPINA: Uhh, yes. So eat up!

ANNA: I have to go.

AGRIPINA: Yes, I suppose you do. (AGRIPINA *helps* ANNA *with her things prior
to exit.*) He's waiting for you, Anna. And my sisters will help.

ANNA: But I'll never find my way through the mountains . . .

AGRIPINA: Oh! I almost forgot! The yarn ball! (AGRIPINA *takes a red ball of yarn
from an inside pocket and hands it to* ANNA.) Here.

ANNA: Yes?

AGRIPINA: Throw it. That way. (ANNA *throws ball offstage; it boings as it bounces
away, and keeps boinging.*)

AGRIPINA: Quick! Follow it! Never let that ball out of your sight!

ANNA: (*Running out.*) Yes, Ma'am!

AGRIPINA: And tell my sisters to stop by sometime . . . (AGRIPINA *watches*
ANNA *go, then exits the other way.* FATHER *and* MARTA *enter.*)

STORYTELLER: Anna went on—over the second mountain, past the third,
around the fourth.

MARTA: I wish she'd hurry up. And why did this silly bird have to go so far
away? He could have perched in the forest nearby. I know lots of men who
do that.

FATHER: And just exactly what does that mean?

MARTA: Oh, never mind. It's personal. And you; go on! (FATHER *and* MARTA
exit.)

STORYTELLER: In the evening of no one knows what day, Anna could go no
farther.

(*Ball bounces through and offstage the other side.* ANNA *enters, exhausted. The
staff breaks, and she stumbles badly.*)

ANNA: Please . . . wait for me . . .

(Ball rolls back in; ANNA *sinks to her knees to gather it in, clutches it to her, and then curls up, asleep.* AGRIPINA, *as Sister Two, enters behind her, looms over her, picks up the ball, pets it, and puts it in an inside pocket.* ANNA *suddenly wakes, looks up and sees* AGRIPINA.*)*

No!

AGRIPINA: No?

ANNA: It's you! Is it you?

AGRIPINA: How do you answer a question like that? Of course, it's me!

ANNA: Then I haven't gone anywhere! Your silly ball has been leading me in circles!

AGRIPINA: Just a moment here . . .

ANNA: Where is it? I'm going to unravel it! (ANNA *begins a frantic, furious search for the ball, with* AGRIPINA *clucking along behind her.)* The Three Sisters will help you, Fenist said. Ha!

AGRIPINA: Fenist! Then you're Anna!

ANNA: Yes! And you're the first sister going THAT way!

AGRIPINA: I am not! I'm the second sister going both ways!

ANNA: *(Giving up.)* I'm not going to make it. I . . . I'm never going to find him . . .

AGRIPINA: Don't cry, little one. We're triplets.

ANNA: What?

AGRIPINA: The three sisters. We're triplets. Didn't Sister One tell you?

ANNA: Oh, my . . .

AGRIPINA: We look exactly alike. Well, not exactly. Sister One's got a mole right here. And Sister Three—Three dyes her hair.

ANNA: I'm so sorry.

AGRIPINA: I hear it's pink this month.

ANNA: I've been a fool.

AGRIPINA: Nonsense. You've had a lot on your mind. Ouch! (AGRIPINA *pulls the ball from her pocket, holding it in her hand, where it seems to be trying to jump away.)*

ANNA: The ball! I have to go!

AGRIPINA: *(To struggling ball.)* You just be patient! *(Ball subsides and just throbs in her hand.)* I cannot abide impolite knitting. (ANNA *picks up her pack)*

ANNA: This seems to get heavier every day.

AGRIPINA: It is heavier. I put a silver spinning wheel in there for you.

ANNA: When did you do that?

AGRIPINA: Uh . . . earlier.

ANNA: Why do I need a spinning wheel?

AGRIPINA: Don't ask so many questions, dear. It's unbecoming. You'll need the wheel later on. And the golden spindle.

ANNA: But . . .

AGRIPINA: *(Tossing the Ball in appropriate direction.)* Go, child.

ANNA: *(Leaving.)* Thank you . . .

AGRIPINA: GO! (ANNA *and* AGRIPINA *exit in opposite directions.*)

STORYTELLER: Anna was halfway across the mountains now. And as she got closer to Fenist, she could almost hear him, calling to her. Back home, her father was frantic. He searched throughout the country for days. But no one had seen his beautiful daughter. Finally, heartbroken, he went home to wait for his Anna and deal with his Marta and Agripina. (STORYTELLER *exits as* FATHER *enters, carrying a broom.*)

FATHER: (*Shouting into wings.*) And you expect me to believe she's out there somewhere, chasing a bird? (AGRIPINA *and* MARTA *enter, terrified.*)

AGRIPINA: A magical bird!

MARTA: (*Whispering.*) I thought we killed the bird!

AGRIPINA: Hush!

FATHER: I don't care about any bird! It's your fault she's gone, and may God have mercy on you if she doesn't come back! (AGRIPINA *and* MARTA *start to leave.*) Stay where you are, both of you! (FATHER *charges them,* MARTA *hides behind* AGRIPINA. FATHER *holds the broom up to* AGRIPINA.) Take this! You know what it is, don't you?

AGRIPINA: It's a broom.

FATHER: Excellent! Use it!

AGRIPINA: But I don't know how to broom!

FATHER: Learn! This house is going to be spotless when Anna comes back, and since we don't know when that will be, it's going to be spotless all the time!

AGRIPINA: Ha! (AGRIPINA *sweeps away, exposing* MARTA *to* FATHER.)

FATHER: You!

MARTA: What!?!?

FATHER: Get out to the kitchen and cook something!

MARTA: Cooking? Me? I think not!

FATHER: Oh, yes, you will, or . . . or I'll give every dress and jewel you two own . . . to the Chedia sisters!

MARTA: You wouldn't!

FATHER: COOK!

AGRIPINA: (*Sweeping in.*) Papa, I keep sweeping the dirt around, but it doesn't go away. I think there's something wrong with your broom. (FATHER *charges them, chasing them offstage.*)

FATHER: Ahhhhhhhhhhhhh!!!

(ANNA *enters, the Ball rolling before her and stopping.* ANNA *comes up to the Ball, looks at it for a moment.*)

ANNA: What? Lunch? Good idea. (ANNA *sits near Ball, takes a stone loaf from her pack, starts to take a large bite, then stops and looks at Ball.*) You sure you don't want to try a little of this stone loaf? It really fills you up. I know how you feel.

(ANNA *looks around furtively, then tosses the loaf away into the wings with some vigor.*) Well that's the last one! And the iron shoes are almost gone, too. We must be close.

(Pink hair of Sister Three appears behind her—and peeks through the following.)

ANNA: But close to . . . what? I've come all this way, and I don't know who, or what, I'm coming to. Do you know? No, huh? Then take me to the Third Sister. Let's go, I'm ready. (ANNA *nudges the ball.* AGRIPINA *as Sister Three appears quietly behind her.*) The Third Sister!

AGRIPINA: Yes?

ANNA: Ahhh! (ANNA *turns quickly.* AGRIPINA *goes for the ball, picks it up, pets it.*)

AGRIPINA: Yes, I love you too. Hush, now.

ANNA: You're the Third Sister!

AGRIPINA: That depends. Which way are you going?

ANNA: That way.

AGRIPINA: Then I'm the Third Sister. (*Suddenly bowing deeply.*) And you are the Princess Medea of Kolchis. Your highness!

ANNA: Uh, no. I'm Anna from the Great Forest.

AGRIPINA: Anna? Anna! Help me up! (ANNA *reaches for the pink hair, the closest thing to her.*)

AGRIPINA: NOT THE HAIR! (AGRIPINA *finally rises.*) Thank you. Anna. (AGRIPINA *pulls a list from her pocket.*) Anna. Anna. Ah, here we are. You're earlier than expected. You must be very enthusiastic.

ANNA: I . . . I can feel him. Near me.

AGRIPINA: Him? (*Checking the list.*) Of course. The Falcon.

ANNA: Yes! Fenist! Do you know where he is?

AGRIPINA: Behind you. (ANNA *turns, and as she does so the third staff breaks. She looks around in confusion.*)

ANNA: Where . . . ?

AGRIPINA: Not down here. Up there. (AGRIPINA *points high offstage.* ANNA *looks.*)

ANNA: It's a castle! He's in that castle?

AGRIPINA: Yes.

ANNA: Is it HIS castle?

AGRIPINA: Hardly. It's the castle of the Tsarevna.

ANNA: The Tsarevna!

AGRIPINA: He's her prisoner.

ANNA: Why? What has he done?

AGRIPINA: It's what he hasn't done. He refuses to marry her.

ANNA: Marry her!? But she can't keep him prisoner for that!

AGRIPINA: Ha! She can do anything she wants. She's the Tsarevna!

ANNA: It's not right!

AGRIPINA: No. It just is. (AGRIPINA *gets* ANNA's *bag, gives it to her.*) Anna, you have what you need to rescue Fenist.

ANNA: You mean the spinning wheel?

AGRIPINA: Yes, but more than that. You have a good heart, and a good mind. Use them—use everything. And hurry. A caged falcon can't live long. He has to FLY.

ANNA: How are we going to do it?

AGRIPINA: *You're* going to do it. I'm going to find the Princess Medea. (AGRIP-INA *starts to exit.*) The twit . . .

(ANNA *watches her go, then turns back, looks toward the castle and exits toward it.* STORYTELLER, MARTA, *and* TEVDORE *enter.*)

MARTA: You mean this Fenist can marry a Tsarevna if he wants to, and he'd still rather have this . . . this peasant? He's as crazy as she is!

TEVDORE: But he . . . he loves the peasant.

STORYTELLER: You're right, Tevdore. He does. And does she love him?

TEVDORE: She must. She's gone a long way to prove she loves him. A long way.

(TEVDORE *and* MARTA *exit.*)

STORYTELLER: And now, she's at the threshold of her final adventure.

(ANNA *enters with the spinning wheel outside the castle. She sits and begins spinning, turning out a golden thread. After a moment* FATHER, *now dressed as Ivane, enters from the castle, shaking out his mop. He sees* ANNA *and cautiously approaches her, looking very intently at the thread.*)

FATHER: Gold! That's gold you're spinning there, young woman. Gold from flax! Did you know?

ANNA: Yes. It's such a dull color, though. If only I could spin something in a nice, dark blue.

FATHER: Gold is nice. I rather adore gold.

ANNA: Some people do like it.

FATHER: Who are you?

ANNA: I'm Anna. The Spinner.

FATHER: Spinning gold! Outstanding! Incredible! Really nice!

ANNA: And you are . . . ?

FATHER: I am Ivane, personal aide to the Tsarevna herself. (FATHER *throws down his mop.*) You know the Tsarevna?

ANNA: No. What's she like?

MARTA: (*Offstage, but very loud.*) IVANE!!

FATHER: Forceful. Personally, I would describe her as forceful. (FATHER *runs like mad for the castle door.* MARTA, *now dressed as the Tsarevna, enters just as he gets there.* FATHER *throws himself to the ground at her feet.*) A thousand pardons, your highness.

MARTA: What have you been doing?

FATHER: Just a potload of pardons.

MARTA: Rise! Why were you out here, when *I* was in there?

FATHER: I was questioning an intruder, your highness. A spinner.

MARTA: A what?

FATHER: A spinner. She spins flax into gold.

MARTA: Gold!

FATHER: Yes. Personally, I was very impressed.

MARTA: I will speak to her.

FATHER: That will be the greatest thrill of her miserable life, your highness.

MARTA: Indeed! (MARTA *approaches* ANNA. *They look each other in the eye for a moment, then* ANNA *bows.*)

ANNA: Your highness.

MARTA: What are you doing here, girl?

ANNA: Spinning, if it please your majesty.

MARTA: How can it please me if I don't know anything about it? I don't trust things I know nothing about.

FATHER: Her highness trusts very little.

MARTA: Indeed, again!

ANNA: I'm sorry if I displeased you. I thought the castle was deserted. You usually see more people around a castle. Soldiers, servants . . .

MARTA: Servants! Ha!

FATHER: We have no servants. Her majesty's personality is so forceful, as I said before, that the servants just disappear, usually in the middle of the night, usually with one of our horses.

ANNA: Then why do you stay?

FATHER: I'm not a servant. I'm a Personal Aide. Big difference.

ANNA: I see.

FATHER: And we're all out of horses.

ANNA: You two must be very lonely.

MARTA: Ah! I'm doing something about that. At this very moment, up in the tower . . .

ANNA: Yes?

MARTA: Never mind! How do you spin flax into gold?

ANNA: With this magic spinning wheel.

MARTA: That's nice. I'll buy it from you.

ANNA: How much thread would you like?

MARTA: Not the thread; the spinning wheel. Ivane, get the wheel. (FATHER *quickly gathers up the spinning wheel.*)

ANNA: But if you take my wheel, what will I do? All I know is spinning, and cooking, and cleaning, and lady-in-waiting work.

MARTA: Say! I have an idea!

FATHER: Another breakthrough for her highness!

MARTA: You come work for me!

ANNA: I never thought of that.

FATHER: Uh-huh.

MARTA: Then you can spin, cook, clean—all those fun things, all the time!

ANNA: Wonderful.

MARTA: Do you like horses?

ANNA: I'm allergic to horses.

MARTA: Perfect. And that's enough thinking for one day. Ivane, attend.

(MARTA *and* FATHER *exit.* ANNA *looks up toward the tower.* FATHER *returns, whistles for her.*)

ANNA: Coming! (ANNA *clanks by* FATHER *in her iron shoes, which he notices.*)

FATHER: Nice shoes! (FATHER *and* ANNA *exit;* STORYTELLER *enters.*)

STORYTELLER: Days went by, and though Anna was inside the castle, she saw no sign of Fenist. But she felt his presence; she knew he was only a few hundred feet away from her—but in which direction?

(ANNA *enters, scrubbing the floor of the Tsarevna's bedroom. A door leads off-stage.*)

Then one morning . . .

(MARTA *enters with a large, covered tray, walking toward* ANNA, *who sees her and jumps up to help.*)

ANNA: Good morning, your highness.

MARTA: Uh, yes.

ANNA: (*Reaching for the tray.*) Let me help you with that.

MARTA: No! (MARTA *jerks the tray away; the cover comes off, revealing three dead mice.*) I have it. (MARTA *brings the tray back in front of her; Anna stares at the mice.*)

ANNA: Mice!

MARTA: Yes. For . . . for the cat.

ANNA: Our cat always brought mice to us, never the other way around.

MARTA: This is a *royal* cat! Now, get back to your work.

ANNA: Yes, Ma'am.

(ANNA *drops to the ground at* MARTA's *feet, cleaning, moving with* MARTA *under the tray as she goes to the tower door.* MARTA *sets the tray down on* ANNA *as she gets the key; unlocks the door, picks tray up and goes through, closing the door behind her.* ANNA *immediately listens at the keyhole.* FATHER *comes in behind her, sees her in this posture, and exits. Sound of key in other side of lock;* ANNA *throws herself to the floor as* MARTA *reenters, without the tray, holding a falcon feather in her hand.* ANNA *sees the feather and gasps.*)

MARTA: (*Hearing the gasp, looking down.*) What? What is it?

ANNA: Nothing, your highness. I was just admiring that lovely feather.

MARTA: A gift . . . from an admirer.

ANNA: A falcon feather, isn't it?

MARTA: Yes! How did you know?

ANNA: I'm very fond of falcons. I won't allow them to be hurt . . . by anyone.

MARTA: I'll keep that in mind.

(MARTA *sweeps out,* ANNA *watching her go. Then* ANNA *returns to the tower door, listening.* FATHER *enters, comes up quietly behind her. As he gets there,* ANNA *stands, not turning to him.*)

FATHER: You would be making a grave mistake to underestimate the Tsarevna. (ANNA *turns.*) With a snap of her fingers she can summon up forces that will crush you like the smallest spider. She'll do it, too, if she thinks you are a threat to her.

ANNA: I'm not afraid of her.

FATHER: *(Indicating the door.)* Then be afraid for him.

ANNA: You know—he's here—the falcon?

FATHER: Of course. And he'll stay here, until he marries her, or he dies.

ANNA: No!

FATHER: And soon her highness won't care which comes first, a wedding, or a funeral. *(ANNA turns back to the door, as FATHER exits quietly.)*

ANNA: Then we have to save him. She has the key to this door—do you know where she keeps it? *(ANNA, not hearing any answer, turns, finds FATHER gone.)* Ivane?

(ANNA turns back to the door. MARTA enters in her nightgown, carrying the spinning wheel, which she puts beside her bed and gets into bed. ANNA sees her, goes and sits by her.)

STORYTELLER: The day passed slowly. Finally, it was evening. Time for bed, time for rescue.

(STORYTELLER takes an old book, hands it to ANNA, and exits.)

ANNA: *(Reading.)* . . . and so the brave, handsome Prince lifted the wicked Tsar by his greasy beard and tossed him into the sea. Then he took the beautiful maiden in his arms and carried her happily into his new castle. The End.

MARTA: Where did you find this horrible book?

ANNA: In the old servant's quarters. Isn't it wonderful?!

MARTA: No!

ANNA: Would you like to hear the one called "The Tsarevna and the Twelve Pigs"?

MARTA: NO! Why haven't you spun any gold yet?

ANNA: I've been too busy. Frankly, your highness, this castle was a shambles. I still haven't cleaned the armory, six bathrooms, the tower . . .

MARTA: You stay away from the tower!

ANNA: Yes, Ma'am.

MARTA: And spin something, right now. Something I can wear tomorrow.

ANNA: Yes, your highness. *(ANNA starts the spinning wheel, which hums quietly.)*

MARTA: The tower is very dangerous. I wouldn't want you to fall and BREAK YOUR NECK.

ANNA: I understand, your highness.

MARTA: *(As humming gets louder.)* Good. Ah, that humming sound . . . yawn . . . It makes me sleepy . . .

ANNA: Would you like me to stop?

MARTA: No . . . keep working . . . fill the room with gold . . . yawn. . . . Just ignore me . . . if that's possible . . . *(Humming increases; MARTA begins to snore. ANNA stands to look into her face.)*

ANNA: Your highness! Yoo hoo! (ANNA *quickly starts to search the bed, looking for the key.* MARTA *snorts awake.*)

MARTA: What? What's going . . . (MARTA *sinks back to sleep.*)

ANNA: All right, you bonehead, where's that key? (ANNA *gets idea, dives under* MARTA's *covers, burrowing around.*) Aha!

(ANNA *pushes* MARTA's *leg out from under the quilt. Tied around her big toe is the key. Anna unties the key, goes to the tower door.* MARTA *snorts in her sleep.* ANNA *looks back, returns to the bed, takes some gold thread from the spindle and ties* MARTA's *hands with it.*)

Did I happen to mention this is the strongest thread on earth?

(With MARTA *tied up,* ANNA *goes to the tower door, unlocks it, gets a lantern and passes through the door.* STORYTELLER *enters, speaks directly to the audience, as* FENIST *unobtrusively assumes the dead position in the cell behind.*)

STORYTELLER: The last threshold crossed, the last climb up the tower staircase. There are no sisters to help her now, no magic spinning wheel either; no strange old man by the side of the road. In the greatest moments of our lives, we always are and always will be . . . alone.

(ANNA *enters the cell with her lantern, looking around.* FENIST *is center, unmoving.* ANNA *sees him, runs to him.*)

ANNA: Fenist! It's me! You're so cold! Please, please wake up! This is our only chance! I won't leave without you! I've come so far . . . Fenist, I do love you . . .

(ANNA *gently kisses his cheek, puts her head on his shoulder.* FENIST's *hand comes up and strokes her cheek, as in their first scene together.*)

FENIST: Don't cry, Anna . . .

ANNA: Thank God! I thought I'd lost you!

FENIST: (*As if this is a plausible answer.*) I am Fenist.

ANNA: I know.

FENIST: Where is SHE?

ANNA: I've taken care of her, for a while. Can you . . . fly?

FENIST: I'm too weak.

ANNA: Then we'll walk out—across the nine mountains.

FENIST: Anna, I've never crossed the mountains as a man. On the ground . . . I don't think I can do it.

ANNA: We must!

FENIST: We will get lost—or she will catch us.

ANNA: Never try, never know . . . (*Boinging sound heard faintly, getting louder.*)

FENIST: Anna . . . Anna? What's that sound?

ANNA: What sound?

FENIST: That sound? Is that your heart?

ANNA: (*Jumping up, looking out window.*) It's my ball!

FENIST: Pardon?

ANNA: The three sisters have sent the yarn ball! We can follow it across the mountains!

FENIST: Dogs chase balls. Birds do not.

ANNA: *(Taking charge.)* Nonsense. Get up, get ready. *(Shouting to ball.)* Wait there! We're coming! *(To FENIST.)* We're almost free!

FENIST: I am for you, Anna . . .

ANNA: And I am for you, Fenist. *(They kiss.)* You kiss very well, for a bird.

FENIST: Birds invented kissing. Let us go.

ANNA: Together.

(ANNA and FENIST exit. STORYTELLER enters, family fills in behind him.)

STORYTELLER: The Tsarevna finally got free and went after them. But in the mountains, in the dark, she found her heart wasn't in the chase. She let them go—and went back to her castle, to wait for the next falcon passing by. In a few days Anna and Fenist were home again.

(FATHER, AGRIPINA, MARTA, and ANNA now as we first saw them. TEVDORE is missing.)

MARTA: Well?

STORYTELLER: Well, what?

MARTA: What happens?

STORYTELLER: That's the end of the story.

ANNA: No, it isn't! What did her father say? What do her sisters do? Do Anna and Fenist marry? Are they happy together?

STORYTELLER: What do you think?

ANNA: I think her father was overjoyed to have them back and gave his blessing to a beautiful wedding, and they lived especially happy ever after.

AGRIPINA: Happy? Eating mice? Watching him fly away into the forest every night to hunt?

MARTA: And eventually having a few little chicks of their own? She'll be miserable.

ANNA: No. They WILL be happy.

AGRIPINA: Why?

ANNA: Because she will teach him how to love. And he will teach her how to fly.

STORYTELLER: And you, sir. Is that how the story ends?

FATHER: I don't know. Happy ever after is a very long time. We try as best we can. That's all we can do.

ANNA: Yes, Papa.

FATHER: Thank you for your story. But it's late, and morning is near. *(All rise; MARTA and AGRIPINA exit.)* Would you like to stay the night?

STORYTELLER: Thank you, no, I still have a long way to go.

FATHER: Mog zan dee; good-bye then. *(FATHER begins to exit.)*

ANNA: Wait! Where's Tevdore?

FATHER: *(Stopping, taking her hands.)* He went home awhile ago. He said he knew how the story ends. And there are cows to milk.

ANNA: Oh.

(FATHER looks for a long moment at ANNA and the STORYTELLER, realizing that he's lost her to whatever the STORYTELLER represents, that they are waiting for him to leave before they conclude their business. FATHER smiles sadly and exits. ANNA turns to face the STORYTELLER, who stands with his back to the table.)

What should I do?

STORYTELLER: I can't tell you that. I can only tell you what others have done before you.

ANNA: Tevdore is very sweet . . .

STORYTELLER: Yes, he is. And he will love you and take care of you, and work hard all his life to make you happy. You mustn't blame him for that.

ANNA: I know. Still . . .

FATHER: *(Offstage.)* Anna! Are you coming?

ANNA: Yes . . . I . . . I'm looking for something.

STORYTELLER: I'm going, Anna.

ANNA: Please . . .

STORYTELLER: The moment to decide comes without warning for most of us, and we miss it. Some day you'll realize how lucky you were.

(STORYTELLER moves around her; ANNA turns to watch him go. STORYTELLER exits. Behind ANNA, on the table, is the glowing box. She senses it, turns to look at it. She picks up the box, looks closely at it with wonder. Behind her the STORY-TELLER opens the door and ushers in TEVDORE, holding the same flower FENIST had earlier. TEVDORE walks quietly up behind ANNA, takes off his hat and holds the flower out to her.)

TEVDORE: Anna . . .

(ANNA looks up from the box, but doesn't turn to face him.)

CURTAIN

THE MAN-CHILD

by

Arnold Rabin

With two degrees from the University of Pennsylvania, Arnold Rabin spent the early years of his professional life as a writer, producer, and director of network television. He also served as Director of Public Affairs for WCAU-TV in Philadelphia, as Chief of English Language Television services for the United Nations, and as Administrator of Special Projects for Channel 13, the PBS station in New York. During these years his documentaries and TV plays received such commendations as a Harcourt-Brace Best TV Play Citation, an Emmy nomination for *The Little Orchestra*, an Edinburgh Film Festival showing, and Ohio State and *Variety* awards.

Rabin then left television to concentrate on his own writing projects. His short stories and essays have appeared in such commercial and literary quarterlies as the *Ladies' Home Journal*, *Journeymen*, *Changing Men*, the *Chicago Review*, the *Massachusetts Review*, *Descant*, *Brushfire*, and *Folio*.

As a playwright he was selected as a Fellow to the Edward Albee Foundation for his play, *Friends and Relations*. He is the recipient of a Distinguished Play Award from the American Alliance for Theatre and Education for *The Man-Child*, which premiered at the Henry Street Settlement House in New York City in 1976. His other play for young audiences, *The Outing*, was originally written for television and was produced twice on NBC.

Other honors include: the Denver Drama Critics Circle Best New Play Award, Drama League of New York Playwrights' Award, and the First Prize at the Aspen Playwrights' Festival for *Henry Apples or The Powers of Love Attested*. He has received a playwriting grant from the New Jersey State Council on the Arts and a creative writing grant from the National Endowment for the Arts. He is the author of the children's book, *The Christmas Bunny*, and the recently published novel, *The Rat and the Rose,* which was written while he held the grant from the National Endowment.

Rabin has taught and lectured at several colleges and universities and was for many years adjunct professor of English at Seton Hall University, South Orange, New Jersey, where he taught a variety of courses from creative writing to world drama. Among his latest adult plays are *Lady I and Lady II Talk Like Pigeons, They Dooooo . . . They Dooooo . . .* , which he calls A Play/Vaudeville, and *The Queen of Thebes.*

Having been interested in drama since I could breathe, I know the power of the theatre. I was born and raised in Philadelphia, where I began my writing and directing career in the second grade, with the cloakroom playing an integral part in the staging of *Beauty and the Beast.*

By the fifth grade I directed *Aladdin* because I wanted to play the wicked uncle, and in high school I wrote a radio play which, after winning a contest, was broadcast on the local radio station. These and many other experiences were central to my development, and so I believe it is our responsibility to give children the extraordinary world of theatre very early on.

To watch an audience of children, to watch their fascination and the delight in their eyes is pure joy. One such experience occurred when *The Man-Child* premiered before a very diverse audience on the lower East Side of New York City. Performance after performance the children, as one, were completely engrossed during the climactic moment and responded with exuberant release when the young boy Allen admits that he has lied to his mother. I want children to have such experiences apart from their everyday existence—theatre experiences which enflame their imaginations and make them lifelong audience members.

—ARNOLD RABIN

The plays printed in this anthology are not to be used as acting
scripts. All inquiries regarding *The Man-Child* performance
rights should be addressed to:

Baker's Plays
100 Chauncy Street
Boston, Massachusetts 02111-1783

THE MAN-CHILD

CHARACTERS

(In order of appearance)

Mrs. Wishnefsky: the grandmother
Miriam (Mimla): the mother
Pearl Gardner: a neighbor
Allen: Miriam's son
Herb: a friend of Allen
Voice of Western Union Boy
Uncle Frank
Aunt Sheila
The Cantor
Man in Service (nonspeaking)

The play is divided into three parts to be performed without intermission.

PART I

THE RING

The stage is divided into three sections. The main area is in two parts: a crowded kitchen and living room arrangement; the second is a small bedroom, well kept, even though it is full of mementoes, souvenirs, books, athletic equipment, all those things precious to a thirteen year old boy; the third area is the pulpit of the synagogue.

It is Friday afternoon in spring. The year, 1910. The place, the Lower East Side of New York.

It is in the main kitchen living room that we find MRS. WISHNEFSKY *welcoming the audience even as the lights come up. She is a delightful woman in her late sixties with a homespun wisdom of which she gives as heartily as she does of the joy she finds in living. She is open to the point of being confidential, but her innate common sense and her old world pride never allow her the indulgence of gossip.*

MRS. WISHNEFSKY: *(Generously to the audience.)* Hello—what a day for you to visit! So much excitement is going on! You wouldn't believe it! That's why I'm staying with my daughter Mimla, so I can help her. I usually live with my son Frank and his wife Sheila in Philadelphia. But my daughter needed me, so I came on a train to New York.

    Mimla, my daughter, isn't here now, but she'll be back in a few minutes. She's finishing some last minute shopping. Four more people said they could come to the dinner, and suddenly Mimla was afraid she wouldn't have enough food. I told her she's just making herself nervous. She's got enough food to feed an army, although thank God! there's no armies to feed. We had enough with the armies in the old country.

    But Mimla doesn't want to take chances. Everything's got to be right, absolutely and perfectly right for my grandson Allen's Bar Mitzvah. That's why we're turned upside down today. Tomorrow's my grandson's Bar Mitzvah, and what a time we're going to have! Maybe even you can help celebrate with us.

MIRIAM: *(Offstage.)* Mom, can you open the door? My arms are full. Did Frank and Sheila get here yet?

MRS. WISHNEFSKY: *(Calling to her.)* Not yet, Mimla. *(As she goes to open the door, she turns once again to the audience.)* Mimla's back. I'll tell you more about the Bar Mitzvah later. (MIRIAM *rushes in with three bundles which she sets down on the table. She is a woman in her late thirties.)* Look at you—a walking grocery store.

MIRIAM: *(Excitedly, flushed.)* I think I have everything now. I bought four more chickens and another three pounds of meat . . . more carrots and onions and another bunch of celery. I even bought some more tea. And I stopped by and told Mr. Gerstein to bring me another half dozen bottles of seltzer and soda.

MRS. WISHNEFSKY: Mimla . . . Mimla . . . it's like a fire under you. You have plenty of food, everything's going to be all right. It couldn't be better!

MIRIAM: It'll only be good if I make sure . . . if I check and double check. *(Sud-*

denly she looks at her mother who smiles back at her and self-consciously touches her hair.) Momma . . . your hair looks beautiful . . . I just noticed.

MRS. WISHNEFSKY: Do you like it?

MIRIAM: Pearl did a wonderful job.

MRS. WISHNEFSKY: On my head Houdini I should have setting the hair. I told Pearl, I said, "Houdini, you should be, Pearl. If it doesn't look so good, I won't blame you. I'm not the beauty I used to be."

MIRIAM: *(She kisses her mother gently.)* You are a beauty, Momma. I don't know what I'd do without you here. *(Slight pause.)* I just wish you could have managed to get that son of yours here already. Allen's going to be so upset when he gets home from school and finds Frank and Sheila haven't arrived yet.

MRS. WISHNEFSKY: They'll be here. My Frank is a dependable boy. He has never yet disappointed me—ever! (PEARL GARDNER *bursts into the room. She is about forty, perhaps slightly taller than* MIRIAM. *She is a pleasant woman, who speaks quickly and positively.)*

PEARL: Mim dear, if you have time now, I can pin up your dress.

MIRIAM: Thanks, Pearl.

PEARL: *(She looks at* MRS. WISHNEFSKY, *but speaks to* MIRIAM.) How do you like your mother's hair? How do you like what I did to her?

MIRIAM: I was just telling her it looks beautiful.

PEARL: I told her, I said, "Mrs. Wishnefsky, I think all the men will fall in love with you tomorrow."

MRS. WISHNEFSKY: *(With a laugh first and then pride.)* It won't do them any good, I'm afraid. Tomorrow I'll only have eyes for one man, my grandson, Allen.

MIRIAM: *(To* PEARL.) I just went out and bought a few more things.

PEARL: It must be costing you a fortune. You should have let good enough alone with just a kiddush—a little cake and wine, and you don't have all this headache.

MIRIAM: It's not a headache, Pearl I saved for it. I've put a little away each week for the past year. And last week, Mr. Tannenbaum gave me a bonus. He said, "I never had a son, Miriam, and I watched you raising Allen, and you're a good bookkeeper, so I want you to have this."

MRS. WISHNEFSKY: Fifteen dollars he gave her. And she's worth every penny of it.

PEARL: Well, I'm really glad you're doing it. We need a party around here.

MIRIAM: And I couldn't do it without you, Pearl—the cooking you're doing, and letting us use your apartment, and your dishes—

PEARL: So what else is new?

MIRIAM: I think I'll need a vacation when it's over. (ALLEN *comes bursting into the room carrying his school books.)*

ALLEN: *(With great excitement as if it were the most important thing in the world.)* Is it here yet? Did they come with it?

PEARL: *(Before anyone can answer* ALLEN's *questions.)* Well, here he is! Congratulations, Allen!

ALLEN: *(Swallowing his impatience.)* Thank you, Mrs. Gardner.

PEARL: Do you know everything perfectly for tomorrow?

ALLEN: *(Still polite in spite of his anxiousness.)* I hope so.

PEARL: I'll be listening carefully to every word. Remember what happened to my son, Carl. *(To MIRIAM.)* I'll get my pins and my yardstick. I'll be back in a few minutes.

MIRIAM: It's a big hem, Pearl. I have to finish it before sundown. I won't sew on Shabbos.

PEARL: I'll be back in no time. *(She leaves.)*

ALLEN: Did the suit come? Didn't Aunt Sheila and Uncle Frank get here yet?

MIRIAM: Not yet, dear. I expect they'll be here soon.

ALLEN: I wish they would have taken the train.

MIRIAM: Uncle Frank's very proud of his Model-T, and he was looking forward to driving it from Philadelphia. They wrote in their letter they'd be here by four, and you know Uncle Frank. When he says something, he usually lives up to his word.

ALLEN: But Mom, suppose they're not here by then. What if they're not! And if anything's wrong with the suit!

MRS. WISHNEFSKY: Already's he worrying like an old man!

ALLEN: But grandmom, it's Friday night! Who's gonna fix it!

MIRIAM: Allen, don't fret so. We sent Uncle Frank the exact measurements. You'll be able to walk out the door in the suit.

ALLEN: We should have told them to send it!

MIRIAM: When they're coming here themselves! What a thing to say! They want to give it to you personally.

MRS. WISHNEFSKY: It's their pleasure, Allen.

ALLEN: But suppose they're in an accident!

MRS. WISHNEFSKY: God forbid! If they were in an accident, the suit would be the last thing to think about!

ALLEN: I'm sorry grandmom!

MRS. WISHNEFSKY: What a way to talk! And you a Bar Mitzvah *bauchur!*

(The light fades on this part of the set as MRS. WISHNEFSKY walks out of the scene to share her feelings with the audience.)

MRS. WISHNEFSKY: It's my pleasure to explain to you what's a Bar Mitzvah *bauchur.* It's the Bar Mitzvah boy! And like I started to tell you before, tomorrow's my grandson's Bar Mitzvah!

When a Jewish boy is thirteen years old, he has a Bar Mitzvah. According to tradition he's old enough now to become a man, to take on a man's responsibilities. In the synagogue is a ceremony. For the first time my grandson will be called up to the pulpit to read from the Torah, the holy Scroll of Jewish law—the five books of Moses! He'll stand at the pulpit with the other men, and he'll speak aloud the word of God! *(She takes a breath of pride, and then she comes back to ALLEN's immediate concern over the suit.)*

That's why Allen's so upset about the suit! To go into manhood, you have to have a new suit! With, for the first time, long pants, if you please! But believe me, he doesn't have to worry like that! He'll have his suit. And it'll be a fine suit. If his Uncle Frank gets something, it's got to be the best! Wait till you meet my son, Frank, a wonderful boy—successful, too. When he told my daughter, Miriam, that he wanted to give Allen the Bar Mitzvah suit for a present, I said "Miriam—you should be quiet and don't argue. Frank has taste like a king!" *(The bedroom slowly lights up.)* But I have to interrupt myself now, or you'll miss an important part of the story that's going on in Allen's room. *(In the bedroom,* ALLEN *is getting some books together. His mother enters.)*

ALLEN: Hi, Mom. I promised the rabbi I'd be there at three o'clock.

MIRIAM: Good, remember to go over everything with him, Allen. If you have any doubts—

ALLEN: He said the other day I had it perfect.

MIRIAM: Still it never hurts to double check. Like they say, this is your dress rehearsal.

ALLEN: Don't worry, Mom.

MIRIAM: *(After the briefest pause.)* Allen . . .

ALLEN: Yes, Mom . . .

MIRIAM: I'd like to talk with you a minute.

ALLEN: Sure, Mom, what's the matter?

MIRIAM: *(Slightly self-conscious.)* Nothing's the matter. Does something have to be the matter for me to talk with you?

ALLEN: I didn't mean—

MIRIAM: *(Realizing herself.)* I know you didn't. I—I guess I—*(And now she begins to find her words.)* Allen, this will probably be the last chance I have to talk quietly with you—without all the people around—and before you'll be too excited to know what I'm saying.

ALLEN: I'm not nervous about tomorrow, if that's what you mean.

MIRIAM: *(Her assurance back with her—and with an encouraging mother's pride.)* You shouldn't be nervous. You should be sure of yourself! You're not a little boy anymore! *(A slight pause as she herself grasps the idea. Then, quite simply . . .)* In a few hours, you'll be a man. *(Gently chiding him.)* Why, you may not even want to listen to me then!

ALLEN: Mom, you know that's not true.

MIRIAM: *(Teasing.)* All right. Maybe I won't know how to talk to you.

ALLEN: You can talk the same. I'll know what you mean.

MIRIAM: I'm not so sure. Things don't mean the same to a man as they do to a boy.

ALLEN: *(Half curious, half not believing.)* Do you think I'm going to change that much?

MIRIAM: Not right away—but gradually—slowly by degrees you should. From inside you'll have to grow to fit into yourself. You should even grow bigger inside than out. For some people it takes longer than for others.

ALLEN: But as you get older, things happen faster, don't they?

MIRIAM: They happen too fast, sometimes. At least it seems that way. I guess it's because as you get older, you're planning more and more things, and suddenly you begin to worry if you'll get them all done.

ALLEN: How do you get everything done before you die!

MIRIAM: You never do. It's a kind of death if you think you have.

ALLEN: Mom . . . *(There is a pause.)* Did Daddy leave many things unfinished when he died?

MIRIAM: *(Quietly as she thinks of so many things.)* All the things he had hardly begun. And he would have done so many of them, Allen. *(MIRIAM gathers the memories together.)* That's one of the reasons I came here to talk to you. He could have done so much for you that I haven't been able to do. Like tonight—you and he could have spoken together. It would have been different from the way it is with me. *(As if to excuse herself.)* Not that there's any one magic word that'll bring wisdom, but—*(For a moment she is at a loss. Then MIRIAM takes a small box from her apron.)* There was something else. I came up here to give you a present from him. If he were alive, he would have given it to you himself. *(She gives ALLEN the box.)* Go on . . . open it.

ALLEN: *(Slowly he opens it.)* It's a ring!

MIRIAM: It's your father's ring! His own Bar Mitzvah ring! He said he wanted to give it to his son some day. It was one of the things he couldn't do before he died.

ALLEN: It's gold! Mom, is it real?

MIRIAM: As real as he was. *(Pause.)* Try it on.

ALLEN: *(He holds the ring in his hand. He looks at it. He looks at his mother. Just a touch of awe is there in his voice.)* Now? *(MIRIAM nods. Slowly ALLEN puts the ring on his finger. It fits. He holds the ring hand clenched in the other hand, staring down at it.)* It fits! And it's gold! Is it fourteen karat gold?

MIRIAM: *(Smiling.)* It's fourteen karat gold—at least—maybe more. It was one of the few things your father brought with him when he and his family left almost everything else they had in the old country to come here.

ALLEN: I never had anything real gold before. *(Covering the ring finger with pride.)* It's a precious thing! Is it an antique too? How old is it?

MIRIAM: Well, your father died when you were three. He was twenty-nine. He had the ring for sixteen years, and you've lived for ten years after him.

ALLEN: *(After a moment.)* It's twenty-six years old. *(Pause . . . then . . .)* Mom, thirteen and thirteen are twenty-six. The ring is two Bar Mitzvahs old.

MIRIAM: I never looked at it that way. But you're right—

ALLEN: It'll have its second Bar Mitzvah tomorrow—one for me—and one for my father. *(MRS. WISHNEFSKY's voice is heard from the living room.)*

MRS. WISHNEFSKY'S VOICE: Miriam! Pearl's back to pin up your dress for you.

MIRIAM: *(Calling to MRS. WISHNEFSKY.)* All right, I'll be right there!

ALLEN: Mom, can I wear the ring outside?

MIRIAM: It's yours, Allen. From now on you can wear it always.

ALLEN: I'll never take it off, Mom. I'll never take it off.

(The light in the bedroom slowly fades as the living room set is lighted. PEARL and MRS. WISHNEFSKY are talking.)

PEARL: You should be very proud, Mrs. Wishnefsky.

MRS. WISHNEFSKY: I am. Allen's my only grandson.

PEARL: *(Going on as if she has not been interrupted.)* When my Carl was Bar Mitzvahed, everyone in the family was worn out already. My sister Rose's boy had been Bar Mitzvahed on March 10, my other sister's son two weeks later, my brother's boy April 14, and my Carl on April 21. *(Pause.)*

But my Carl was something to remember! Did Miriam ever tell you about it. You would not dream what happened. Mrs. Wishnefsky! In the middle of the Torah reading my Carl suddenly stopped. My heart skipped a beat. I thought he lost his place or was mixed up. My husband grabbed my hand. The whole synagogue was tense. We watched Carl staring at the Torah and then we saw him whisper something to the rabbi. I was sure he couldn't read the word! I was so embarrassed! I was disappointed! I thought I would cry! After all those lessons—that my Carl should forget in front of everybody! But how wrong I was, Mrs. Wishnefsky! How wrong I was! Do you know what happened? You'll never believe it! My Carl found a mistake in the Torah!

MRS. WISHNEFSKY: *(Supreme disbelief.)* No! a mistake in the Torah!

PEARL: *(Carried right on.)* You know how each Torah is copied by hand, each little word painstakingly. Well, there was a mistake in the copying—the scribe made an error! It's very rare! And for a boy only thirteen to be able to tell it! You know they have to get rid of the Torah when something's wrong with it—because it's so sacred. In all the time that this one had been used, no one had discovered the mistake! Everyone said right then and there that my Carl should be a rabbi!

MRS. WISHNEFSKY: I never heard of such a thing!

PEARL: It was thrilling—to see everybody looking at my son Carl in amazement. It was like the hand of God was right there. The rest of the service went on as if the synagogue was now in heaven!

MRS. WISHNEFSKY: Such a miracle on such a day! (MIRIAM *enters the room in her dress.* PEARL *turns to her.)*

PEARL: Oh, Miriam, the dress is beautiful. You did a perfect job.

MIRIAM: *(Turning around.)* Do you really like it? It's a little light, I suppose, but I want the extra color.

PEARL: It's a lovely color for you.

MIRIAM: I thought of Max when I picked the fabric. He always liked cheerful colors. *(A moment's awkwardness.)* I didn't want anything dark tomorrow, Pearl. If I feel cheerful, I'll be able better to go through it alone. I've been thinking about it all day! I don't want to cry, it's a happy occasion, and yet I miss Max. I miss him more than I ever did. I wish he could see Allen tomorrow.

MRS. WISHNEFSKY: *(Gently.)* Mimla, you should hurry with your dress.

MIRIAM: *(Smiling and taking control of herself.)* You're right, Mom.

MRS. WISHNEFSKY: In the meantime, I'll start supper.

MIRIAM: No, Mom, don't bother. You don't have to. I'll take care of it.

MRS. WISHNEFSKY: What's the matter! I can't do something to help! I don't have to sit around the whole time with my hands folded! And if I don't do anything, I'll only be nervous. So take care of your dress with Pearl, and let me make supper. *(She starts towards the kitchen.)* And take your time with her, Pearl. I can manage fine. *(She goes to the kitchen.)*

PEARL: What a wonderful woman!

MIRIAM: She's a blessing!

PEARL: *(Stepping back and looking at* MIRIAM's *dress.)* It needs just an inch, maybe an inch and a half.

HERB'S VOICE: *(Offstage.)* Mrs. Samuels, is Allen home? *(He stands framed in the doorway.)*

MIRIAM: You can come in, Herb. You don't have to shout at the door. Yes, he's home.

HERB: *(Entering.)* Hello, Mrs. Samuels. Did you say Allen was home?

MIRIAM: *(Patiently.)* Yes, I did. *(Coaching him to say hello.)* Mrs. Gardner's here, Herb.

HERB: Hello, Mrs. Gardner. *(To* MIRIAM.*)* Is that your dress for tomorrow?

MIRIAM: Why yes, do you like it?

HERB: It's pretty. You know that's why my mother said she wished I had a Bar Mitzvah every week. She said it was the only time my father let her have a new dress without arguing. *(*MIRIAM *and* PEARL *laugh.* HERB *looks around.)* I thought you said Allen was here.

MIRIAM: He's in his room getting his things for his lesson. He's got to go to the rabbi's. His final rehearsal—

HERB: I'll walk him.

MIRIAM: I'm sure he'll like that.

HERB: I'll give him confidence, even though a Bar Mitzvah's not really so bad. It's just before that you worry. When it's over, you see the whole thing was nothing.

MIRIAM: I wouldn't say it was nothing.

HERB: Well, you know what I mean, nothing to worry about. *(*HERB *is distracted as he spots a seltzer bottle. To* MIRIAM.*)* I hear you're going to have seltzer at the Bar Mitzvah.

MIRIAM: Of course.

HERB: I like seltzer.

MIRIAM: Do you want some, Herb. Is that what you're asking? There's a bottle here. I'll give you a glass.

HERB: Can I take it myself, Mrs. Samuels?

MIRIAM: Sure, if you want to.

HERB: Thanks. *(He takes the glass, presses the lever on the seltzer bottle, and sprays the seltzer into the glass.* MIRIAM *watches him.)*

MIRIAM: *(As* HERB *fills his glass.)* You must be thirsty, Herb. *(When he has filled his glass, he looks at it.)* Aren't you going to drink it, Herb?

HERB: Huh?

MIRIAM: I said you poured such a big glass, why don't you drink it before the fizz goes out. *(*HERB *takes a sip.)* Is that all you're going to drink? I thought you said you liked seltzer.

HERB: *(Pressing the seltzer bottle lever again.)* I just like to watch it spritz, Mrs. Samuels. *(*MIRIAM *and* PEARL *laugh.)*

MIRIAM: (*Calling to* ALLEN.) Allen, Herb's here. He's going to walk you to the rabbi's.

ALLEN'S VOICE: Tell him to come up. (*Pause, then—*) Come on up, Herb. I want to show you something.

HERB: O.K. (*He starts to* ALLEN's *room. Then he turns to* MIRIAM *and* PEARL *as if they couldn't possibly have heard the conversation he has been having with* ALLEN.) Excuse me, please. Allen wants me to come to his room. He wants to show me something. (*He leaves for* ALLEN's *room.* MIRIAM *turns to* PEARL.)

PEARL: I think the best thing, Miriam, would be if you stood on a chair. Then I could sit on the stool and be comfortable while I pin.

MIRIAM: (*As she steps up onto a chair.*) Do you see what I mean, Pearl, about it being such a big job? The skirt is so full. (*The light fades in the living room as* HERB *enters* ALLEN's *bedroom. Immediately* ALLEN *puts his hand behind his back.*)

ALLEN: Hi, Herb—

HERB: Hi—you nervous?

ALLEN: Not too . . . (*A slight pause.*) Guess what.

HERB: I don't know. (*Pause.*) What do you have your hand behind your back for?

ALLEN: That's part of it.

HERB: Is it in your hand what you want to show me?

ALLEN: You're getting hot! Not "in" my hand.

HERB: Is it one of those new kind of watches that you can put on your wrist?

ALLEN: No . . . that's for millionaires. But it's almost as good.

HERB: What is it then?

ALLEN: (*Taking his hand from behind his back.*) It's a ring. It belonged to my father. It's his Bar Mitzvah ring. And it's gold!

HERB: Real gold?

ALLEN: Real gold!

HERB: (*A shot of envy races through him.*) How do you know it's real gold?

ALLEN: My mother told me when she gave it to me!

HERB: Does it say so on the ring?

ALLEN: What do you mean?

HERB: It says so if it's real gold.

ALLEN: Yeah, I didn't look.

HERB: Sure, my brother got a ring from my uncle when he graduated, and inside it had 14K. It stands for fourteen karat.

ALLEN: That's what my mother said this was.

HERB: It should say so inside. If it doesn't say so, it's not real gold.

ALLEN: Well, I'm not worried. I'm sure it is.

HERB: I'll show you where it said so on my brother's ring. It was right on the side—underneath.

ALLEN: (*Covering the ring hand again.*) I don't want to take it off.

HERB: You're going to have to take it off sometime. When you wash your hands you'll have to take it off.

ALLEN: Maybe—but I don't want to take it off just like that.

HERB: You could, just for a second. It wouldn't hurt. See if it says 14K like my brother's. That's the real test. You can put it right back on.

ALLEN: I don't have to test it. I know it's real gold!

HERB: Well, I don't. You're asking me to take your word!

ALLEN: It's not my word! It's my father's ring! And my mother wouldn't tell me it was fourteen karat if it wasn't.

HERB: How do I know she told you it was! You might have just made it up. You might have made up the whole story.

ALLEN: *(Hurt at the insinuation.)* I didn't make it up! Why would I do that!

HERB: Lots of reasons. So I should think you had something that was real gold when you didn't.

ALLEN: But it is real gold! How many times do I have to tell you!

HERB: Then let me see it where it should say so. That's all I'm asking. If it has the 14K—*(Impulsively* ALLEN *removes the ring from his finger. He looks inside.* HERB *immediately tries to look too.)* Do you see it?

ALLEN: Take it easy.

HERB: If the ring's old like you say, it might be a little black from time. Hold it to the light. *(ALLEN raises the ring.)* Can you see it now?

ALLEN: *(Nervously.)* I can't tell.

HERB: It's hard sometimes. *(ALLEN turns the ring in several directions. Then* HERB *grabs it from him.)* Let me look. I got better eyes. *(He studies the ring carefully.)* I don't see nothing. *(ALLEN takes the ring back. He looks again himself.)*

ALLEN: It's probably rubbed off. It's old. Twenty-six years old. And I guess those things rub off after a while. I know a cousin of mine had a ring with his initials on the side, and after a couple of years they were all rubbed away.

HERB: They scratch the 14K pretty deep. It's important for them, so even if you couldn't read it clear, there should be some sign of it. And I don't see any sign.

ALLEN: It is real gold! I know it is. My mother wouldn't have told me otherwise!

HERB: You don't think she'd give you a ring and tell you it was a fake, do you!

ALLEN: It's not a fake!

HERB: All I know is—it doesn't say 14K!

ALLEN: They could have left it off, couldn't they! There's no law that says they have to put it on, is there?

HERB: *(Deliberately.)* I don't know if there's a law, but if it's real gold, jewelers put it on!

ALLEN: Well, my ring's from the old country. Maybe there—

HERB: It doesn't matter where it comes from.

ALLEN: *(Not really knowing how—)* I can prove it's gold.

HERB: How?

ALLEN: *(Hedging.)* There are ways to prove it's gold without it saying 14K.

HERB: If there is, I don't know it.

ALLEN: Then that shows how much you know! There's got to be a way! Else how could a jeweler know it's fourteen karat before he puts the 14K on it! There must be a test! Somebody's got to have a way to find out in the beginning!

HERB: Maybe. I guess they do have some kind of test. (Pause.) Maybe they try to dent it. You know like they do with coins! You've seen them put the coins between their teeth!

ALLEN: Do you think that would be a test?

HERB: It works with coins. Try it!

ALLEN: If it doesn't dent, will you believe it's fourteen karat even if it doesn't have the 14K?

HERB: I guess so. It would be proof! (ALLEN stares at the ring. He takes it between his fingers. Slowly he brings it to his mouth. There is one last hesitation.)

ALLEN: I know it's real gold!

HERB: Prove it—go ahead—Bite it! See if it dents! (ALLEN places the ring between his teeth and closes his teeth down on the ring. Then he cups his hand over his mouth and lets the ring drop into it. Slowly he opens his fist.) It's dented! I told you it wasn't real gold! I told you it had to say 14K! I told you it was a fake! (ALLEN stares at the dented ring. The light fades.)

PART II

THE LIE

The living room.

MIRIAM *is standing at an ironing board putting the final pressing strokes to her dress. Then she lifts the dress carefully from the board and places it on a hanger.*

Her mother watches.

MIRIAM: There! It's finished! And it's only four-thirty.

MRS. WISHNEFSKY: And you have time to spare before Shabbos.

MIRIAM: (She holds up the dress.) What do you think, Mom?

MRS. WISHNEFSKY: I think it's beautiful. You should wear it beautiful tomorrow.

MIRIAM: I've got a good son who'll make sure of that. (As she goes out with the dress.) I'm going to hang it in the bedroom.

MRS. WISHNEFSKY: (Turning to the audience.) You want to know about the Shabbos? And why it's important! It's the holy day of the week for the Jews, a day of rest and worshipping God. Nobody goes to his business, only to synagogue. That's why Mimla won't sew on the Shabbos. We even have to find a way to get the Bar Mitzvah meal ready without cooking on Saturday. So we made some of it ahead of time, and some other things we'll put on the stove before sundown tonight, and they will cook slowly all day tomorrow. On Friday night the Shabbos starts because the Jews really believe a new day begins on the night before.

PEARL: (Rushing in, breathless.) Hello, Mrs. Wishnefsky. Is Allen here?

MRS. WISHNEFSKY: So what's the matter, Pearl, you're running so fast? All the time is plenty of time.

PEARL: *(Insistently.)* Is Allen here?

MRS. WISHNEFSKY: You know he's still with the rabbi.

PEARL: But he isn't, Mrs. Wishnefsky.

MRS. WISHNEFSKY: What do you mean he isn't?

PEARL: I just passed the synagogue and one of the boys outside asked me where Allen was. He said the rabbi was annoyed that Allen hadn't kept his appointment. So I went in, and the boy was right. The rabbi said Allen hadn't come for his lesson.

MRS. WISHNEFSKY: What are you saying?

PEARL: You heard me, Mrs. Wishnefsky. Allen never showed up for his lesson.

MIRIAM: *(MIRIAM comes back into the room.)* Pearl! I just hung the dress up. It looks wonderful.

PEARL: *(Quietly and with a forced smile.)* I'm glad.

MIRIAM: You don't sound glad.

PEARL: *(Nervously.)* I'm glad, I'm glad. Why shouldn't I be glad! I fixed it for you, didn't I?

MIRIAM: What's the matter with you, Pearl? Why are you talking like this? Is something wrong? *(PEARL looks at MRS. WISHNEFSKY.)* Something's wrong!

MRS. WISHNEFSKY: Nothing's wrong, Mimla. It's just that Allen hasn't shown up at the rabbi's.

MIRIAM: But he was supposed to be there two hours ago!

MRS. WISHNEFSKY: He's so excited. He probably stopped on the way to talk to somebody.

MIRIAM: Not for two hours! You know when he left here! Why in the world does he have to go wandering around. On the day before his Bar Mitzvah, I don't need any more headaches.

MRS. WISHNEFSKY: You don't have to get headaches! There's nothing to worry about.

MIRIAM: Mom, from here to the synagogue should take him ten minutes!

MRS. WISHNEFSKY: When you get excited you forget about time.

MIRIAM: Herb was going to walk him over. I'm going over to his apartment and see if he's home yet— *(She starts out.)*

MRS. WISHNEFSKY: Maybe they stopped to play baseball.

MIRIAM: *(Turning back into the room.)* Baseball! I don't want him to play baseball! He'll break a leg yet.

PEARL: Relax, Miriam. For goodness sake—you just gave him Max's ring. He's probably showing it to everybody he meets.

MIRIAM: He and the rabbi were going to go over everything this afternoon.

PEARL: He knows it all fine.

MIRIAM: I've been worried all day. I've been worried something wrong would happen, something terribly wrong. It started this morning when I couldn't stop thinking of Max. My mind raced—I thought, God Forbid! what if something should happen to Allen, too. And then, before I knew it, I went from thinking—*suppose* something happened to Allen to thinking that something would happen!

MRS. WISHNEFSKY: Why should something happen! Except in your head is—

MIRIAM: It seems there's always something that takes away. You can never have just *joy*, as if God doesn't want you to forget—as if He thinks when everything goes well, you won't appreciate it. This morning I thought my reminder was that Max wasn't here to share tomorrow with me! I'm afraid, Mom! I hope it isn't anything more!

MRS. WISHNEFSKY: You shouldn't say such a thing!

PEARL: I'm sorry I even told you—I'm sure he's all right!

MIRIAM: Suppose something did happen to Allen!

MRS. WISHNEFSKY: Look how you're working yourself up!

MIRIAM: Suppose—

MRS. WISHNEFSKY: Suppose! Suppose! Oh, how your mind works!

MIRIAM: You said yourself he was excited! And you know how he is when he's excited! He doesn't know what he's doing! He doesn't look where he's going—

MRS. WISHNEFSKY: Already in your head is the worst!

MIRIAM: (*Beside herself.*) It's not like Allen to be two hours late! (ALLEN *enters the room and quietly moves towards his bedroom hoping to avoid the family.*)

MRS. WISHNEFSKY: (*First to spot him.*) Allen! (*Quietly.*) Oh, thank God!

MIRIAM: (*Turning swiftly and going to him as he watches her coldly. Relief and impatience are there with one another.*) Where were you, Allen? You had everyone so worried. The rabbi was expecting you. Where did you get to? (ALLEN *does not move. He does not answer. He has hardly looked at her.*) Are you all right? What's the matter! Why do you look like that? What's wrong?

ALLEN: Nothing.

MIRIAM: Did something happen? You look like you've been crying. You'd better get right over to the rabbi. He's waiting for you.

ALLEN: That's all right. Herb was passing the synagogue. I told him to tell the rabbi. He probably knows by now.

MIRIAM: What do you mean you told Herb to tell the rabbi? Why didn't you go there like you were supposed to?

ALLEN: I—I wasn't feeling good.

MIRIAM: (*Immediate concern.*) You mean you're sick?

ALLEN: I'm better now.

MIRIAM: I don't understand you. You were supposed to go over everything for tomorrow.

ALLEN: It doesn't matter.

MIRIAM: What doesn't matter! What are you trying to say? (*The doorbell rings.*)

PEARL: I'll see who's there, Miriam.

BOY'S VOICE: Western Union. Are you Mrs. Samuels?

PEARL: I'm Mrs. Gardner, but I'll take it for Mrs. Samuels.

MIRIAM: *(Still distressed with* ALLEN.*)* I don't understand, Allen. You were so excited before. *(*PEARL *comes back into the room with the telegram.)* Who was it, Pearl? *(*PEARL *extends the telegram.)* What's that?

MRS. WISHNEFSKY: It's a telegram, my God! Somebody died! *(*MIRIAM *tries to open the telegram, but she fidgets.)*

PEARL: Let me open it for you.

MIRIAM: Something's happened to Frank!

PEARL: *(Tearing the telegram open.)* Not every telegram has bad news.

MIRIAM: Read it to me, Pearl.

PEARL: He's all right. Everything is all right.

MRS. WISHNEFSKY: *(Excitedly.)* So who's all right, Pearl?

PEARL: Your son, Mrs. Wishnefsky. He's had a little trouble with his motor car. But he says he's near Newark, and he should be here in a few hours.

MRS. WISHNEFSKY: Such a thing, an automobile! I told him he shouldn't buy an automobile. So much money he spent! And they're so dangerous! But my Frank had to buy one! *(In the confusion,* ALLEN *slips from the room.)*

PEARL: It was only a small problem.

MRS. WISHNEFSKY: Who takes a chance and drives such a thing as an automobile to a Bar Mitzvah! To a Bar Mitzvah you take a train!

MIRIAM: *(Taking the telegram from* PEARL *and reading.)* It's all right, Mom, he says everything's all right! He just didn't want us to worry!

MRS. WISHNEFSKY: What a way not to worry! He should be here, and I wouldn't worry.

MIRIAM: He says everything's all right, and Allen's suit is handsome.

MRS. WISHNEFSKY: Just like Frank—to think of his nephew when he has his own problems.

MIRIAM: *(She notices* ALLEN *has left the room.)* Where is Allen?

MRS. WISHNEFSKY: *(Also for the first time realizing that* ALLEN *has left.)* I guess he went to his room.

MIRIAM: I don't understand what's the matter with him.

PEARL: Be patient, Miriam. You'll see it's nothing—a little bit of nerves. I had the same thing with my Carl. Your Allen should give you the same pleasure my Carl gave me. *(*MIRIAM *leaves.)* It'll be all right, Mrs. Wishnefsky. Everything will be all right. There's always a problem. Remember, the sun never shines on a happy bride. *(She leans and kisses her and leaves.)*

MRS. WISHNEFSKY: *(To the audience.)* Like Pearl said, there's always a problem. All the time when there's a *simchah*—a celebration—there's a problem, too. At the last minute, no matter how many worries you think you have, some new ones come up. You can never anticipate everything! But maybe in a way it's good. You shouldn't expect everything to fall in your lap. You should remember you have to work for joy. Making joy is like making any other thing! You have to earn it! There is no business success, but the man doesn't work to make the success; there's no happy marriage, but the couple doesn't try for it. Nothing in life comes without trying, without working! And whenever it looks like it's coming too easy, God reminds you. There's a saying, "God sits on high and plays with things below." *(The light goes out in the living room and up in the bedroom as* MIRIAM *enters.* ALLEN *lies stretched across the bed.)*

MIRIAM: Allen—(ALLEN *doesn't look up.*) Allen, I'm talking to you. I think I deserve the courtesy of your looking at me. (ALLEN *slowly lifts his head barely acknowledging her.*) Why did you walk out of the room like that—in the middle of our conversation?

ALLEN: *(Barely audible.)* I'm sorry.

MIRIAM: The telegram was from Uncle Frank. He and Aunt Sheila were delayed with car trouble. But they'll be here soon, and he said your suit is handsome. (ALLEN *doesn't answer.*) I thought you'd be happy. You don't have to worry anymore.

ALLEN: *(Almost grimly.)* It's like what I thought would happen.

MIRIAM: Allen!

ALLEN: They won't be here till late, till after dark, will they?

MIRIAM: No—but—

ALLEN: And I know something else. The suit won't fit either, and there won't be anybody to fix it.

MIRIAM: Why are you talking this way?

ALLEN: There's nothing good about this Bar Mitzvah.

MIRIAM: Now look here, Allen! What's gotten into you!

ALLEN: *(With a slow deliberateness.)* You told me the ring was real gold!

MIRIAM: *(For the first instant confused.)* The ring? You mean your father's ring!

ALLEN: The Bar Mitzvah ring!

MIRIAM: Well, it is real gold!

ALLEN: It's not!

MIRIAM: What do you mean it's not!

ALLEN: It's not real gold!

MIRIAM: *(Impatient with him.)* Allen, please stop this game! You're supposed to be a man now! What gave you the idea the ring isn't real gold!

ALLEN: It doesn't say 14K!

MIRIAM: What's 14K?

ALLEN: Fourteen karat! If a ring is real gold, it has 14K carved on it. And this ring doesn't. Herb showed me!

MIRIAM: *(Quietly, evenly.)* Where is the ring? (ALLEN *is silent.* MIRIAM *does not raise her voice.*) Allen, I'm asking you a question. What did you do with the ring? *(He still does not answer. She goes on, not angrily, but attempting to get to him.)* Did you lose the ring?

ALLEN: *(Slowly.)* No, I didn't lose it. I have it.

MIRIAM: *(Still controlling herself.)* Let me see your hand.

ALLEN: *(He hesitates. Then he covers his left fingers with his right hand.)* It's not on my finger! I took it off!

MIRIAM: *(Still keeping control.)* Why did you take it off?

ALLEN: *(Silence. Then—suddenly—)* Because . . . Because it's a *fake!* The ring's a fake! *(The movement of air in the room seems to stop.)*

MIRIAM: (*Still evenly, still quietly.*) Would you give it back to me then. (ALLEN *does not move.*) If you think it's a fake, please give it back. I don't want you to keep anything you believe is a fake!

ALLEN: (*Bewildered. A little frightened by her calm.*) You said it was real.

MIRIAM: It is real.

ALLEN: Then why isn't it marked real?

MIRIAM: (*Almost without emotion.*) I don't know why it isn't. But I'm sure that it's not the only real gold ring in the world that isn't marked. It may have been an oversight. The numbers may have worn off.

ALLEN: (*Interrupting.*) Herb said they couldn't wear off!

MIRIAM: (*Going right on, ignoring this interruption.*) As I remember, your father said the ring had been too big for him, and I believe they had to make it smaller—perhaps in making it smaller, they rubbed the markings off. Now, would you give me the ring!

ALLEN: (*Treading the green grass softly.*) If—if it was real gold—it wouldn't dent!

MIRIAM: Gold is a soft metal. A gold ring will dent easily under pressure. (*The slightest pause.*) And how do you know this ring dents?

ALLEN: (*Panic crosses his face. He blurts out three carefully chosen words.*) Because it dented!

MIRIAM: (*Firmly, emphasizing* ALLEN'*s last words.*) What do you mean—*it dented?* (ALLEN *has no answer.*) Allen, please give me the ring.

ALLEN: It dented . . . it dented!

MIRIAM: How did it dent?

ALLEN: It—it—fell off my finger—it fell—and before I could pick it up—it fell off my finger and before I could pick it up, Herb—Herb—accidentally stepped on it.

MIRIAM: (*Almost a command.*) Let me see the ring! (ALLEN *does not budge. And now his mother makes a strong command.*) Let me see the ring! (*Slowly* ALLEN *takes the ring from his pocket. He gives it to his mother.* MIRIAM *looks at it.*) It doesn't look like it was stepped on. (*She examines it closely.*) It looks more like teeth marks. It looks almost as if someone bit it! (*Pause—Suddenly.*) Allen! Did you bite the ring?

ALLEN: (*A fierce cry.*) No!

MIRIAM: (*The pieces falling into place.*) Were you testing the ring? Did you bite it to test it? To see if it was real gold!

ALLEN: (*Hating his own lie.*) I didn't bite it!

MIRIAM: (*Slowly understanding.*) You didn't believe me! Did you think I was trying to fool you! Did you think I would deliberately tell you something was real gold when it wasn't.

ALLEN: (*Burning with shame.*) No—it fell off my finger, and Herb stepped on it before I had a chance to pick it up.

MIRIAM: It couldn't have just fallen off your finger. It fit too well. You had to take it off.

ALLEN: That's what I mean. I took it off—I took it off to show to Herb—to prove to him that it was real gold. He wanted to see the 14K! And then it fell, and before I could pick it up, he stepped on it by accident.

MIRIAM: You're not telling the truth.

ALLEN: *(Unable to stand hurting her but unable also to take back his words.)* I am!

MIRIAM: *(Afraid of more than this ring.)* Allen, please don't lie. I won't punish you if you tell me the truth! Just answer me. When you took off the ring to show it to Herb—to examine it—when you saw it didn't have the 14K— then did you try to test it by biting it!

ALLEN: *(Desperately ashamed of hearing the truth.)* No!

MIRIAM: Allen . . . Listen to me. It's one thing to do something you may be ashamed of. It's quite another not to be willing to admit it.

ALLEN: I am admitting it. I told you I took it off—

MIRIAM: *(Trying to reason with him.)* Allen, honey, I can see the teeth marks. A blind man could tell they were teeth marks! The ring is just a ring! It can be fixed! It can be put back into shape! But you can't be, Allen! If you find it so easy to lie, you can't be put back into shape so easily as the ring.

ALLEN: *(His shame driving him still further into the lie.)* I—I didn't bite it!

MIRIAM: *(Once again quietly, evenly, trying to cover her hurt and disappointment.)* I'll keep it, Allen. I'll keep the ring till you deserve to have it back. *(She starts to leave the room.)*

ALLEN: Mom!—I—(MIRIAM *turns back to him. The moment is lost. There is silence.)*

MIRIAM: We'll have supper in about fifteen minutes.

ALLEN: I don't want any supper.

MIRIAM: I'll expect you at the table. I want to say a special prayer when I light my Shabbos candles—a prayer for your Bar Mitzvah. Now you'd better wash your face and hands. (MIRIAM *leaves.* ALLEN *starts to cry bitterly, one terrible outburst. A moment later,* MRS. WISHNEFSKY *enters his room, a package in her hand.)*

MRS. WISHNEFSKY: All right if I come in?

ALLEN: *(His back is to her as he tries to wipe his eyes.)* Sure, grandmom.

MRS. WISHNEFSKY: It may be the wrong time, but I brought up my Bar Mitzvah present for you. (ALLEN *manages a smile.)* I bet you thought I wasn't giving you a present. I never even asked you what you wanted. You know why! There was something I knew I had to give you. I even made part of it myself. Here Allen—*(She hands* ALLEN *the package.)*

ALLEN: Do you want me to open it now?

MRS. WISHNEFSKY: It's my pleasure. I should see if you like it. *(Slowly* ALLEN *undoes the string. And then he opens the package. He takes from it a small red velvet bag.)*

ALLEN: *(Genuinely moved.)* Grandmom! My own *tallis!* *(Immediately he takes from the velvet sack the long silk fringed prayer shawl, the tallis.)*

MRS. WISHNEFSKY: You should pray well in it. You should wear it proudly on your shoulders when you say your prayers. It should bring you not only manhood, but goodness and happiness, too. Like the mantle of God, it should bring you peace. *(She picks up the red velvet sack from the bed where* ALLEN *placed it after removing the shawl.)* I made the bag myself. I bought the softest velvet and real gold thread. The star is real gold thread. I embroidered it myself. (ALLEN *holds his grandmother tightly to him.)* Try it on . . . Let me see it on . . . Let me see how my handsome grandson is going to look. Let me hear you say the blessing, and let me see you put the *tallis* on your shoulders.

ALLEN: *(He cannot bring himself to put the holy shawl on.)* Not now, grandmom. Please, not now. I can't put it on now.

MRS. WISHNEFSKY: For me! you can't let me see you in the *tallis!*

ALLEN: Not now, grandmom. It's holy. Don't make me do it now.

MRS. WISHNEFSKY: All right, Allen—whatever you say.

ALLEN: *(Not wanting her to misunderstand.)* Please, grandmom. I like it! It's not that I don't like it. I just can't put it on now. Please, please, don't make me put it on now.

MRS. WISHNEFSKY: I won't make you put it on. A *tallis* you have to want to put on. Come, Allen, let's go to the table. Your mother is ready to light the Shabbos candles. *(The two of them leave the bedroom. The light slowly fades.)*

(For an instant the stage is black. Then at the kitchen table MIRIAM *lights the two white candles set in the silver candlesticks. By this light and by the barest minimum of fill-light, we see the outline of the figure of* MIRIAM *with her lace shawl on her head as she stands over the candles.* MRS. WISHNEFSKY *sits on one side of the table,* ALLEN *on the other.* MIRIAM *waves her hands gracefully in ritual movements over the burning candles, bringing her hands finally over her face in the ceremonial prayer position. And now she recites the traditional Friday night Shabbos blessing, first in Hebrew and then in English.)*

MIRIAM: Boruch ataw adony elohanoo melach ho'olom, asher kidishawnoo bemitz-vo-sov vitzi vawnoo lehadlick nair shal Shabbos. Blessed art Thou, O Lord our God, King of the Universe Who Commandest us to kindle the Sabbath lights. *(She pauses a moment.)* On this Sabbath of my son's Bar Mitzvah, we thank Thee God for the Blessing of his life. Help him to make it a good one! Grant peace, O Heavenly God, to his father who is with You. And God, before the hour when my son becomes a man, let him know the blessing of truth. Amen. *(Quietly she says.)* "Good Shabbos . . ." *(She leans to her mother who returns the greeting and then kisses her. She leans to* ALLEN, *who barely whispers the "Good Shabbos" and barely kisses his mother. The Sabbath greeting over,* ALLEN *murmurs an excuse and leaves the room as the light fades . . .)*

PART III

THE MAN-CHILD

It is after supper. The kitchen living room area is lighted. Glassware and dishes are set out, and MIRIAM *looks over them, touching, inspecting—but all of her actions obviously being done with something else on her mind.*

MRS. WISHNEFSKY *seems to be reading a Jewish newspaper, but it is obvious that she too is unable to concentrate.*

There is a strain between the two women which MRS. WISHNEFSKY *tries tentatively to break.*

MRS. WISHNEFSKY: I only hope Frank and Sheila didn't have any more trouble. It's already so late. From Newark they should have been here already, shouldn't they?

MIRIAM: *(Dryly.)* I'm sure they're all right. *(The conversation goes no further. There is silence between them.)*

MRS. WISHNEFSKY: *(A careful, quietly stated suggestion.)* Mimla, the Friday night before Allen's Bar Mitzvah you should be at services.

MIRIAM: *(The pretense of an excuse.)* Someone has to be here when Frank and Sheila come.

MRS. WISHNEFSKY: But I can be here so simple. You and Allen should go to synagogue together. You have a lot to be grateful for. *(MIRIAM says nothing.)* Mimla—it's none of my business, but—

MIRIAM: Please, Mom, don't let's talk about it.

MRS. WISHNEFSKY: But it should be a house of joy tonight! *(MIRIAM does not answer.)* He didn't even eat any supper. He'll be sick. And tomorrow—

MIRIAM: He won't be sick. Missing one meal won't make him sick. *(There is a pause.)*

MRS. WISHNEFSKY: *(Gently trying to reason with MIRIAM.)* He's sorry—he's ashamed. What more do you want?

MIRIAM: I want him to admit to a lie.

MRS. WISHNEFSKY: Does he have *to say it*, Mimla! He's tried to tell you in so many ways.

MIRIAM: He's got a problem, Mom. It's one of the first big problems he's faced. He's done something he's ashamed of, and he's done it on a very important night. I know he wants to undo it—to change it—to make it right—and he's got to have the chance. I've got to let him alone—he must do it himself—he must work the whole thing out himself.

MRS. WISHNEFSKY: But he's so afraid.

MIRIAM: He shouldn't be. I won't punish him. I told him that. He's got nothing to be afraid of but telling the truth. And if he's afraid of that, it's an awful thing.

MRS. WISHNEFSKY: But Mimla, don't you see how it gets worse for him. As the minutes go by it gets harder.

MIRIAM: He should understand that too. He should learn from it. He should know that this is exactly what happens. Nothing gets easier when you push it aside, when you close your eyes to it—the truth most of all.

MRS. WISHNEFSKY: *(At her wit's end.)* Uh! You talk philosophy! *(With a gesture which pleads for understanding.)* Mimla, he's a baby—

MIRIAM: He's not a baby anymore. He's old enough so that tomorrow he's going to be considered a man. He's going to believe he's a man. I can't just hold him in my arms and say this doesn't matter, that it's going to be all right. He's supposed to be able now to assume the responsibility for himself. Now he's supposed to be able to tell right from wrong. Do you want me to deprive him of that tonight! Mom, if I don't let him work this out, I'll fail him. Maybe I've failed him already. I thought there was something so strong between us. Something that could stand up. Something that couldn't be damaged so easily.

MRS. WISHNEFSKY: How you talk! Nothing's been damaged!

MIRIAM: He needed a father! If Max was alive—

MRS. WISHNEFSKY: Mimla, you've done everything for him. You've given him—

MIRIAM: I've done too much for him. I haven't let him stand on his own feet—

MRS. WISHNEFSKY: Don't blame yourself like this.

MIRIAM: After Max died—

MRS. WISHNEFSKY: Mimla—

MIRIAM: I was so afraid something would happen to Allen that I drew him closer and closer to me. I tried to protect him from—

MRS. WISHNEFSKY: How can you think you protect him when you can stand to see him unhappy like this. I never saw such a thing! It's cruel!

MIRIAM: *(Reminding her mother of a story.)* Mom, when I was a little girl and you and Pop had the grocery store on Royden Street, you remember you asked me once to deliver a bag of potatoes to Mrs. Foreman, and you remember I was so ashamed to walk in the street with the order when all my friends were playing that I opened the bag and threw the potatoes into the sewer. Do you remember what you did! You said you and Pop earned a living in that grocery store and that if I was willing to eat the food and wear the clothes the money brought, I shouldn't be ashamed to be seen delivering the potatoes. And then you made me deliver a few light orders every day after school just so I should never forget it! I thought you were so cruel then.

MRS. WISHNEFSKY: I guess maybe it's easier for a mother to teach than for a grandmother to watch her do it. *(She pauses and then, with a slight shrug of humor, as if good-naturedly invoking the help of heaven.)* But he should only learn before tomorrow morning! *(The doorbell rings.)* Thank God! They're here! Frank and Sheila, they're here!

*(*MIRIAM *rushes to the door. She opens it.* FRANK *and* SHEILA, *dressed in their driving outfits, replete with dusters and goggles, enter with their valises and a large box.* FRANK *is a tall handsome man in his early forties, with a sureness that comes from his professional success.* SHEILA *is a few years younger and she enjoys the fact that she knows the family thinks she is someone special.* MRS. WISHNEFSKY *takes her son in her arms.* SHEILA *and* MIRIAM *embrace. Conversations overlap.)*

MRS. WISHNEFSKY: We were so worried.

MIRIAM: Sheila! what an outfit!

FRANK: You shouldn't worry so much, Mom. The car is perfectly safe, and we had it up to forty miles an hour.

SHEILA: It's my driving costume! It's the only thing I like about the automobile. I'm aching from the ride.

MRS. WISHNEFSKY: You feel like you lost weight, Frank.

MIRIAM: But you look extravagant! it's wonderful, absolutely wonderful!

FRANK: In a week, I couldn't lose weight.

MRS. WISHNEFSKY: You've been working too hard.

SHEILA: That brother of yours! I should have taken the train and let him drive.

FRANK: *(With great relish.)* Don't listen to her! Miriam, you should ride in it.

SHEILA: Save yourself the pleasure, Miriam.

FRANK: *(Taking* MIRIAM *to the window.)* Look at it. Just look at that automobile.

SHEILA: You should ride in it.

MIRIAM: It's splendid!

FRANK: Let me take you for a ride. I'll take you and Mom for a ride.

SHEILA: I can't believe he would do that to his mother.

MIRIAM: It's Shabbos, Frank, I wouldn't ride. Here, give me your coats. *(Helping both of them.)* You both must be exhausted.

FRANK: *(Taking off his coat.)* Where's Allen? Where's the Bar Mitzvah *bauchur?* I thought he'd want to rush to see the automobile.

SHEILA: I told Frank I thought you'd all be at services by now.

MIRIAM: Someone had to be here to meet you.

SHEILA: *(While taking off her coat.)* Where *is* Allen? We have his suit. *(Suddenly to* FRANK.*)* Frank, where's the suit?

FRANK: *(Reaching for the box which he has laid on a chair.)* Let's get him to try it on.

MIRIAM: He's—he's in his room.

FRANK: *(Eagerly.)* Well, call him—

SHEILA: *(In amazement.)* What's he—in bed?

MIRIAM: *(Calling.)* Allen! Uncle Frank and Aunt Sheila are here! *(She waits.)* Allen, can you hear me?

ALLEN: *(Fighting to answer.)* I'm coming. *(*SHEILA *looks about and sees dishes stacked and glasses.)*

SHEILA: It looks like you have everything all set. Am I too late to do anything?

MIRIAM: Thank you, Sheila. Mr. Tannenbaum told me to take the day off from work—and Mom's been a lifesaver.

MRS. WISHNEFSKY: She only let me watch! Don't let her fool you! She's been— *(*ALLEN *enters quickly.)*

FRANK: *(Enormously, and extending his hand.)* Hello, Allen! Congratulations!

ALLEN: *(Shaking his uncle's hand.)* Thanks, Uncle Frank.

FRANK: I know—you're worried about your suit. *(Handing him the box.)* Here it is. You see, safe and sound! Good luck and wear it in the best of health.

SHEILA: Open it, Allen. I'm dying to see you in it. *(*ALLEN *looks at his mother.)*

FRANK: *(Misunderstanding.)* It's your present! You don't need her permission to open it! *(Very slowly ALLEN opens the box. He pushes back the tissue paper. From his lips escapes an admiring and hushed, "Oh, wow—!" He takes a vest out of the box.)*

ALLEN: It's got a vest!

FRANK: It's got everything. What do you mean—you'll be a regular Beau Brummel! *(ALLEN buttons the vest quickly.)*

MRS. WISHNEFSKY: Look how he buttons the vest! Like he always wore one! *(Now ALLEN takes the jacket out of the box.)*

MIRIAM: Frank, it's handsome!

MRS. WISHNEFSKY: Such a suit! Such a beautiful suit I never saw!

ALLEN: *(He slips into the jacket. It fits exactly.)* I—I couldn't have picked a better one.

SHEILA: I'm glad you like it.

MRS. WISHNEFSKY: So handsome! Like a prince!

ALLEN: *(Turning to his mother.)* Do you like it? Do I look all right?

MIRIAM: *(Proudly and wishing what happened wasn't still there between them.)* The jacket looks fine on you, Allen.

ALLEN: No suit I ever had looked this good. It's so soft.

FRANK: I had my own tailor make it.

MRS. WISHNEFSKY: The pants. Put on the pants, too. Your first long pants.

ALLEN: *(He goes for the pants. Then, with slight embarrassment, he picks up the box.)* Excuse me. I'd better put these on in my room.

SHEILA: It's all right. I diapered you. *(Then she catches herself.)* But I guess it's different now.

FRANK: You don't have to go to your room. We can all turn around. *(Slowly they all turn around. There is a wonderful moment of awkwardness which SHEILA breaks.)*

SHEILA: *(Her back to the audience.)* How many people are you finally having to dinner?

MIRIAM: About thirty.

SHEILA: Where are you going to put them all?

MIRIAM: Pearl's letting us use her apartment, too. We're making use of both apartments, like one big hall.

SHEILA: I've got to hand it to you. How in the world you managed all this. *(ALLEN has now removed his knickers. Carefully he starts to take the new pants from the box.)*

FRANK: *(Impatient to turn around and see ALLEN dressed.)* Hurry up, already, Allen. Wait till you see the pants, Miriam. I made them line the knees, the same lining as the jacket.

ALLEN: *(As he pulls the new trousers on, with a panic to his voice.)* Uncle Frank! *(They all turn around. ALLEN has the pants on, but—)* They don't have cuffs! *(The extra material—about ten inches extends beyond ALLEN's shoes.)*

MIRIAM: Frank! We sent you all the measurements. How could you leave all that fabric. It looks like a bridal train, not a Bar Mitzvah suit!

FRANK: *(Not understanding all the consternation.)* I know, but I wouldn't have the cuffs put on just like that! Cuffs are a last minute proposition! Anything else I would take a chance with. But the cuffs have to be just right. You got enough tailors around here.

MIRIAM: But Frank—

FRANK: What's the matter? It takes five minutes! *(Pause. Then a slight trace of apology.)* I will say I thought we'd be here earlier, but—

MIRIAM: Who's going to fix them?

FRANK: In a neighborhood where everyone's a tailor, what kind of a question is that?

MIRIAM: There's not a tailor around who would sew anything tonight.

FRANK: For a dollar, any tailor will put on a pair of cuffs.

ALLEN: Uncle Frank, it's Friday night.

MIRIAM: No one will sew cuffs on *Shabbos.*

FRANK: But it's an emergency!

MIRIAM: Maybe where you live it doesn't matter. In our neighborhood, you couldn't find a tailor now.

FRANK: I don't believe it! Everyone's a tailor, and no one will sew! Making a pair of cuffs is practically no sewing.

MIRIAM: It doesn't matter.

FRANK: All right! So we'll take a ride in my Model-T and find a tailor somewhere out of the neighborhood! It's not a catastrophe!

MIRIAM: You should have had the cuffs put on in the first place. Why do you think I sent you all the measurements!

SHEILA: I warned him. I said he shouldn't leave anything till the last minute. But your brother knows everything. He had it all worked out! Like with the automobile, he was sure nothing could go wrong!

FRANK: It was only a minor mechanical difficulty! Don't get so excited.

SHEILA: *(Ignoring his interruption.)* For Frank, the world is always supposed to run smoothly! Nothing unforeseen will ever occur. (ALLEN *takes off the jacket. He puts it in the box again.)*

ALLEN: It's not his fault, Aunt Sheila. I knew something would be wrong. It had to be. It's purposely the best suit I ever had—the thing I most wanted to be right. *(Not concerning himself now with who may be looking, he takes off the slacks.)*

FRANK: It's a cuff! A simple cuff! Anybody can make a cuff!

ALLEN: *(Emphasizing the inevitability in his mind.)* But nobody can tonight! Don't you see—everything's wrong!

FRANK: Nothing's that wrong! Everything in life should be this easy to solve! You don't even need a professional tailor. If I could sew, I would do it myself. Why even your mother can do it.

SHEILA: That's right, Miriam. I forgot how beautifully you sew. You can make the cuffs.

ALLEN: Mom never sews on Shabbos. She hardly got her dress done in time today.

FRANK: *(Looking at his sister in surprise.)* Is that right, Miriam?

MIRIAM: *(Quietly.)* That's right, Frank.

FRANK: I didn't know you worried about things like that! You were born in America.

MIRIAM: I don't worry about it. I just don't do it!

FRANK: But this is an exception. After all we're not still living in the dark ages.

MIRIAM: That has nothing to do with it. I've made it a practice never to have to sew on the Sabbath. There are six other days.

FRANK: I don't understand, Miriam. You're a modern woman. Mom's from the old country. I can see tradition's important to her. I know she doesn't sew, but for you—

SHEILA: Couldn't you pin it, Miriam? Catch it up with a couple of pins?

MIRIAM: *(Nicely with a gentle laugh.)* Pinning or sewing, I'm afraid it's the same thing, Sheila.

FRANK: Believe me, God will forgive you! Your son has only one Bar Mitzvah! It's his first pair of long pants. You can sew for this occasion. *(Turning to* MRS. WISHNEFSKY.*)* You're her mother! Tell her the world won't come to an end this time.

MRS. WISHNEFSKY: I can't tell her what to do. Miriam has a mind of her own.

FRANK: Look, I had the suit made by my own tailor. Like my own suit! I brought it all the way from Philadelphia. It's ridiculous he wouldn't be able to wear it! There are extenuating circumstances. It's the least you can do for your son!

MIRIAM: *(The ring incident in her thinking.)* Don't tell me what I can do for my son. I know all about what I can do for him. You don't have to remind me.

FRANK: *(An order to* ALLEN.*)* Put on the pants! Put on the jacket! Come on! We'll find a tailor somewhere. *(*ALLEN *frantically hesitates.)*

MIRIAM: Frank, what's the difference if I give it to a tailor or do it myself! God didn't mean for you to farm out a sin! If it's wrong for me to sew, it's no better for me to ask anyone else. Just because I don't put the needle through the cloth myself doesn't mean—

FRANK: Then for once you can put the needle through the cloth. It's got to get done! The boy's got to have a suit! You have no choice!

MIRIAM: *(She looks at* ALLEN *who barely looks up at her. And quietly she speaks.)* Allen, put on the pants again.

FRANK: Now, you're making sense!

MIRIAM: *(His logic not concerning her.)* Please, Frank! *(*ALLEN *stares at his mother.)* Go on, Allen. Put on the pants.

ALLEN: *(Wanting the suit, but concerned about what his mother is about to do. He hardly gets the word out.)* Now?

MIRIAM: *(Moving to get her sewing things.)* Now! I'll get my sewing basket.

ALLEN: But Mom—you never—

MIRIAM: *(Almost business-like.)* Hurry up. Put on the pants. *(She has reached the shelf. She gets down her sewing basket.* ALLEN *slowly puts on the new trousers.)*

SHEILA: You're going to look fine, Allen. Your mother will do a better job than any tailor, believe me. With your mother, it's a labor of love.

ALLEN: *(Trying to know what to say to his mother.)* Mom—you—don't—have to—not just for me—

MIRIAM: *(The same quiet business-like tone.)* You want to wear the suit, don't you?

ALLEN: Yes, but—

MIRIAM: *(Simple facts.)* Then no buts. The trousers need a cuff. So we'll put on a cuff.

ALLEN: You never sewed on Shabbos.

MIRIAM: There are lots of things I never did till today. *(The room is still. MIRIAM kneels on the floor and starts to fold up the cloth on the outside of the trouser leg to get an idea of length.)* Stand still.

ALLEN: *(Beginning to break down.)* Mom, let's take the suit to a tailor. It's not so bad if a tailor does it.

MIRIAM: *(Matter-of-factly.)* There's no tailor open. You know that as well as I—and anyhow—

ALLEN: *(Fighting himself.)* We can find one.

MIRIAM: I can't get the right length if you don't stand still.

ALLEN: *(The tears springing to his eyes.)* Mom, please—we can find a tailor! Uncle Frank has an automobile, and he said we could drive around.

MIRIAM: *(Evenly.)* What's the difference if I do it or a tailor?

ALLEN: *(Desperately.)* There is a difference. Then it's not you!

MIRIAM: The difference is only in your eyes I'm afraid.

ALLEN: But Mom—

MIRIAM: You want to wear the suit. It has to get fixed. I'm the one who can fix it.

ALLEN: *(The tears on his cheeks.)* I want the suit! But I don't want you to have to fix it.

MIRIAM: *(Calmly.)* Stand still. No, better get up on the stool! *(She pushes the stool to him.)*

ALLEN: *(Violently.)* It's a sin for you!

MIRIAM: You forget something, Allen. Till tomorrow I carry your sins as well as my own. And I took on a big one today.

ALLEN: Mom—please!

MIRIAM: One more sin on my shoulders can't matter that much!

ALLEN: *(A final appeal.)* I can wear my other suit!

MIRIAM: Allen—please stand still!

ALLEN: *(He will not let her take on another sin; he will release both of them.)* Mom! I lied! I lied, Mom! I lied! *(MIRIAM looks up at him. His words rush on in an outburst.)* I bit the ring! I wanted to test it! Now, you know! And you don't have to sin anymore! And you don't have to give yourself another one! It doesn't matter! I can wear my old suit! *(Weeping bitterly he holds his mother. After a moment, they embrace in tears of release and understanding.)*

MRS. WISHNEFSKY: Frank! *(She throws her arms around him and kisses him.)* It's so good the pants didn't have cuffs.

FRANK: What's going on here! What happened!

MRS. WISHNEFSKY: It's like it was planned that way!

FRANK: What was planned! Why is everyone crying!

MRS. WISHNEFSKY: It's a miracle! Who understands the ways of God!

FRANK: Can he wear the suit? That's all I want to know. Is he going to be able to wear the suit?

MRS. WISHNEFSKY: Yes, Frank. He'll wear the suit. It will fit him better than ever.

SHEILA: But what about the cuffs? He can't wear the pants without cuffs!

MRS. WISHNEFSKY: *(Suddenly.)* That's it! Why can't he wear them without cuffs! All the time I'm looking, and it's not till now I see! The pants don't need a cuff. They can be like a tuxedo! Straight down they can hang like a tuxedo. We can fold the material up under the trouser leg.

SHEILA: What's the difference if you fold or sew?

MRS. WISHNEFSKY: What's the difference! All the difference in the world! No one ever said anything about folding! They even fold the *tallis*. Folding is no sin, no matter which way you look at it. *(She gets down on her knees and bends the material up under one trouser leg. She presses it hard with her hand.)*

FRANK: But if he walks three steps, it'll fall!

MRS. WISHNEFSKY: We can dampen it. And set it under a heavy book all night. There's plenty of material for it to stay inside. But Allen, you mustn't walk fast!

ALLEN: It'll work. It's like you said, grandmom, a miracle.

SHEILA: Well, I'm glad we got that settled. I'd love to wash up.

MRS. WISHNEFSKY: I'll take you over to Pearl's. You're going to sleep at Pearl's. Her boarder and his wife went to Mrs. Liebman's. Come Frank, you can bring the valise. Fix the other leg, Mimla. *(FRANK, SHEILA, and MRS. WISHNEFSKY leave. MIRIAM gets down on her knees again. Slowly she turns up the other cuff, folding the material up under ALLEN's trouser leg.)*

MIRIAM: It'll look fine, Allen.

ALLEN: We can put it under a book like grandmom says. It'll be like pressing. And I can walk slowly tomorrow.

MIRIAM: Slowly—and proudly, Allen.

ALLEN: Mom?

MIRIAM: What is it, Allen?

ALLEN: Can I—have the ring back?

MIRIAM: We'd better have it fixed first.

ALLEN: That's all right. For tomorrow let me wear it dented. *(MIRIAM takes the ring from her apron pocket.)*

MIRIAM: I don't know if you can get it on your finger. *(She helps him slip it on. Though it is out of shape, it does stay on his finger.)* Well, I will say, you'll be wearing a lot tomorrow that has to be fixed.

ALLEN: It's O.K., Mom. I'll remember the things inside of me that have to be fixed, too. *(Slowly the light fades. MRS. WISHNEFSKY steps out to the audience in her simchah dress.)*

MRS. WISHNEFSKY: *(To the audience.)* My Mimla was wondering if her son would know what it is to be a man. God moves in strange and wonderful ways. And it's all all right—the ring—the pants—the whole Bar Mitzvah has become like a miracle. *(Confidentially.)* I know you probably don't have time now to see the whole service in the synagogue. It's over two hours long—and we have only a few more minutes to be with you. But I would like you should see the part where they call my grandson Allen to the pulpit to read from the Torah. You should see him in his new suit and *tallis* and you should hear him at least say the blessings. *(With* MRS. WISHNEFSKY's *last words, the back area of the stage lights up revealing the pulpit of the synagogue. The ark is opened and the cantor, standing with the rabbi and two other men [one of them* UNCLE FRANK*], holds the Torah and sings.)*

THE CANTOR: Sh'ma yis-ro-el a-do-noy e-lo-hay-noo a-do-noy e-chod. E-chod e-lo-hay-noo, go-dol a-do-nay-noo ko-dosh-sh'mo. Gaf-loo la-do-noy ee-tee un'-ro-m'-moh sh'mo yakh-dov. *(More light reveals the cast serving as congregation. As* MRS. WISHNEFSKY *joins them, she explains.)*

MRS. WISHNEFSKY: They were holy words the rabbi just chanted—the watchword of Israel. Hear O, Israel: the Lord our God, the Lord is One. One is our God; Great is our Lord; Holy is His Name. Extol the Lord with me, and together let us exalt His Name. *(The* CANTOR *has set down the Torah and with the help of the two men, he removes the elaborate coverings, unties the band around the scrolls and opens the Torah.)*

THE CANTOR: *(Chanting.)* Ya-mod habauchur ha Cohen, Abrum den Morde-cai v'yaaley al aumood.

MRS. WISHNEFSKY: He says, Let the young man, the Cohen, Allen, son of Max, arise and ascend to the pulpit. *(*ALLEN*, wearing his new suit, tallis, and skull cap, walks slowly down the center aisle of the theatre. He is watchful of the trouser leg, and he very carefully ascends the one or two steps to the reading desk. He takes the fringed edge of his tallis and places it to the portion of the text which* THE CANTOR *indicates; he then kisses the fringed edge in the traditional ritual. Finally, he straightens himself up and begins the chanting of the blessings.)*

ALLEN: *(Chanting.)* Borichu es adony ham'voruch . . . *(As members of the congregation, the cast now chants the response.)*

CONGREGATION: Boruch adony ham'voruch l'olom vo'ed.

MRS. WISHNEFSKY: Bless the Lord who is to be praised. Praised be the Lord who is blessed for all eternity.

ALLEN: *(Repeating in chant.)* Boruch adonoy ham'voruch l'olom vo'ed. *(Then going on with the blessing.)* Boruch ataw adonoy elohanoo melach ho'olom asher bocharbawnoo mecawl hawamim vi-nawsahnlawnoo es-torahso. Boruch ataw adonoy no sain ha torah.

MRS. WISHNEFSKY: Blessed art Thou, O Lord our God, King of the Universe who didst choose us from among all the people by giving us the Torah. Blessed art thou, O Lord, Giver of the Torah.

CONGREGATION: Amen.

MRS. WISHNEFSKY: It's a beautiful service. If you had time, you should see the whole thing; but since you can't. I wish you well, and I thank you for visiting me on such a happy occasion.

(The lights fade, and after a moment of applause, they go up again, and MRS. WISHNEFSKY *raises her hands to talk once again to the audience)*

MRS. WISHNEFSKY: I forgot an important thing. After the service is a Kiddush—you remember Pearl was talking about it—when the family of the Bar Mitzvah *bauchur* serves all their friends and relatives cake and wine—fruit juice for the young people. And *that* you should take a minute for because my Mimla asked me to invite you to have some—And it's my pleasure . . . (*And the Kiddush is served.*)

CURTAIN

HUSH:
AN INTERVIEW
WITH AMERICA

by
James Still

JAMES STILL, a writer whose work is primarily for family audiences, is the recipient of the Charlotte B. Chorpenning Playwright Award for Distinguished Body of Work. His award-winning plays have been produced at theatres throughout the United States, Canada, and Puerto Rico. In addition to his work in the theatre, Still writes for the Nickelodeon television series, *Maurice Sendak's Little Bear*.

Hush: An Interview with America was cocommissioned by Childsplay in Tempe, Arizona, and Metro Theater Company in St. Louis, Missouri, and premiered at both theatres with development and production support from the New Works for Young Audiences program underwritten by the Lila Wallace–Reader's Digest Fund.

A musical theatre adaptation of John Gardner's novella *In the Suicide Mountains*, originally commissioned by The Mark Taper Forum in Los Angeles and developed at New Visions/New Voices of the Kennedy Center in Washington, D. C., and at the Sundance Playwrights' Lab in Utah, premiered at the Honolulu Theatre for Youth in 1997. An oral history/theatre/video project about teenagers during the Holocaust, entitled *And Then They Came for Me*, opened in 1996, at the George Street Playhouse in New Brunswick, New Jersey, and at Indiana Repertory Theatre in Indianapolis.

Other original plays include *Amber Waves*, which premiered at the

Kennedy Center and received several awards including the Distinguished Play Award from the American Alliance for Theatre & Education; The *Secret History of the Future*; *Just Before Sleep*; *Dreaming on Tiptoe*; and the musical *The Clouds on Highway 40*.

Still's adaptations include *The Velveteen Rabbit*, *The Ugly Duck*, and *Harriet the Spy*, all of which have been produced Off-Broadway and on national tours of Theatreworks/USA, New York City. His other dramatizations for young people include *The Adventures of Madeline*, *Jack Frost*, and *King of the Golden River*.

Since its premier in New York at the Ensemble Studio Theatre James Still has performed his solo performance piece for adults, *The Velocity of Gary (Not His Real Name)*, at theatres across the country. In addition to his work in the theatre, Still is currently working on a number of film and television projects including a feature film based on *The Velocity of Gary*.

James Still has been a visiting professor at a number of university theatre departments, most recently at The University of Texas at Austin. He grew up in Kansas, where he graduated from the University of Kansas. After living in New York for many years, he now lives in Venice, California.

I don't consciously think about the audience while I am writing a play; the challenges in rehearsal seem to always be specific to the particular project—not the intended audience. Once in performance, however, I love the sense of "event" that seems to define a child's theatre-going experience— the play really begins the moment they step into the lobby of the theatre. One of my favorite things to do is to stand at the door and watch kids walk into the theatre. I love the way they spontaneously scream when the house lights go to black at the top of the show. I'm amazed every time by their hushed silences and jazzed by their raucous laughter. As an audience member I appreciate their willingness to put themselves in unfamiliar worlds, and as a playwright I love and admire their demanding yet open sense of story.

Finally, in talking with children after a play, I'm always reminded that they are smarter, more savvy, more demanding, more willing to be surprised, and more direct than grown-ups ever give them credit for. In writing for family audiences I especially like the idea of several generations coming together and having a community experience as well as individual experiences. I've always wished I could hear the conversations in the cars on the way home as children and parents and grandparents talk about a play they just saw together.

—JAMES STILL

HUSH: AN INTERVIEW WITH AMERICA

CHARACTERS

Maggie Parks: an almost twelve-year-old girl.
Frank Parks: Maggie's dad.
Jana Roberts: a television news reporter.
Newscasters
The Lion: a lion from the Los Angeles zoo.
Statue #1 (lion)
Statue #2 (lion)
Sound Man
Pilgrims
Strangers
Eve: a spirit.
The Lamb: a lamb in Illinois.
FBI: an FBI Agent.
T-Shirt: a twelve-year-old girl.
Phone: a persistent, ringing telephone.
Voices of America: people from towns across the United States.

The place is Hush, Kansas.
And throughout the United States.

The time is now.

THE BEGINNING

(Sounds of a wind chime. In darkness we hear the joyful laughter of a young girl. It is a sound that comes from somewhere deep inside. The laughter builds and then fades to quiet.

Lights come up slowly on an evening sunset. Late May. A back yard in Hush, Kansas. An apple tree. A twelve-year old girl. She spies, plays hide-and-seek, searches with intense curiosity. When she senses something nearby, she interacts fearlessly and begins to laugh again. The interaction evolves into free-spirited movement between her and an unseen presence. Through her, we see what she sees. For us, it is like witnessing a private moment, watching someone who doesn't know they're being watched. Her laughter builds to genuine release and continues as:

Suddenly we hear loud noises from another part of the world. The sounds of an angry riot. Screaming. Shattering glass. A LION *enters, looks at the audience in fear. The* LION *nervously crosses the stage looking in all directions. His movements resemble a dance—fear, apprehension, the hunted.*

The girl stops, startled, as if she, too, can hear the sounds of the riots. Without looking at the LION, *she holds her hands out, a simple gesture suggesting safety. The* LION *sees her—the dancing light in the sky—and roars from deep inside. It is not an angry roar, but one filled with loneliness. Then he disappears.*

Suddenly alone again, MAGGIE *seems disturbed, shaking herself out of a dream. A voice from offstage interrupts:)*

FRANK: *(Calling out.)* Maggie! Time for dinner!

*(*MAGGIE *does a jig and exits inside the house.)*

DINNER IN AMERICA: PUBLIC/PRIVATE

PUBLIC VOICE OF AMERICA #1: . . . Rocky Face, Georgia, is reporting 92 degrees . . . in the shade!

PRIVATE VOICE OF AMERICA #1: What's for dinner?

FRANK: *(Coming into the house.)* Anybody home?

PUBLIC VOICE #2: . . . This late-breaking story from Gualala, California:

FRANK: *(To himself.)* Maybe we should just go for pizza.

PUBLIC VOICE #3: . . . A bank robbery in the neighboring town of Sleepy Eye, Minnesota . . .

PRIVATE VOICE #2: Don't you want to eat first?

FRANK: *(Calling outside.)* Maggie?

PUBLIC VOICE #4: . . . the residents of Texico, New Mexico, are preparing for their first visit from the—

PRIVATE VOICE #4: Why can't we have one meal where no one leaves the table crying?

VOICES OF AMERICA: AND—in the little town of Hush, Kansas . . .

VOICES OF AMERICA: . . . little town of Hush, Kansas . . .

VOICES OF AMERICA: . . . Hush, Kansas:

(MAGGIE *rushes into the kitchen, out of breath.* FRANK *ceremoniously presents* MAGGIE *with a plate of food from the microwave.* MAGGIE *rushes by:*)

MAGGIE: Fruit Loops please!

(FRANK *gives in, gives* MAGGIE *a giant box of Fruit Loops, which she devours by the fistful. They are easy with each other, the conversation is simple, chaotic, family.*)

FRANK: What would people think if they knew all you ate was Fruit Loops?

MAGGIE: You worry too much about what people think, Dad.

FRANK: (*Defensive.*) I do not. (MAGGIE *gleefully eats more Fruit Loops and starts to exit back outside.*) You know, Man cannot survive on Fruit Loops alone.

MAGGIE: (*Laughs.*) I'm not a man, Dad. I'm a woman.

FRANK: (*Automatic.*) Girl.

MAGGIE: Woman.

FRANK: Girl.

MAGGIE: Woman.

FRANK: Girl.

MAGGIE: (*Roaring, like a lioness.*) Woman.

FRANK: (*Flustered, rattled.*) Right. I know. I was—whatever.

MAGGIE: Do you know the story about the girl who got lost in the woods?

FRANK: (*Launching into his own version of the story.*) Once upon a time there was a girl—

MAGGIE: Come on, Dad. This is my story. This girl was lost in the woods and the only thing she had to eat was a box of Fruit Loops. She survived for a whole week by eating one little Loop at a time. And when the cereal was gone, she ate the box. Except she saved the box TOP; and when she was rescued she mailed it in and got a free pen with invisible ink. (*She tears off a piece of the cereal box and offers it to* FRANK.) Want some? (FRANK *laughs, refuses her offer.*) Suit yourself. (*Eating a piece of the box, exaggerating.*) Yummmmmmm.

FRANK: (*Thrown, not sure what to say.*) Where do these stories come from?

(MAGGIE's *attention drifts out the window where* EVE *appears dancing joyfully in the night with a giant full moon as her partner.* EVE *is dressed in a full skirt with jeans underneath and boots, a potato chip bag on her head.*)

(*The* LION *appears, out of breath, running. Stands nearby, as if holding his breath, listening to* MAGGIE's *story.*)

(EVE *tosses the moon up into the sky, and it sticks—as if dramatically/theatrically rising against*

MAGGIE: So: this girl wrote down her greatest most private thoughts with this invisible ink—secrets that filled an entire book. And hundreds of years later when somebody found it they thought it was nothing but a bunch of blank paper.

(FRANK *stares at* MAGGIE.)

MAGGIE: Sometimes I'm dancing or making up a poem or even just

the starry summer night. The moon throws light into the house, across MAGGIE's *face which makes her laugh as if she's been tickled.)*

*(*EVE *dances into darkness and disappears.)*

*(*THE LION *cowers in a corner, hiding from danger in the safety of darkness.)*

dreaming—and I think—here I am, full of all this stuff, like all my secrets are written in invisible ink—

FRANK: Invisible ink?

MAGGIE: —and who would ever know just by looking at me?

FRANK: Are you okay, Maggie?

MAGGIE: I'm fine, Daddy. Really.

*(*FRANK *isn't sure how to respond to* MAGGIE's *insights. He picks up the remote control and switches on the television news. Behind a large frame suggesting a TV screen,* JANA ROBERTS *delivers the day's news.)*

JANA ROBERTS: *(Immediately assuming a slick, professional pose.)* Good evening, I'm Jana Roberts with What's News Around The World. Tonight's top story . . . Welfare Reform. The Clinton Administration continues to—

*(*EVE *disappears,* MAGGIE *gets up to leave the room as if to find* EVE *and* THE LION. FRANK *turns off the TV.)*

FRANK: Woah, woah, woah! Where's the fire?

MAGGIE: I'm going outside!

FRANK: Every night this week you've run a race to get outside.

MAGGIE: *(Weary.)* Dad, it's almost summer . . .

FRANK: Maybe we should talk more.

MAGGIE: About what?

FRANK: I don't know. Things, stuff, whatever . . .

MAGGIE: Things, stuff, whatever?

FRANK: Ask me a question.

MAGGIE: How was work?

FRANK: The same. *(Thinks.)* It's always the same. *(Pause.)* How was school?

MAGGIE: *(Mimicking her father.)* The same. It's always the same. *(Strains to engage her father.)* In science class we're learning about snow.

FRANK: *(Relieved.)* Great! Let's talk about the weather. Now, snowflakes have six sides and each one is totally unique.

MAGGIE: *(Suddenly very passionate, putting her own spin on "snowflake," making up a poem/song, engaging* FRANK *who joins in with goofy glee.)*
> The skies open like a big, big mouth
> Like words to a song, see the snowflakes pop out
> Floating/floating/floating little heroes in the sky
> Landing next to snowflakes in a crowd.
> Snowflakes piling high
> Now becoming round
> Not another sound.
> If a snowflake doesn't dance,
> It becomes a piece of lost,
> Dull,
> Ice.

(FRANK *collapses dramatically in a heap on the floor. Seizing her opening,* MAG-GIE *quickly jumps up and heads for the door.*)

MAGGIE: Your turn to do the dishes!

FRANK: Maggie—

MAGGIE: I'll be out back, Daddy!

(MAGGIE *runs to the backyard. Running free toward the tree swing.*)
> Swing, king!
> Sing-ping-spring-thing
> Wing! wing! wing!

VOICE OF AMERICA: Yeah, I'm from Friendship, Tennessee—and I read some-where that Americans would pay about $15 to see live dinosaurs. I would!

MAGGIE: (*Calling out.*) You want to dance with me? (EVE *appears and accepts* MAGGIE's *invitation. They dance a playful, dramatic tango together accompanied by* MAGGIE's *spontaneous poetry:*)
> A little dancing
> After dinner
> Helps you digest
> What you didn't.
> Do you dare me like the darkness in the dawning of the deep?
> To ding the dipping dilly like the drummer in my dreams?

(A NEWSCASTER *appears out of nowhere and addresses an invisible camera.* MAG-GIE *stops dancing as if to listen.*)

NEWSCASTER #1: ". . . Back in the 1870s, Wyatt Earp was called into Wichita, Kansas, because the cattle town was averaging one homicide a year. . . . That was the Wild West, folks!"

(MAGGIE *returns to her dance with* EVE. *Suddenly another* NEWSCASTER *appears and seems to address another camera.*)

NEWSCASTER #2: ". . . Last year in Wichita there were twice as many murders as in Belfast, Northern Ireland . . ."

(MAGGIE *is affected by the information but tries to return to her innocent dance with* EVE. *Suddenly a third* NEWSCASTERS *appears.*)

NEWSCASTER #3: ". . . A recent study shows that one of every three Ameri-can teenagers believes he or she will be shot to death before reaching old age . . ."

(The NEWSCASTERS *disappear.* EVE *invites* MAGGIE *to resume their dance.* MAG-GIE *can't.* EVE *disappears.* MAGGIE *looks up into the tree.*)

MAGGIE: (*Whispering.*) Hello? Hello? (*She shines a flashlight into the tree.*) Can you see me? (*She waves the flashlight around impatiently and leans back against the tree.*)

THREE LIONS SITTING AROUND TALKING

(Three lions sit facing the audience. Two of them are STATUES and stare straight ahead, stiff and regal. The other one is THE LION we've seen earlier—obviously real *though he is pretending to be a statue; his eyes move impatiently from side to side.)*

THE LION: *(Tense.)* This has been the longest day of my life. *(The other two lions do not move. They are real statues.)* How do you do it? *(The* STATUES *do not respond;* THE LION *grows more agitated.)* How do you just SIT here—all day? The rain, the people, the birds . . . *(Looking up at the sky.)*

STATUE #1: We don't feel a thing.

STATUE #2: We're statues, remember?

THE LION: *(Frustrated.)* Well, I'm NOT a statue, remember? And I don't like pretending to be something that I'm not. I'd rather go back to the zoo— *(Looking around anxiously.)* I didn't mean that. Oh, man, what am I gonna do? If I hang around you guys much longer, my brain is gonna turn into rock.

STATUE #1: Worse things could happen.

THE LION: Don't you ever dream about going home?

STATUE #2: Home?

THE LION: Home: Africa!

STATUE #1: *(Explaining to* STATUE #2.*)* He means the rock quarry.

STATUE #2: We don't dream.

STATUE #1: We're statues, remember?

THE LION: You guys are gonna drive me nuts! I gotta get outa here.

STATUE #1: Where will you go?

THE LION: *(Despairing.)* I've been to every state but Hawaii, and I'd go there if I could swim that far. I'm so sick of wandering around with no idea where I'm going, no reason to stop, no one to trust. *(Paranoid.)* Men. With guns. *(Looking around.)* Aren't there any decent human beings left in this country? *(Looking in the distance.)* I'm so tired of running. I don't know where to go anymore . . . so I just keep running. *(Knocks on the head of one of the* STATUES *as he sneaks into the darkness.)* Think of me.

(The two STATUES *look straight ahead, staring, blank.)*

STATUE #2: Will you miss him?

STATUE #1: No. Will you?

STATUE #2: No. He talked too much.

(The two STATUES *stare blankly straight ahead.)*

FRANK: *(calling from the house.)* Maggie? You want dessert?

FRANK: Maggie?

FRANK: Everything okay?

FRANK: Okay.

*(*MAGGIE *looks up into the tree again.)*

MAGGIE: Nobody's gonna hurt you. *(She looks around slowly.)* I'm right here.

MAGGIE: *(To the tree.)* You're safe with me.

MAGGIE: *(To the tree.)* Forever.

MAGGIE: *(To the tree.)* Okay? *(*MAGGIE *sits back against the tree with the flashlight illuminating her face.)*

GUNS, THE PENTAGON, AND APPLE PIE

(In the house, FRANK *uses his remote control to turn on the TV.)*

FRANK: Talk to me, Jana!

JANA ROBERTS: *(On TV.)* ". . . In 1990, 10 people were killed in Australia by handguns, 22 in Britain, 68 in Canada and according to Handgun Control, Inc., 10,567 people were killed in the U.S. in 1990." (JANA *stops and looks over what she's just read, troubled.)* 10,567 . . .

FRANK: *(Talking to the TV.)* Is that true?

JANA: What else is there to say after that? *(Looking through her notes.)* One out of four supermarket customers in the express checkout line have more than the allowed number of items. Let's see . . . of the four cats who've lived in the White House since 1933, only one of them has belonged to a Republican. That's especially interesting because in another study it shows there are two rats for every person in Washington, D.C. Here's one that really speaks to me tonight: Americans are in a bad mood on the average of 110 days a year. *(Tossing the papers on her desk.)* Where are all the good stories these days? (FRANK *is staring at the TV, fork frozen in the air.)* Every night I sit here in New York doing the news while all of you eat dinner right in front of me. And then I go to MY home and eat dinner alone. Do you see the irony? I mean, it's pretty damn lonely here on television.

FRANK: *(Talking to the TV.)* Yeah, but you make a million dollars . . .

JANA: Sure, I make a lot of money, I meet a lot of famous people—but *so what?* Is it just me, or does the world seem really crazy right now? Nothing adds up. *(Suddenly, directly to* FRANK.*)* What kind of pie is that?

FRANK: *(Answers instinctively.)* Apple.

JANA: Yummy. (JANA *suddenly steps through the television screen into* FRANK's *kitchen. He is stunned.* JANA *is just as surprised as* FRANK.*)* I never knew I could do that. *(She recovers, smoothes her dress, fixes her hair, and then smiles at* FRANK.*)*

(FRANK *drops his fork. He stares at* JANA, *speechless.)*

(Under the apple tree, MAGGIE *makes contact with an invisible presence and explores the relationship through the physical and vocal interaction which continues under the scene:)*

JANA: *(To* FRANK, *extending her hand.)* Jana Roberts—What's News Around The World.

FRANK: *(In shock.)* I know, I—watch you—every night. On the news, IN the television.

JANA: Are you the guy with the apple pie?

FRANK: *(Modest.)* That's me. My name's Frank.

JANA: *(Looking around.)* You keep a very clean house, Frank. What do you do for a living?

FRANK: I'm a janitor.

JANA: Where do you work? Do you like your job? How long have you worked there?

FRANK: You ask a lot of questions.

JANA: Do I?

FRANK: That's another question.

JANA: Frank, can we cut to the chase?

FRANK: The chase? *(Confused.)* I don't even know you.

JANA: *(Extending her hand.)* Jana Roberts—What's News Around The World.

FRANK: No, I know what you do—but I don't know who you are . . . I don't know what you're doing in my living room.

JANA: I don't know, either. *(Looking around.)* Just where the hell IS your living room?

FRANK: Hush—Kansas.

JANA: Hush, Kansas? Why are we in Hush, Kansas?

FRANK: Well, I live here.

JANA: *(Letting it sink in.)* Hush, Kansas. Sounds like a corporate euphemism for Siberia. I mean, if they wanted to fire me couldn't they just send a memo? *(She yells into the television set:)* I can take a hint! *(Switching gears, turning to FRANK; MAGGIE is at the door in time to hear:)* Frank! My ratings are down, they're trying to get rid of me . . . *(Desperate.)* I need a story!

FRANK: A story?

(MAGGIE enters.)

MAGGIE: Dad, who are you talking to?

JANA: *(Extending her hand.)* Jana Roberts—What's News Around The World.

MAGGIE: I recognize your smell. My dad watches you on TV all the time.

FRANK: *(To JANA.)* This is my daughter, Maggie.

JANA: Maggie.

MAGGIE: *(Direct.)* What are you doing in our living room?

JANA: *(Shrugs.)* Having dessert.

MAGGIE: *(To JANA.)* My dad is single. And he made that pie from scratch.

JANA: *(Smiling.)* It's as light as a dream.

MAGGIE: I remember my dreams almost before they happen.

JANA: What?

MAGGIE: In my dream I was floating like a Frisbee in slow-motion. And it was weird because I kept running into astronauts.

FRANK: *(To JANA.)* She's got quite an imagination.

JANA: *(Impatient, looking around.)* Really . . .

MAGGIE: *(Trying to suggest romance between FRANK and JANA:)* But the astronauts didn't have a ship, and they were falling through space. So I got this funny idea that if I was going to save the astronauts I'd have to go to Venus. *(Giggles.)* The planet of love. I blinked—and I was there!

JANA: *(Condescending.)* On Venus . . .

FRANK: She likes to make up stories—

MAGGIE: In my dream my teacher was that woman on the Challenger—you know the space lab—

JANA: *(To FRANK.)* I was eating Chicken McNuggets when it blew up.

MAGGIE: Christa—that was her name—and she was teaching all of these Venus kids how to read, and they totally loved her. What do you call people from Venus? Venuses? Venuslings?

FRANK: Veenie-weenies?

JANA: Venusians.

FRANK/MAGGIE: Venusians???

JANA: I do crossword puzzles.

MAGGIE: Christa just looked at me with this smile and said, "Angels and astronauts both begin with the letter A."

JANA: *(Looks at her with sudden curiosity.)* Angels?

MAGGIE: That was the end of the dream. My dad says if you eat three unwashed fish tails, all your dreams will come true.

(JANA looks at MAGGIE who shines the flashlight on herself.)

JANA: *(Intrigued, referring to the flashlight.)* What are you doing now?

MAGGIE: *(Concentrating.)* Trying to be seen. Like the lights at an airport that show the planes where it's safe to land.

JANA: *(Genuinely curious.)* But what do you think will see you?

MAGGIE: *(Guarded, looking around.)* Oh, you know—just whatever's—out there. *(Dismissing JANA.)* It was nice meeting you.

(MAGGIE continues outside to the apple tree.)

Hello?

JANA: *(Suddenly looking right at her story.)* Hello.

FRANK: *(Trying to flirt with JANA.)* Hello.

(MAGGIE tries to make contact with her Vision, tries to draw it out. JANA watches MAGGIE who is deeply engaged with her Vision. JANA is mesmerized, curious, puzzled. The wheels turn.)

JANA: Angels and Astronauts both begin with the letter "A."

FRANK: I thought you needed a story—

(Grant Wood's "American Gothic"—a MAN and WOMAN on the "street" stop and address the audience. They finish each other's sentences:)

WOMAN/VOICE OF AMERICA: We're from Coosawatchie, South Carolina—

MAN/VOICE OF AMERICA: —and I've been in a much better mood ever since we stopped reading the newspaper—

WOMAN/VOICE OF AMERICA: —watching the television—

MAN AND WOMAN/VOICE OF AMERICA: —and talking to our neighbors. *(Beat.)*

MAN/VOICE OF AMERICA: 'Course we're pretty lonely. *(Beat.)*

WOMAN/VOICE OF AMERICA: But we're in a much better mood.

(They both stare out expressionless at the audience and then disappear.)

JANA SPILLS THE BEANS

(In the kitchen. JANA *goes over her notes.)*

JANA: *(Reading from her notes.)* Maggie Parks lives in Hush with her father, Frank.

FRANK: *(Flirtatious.)* That's me! *(Self-important.)* Shall we begin?

JANA: *(Direct.)* May I be frank, Frank?

FRANK: *(Trying to be witty.)* Please, please.

JANA: I know about your daughter—

MAGGIE: *(Under the apple tree.)* Hello?

JANA: I have a hunch her story is going to be very, very . . . big.

FRANK: *(Confused, anxious.)* What did she do now?

JANA: Then—you don't know.

FRANK: *Know what?*

JANA: About your daughter.

FRANK: What's to know? She's a little girl!

MAGGIE: Hello???

JANA: What's Maggie's favorite music group?

FRANK: I can't remember.

JANA: Does she like girls?

FRANK: Sure.

JANA: Does she like boys?

FRANK: *(Faster.)* Some—

JANA: Was she ever fat?

FRANK: *(Flustered.)* Depends what you—

JANA: Has she had the measles?

FRANK: *(Losing ground.)* Measles?

JANA: Does she ever tell lies?

FRANK: *(Indignant.)* Not that I know—

JANA: What does she eat for breakfast?

FRANK: *(Very quick.)* Fruit Loops.

JANA: What does she eat for lunch?

FRANK: Fruit Loops!

JANA: What does she eat for dinner?

FRANK: Fruit Loops!!!

JANA: Have you noticed that your daughter's growing up?

FRANK: FRUIT LOOPS!!! *(He stops when he realizes what she's said.)*

MAGGIE: *(Calling out.)* I'm here now.

FRANK: *(To* JANA.) What did you say?

JANA: I said: Have you ever seen the angel that she sees behind your house? *(*FRANK *stares at her, stunned.)* Your daughter sees an angel.

FRANK: That's impossible. She can't see.

JANA: What do you mean?

FRANK: Maggie's blind.

MAGGIE: Can you see me?

JANA: *(Almost to herself.)* A blind girl who sees angels . . .

FRANK: Who said anything about angels?

JANA: This will be the biggest story of the year!

FRANK: Nobody said anything about angels.

JANA: I found it!

FRANK: So she likes to tell stories, she makes up poems—

JANA: *(Struggles to crawl back inside the TV.)* I FOUND MY STORY!!!

FRANK: *(Pulling JANA back out of the TV.)* What exactly did she tell you?

JANA: *(Tearing up her notes and throwing them aside.)* Frank—do you think I just popped out of that 19-inch box of scrambled electromagnetic waves by accident? Right now, I'm a recipe for all my unsatisfied creative juices cooking in the boiling doubters who never thought I'd amount to three-quarters cup of anything tasty! I'm reinventing myself, Frank! I'm rattling my cage, shattering those tiny bits of light and reconverting them into something more than a static picture bounced off satellites that fill the heavens with pictures of my smiling face! I'll show the network once and for all: Jana Roberts not only talks the talk, but Jana Roberts walks the walk! *(Laughs victoriously.)*

FRANK: *(Dizzy.)* You seemed so normal on TV.

JANA: *(Sensing a weakness in FRANK.)* Frank! Do you have any idea what kind of crackpots will be calling you?

FRANK: You're blowing this out of—

(The TELEPHONE—played by an actor—begins to ring, slowly creeping into the room, ringing impatiently as:)

JANA: Reporters, historians, agents, talk show hosts, movie producers, borderline quacks—Frank, trust me when I tell you that none of those clowns will be interested in your daughter. Do you know what it's like to have people crawling outside your house, hiding in the bushes, peeking in your windows, following your daughter around town—

FRANK: Wait a minute—

JANA: Talk to her, Frank. Before everyone else does. *(She feeds FRANK a bite of his pie; the phone keeps ringing.)* Or let ME talk to her.

(FRANK blocks the door so JANA can't get to MAGGIE in the back yard.)

FRANK: *(Desperate.)* Couldn't we just keep this between you and me?

JANA: There are no secrets, Frank, there are only stories.

FRANK: She's a little girl.

JANA: *(Correcting him.)* A little girl with a story. MY story.

(JANA exits through the door and FRANK watches her go. The phone rings. FRANK finally picks it up in a rage:)

FRANK: We already have AT&T!!!

(FRANK exits and a VOICE OF AMERICA takes the phone on his entrance.)

VOICE OF AMERICA: *(On the phone.)* Hi! I'm calling from Tivoli, New York: Whose idea was it to "just say no?" We need to be able to say YES to something.

FRANK: *(Enters and takes the phone.)* Who is this? How did you get this number?

(FRANK hangs up the phone and another VOICE OF AMERICA enters and takes the phone.)

VOICE OF AMERICA: Yeah, I'm from Romeo, Colorado. Nobody waves to anybody anymore. Nobody says hello. Nobody talks to strangers.

(JANA enters and grabs the phone away from Romeo, Colorado.)

JANA: *(On the phone.)* Yeah, Mitch—I have a late-breaking story from Hush, Kansas . . .

FATHERS & DAUGHTERS

(Outside, MAGGIE is staring at the tree. The sound of wind chimes. MAGGIE looks up at the tree. FRANK watches her.)

MAGGIE: . . . and I hope you don't think it's weird—but I really can't stop thinking about it so here goes: if I was stranded on a desert island and could ask only one question here's what I'd want to know—How was your date with Jana Roberts?

FRANK: I did not have a date with Jana Roberts!

MAGGIE: *(Shrugs, laughs.)* I think she liked your pie.

FRANK: *(Putting the blanket on her legs.)* Who were you talking to?

MAGGIE: Is there a moon?

FRANK: Uh-huh. It's right above the apple tree. *(MAGGIE looks toward the moon which winks at her. Wind chimes blow in the breeze. FRANK looks around nervously.)* Are we—alone?

MAGGIE: *(Cautious.)* What do you mean? *(Tentative.)* Do you see something?

FRANK: *(Looking around.)* There's nothing here, Maggie.

MAGGIE: Are you sure?

FRANK: A tree, the sky, the moon—what else is there?

MAGGIE: It's just—something—a feeling, something—so beautiful.

FRANK: *(Not sure how to respond.)* Sometimes you just have to be like everybody else.

MAGGIE: Why?

FRANK: Maggie, people are gonna talk.

MAGGIE: People might see something if they know where to look!

FRANK: Just sometimes, Maggie.

MAGGIE: But why?

FRANK: Because . . .

MAGGIE: Because why?

FRANK: Because—I don't know, Maggie!

MAGGIE: Then why did you say I have to be like everybody else?

FRANK: Forget it.

MAGGIE: Are you saying I SHOULD be like everybody else?

FRANK: Maggie—it would just be easier.

MAGGIE: Easier? It's not easier to be like everybody else if you're NOT like everybody else.

FRANK: You could try.

MAGGIE: (*Hurt, insecure.*) What's wrong with the way I am?

FRANK: Nothing is wrong—

MAGGIE: (*Panics, sensing something moving.*) Where did it go?

FRANK: What?

(*Chaos.* EVE *and* THE LION *run on, confused; their movements are fearful, disconnected. They disappear.*)

MAGGIE: (*Struck.*) Where did it go!?!

FRANK: What do you mean?

MAGGIE: (*Upset.*) It was here. It was here, and now it's gone. (*Looking around.*) Where did it go? Hello? Please come back!

FRANK: Maggie!

MAGGIE: (*Running around the yard, calling out.*) Please, come back! I won't let them hurt you!

FRANK: Maggie, stop it!

MAGGIE: (*Calling out to the night.*) I'm not like everybody else!

FRANK: Maggie!

(*The wind chimes make a loud, violent sound like something ripping apart.*)

MAGGIE: (*Staring up into the tree.*) It's up the tree. All the way up in the top of the tree.

FRANK: Maybe you should see a doctor.

MAGGIE: I'm not sick!

FRANK: (*Thinking aloud.*) You could go to your grandma's.

MAGGIE: (*Staring up at the tree.*) It's so far from in here to up there.

FRANK: (*Ignoring her.*) We'll sneak you out in the middle of the night and wait for this whole thing to blow over.

MAGGIE: (*Looking up at the tree.*) I'm not leaving.

FRANK: I'm your father, Maggie. If I say you're leaving, you're leaving!

MAGGIE: (*Emphatic.*) NO!!! (*Upset.*) There was something special out here—in me. (*Yelling.*) And now, it's chased up a tree!

FRANK: (*Paranoid.*) Shhhhhh! Would you just—(*He looks around to see if anyone is watching.*) What if I lose my job?

MAGGIE: Your job?

FRANK: Everybody's gonna wanna know everything about it. What are you gonna tell them?

MAGGIE: (*Shining the flashlight onto her body, then into the tree.*) The truth.

(FRANK *looks around, uneasy. Suddenly, like fog spreading over wetlands, eerie light from the television in the house pours into the back yard.*)

(JANA *enters with her TV* SOUND MAN, *setting up for taping:*)

JANA: We're making history here, guys!

SOUND MAN: She saw an angel?!?

JANA: This'll blow the ratings right through the roof!

SOUND MAN: What does that mean—she "saw" an angel . . . ? I thought you said she was blind. . . . Stand-by, everybody. Roll tape! (*Signaling to* JANA.) Three-two-one:

JANA: ". . . and so a little girl in Kansas has us all looking up at the sky tonight. Hoping. Angels and astronauts both begin with the letter 'A.'"

SOUND MAN: And . . . . cut! (JANA *and the* SOUND MAN *clear out.*) Great stuff, Jana . . .

BLESSED ARE THE MEEK FOR THEY SHALL INHERIT THE EARTH

(*In another part of the country, a* LAMB *wanders onstage having lost his mother. The* LAMB *looks around, makes a "baaaaahhhh" sound.* THE LION, *physically exhausted, creeps up to the* LAMB. *The* LAMB *looks at him and makes another "baaahhhh" sound.* THE LION *roars. The* LAMB *looks at him, curious.*)

LAMB: How do you do that?

THE LION: (*Annoyed.*) I'm a lion.

LAMB: A lion? In Illinois?

THE LION: You got a problem with that?

LAMB: (*Backing down.*) No, no! That's cool. (*Pause.*) But aren't you supposed to be in a zoo?

THE LION: I used to be in a zoo—in Los Angeles—

LAMB: Wow. You're a long way from home.

THE LION: That wasn't my home, man. It's where I lived.

LAMB: (*Watching* THE LION *stake out the place.*) You seem pretty nervous for a lion. Last Christmas my mom was in the Live Nativity—(*Impressed.*) in town. Boy, was she ever nervous. Where are you headed?

(*Looking out into space,* MAGGIE *repeats her "dance" from the opening image.*)

THE LION: Sometimes at night there's a light dancing in the sky. (*Looking off in one direction.*) It's a long way away, but it smells like kindness. (*He turns to the* LAMB *and stares hungrily.*)

LAMB: What are you thinking about?

THE LION: Lamb chops.

(*The* LAMB *stares back at* THE LION *and suddenly roars like a lion.* THE LION *jumps back, frightened. The* LAMB *disappears.* THE LION *looks around confused and exhausted. He watches the* LAMB *as he disappears into the scary sound of speeding cars on a highway.*)

JANA: (*On television.*) And so, in Hush, Kansas—there is no longer a hush in the air. Avon, Alabama?

VOICE OF AMERICA: It was probably one of them UFO's.

JANA: Mashpee, Massachusetts?

VOICE OF AMERICA: Reminds me of a movie about a left-handed spy . . .

JANA: Cactus Spring, Nevada?

VOICE OF AMERICA: Elvis is definitely alive.

JANA: South Heart, North Dakota?

VOICE OF AMERICA: Maybe it's a bird. Or a ghost of a bird.

TONGUES WAG

(FRANK *sits watching TV, empty beer can in one hand, remote control in the other. Awake, his eyes are closed in exhaustion.*)

JANA: (*On television.*) Little Maggie Parks and the angel in her backyard have become the topic of discussion at every breakfast table in America. . . . And so, in the little town of Hush, Kansas—

FRANK: (*Talking to TV, reckless.*) Why don't you tell 'em exactly where we live, too. That way EVERYBODY can come and see the angel.

JANA: "—five blocks from the school on a dead end street called Eden Lane— one angel has found a place to rest . . . for now. This is Jana Roberts in a continuing report for What's News Around The World." Good morning, Frank.

FRANK: (*Without thinking.*) Good morning, Jana.

JANA: (*On television.*) Is there any pie left?

FRANK: (*Realizing he's talking to the TV.*) DO NOT TALK TO ME!

JANA: Okay, Frank.

FRANK: Everybody knows you cannot talk to me when you're on TV.

JANA: Okay, Frank.

FRANK: Don't "Okay Frank" me. (*Switches off the TV.*)

(JANA *doesn't "turn off," she steps through the TV.*)

JANA: Paula from Rattlesnake, Montana:

PAULA/VOICE OF AMERICA: (*Entering the living room through a wall and joining* JANA.) First, I want to say how much I love your show, Jana. My boyfriend and I watch you all the time.

JANA: Thank you.

FRANK: What is she doing in my living room!?!

(JANA *and* PAULA *casually stroll through* FRANK's *living room.*)

PAULA/VOICE OF AMERICA: I trust you, you know? I mean, it's hard to know who to believe anymore. If you ask me, I definitely think the world was in better shape a thousand years ago . . .

FRANK: (*Talking back to the TV.*) You can say that again.

PAULA/VOICE OF AMERICA: (*Finding the camera to talk to.*) I definitely think the world was in better shape a thousand years ago—

JANA: Thank you, Paula.

FRANK: *(Trying to make them disappear.)* Okay, Frank—none of this is really happening. And even if it is—which it isn't—but even if it was—it wouldn't. Nobody watches the news anyway.

(FRANK goes outside to the tree where MAGGIE is sleeping. He makes an obvious noise, and she wakes up. FRANK holds out a box of cereal.)

FRANK: Fruit Loop? *(MAGGIE ignores him. FRANK pushes the box closer until she can't resist. She eats. The phone rings.)* The sound of everybody in town waggin' their tongues kept me awake all night. All of a sudden the paper boy asked about you.

MAGGIE: He's a nerd.

FRANK: He's never even said "boo" before.

MAGGIE: He's always been a nerd.

FRANK: Well, I guess I never noticed. He was just so *curious*, you know? Mrs. Shipley called.

MAGGIE: My science teacher?

FRANK: Yeah. And she didn't have anything to say. She was just "checking in." We talked about the weather, and I told her you really know your snowflakes. *(MAGGIE laughs.)* I didn't know what else to say. I just don't know what to say. *(Glancing up at the tree.)* Anymore. Maybe when you grow up, you'll be a weather girl on TV.

MAGGIE: *(Totally disgusted.)* No way! I'm going to be a poet. Or a painter. Or a dancer. I definitely want to live in Paris. And Caracas. Maybe I'll be a Shakespearean actor. *(MAGGIE uses the blanket as a dramatic cape.)* "This above all: to thine own self be true . . ."

FRANK: *(Trying to be helpful.)* Maybe you'll write your own plays.

MAGGIE: *(Excited by the idea.)* "I'll live forever! The dinosaurs mumbled . . ." *(MAGGIE sees something. The sound of the wind chimes.)* Look!

(FRANK can't see anything. He watches MAGGIE watching:)

FRANK: What?!? *(Frustrated.)* What are you seeing? *(MAGGIE tries to involve FRANK in the interaction but he only gets more confused.)* There's nothing here, Maggie! I can't see anything!

MAGGIE: Then close your eyes!

(FRANK closes his eyes, tries to "see" MAGGIE's vision.)

FRANK: I can't see it. And if I can't see it—how do I know it's here?

MAGGIE: How do I know there's really a moon? How do I know there's really a sky? *(FRANK opens his eyes and watches MAGGIE.)* I believe you when you tell me YOU see things.

(FRANK doesn't know what to say. MAGGIE continues chasing her Vision around the backyard while FRANK stumbles into the kitchen disheveled, disoriented.)

(In another part of the world, THE LION runs through space, fleeing, on a journey. Closer, closer.)

(MAGGIE continues engagement with Vision under the following FRANK/JANA scene:)

SOMEONE'S IN THE KITCHEN WITH DINAH

(In the kitchen JANA wears an apron and greets FRANK warmly as if she belongs.)

JANA: Morning!

FRANK: *(Startled.)* O, man. I thought you were a dream.

JANA: If you eat three unwashed fish tails, all your dreams come true.

FRANK: What are you doing here?

JANA: "Hot baths soothe the soul. Chicken soup and cinnamon rolls." That's what my grandmother used to say. *(She takes a pan of fresh cinnamon rolls from the oven.)*

FRANK: I'm not talking about cinnamon rolls! *(Lowering his voice.)* I'm talking about Maggie!

JANA: *(Passionate, genuine.)* I can't stop thinking about your daughter. I dream about her! I even talk to her in my sleep! *(The phone rings.)* And if I'm thinking about it, that means others must be thinking about her angel also.

FRANK: *(Sharp.)* She never said it was an angel.

JANA: It has to have a name, Frank! It has to grab you, it has to MEAN something. It has to fit into a sentence so I can say it on the news: "A blind girl in a small town in Kansas is seen by an angel in her own backyard."

FRANK: There is no angel!

JANA: Of course not, Frank. But what if there is?

(FRANK stops in his tracks.)

FRANK: It's up a tree.

JANA: *(Looks sharply to FRANK.)* Up a tree?

FRANK: The apple tree.

JANA: An angel in an apple tree? Even the words sound fantastic! I mean it's crazy—but doesn't the possibility give you goosebumps?

BREAKING BREAD

(MAGGIE looks up into the tree in the backyard. From far, far away, miles and miles—she hears the faint sound of drumming. She is suddenly very alert, like an animal.)

(The drumming gets nearer, and MAGGIE responds with her body, with rhythm, with kindness.)

(The drumming is nearer, more urgent. MAGGIE seems to be willing it to come closer, beckoning it like a dancing light in the sky.)

(THE LION suddenly wanders into the backyard. He stares at Maggie, she stares at him. They circle each other, sniff. Two animals in cautious, curious ritual.)

(THE LION suddenly roars in MAGGIE's face, testing her. She doesn't flinch, looks at him with even greater curiosity. She touches his face, puts her head in his mouth.)

(*Seductive.*) Now, what makes my chili so special are the marshmallows. (FRANK *slowly chews the food, savoring the flavors.*) What was Maggie like when she was a baby?

FRANK: Sometimes— . . . her eyes looked so old she seemed more like my grandma than my daughter. It's hard to explain. It's just that . . . (*He stops.*)

JANA: (*Gentle, on the brink.*) What?

FRANK: She scares me. She's like an animal. She just has this way of looking right AT you. For the longest time I didn't believe she was blind. Just between you and me—I think she CAN see.

(JANA *is moved, curious.*)

JANA: Frank! A blind girl in Kansas who sees an angel in an apple tree shouldn't affect me this much. (*She's falling apart; the phone is ringing.*) I must be mad. Animal crackers! I should just go back to New York and face the music. (*She tries to climb back into the TV but gets stuck which makes* FRANK *laugh which enrages* JANA. *The phone continues to ring.*) If I'm not stuck in the TV, then I'm stuck here. But until I talk to Maggie—until I know what she sees, I'm stuck. I'M stuck.

FRANK: (*Barking into the phone.*) HELLO! Oprah who? (*Softens, surprised.*) Oprah! Hi. Thank you. Well—

(JANA *takes the phone and hangs it up.*)

JANA: Please, let ME talk to her. It'll bring the ratings right through the roof! (*She tears the ringing phone out of the wall.*) Please, Frank.

(FRANK *hears the roaring coming from the backyard and runs out followed by* JANA.)

(MAGGIE *and* THE LION *eat Fruit Loops together. It is communion, faith, a deep friendship sealed.*)

(THE LION *roars his approval of* MAGGIE. MAGGIE *is riveted by the sound. She imitates the roar.* THE LION *roars again.* MAGGIE *roars back. They do this back and forth several times until* MAGGIE *sounds exactly like* THE LION.)

(*In shock/horror,* FRANK *and* JANA *watch* MAGGIE/LION *roaring. The wind chimes rustle.* MAGGIE *stops roaring when she senses company. The* LION *looks at them.* FRANK *and* JANA *tense.*)

FRANK: What the—

(*The* LION *roars at* FRANK *and* JANA—*and they jump back in fear/surprise.*)

MAGGIE: Daddy?

FRANK: (*Looking at* THE LION.) Are you out of your mind?

JANA: (*To* THE LION.) Are you a real lion?

THE LION: (*To* JANA.) Are you a real woman?

FRANK: I'm gonna call the Sheriff. (*He starts to exit.*)

MAGGIE: WAIT!!!!

(FRANK *turns and looks at* MAGGIE. *He is exhausted.*)

FRANK: Maggie?

MAGGIE: (*Impatient.*) What?

FRANK: A lion?

MAGGIE: He came a long way to see me.

FRANK: But he's a lion!

MAGGIE: He's nice!

FRANK: What will people say?

MAGGIE: I don't see why they should care! I like him.

JANA: (*Extending her hand to the* LION.) Jana Roberts—What's News Around The World. (THE LION *roars.* JANA *roars right back. To* MAGGIE:) I was hoping you and I could talk. (MAGGIE *roars.*) In English.

FRANK: You don't have to tell her anything, Maggie.

MAGGIE: I know.

(FRANK *looks at* MAGGIE *and then at* JANA. *The phone begins to ring in the house.*)

JANA: Why don't you go answer that phone, Frank.

(FRANK *looks at* MAGGIE.)

MAGGIE: (*Direct.*) I'll be fine, Daddy.

(FRANK *finally exits inside the house and answers the phone.*)

THREE LIONS IN THE JUNGLE

(THE LION *gets closer to* JANA *and smells her.* MAGGIE *is at* JANA's *feet, smelling her.* JANA *is trying not to scream. The scene is like a dance—animals circling each other, sniffing, moving, staking out territory.*)

MAGGIE: You can tell a lot about someone by the way they smell. It's like their fingerprints—it's something you can't hide.

JANA: (*Unnerved but charmed.*) What can you tell about me? From my smell, I mean.

MAGGIE: (*Smelling* JANA's *hand, very intense.*) You're a very hard worker. And you don't play the guitar. (*Mysterious, from the heart.*) I don't think you have any children. (*Smelling.*) You're not very good at keeping secrets. And you hate losing at Monopoly.

JANA: How did you know that? (JANA *stares at* MAGGIE. *Trying to shift back to power.*) Can I ask you a few questions?

MAGGIE: Can you—or may you?

JANA: (*Smiles, beaten at her own game.*) Very good. Should I call you Maggie?

MAGGIE: (*Smiles back.*) Should you—or shall you?

JANA: Would you like me to call you Maggie?

MAGGIE: Maggie's so boring.

JANA: How about . . . Margaritte?

MAGGIE: Margaritte. Sounds like someone who wears lots of scarves and does slow dances. (*Dramatic.*) I like it. It sounds . . . mysterious. (MAGGIE *strikes a dramatic pose with* THE LION.)

JANA: Is that what you wanna be? Mysterious?

MAGGIE: (*Collapsing.*) No.

JANA: You know, I grew up in a small town like Hush.

MAGGIE: Why'd you leave?

JANA: I had visions, too. No angels. Just visions of a bigger world.

MAGGIE: Did everybody think you were crazy?

JANA: A lot of people did. (*Laughs.*) A lot of people still do. (*Pause.*) Is there anything you'd like to tell me?

MAGGIE: Why should I want to tell you anything? I don't even know you.

JANA: But you know why I'm here. (JANA, MAGGIE, *and* THE LION *look up into the tree.*) Do you think HE'D give me an interview?

MAGGIE: Gee, I don't know. (*Exaggerating, testing her.*) Why don't you ask HIM???

JANA: (*She looks at* MAGGIE, *impatient.*) Are you sure there's anything up there?

MAGGIE: Are you sure there's not?

JANA: (*Stares at* MAGGIE, *unsure what she's dealing with.*) What do you think?!?

MAGGIE: I think the wind can sound like an orchestra. Don't you ever want to DANCE???

(MAGGIE *tries to dance, but her body seems strange, unfamiliar. The movements she's always been comfortable with don't make sense. There are parts to her body that feel new, different.* EVE *appears, tries to help* MAGGIE.)

JANA: (*Anxious, demanding.*) Where's the angel, Maggie?

MAGGIE: It used to always be everywhere—in songs I made up, or just sitting on top of stops signs waving at me. (*She looks up into the tree.*) I didn't have to think about it. It was just here (*Referring to her insides:*) HERE! But now things feel—all different. Sometimes, I don't even know if it sees me. (*Realization.*) What if it doesn't come back?

JANA: He probably just needed a little R&R—

MAGGIE: (*Exasperated.*) It's not a "he"—

JANA: I mean, it's probably a drag being an angel, always saving the day and all that—

MAGGIE: It's not an angel!

JANA: What else is there for an angel to do in Kansas?

MAGGIE: It's not an angel, I told you—it's a FEELING, a—

(FRANK *enters from the house.*)

FRANK: Well, I talked to Oprah, Phil, Maury, Geraldo, Leno, Letterman, Regis and Kathy Lee, Jerry, Joan, Carnie, Jenny, Ricki, Charlie, Montel, Sally Jessy, ABC, NBC, CBS, Fox, HBO, CNN—

JANA: And Jana Roberts.

FRANK: Everybody wants an interview.

JANA: I was here first.

FRANK: (*Suspicious.*) What have you two been talking about?

(FRANK *and* MAGGIE *stare at each other. Finally,* JANA *gets up and makes a move to exit.*)

JANA: Well—I've got work to do. It's been very nice talking to you, Margaritte.

FRANK: Who's Margaritte? (*To* JANA.) What did she tell you? (*To* MAGGIE.) What did you tell her?

JANA: She told me everything.

MAGGIE: I didn't tell you anything. Besides, you don't SEE anything.

JANA: (*Looks at* MAGGIE.) Not yet, anyway. (*She starts to exit.*)

FRANK: (*To* JANA.) Wait a minute! So now, you leave? Is that how it works? You squeeze inside our lives and then just WALK AWAY?!? I wanna know what you're gonna do!

JANA: I'm a reporter, Frank. I'm going to report the news.

FRANK: What?!? Wait a minute—

JANA: There's a lion dancing in your backyard. That's news.

FRANK: One measly little dancing lion? (THE LION *roars.*) What about real news? What about welfare and health care and—and education and the war in Bosnia—

JANA: This country needs—a different story. We need a miracle, something other than Prozac to believe in.

FRANK: So it has to be on the six o'clock news?

JANA: Everybody needs to know.

FRANK: But how do you know she's telling the truth?

JANA: Careful, Frank. Let ME be the bad guy.

FRANK: Nobody will believe you.

JANA: Don't screw it up. For your own sake.

FRANK: Maggie! She's telling the whole world that you see an angel in the apple tree!

MAGGIE: I don't care.

FRANK: (*To* JANA.) She doesn't care. (*To* MAGGIE, *realizing what she's said.*) YOU DON'T CARE!?! I—this is not the—(*Yelling.*) WHAT WILL PEOPLE THINK?

MAGGIE: (*Yelling back.*) WHY DO YOU ALWAYS SAY THAT?

FRANK: *(JANA is leaving.)* Where are you going?!?

JANA: I told you, Frank. I have a story to tell.

FRANK: You said you wanted to find out the truth.

JANA: *(Looking at MAGGIE.)* I think she thinks she's telling the truth.

FRANK: *(To JANA.)* Who cares what you think?

JANA: *(Looks at FRANK.)* You really are an innocent, aren't you? *(Looks at THE LION.)* If you're still hungry, there's homemade cinnamon rolls in the kitchen.

(THE LION *roars,* JANA *exits.*)

FRANK: I'm definitely gonna lose my job. Oh, God. Think, man, think! *(He notices THE LION looking at him.)* WHAT ARE YOU LOOKING AT!!!

(FRANK *stumbles into the house, distraught.* MAGGIE *and* THE LION *are all alone.* MAGGIE *pets* THE LION.)

MAGGIE: Sometimes it's lonely being me.

(THE LION *comforts her.*)

J. EDGAR HOOVER WORE DRESSES UNDER THAT COAT

(FRANK *is alone in the house. There is a knock.* FRANK *goes to the door.*)

FRANK: Who's there?

(The microwave oven in the kitchen beeps. FRANK *turns and looks at it. He cautiously opens the microwave door.* FBI *pokes out his head.)*

VOICE: FBI.

FRANK: FBI who?

VOICE: FBI wanna talk to you. *(A man crashes through the door leaving the outline of his body like a cartoon cutout.* FBI *stands staring at* FRANK. *He/She wears dark glasses and all black.)* FBI.

FRANK: *(Extending his hand.)* Frank Parks.

FBI: FBI.

FRANK: Frank Parks.

FBI: FBI

FRANK: Frank Parks.

FBI: FBI—

FRANK: ALL RIGHT! Are you here to see ME?

FBI: I got a hot tip you got a cold thug up a fruit tree.

FRANK: A thug?

FBI: A fugitive.

FRANK: A fugitive?

FBI: America's Most Wanted.

FRANK: Most wanted what?

FBI: *(Flipping through his notes.)* Most wanted by most Americans. In an apple tree. In your backyard. *(Flashes a piece of paper.)* Search warrant.

(FBI *sneaks to the backyard, followed by* FRANK.)

(MAGGIE *and* THE LION *are talking under the tree.*)

LION: There was fire in the sky—and everyone running around Los Angeles not sure where they could go, where it was safe. People, animals everywhere. The smell of smoke. The beautiful April sky—awful, orange—

(FBI *sneaks up on* MAGGIE *and* THE LION, *followed by* FRANK.)

FBI: Freeze! FBI. (THE LION *looks terrified.*) Who's there in lion's clothing?

MAGGIE: He's a real lion. Who are you?

FBI: FBI. (*Looking around, suspicious, eyes the tree.*) What about the tree?

MAGGIE: It's real, too.

FBI: (*To Frank.*) Is she your kid?

FRANK: Yeah.

FBI: (*Secretive.*) Better keep an eye on her. (*Stepping out and looking suspiciously at the audience.*) You got to get 'em when they're young. Nip the smart ones in the bud. Otherwise, they grow up to be—you know—trouble. (*Looking at* MAGGIE.) Big trouble.

FRANK: (*Reminding himself.*) She's a good kid.

FBI: What about the lion?

MAGGIE: Friend of the family.

FRANK: Sort of.

FBI: Right. (FBI *looks up into the tree, suddenly looks around an imaginary corner.*) Well. I don't see anything.

FRANK: (*Looking at* MAGGIE.) Join the club.

FBI: In the future if you notice anything that braids the hairs on the back of your neck, here's my card. I got a FAX, modem, beeper, and cellular phone. I never sleep.

(FBI *starts to exit.*)

FRANK: Uh—FBI? (FBI *turns and looks at* FRANK.) How did you hear about the uh—(*Looks at tree.*) You know.

FBI: I watch the News.

(FBI *exits. The phone begins to ring in the house.*)

JANA: (*On camera.*) Earlier today all major airlines announced special fares to Hush, Kansas. Tickets sold out nationwide in an unprecedented fifteen minutes. An anonymous tip reports that a new international airport is being considered to accommodate the unexpected popularity of Hush. Funkstown, Maryland?

VOICE OF AMERICA: I used to always look at the ground when I walked. Thanks to Maggie Parks, now I look up at the sky.

JANA: Sour Lake, Texas?

VOICE OF AMERICA: Yeah, I just want to say that I think Maggie Parks is the best thing that's happened to this country since they started showing reruns of *The Partridge Family*—

JANA: Halfway, Kentucky?

VOICE OF AMERICA: Um, hi Jana. We've been listening to your show here in the hospital, and we've decided to use some of our retirement money to come out to Hush, to see—you know, if maybe the angel can't heal my wife. You always hope for a miracle.

(The sound of honking horns.)

MAGGIE: Daddy? What is it?

FRANK: *(Looking around.)* I'm not sure.

JANA: *(On camera.)* The sale of Fruit Loops have risen 839 percent in the last week alone—

MAGGIE: Daddy?

FRANK: *(Looking out at the horizon.)* Hundreds—no thousands of cars—bumper to bumper . . .

MAGGIE: Where are they headed?

SEEKER: I know someone who knows someone who knows someone who knows someone who knows someone who knows someone who knows someone who knows someone—and they actually touched little Maggie Parks.

FRANK: *(Looking out.)* I've never seen so many cars in my life.

JANA: The name "Maggie" has suddenly become the most popular name for both girls and boys—eclipsing favorites "Hillary," "John," and "Spot."

FRANK: *(Looking up at the sky.)* Helicopters! The Fuji blimp! All of these people . . .

MAGGIE: They're coming to be seen.

SEEKER: My husband's mother's second cousin's college roommate's ex-wife's attorney's part-time secretary once saw little Maggie Parks buying a slushie at the 7-Eleven.

MAGGIE: *(Feeling all of the people arriving.)* Dad, do you believe in miracles?

FRANK: *(Confused.)* I don't know what I believe.

MAGGIE: *(Peaceful.)* I do.

(The sound of the pilgrimage getting nearer.)

MAGGIE: *(Excited.)* Hello!

PILGRIMS: Caio! Allo! Hola! Bon Jour!

MAGGIE: Daddy?

PILGRIMS: Maggie! Maggie!

MAGGIE: Daddy . . .

PILGRIMS: Say something, Maggie!

MAGGIE: Snowflake?

PILGRIMS: Ooooooooooo!

PILGRIM: *(Touching MAGGIE.)* You are the sunshine of my life!

PILGRIM: Say something, Maggie!

MAGGIE: LIKE WORDS TO A SONG—

(SEEKERS/PILGRIMS shove to get closer to MAGGIE.)

PILGRIMS: Ooooooooo! We love you, Maggie! We love you, Maggie! We love you, Maggie!

PILGRIMS: Mama, I want to see the angel, too!

PILGRIMS: *(Demanding.)* Say something, Maggie!

MAGGIE: Invisible ink—

(Seekers/Pilgrims shove to get closer to MAGGIE.*)*

PILGRIMS: Ooooooooooo! Save us, Maggie! Save us! Save us!

(Out of the crowd there is a bright flash from a camera. A young girl wearing a "Maggie T-Shirt" roars until MAGGIE *has to look in her direction. Throughout the scene* T-SHIRT *is constantly taking flash-pictures of* MAGGIE.*)*

T-SHIRT: Maggie Parks.

MAGGIE: *(Looking toward* T-SHIRT, *exhausted.)* Who are you?

T-SHIRT: *(Snapping a picture.)* Just a kid.

MAGGIE: *(Relieved.)* Good.

T-SHIRT: Just like you. Well, not JUST like you. I'm not up for the Nobel Peace Prize. *(Comforting* MAGGIE, *who accepts her kindness;* THE LION *is nervous.)* I knew you'd be even better in person. That's why I came to see you, to see for myself. *(Snaps another picture.)* Proof.

MAGGIE: I'm not nearly as interesting as they think I am.

T-SHIRT: I've been cutting out every story about you in every newspaper and magazine that money could buy.

MAGGIE: I'm sorry you went to all that trouble.

T-SHIRT: I already have over a hundred scrapbooks filled with you.

MAGGIE: You mean *pictures* of me.

T-SHIRT: I knew if I could get THIS close to you that I'd feel better, that I'd be somebody really important. *(Holding tighter to* MAGGIE.*)* Sometimes, it's lonely being me.

MAGGIE: *(Gently.)* I'm sorry to hear that. I really am.

T-SHIRT: I came a long way to see you.

MAGGIE: I need to go inside now. *(*T-SHIRT *flashes the camera.)* Good-bye.

*(*MAGGIE *walks away and doesn't know that* T-SHIRT *follows her, imitates the way she moves.* MAGGIE *goes inside the house.)*

MAGGIE: Daddy? *(*T-SHIRT *steps into the house. She looks around. It is creepy, invasive. She finds a paper snowflake, treasures it, puts it in her pocket. She sits in* FRANK's *rocking chair, and it creaks.* MAGGIE *looks up, startled.)* Daddy?

T-SHIRT: It's me.

MAGGIE: What are you doing in my house?

T-SHIRT: I didn't come all this way to see an angel—I came to see you. I want you to autograph my T-shirt. Sign it, "To my best friend"—no, "To my VERY best friend in the whole world"—

MAGGIE: I'm really tired—

T-SHIRT: *(Stopping* MAGGIE.*)* You owe me!

MAGGIE: Owe you?

T-SHIRT: You're my hero.

MAGGIE: Look, you can't believe everything they tell you on TV. I'm not—

T-SHIRT: I want to be your best friend.

MAGGIE: I don't even know you.

T-SHIRT: But I know YOU!

MAGGIE: No, you don't!

T-SHIRT: I do! I have video tapes full of stories about you on the news.

MAGGIE: But that isn't really ME!

T-SHIRT: You're on every channel of every television in every house in America.

MAGGIE: (Frustrated, scared.) I'm not that interesting—

T-SHIRT: Are you saying you don't want to be my friend?

MAGGIE: No! But if we're going to be friends, we have to KNOW each other first.

T-SHIRT: I DO know you. Are we friends or not?

MAGGIE: You're not listening to what I'm saying.

T-SHIRT: (Irrational.) I WANT TO BE YOUR FRIEND!

MAGGIE: I'm not trying to hurt your feelings—

T-SHIRT: I WANT TO BE YOU! (T-SHIRT tries to literally get inside MAGGIE's skin, and instantly THE LION jumps at T-SHIRT.) I WANT TO BE LOVED! I WANT PEOPLE TO PAY ATTENTION TO ME!

THE LION: RUN! (MAGGIE looks at THE LION, unsure what to do, where to go.) Maggie, GO! RUN!

(MAGGIE begins to stumble off. She is disoriented, frightened, insecure.)

T-SHIRT: (Pinned to the ground by THE LION.) He's trying to eat me! Get him off! She's getting away! (FRANK and JANA pull THE LION off of T-SHIRT who jumps up and runs after MAGGIE.)

FRANK: Maggie! Maggie—come back! Maggie!

(FRANK runs off after MAGGIE.)

T-SHIRT: (Into JANA's camera.) Maggie Parks is a FAKE!!! (T-SHIRT runs off followed by the crowd.)

(JANA turns to THE LION.)

JANA: (Sympathetic.) I hope you have a good lawyer.

THE LION: (Into JANA's camera.) I'd rather sing one day as a lion than 100 years as a human being.

(THE LION runs off after MAGGIE, T-SHIRT, and FRANK.)

JANA: (Excited, victorious.) I'm Jana Roberts reporting in a special LIVE edition of What's News Around The World. (JANA rushes after them.)

WHEN MAGGIE PARKS ISN'T MAGGIE PARKS ANYMORE

(Voices from MAGGIE's past chase her as she runs on out of breath.)

VOICES IN MAGGIE'S HEAD: Sometimes you have to be like everybody else. What's wrong with the way I am? Can I ask you a few questions? What would people think??? I used to be in a zoo. You are the sunshine of my life! Is there anything you'd like to tell me? What if I lose my job? You owe me!

(MAGGIE *stops, looks around, unsure where she is. Her clothes are sweaty and soiled. Her hands are dirty, her face is dusty. She looks like a stereotypical image of a homeless person. She finds a hiding place and huddles alone. She speaks some of her poetry in the present, trying to hold on to any reality. The feeling is scary, loud, faraway, close, disorienting.*)

MAGGIE: Help me!

STRANGER #1 VOICE: Get your filthy hands off of me before I call the cops!

MAGGIE'S VOICE: But I'm lost and need help.

STRANGER #2 VOICE: Look, I'm just a normal, disinterested, self-absorbed person.

MAGGIE'S VOICE: My name is Maggie Parks—

STRANGER #3 VOICE: You're the fifth person today who's used that line.

STRANGER #4 VOICE: You're not Maggie Parks—

STRANGER #5 VOICE: None of you are Maggie Parks—

STRANGER #6 VOICE: Even Maggie Parks isn't Maggie Parks anymore.

MAGGIE'S VOICE: You have to believe me.

STRANGER #7 VOICE: Get away from me!

MAGGIE'S VOICE: I'm Maggie Parks.

STRANGER #8 VOICE: And I'm George Jetson.

MAGGIE'S VOICE: I'm Maggie Parks.

STRANGER #9 VOICE: Set your goals, honey. But know your limitations. And never compromise your personal hygiene.

MAGGIE'S VOICE: Call my father—please!

STRANGER #10 VOICE: I'm late for work.

(MAGGIE *huddles alone, scared. Tired. Stunned.*)

MAGGIE: Daddy??

(THE LION *crosses the stage, looks out at the audience and then disappears.*)

MAGGIE: I AM A BEAUTIFUL SNOWFLAKE IN AN AWFUL BLIZZARD.

TALK SOUP/INVISIBLE INK

(JANA *is conducting an impromptu talk show at the Angel Tree.* THE LION *is lying on the ground.*)

JANA: Callers? Are you there? Zafra, Oklahoma: go ahead.

CALLER #1: Yeah, Jana, I just want to say that I don't think it's right they had a lion living over there.

JANA: Paris, Maine?

CALLER #2: This is what happens when humans and lions get to be too friendly.

JANA: Dead Horse, Alaska?

CALLER #1: Next thing you know, lions are gonna want the same rights as humans.

CALLER #2: It's wrong.

CALLER #1: It's perverse is what it is.

CALLER #2: As long as there are lions, none of us are safe.

JANA: Hot Coffee, Mississippi?

CALLER #1: Yeah, I'm calling from Hot Coffee, Mississippi, and me and my husband went all the way up there to Hush, Kansas, and we didn't see any angels.

CALLER #2: I read that Heather Locklear is gonna play Maggie Parks in the TV Movie of the week!

CALLER #1: I think that Tom Hanks should play Frank—

CALLER #2: Or Denzel Washington!

CALLER #1: And I don't buy this business that a lion is born that way—that he has to eat humans.

CALLER #2: If they're gonna make lions legal, then I say there's something sick about this—

(JANA *disconnects all the callers. She is chilled by their hatred.*)

JANA: Thank you for calling in. (*Looking at the camera.*) You know, since I've known Maggie Parks, I add wings to everything I see. It makes a difference. I don't know—maybe everything's an angel.

(MAGGIE *is alone, lost, huddled in a doorway.*)

MAGGIE:

> And the hands are cold and the fingers are long
> And the light is dark
> And the ice that hangs from my eyelashes tells my future

FRANK: (*Far away in the distance.*) Maggie! Come home!

MAGGIE:

> But I cannot see it!
> So I touch my face
> To prove that I am alive.
> And then, even then, even now, now,
> I want to live forever.

(THE LION *enters searching for* MAGGIE. *He roars, listens for a response, roars again, and disappears.*)

COUNTING SHEEP

(MAGGIE *is running—in her sleep. Exhausted, dirty, tragic, nearly delirious. She comes across the same* LAMB *that* THE LION *met earlier.*)

LAMB: Maggie? Little Maggie Parks?

MAGGIE: Where?

LAMB: Aren't you Maggie Parks?

MAGGIE: Am I?

LAMB: Are you all right?

MAGGIE: Am I still on Earth?

LAMB: Of course. *(Not believing he's actually meeting her.)* Little Maggie Parks! My friends are going to have a cow when I tell them I met you. *(The LAMB tries to get MAGGIE to play, but MAGGIE is too exhausted.)* What's the matter? You look beat.

MAGGIE: I haven't slept since I was eleven.

LAMB: Lay your head against my soft wool. *(She collapses to the ground next to him.)* Do you know what helps me when I can't sleep? *(MAGGIE shrugs.)* Counting sheep.

MAGGIE: *(Looking at the lamb.)* One. *(Feeling drowsy.)* One. *(Seeing only one lamb.)* One. One. One. One.

LAMB: Shhhhhhh.

(MAGGIE sleeps.)

(MAGGIE sleeps in the LAMB's arms.)

(JANA reporting from the Angel Tree.)

JANA: Still no news about little Maggie Parks. But in related news, today the neighboring State of Colorado passed sweeping new laws making lions and angels illegal. So as not to seem exclusive, the laws also state that anything else that doesn't meet the approval of Colorado can also be made illegal. *(JANA stops and considers what she's said.)* What's going on here? I don't like this story. These are stupid laws. I'm afraid I've made a terrible mistake . . . *(FRANK joins JANA and speaks into the microphone.)*

FRANK: Maggie, if you're out there—come home.

JANA: ". . . that number again is 1-800-FOR-MAGGIE—

FRANK: *(Interrupting JANA.)* Why couldn't you just have believed her?

JANA: Did YOU? *(FRANK doesn't answer.)* It mattered too much, Frank. We all want to feel special. We all want to be able to SEE like Maggie. *(Pause.)* I'm up for a Pulitzer. Who'd a thought? I mean a human interest story no less. Maybe that's what people really

(MAGGIE *stirs, suddenly wakes up like she's remembered something from long ago.*)

want. Well. (*She exits back inside the TV.*) For What's News Around The World, I'm Jana Roberts. Good night, America. Good night, Frank.

FRANK: Good-bye, Jana.

(FRANK *reaches out to touch the TV screen and* JANA *disappears.* FRANK *takes the box of Fruit Loops, a blanket and pillow, and exits the house. He leaves a trail of Fruit Loops, deliberately dropping one loop at a time. It is the only sound.*)

MAGGIE: Invisible Ink!

LAMB: (*Waking up, groggy.*) What?

MAGGIE: (*Reading from her soul.*) "This above all: to thine own self be true . . ."

(MAGGIE *looks at* LAMB *who shrugs, smiles.* MAGGIE *does a wild, dance full of every part of herself.*)

(THE LION *dances on and sees* MAGGIE. *They do a wild primitive dance together until there is nothing else to say. They stand looking at each other.*)

(THE LION *roars,* MAGGIE *roars back. They look out at their separate roads and part. The* LION *disappears into the shadows.* MAGGIE *dances home.*)

(MAGGIE *returns to her backyard.* FRANK *enters still leaving a trail of Fruit Loops behind him. He doesn't see* MAGGIE.)

MAGGIE: (*To* FRANK.) Have you ever noticed that all animals have human eyes?

(FRANK *turns and looks at* MAGGIE. *He doesn't know what to say. He looks at her and waits for her to make the first move. She moves to him and embraces him.*)

FRANK: Maggie? Maggie! (*Embracing her.*) Are you okay?

MAGGIE: I'm home, Daddy. (*They embrace.*) I'm finally home.

(*The chimes blow gently in the breeze.* FRANK *looks around at the damaged yard, the ruins.*)

FRANK: Fruit Loop? (*Suddenly grabbing her and hugging her.*) Tell me a story?

(MAGGIE *looks at* FRANK, *surprised and pleased.*)

MAGGIE: (MAGGIE *begins to eat Fruit Loops.*) Once there was this girl—

FRANK: How come all your stories start the same way?

MAGGIE: Because I'm the storyteller, and the storyteller gets to tell it any way she wants. (MAGGIE *tries to soften up her pillow.*) Once there was this— young woman! who lived with her dad in a small town in America— (MAGGIE *tries to fluff up her pillow, hitting it against the tree. It breaks. Feathers go everywhere,* MAGGIE *feels them falling around her.* FRANK *begins to laugh.*) It's snowing!

FRANK: *(Laughing.)* Hey, everybody! Look at us! It's snowing in our backyard.

(MAGGIE *and* FRANK *begin to play in the "snow.")*

MAGGIE: It's snowing in July!

(MAGGIE *and* FRANK *pretend to have a snowball fight.* MAGGIE *suddenly looks in the sky.)*

FRANK: Maggie? What is it? What do you see? (MAGGIE *smiles and shakes her head. She stares at the sky.)* Maggie? *(He looks at the sky.)* Whatever you see— hold on to it. Hold it tight. Don't ever let go. (FRANK *is behind* MAGGIE *holding onto her, holding tight, looking up at the sky.)*

(MAGGIE *touches her heart and closes her eyes. She takes a step out, gently pulling away from her father, standing on her own. She sings a simple made-up song.)*

MAGGIE: AND TOMORROW IS NOW STANDING WITH ARMS SPREAD OPEN WIDE HUGGING ME, HUGGING ME, HUGGING ME . . .

(There is the sound of wind chimes. EVE *dances in the distance. A* LION *roars.* MAGGIE's *face radiates with joy as the lights fade slowly, a tiny spotlight on* MAG- GIE's *face is the last bit of light. The play is over.)*

CURTAIN

BOCÓN!

by
Lisa Loomer

LISA LOOMER began her career as an actress, character comedienne, and stand-up comic. Her first work for theatre was a collaboration called *A Crowd of Two* at The American Place Theatre, New York City, in 1981. *All By Herselves*, a one-woman show, followed at the Westside Arts Theatre. In 1985, she spent a year as a writer-in-residence at Intar in New York City. Her first play, *Birds*, was produced by South Coast Repertory, Costa Mesa, California. Subsequent works, including *The Waiting Room, Looking for Angels, Cuts, Chain of Life*, and *Accelerando*, have been produced at such theatres as The Mark Taper Forum, Los Angeles; Arena Stage, Washington, D.C.; Intar, New York City; the Public Theatre, New York City; Trinity Repertory, Providence, Rhode Island; the Los Angeles Theatre Center; the Williamstown Theatre Festival in Massachusetts; the Vineyard Theatre, New York City; and the Odyssey in Los Angeles.

Bocón!, her political fable for young audiences, was commissioned by The Mark Taper Forum in 1989. Since then it has been seen nationwide from the Kennedy Center to the Group Theatre in Seattle; at the Open Eye, New York; Childsplay, Tempe, Arizona; MUNY, St. Louis; Stage Left, Chicago; the LaJolla Playhouse in California, as well as in Alaska, Germany, and Mexico. It was revived by The Taper in 1997.

Her newest play, *Maria! Maria! Maria! Maria!*, a multicultural farce, was commissioned by The Taper and a reading was presented as part of its 1996 New Works Festival.

Loomer is an alumna of New Dramatists and the recipient of two grants from the National Endowment for the Arts and a grant from the New York Foundation for the Arts. Her awards include The Jane Chambers Award, The Susan Blackburn Prize, and The American Theatre Critics Association Awards. She has also been nominated for a Pulitzer Prize.

Lisa Loomer's first film, *Looking for Angels,* was chosen by Robert Redford's Sundance Institute for its first collaboration with the Latin American Film Institute in Cuba. There, she had the opportunity to work with Gabríel García Márquez. Other films include *Girl, Interrupted* for Sony, *Just Desserts* for Paramount, and *Dreaming* and *Brothers and Sisters* for Fox 2000.

Writing a play for children was one of the most gratifying things I have done. Most of the kids who come to see *Bocón!* have never been to a play before, so I have the joy of watching children raised on television see their first live show. They are the most responsive audience a writer can have. They're not jaded, they're not proper . . . they talk back, they scream when they're scared, they cheer for the hero—a boy of their own age undertaking a transformation they might undertake themselves.

What I'm really interested in is getting to their still open minds. Get to them early enough, you can raise questions, you can plant an awareness, you can give them an experience that might actually have some impact on their lives. And, who knows, maybe I've given a future Williams, or Sondheim, or August Wilson, or Eddie Olmos the crazy idea to go out and do a play. I suspect that, at the end of my career, when I am wise like La Llorona, I will treasure the letters I've gotten from kids—and trust them—more than the raves from *The Times.*

—LISA LOOMER

BOCÓN!

CHARACTERS

Miguel: "Bocón" (Big Mouth), a storyteller of twelve. A kid with a wild imagination and reasonable fears in an unreasonable world.

Border Guard: American. An offstage voice.

The Judge: Doing the best he can with the misinformation he's got. American. A voice.

Ana: Miguel's mother. Superstitious and loving. One minute she's scaring the daylights out of you, the next she's tucking you in.

Luis: Miguel's father. Proud and big hearted, with a great laugh.

Cecilia: Miguel's aunt, in her forties. A pragmatist.

Rosita: Her daughter. A wild child. Loves to eat.

Kiki: An old Indian. Part spirit. A wizard of the dance.

La Llorona: "The Weeping Woman" . . . and a great comedienne. The Boogey Woman and Mother Earth. A woman of quick changes, with the stature of a myth and human concerns.

Viejitas: Crazy old crones.

The Voice Keeper: An elegant, smooth, smiling fascist. Knows flamenco. A Spaniard with a sash of medals.

The Voice Picker: A slightly touched, raggedy and strange old woman who's caught in a net and talks to shells. She's also caught in the web of war.

La Calavera: A skeleton. A nightmare in boots.

Duende: A trickster, short and green, and a Coyote.

Guard Dogs: Fierce, but funny.

PLACE

A judge's chambers across the U.S. border; a village in Central America; and a forest in between.

TIME

Anytime there is war and refugees.

THE STORY OF LA LLORONA

Legend has it that she was an Indian woman who drowned her own children after their father, a Spanish conquistador, left her for a rich Spanish lady. They say she still goes all over the world crying "Ay, mis hijos!"—"Oh, my children!" In Mexico and parts of Central America, she's thought of as a witch, a Boogie Woman . . . but maybe she's been misunderstood.

Maybe under the Boogie Woman mask is the Mother who is out to keep her children—all the earth's children—safe from the Soldiers of War. What if Medea got over her personal grief and walked among the Mothers of the Plaza de Mayo?

SOME NOTES ON PRODUCTION . . .

CASTING

Six actors play all the characters. The actress who plays LA LLORONA can also play CECILIA. MIGUEL is usually played by an actor in his twenties.

Ideally, casting should reflect the fact that the main characters are Central American. On the other hand, since MIGUEL's story happens all over the world, casting is one way to encourage children of other ethnicities to relate to it.

THE SET

The set should be minimal, flexible, and evocative rather than literal so it can suggest three different worlds: a courtroom in America; a village in Central America; and a mythical forest which is the setting for an interior journey. The village should be warm and beautiful, like all our remembered homes. The forest can be scarier.

The set might have different levels. The Military Calavera should come up out of the ground. Rope ladders might be used for trees. Especially on the journey, actors need not always be on the ground.

There might be modular, reversable pieces suggesting the topsy-turvy nature of MIGUEL's world. A set piece might have stars and stripes on one side, an altar on the other, and the face of a wild monkey on the third. Flowing fabric might be used by the actors to create a river. The marketplace might consist of fruits and wares glued to colorful blankets and unfurled.

SOUND AND MUSIC

The original production had a lot of taped music with a distinctly Latin feel. There was a live musician with a variety of ethnic and percussion instruments underscoring and accenting moments throughout the play.

THE JUDGE's voice on mike might have some distortion—because his language is strange to MIGUEL. The journey is filled with the sounds of the elements and the howling of wild animals. THE BOOT is the sound of oppression. Could be hard as stone, or clanging and metallic like a prison door.

COSTUMES

Because this is a tale, ethnic costumes work well in the village. In reality, Americanized dress might be more common, but the village should feel like a distant world. On the journey, the sky's the limit. The CHORUS has worked well in natural cotton, capesino-style shirt and pants.

MASKS

If masks are used, only the characters on the journey should be masked. Masks give a magical lift—but they can also be distancing, so half masks work well. The masks should be achingly human. See Guatemalan and Mexican masks for inspiration. LA LLORONA's mask should make her huge, ten feet tall, and when she loses it, she's not masked at all.

(The play opens with a rhythmic spoken piece—an invitation and a challenge to the audience. The actors are in simple white clothes, suggesting a chorus of campesinos. They each have two sticks which are beaten against each other, against the floor, in the air, or against the sticks of another actor, creating rhythm and movement.)

CHORUS: Imagine a land—

ACTOR #1: Fijate, imagine!

CHORUS: Jaguars, papagallos—

ACTOR #2: Yellow corn in the fields—

CHORUS: Imagine a land—fijate, imagine!

ACTOR #3: Oye marimba!

ACTOR #4: Quieres sandias?

ACTOR #5: Mira—Quetzal en las ceibas alli!

CHORUS: Imagine a place—WAR in the mountains!

ACTOR #1: There's war in the mountains!

ACTOR #2: Fire in the sky!

CHORUS: Imagine this place—not far from here . . .

ACTOR #3: *(Whispered.)* Fijate, imagine—

(Faster now, imploring.)

ACTOR #1: Cross the borders!

ACTOR #4: Take my story—

CHORUS: Cross the borders—

ACTOR #5: Take my hand!

CHORUS: *(Fading.)* Take my story, take my story . . . Fijate, imagine . . .

SCENE 1

(Night. The stage is bare and dark. Sound of HELICOPTERS. MIGUEL *enters and begins to run from a* BORDER GUARD *we do not see. The* CHORUS *creates a border with their sticks, stopping him. As soon as he speaks, the* CHORUS *vanishes.)*

BORDER GUARD'S VOICE: *(Out of breath.)* Stop! That's it, kid. Now, you hold it right there.

*(*MIGUEL *stops. It is as though a bird were being captured. One of* MIGUEL's *arms is lifted up, then the other, like wings. Then both are brought down and back behind him, and the chase is over.*

THE JUDGE *appears behind a scrim, or he may be a shadow cast over* MIGUEL, *or a just a Voice over a microphone.)*

JUDGE: What's your name son?

*(*MIGUEL *is too frightened and confused to speak.)*

Where do you come from? Guatemala? Mexico? El Salvador? *(Waits.)* Who brought you here? Your parents? Where are your parents, son? *(Louder,*

slowly.) Sus padres? Donde estan sus padres? *(Clears throat.)* Look. I am a
judge, son. How am I supposed to know where to send you back to, if I
don't know where you're from? *(Faster, more insistently.)* What are you afraid
of? Where are your parents? WHERE ARE YOU FROM?

(The last line echoes. THE JUDGE *bangs his gavel—and we hear* THE BOOT SOUND
that MIGUEL *hears in his mind.)*

SCENE 2

*(*MIGUEL *starts to tell* THE JUDGE *his story, awkwardly at first. As he gets more
comfortable, it is directed more and more to the audience.)*

MIGUEL: Yo vengo de . . . es un pueblito . . . I come from a small village, San
Juan de La Paz, in the middle of my country . . . by the river they call La
Ballena—because the river swells up sometimes like a fat green whale!
And we—all the people there work for Don Madera, picking his coffee for
him in the fields and— *(Remembers, smiles.)* My father says he can't pick his
own coffee 'cause his belly is so big, he—*(Sticks belly way out.)* Can't find
the basket! *(Laughs at his joke—then explains it.)* To put the coffee beans in,
pos . . . *(Embarrassed.)* Bueno, after you're done working, you could go to
the Plaza—where there's always people selling . . .

(From offstage, we hear the VENDORS *selling their wares, softly beckoning*
MIGUEL's *memory.)*

VENDOR #1 (ROSITA): *(Singsong.)* Pupusas!

VENDOR #2: Bananos!

VENDOR #3: Flores!

*(They enter and spread out their wares—which are glued to blankets and un-
furled, as memory is unfurled, in a swirl of color and movement.)*

VENDOR #4 (CECILIA): Tamales!

ROSITA: Aguacates!

VENDOR #3: Pinas!

ROSITA: Manzanas!

VENDOR #2: Aguas frescas!

*(*MIGUEL *takes a bunch of firecrackers from his pocket—a self-styled vendor.)*

MIGUEL: *(To the plaza.)* Firecrackers! Cohetes! Para La Fiesta de San Juan! The
Saints love firecrackers—that's how they know there's a fiesta. *(To the sky.)*
Saints—come down from the sky, and bring a fat juicy pig for Rosita! Que
vengan a la fiesta—todos los Santos gordos—all the fat saints!

ROSITA: Miguel!

MIGUEL: Come down before Rosita eats all the food in the village!

CECILIA: Ay, he's got a big mouth—

ROSITA: *(Eating a pupusa.)* Bocón!

MIGUEL: Come sing!

CECILIA: Not so loud, Bocón, or the Soldiers will hear you!

(But this makes him more rambunctious—and he sings a rhythmic child's song to which he's changed the words to mock the Soldiers.)

MIGUEL: *(Sings defiantly.)*

> Chanca barranca, hojitos de laurel,
> Soldiers of my village—soldados de papel!

CECILIA: Callate! Quiet!

MIGUEL: *(To audience; still giddy.)* The Soldiers didn't like us to shout or sing . . .

(KIKI enters and prepares for his ritual dance.)

(Serious now.) Or dance.

(The tone of the scene changes, as KIKI's as much a part of the spirit world as this one.)

But there was an old Indian, Kiki El Loco, who used to dance all the time at fiestas—right in the plaza! They say he was deaf—but he could hear music right through the ground—like a radio!

(KIKI begins to dance. It's part folk dance, part wizardry, part protest. The others watch in awe—and some fear.)

CECILIA: Mira ese Kiki El Loco—how many times have they told him, "Don't dance!"

MIGUEL: He's not afraid of nothing! Mira—the Dance of the Quetzal! The Bird of Freedom!

(Suddenly we hear the sound of THE BOOT.)

Los Soldados! The Soldiers!

(The VENDORS run off, frightened.)

ANA: *(Offstage. Calls.)* Miguel!

MIGUEL: *(Calls, without moving.)* Si, ahorita vengo Mama! Coming!

(We hear THE BOOT, closer.)

(Fierce whisper.) Kiki! Alli vienen los soldados, Kiki! The Soldiers!

(KIKI stomps into the ground, defying the soldiers. As he dances off, he gives MIGUEL a magnificent red and green feather. THE BOOT fades.)

(To audience; with wonder.) The feather of the Quetzal! The Bird of Freedom . . . Kiki—he danced the Soldiers away. He's not afraid of nothing! *(Sings, fearless.)* CHANCA BARRANCA HOJITOS DE LAUREL, SOLDADOS DE MI TIERRA, SOLDADOS GO TO—

ANA: *(Offstage.)* Miguel! Come in now. La Llorona's gonna get you!

MIGUEL: *(Terrified.)* La Llorona . . . !

SCENE 3

(ANA runs on and pulls MIGUEL to another part of the stage, and we are in their house. She lays their petates (mats) and blankets on the floor, then begins to wash MIGUEL in a basin, as he continues to the audience . . .)

MIGUEL: La Llorona! "The Weeping Woman." Everybody in the village says she's a witch. They say—

ANA: She killed her own children!

(ANA is killing MIGUEL's ears, scrubbing.)

MIGUEL: Verdad, Mama?

ANA: They say she drowned them in the river!

(She nearly drowns MIGUEL.)

MIGUEL: Ay, Mama, por favor!

ANA: And then—was she sorry! She was so sad, she's been going all over the world for hundreds of years crying— *(Bloodcurdling.)* "Ay, mis hiiiiijos!"

MIGUEL: *(Wails.)* "My children! My children!"

(ANA gets him under the blankets. The basin is turned over and covered with a cloth, becoming an altar.)

ANA: *(Scary.)* And if you're outside after dark, she'll think you're one of her children—and she'll grab you and take you down to the river, too!

(Her tone changes completely, and she's just a regular loving mom.)

(Sweetly.) Good night, Miguel.

(ANA lies down beside him and sighs, content. And then we hear, in the wind—)

LA LLORONA'S VOICE: *(Really bloodcurdling.)* Ay, mis hiiiiiijos!

(The altar shakes. MIGUEL jumps three feet in the air.)

MIGUEL: Mama! I saw her! La Llorona—right outside, alli! She was all dressed in black, and she was ten feet tall—and she was floating on the air, Mama! She had a face like death, como la Calavera— *(Makes a deathly face.)* Asi! And yellow teeth like a dog—and snakes for hair—and she put a magnet in me— *(Hand to his heart.)* Here! And she was pulling me. . . . Right down to the river. And she was crying, "Ay, mis hiiiijos!"

ANA: *(Calmly.)* Calmate, Miguel.

(She pulls him down beside her on the mat. Shakes her head and sighs, "What a nut." She crosses herself. They go to sleep. And then—)

LA LLORONA'S VOICE: Ay, mis hiiiiijos!

(The house, the mountains—the whole set shakes. ANA and MIGUEL sit straight up, crossing themselves madly.)

ANA: *(Trying to convince herself.)* It was just the wind, m'hijo, nada mas. Duermete con los angeles—sleep with the angels, si?

(She begins a lullabye.)

A la ru-ru, nino, a la ru-ru ya . . . duermese mi nino . . .

(LUIS enters.)

LUIS: *(Gravely.)* Ana—

> *(ANA goes to him.)*
> Kiki El Loco has disappeared.
>
> *(MIGUEL pops up.)*

MIGUEL: *(Straight out.)* Kiki? He disappeared? *(Cries.)* No!

SCENE 4

(A ROOSTER crows and it is dawn. MIGUEL comes downstage to the audience.)

MIGUEL: A lot of people were disappearing in my village.

(LUIS sharpens his machete. ANA rolls up the blankets and prepares tortillas, patting rhythmically.)

(To Luis.) But how do people disappear, Papa? Does the earth just open up and suck them in? Or—or maybe it's the duendes, the little green people that trick them into their caves—or one of those ships that come down from the sky!—or maybe it's the—

(LUIS puts a gentle hand over his son's mouth.)

LUIS: Soldiers.

MIGUEL: *(Softly.)* I know . . .

LUIS: Vamanos.

(ANA sprinkles holy water in the four corners of the house and exits. MIGUEL gets his machete and his guitar. He starts to go in the wrong direction. LUIS turns him around for the hundredth time.)

Norte, Miguel. North.

(They walk, circling the stage, to the fields.)

MIGUEL: But why are the Soldiers so angry with us, Papa? If the Soldiers are supposed to protect us, why is everybody afraid of them?

LUIS: It's a long story.

MIGUEL: *(To audience.)* A lot of my father's stories were long, but it was a long walk to the fields . . .

LUIS: When the earth was about your age, there was only one man. Adam.

MIGUEL: *(Cuts in.)* I know—the guy who ate the apple. And then he said, "This apple is so good I'm going to—"

LUIS: *(Hand over MIGUEL's mouth.)* "Sell it."

(A line of CAMPESINOS appear upstage, working the fields in a slow rhythmic movement across the stage. LUIS's story is punctuated by the sound of their machetes. downstage, LUIS and MIGUEL work too.)

Well, God didn't like Adam selling his apples, because they weren't Adam's apples.

MIGUEL: *(Cracks up.)* "Adam's apples—"

(LUIS *gives him a look.*)

LUIS: They were the earth's apples. And God was so angry he took his machete and chopped Adam in three—

(*He chops with his machete, illustrating.*)

MIGUEL: Como una manzana—

LUIS: Like an apple, si. And God said, "Adam—I'm going to take your head, Adam, and out of your head I'm going to make the Rich Man. Just a Big Head—and a pair of hands for grabbing. Then I'm going to take your arms and your back, Adam, and make the Poor Man. And the Poor Man will work the fields to put food in the Rich Man's mouth. (*Pause.*) A ver, que falta? What's left . . .

MIGUEL: The foot! Si! And—and God said, "Adam, I'm going to take your foot, and out of your foot I'll make . . ."

LUIS: "The Soldier. And the Soldier will kick the Poor Man to do the Rich Man's work forever!" (*Laughs.*) Y ya, m'hijo, that's the world. (*Beat.*) Pos, Adam forgot that he used to be one man, and all that's changed in thousands of years—is now the Soldier's got a BOOT! (*Laughing.*) And a dirty one, too! Y fea y cochina tambien!

MIGUEL: (*Frightened.*) Papa, not so loud, Papa—the Soldiers will hear you, they'll think you're laughing at them!

LUIS: (*Laughing.*) But I am—I am laughing at them! Big ugly boot y apestosa, smelly, tambien! (*Beat.*) But one day, m'hijo, the Poor Man's going to put down his machete . . . (*Raises his arms.*) and use his arms to tell the Boot, "NO MORE! Si?

MIGUEL: Si, Papa.

LUIS: No mas. Eso. Soon. A trabajar . . .

(MIGUEL *takes the feather from his pocket.*)

MIGUEL: (*Tentatively.*) Mira, Papa—

LUIS: The feather of the Quetzal—the Bird of Freedom! Vete—run, Miguel, show your Mama—tell her it's good luck!

MIGUEL: (*Starts to run.*) Si, Papa!

(LUIS *exits, singing, chopping with his machete.*)

LUIS: (*Sings.*) Brazos para trabajar . . . corazon para amar . . . semillas para plantar . . . esta voz para gritar . . .

(ANA, CECILIA, *and* ROSITA *appear washing clothes and sheets in the river. The sheets billow in the wind.* MIGUEL *rushes to* ANA.)

MIGUEL: Mira, Mama—

(*But the women are busy talking about . . .*)

CECILIA: (*Waving an envelope.*) Mira, Miguel, we got a letter from my daughter—

ANA: En Los Angeles!

ROSITA: The City of Angels! (*Incredulous.*) She's got two jobs! And she eats every day!

MIGUEL: Si, pos— *(Tries to show them the feather.)* mira—

ROSITA: She said all the kids there got BIG MOUTHS—just like you. Everybody in Los Angeles makes a lot of noise!

CECILIA: They got radios in their cars, and they ride around all day in their villages playing music—

ROSITA: LOUD—so the angels can hear them in the sky! And they got radios on their heads—and telephones right in their pockets!

MIGUEL: *(Cracks up; to audience.)* What a nut, eh? *(Tries to show ANA the feather.)* Mira—Papa said—

CECILIA: Ay, you could hear your Papa laughing all the way to the river. He better be careful—

ANA: He's a brave man, Cecilia.

CECILIA: Brave like Kiki El Loco. Y bocón, Ana, como you know who—

MIGUEL: Si! Mama, mira— *(To audience.)* But I never got to show her, porque . . .

(ANA hears something in the distance and turns upstage, frightened.)

My mother wasn't listening, porque . . . *(Pained; frightened.)* My mother—she can hear a baby cry in the next village—

(We hear THE BOOT, and LUIS is propelled onto the stage by the unseen SOLDIER. His hands are pulled behind him and tied.)

ANA: *(Running to LUIS.)* No! Dejele por el amor de dios! NO, YOU CAN'T TAKE HIM! NO!

(We hear THE BOOT. One of ANA's arms is lifted, then the other. Then both are pulled down behind her by the invisible SOLDIER. We should feel that a bird is being taken. The capture is the same as MIGUEL's in Scene 1.)

MIGUEL: *(To audience, with great difficulty.)* And the Soldiers took my mother for talking loud, too. And I wanted to scream at them, I wanted to yell—

(He tries to yell—but his voice flies away in terror. We hear his "NOOOO!" on tape, flying away, echoing, fading . . .)

(Mouths silently, wildly.) No! No!

ROSITA: *(To CECILIA.)* His voice, Mama—IT FLEW AWAY!

(She runs off scared. ANA and LUIS are taken off, THE BOOT sound dragging them. They recede upstage, facing the audience.)

ANA: Run, M'hijo, run! I love you . . . !

MIGUEL: *(Mouths voiceless.)* No!

(CECILIA grabs MIGUEL and thinks with lightning speed.)

CECILIA: *(Urgently.)* You have to run, Miguel—the Soldiers will be back! They'll make you join up with them, or they'll make you disappear—

(MIGUEL shakes his head wildly, "No!" CECILIA takes the envelope from her apron and stuffs it in his pocket.)

Here—take this. A hundred dollars my daughter sent me from Los Angeles. Al norte! Si! They don't got Soldiers there, they got—angels! That's where my daughter went, y tu tambien, that's where you'll go—

(He starts to run from her. She grabs him.)

(Frantic.) The Soldiers don't want us here, Miguel—we're not wanted in our own home! You tell the people in Los Angeles—we just want to work our land in peace! M'entiendes? Speak to me, Miguel—speak! *(Finally realizing.)* Ay, no, por dios! Your voice—the Soldiers scared it away!? *(Hugs him.)* It's hiding, m'hijo; it's frightened. You've got to find it. Don't let the Soldiers get your voice, Miguel! Don't let it disappear!

(She hugs him and runs off. MIGUEL *starts to run all around the stage, through the village. The* CHORUS *appears, as* VILLAGERS, *offering directions as he runs by. If they can unfurl a river or cause a mountain, all the better.)*

VILLAGER #1: There's a forest . . .

VILLAGER #2: Full of dangers—

VILLAGER #3: Then a Border of Lights—And the City of Angels!

VILLAGER #2: Tell the people there—

VILLAGER #1: *(Cries out.)* We got no more angels!

VILLAGER #2: *(Imploring.)* Tell our story!

ALL: Tell our story. . . . Tell our story. . . . Tell our story . . .

SCENE 5

*(*MIGUEL *runs and runs. When he stops, he's in a strange new world. The forest. All the characters here are masked. He looks around. Suddenly, he hears . . .)*

LA LLORONA'S VOICE: Ay, mis hiiiijos!

VOICES: *(Offstage.) (Frightened.)* La Llorona . . . La Llorona!

*(*MIGUEL *has no idea which direction to go in. He starts to go in one direction— and a refugee runs by, carrying her house on her back.)*

REFUGEE: Not that way—the Soldiers!

(He starts in another direction. A DUENDE *coyote runs on, a short green, fast talking trickster.)*

DUENDE: Oye, going North? Need a coyote?

*(*MIGUEL *nods.)*

(Spins him.) Iiiit's . . . that way! *(Spins him the other way.)* Not that way—that way! *(Spins him again.)* No, not *that* that way—THAT WAY!

(The DUENDE *runs off with his money.* MIGUEL's *still reeling. When he checks his money, it's gone. He tries to shout after the* DUENDE, *but has no voice for his rage.*

He tries calling his voice, summoning it with his guitar.

An old woman enters, making tortillas. We do not see her face. MIGUEL *goes to her. Suddenly she turns, rising to her full height—ten feet tall. It's . . .)*

LA LLORONA: *(Wails.)* Ay, mis hiiiijos! Correle!

(MIGUEL is too scared to move.)

VOICES: *(Offstage.)* La Llorona . . . La Llorona . . . !

LA LLORONA: Ay, mis hiiiijos! Run hoooome!

(MIGUEL looks back toward home. He can't go there!)

Ay, mis hiiiijos! CORRELEEE!

(MIGUEL gathers all his strength and shakes his head "no." La Llorona tears off her mask, incredulous. No one has ever refused to run from her. She's completely thrown. In fact, she sounds just like a regular woman.)

Oye, tonto, que te pasa a ti? What's the matter with you? Crazy kid—ay, ay, ay, ay, ay . . .

(MIGUEL can't believe his eyes and ears.)

What does it take to send you home?

(He starts to explain without words . . .)

You can't go home? *(Responding to his gestures.)* You'll DIE if you go home!? *(Responding to more gestures.)* The Soldiers took your parents!?

(She bursts into tears. They don't call her The Weeping Woman for nothing. There's an elaborate ritual to her crying—a beginning, a build, then an explosion, so that each time we hear it, we know exactly what's coming, and it's increasingly comical.)

(Sputtering through tears.) I try to scare you kids home, so you'll be safe from the Soldiers. *(Incredulous.)* Now you're too scared to go home—'cause there are Soldiers there too!?

(MIGUEL gestures, "Please stop crying.")

Que? You think it's easy going all over the world crying—*(Wails.)* Ay, mis hiiiijos! *(Beat; regular gal.)* Ay, it hurts. My throat's been killing me for a century. I'm up all night scaring children into their houses—I haven't had a good night's sleep in four hundred years! Not since the Conquistadores. Well, who else is gonna do it, eh? *(Waits.)* Oye, say something already or— *(This usually gets 'em.)* I'll drown you in the river!

(MIGUEL mimes "I've lost my voice!")

You've lost your voice?

(He gestures about the SOLDIERS.)

The Soldiers . . . scared it away?

(He nods "yes." She starts the build to tears—then stops abruptly, mid-wail.)

No. There's no time. *(Thinks out loud.)* You can't go home. . . . You've got to find your voice—*(Tentative.)* Pues, maybe I could help him . . .

(The thought terrifies her. After all, she's gone alone for hundreds of years.)

(Paces; to herself.) Ay, no . . . Pues, si . . . Pues, no . . . Pues, si . . . Pues—just till he finds his voice? Okay. *(Goes to him.)* Oyeme bien. The voices are trapped. Locked up in the Palace of the General. No one can get in. There's a gate of iron—high as the sky. And wild dogs with teeth as sharp as razors. But the most dangerous of all is the Voice Keeper. He will trick you and trick you—till you forget why you came. Pues—you must not listen to him!

(MIGUEL gestures, "Not me.")

Not you, good. Apurete, pues! And be careful! Show me you can't be tricked, and I'll lead you to the Border of Lights!

(MIGUEL starts to go in the wrong direction. She turns him around.)

Ay, por dios—Norte, North—alli!

(She runs off. MIGUEL starts to walk, calling his voice tentatively with his guitar. Two VIEJITAS with creaky voices, enter arguing.)

VIEJITA #1: Over that fence, mujer, under the volcano . . .

VIEJITA #2: No, mujer, in the General's Garden—that's where I've heard the voices . . .

VIEJITA #1: *(Noticing MIGUEL.)* Why is he playing that guitar for? Dangerous! Peligroso!

VIEJITA #2: He's calling his voice, mujer!

VIEJITA #1: Con la guitarra, mujer? Muy loco! *(To MIGUEL.)* You'll never get behind that gate—

VIEJITA #2: But if you do—

BOTH: Watch out for the dogs!

VIEJITA #1: Los perrrros, si!

(They go off laughing, howling like dogs.)

MIGUEL *arrives at the Palace. He bangs on the iron gate so hard he hurts his hand. The* VOICE KEEPER *appears with a metal box full of voices. And two huge guard dogs, one red, one blue.)*

VOICE KEEPER: *(Smooth as silk.)* Why all the noise, hermano? The General is sleeping. Sssshhh!

(MIGUEL bangs on the gate.)

No, no, hermano! You don't want your voice. They're nothing but trouble!

(MIGUEL keeps trying to get through.)

That's why we keep them locked up—*(Pats box.)* in here. The loud ones. The ones that talk too much. *(Bows.)* I'm the Voice Keeper. I keep things nice and quiet. For the General.

(He salutes in the direction of the Palace. MIGUEL bursts through the Palace Gate. The dogs growl. The VOICE KEEPER *tries to seduce MIGUEL with his words.)*

The voices lie, hermano. . . . They tell stories about the General. They get together, one voice starts in—and before you know it, every one of them has an opinion. There's a racket in the garden. The General can't sleep.

(MIGUEL *tries to get the box. The* VOICE KEEPER *sidesteps, doing flamenco.*)

Always complaining . . . crying "I'm hungry!" Whining, "It's not fair!" Well, that's not our fault. We didn't make the world!

(MIGUEL *manages to get the box open for a moment. A murmur of* VOICES *flies out. The* KEEPER *closes the lid.*)

(*In a rage.*) Infeliz! (*Quickly smiles.*) Oyeme, hermano, the voices are happy now . . . content. Listen for yourself—

(MIGUEL *listens. He hears silence.*)

No more shouting, no more tears. . . . A kinder, gentler garden.

(*He takes a shiny metal coin from his sash and starts to hypnotize* MIGUEL.)

You don't want your voice, hermano. You don't want to tell bad stories about the General's Soldiers. . . . Promise?

(*He is inadvertently hypnotizing the dogs, too.*)

The General loves you, hermanito! You're a good boy. . . . A quiet boy. . . . Good. Si?

(*He teaches* MIGUEL *a gesture—a "ssshhhh" and a thumbs up.* MIGUEL *repeats the gesture, like a dazed, smiling Moonie. The voice* KEEPER *waves and gestures, exiting. The good Moonie waves and gestures.*)

LA LLORONA *enters.* MIGUEL *repeats the gesture to her, smiling dumbly.*)

LA LLORONA: (*"Oh, for God's sake."*) Ay, mis hijos, que te pasa a ti? Ay, ay, ay, ay, ay . . . You give up your fight? For a pretty speech and a smile?

(MIGUEL *smiles and does the gesture.*)

And what will it be like when the whole world is silent? Will you miss the voice of your guitar? The song of the wind—the rain? The sound of your own voice telling the Soldier, "No! No mas"?

(MIGUEL *smiles and gestures, thumbs up, again.*)

No!?

(*She starts to cry. It builds and builds. But again, she catches herself mid-wail.*)

No. There's no time.

(*Her crying has broken the spell, but good.* MIGUEL *is* MIGUEL. *The dogs have awakened as well. Suddenly she hears something.*)

Listen!

(*He looks at her like she's nuts. She puts her hands to his ears, and we hear a murmur of* VOICES.)

In the wind . . . the voices are flying away! They're frightened. . . . They're hiding . . . *(Listens.)* At the edge of the earth? No— *(Listens again.)* The Edge of the Sea!

(We hear THE BOOT, *faintly.)*

The Soldiers! You've got to find your voice before the Soldiers do! Don't let them scare you!

(The dogs growl. She growls back, and they run off.)

Oye—show me you can be brave, and I'll lead you to the Border of Lights! Apurete—to the Edge of the Seaaaa!

(He starts to go in the wrong direction. She turns him around.)

Al Norte! North! Alli!

(She calls up the OCEAN, *and leaves. We hear* WAVES. MIGUEL *plays his guitar, calling his voice. Instead, he catches a song.)*

THE VOICE PICKER: *(Offstage.) (Singing.)* Nonatzin ih caucnimiquiz notle cuilpan xinechtoca . . .

(The VOICE PICKER *comes on, caught in, and dragging a large net filled with seaweed, driftwood, and shells. She speaks partly to* MIGUEL, *partly to herself, partly to her shells.)*

Sigue, play—I like the old songs . . . *(Laughs.)* Don't tell the Soldiers! *(Searching the stage.)* You heard any voices by here? *(Whispers.)* In the shells— that's where they like to hide. I got a sack full already, but the Soldiers won't be happy till I got 'em all. Greedy. And what do they pay me? Beans. *(Laughs crazily.)* Frijoles, si. Maybe a tortilla.

(MIGUEL follows her, curious.)

(To her net.) Ay, break the back of an old woman. *(Yells at* MIGUEL.) Pos, what else am I gonna do? Find another husband to bring home the frijoles? I had three husbands! *(Rustles her net.)* Dragged off to the wars, all of 'em! Now I got shells. *(Takes one from pocket.)* This one I'm keeping, eh? Listen . . .

(From the shell we hear the VOICE *of an amorous man. The shell lights up when it speaks.)*

VOICE IN SHELL: Ay, mi amor, chula, preciosa, I adore you my love, I want to . . .

VOICE PICKER: *(Puts shell back fast.)* Don't listen to that. You're too young.

(MIGUEL dives into the net of shells, looking for his voice.)

Oye—stop that! What are you doing? Muchacho feo, mocoso—

(MIGUEL mimes, "I'm looking for my voice!")

You're looking for your voice? Why didn't you say so? Maybe I'll help you . . . *(Beat; wary.)* Wait a minute—there's a war out there. Which side are you on—our side or their side?

(MIGUEL *doesn't know.*)

What do you mean, you don't know? Muchacho estupido, tonto . . . On our side, we look like us, and on their side, they look like them!

(*If she has a mask on the back of her head just like the one on the front, maybe in a different color, she can make her crazy point, if not clearer, crazier . . .*)

And even if they look like us—they dress like them, and they pray like them, and they dance like them, and they EAT like them, and we HATE them like them—BECAUSE THAT'S WAR!

(MIGUEL *mimes, "I'm like you! I'm like you!"*)

(*Laughs; arm around him.*) You're like me, eh? Good. Good boy . . . (*Under her breath.*) Y chulo, y precioso tambien . . . (*Holds out net.*) Okay. But don't tell the Soldiers—

(*In case there are Soldiers around, she pretends she's being robbed.*)

Ay, steal from an old woman, aaaah! (*Sotto; to* MIGUEL.) Just one, eh?

(*He picks up a shell—and out flies his voice.*)

MIGUEL'S VOICE: (on tape):
> Chanca barranca, hojitos de laurel,
> Soldados de mi tierra,
> Soldados go to—

VOICE PICKER: (*Laughs wildly.*) La voz de un loco, si? A crazy one!

(MIGUEL *holds the shell in the air, thrilled. He tips it and tries to pour the voice down his throat.*)

Ay, that's your voice? (*To herself.*) He's got a big mouth—

(*Suddenly we hear* THE BOOT.)

The Soldiers! Don't tell the Soldiers where you got it! (*Running off.*) Don't say a wooooord!

(*She's gone. We hear* THE BOOT—*and* MIGUEL *is so frightened, he throws the shell in the air. He dives for it as it falls—but he misses, and the shell shatters on the ground. He tries to catch his voice, but it's flying away, fading.* THE BOOT *retreats. Silence.*

MIGUEL *is alone.* NIGHT—*which could be an actor in black—turns the stage dark.* MIGUEL *cries, but hears no sound. He touches his cheeks . . . no tears. He takes the feather of the Quetzal from his pocket and throws it on the ground in despair. Then he plays a line of* ANA's *lullaby on his guitar to comfort himself.*

LA LLORONA *enters upstage, unseen by* MIGUEL. *She picks up the feather and tucks it in her rebozo.* MIGUEL *stops playing. It's too painful to remember his mother.*)

LA LLORONA: Don't stop. That's a pretty tune. I remember I used to sing it to my own children. After a story . . .

(He looks at her, amazed.)
What? Que? You think I can't tell a story?

(He shakes his head, "no.")
Pues, it's been a long time . . . three or four hundred years . . .

(She'd like to comfort him, but she's been scaring people so long, she's scared herself now to get close.)
Bueno. Eh . . . Once upon a time. . . . That's how they start, si?

(He shrugs and walks away.)
Well, anyway, once upon a time, there was a boy who lost his voice. And he went aaaall the way to the Gate of the General—and he was very stu— *(Catches herself.)* Very brave—but still he couldn't find it. So he went to the Edge of the Sea—and he found his voice! But the Soldiers came, and the boy was very scar—

(MIGUEL shakes his head, "no" on "scared.")

(Corrects herself.) Very brave. . . . But his voice got scared and flew away. And the boy was very sad, and he cried.

(MIGUEL is very insulted.)

(Exasperated.) All right, he almost cried. And it was a good thing he didn't because his voice wasn't lost—it was just trapped somewhere—caught like a bird, waiting for the boy to set it free.

(She gets up and starts to leave. He grabs her leg as if to say, "Wait—what then?")
Well, what do you think happened? He kept looking—porque—who can live without a voice in this world? Without a voice, you have no story. No one knows where you come from, why you're here. Without a voice, you disappear! Is that what you want?

(He shakes his head, "no.")
Okay, it's your story. You find your voice, and you tell me how it ends.

(MIGUEL gestures, "But where do I look?")
You must look where you're most scared to go. Even in your darkest dreams. *(Starts to leave again.)* Oye, show me you have the courage to dream . . . and I'll lead you to the Border of Lights!

(He lies down and tries to dream. But he can't sleep.)

(Throws up her hands.) Oh—now he wants a lullaby! Mira, I haven't sung in a couple of hundred years . . . *(Sighs.)* Okay.

(She clears her throat and starts to sing "La Llorona," the sad song men have sung about her for centuries.)

> *Dicen que no tengo duelo, Llorona,*
> *Porque no me ven llorar,*
> *Dicen que no tengo duelo, Llorona,*
> *Porque no me ven llorar—*

(In the wind, the VOICES *join in . . .)*

LA LLORONA and VOICES:
> *Hay muertos que no hacen ruido, Llorona,*
> *Y es mas grande su pena . . .*

(LA LLORONA tiptoes away.)

LA LLORONA: Go now, m'hijo, to your dreams . . .

(MIGUEL sleeps. ANA enters upstage in his dream.)

ANA:

(Sings.)
> *A la ru-ru, nino, a la ru-ru ya . . .*

(LUIS enters, puts down his machete, and joins ANA.)

LUIS and ANA:

(Singing.)
> *Duermese, mi nino . . .*

(A military CALAVERA comes up out of the earth, dancing to the lullaby. He's a skeleton in an army jacket and giant boots. He puts a hand over MIGUEL's parents' mouths to silence them. MIGUEL runs to stop him. La Calavera turns on MIGUEL with his machete.)

ANA: No! Dejelo por el amor de dios!

(MIGUEL grabs a branch and he and LA CALAVERA duel. LA CALAVERA is winning. Just as LA CALAVERA is about to strike a final blow—just as MIGUEL's parents are about to disappear—MIGUEL finds his voice! Pulls it up out of the depths of his own being and sets it free.)

MIGUEL: NO! NO, YOU CAN'T TAKE US! NO, YOU CAN'T STOP US! NO MAS!

(The fight resumes, and MIGUEL wins! LA CALAVERA goes back down under the earth. MIGUEL's parents raise their arms in slow motion in exultation. LA LLORONA runs on and shakes MIGUEL, and his parents recede, triumphant.)

LA LLORONA: Wake up now—despiertate, Miguel!

(He comes out of his dream, talking a mile a minute.)

MIGUEL: I did it! Yo gane! Tengo mi voz! My voice! *(Spins LA LLORONA.)* Chanca barranca hojitos de laurel! Vamanos—apurete—to the City of Angels. Got to tell the people there—we can stop the Soldiers! Got to tell our story loud—so the angels can hear it in the sky!

LA LLORONA: Ay, he's got a big mouth. Bocón, verdad?

MIGUEL: Bocón! Sí! Ay, what did they tell me? Which way? There's a forest—and then a Border. The Border of . . .

(He's shown her he has the courage to dream. With the wave of an arm, she shows him the Border of Lights. In fact, the entire downstage area fills with light.)

The Border of Lights! Ay, look at all those lights! Vamanos! Let's go!

(There is a pause.)

LA LLORONA: *(Sadly.)* I can't go with you, Miguel. I can't cross this border.

MIGUEL: Como que no? You can do anything!

LA LLORONA: They don't believe in me up there. *(Beat.)* The only way I can cross is in your heart. *(Practical.)* Besides, I got children to scare all over the continent—

MIGUEL: No lo creo, I don't think you want to scare children—

LA LLORONA: Pues, it's a lousy job, m'hijo, but somebody's got to do it—so they'll run in their houses and be safe from the Soldiers! En Guatemala y El Salvador . . . y ahora Chiapas, Mexico— *(Sighs; rattles off.)* Y Bosnia, y Ireland, y Rwanda . . .

MIGUEL: *(Takes a few steps away.)* Pos, I'm not going to cry—

LA LLORONA: Mira, do the clouds say, "I'm not going to rain?"

(For the first time in his journey, MIGUEL cries.)

MIGUEL: I don't want to go alone.

(She nods. Thinks.)

LA LLORONA: *(Thinks.)* Pues . . . listen . . . *(He listens hard. In the wind, he hears . . .)*

ANA'S VOICE: Miguel! Come in now, or La Llorona's gonna get you!

(MIGUEL and LA LLORONA smile.)

MIGUEL: Mama—

LA LLORONA: Remember . . .

(He listens again and hears . . .)

LUIS'S VOICE: But one day, m'hijo, the Poor Man will raise his arms and tell the Boot, "No mas!" "No more!"

MIGUEL: Papa!

LA LLORONA: Take them with you. Remember. Like I remember my own children. Porque, when we remember, we keep them alive . . . and free. Go now. Tell your story.

MIGUEL: Gracias.

LA LLORONA: No, m'hijo, gracias a ti—

MIGUEL: No, pos, a usted gracias—

LA LLORONA: No, no, gracias a ti—

MIGUEL: No, digo, a usted gra—

(She starts to cry—but catches herself.)

LA LLORONA: No. There's no time.

(She takes the feather of the Quetzal from her rebozo and hands it to MIGUEL.)
Correle, m'hijo. Fly!

(Slowly she recedes upstage, her feet never touching the ground. MIGUEL turns to the Border of Lights and gets it right this time.)

MIGUEL: NORTH!

(He raises his arms in exultation and, in slow motion, starts to cross the Border. We hear the sound of HELICOPTERS. His body goes from exultation to fear. He starts to run. The CHORUS runs on with their sticks, making the border, as in Scene 1.)

SCENE 6

(There is a light change to indicate that we are back in the courtroom where we began. If THE JUDGE appeared behind the scrim in Scene 1, he will reappear. We hear the sound of the gavel.)

MIGUEL: *(Still out of breath.)* And then—and then, señor—a man in a uniform caught me—and took me here.

THE JUDGE: *(Chuckles.)* Well. That's quite a story. I've got to hand it to you, son; you kids have some pretty wild imaginations. Things you kids come up with . . .

(MIGUEL touches the feather of the Quetzal, the rebozo LA LLORONA gave him—both quite real.)

MIGUEL: Señor—Judge, digo—are you going to send me back?

(A pause.)

THE JUDGE: *(Sighs.)* Son . . . thing is, we just don't have a whole lot of room. No room in the playgrounds, no room in the schools—

MIGUEL: But the Border of Lights—it's so bright, it—it puts a magnet in you— *(Touches his heart.)* Right here!

THE JUDGE: We're turning the lights down, son. Light's expensive—

MIGUEL: Wait! Just one question—one question, por favor—

THE JUDGE: *(Very patiently.)* Yes?

(We hear an echo of THE JUDGE's first questions to MIGUEL, "Where do you come from? Where are your parents? Where are you from?")

MIGUEL: Judge . . . *(Simply.)* Where are you from?

THE JUDGE: *(Chuckles; awkward.)* Well, uh . . . I'm from right here, son. And my parents are from right here, too. And their parents came when they were just children. *(Proud.)* Came from halfway across the world!

MIGUEL: *(Softly.)* Like me?

(Pause.)

THE JUDGE: *(Caught.)* Well ... uhm ... uh ...

MIGUEL: If you send me home, I'll just come back again. I'm not going to disappear.

THE JUDGE: I'm sorry, son.

(He bangs his gavel. We hear the echo of THE BOOT *sound that* MIGUEL *hears in his mind.)*

MIGUEL: NO!

*(*MIGUEL *stomps into the ground in protest—and up comes a strain of* KIKI'S MUSIC.)*

THE JUDGE: What did you say?

*(*MIGUEL *stomps again—*MORE MUSIC.)*

MIGUEL: Kiki—right through the ground like a radio!

*(*KIKI *appears behind the scrim, dancing.)*

THE JUDGE: *(Mutters.)* Kid's loco ...

(In front of the scrim, MIGUEL *does a few steps of* KIKI'S *dance.)*

MIGUEL: The music—you heard it didn't you?

THE JUDGE: Nope—

MIGUEL: It followed me! It flew across the border! You can't stop it, señor—it's right here—in my story! And my story's spreading! It's catching—*(Points to girl in audience.)* She's got it, señor, and she's got a BIG MOUTH! *(To girl.)* Una Bocóna, si? She's going to tell it on the buses, so it rides all over the city! Tell it loud so the ANGELS can hear it! And then—

(We hear THE WIND, *and in the wind ...)*

LA LLORONA'S VOICE: Ay, mis hiiiijos!

*(*LA LLORONA *laughs.)*

MIGUEL: My story's in the wind! *(Yearning.)* It's flying home, Mama! It's in the plaza and in the fields! It's in the Big Head of the Rich Man. It's in the arms of the Poor Man, Papa! And he's putting down his machete, and he's telling the Soldier, "No Mas!" "No More!" And he's singing ...

*(*MIGUEL *sings* LUIS'S *song, translating for the people in his new village.)*

> *Brazos para trabajar—*
> *(Spoken.)*
> *Arms to work, eh Papa?*
> *(Sung.)*
> *Corazon para amor—*
> *(Spoken.)*
> *And a heart to love ...*
> *(Sung.)*
> *Semillas para plantar—*
> *(Spoken.)*
> *Seeds to plant—*

> *(Sung.)*
> *Esta voz para gritar!*
> *(Spoken.)*
> *And a voice to cry out and sing—*

(The CHORUS *comes on and sings the entire song, upbeat now, with Miguel, ending with . . .)*

ALL:

> *(Singing.)*
> *Canta verso a verso,*
> *Y baila paso a paso,*
> *Oye, mi bocón—*
> *El canto volera!*

(The CHORUS *finishes with a rhythmic triumphant beating of their sticks. Then—)*

CHORUS: Fijate, imagine!

CURTAIN

THE CRANE WIFE

by
Barbara Carlisle

A Folktale from Japan

BARBARA CARLISLE, who received her B.A. from Ohio State University, her M.A. in comparative literature from Michigan State University and her Ph.D. in history of art from The University of Michigan, is a professor of Theatre Arts at Virginia Tech, Blacksburg, Virginia, where she teaches playwriting, serves as Director of the Women's Studies Program, and is on the faculty of the Graduate Arts Management Program. From 1985 to 1989, she was Associate Dean of the School of Fine Arts at Miami University, Oxford, Ohio, and concurrently, Literary Manager of Cincinnati Playhouse in The Park. From 1977 to 1982, Carlisle was the coordinator of arts programs in the Michigan Department of Education, heading the arts in Michigan schools.

She has taught art history and humanities courses and has studied art education in China. She has published articles on art history, the arts in education, and the art of children in China. In 1990, the W. K. Kellogg Foundation released her book, *The Making of a Grass Blade*, a longitudinal study of twelve arts organizations and their work in schools.

Carlisle worked in university, community, and regional theatres for many years. During that time she created two story theatre pieces for the Michigan Council for the Arts. She then directed professionally in regional theatre for fifteen years at such theatres as BoarsHead: Michigan Public Theatre. She has choreographed a number of pieces for ballet and modern dance companies as well as a long list of musical comedies.

In 1989, she directed the workshop production of her play *I Don't Want to Die in China*. It was subsequently a finalist in the New Play Competition of the Virginia Festival of New Works and was produced at the Gunston Arts Center in Arlington. During the last twenty years she has been working in the field of drama for young people, producing pieces and giving workshops for teachers. With Don Drapeau she wrote *Hi Concept-Lo Tech: theatre for everyone in any place*, published by Heineman in 1996.

Currently, her works in process include *Abigail*, a play about an elementary school principal, who believes in magic, and a series of plays for adults based on a character named "Louise." In 1991, her adaptation of *The Crane Wife* was produced at Virginia Tech and other universities before its publication in 1997.

When children and adults—their parents or friends—experience an imaginative transformation together, in the presence of each other, they share deep common understandings. Theatre that is satisfying to both adults and children has the possibility of revealing the fundamental humanity that binds us as a species. For this reason I choose to write for a multigenerational audience.

—BARBARA CARLISLE

This script owes its origins to reading the children's book, *The
Crane Wife*, as told by Sumiko Yagawa, and translated by
Katherine Paterson, Mulberry edition, 1987. Other useful
renditions of the story were found in *The Yanagita Kunio Guide
to the Japanese Folk Tale*, translated and edited by Fanny Hagin
Mayer, Indiana University Press, 1986, and *Folk Tales of Japan*,
edited by Keigo Seki, translated by Robert J. Adams, The
University of Chicago Press, 1963.

THE CRANE WIFE

CHARACTERS

Narrators
The Signer (American Sign Language)
Musician
Villager Chorus
Dancers
Kokuro
The Crane Wife
The Neighbor
The Samurai

THE SETTING

The stage is open and unencumbered. It may have platforms and needs a space where KOKURO's *hut can be identified. There needs to be a way for* THE CRANE WIFE *to appear to be hidden from* KOKURO *while she is weaving. In the original production the crane* DANCERS *created weaving dances in shadow behind a large white cloth which they hung on a Tori gate.*

As the audience enters: The MUSICIAN *is tuning up, the* DANCERS *are doing warm up exercises, the* VILLAGERS *are seated in* KOKURO's *hut;* THE NEIGHBOR *and* KOKURO *are seated. They may be chatting softly.*

The Crane Wife is an ancient Japanese folk tale. This retelling for the theatre is based on a reading of several versions of the story. It borrows Japanese theatre conventions, particularly a narration, a very presentational style, and the use of symbolic objects to signify necessary props, but is not intended to replicate a Japanese theatre experience.

There are many Japanese words in the script to give color to the performance. Assistance should be sought from a Japanese speaker to give these words their correct pronunciation although American speakers will inevitably have American accents. The meaning of the words is given within the context of the speeches.

The story is told by a narrator or a group of narrators who divide the narration among themselves, sometimes speaking single lines, sometimes speaking in unison, sometimes dividing up phrases or words for particular emphasis. This division should be determined for each production. The narration is omniscient, kindly, and understanding, existing in the present. The performers should create their own divisions of the text according to their own rhythms and emphases. A single narrator is also a valid choice.

The VILLAGER CHORUS acts as an intermediary for the audience and creates the antique world of the story, reacting as the villagers, and as spirits of the village, and occasionally taking other roles—the hunters and buyers of the cloth. The villagers in the original production carried masks which they wore to change themselves into hunters, and then carried as puppets, to suggest a multitude of villagers gossiping, or malicious village voices speaking in KOKURO's head. They, too, divided up the VILLAGER CHORUS lines among themselves as they created the performance. This script suggests five villagers, but any number could be used, and they could be mixed male and female, all male or all female.

The named characters—KOKURO, THE NEIGHBOR, THE SAMURAI, and THE CRANE WIFE—stick to their single roles. THE SAMURAI is not seen until he makes his entrance during the action. He is conceived as a full-blown Kabuki samurai, complete with swords, painted face and geta. His entrance is a surprise and however elaborately or simply he is created, he needs to be treated as powerful and frightening.

Properties should be very limited. No attempt should be made to disguise the materiality of any object. There might be a crock for bean curd, a kettle and a broom in KOKURO's hut, swords for THE SAMURAI. A set of poles or 4-foot dowels carried by the villagers and passed around as needed, become bows, arrows, wood to make the loom, and loom elements in the weaving dances. Simple ribbons of red cloth can represent the blood of the wounded crane, both in the beginning and at the closing revelation.

Dancers, dressed in white, do not speak. They become the snow, the crane flock, and the weaving. They also manipulate the great snow crane, who in the original production was acted by a large-scale puppet. The crane could be a folded paper crane as well. The play has also been done with only an imagined crane. If there is a puppet, there should be no attempt to hide the fact that the puppet is just that. Her manipulators are crane dancers, fully in view. One production used four dancers, another five. A single dancer would work as well.

THE CRANE WIFE is one of the puppet's manipulators, and she is not disguised as anything else when she returns to become KOKURO's wife. She is distinguished, however, from the other puppet dancers and manipulators by her traditional kimono.

THE SIGNER, using American Sign Language, was part of the original company. She entered with the narrators, and began independently, but eventually interacted with the VILLAGER CHORUS and the characters as part of the action, returning to her platform at the close of the play.

All these performers—villagers and narrators—may play percussion instruments—bells, wood blocks, bamboo sticks, ratchets, and drums, to underscore the action. In another production a single percussionist accompanied the action in performance and recorded music accented many moments. In the original production two of the villagers played flute accompaniment. The musical score in this script is written for koto and flute and can be produced with a synthesizer or played on original instruments. The music accompanied the movements of each character. The musician may be a member of the VILLAGER CHORUS. Music is a valuable element of the script.

THE PROCESSION AND PREPARATION

(The NARRATORS *and* THE SIGNER *enter in street clothes and cross to the stage. The villagers and* DANCERS *bring them their kimonos or some form of dress that signals that they are becoming part of the company. The company then moves to preset all of the props. Once the stage is set the company bow to each other and take their places. The* VILLAGER CHORUS *and the* NARRATORS *are always on stage in view of the audience, though each has a neutral place to which they can return when they are not the focus of the action or narration. Other characters may wait in view of the audience for their entrances, or they may be offstage. The important thing is to treat the whole event as theatrical and not illusionistic. These people are making a story for the audience and the audience must participate in imagining the events, the scenery, and the characters.)*

PROLOGUE

NARRATORS: *(Drums or percussion sound.) Mukashi mukashi,* once upon a time, *aru tokoro ni,* there was a place. In the shadow of Myoko mountains in the province of Echigo, the snow falls for nine months.

(The DANCERS *in white dance the snow to music of the flute, and unfold a large white cloth on to the ground.)*
It covers the thatched *kayabuki* and fills the village streets.

VILLAGER CHORUS: *(Interacting among themselves.)*
1. Dig, good neighbor, dig, and make a tunnel.
2. Come to my house. We will smoke a pipe.
3. They will only tell each other tall tales.
4. And fill the house with smoke.
1. The snow has covered the treetops
2. The mountain spirits whistle in the wind.
5. The great bear will come out of her house.

NARRATORS: When the snow comes the young women, *musume,* go into the weaving room to weave the beautiful Echigo cloth. Alone behind the screen, sitting straight at the loom, the women weave ramie into long strips of soft white crepe.

(During the next speeches DANCERS *lift and move the white snow cloth, and others make movements of sitting on their knees and weaving.)*
VILLAGER CHORUS:
1. Weave well, my dear.
2. Breathe deeply. In and out.
3. Keep it even, young one.
4. The crepe buyers will pay a high price.
5. Echigo cloth is famous.

NARRATORS: In March, when the snow is still deep and white upon the ground, the long strips are laid out and bleached in the snow and sun.

(The villagers hang the snow cloth on a frame where it will be a backdrop and a screen for the shadow weaving dances. The DANCERS *exit.)*

NARRATORS: *Mukashi, mukashi, aru tokoro ni.* A long time ago the cranes lived each summer with the farmers of Echigo.

(The DANCERS reappear as the graceful shapes of the cranes, as the musician plays the crane theme on a bamboo flute.)

VILLAGER 1: We fished together in the waters of the Uono River.

VILLAGER 2: And the cranes kept the mice from the rice bin.

NARRATORS: But when the sun hides behind Komagatake mountain, and heavy snow falls from the burdened sky, the white, long-necked cranes rise from the icy stream and fly to their nests in the grassy meadows by the sea.

(The crane DANCERS dance out of sight.)

VILLAGERS:
1. Fly, *tsuru*, fly.
2. Go to the ocean marshes.
3. Come back to Echigo.
4. Summer will come.
5. The snow will pass again.
All: Fly, beautiful cranes.

NARRATORS: The great snow crane leads her flock up out of the valley.

(The crane DANCERS raise the crane puppet and animate it throughout the narration and music that follows. They circle the stage and fly off up the aisle and out.)

One by one and two by two they fly, casting shadows on the frozen earth. They swoop to catch an unsuspecting field mouse, and circle away, thin legs stretched long under their sleek bodies, suspended on the wind, wide wings carrying them to the ocean shore.

MARCH OF THE HUNTERS

NARRATION: When the cranes fly out of their houses, come the hunters.

(Drum sounds. The villagers enact the hunters with masks and sticks as bows.)

VILLAGER CHORUS:
1. Food must be gathered.
2. The winter is long.
3. We need new feathers for the comforter.

NARRATORS: Strong arms lift the heavy bows and draw arrows from the quiver. The hunters take aim.

VILLAGERS: Flash.

NARRATOR: The bow string snaps.

VILLAGERS: Zing.

NARRATORS: The arrow flies. Swift and sharp, seeking its mark, it crosses the sky. Arrow and crane, crane and arrow.

(The "arrow" is carried out of the theatre in the direction of the crane by one of the villager hunters. The crane music theme is heard briefly as the hunters return to their spot on the stage and put down their "bows.")

THE STORY

NARRATORS: *Mukashi mukashi. Aru tokoro ni.* A poor young peasant named Kokuro lived alone in his little kayabuki hut at the foot of the mountain.

(KOKURO enters. There is a tune played for him, which becomes his theme.)
One day, when the hunters had gone home, he went to the woods to gather twigs to keep his tiny fire alive. He walked and walked, until his bundle was full upon his back. It was cold and nearly dark when he set out for home. The snow, *yuki,* had begun to fall.

(The crane enters, wounded.)

VILLAGER CHORUS: Bata bata, bata bata, bata bata. *(Making percussion sounds to imitate the beating of wings.)*

NARRATORS: Behind him, Kokuro heard a rustling sound.

VILLAGER CHORUS: Bata bata, bata bata, bata bata.

NARRATORS: And suddenly a crane swooped down and landed on the path.

VILLAGER CHORUS: *I tai. I tai. I tai. (A cry of pain.)*

(The crane lands. THE CRANE WIFE *is manipulating the head as it sinks in pain to the ground. She carries the "arrow" pole with a ribbon of red attached to it.* KOKURO *comes to the fallen bird as the narration continues.)*

KOKURO: Oh, my beautiful friend. The arrow has pierced your wing. How you must suffer. Surely you will freeze to death if the snow continues to fall.

NARRATORS: Kokuro put down his bundle of sticks and went to the milky white bird.

KOKURO: Quiet, my beautiful creature. Softly, softly. There, it is free. The terrible arrow is gone. *(Taking the pole from* THE CRANE WIFE.*)* Here, let me seal the wound with this pure fresh snow. Lie down, lovely bird.

NARRATORS: He cradled the crane's beautiful body in his arms until he felt the heart beat strong again, and the proud head rise up. He watched the crane stand upon its long legs and stretch its wings. It lifted its huge silvery body and flew off into the night circling once over his head.

(The healed crane rises and flies away.)
Kokuro gathered up his pack and walked back to his cold, gray hut.

KOKURO: *(Singing.)*   *The snow falls again*
                          The night is dark
                          The path is long
                          A tiny fire will warm my heart.

KOKURO: Fly, *tsuru,* fly.
         Fly, *tsuru,* fly.

NARRATORS: The stars and moon were hidden by great black clouds. The wind whistled down the mountain. Snow fell thickly in the woods.

(KOKURO enters the area that will be his hut.)

KOKURO: *(He blows on "coals" and adds sticks to his "fire.")* Come, little flame. Burn brightly, my friend. The blanket is thin, and it will be a long cold night. *(KOKURO wraps himself in his blanket and lies down to go to sleep.)*

(The crane DANCERS enter in black kimonos, shrouding THE CRANE WIFE. They bring her down the aisle, deposit her at the hut and circle off behind the screen.)

NARRATORS: It was the middle of the night. . . . Suddenly!

(The VILLAGER CHORUS makes three sharp knocks on the wood block.)
A knock came at the door.

KOKURO: What is this? Who can be knocking at this time of night?

(Three knocks.)

NARRATORS: Kokuro hid in a corner of the hut.

KOKURO: Who can be coming for me? What have I done?

CRANE WIFE: Kokuro. Please. Come answer my knock.

VILLAGER CHORUS: *(Three knocks.)*

NARRATION: The voice was beautiful. The voice was elegant. The voice called again.

THE CRANE WIFE: Kokuro, I beg you, come answer my knock.

VILLAGER CHORUS: *(Three knocks.)*

NARRATION: Kokuro went to the door. When he slid it open to look out, there before him stood a beautiful woman with gleaming, golden skin and glistening, black hair, sparkling with crystal flakes of snow.

THE CRANE WIFE: Kokuro. Kind, gentle man. Please. Let me in. It is cold and dark and the snow will soon cover my head.

NARRATION: Kokuro was struck dumb. The woman spoke again.

THE CRANE WIFE: Kokuro, please. Let me enter the hut. I wish to stay with you. I wish you to allow me to become your wife.

NARRATION: Kokuro could not believe his ears. He could not move. He could not speak.

THE CRANE WIFE: I am sorry to disturb you. Please. If you wish, I will go away. I shall only ask you once again. Will you let me become your wife?

(She steps back, and KOKURO runs after her, bowing low, but trying to keep her from leaving.)

NARRATION: At last Kokuro found his voice.

KOKURO: Please. Come into my sad little hut. It is empty and poor, but dear beautiful lady, if you truly wish it, I am honored to receive you as my bride.

NARRATION: Bowing low, Kokuro took her hand and led her, step by step, inside his dark and dingy hut.

KOKURO: I have only this tiny fire and a thin blanket. You are very fine and beautiful . . .

THE CRANE WIFE: I have enough to be happy. Please, let us go to sleep.

NARRATORS: Very soon the village was full of gossip.

(Lights come back to full.)

The First Gossip Gavotte

VILLAGER CHORUS: (*Chattering among themselves. The masks become puppets to accompany the villagers. The final line is punctuated by all looking at* KOKURO *in an accusing and suspicious pose.*)
1. Have you seen that boy, Kokuro?
2. Young Kokuro has a wife.
3. The *ujigami* have smiled on him.
1. That young man has a fine wife.
2. Have you ever seen such a handsome bride?
4. Where did Kokuro find such a wife?
5. Kokuro has a better wife than he deserves.

NARRATION: Indeed Kokuro had a fine wife.

(*During this narration* THE CRANE WIFE *fixes up the hut by hanging cloth screens and sweeping.*)
She swept the mud from the *tatami* mats. She cleaned the crocks and scoured the kettle. She mended the paper *shoji* with beeswax. She patched the straw and put pitch between the logs to keep out the wind.

KOKURO: (*Praying before the hearth.*) *Ujigami*, protectors of my little house. You have given me a great gift. I do not deserve it. I offer this little rice cake. It is all I have. I know I have not thanked you properly since I was a boy. Please, spirits, accept my gratitude. Do not mock me with this honor and take it from me as strangely as it came.

THE CRANE WIFE: You are simple and kind, dear husband. You are humble, and generous. I am honored to be at your side.

NARRATORS: But it was not an easy time. Kokuro was the poorest of the poor among the peasants.

VILLAGER CHORUS: (*Mockingly.*)
1. Winter is here, foolish Kokuro.
2. It is cold.
3. There is no work for you.
4. What will you feed your pretty bride?
5. Two mouths to feed instead of one. How will you manage that?

NARRATION: Each day when Kokuro looked at what he had stored away, he was poorer than the day before. His heart was heavy. Each day his wife saw his face grow darker and darker. Finally she said to him.

THE CRANE WIFE: *Anata*, dear husband. I see that you are troubled.

KOKURO: I am ashamed. I cannot care for you. The bean curd is gone. We have eaten the carrots. The rice is gone. The hunters have taken all the animals from the woods.

THE CRANE WIFE: *Anata*, dear husband. You must share your worries with me. You must not be too proud to accept my help.

KOKURO: *Omae*, dear wife. I confess. I cannot find a way. I am grateful for your offer, but what can you do?

THE CRANE WIFE: I see the village women weaving the Echigo cloth to sell in the market. Please, dear husband, if you will build me a loom from the wood you find in the forest, perhaps you will permit me to weave for you. I am not of this village, but I can weave one time for you if you will allow it.

KOKURO: Dear Wife. It is true. The village women are weaving. If you like, I will build you a loom such as my mother used when she was a girl.

NARRATION: (KOKURO *gathers the sticks from the villagers and returns to the hut with them.*) So Kokuro gathered the wood from the forest at the top of the mountain, and with his mallet and chisel he built a loom, just as his wife had asked him to do. When it was finished, he gave it to her.

THE CRANE WIFE: And now dear husband, you must put the loom behind the *shoji* at the back of the hut. There I will weave, and you must promise never to look at me behind the screen while I work.

(KOKURO *takes the sticks behind the screen where he hands them to the* DANCERS *who will use them to create a "loom" and weaving movements.*)

KOKURO: I will do as you say, my wife, but why must you hide behind the screen?

THE CRANE WIFE: Please, I beg you. That is my request. You must never look upon me while I am weaving.

NARRATION: And so Kokuro's wife prepared herself with bathing and offerings, and went to work.

(THE CRANE WIFE *exits behind the screen.*)

The First Dance of the Weaving

(*Lights dim. A light comes up upstage. We see* THE CRANE WIFE *in silhouette with* DANCERS *who "weave" in shadow using the sticks in the dance as abstractions of the loom. This is not so much literal imitation of weaving as capturing the rhythm and flow of weaving in the dance as the chorus recites.*)

VILLAGER CHORUS: (*Reciting in rhythm and using percussion beats.*)
> Kattan Coton Kattan Coton
> Over and under, the shuttle is passed.
> Over and under the fragile thread,
> Over and under the cloth is made.
> Over and under the weaver works.

> Kattan Coton Kattan Coton
> Days and nights the weaver works,
> Days and nights she doesn't sleep.
> Over and under the shuttle goes,
> Days and nights she doesn't eat.

> Kattan Coton Kattan Coton
> Three days, three nights she works alone.
> Three days, three nights the shuttle goes.
> Over and under the cloth is made.
> She weaves and works and then is done.

(*The shadows dance with the cloth, then lights go down on them and return to full on stage.*)

KOKURO: How lonely it is when she is gone. What does she do that I cannot see? But she asked me to wait, and I shall wait.

NARRATION: On the fourth day his wife appeared.

KOKURO: My wife. My beautiful wife. How pale you look. Your skin is clear as glass.

THE CRANE WIFE: Here, dear husband. I have made you a cloth.

KOKURO: You have worked too long behind the screen. You have become ill. I swear, I shall never ask you to weave again.

THE CRANE WIFE: The cloth is yours. Please, take it to the market.

KOKURO: It is beautiful, my dear wife. It is finer than anyone has ever seen.

THE CRANE WIFE: Take it to market, and our troubles may be ended.

NARRATORS: On the next day he took the cloth, folded it carefully in the sleeve of his ragged kimono, and set out for the market in the town.

(VILLAGERS *and* NARRATORS *travel, playing tunes and making noises of the market.*)

Along the road the dogs barked. The oxen pulled carts piled with baskets of turnips and pigs tied up for the slaughter. The roadway filled with chatter. Kokuro could not resist showing his neighbors the cloth his wife had made.

A Second Gossip Gavotte

VILLAGER CHORUS: *Hiso, Hiso.* ("gossip gossip" *They pull at the cloth and stretch it out as they talk. The cloth is a long strip, about 18" wide and 8–10′ long. It should seem pure and white and light weight*)

1. That cloth is very rare.
2. It is white without bleaching.
3. It is soft as the first snow.
1. How can this be?
2. Where did she learn to make such stuff?
4. What a lucky man with a wife like that.
5. I would not want such luck. She has the help of the *bakemono.* (*Bakemono*—evil spirit.)
1. Luck like that comes at a great price.
2. After good fortune comes only bad.
4. The cloth is too fine for Kokuro.
5. He doesn't deserve a piece of cloth like that.

NARRATION: At the market the bidding was very good. The *choja* hunters came from their houses with their wives. Each one wanted the cloth for himself.

VILLAGER CHORUS: *(As buyers.)*
1. I say ten *ryo.*
2. I shall make it twenty.
3. I'll take the whole piece for thirty-five.
4. I shall have it for myself.
5. I say fifty *ryo* and I'll not pay a *sen* more.
2. Fifty *ryo.* I cannot match it.
3. Nor I.
4. Nor I.
5. Fifty *ryo.*

(KOKURO *gives the cloth to a villager and receives a bag of coins.*)

NARRATION: And so the cloth was sold. Kokuro returned to the hut filled with joy.

KOKURO: *(Singing.)*

> *Money, silver, money, gold,*
> *Kokuro is a rich man.*
> *Kokuro is a fine man.*
> *Money, silver, money, gold,*
> *What a blessing for Kokuro.*

(In the hut.) Look at this. We shall have the finest food and the warmest fire for days and days. Blessings on the *ujigami* for this good fortune.

THE CRANE WIFE: I am glad to see your brow is free of care.

KOKURO: You are a fine wife. And you make me into a fine husband. Fifty ryo. I have never seen such a fortune.

THE CRANE WIFE: If we are wise, it will serve us well.

KOKURO: If we are wise, indeed. We shall manage it.

THE CRANE WIFE: You are a kind and humble man, dear husband.

NARRATION: *Nigatsu.* February passed. And then *sangatsu.* March. And still the snow fell.

VILLAGER CHORUS:

1. The Echigo winter is cold.
2. The Echigo winter is long.
4. Fifty ryo will not last forever.
5. Do not be too proud, young Kokuro.
3. Do you make your offerings on the *kamidana*?
4. Did you pay the *nengumai*?
1. Two mouths to feed.
2. What will you do when your coins are gone?

NARRATION: The crock of bean curd was nearly empty. But Kokuro said nothing. He did not wish to trouble his gentle wife. He looked at the sky for the spring rains that would bring the garlic shoots up through the earth. But the *harusame* did not come. Still Kokuro said nothing. Each day he went to the village to buy some rice and a piece of dried fish.

(KOKURO goes to a market created by the villagers.)
One by one the fifty ryo slipped away. But still, Kokuro could not speak. Finally his wife said to him:

THE CRANE WIFE: Dear husband. I see that you are troubled.

KOKURO: I do not wish to speak of it.

THE CRANE WIFE: Are you not my husband? Do I not share your sorrows as well as your joys?

KOKURO: Yes, my wife. It is true.

THE CRANE WIFE: Then speak to me, dear husband. What makes your face so dark?

KOKURO: The winter will not end. The rains do not come. The *tofu* is gone.

THE CRANE WIFE: I see, dear husband. And the money for the cloth. That is gone as well?

KOKURO: Yes. It is true. I have nothing left. I cannot buy even a tiny bowl of *miso* to make the soup. What will we do?

THE CRANE WIFE: It is possible for me to weave one more time.

KOKURO: I dared not ask you. It mades you so pale. I cannot bear to make you ill.

THE CRANE WIFE: Bring the loom. I will weave again. But please, I beg you, this must be the last.

KOKURO: Dear wife, I am grateful. I will bring you the loom. This will be the last. I will not ask you again.

NARRATION: Kokuro brought the loom pieces into the hut. His wife scoured away the dirt and snow.

(KOKURO *brings the sticks from behind the screen.* THE CRANE WIFE *brushes them with a broom.*)

THE CRANE WIFE: I will set up the loom behind the *shoji*. Take the pieces there. I will prepare myself to weave. And now, I beg you, please, never to look at me while I am weaving.

KOKURO: Yes, my wife. I know. I do not understand, but I shall do as you say.

NARRATION: Once again, Kokuro sat down to wait as his wife disappeared from sight.

(THE CRANE WIFE *goes behind the screen. Lights as before. We see the shadow dance.*)

THE SECOND WEAVING DANCE

(New movements echoing the previous ones.)

VILLAGER CHORUS: *Kattan Coton Kattan Coton (With rhythm instruments as before.)*

VILLAGER CHORUS: *(Rhythm sounds continue "kattan coton" beat.)*
              Days and nights the sound of breath,
              Days and nights no food or sleep,
              Over and under the shuttle glides.
              Days and nights the weaving goes.

(Soft rhythm sounds only as the dance continues under the narration.)

NARRATION: Kokuro waited. One day.

VILLAGER CHORUS: *Ichi Nichi*

NARRATION: Two days.

VILLAGER CHORUS: *Futsuka*

NARRATION: Three days.

VILLAGER CHORUS: *Mikka*

NARRATION: Four days.

VILLAGER CHORUS: *Yokka*

NARRATION: Five days.

VILLAGER CHORUS: *(Gossip that is directed at* KOKURO, *as if buzzing in his mind.)*
1. Simple man.
2. What does he think?

3. She weaves for him.
4. What is she doing?
1. Who is this woman?
2. What thread does she use?
5. There is a *bakemono* in the village.
4. Who is it weaving behind the screen?

NARRATION: On the fifth day Kokuro's wife came out from behind the screen. In her hands was the most beautiful piece of cloth he had ever imagined.

VILLAGER CHORUS: *(Villagers pull the cloth from* KOKURO *and watch it float.)*
1. What is this cloth?
2. It is lighter than silk.
4. This is not the village cloth.
3. It is made of air.
5. It is made of the wind. Who has made this cloth?
4. There is a *bakemono* in the loom!

(VILLAGERS *quickly toss cloth back to* KOKURO *who folds it over as he looks at it.)*

NARRATION: The cloth seemed to breathe with a life of its own. Kokuro stood and gazed at it in amazement.

KOKURO: It is magnificent, my wife. There is nothing like it in the world. I shall take it to market today.

THE CRANE WIFE: It is yours, dear husband.

NARRATION: The thin voice surprised him. She was even paler than before. Her cheek bones pressed through her skin, she had dropped to her knees, her chin fallen to her chest, and her hands dropping limply to rest at her sides.

KOKURO: Dear wife, you are tired. But the cloth. The cloth shimmers and glows.

THE CRANE WIFE: I'm glad you are pleased.

KOKURO: Rest yourself, and I shall go to market. I shall sell the wonderful cloth. Thank you, my wife. Now rest. Thank you.

NARRATION: Kokuro quickly wrapped the cloth, tying the four corners of the *furoshiki,* and set off for town. Once again he could not resist showing the cloth to his neighbors.

THE GOSSIP MARCH TO THE TOWN

(Travelling with music and sounds.)

VILLAGER CHORUS: *Hiso, hiso.*
1. That cloth is very rare.
2. Much too rare.
3. What a lucky man with a wife like that.
4. I would not want such luck. That wife is a *kappa* from the swamp.
5. She is an *obake* in disguise. Beware such good fortune.
4. After good fortune comes only bad.
All: Beware, Kokuro.

NARRATION: Kokuro hurried on to the market. The hunters came out of their houses. The wives came out with the hunters. A merchant had come from across the mountain. Everyone wanted the cloth of Kokuro.

(VILLAGER CHORUS portray the buyers.)

VILLAGER CHORUS: *(As buyers.)*

1. Thirty ryo, I say.
2. I shall make it forty.
3. The last piece sold for fifty, and it was not so fine as this.
4. One hundred ryo. I shall have it for myself.
5. *(The merchant from across the mountains.)* I say one hundred fifty ryo, and I'll not pay a sen more.

VILLAGER CHORUS:

4. One hundred fifty ryo.
1. I cannot match it.
2. Nor I.
3. Nor I.
5. There it is. One hundred fifty ryo.

(Once again, the cloth is exchanged for a bag of coins.)

NARRATION: Kokuro soon had a heavy bag of coins for the long walk home. But it was a burden he was happy to carry.

(KOKURO does a little song and dance of joy as his theme music plays.)

NARRATION:

> Money silver, money gold,
> Kokuro is a rich man.
> Kokuro is a fine man.
> Money silver, money gold.
> Who has seen such a fine man.

KOKURO: One hundred fifty ryo . . . and spring will soon be coming. I can buy an ox, and three chickens, and seed for the corn, perhaps a tiny piece of land. *(KOKURO returns to the hut.)*

KOKURO: Look, dear wife. We are rich. I will buy rice from the farmers, and chickens, and salt and beet sugar. We will plant a little corn, and we will live better than ever before.

THE CRANE WIFE: Yes, my good husband.

KOKURO: When summer comes, we will put up food for the next winter.

THE CRANE WIFE: Yes, my good husband.

KOKURO: Our worries have surely come to an end.

NARRATION: But it was not to be so easy. News of the beautiful cloth spread quickly. Every wagging tongue in the town had something to add to its fame.

A GOSSIP RONDO

VILLAGER CHORUS:

1. They tell me the cloth is magic.
2. I have heard the mountain *yamauba* made the cloth.
3. If you touch the cloth to your daughter's nose, she will surely marry a rich man.
4. I am told if you wrap yourself in the cloth, it will make you young again.

5. Make your wife a kimono of that cloth, and she will bear only healthy sons.

NARRATION: And so it went, from hunter to hunter, from town to town, each gossip forging a tale more fantastic than the last. It travelled on the wind until news of the cloth covered the mountains of Echigo like a blanket of new fallen snow. In the tiny mountain village Kokuro's neighbor came over the snow to see him. The neighbor had heard of Kokuro's good fortune, and he longed to share in it.

(*Enter* THE NEIGHBOR.)

THE NEIGHBOR: *Kokuro-don*, my neighbor. Good friend. I see you've bought an ox and some chickens. And now, you have your land. Tell me, how has such a lad as you been able to do all of that with just a little weaving of cloth?

NARRATION: Kokuro was an innocent fellow. He answered his neighbor with the truth of the matter.

KOKURO: You see, my neighbor, my good wife has woven the cloth, and when I took it to town, the hunters paid a fine price for it. One hundred fifty ryo. Can you imagine?

THE NEIGHBOR: Now, that is quite a story, *Kokuro-don*, my friend, my neighbor. The ramie cloth of my wife has never brought such a price. What thread is it that your wife uses?

NARRATION: Still the honest man, Kokuro explained.

KOKURO: I have no answer to that question, you see, because my wife will not let me watch her while she is weaving.

THE NEIGHBOR: You cannot watch her? You believe that old wives' tale? You think there are demons in the weaving room?

KOKURO: It is her wish that I not watch her. I do not know why.

NARRATION: The neighbor saw that simple Kokuro was not the man to manage such a piece of good fortune.

THE NEIGHBOR: *Kokuro-don*, my friend, my neighbor. If your wife can make such remarkable cloth, then it should not be wasted on the hunters. The hunters indeed. What do they know of fine things? Why you should take it to the capitol, to the palace. It is cloth for a shogun or a nobleman at least. You must tell your wife to weave a new supply.

KOKURO: Oh, no. I cannot do that. My wife has said that she cannot weave again. I dare not ask.

THE NEIGHBOR: *Kokuro-don*, my neighbor, my friend. Are you not master in your own house? Do you let your wife tell you what to do? Order her to make more cloth, and we shall take it to market.

KOKURO: Oh. I could not do that. I do not know the way to the palace. I have never travelled beyond the town.

THE NEIGHBOR: *Kokuro-don*, my neighbor, my friend. That is what I can do for you. I know the way. I will take it for you. You tell your wife to weave the cloth. I will find a rich buyer in the castle town and sell it for ten, no twenty, no one hundred times what the hunters will pay. Just think of it, my friend. Money for the rest of your life. No more work. The profit will be so great we will each take half and be rich as noblemen. We will sit back and watch while others chop the wood.

NARRATION: That was an idea that pleased the simple peasant.

THE GREED DANCE (*JINGLING BELLS.*)

VILLAGER CHORUS: (*Chanting and taunting.*)
> *Money, gold, okane, kin.*
> *A fine house. Servants.*
> *Money. Gin.*
> *Sit and sit the whole day long.*
> *Gold. Money. Money. Gold.*
> *Kokuro, the rich man*
> *Kokuro, the landowner.*
> *Silver. Money. Money. Gold.*
> *Why not you,*
> *Kokuro?*

NARRATION: What an idea. Kokuro could not say no, and off went the neighbor to find his wealthy buyer.

(*They bow to each other, and* THE NEIGHBOR *exits through the theatre.*)
But what should he tell his wife? The poor peasant was frightened. What if she could not weave again? He went to the forest to gather wood for the fire. When he returned to the hut, his head was full of confusion.

THE CRANE WIFE: What distresses you, my husband. What worries your mind?

KOKURO: It is late, and I must sleep.

THE CRANE WIFE: Your brow is furrowed, and the corners of your mouth are turned down.

KOKURO: I have much to consider.

THE CRANE WIFE: Cannot I not share your trouble as I have shared your joy?

KOKURO: This is not for a woman to decide.

THE CRANE WIFE: I am sorry to be of no use to you.

NARRATION: How was he to explain? He rolled out the futon and fell into a sleep of troubling dreams.

VILLAGER CHORUS: (*Voices in his dreams taunting him.*)
1. *Kokuro-don,*
2. neighbor,
3. friend.
1. What have you done?
2. How will you tell your wife.
4. What if she refuses to weave?
5. What will become of you?
1. *Kokuro-don*, will you be rich?
2. Will you be poor the rest of your life?
5. The day will come, and you must tell your wife.

NARRATION: In only a few days the neighbor returned.

(THE NEIGHBOR *runs down the aisle.*)

THE NEIGHBOR: *Kokuro-don.* Come out. My neighbor, my friend. See what I have brought you!

THE ENTRANCE OF THE SAMURAI

(THE SAMURAI *appears in the theatre. He comes to the center of the house and pulls out his swords. The villagers run in fear.*)

THE SAMURAI: (*Using the exaggerated speech patterns of the Kabuki performer and striking fine poses.*) Ho! Ho! Ho! Ho!

NARRATION: And there he was. A fine rich Samurai lord.

THE SAMURAI: Ho! Ho! Ho! Ho!

NARRATION: The blinding sun glanced off his sharp silver sword. His bag of silver coins clanked noisily as he dropped it on the hard packed snow. It was a frightening sight.

VILLAGER CHORUS: (*Scattering, and then clinging together to both hide and see what is going on at the same time.*)
1. See who comes to the village.
2. He is a king.
3. He is a god.
4. He is sent by the *tengu*.
5. He is sent by the *oni*.
1. Beware of the rich man.
2. Beware of the soldier.
3. He will surely kill us all.
All: What has Kokuro done to us?

NARRATION: The Samurai shouted in a mountainous bellow.

THE SAMURAI: Where is the man who will sell me the magic cloth?

(*The* VILLAGERS *point to the hut.*)

NARRATION: Kokuro hid in his hut, trembling with doubt and fear.

THE NEIGHBOR: *Kokuro-don,* my neighbor, my friend. Where are you?

THE SAMURAI: Kokuro, young peasant, come out. I will not harm you. I have brought you two thousand ryo to buy me some magical cloth.

NARRATION: Finally Kokuro came forward, bowing to the ground.

THE NEIGHBOR: *Kokuro-don,* my neighbor, my friend. Here he is, my lord. Look, Kokuro. There are the silver ryo. Two thousand of them. Tell your wife to bring this fine warrior his cloth.

KOKURO: I fear I cannot, my lord. She says she cannot weave again.

NARRATION: The warrior's face grew fat with rage.

THE SAMURAI: What is this? You have brought me here, and there is no cloth? I will take your skin before I will be dishonored so.

(THE SAMURAI *threatens* THE NEIGHBOR *with his sword.* THE NEIGHBOR *is thrown to the ground and scurries around on his knees to avoid* THE SAMURAI's *sword.*)

THE NEIGHBOR: No, no, no, my lord. Kokuro, will you see me cut in two? What about the fortune? Look. Two thousand ryo! Tell your wife to weave some more. Are you not master in your own house? He will deliver the cloth, my lord. I swear by my right arm.

KOKURO: The weaving is slow, my lord. It is such a fine cloth.

THE NEIGHBOR: That is it, my lord. The weaving is slow. Return to the city. Leave the money here. She will make the cloth, and I will bring it to you. Kokuro is an honest lad. He will make his wife obey.

THE SAMURAI: Ho! Ho! Ho! You scheming peasant. You think I am such a fool as that. No.

(THE SAMURAI *pushes* THE NEIGHBOR *down on his back and catches his up-thrust legs on his sword.*)

You will go to town with me. At the end of ten days, Kokuro will bring the cloth.

(THE SAMURAI *pulls the sword out, and* THE NEIGHBOR *falls flat on his back.*)

THE SAMURAI: Come, boy, open the bag of silver. Look at it dance in the sunlight. That will make your wife happy. She will do whatever you say.

(THE SAMURAI *catches* THE NEIGHBOR's *upstage arm with his sword and pulls him to his feet.*)

I will take this friend of yours with me for ransom. If you bring the cloth in ten days, he gets his own reward of silver. If not, we will see what a good farmer this friend will make with only one arm.

(THE SAMURAI *traps both of* THE NEIGHBOR's *arms with his sword. Then places* THE NEIGHBOR *over his shoulder.*)

THE SAMURAI: Do not disappoint me, Kokuro. I have a fierce temper.

(THE SAMURAI *exits through the theatre as he came, carrying the protesting* NEIGHBOR.)

THE NEIGHBOR: (*His words are heard trailing off as he is carried out of the theatre.*) Kokuro-don, take the silver. Tell your wife to weave the cloth. Ten days, Kokuro. Come. This getting rich. It was your idea, you know. I only offered to help. Make her do it. Don't lose the chance, Kokuro. Once in a lifetime, foolish boy. We will both be rich.

NARRATION: Kokuro looked into the bag. What a blinding sight. His mind began to spin. He felt the intoxicating weight of the coins.

KOKURO: Surely, she will not refuse me. But what am I to tell her?

NARRATION: His thoughts raced as he hid the silver under the corner of the hut.

THE GREED DANCE

VILLAGER CHORUS: (*Surrounding* KOKURO *with temptation.*)
        Money. Silver.
        Money. Gold.
        Sit and sit the whole day long.
        Money. Silver. Money. Gold.
        Kokuro, the rich man
        Kokuro, the landlord.

> *Silver. Money. Money. Gold.*
> *Why not you, Kokuro?*
> *Kokuro, why not you?*

KOKURO: Oh, my wife, what I have seen.

THE CRANE WIFE: You have seen a fine Samurai lord, I believe.

KOKURO: Oh, to have a sword like that. Oh, to shout commands in a fine loud voice.

THE CRANE WIFE: The Samurai are rich and powerful.

KOKURO: Oh, to have a such a fine bag of silver. Two thousand ryo!

THE CRANE WIFE: Are we not happy, dear husband?

KOKURO: We are, my wife, we are.

THE CRANE WIFE: Have we not food to eat and fire to keep us warm?

KOKURO: We have, my wife, we have.

THE CRANE WIFE: Have we not a hut to keep us from the wind? Do we not care for each other?

KOKURO: We do, my wife, we do.

THE CRANE WIFE: Then why would we ever need so much money as that?

NARRATION: But you have not seen the fine warrior. You have not seen the bag of silver.

THE CRANE WIFE: You have promised him the cloth?

KOKURO: It is our neighbor . . .

THE CRANE WIFE: I see.

KOKURO: With that money a man could have his own rice fields. He could give the orders for others to work.

THE CRANE WIFE: Is it not enough to do our own work together and to make each other happy?

NARRATION: Kokuro saw he could not make his wife understand. So, it was clear. He would have to return the bag of silver. He gave up his entreaty. He went to the fire to boil snow water for the tea. He rolled out the futon for the night. But the jangle of the silver coins echoed in his ear.

THE FINAL DANCE OF GREED

VILLAGER CHORUS: *(Voices in his mind.)*
> *Money. Silver.*
> *Money. Gold.*
> *Sit and sit the whole day long.*
> *Kokuro, the rich man*
> *Kokuro, the landlord.*
> *Money. Silver. Money. Gold.*
> *Why not you?*
> *Kokuro, Kokuro*
> *Why not you?*

NARRATION: One day went by. Kokuro grew silent. Then two. Kokuro kept count with marks on the wall of the hut. Ten days would soon be gone. He brooded in a corner. He did not speak. Finally his wife could not stand his unhappiness any longer. On the third night she came to him.

THE CRANE WIFE: Dear husband. I cannot bear your distress. I will weave for you. One more time. But this must truly be the last. I shall never weave again.

KOKURO: Thank you, my wife. My beautiful wife. Thank you. I shall get the loom. Where is the loom? I shall bring you the loom. (KOKURO *runs to get the sticks from behind the screen.*)

NARRATION: Kokuro dashed from the hut and returned with the loom. Before she could say a word, he brought the screens as well.

(*He dashes out to take the sticks to the* DANCERS.)

KOKURO: I know, my wife. I am not to look. I do not understand, but I am not to look.

THE CRANE WIFE: No matter how long I may weave, you must not look at me. You understand. Do not watch me.

KOKURO: I know. I know. I must sit and wait. I will do as you say. You see? I am sitting. (*He sits.*)

NARRATION: Kokuro's wife went behind the screen. Soon the sounds of the weaving began again.

(THE CRANE WIFE *exits behind the screen. Again the lights shift, and we see the shadow dance.*)

The Third Dance of the Weaving

(*Slow and deliberate; more lyrical.*)

VILLAGER CHORUS: *Kattan Coton Kattan Coton*
     Over and under, she weaves alone.
     Over and under, the thread is drawn.
     Over and under, the groaning loom
     Days and nights with mysterious thread.

NARRATION: Kokuro looked at the marks on the wall. One day she has been weaving. Two days.

VILLAGER CHORUS: (*Kattan Coton Kattan Coton–rhythm sounds under.*)
     Why take so long?
     What is so secret behind the screen?

NARRATION: Three days. Four days.

VILLAGER CHORUS: (*Kattan Coton Kattan Coton–rhythm sounds under.*)
     What does she do with the secret loom?
     Over and under, the cloth is made.

NARRATION: (*They close in upon him as all become more intense.*) And still it goes on. Five days. He marks the days on the wall of the hut. He paces around the room.

KOKURO: Only two more days left and I must take the cloth to town. What is she doing?

NARRATION: He sits upon the ground. He chews a stick of sugar cane.

(KOKURO *throws down one hut screen.*)

KOKURO: What does she do for so many hours?

NARRATION: Why must he wait and wait? Kokuro's patience ran thin. He bit his thumb. He pulled his hair. He must know.

(KOKURO *throws down the other hut screen.*)

KOKURO: When will it be done? Why does she keep me out? I am her husband. I deserve to know. What is the secret of the thread?

NARRATION: And finally, it was too much. His simple peasant mind gave way. His patience failed him. His curiosity drove him mad, and on the evening of the sixth day he put his hand upon the paper door.

(KOKURO *tears down the huge white cloth on which the dancers had been shadow figures. Behind it we see* THE CRANE WIFE *in her under garments which are covered in red ribbons hanging like strips of blood. The cranes stand around her holding above her head a long white strip of cloth with a red ribbon running through it.*)

VILLAGER CHORUS: (*Scream and draw back on the ground.*) Aaaaaaagh.

NARRATION: A piercing cry threw him back. And then Kokuro screamed himself.

KOKURO: (*Scream.*) Aaaaaaaaaaagh.

NARRATION: What he saw was not human.

VILLAGER CHORUS:
1. Look what you have done.
2. This is the price you pay.
3. Curiosity got the best of you.
4. The *oni* have come for you.
5. Greed is your enemy, peasant boy.
4. See what has become of your good fortune.
5. You see the demon weaving in your hut.
1. You don't deserve the silver coins.

NARRATION: What he saw was not the *oni*, not *yamauba*, the mountain demon. What he saw was not the *nushi* from the swamp. No. What he saw was a crane,—but no. . . . Once a beautiful crane, now the bird's long neck and sleek body were naked, bald, the white body smeared with blood. Three times, there behind the screen, three times, with its own beak it had plucked out each of its beautiful feathers to weave upon the loom. The sight was too much for the simple Kokuro. He fell to the floor in a deep faint. There, while his mind lost touch with his body, he heard a sad and terrible voice.

THE RETURN OF THE CRANE FLOCK AND THE CEREMONY

THE CRANE WIFE: (*During this speech and the previous narration two of the crane* DANCERS *exit to retrieve the crane puppet. The other two dress* THE CRANE WIFE *in her kimono—now inside out, revealing the lining, which is covered with a red blood-like pattern. They ceremoniously tie her obi while she speaks.*) My dear husband. For your sake, I did as you asked. I had hoped you would be able to honor my request. I begged you not to come behind the screen. But now you have looked upon me in my naked suffering. You have seen my sorrow. I have sacrificed my honor. My dignity is lost. And now I can no longer remain in the human world, the sad human world of envy and distrust. I am the crane you saved from the snow at the threshold of the winter. I fell in love with your simple kindness and your gentle heart. I trusted your tenderness and I left my home to come to live by your side. But now I must go back to my flock. You know my sad disgrace. Our future together is lost. Farewell. I pray that your life will be long and happy.

(The crane DANCERS *have reentered with the inert body of the crane puppet.* THE CRANE WIFE *and other two cranes join them, reanimate the crane, and fly out through the house, while the musician plays a melancholy theme.)*

NARRATION: When Kokuro came to his senses he looked about him. The room was empty except for a length of cloth lying at his feet. And what a piece of cloth it was!

THE FINAL DANCE OF THE CLOTH

(The VILLAGERS, *who have watched the exit of the crane, now go to the cloth and pick it up.)*

VILLAGER CHORUS:
1. Lighter than air.
2. Whiter than snow.
3. It glows.
4. Made of breath.
5. It floats.
4. But look.
2. But look.
3. But look.
1. See the crimson thread.
2. Deeper than blood.
3. Deeper than blood and whiter than snow.
1. It is magnificent.
5. It is a gift of life and blood.

NARRATION: Kokuro looked wildly about him. Out he ran into the crisp night air that smelled of the birth pangs of spring.

KOKURO: Wait. Wait. Wait.

*(*KOKURO *runs after the puppet that is moving out of the theatre.)*

VILLAGER CHORUS:
1. No use, foolish boy.
2. She is gone, Kokuro.
3. She is gone.

*(*KOKURO *sits on the edge of the stage. Lights have come up to suggest spring.)*

NARRATION: Beyond the crest of the mountain a flock of cranes filled the sky with beating white wings.

(The MUSICIAN *plays, the crane* DANCERS *appear to dance the final movements of the crane flock.)*

Up from the valley, toward them, flew a single bird. They gathered her into the flock. Kokuro could barely see it. The tiny form of a single crane, swallowed up in a mist of snowy birds, carried farther and farther away.

(The crane DANCERS dance out of sight; lights fade on them as the VILLAGER CHORUS drapes KOKURO's shoulders with the cloth and spreads it out along the stage.)

VILLAGER CHORUS:

> The cranes are flying.
> See them go, Kokuro.
> Look at the cloth,
> The beautiful cloth.
> Kokuro is a rich man.
> Money. Silver.
> Money. Gold.
> Where is Kokuro's wife?
> Kokuro is a rich man.
> Money. Gold.
> Look at the crimson cloth,
> The white and crimson cloth.
> Kokuro had a wife,
> Where is she now?

(The VILLAGER CHORUS goes to their knees, heads bowed.)

NARRATION: It is done.
  Itte shimaimashita
  The story is done.

(Lights fade to black as the NARRATORS and THE SIGNER bow to the last phrase of music.)

CURTAIN

JUNGALBOOK
by
Edward Mast

Adapted from Rudyard Kipling's
The Jungle Book

EDWARD MAST was born in California and now lives in Seattle. He began writing poetry in high school, and by age twenty he was writing plays. Mast received his undergraduate training at California State College at Sonoma and his MFA in theatre (playwriting) at the University of California at Los Angeles. In addition to being a playwright he has been a theatre director and actor; a screen writer; a writer/director for television and radio; and an installation writer/producer.

His awards include first place for *Sacrilege* in the Native American Play Contest and the 1991 Distinguished Play Award for *Jungalbook* from the American Alliance for Theatre and Education.

Among his nine original plays are *Wolf Child: The Correction of Joseph*, and *Dinosaurus* (with Lenore Bensinger). Besides *Jungalbook*, his adaptations include such stories as *Ramayana, The Hobbit*, and *A Wrinkle in Time*.

Mast's plays, as well as his own solo performances, which he has also written or adapted, have been seen in New York, Chicago, Los Angeles, San Francisco, Seattle, Washington, D.C., Dallas, Honolulu, and other major cities in the United States.

His two latest works will be published soon: a book of poems, *Suzy and Her Husband*, and *The History of Eastern Europe for Beginners*.

Jungalbook was my first play for young audiences, and at the time, I might have guessed it to be my last. I wrote the play because I wanted to see it. The images of boy and monkey and wolf, and then the invented sound of jungaltalk, had become a private haunt of mine, only to be exorcised by watching them on stage.

I had come to love Kipling's *Jungle Books* as an adult in my early twenties; however, when I came to imagine an audience for a dramatization, I naturally thought of children. This was partially because the stories spoke to my own childhood world of loyalty, adventure, and betrayal, but also because I feared that an audience of grown-ups would require a snicker or sidelong glance from actors pretending to be bears and hyenas. At the same time, I feared that children might find the themes of the play too merciless or harsh.

I was wrong on both counts. Adults were challenged by the grimness of the play much more than children, though many seemed to respond to the same qualities of the stories that I did. The young people, on the other hand, taught me that the younger the audience, the more it is filled with passionate extremists, hungry for actions of inevitability and consequence, eager to witness the workings and misworkings of justice, emotion, and responsibility. Why any of this should have surprised me, I don't know; as a child, I was much more enthusiastic about grappling with grown-up issues than I am as a comparative grown-up.

Audiences of young people do not always demonstrate their approval through attentive silence; and even that attentive silence is harder to earn and maintain than that of polite theatregoing adults. I'm daunted by the more exacting discipline required to compel the attention of a young audience, but I've also found that, while there are some stories I would not choose to direct at young people, there are some that are best when told for them. I'm not sure if this is a function of young people versus older, or if it grows out of prejudices our industrial culture has about make-believe. When we accompany children, we are sometimes able to risk unusual intimacy with primal events and dances— people dressing up like animals, for example—which are usually required to keep a safe distance. Working for younger people has allowed me to take similar risks and has served to open and reopen my senses to possibilities from which I might otherwise have been lethally and sadly corrected.

—Edward Mast

JUNGALBOOK

CHARACTERS

Baloo, the bear
Bagheera, the panther
Sherakhan, the tiger
Mowgli, the human boy
Akela, leader of the wolf pack
Grab, a wolf
Hathi, the elephant
Grey, a wolf
Kaa, the python
Perchy, the monkey
Chil, the vulture
Hyena
Buffalo
Humans

[THE CHARACTER GROUPINGS ARE SUGGESTED DOUBLING FOR EIGHT ACTORS.]

Only HUMANS wear masks, excluding MOWGLI. Different animals are suggested by posture and voice. Costumes are playground clothing, grade-school level, with suggestions of jungle: shorts, tennis shoes, etc., with maybe a claw or two.

Several actors can play HUMANS as well as part of the ELEPHANT. Even though the characters are all referred to as "him's," most of them can be played either male or female, with pronouns changed to match. MOWGLI is a boy, and BAGHEERA seems to me more moving as male; but SHERAKHAN, for example, was played by a woman in our original production, and the effect was striking. AKELA might be a she-wolf, as well, especially since wolf packs are sometimes led by the female.

SETTING

Not a jungle, but a jungle gym: an arch of monkey bars, say eight feet tall at apex, spreading sideways across the stage. These can be straight and businesslike, real jungle gym bars; or they can be tangled and intertwined at odd angles. The structure is fully naked, not decorated by vine or leaf or painted ornament, not representing jungle in any pictorial way.

The other item of scenery is a long, frail, light blue fabric, which at rise is absent. This fabric will be unfurled at the proper time by two offstage actors to become the River.

(Jungalsounds in the darkness. Roar, monkey's chatter, snarl. Increasing, louder and louder, till the jungal is close and loud. Lights up on the playground of the jungal. Kid-dressed animals, all shapes and sizes, changing shape, all playing children's games. Not jump rope or jacks; rather, chasing, tossing, surrounding, scuffling, attacking, and defending. One large animal doesn't move quickly. Lumbers toward us, speaks.)

BALOO: To eat in the jungal
   ya must kill.
   Therefore it's law in the jungal:
   Never kill for pleasure.
   The Law uv the Jungal is older than I am
   and I'm pretty old.
   I'm Baloo the baare.
   I teach the Law uv the Jungal to baarcubs, wulfcubs,
   all uv'em.
   If yoo live as long as me,
   yoo will see
   none uv these animals survive
   without
   the Law uv the Jungal.

(A fight breaks out over a prize. BALOO steps over, breaks it up. To the fighters:)
   Law uv the Jungal:
   The meat belongs to the killer.
   Steal it from him, yoo die.

(Two wolves fight: BALOO breaks them up.)
   Fight if yoo must,
   but cat may not kill cat,
   nor wulf kill wulf.

(The two wolves obey silently, move apart. A big creature is lurking around: BALOO faces it.)
   Hunt on your own ground.
   Otherwise some may go hungry.

(A HUMAN—masked, with robot movements—walks across the stage. Animals hide.)
   (To us.) Stay clear uv Man.
   If yoo kill one man,
   men and men and men will return
   to murder your people.
   Seven times over.
   Never kill Man,
   and never kill for the pleasure uv killing.

(Two wolves—who will later be GRAB and GREY—are tussling over a small bundle. As they toss and snatch it from each other, it emits baby cries—made by MOWGLI offstage.)
   Wulfs may not—*(They're not listening; BALOO shakes head wearily.)*

Wulfs are slow learners.

(Turns to another wolf who's playing elsewhere.)
Akela!

(AKELA looks at him: BALOO gestures toward the fight. AKELA leaps down, breaks up the scuffle.)
AKELA: Hey! Break it up! Cut it!

(GRAB and GREY kneel, bend heads to ground.)
GRAB: Sorry, Akela.
GREY: *(Points at GRAB.)* He stole my meat!
AKELA: *(To GRAB.)* Put it down. Yoo hear me?
BALOO: Law uv the Jungal:
  Obey the Leader of the Pack.

(GRAB sets bundle down.)
AKELA: *(Sniffling at bundle.)* What kind uv meat is it?
GRAB: Mancub.
AKELA: *(Recoils.)* Human meat?
GREY: Still alive.

(AKELA sniffs at the bundle, nudges it with his paw: a loud baby cry comes from it, making all of them jump back.)
  I saw it first.
GRAB: Nuh-uh. I saw it.
GREY: I did!
GRAB: I did!
GREY: Me!
GRAB: Me!

(They jump together; AKELA shoves them apart. He stares at the bundle, puzzled.)
BALOO: Word uv the Leader of the Pack is law,
  but the law also says
  seven times over, never kill Man.
AKELA: Yeah, yeah.
GRAB: So who gets it, me or him?
AKELA: *(Annoyed, confused: cuffs him.)* Shuddup for a minute, willya?

(BAGHEERA appears.)
BAGHEERA: Akela.

(GRAB and GREY huddle behind AKELA as BAGHEERA the panther approaches, powerful and polite.)
  Good hunting, Akela.
AKELA: Good hunting, Bagheera.

BAGHEERA: *(Calm, smooth.)* I am a panther
and have no right to meddle in
wulf business.
But Jungal Law states that
a hunter's meat may be bought
for a price.
Am I right, Baloo?

BALOO: Bagheera knows the Law.

AKELA: You wanna buy this mancub meat from us?

BAGHEERA: Close by here
is a freshkilled bulllll,
fatter and juicier than this little bundle.
For this price
will the wulfpack let the mancub live?

AKELA: Trade a whole big bull for a little mancub?
Sure. Right?

GRAB: Sure! Bull's better than mancub.

GREY: Yoo bet!

AKELA: Yoo got a deal, Bagheera.

BAGHEERA: Will yoo also
let the mancub run with yoor pack?

AKELA: *(Puzzled again.)* Yoo want us
to raise the cub?

BAGHEERA: I want the cub to live.
A panther is no animal to
nurse
a cub. You have motherwulfs in your pack
who will care for a humancub.
Will you raise the mancub?

AKELA: *(Looks at GRAB and GREY, who grumble.)*
I dunno about that part—

(Snarl offstage.)

SHERAKHAN: *(Off.)* Wheeere's my meeeet!

(BAGHEERA steps back slightly; wolves pack up behind AKELA as SHERAKHAN the Tiger springs on.)
Where is it!

BAGHEERA: Where is what, Sherakhan?

(SHERAKHAN stops, crouches to fight when he sees BAGHEERA. But then he sees the bundle.)

SHERAKHAN: That's my kill. Get away from it.

AKELA: We're makin a deal here—

SHERAKHAN: *(Shoves him away.)* Outta my way.

AKELA: *(Standing firm before the bundle.)*
　Hey!
　We don't take orders from tigers.
　We're makin a deal with the panther
　so yoo go mind yoor own
　tigerbusiness.

(SHERAKHAN is wary of BAGHEERA, who also takes a stance of defense.)

SHERAKHAN: That meeet is mine, Bagheera.
　That mancub's mother and father
　arr in my stomach.

BAGHEERA: *(Angry.)* You killed the parents?
　(Stops himself; calm.)
　Shouldn't eeat Man, Sherakhan.
　You'll lose your teeth.

SHERAKHAN: You just back away, Panther.

AKELA: The mancub belongs to the Freepeople Wulfpack, Sherakhan.
　Back away yourself.

SHERAKHAN: Yooo
　watch yoor tail, Bushyface.
　That meet belongs to me.

AKELA: Bushyface? Bushyface, huh?
　Well, I
　Akela
　Leader uv the Freepeople Wulfpack
　have accepted Bagheera's bargain
　and will take this mancub
　to grow up part uv my pack.
　That's my word;
　my teeth defend it.
　And also: *(Snaps fingers.)*

GRAB: My teeth!

GREY: My teeth!

BAGHEERA: And mine, oh mighty tiger.

SHERAKHAN: *(Looks at them all together.)* Eeeeeeeasy talk,
　One by one yoor not so brave.

BAGHEERA: Sneak up behind them one by one:
　that's yoor way,
　brave tiger.

SHERAKHAN: Oooooooh, unbeaten panther.
　Afraid for yoor little baby mancub?
　Mommy? MommyMommyMommyMommy

(BAGHEERA's back coils to spring, but the fight is stopped by BALOO's words.)

BALOO: Cat may not kill cat
　nor wulf kill wulf,
　Law uv the Jungal.

(The two cats freeze; slowly BAGHEERA pulls away.)

BAGHEERA: Yoo kill defenseless dangerous Man
  and make trouble for the whole Jungal.
  I can't punish yoo myself,
  but I will live to see yoo pay the price.
  Go feed on rats and porcupines, Tiger.

SHERAKHAN: I am Sherakhan
  and I feed wherever I choose.
  That mancub will come to my teeth in the end
  when yoo bushtailed thieves grow tired uv toying with it.
  Take good care uv him,
  mommy Bagheera.

(TIGER *springs away and off.*)

AKELA: Showed that Tiger.

GREY: Do we eat the mancub now?

AKELA: *(Punches him.)* No, stupid. We get the bull.

GREY: Oh. Yeh.

BAGHEERA: What will you name the mancub?

AKELA: Name? Oh, right.
  We'll call him
  uh
  let's see.
  He's got no fur on his skin
  so we'll call him
  Mowgli.

(*Wolves laugh.*)

BALOO: *(To us.)* Means Little Frog.

BAGHEERA: Keep him safe.

AKELA: He's safe as long as I'm leader.

BAGHEERA: Nobody's leader forever.

(AKELA *stares at him, silent. Then turns away, uncomfortable.*)

AKELA: So where's this bull?

BAGHEERA: Top uv the hill. Over there.

AKELA: *(Tosses his head in gesture to the wolves.)* Let's go.

(*The wolves leave.* BAGHEERA *stops* AKELA.)

BAGHEERA: Akela!

(AKELA *stops:* BAGHEERA *points to bundle.*)

AKELA: Oh. Yeah.

(AKELA *picks up bundle awkwardly, leaves to follow wolves.*)

BALOO: If I were you, Bagheera,
  I'd keep one eye on that wulfpack
  and that little frog.

BAGHEERA: I'm not a mother for cubs! *(Pause.)*
But I will watch.
Will you teach him the Law?

BALOO: I'll teach him, till he grows and returns to Man.
Time will come, if I know humans,
for that little Frog Mowgli
to teach that tiger some manners.
He may even be some help to yoooo
someday.

BAGHEERA: Nobody helps Bagheera.

(BAGHEERA springs away. BALOO, alone, turns to us.)

BALOO: Seasons pass by quick
to an old baare
like me.
As many years as *(Holds up hand.)*
toes on my paws
pass by me like nothin.
But this many years
are plenty
for a prime wulf
even a wulf leader
to get old and get slow.

(GRAB and GREY enter, hunting. AKELA enters with them; but when GRAB and GREY scurry across and off, AKELA stops, panting and tired. He walks after them.)
And this many years to a
little human kid
well
that's his whole life,
enuff years to grow up from baby frog to
Mowgli the Mancub,
walkin on two feet like a human
or a baare.
Nuff years for him to learn
all the special ways uv the Jungal,
all the language uv
batsplash, grassrustle, footprint,
all the slow secret signals uv the Jungal—

(MOWGLI has entered behind BALOO, silent and crouching; he now jumps up, screeching "CAW" in BALOO's ear. BALOO whirls around ready for battle with some great pterodactyl. MOWGLI laughs uproariously.)

BALOO: Mowgli!
How many times have I tooooold yooo
the Jungal is no place for playing at danger?

MOWGLI: As many times as there are nutts on the palm tree.

BALOO: I've squashed bigger creatures than yoo
for less uv a scare.

MOWGLI: Yoo deserve it
for making me,
King uv the Jungal,
spend all morning listening to yoor silly old
junnnnngalll Laaaaaaws.

(*Enter* PERCHY *the Monkey, chased by* GRAB *and* GREY. MOWGLI *leaps to join them.* MOWGLI *and the three wolves surround* PERCHY, *who tries to escape, but the delighted wolves and* MOWGLI *taunt him fiercely, dancing round in a ring.*)

BALOO: Mowgli—(*Sighs: to us.*)
And of course,
he has plenty of time to play with his packmates
the wulfs.

GRAB & GREY & MOWGLI: Monkeeface, Monkeeface
uggllee you!
Bull butt stinks,
and yoo doo too!

(PERCHY *tries to get away, but* GREY *blocks him and* MOWGLI *imitates his funny walk. Wolves laugh.* PERCHY *tries to run:* MOWGLI *imitates.*)
Monkeeface, Monkeeface
ugggleee yoo!
Snakes are skinny
and yoo arr too!
Monkeeface, Monkeeface
ugggggleeee yoo!
Spiders got long arms,
and yoo doo too!

(PERCHY *waves arms and shouts, trying to scare them; wolves recoil slightly, but* MOWGLI *imitates, and the wolves scream with laughter.* BALOO *shakes head wearily, lumbers toward them.*)

BALOO: Awwwwwwllllllright.
Leave him alooooooone.

MOWGLI: We're just havin fun!

BALOO: Perchy, go way.

(PERCHY *the Monkey hops away; stops, gives a raspberry to wolves, exits fast. Wolves bark, but* BALOO *silences them.*)
Yoo got nothin better to do?

GREY: Better than listnin to fatt bayerrrrrs—

BALOO: (*To* GREY.) Now listen, Grab—

GREY: I'm *Grey!*

GRAB: *I'm* Grab!

GREY: *He's* Grab!

BALOO: Whichever. This fatt old bayer
has fat old paws, so careful
with your loose tongue.
Hear me?

GRAB: Yeh, yeh.

GREY: Sure, sure.

BALOO: Go play. Play good.

(GRAB *and* GREY *run off.* MOWGLI *starts to follow.*)
Mowgli!

MOWGLI: Whaaaat?

BALOO: Not so fast. Ya got lessons to learn.

MOWGLI: Awwww!

More stupid old Jungal words?

BALOO: Yoo gotta learn
yoo're too small to go
tantalizing monkees.

MOWGLI: Aww, Perchy the Monkee's just silly and stinky.

BALOO: Monkey can bite just like everybody.

MOWGLI: *(Pointing off.)* Grab and Grey getta go play.
How come I gotta sit arownd reciting yoor old lessons?

BALOO: Grab and Grey got wulfteeth and wulf claws.
Yoo have mancub babyteeth and no claws.
I teech yoo Masterwoords
for yoor own safety.

MOWGLI: What's a mancub?

BALOO: Yoo.

MOWGLI: *(Clambering about on the bars.)* Aaa! I'm a wulf.
I run as fast as any wulf,
I climb better than I run,
I swim better than I climb;
wulf like me got nothing to be safe from.

BALOO: The jungal will teech yoo feeer
someday.

MOWGI: Jungal's my playgrownd.
What's "feeer"?
I don't know that word "Feeeeer."

BALOO: You should feer this jungal.
The rain is late this year.
Jungal gets dry, food gets scarce,
tempers get brittle as sticks.
If that tiger Sherakhan catches you alone
you'll learn feeeer real quick.

MOWGLI: Stupid old tiger. I'll stare in his eyes.
Like this.

(*Stares in* BALOO's *eyes.* BALOO *must turn away.*)

BALOO: Yoo have
human eyes.

MOWGLI: Nobody meets my eyes.
Not yoo,

not Akela,
not Sherakhan.
That's why I'm the biggest, best wulf,
and I'll have my own pack someday
and do whatever I want
all day long.
Mowgli, Ruler uv the Jungal!

BALOO: Is that what yoo arr?
Well, Baloo wishes to speak with yoo,
O Master uv Birdnests.

(BALOO *has walked to the bottom of the tree where* MOWGLI *is climbing. He now gives it a solid rap with his fist: the tree shivers and shakes;* MOWGLI *loses balance, topples, falls tumbling to the ground at* BALOO's *feet.* BALOO *picks him up by the ear.*)

Jungal is wide,
and yoo
arr tiny.
Jungal is mighty,
yoo
arr weak.
Jungal is thick,
yoo
thin.
Jungal is full uv creatures
could swallow yoo
without chewing.
Does Mowgli hear?

MOWGLI: (*Sulky and bruised.*) I hear.

BALOO: Yoo will learn feeer
soon enuff.
Meanwhile
I teach yoo Masterwoords so yoo
can stay alive.
What arr the Masterwoords?

MOWGLI: One blood,
yoo and me.

BALOO: (*Lets go of his ear.*) Good.
Mowgli is wise and learns quick. (*Ruffles the boy's hair.*)
And why do I teach yoo the woords?

MOWGLI: 'Cause Mowgli is tiny
while Jungal is wide.

BALOO: Correct.

MOWGLI: Mowgli is weak
while jungal is mighty.

BALOO: Correct.

MOWGLI: Mowgli is thin
while Baloo is fat.

(BALOO *looks at him, raises paw to cuff him;* MOWGLI *covers head.* BALOO *lowers paw.* MOWGLI *uncovers, sighs with relief; thus is offguard when* BALOO *cuffs him gently, just enough to send* MOWGLI *rolling across the ground smack into the tree-bottoms.* BAGHEERA *appears.*)

BAGHEERA: Baloo.

> (BALOO *stops.* MOWGLI *rubs his head.*)
> *(Calm, detached.)* Is the mancub some
> coconut
> to bat abaaaowt
> with yoor flat feet?

BALOO: We cannot spoil the boy, Bagheera.
He must learn the Law uv the Jungal . . .

BAGHEERA: *(Gently scornful.)*
Oooooh, naaaaow, how can his little head carry
awwwwll your looooooong talk?

BALOO: Is anyone too little to be killed?
No. So I teach him strict,
so I discipline him,
veeeeery softlee,
when he forgets.

BAGHEERA: *(Chuckling.)* Where did you learn "softly,"
Old Ironfeet?
He's battered head to foot by your "softly."
The boy is no treetrunk to
sharpen your blunt claws upon.

BALOO: He will remember and thank me someday.

MOWGLI: If I live.

BAGHEERA: Are you in one piece, Mancub?

> (MOWGLI *is silent, uncertain.*)

BALOO: Yoo may speak, Mowgli.
Yoo know Bagheera the Panther?

MOWGLI: I have seen Bagheera.
I have heard that Bagheera
never misses his hunt.

BAGHEERA: *(Chuckles.)*
Well, I don't hunt mancubs
tonight, so have no fear.

MOWGLI: *(Stands.)* That "fear" again.
What is feeer? Will you tell me?

BAGHEERA: *(Pauses.)* Yoo'll find it. Soon enough.

> (CHIL *the Vulture screeches on overhead.*)

CHIL: Yaaa! Yaaa!
Draaaaaooooowt!
Yaa! Yaa!

BALOO: What are yoo screeeeeeeeching abowt, Vulture?

CHIL: *(Hopping about, rather happily.)* No rain! Drought!
No rain!

Jungal people thirsteeeee!
Chil the Vulture feeeds well!

MOWGLI: What's drought?

BALOO: Waterholes dry up,
  food gets scarce,
  we all get hungry
  and Chil that vulture gets happy.

CHIL: Draaaaaaoowwt!

BALOO: *(To* BAGHEERA.*)* Come to the River with us?

BAGHEERA: I will be there. *(*BAGHEERA *exits.)*

BALOO: All the Jungal obeys this one law, Little Frog.
  And it is not a pretty sight.

*(*BALOO *and* MOWGLI *exit.* CHIL *continues to shout.)*

CHIL: Pritty for Chil! Pritty for Chil!
  Lotsa food for Chil!
  No water, no eating for everyone else,
  everyone starves,
  lotsa food for Chil!
  Pritty for Chil!
  Pritty for Chil!

(As CHIL *speaks, the long, light blue fabric of the River unfurls across the stage. At first it ripples high, then settles, till it barely moves, till it lies flat and motionless.* CHIL *inspects the River.)*

(Hopping, happy.)
River all dry!
All mud!

(Enter AKELA *leading* GRAB *and* GREY. AKELA *is older, slower, wearier.* CHIL *screeches at them.)*
Yaa! Chil feeeds! Yaa!

AKELA: Get outta here, Chil.

CHIL: Oooooold Akela! Yaa!
  See how long you live in drowwt,
  oooold and tired Akela!
  Yaa! Yaa!

*(*AKELA *gestures:* GRAB *and* GREY *bark and jump at* CHIL, *who flurries away and exits.)*

GRAB: Showed him.

AKELA: Shuttup and drink.

*(*AKELA *laps at the River.* GRAB *looks at* GREY; *they kneel and drink.* BALOO *and* MOWGLI *have entered.)*

BALOO: The River's fallen. Drying up.
  Summer heeet will turn owr green jungal black

and we awl go hunnngry.
Time for Water Truce.

GRAB: Whatsatt?

AKELA: *(Punches him quiet.)* Shh! Lissen.

BALOO: Until the rayne comes again,
anyone can drink at this river
free from harm.
While the Truce lasts,
to kill any animal beside this river
will be punisht
by death.

AKELA: Everybody hear that?

GRAB: Sure.

GREY: Yeh. Swell.

MOWGLI: Do all the meat eeters really follow this troooce?

BALOO: Everyone's thirsty:
everyone obeys.

AKELA: Ugly time, Little Frog,
We all gotta watch for ourselves,
so yoo be careful.
First to drop are ones like yoo,
small and weak.

GRAB: And hairless.

GREY: And skinny.

(GRAB and GREY laugh. AKELA frowns.)

MOWGLI: I'll get by.
Maybe I'll just staaare the river in the eye.
Like this:

(He stares at GRAB, then at GREY: both must turn their eyes away from his. They growl.)
Till the water comes back.

(Enter SHERAKHAN. Behind the tiger, a giggling hyena.)

SHERAKHAN: Staaare in my eyes, Manling.

(Wolves tense, pack together.)
Look in my eyes and see if
you'll live.

HYENA: Yeh, yeh, staare in his eyes. Yeh, yeh, yeh.

BALOO: We're under the Water Truce here, Sherakhan.

SHERAKHAN: Good hunting
to the teeeeecher uv the law.
Good hunting to the Freepeeple wulfpack.

(HYENA punctuates with laugher.)
And especially to Akela, leader uv the pack.

How is your limp, Akela?
How is your naked mancub?

MOWGLI: I'm a wulf.

HYENA: Mancub's a wulf! Hahahahahahaha

SHERAKHAN: Well, yoo're safe by this river, little wulfee.
Leave this river, though . . .

(SHERAKHAN flexes claws, staring at MOWGLI.)

HYENA: An I get the scraps! Hahaha!
(Hopping toward MOWGLI.)
I get all yoor scraps.
How do yoo taste? Heee heehee

(Tries to lick/bite MOWGLI.)

(AKELA, who has been growling, steps in, kicks the hyena over on his back.)

AKELA: Grubby, foot-licking hyena.

(HYENA cowers, whimpers as AKELA stands over him.)
Mowgli's in my pack.
Yoo go follow yerrr mangy tigerr
and keep cleer uv Mowgli
and me.

BALOO: *(Quiet, urgent.)* Akela. Cool off.

AKELA: Pick yer friends better, Tiger.
Hyeena stinks.

SHERAKHAN: Hyena's got doggie smell. Just like yoo. *(Advances on Akela, pushes him.)*
Wanna pick on meee
instead uv hyeeena? Huh?

(Pushes AKELA again, who looks away, tense: used to fighting back, but unsure and hesitant. HYENA picks himself up, starts giggling.)

AKELA: Don't do that.

BALOO: Water Truce, Sherakhan.

SHERAKHAN: Nobody's killing heer.
Arrrr we, Akela?

(Pushes him again. SHERAKHAN advances; AKELA backs away, avoids, trying to cool it off.)
Arrr we, oold limpwulf?

AKELA: *(Furious, ready to spring but frightened.)* Eennnnnnuff!

SHERAKHAN: Nuff what, Mancub likker?

AKELA: We're at the River.

SHERAKHAN: Ho ho.
Yer brayve by the truce river.
I'll meet yoo

anywhere you like, Bushfoot.
And then I'll meet yoor little pet Mancub.

AKELA: *(Fierce growl.)* Nuff!

SHERAKHAN: Stop me. (AKELA *growls, desperate;* SHERAKHAN *keeps advancing. Suddenly* AKELA *stops, stands his ground, is about to spring.* BAGHEERA *has appeared behind them.)*

BAGHEERA: *(Calm; cleaning himself.)* Heeet
makes everyone nervous.
Doesn't it, Sherakhan.

(SHERAKHAN *whirls to face* BAGHEERA. GRAB *and* GREY *appear frightened of the panther.* AKELA *only slowly relaxes.* BAGHEERA *lounges forward slowly.)*

BALOO: *(Relieved.)* Good hunting, Bagheera.

BAGHEERA: Good hunting, Baloo.
Good hunting, Sherakhan.
Do yoo evrrrr hunt anyone
yoor own size?

(BAGHEERA *is face to face with* SHERAKHAN. *Silence: the two cats do not take eyes off each other. Finally* SHERAKHAN *steps back, snorts, chuckles.)*

SHERAKHAN: I'm hungry.
Got no more time to play.
But yoo and that crusty wulf
can't watch that manboy forever.

HYENA: An I'll get the scraps!

(SHERAKHAN *cuffs him silent; starts to go, turns back.)*

SHERAKHAN: That bull
that paid for this boy's life
tenn yeeeers back
is long since eaten.
If any wulfs get hungry,
I usually have food to spaaare
at my meals.
Anyone come with me?

(GRAB *and* GREY *look at each other, start to follow the tiger.* AKELA *cuts them off, facing* SHERAKHAN.)*

AKELA: Not a chance.
We aren't hyenas
to pick at your scraps.

(SHERAKHAN *looks at him, at the wolves; the* HYENA *starts to laugh, and the tiger joins in. They exit, laughing.* GRAB *and* GREY *grumble.)*

Lucky for that tiger
we're at this river.
Let's go.

(Starts to walk off opposite. GRAB *and* GREY *don't move.* AKELA *stops, turns to them. Furious.)*

Let's go!

(GRAB and GREY hesitate, then follow AKELA, who stomps off.)

MOWGLI: I don't understand.
I don't understand.
What's Sherakhan got so much against me?

BALOO: Look at yourself in the water,
and you'll see.

MOWGLI: I've seen what I look like. *(He looks at his reflection anyway.)* Lotsa times.

BALOO: Then don't you see
ya got no fur? No claws? No fangs?
Yoo arr no wulf?

(MOWGLI is staring down at the River, puzzled as though seeing something strange.)

MOWGLI: I'm just different looking, is all.

BALOO: Yoo have fingers.
Yoo stand on feet like me.

MOWGLI: *(Trying to laugh it off.)* What am I? A bayer?

BALOO: Told yoo already.
Yoo were born human,
and the tiger hates all humans.
Yoo're only alive in the jungal
because yoor life was bought from the wulf pack
for a just-killed bull.

MOWGLI: Who killed the bull?

BAGHEERA: *(Cuts BALOO off.)* Doesn't matter.
That's long past.

MOWGLI: *(Looking at him.)* Thanks for sticking up for AKELA.

BAGHEERA: *(Quickly.)* I don't protect wulfs.
(Then more slowly.) Sherakhan's a bully.
Hunts cattle and slow little animals
smaller than himself. A coward.
Got catblood like me
so I don't like watching him
bully old wulfs and little mancubs.
That's all.

MOWGLI: You're right.
Sherakhan's all talk. Big wulf like me . . .

BALOO: Yoo're not a wulf.

MOWGLI: Big old BAYER like me,
I'll just staare in his eyes, he'll run away
biting his tayle.
Ha! Let'im pick on me some time.
(He starts to walk off, lumbering like BALOO.)

BALOO: Where're yoo goin?

MOWGLI: Gonna teach lessons to the pack.

BALOO: Don't go alone.
Sherakhan's still around.

MOWGLI: So? Think I can't handle that notooth bully?

BALOO: Doo what I tell yoo.

BAGHEERA: Let him go, Baloo.

(BALOO *glares at* BAGHEERA.)
Mowgli is Ruler uv the Jungal.
He can walk where he pleases.

(MOWGLI *sticks his tongue out at* BALOO, *turns, lumbers off like a bear.* BALOO *turns to* BAGHEERA *with exasperation.*)

BALOO: Yoo spoil him. This is dangerous.

BAGHEERA: He's just a cub. Why not let him play?

BALOO: Just a cub, and the tiger nearby.

BAGHEERA: He is watched.
Been safe these ten years.
Why arr yoo all uv a sudden afraid?

BALOO: Akela's old, gonna miss his kill one time soon,
and those wulfs will turn on him.
They'll forget yoor bargain
and leave nothing between Mowgli and Sherakhan.

BAGHEERA: Nothing but me.

BALOO: Even yooo
can't protect him forever.
(*Pause.*) Why do you keep this secret?

BAGHEERA: I am not one to nurse cubs.

BALOO: This cub believes the whole jungle is safe for him.
He's gotta know who guards him,
and who's been guarding him.
I'll tell him if you want.

BAGHEERA: No.
Don't yooo
tell him.

(BAGHEERA *leaves, running after* MOWGLI. BALOO *shakes his head, grumbles to himself as he exits. The River furls up and away. When it's gone, enter the wolves,* GRAB, GREY, *and* AKELA, *playing, jumping, pawing, cavorting.*)

GRAB: Why do we gotta keep with that Littlllllle Frog?

GREY: Get Sherakhan all mad at us.

AKELA: The pack made a promise, that's why.
Beforr yoo were born.

GREY: Bet yoo were there, hun?

GRAB: Beforr we were born.

GREY: Yer old enuff.

(GRAB *and* GREY *laugh.* AKELA *is stung: covers it by attacking them playfully. They scuffle and yelp with delight. Enter* MOWGLI, *lumbering and rolling like* BALOO. *Speaks in low Baloovoice.*)

MOWGLI: Hullooo. I'm Mowwwwgli the bayer!

(He jumps in, roaring like a bear. They scuffle and laugh, till suddenly GRAB and GREY step away. Slowly they begin to circle and chant, with AKELA standing by, annoyed.)

GRAB & GREY: Mannncubb
   Mannncubb
   uggggleee yoo
   Pigs arrr naked,
   and yoo arr, too.

(MOWGLI laughs uncertainly; is worried by their growing ferocity.)
   Manncub Manncub
   ugggggleee yoo
   Birdies arr toothless,
   and yoo arrr, too.
   Mannncubb Manncubb
   ugggggggleeee yoo
   Humans arrrr stinky,
   and so arrrrrr yoo!

AKELA: *(Steps in.)* Nuff. Knock it off.

(GRAB and GREY hesitate; till GREY starts circling AKELA. GRAB joins in.)

GREY: Kela Kela
   ooooold yoo
   Buffaloes limp
   and yoo doo, too.

AKELA: *(Restrained.)* Hey . . .

GREY & GRAB: Kela Kela
   ooooold yoo
   Deer walk backwards
   and yoo doo, too.
   Kela kela
   ooooooooooold yooo
   Oldies get hurt
   and yoo will, tooo!

(GRAB and GREY scream with laughter, run off. AKELA stands, shaken. MOWGLI approaches, touches him.)

MOWGLI: Why'd they do that?

AKELA: *(Shakes him off.)* Get away, willya.

(Pause. AKELA lowers head. MOWGLI sulks.)

MOWGLI: Thought I wuz one uv the pack:

AKELA: Yoo're just young.
   Like them.
   Tiger makes'em strange,
   say stuff they don't
   mean.

MOWGLI: Tiger's after me, not them.

AKELA: Nobody gets yoo while
I'm around.

MOWGLI: *(Pauses.)* Would I be in yoor pack even if I wasn't a wulf?

AKELA: *(Looks at him, chuckles wearily.)* Even if yoo were a tigercub, Flatface.
(Shoves his head playfully.) Wulf keeps a promise.
No big deal.

(AKELA *looks at* MOWGLI; *then turns, follows wolves.* MOWGLI *sits, sulks.* PER-CHY *the monkey enters behind him. Walks up, staring at* MOWGLI. MOWGLI *notices.)*

MOWGLI: Get away.

(MONKEY *stares. Dances around* MOWGLI. MOWGLI *scowls.* MONKEY *sits beside* MOWGLI, *imitating scowl and sulk.* MOWGLI *turns glaring at the* MONKEY. MONKEY *imitates, glaring back.* MOWGLI *stands threatening;* MONKEY *stands threatening back.* MOWGLI *roars;* MONKEY *screeches.* MOWGLI *shoves;* MONKEY *shoves back.* MOWGLI *beats fists on the ground;* MONKEY *likewise.* MONKEY *imitates* MOWGLI's *every action until suddenly* MOWGLI *stops, stands, listening. Pulls the* MONKEY *with him, and they climb up behind trees to watch.)*

Enter SHERAKHAN *the Tiger, strolling, looking about. Stops, pauses; listens. Smells something.* MOWGLI *and the monkey are very still.*

Enter opposite, GRAB, *running from some fast game. He almost collides with the* TIGER.)

SHERAKHAN: Good hunting.

GRAB: *(Freezes with panic.)* Good hunting, Sherakhan.

SHERAKHAN: *(Lounging catlike.)* Relllllllaaaaaax.
I'm not hunting
young wooooooolves . . .
right now.

GRAB: Good thing.

SHERAKHAN: Though I do wonder how
such fine hunters as you Freepeepul
are content to be led by a
dying old wulf—what's his name?—
and a hairless mancub.

GRAB: Akela is pack leader.

SHERAKHAN: I hear that even
Akela yoor old leader
cannot look this manling in the eyes.

(GRAB *growls, nods.)*
Does this manling
belooooong
in the Jungal?
With his fingers
and staaaaaaaring eyes

and furless skin?
Is he one uv us?
Arrr therr no brayve wooooolves
to tayke
back
the pack
from this naked Manboy?

GRAB: He grew up with us.
Akela protects him, is all.

SHERAKHAN: Akela protects him,
while Akela's alive.

(MONKEY's *getting bored with being silent; he's been hanging by one hand. He slips, catches himself, laughs briefly before* MOWGLI *can slap a hand over his mouth.* SHERAKHAN *looks up, but cannot see them through the trees. Silence.* GRAB *takes this opportunity to turn away, but* SHERAKHAN *notices.*)
Wait.

(GRAB *freezes.*)
I have fed full tonight
on a large buck.
Come with me.
I will take yoo too it,
and you can feed with me.
And we'll talk
about Akela
and about a leader for yoor Pack.

(SHERAKHAN *starts to walk off, turns, looks at* GRAB. GRAB *looks around, follows.* SHERAKHAN *lifts a paw to pat* GRAB's *head;* GRAB *pulls away.* SHERAKHAN *smiles, leaves.* GRAB *follows.* MOWGLI *makes sure they're gone before letting go the* MON-KEY, *who chatters angrily.* MOWGLI *climbs down, stares after the wolf and the tiger.*)

MOWGLI: (*Holds up hand, looks at it.*) Stupid ugly fingers.
Ugly crummy bare skin.
Why do I have to look like this!

(*He's clenching his fist, furious.* MONKEY *imitates.* MOWGLI *notices.*)
Yoo have others who look like yoo?

(MONKEY *doesn't understand.*)
Thought I did. I guess
I was wrong.

(MOWGLI *looks sad.* MONKEY *mimics sadness.* MOWGLI *giggles. They begin to mimic each other, ending by pulling tail and hair, laughing and chattering. Enter* KAA *the Python, moving sinuously and silently until he is just behind them. Emits a long hiss.*)

KAA: YYyyyyyyyyyyyyyyyyyaaaaaaaaaaaaaaaaaaasssssssssssss.

(MOWGLI *and* MONKEY *turn to see him.*)
MOWGLI: Rock snake!

(They dive for the trees. KAA *follows them with eyes, calm.)*

KAA: Sssssstayy yoo sssssssssso!

*(*MOWGLI *and* MONKEY *freeze, looking at* KAA. KAA *holds their gazes with his eyes, moves slowly toward them.)*
    Kaa ssss seeeeees.
    Kaa seeeeeees
    hayyyyyrrlesssss monkeeeee,
    Kaa feeeeeeeds.

*(*MOWGLI *and* MONKEY *are hypnotized, as* KAA *moves in. Enter* BAGHEERA *behind the snake.)*

BAGHEERA: Good hunting, Kaa.

(The moment is enough for the MONKEY *to snap out and scurry away.* MOWGLI *shakes his head, but* KAA *looks back and hypnotizes him.)*

KAA: Ssstay!

MOWGLI: *(In the instant of consciousness.)* One Blood, yoo and mee.

*(*KAA *stops, stares at him, puzzled.)*

KAA: Whaaat monkeee is thisss
    who speeeeks Masssssterrr woooords?

BAGHEERA: No monkey, Kaa
    A friend uv mine.

KAA: Friend uv Bagheera?
    This creature isss noo catt.

BAGHEERA: This is the manncub, Kaa.
    Ward uv the Freepeepul wulfpack.

KAA: Aaaah!
    Ward uv Bagheera.
    Kaaa knoooows.

BAGHEERA: Must be
    good hunting elsewhere,
    Kaa.

KAA: I spaare this mancub
    for his Massssstrrr woords.
    That other monkee
    is not passst my chase.
    But have caaaaare, manling.
    Kaa feeeds on monkeeees
    whoo look
    like
    yoo.
    Kaa seeeeeeees,
    Kaa knoooooooooooooooooooooooooowwwwwwwsssssssssssssss.

*(*KAA *moves off after the* MONKEY.)*

MOWGLI: Good hunting, Kaa.
    Somewhere else.

BAGHEERA: Kaa will feed well enough.
No monkey survives the stare uv the python.
What did you see in his eyes, Little Frog?

MOWGLI: *(Looks at* BAGHEERA, *then away; shudders.)* Feeer.

(Pause. Jungalsounds.)
You saved my life.

BAGHEERA: The Masterwoords saved yoo—

MOWGLI: You saved me.
I'm lucky yoo were here.

BAGHEERA: *(Considers saying something, decides against it.)* Yoo should be more careful.

MOWGLI: Baloo taught me
always repay a favor.
Don't know how a little guy like me
can pay back a life to Bagheera the Panther.

*(*MOWGLI *reaches out tentatively to touch* BAGHEERA'*s back.* BAGHEERA *pulls away, awkward.)*

BAGHEERA: I didn't ask for payment. *(Pause.)*
I am not one to be
petted.

MOWGLI: *(Thinks, then smiles.)* I wasn't gonna pet.
It's just that
most uv my friends in the jungal
can't quite reach back to scratch the
itch
they get
right here—I'll show yoo—
right here between the shoulderblades.
But I have these. *(Holds up hand.)*
Maybe these ugly fingers uv mine can
be some good.

BAGHEERA: *(Cautious.)*
I have
had
an itch
there . . .

*(*MOWGLI *reaches back;* BAGHEERA *warily lets him scratch his back near the neck.* BAGHEERA *is tense at first, but quickly relaxes, lounges, even purrs and stretches at the scratching. Howl offstage.* BAGHEERA *coils up.)*
I smell the tiger.

*(*BAGHEERA *leaps off into the jungal; opposite,* GRAB *scrambles on, watching behind him.* MOWGLI *confronts him.)*

MOWGLI: Grab!

GRAB: *(Whirls.)* Whaddya want?

MOWGLI: Been talking to Sherakhan, have ya?

GRAB: What about it?

MOWGLI: Hyeeenas talk to him, too.

GRAB: Get outta heer, Goggle-eyes.
 Yoo're no part uv the jungal,
 furless, funnyface manbaby.
 Go back to yoor human village
 where yoo belong.

(*Behind* GRAB, *enters a tired or wounded buffalo, groaning.*)
 Beat it, manbaby!

MOWGLI: What for?

(MOWGLI *is pushed aside by* GREY *entering opposite. With him is* AKELA.)

GREY: Heeer it is! The buffalo! Heer, Akela!

GRAB: Stand back for Akela!
 Leader uv the Pack show yoor stuff!

(MOWGLI *steps away, inconspicuous.* AKELA *is puzzled and confused, looking at* GRAB *and* GREY.)
 We saved this kill for yoo.

AKELA: Why'd ya do that?

GREY: Get him!
 Arr yoo still
 Leeeeder? Spring, Akela!

(AKELA, *flustered and confused, crouches and springs on the buffalo, which bellows. As he does so,* SHERAKHAN *steps onstage behind the buffalo.*)

SHERAKHAN: Steal my kill, Akela?

(*Claws out,* SHERAKHAN *cuffs* AKELA *powerfully across the face, sending the* WOLF *sprawling on his back, badly hurt.* SHERAKHAN *moves at him.*)
 Jungal Law forbids that. Yoor punishment—

AKELA: (*Trying to pull himself up.*) Wulfs! Defend me!

(GRAB *and* GREY *stand stock-still.* AKELA *looks at them. The buffalo has escaped.*)

SHERAKHAN: Defend yoorself, dead wulf.

MOWGLI: Ambush cowards! (*He jumps out, tries to pull* AKELA *away.*)
 Akela, get away from here—

AKELA: (*Shoves* MOWGLI *aside.*) Outta my way.
 I'm no dog
 like them.
 All I need is one bite at yoor throat—

(*He swipes weakly at* SHERAKHAN, *who cuffs him down again.*)

SHERAKHAN: Gooood!
 Dead wulf and manboy,
 both in one meal.

(BAGHEERA *springs on, flinging* SHERAKHAN *down, standing over him poised to kill the* TIGER *with one blow.*)

BAGHEERA: *(Agonized and furious.)* Yoo sicken me.
 Yoo make me ashamed.
 Make stupid young wulfs betray their leader
 so yoo can sneak up on one who's dying.
 Is there no
 coward snake-thing
 yoo won't do?

(BAGHEERA *will kill him; but stops, hesitates, lowers paw just slightly. The* TIGER *sees the chance, hurls himself against* BAGHEERA'*s side. The* PANTHER *falls back, the* TIGER *leaps up; the two cats face off like two karate masters.*)

SHERAKHAN: Agayn
 and agayn
 yoo keep me from my meat.
 The buffalo was my kill. I'll catch it,
 and let yoo protect yoor wooooolfes,
 O untamed Bagheera.
 But watch yoor mancub closely.
 I taste him;
 my teeth sharp at the feel uv his flesh.
 Ride on this panther's *back* now,
 boy.
 If I meet yoo alone,
 truce or no truce,
 yoo will end where yoo should have begun.

(SHERAKHAN *roars, exits.*)

GRAB: *(Innocent.)* Is Akela hurt?

(MOWGLI *screams, hurls himself at the wolves, who run off; he starts to follow, but* AKELA, *who has pulled himself up partially, moans and crumples.* MOWGLI *runs to him.*)

MOWGLI: I saw them plant the trap.
 I saw it. I'm stupid and blind . . .

AKELA: Good thing yoo didn't
 fight the tiger for my sake.
 We'd both be gone, instead uv
 just me.

MOWGLI: Yoo're not hurt that bad.

AKELA: Long time
 since the old days uv
 mancub
 rolling naked in the dust.

MOWGLI: I'm a wulf.
 No fault uv mine I was born human.
 I'm one skin with the Freepeeple wulfpack.

AKELA: Wulfpack
 is no wulfpack.

They follow the Tiger.
Lick his hindpaws.
Eat his scraps.
Led me to his ambush.
This hunting is ended;
Yoo arr human.
Go to man.

MOWGLI: I won't go.
I'll hunt alone in the jungal.

AKELA: Can yoo help me up,
Little Brother?
I was Leader uv the Pack
when the wulfs
were
a pack.

(MOWGLI *helps him to his feet.* BALOO *has entered behind.*)
Feet in the dark that leave no mark,
Silent blow uv paw,
This is the hour uv pride and power.
Talon, Tooth, Claw
Hear my call: Good Hunting All
that keep the Jungal Law!

(*He leaps in the air, falls limp to the ground.* MOWGLI *touches him*)

BAGHEERA: Good hunting, Akela.

BALOO: Good hunting, Akela. (*Pauses.*)
I heard the ruckus.
Is this Sherakhan's work?

(BAGHEERA *nods.*)

MOWGLI: By my small and weak and clawless hands
I swear
Sherakhan will pay for this.

BALOO: Mowgli.
Yoo must decide now.

MOWGLI: (*Still kneeling to hold* AKELA.) Decide what?

BALOO: Akela
can't protect yoo anymore.
All yoor protectors will be gone
some night.
Yoo can wait for Sherakhan to catch yoo
alone.
Yoo can hide, or run to some other Jungal,
or run to the manvillage.
Or yoo can face Sherakhan.
What will yoo do?

MOWGLI: Why do I
have to face the Tiger?

BALOO: Tiger wants yoo dead—

MOWGLI: *(To* BAGHEERA.*)* Sherakhan ambushed Akela.
  Yoo are Master.
  Can't yoo punish Sherakhan?

BAGHEERA: Me?

MOWGLI: Kill him.

BAGHEERA: *(Stunned.)* Me, kill Sherakhan?

BALOO: *(Shaking head.)* Mowgli,
  don't you see Bagheera?
  Don't yoo see Sherakhan?
  Panther and tiger,
  they are the same kind.

BAGHEERA: I can fight Sherakhan,
  I can defend yoo from his teeth,
  but kill him?

BALOO: It is against the Law.

MOWGLI: Aren't you Master uv the Jungal?

BALOO: Not uv the Law.

BAGHEERA: The Law is my master. And yoors.

MOWGLI: *(Bowing head.)* Leave me alone then.
  My last friend is gone,
  and I'm alone.

BALOO: Mowgli—

MOWGLI: No one left to defend me.
  Let Sherakhan ambush me. Let him catch me alone—

BALOO: *(Roaring.)* Stop it!
  Yoo're too old to insult
  yoor true guardian.

  (BAGHEERA *has turned his back.*)
  Akela was not yoor only protector.
  There is another
  who has watched yoo closely
  from the day yoo were born.
  He has kept yoo from trouble
  and given yoo
  yoor life
  more times than yoo or I can count.
  He would never tell yoo,
  but Akela is gone
  and yoo must know
  who has guarded yoo ever since he
  bought yoor life
  for the price uv a bull
  ten yeers back.

MOWGLI: *(Looks at* BAGHEERA, *who stands unmoving with his back turned.)* But I
  never hardly saw yoo.

BAGHEERA: *(Slowly.)* I smell
  and I hear
  farther than yoo can see.

BALOO: The Jungal is careful uv whatever Bagheera protects.

(MOWGLI *rises, approaches* BAGHEERA.)

MOWGLI: *(Softly.)* All my life?

(BAGHEERA *turns, raises head, bends back to show his neck.*)

BAGHEERA: What dyoo see here?

MOWGLI: *(Peering.)* A spot without fur. What is that?

BAGHEERA: The mark uv a collar.
Only Baloo
and now yoo
have seen it.
I was born
in
the cages uv the King's Palace at Oodyepoor.
My mother was trapped in the jungal
by men using the stranglevine
which they call rope.
I was raised with this
rope
around my neck,
fed with an iron pan in a cage.
When I grew,
I felt my strength
and bit the vine in two with my jaw.
I returned
and became most terrible in the Jungal.
Am I not, Baloo?

BALOO: All the Jungal fears Bagheera.

BAGHEERA: Terrible and
alone.
Yoo are like me,
Little Frog.
I grew up like yoo
alone
and different
in a world uv strange creatures.
The humans fed me and cared for me,
and I pay them back
with your life.
But kill that tiger . . . I can't doo that.
Not even for yoo.

(MOWGLI *steps away, stunned by all this.*)

MOWGLI: This is
feeer
I guess.
Huh?
Grow up a wulf,
whole jungal is my big friend,

till all uv a sudden I'm no wulf,
I'm no baare,
I'm not even a silly stinky monkey.
What am I?
Some hoooman with no fur?
Where do hooomans live?

BALOO: Manvillage. At the edge uv the jungal.

MOWGLI: Will they protect me?

BALOO: Don't know.

MOWGLI: They have to.
Wet dark jungal is all my enemy,
all ambush and teeth and tiger.
Hooomans have to protect me!

(MOWGLI *runs off.* BAGHEERA *starts to follow;* BALOO *blocks him.*)

BALOO: Bagheera!
This time I tell yoo:
let him go.

BAGHEERA: (*Looks after* MOWGLI, *then back at* BALOO; *plaintive.*) Will he come back?

BALOO: It's up to him.

(CHIL *the Vulture caws in the distance.*)
No need to leave Akela for that vulture.
The River will take his body.

(BALOO *picks* AKELA *up by the feet, carries him away over his back.* BAGHEERA *still looks after* MOWGLI; *then follows* BALOO *off.* MOWGLI *enters opposite, skulking about.*)

MOWGLI: This whole manvillage is like
one big panther cage.

(*Noises off.* MOWGLI *hides, watches as* HUMANS *enter, leading* ELEPHANT. *The robotlike* HUMANS *wear neutral masks; they carry whips, snapping them at the elephant to goad him into place.* ELEPHANT *is also led by rope, which they tie to a tree. One of the whips gets snapped too close to the* ELEPHANT's *face; the* ELEPHANT *panics, skitters.* HUMANS *snap whips, taunt* ELEPHANT *to get him to stay still;* ELEPHANT *grows more frightened as they taunt, till* ELEPHANT *screams—a big scream made of two voices.*)
(*Jumps out.*) Leave him alone!

(*He leaps toward the* HUMANS, *waving his arms and screaming monkeylike to scare them. They are taken aback by this wild creature, but they try to fend him off with their whips.* MOWGLI *grabs the whips out of their hands, shouting. He snaps at the* HUMANS *who turn and clipclop terrified offstage.* MOWGLI *hurls the whips after them. Turns to* HATHI *the* ELEPHANT, *who is staring at him oddly.*)
You're safe. They're gone.

HATHI: (*double-voice   scream.*)   WHOOOOOOOOOOOOOOOOOOOO-
OOOOOOO're YOOOOOOO?

MOWGLI: *(Jumping back.)* One blood, you and me!

HATHI: Jungaltalk!
  WHAAAAAAAAAAAT AAAAAAArrr YOOOOOOO?

MOWGLI: I'm Mowgli the wulf.

HATHI: DOOOOOOOOOOOOOOOOOOOOOOOOOOOOOOOON'T gimme
  that.
  You're no wulf. What are ya?
  Yer sure funny-lookin.

MOWGLI: What're yoo?

HATHI: *(Proud.)* I'm Hathi the Elephant.
  You never seen an elephant?

MOWGLI: Only in the jungal.

HATHI: I didn't know little boys lived in the jungal.

MOWGLI: I'm no boy. Have yoo even been
  to the jungal?

HATHI: BEEEEN THERE?
  My father's father's father MAAAAAAADE the jungal, boy.
  PULLED the jungal owt uv the ground with his trunk
  DUG with his TUSK to make rivers
  STRUCK with his foot to make ponds and trees.
  I am LOOOOOOORD uv the jungal,
  boy.

MOWGLI: If yoo're Lord uv the Jungal,
  how come yoo're trapped to that treee?

HATHI: *(Hesitates; gestures after HUMANS.)* Humans.

MOWGLI: *(Looking after them, astonished.)* Those are hoomans?

HATHI: Trapped me in the jungal when I was
  no bigger than yoo.
  Brought whips, brought this *(Pulls at rope with his neck.),*
  made me
  carry their wood.

MOWGLI: Those ugly silly animals
  arr hoooomans?
  Well I'm not one uv them. *(Imitates their robot walk.)*

HATHI: Yoo look like them.
  They forget
  whooo I am.
  But I don't forget.
  I will leave this human place
  and go back to the jungal
  before I die.

MOWGLI: How do they keep yoo here?

HATHI: With this. (HATHI *strains at the rope.)*

MOWGLI: Well, I'm no human. *(He goes to fiddle with the rope.)*

HATHI: What're yoo doing?

  (With one or two tugs, MOWGLI *figures out how the slipknot works; he takes the rope off* HATHI's *neck, stands holding it.)*

MOWGLI: See?
  Humans trap yoo. I'm Mowgli
  and I set yoo free.
  I'm no human.
  Yoo can go back to the jungal now.

(HATHI *steps away, awkward; twists neck; staggers away and stares at* MOWGLI, *amazed.*)

HATHI: What are yoo, anyway?
  Yoo look just like 'em, but yoo set me freee.
  Yoo say yoo're not human,
  but yoo know how to use rope.

MOWGLI: What's rope?

HATHI: Yoo're holding it in yoor fingers.

MOWGLI: This is rope?

HATHI: Fingers, skin, eyes; ya use the rope.
  Sorry, boy. Yoo're human,
  and stuck with it.

(MOWGLI *stands staring at the rope.*)
  I owe you my freedom.
  Yoo got enemies?
  I'll step on 'em for ya.

MOWGLI: (*Slow.*) No.
  I take care uv my own
  enemies.
  From now on.

HATHI: Okay then. (*Turns to go, stops, turns back.*)
  Good hunting,
  jungal boy.

MOWGLI: Good hunting,
  Lord uv the Jungal.

(HATHI *gives a final trumpet shriek, exits.* MOWGLI *looks at knot on tree; fiddles with it, unties it, throws rope over his shoulder. Carries it off as he exits.*)

As MOWGLI *circles around behind the set, jungal sounds arise from offstage, and the River unfurls in front; when* MOWGLI *comes back around, he is in the Jungal.* MOWGLI *kneels at the River. Bends down, cups hands, drinks/touches lips to fabric.*

Behind, enter KAA. MOWGLI *turns quickly, sees* KAA. KAA *writhes sensuously, dancing slowly, not especially noticing* MOWGLI.)

KAA: Yyaaaaa shhhhh sssss

MOWGLI: One blood,
  you and me.

KAA: (*Draws up startled; sees the boy, continues dancing.*) Sssss!
  Mannnnling.
  Ssssssmmmmmmmmmelll

watrrrrrr
Is watrrrrrr
gooooood?

MOWGLI: Water is good,
what there is uv it.

KAA: Watrrrr
is in the air.
Sssssssmmmelll!
Look up!

MOWGLI: *(Looks up.)* Clouds!

KAA: Claaaowwwds.
sss
full uv rayyyyn
dripfullll
sssss
Kaaaaaa
will make
rayyyynnn.

MOWGLI: Yoo
will bring rain?

KAA: Kaaaa
will daance,
daaaaaaaaaaaaansssssss
at the top
uv the mowntayn
and make
rayyyyn.

MOWGLI: Soon?

KAA: Nowwww.
Rayyyyn
will covrrr the mowntayn
and choke the riverrrrr
when Kaaa
danssss esss.

MOWGLI: The rain will flood this river?

KAA: Kaaa
will dansssss,
and the River
will rise
to draaaown
bear and elephant and giraffe
if they stand in its paaaath.
When Kaa
daaaans esss
atop
the mowntayn
Yaaaaaaaaaaaaaaaaaaaaaa shhhhhhhhhhh sssssssssssssssssss.

(KAA *circles behind the set, still writhing; climbs up the rear of the set very slowly, almost imperceptibly, throughout the following scenes.*

MOWGLI *inspects the area; stands thinking. Tugs at the foot of a tree, then sits, thinking, looking at the rope.* BAGHEERA *enters behind him silently.)*

BAGHEERA: *(Slowly.)* The humans
    won't help yoo?

MOWGLI: *(Rises to meet him.)* No.
    Nobody helps me
    more than yoo.
    And yoo've done all yoo can.

BAGHEERA: I have decided.
    Yoo can stay in the jungal
    and be safe.
    I will kill Sherakhan.
    I'll hunt him and jump on his back
    and kill him.
    Than you can stay.

MOWGLI: What about the Law?

BAGHEERA: Law's not the only master in the Jungal.
    I will leave the jungal if I have to
    or die, or be punished.
    But I will kill Sherakhan,
    and yoo will stay.

MOWGLI: I owe my life to you.
    I owe yoo more than I can pay back
    ever.
    I'll face the tiger myself.

BAGHEERA: Yoo're just a cub.

MOWGLI: Yoo
    belong in the jungal.
    More than me.
    I will face Sherakhan.

(MOWGLI *picks up the rope.* BAGHEERA *leaps away, tense at the sight of it.* MOWGLI *kneels, ties one end of the rope to the foot of a tree.)*

BAGHEERA: *(Hissing.)* No one in this jungal uses that.

MOWGLI: *(Calm, still tying rope.)* No one's *able* to use it.
    But me. I have fingers. See?
    I have human eyes. And skin.
    Makes me different, for all time.
    And makes this rope mine.

BAGHEERA: Law as old as
    human kind
    says
    when manthing enters the jungal,
    animals must disappear
    for their lives.
    You can't live in this jungal
    if yoo use
    that.

(*Silence.* MOWGLI *is finished tying the rope, leaving the rest with the lasso coiled, inconspicuous behind the tree. Stands now to face* BAGHEERA.)

MOWGLI: I know.

(Pause.)

BAGHEERA: I will be close by.

(BAGHEERA stalks away. MOWGLI looks around once more. He goes to the River, sits beside it. Relaxes, looking at us. Begins to sing, carelessly, in a cheerful tune that belies the words. Sings overloud, for distant ears.)

MOWGLI: Before the peacock flutters
   before the monkees cry
   before the vulture swoops a furlong clear,
   through the Jungal very softlee flits a shadow and a sigh—
   he is fear, O little hunter, He is Fear.

(Stops, listens a moment; continues.)

   Very softly down the glade
   runs a waiting watching shade
   and the whisper spreads and widens far and near;
   and the sweat is on the brow
   for he passes even now—
   he is fear, O little hunter, he is Fear . . .

(SHERAKHAN has entered behind him. The TIGER stalks on ready to spring, but seeing the boy's helpless posture, stops, chuckles.)

SHERAKHAN: I seee
   your protectors
   sleeep,
   Manling.
   Yoo and I arr alone.

(MOWGLI turns, casually; rises to face the TIGER, though some distance away, and always between the TIGER and the unseen rope.)

MOWGLI: *(Friendly.)* Welcome,
   Murderer.

SHERAKHAN: We all murderrr, Manling.

MOWGLI: *(Still calm.)* Yoo murderrred Akela
   on his homeground.

SHERAKHAN: All grownd is hunting ground for me.

MOWGLI: Yoo did not kill for food
   but for revenge
   and for sport
   and for the pleasure uv killing.
   Only the coward Tiger
   breaks Jungal law.

SHERAKHAN: Jungal Law is made
   to keep safe old bears
   and young foolish manboys.
   I am Sherakhan the Tiger:
   I ask no safety uv law
   nor do I give it.

MOWGLI: Do you respect the Water Truce
  by this River?

SHERAKHAN: *(Chuckling.)* Baloo your bumblebear is farrr away
  with his laws and troooces.
  My stomach
  has growled
  ten seasons for yoo.
  No speech saves yoo now.

MOWGLI: I must dance my death then.

(MOWGLI *starts hopping, dancing, skipping about.* SHERAKHAN *puzzles.*
MOWGLI *skips close to him, past him;* SHERAKHAN *makes a grab, misses because he
cannot turn as fast as* MOWGLI. MOWGLI *smiles.* SHERAKHAN *laughs, revolving to
watch* MOWGLI *dance.)*

SHERAKHAN: Run, boy,
  climb.
  Run, and I catch yoo.
  Climb, I catch yoo.
  Swimm, I catch yoo.
  But runn, dooo runnn.
  I enjoy the sport.

(MOWGLI *slows, stops, standing before the tree under which the rope is coiled. He
lets out a breath, sinks to his knees as if exhausted.)*

MOWGLI: Yoo are right.
  I have from yoo
  ten years uv life.
  I can run no longer.
  Will you have mercy on me,
  O terribal Sherakhan?

SHERAKHAN: I have hunting to finish tonight.
  Yoo weary me.

(MOWGLI *has gripped the rope behind him, now stands, steps toward the* TIGER.)

MOWGLI: Take me then
  and
  CHOKE!

(SHERAKHAN *leaps;* MOWGLI *leaps to meet him, noose out, straight at the* TIGER;
slips the rope over SHERAKHAN'S *head as he ducks down under the* TIGER'S *too-high
swing, scurries past and away before the* TIGER *can turn.* SHERAKHAN *jumps after
him, away from the bars; the loop tightens round his neck. Pulls angrily.* MOWGLI
stands out of reach. TIGER *rages, growls.)*

SHERAKHAN: No gooooood,
  clevrrrrrr mannboy.
  I chew through this vine
  and run yooooooo
  down!

MOWGLI: Will you? Look then!

(*Points up to where* KAA *has reached the top of the bars;* KAA *begins to dance. Thunder.*)
See where Kaa daaaaaansssses
atop the mowntayn?

(MOWGLI *laughs and dances. The* TIGER *is hypnotized.*)
Hear, Sherakhan?
Rain?
Have yoo seen the rise uv this river?
When the new rain
floods off the mowntayn?

(MOWGLI *climbs a tree out of reach, shouts over the thunder.*)
Have you drunk tonight?
Drink yoor fill,
Sherakhan!

(*The River starts rippling, breaking* SHERAKHAN *out of his trance. He runs, tugs at the rope, tries to climb. The rope holds him back. Claws at it. His paws can't quite reach the neck. Lurches, hurts his neck, struggles snarling left and right. The River is rippling higher and higher.* SHERAKHAN *hurls himself at the tree, staggers back, stands, raises two paws, roars loud and long—till the River fabric snaps up high in the air, covering the* TIGER *from sight.*

KAA's *dance has ended: The* SNAKE *leaves. The fabric floats down descending slowly, till the River settles to level, subsides. The* TIGER *has disappeared.*

The thunder has stopped. Distant howl of wolves.)
GRAB & GREY: (*Off.*) Sherakhan! Sherakhan!

(*Wolves enter.*)
GREY: Sherakhan!
GRAB: Save us from the thunder!

(MOWGLI *jumps down, faces the wolves.*)
MOWGLI: I AM SHERAKHAN!

(BAGHEERA *has entered with* BALOO, *watching.* MOWGLI *is breathing hard and fast, pacing catlike with bared teeth.*)
Master uv the Jungal,
me, Sherakhan!
I kill, I eat, I murder where I please!
I rip the Jungal with my teeth,
I crush the sky with my jaw!
Sherakhan!
Hyenas and dogs
follow me, lick my feet for scraps.
Dogs! Fangmouth dogs with lolling tongues
I'll slash with my talon!
Sherakhan!

(Leaps at the wolves, swinging fists over head like a little boy trying to fight. GRAB *and* GREY *are terrified; they run off.* MOWGLI *stops, panting, wild-eyed.)*
I am Sherakhan
and the ants at the bottom uv the river
have my hide for a gift.
Sherakhan!

(Sees BALOO *and* BAGHEERA*; he attacks them, leaping and clawing.* BAGHEERA *fends him off,* BALOO *catches and hugs him. He beats furiously at* BALOO*; stops; hands go to head, eyes clenched tight shut.)*
Ww
what
is it—
Baloo
Bagheera, help me . . .
am I dying?
Some insect is stinging my eyes.

BALOO: Yoo make tears.
Tears like men use.

MOWGLI: The jungal hurts me,
but I don't want to leave it.
I'm two Mowglis.

BALOO: Man goes to man.
Let them fall, Mowgli.
They arr only tears.

MOWGLI: I broke the Law.
Used manthing.
Dost the jungal cast me out?

BALOO: Yoo killed the Tiger.
No one but Mowgli commands Mowgli now.

MOWGLI: I'll stay then.
Can I stay?

BALOO: Stay
if yoo can.
But the jungal is full uv wulfs
and tigers.
Will yoo spend yoor life
killing them all with rope
just to show yoo belong heer?

MOWGLI: Bagheera?
Yoo bought my life from the Pack.
Yoo are Master uv the Jungal.
Will yoo command me to stay?

BAGHEERA: *(Head is bowed.)* When I was grown,
the cage uv my youth
could not hold me.
Yoo are grown
now,
Little Brother.
This Jungal

uv yoor youth
cannot hold yoo.
Baloo knows more than I do,
and his woord
is my woord.
By the bull that bought yoo
I set yoo free.

(BAGHEERA *steps away, facing away from them.* MOWGLI *looks after him, then down.*)

MOWGLI: I'll live in that village then.
But I'll never be human like them.
I am Mowgli
and the Jungal is my home.

BALOO: No more to say.
Just hold a thought
at night
sometimes
for this fatt
old baaare.

MOWGLI: I will.
Bagheera?

(BAGHEERA *can't speak, can't look at him.* MOWGLI *waits for an answer; then turns away, dries eyes. Walks away. Only when* MOWGLI *is almost off does* BAGHEERA *speak, painfully, without turning.*)

BAGHEERA: *(Can hardly bear to say these words.)* Remember Bagheera!

(Still can't look at MOWGLI; *steps farther away.)*
Remember
Bagheera loved yoo!
Good hunting on a new trail.

(Another step away.)
Remember Bagheera!

(The PANTHER *leaps off and is gone.* MOWGLI *looks after him; turns; leaves the jungal.* BALOO *watches him go.*)

BALOO: *(After he is gone.)* One blood
yoo and me.

(The words "one blood, yoo and me" are taken up in whispers by the whole cast. The chanting of the words grows as BALOO turns, walks off. Chanting modulates to chattering, cawing, snarling. Jungalsounds loud for a moment; then quick silence.)

CURTAIN

A THOUSAND CRANES

by
Kathryn Schultz Miller

KATHRYN SCHULTZ MILLER, who has a B.A. from the University of Cincinnati, has written plays for young audiences since 1976. She served for twenty years as Co-Founder and Artistic Director of ArtReach Touring Theatre, a professional touring theatre based in Cincinnati, Ohio. During the time of her administration ArtReach often performed as many as one thousand times a year to an annual audience of 300,000. The company performed in theatres and schools all across the country, including the John F. Kennedy Center in Washington, D.C. In 1983, ArtReach was awarded the Zeta Phi Kappa Award of the national children's theatre association for "the best new children's theatre in the United States."

Miller is the recipient of three Playwriting Fellowships from the Ohio Arts Council for her plays, *The Shining Moment*, *A Thousand Cranes*, and *Island Son*. She also received an Ohio Arts Council Fiction Fellowship in 1994, and a National Endowment for the Arts Fellowship in 1992.

Fifteen of her scripts including dramatizations of *The Red Badge of Courage* and *The Legend of Sleepy Hollow* have been published. In addition to *A Thousand Cranes*, other published plays that have been produced nationwide include such titles as *Amelia Earhart*, *Blue Horses*, and *Choosing Sides for Basketball*.

Miller is the winner of the 1987 Ohio Theatre Alliance Award for "outstanding contribution to Ohio theatre" and the 1985 Post-Corbett Award "for literary excellence in playwriting." Miller served for six years on the board of the Ohio Theatre Alliance and three terms on the Advisory Panel of the Ohio Arts Council. She continues to serve as administrative and artistic consultant to growing theatre companies in Ohio and Michigan.

In 1996, after twenty years as Artistic Director of ArtReach, Miller retired to spend more time on other writing projects. The administration of the ArtReach was passed from Touring Theatre to Theatre IV of Richmond, Virginia, which has a distinguished, twenty-one-year background of touring theatre for young audiences. Theatre IV oversees the administrative operation, while maintaining a base in Cincinnati.

During my career as a playwright for young audiences, the most rewarding moments were very quiet ones. There is nothing as fulfilling as watching the faces of my audience members and see that they are entirely involved and that the actions on stage have true meaning in their lives. It is particularly challenging to present the kinds of themes that plays like *A Thousand Cranes* present. Love, death, family separation, and even war are concepts that can have great emotional value to young people when they are presented in a caring, thoughtful and gentle way. The most rewarding moments are seeing a child reach toward maturity and understanding.

—KATHRYN SCHULTZ MILLER

A THOUSAND CRANES

A Play in One Act
For One Male and Two Females with doubling

CHARACTERS

Sadako: a twelve-year-old Japanese girl living in Hiroshima
Kenji: Sadako's fourteen-year-old friend (also plays ACTOR 1 and FATHER)
Grandmother Oba Chan: the spirit of Sadako's deceased Grandmother
(also plays ACTOR 2 and MOTHER)

PLACE

Hiroshima, Japan

TIME

1955

AT RISE: *The playing area is a circle of about 20 feet by 20 feet. Audience is seated on three sides of the playing area. Upstage right of the circle will be a musical or instrument "station" with percussion instruments and recorded music arranged in such a way that at appropriate times actors may sit comfortably on a stool and contribute music and sound effects to the performance. Upstage left are standing fans of various pastels and varying heights, the tallest being less than 5 feet. To the left and right downstage are two white masks on each side in tube holders about waist high.* GRANDMOTHER OBA CHAN *will wear a magnificent Japanese mask.* ACTORS 1 *and* 2 *will carry white masks when playing the parts of the* DOCTORS. SPIRITS *will be indicated by red masks on holders but will not actually be worn by actors.* SADAKO, KENJI, MOTHER *and* FATHER, *will not wear masks.* ACTORS 1 *and* 2 *will wear all black.* SADAKO *wears a simple western-style school uniform of a skirt and blouse with a tie.*

The play begins in silence. ACTORS 1 *and* 2 *bow to each other before the music stand.* SADAKO *watches from behind the music stand.* ACTORS 1 *and* 2 *mime lifting a large piece of paper off the floor. In mirrored motions, they carry the paper to downstage center, carefully place it on the floor, and gently smooth it out. They bow again, then turn upstage.* SADAKO *crosses down to paper as recorded folding music begins. The mood of the music is gentle and pleasant.* ACTORS 1 *and* 2 *count with* SADAKO *as she mimes the folding of a larger-than-life crane.*

ALL: *(Punctuating their words with percussion sounds.)* One, two, three, four, five, six, seven, eight, nine . . . *(SADAKO mimes the lifting of the giant bird with both hands. It is very light. She thrusts the bird into flight.)*

SADAKO: Ten. *(SADAKO blows as if to launch it.* ALL *watch it in the sky, from left to right. To* AUDIENCE.*)* My name is Sadako. I was born in Japan in 1943. My home was called Hiroshima. *(Quiet sound effects come from* ACTORS 1 *and* 2.*)* When I was two years old, my mother held me in her arms. She sang a song to me. *(*ACTOR 2 *sings a soothing, quiet melody.)* It was a quiet summer morning. Inside our small house my grandmother was preparing tea. *(*SADAKO *pauses while* ACTOR 2 *sings.)* Suddenly there was a tremendous flash of light that cut across the sky! *(A very, very loud startling* BOOM *noise.* SADAKO *falls into a kneeling position, covering her head. When all is quiet she stands.)* My name is Sadako. This is my story. *(A dramatic rhythm beat, not as loud as before and slowly fading.)*

ACTOR 2: *(Quietly fading away.)* Sixty-seven, sixty-eight, sixty-nine, seventy . . .

*(*SADAKO *and* ACTOR 1, *now* KENJI, *have moved upstage and now* KENJI *comes bounding on to playing area, out of breath and laughing. He wears a black cap to distinguish himself as* KENJI. *He begins to count, determining by how many seconds he has won the race with* SADAKO. *As* ACTOR 2*'s counting fades he picks it up. They say the primary numbers, one and two and three, etc., together.)*

ACTOR 2: *(Fading.)* Seventy . . . seventy-one . . . seventy-two . . .

KENJI: One . . . two . . . three . . . four

*(*SADAKO *runs in out of breath and laughing.)*

KENJI: Beat you by four seconds!

SADAKO: Four? You're lying!

KENJI: *(Laughing.)* It was actually four and a half, but I let you have that.

SADAKO: Oh! You . . . ! (*Slumping.*) You always win! You should let somebody else win sometime.

KENJI: Why, Sadako. You can't mean that I should cheat so that you can win.

SADAKO: Oh, it wouldn't be cheating so much as . . . polite.

KENJI: (*Laughing.*) And I suppose when you run in the girl's contest next month, you'll want the judges to be *polite* and let somebody else win.

SADAKO: Well, no.

KENJI: I thought so.

SADAKO: Oh, Kenji, do you think I have a chance to win?

KENJI: (*Mocking.*) You? You win a race against the fastest girls in Hiroshima? You can't win.

SADAKO: Why not?

KENJI: Because you're a turtle that's why. A great, big, lumbering turtle. (*Mimes slow turtle, laughing at his jest.*)

SADAKO: I am not a turtle!

KENJI: Yes, you are.

SADAKO: Am not.

KENJI: Are, too.

SADAKO: Well, if I'm a turtle, then you're a frog!

KENJI: A frog?

SADAKO: Yes. A great big green one with warts all over it.

KENJI: Sadako, you can't possibly mean . . . croak . . . (*Putting her on.*) Well, where on earth could that have come from? Croak!

SADAKO: Oh, you.

KENJI: Look, Sadako, my hand is turning green . . . croak . . . and it has warts all over it! (*He crouches to a frog position and sticks out his tongue, leaping around, croaking. Uses bill of his cap to indicate the mouth of the croaking frog.*) Croak! Croak!

SADAKO: (*Laughing in spite of herself.*) Now, you stop that. (*She is laughing almost uncontrollably, soon* KENJI *stops and laughs with her. They stop, leaning on each other, gaining composure.*) Kenji, tell me the truth. Do you think I have *any* chance of winning the races next month?

KENJI: Sadako, I will tell you the truth. I believe you will win.

SADAKO: (*Thrilled.*) You really think so? You really, really do?

KENJI: Yes. I really, really do.

SADAKO: Oh, Kenji! (*She hugs him.*) Wait until I tell my father. He will be so proud of me! (*She starts to go.*)

KENJI: Now, don't quit practicing!

SADAKO: Oh, I won't.

KENJI: See you tomorrow?

SADAKO: Tomorrow! (*She moves upstage as if to exit.*)

(KENJI, *now* ACTOR 1, *moves to instrument station and makes music for scene change.* SADAKO *moves upstage as* ACTOR 2, *now* MOTHER, *moves into the scene.*

She is counting out candles and putting them on the table. She wears a kimono.
ACTOR 1 *counts and then fades as* MOTHER *joins in and finally ends the counting.)*

ACTOR 1: One hundred and eighteen, one hundred and nineteen, one hundred and twenty, one hundred and twenty-one, one hundred and twenty-two . . . one hundred and twenty-three . . . *(Again, they speak the primary numbers together.)*

MOTHER: *(Counting candles.)* One . . . two . . . three . . . four . . .

(SADAKO comes running in, very excited.)

SADAKO: Mother, Mother! Wait till you hear! I have wonderful news!

MOTHER: *(Not looking up, continues working.)* Your shoes, Sadako.

SADAKO: Oh. *(She calms down to remove her shoes, puts them by the door, then rushes back to MOTHER.)* Wait till I tell you!

MOTHER: Sadako, show your respect to your elders.

SADAKO: Oh. *(She bows, puts hands together as in prayer and bows her head toward MOTHER.)* Mother, Kenji just told me . . . !

MOTHER: Sadako, show your respect to our beloved ancestors. *(Disheartened, SADAKO kneels before an imaginary shrine, hands in prayer and bowing her head. Returns to MOTHER, somewhat subdued.)*

SADAKO: Mother, I . . .

MOTHER: You must wait for your father to tell this earth-shattering news. Now, it is time to prepare for dinner.

SADAKO: But, Mother . . .

MOTHER: Sushi has been prepared, the rice plates have been set. Sadako, you may warm the saki for your father.

SADAKO: Yes, Mother. *(MOTHER straightens candles on the table.)*

(FATHER enters, takes off his shoes.)

SADAKO: Father! *(She runs to him, grabs him in embrace and almost twirls him around.)* Wait till I tell you!

FATHER: Well, what is this?

MOTHER: *(Not angry.)* This daughter of yours will not learn discipline.

FATHER: Your mother is right, Sadako. You must learn moderation in all things.

SADAKO: But, Father, I have such wonderful news!

FATHER: *(Warm.)* It seems that everything in your world is wonderful, Sadako. *(Kisses the top of her head.)* You may tell us your news.

SADAKO: *(Looks anxiously at them BOTH.)* Now?

FATHER: *(Laughing.)* Now, Sadako.

SADAKO: Kenji says I'm fast enough to win the race next month! Isn't that wonderful? He thinks I can *win!*

FATHER: *(Genuinely impressed.)* You have been practicing very hard.

SADAKO: Oh, yes, Father. Kenji and I run every day.

FATHER: Kenji is a fast runner, an excellent athlete.

SADAKO: Yes, he is, Father. And a good teacher, too.

MOTHER: Even so, you must use discipline to practice very hard if you really want to win.

SADAKO: Oh, I want to win, Mother. I want to win more than anything on earth!

FATHER: We are very proud of you, Sadako. (BOTH *parents hug her.* MOTHER *begins to light candles.*)

SADAKO: Mother, why are you lighting candles on the table?

MOTHER: Soon it will be Oban, Sadako.

FATHER: It is the day of the spirits.

MOTHER: We light a candle for our ancestors who have died.

FATHER: We ask them to return to us and join in our celebration of life.

MOTHER: (*Has lit all but last candle.*) This one is for Oba Chan, your grandmother.

SADAKO: I remember her. I was only a baby, but I remember how warm my grandmother's hands were. (*She kneels before the candles.* MOTHER *and* FATHER *move away. Their lines now sound like statements in a dream.*)

FATHER: Oba Chan died in the Thunderbolt.

SADAKO: She had a gentle voice.

MOTHER: Suddenly there was a great flash of light.

SADAKO: Her smile was like sunshine.

FATHER: It cut through the sky!

SADAKO: Grandmother? Grandmother?

MOTHER: The world was filled with blinding light.

(MOTHER *and* FATHER *spin away with arms up in protecting gesture. They twirl to their places behind the music stand where they make percussion sounds.*)

SADAKO: Can you hear me, Grandmother?

FATHER: It took our friends.

SADAKO: Can your spirit really return like they say?

MOTHER: It took our home.

SADAKO: Are you watching me now? Do you see me when I run?

FATHER: It took your grandmother, Oba Chan.

(MOTHER *and* FATHER *now become* ACTOR 1 *and* ACTOR 2. *They use a percussion sound that builds, and when it stops the silence is startling. They begin to count.*)

ACTORS 1 and 2: One hundred and fifty-one . . .

SADAKO: One. (*Blows out first candle.*)

ACTORS 1 and 2: One hundred and fifty-two . . .

SADAKO: Two. (*Blows out second candle.*)

ACTORS 1 and 2: One hundred and fifty-three . . .

SADAKO: Three. (*Blows out third candle.*)

ACTORS 1 and 2: One hundred and fifty-four . . .

SADAKO: (*Before the candle of her* GRANDMOTHER, *looks up.*) Will I win my race,

Grandmother? Can you hear me now? (*Turns back to candle.*) Four. (*Blows out candle, stands and looks around.*) Grandmother?

(ACTOR 1 *plays a loud dramatic percussion sound that fades.* ACTOR 2, *using the voice she will use later as* GRANDMOTHER *speaks.*)

ACTOR 2 / GRANDMOTHER: (*As she moves slowly, twirling away until she is hidden behind the largest fan.*) I hear you, Sadako!

(*The loud cymbal sound comes again and fades into a new sound. Now a fast, quick staccato sound is heard from the instrument stand.* ACTOR 1 *also is* KENJI, *using only the voice from his location.* ACTOR 2 *turns upstage to put on* GRAND-MOTHER OBA CHAN's *mask.* SADAKO *begins to run in place.*)

KENJI: (*Moving downstage to replace set piece and back to music stand.*) You little turtle, you'll never win at that speed. (SADAKO *speaks as if he is beside her, running.*)

SADAKO: (*Running.*) I am not a turtle!

KENJI: Sure you are, that's how fast turtles run, isn't it?

SADAKO: Croak, croak, croak! (*They* BOTH *laugh.*)

KENJI: I bet I can make it to the river before you!

SADAKO: Bet you can't.

KENJI: Bet I can!

SADAKO: Bet you can't. (*She runs faster in place as percussion sound also speeds up.*)

(ACTOR 2, *who now becomes* GRANDMOTHER OBA CHAN, *turns and raises her arms. Her costume and mask are magnificent. A majestic sound is used by* ACTOR 1 *to accompany her movement.* SADAKO *is becoming out of breath.* GRANDMOTHER *makes a magical gesture toward* SADAKO. SADAKO *trips and falls.*)

KENJI: (*Still out of scene.*) Sadako, are you all right?

SADAKO: (*Rubbing her hip.*) Oooh . . .

KENJI: Here, let me help you up. (*She takes his hand and stands.*) Are you all right?

SADAKO: Yes, I'm fine.

KENJI: All right, then, let's begin again. (*Again,* SADAKO *runs very fast to the music. Again,* GRANDMOTHER *makes her magical gesture.* SADAKO *falls.*) Sadako?

SADAKO: I'm okay. Just a little dizzy, that's all. (*Staccato music begins again very fast, but* SADAKO *is slowing down.*)

KENJI: Discipline, Sadako! (*She speeds up, we can see that she is in pain, but she picks up the pace of the run.*)

SADAKO: I'm trying, Grandmother. I want to win, Grandmother. I want to fly like the wind!

GRANDMOTHER / ACTOR 2: I hear you, Sadako! (SADAKO *moves slowly in a circle, obviously dizzy.*)

(KENJI *and* GRANDMOTHER *become* ACTORS 1 *and* 2. *During the following lines, masks on poles will be carried and moved in the air by* ACTORS 1 *and* 2. *The masks will be stark white and ghostly.* ACTORS 1 *and* 2 *may use many voices and the lines should run into each other to give the impression of many.* SADAKO *tries to escape the floating faces, but they dance around her, bearing down to force her to bed. Recorded music uses a gong sound and heavy beat.)*

ACTOR 1: What is the matter with Sadako?

ACTOR 2: What is the matter with Sadako?

ACTOR 1: Why did she fall?

ACTOR 2: Why did she fall?

ACTOR 1: What could be wrong?

ACTOR 2: What could be wrong?

SADAKO: Nothing! I'm just tired, that's all!

ACTOR 1: X-ray her chest.

ACTOR 2: Examine her blood.

ACTOR 1: Put her in a hospital.

ACTORS 1 and 2: Hospital, hospital, hospital . . .

SADAKO: A hospital? No!

ACTOR 1: Put her to bed.

ACTOR 2: Put her to bed.

SADAKO: But there's nothing wrong with me!

ACTOR 1: Why did she fall?

ACTOR 2: Why did she fall?

ACTOR 1: Take some more tests.

ACTOR 2: Take some more tests.

ACTOR 1: You'll be just fine.

ACTOR 2: Now, don't you worry.

ACTOR 1: Don't you worry.

ACTOR 2: Put her to bed.

SADAKO: But I'll miss the race!

ACTOR 1: Now, don't you worry.

ACTOR 2: You'll be just fine.

ACTOR 1: Put her to bed.

SADAKO: I want to fly like the wind!

ACTORS 1 and 2: *(Holding white masks above their stands.)* Leukemia, leukemia, leukemia, leukemia, leukemia, leukemia . . .

SADAKO: Leukemia?

*(*ACTORS *1 and 2 drop masks into holders with a jarring thud. They become* MOTHER *and* FATHER *speaking with faces forward as if speaking to a doctor.)*

MOTHER: Leukemia? My little girl? But that's impossible! The atom bomb didn't even do so much as scratch her!

FATHER: The atom-bomb sickness? My daughter?

SADAKO: But it can't be true, Mother, can it? *(*MOTHER *and* FATHER *rush to her seated on the bench.)* I don't have any scars from the bomb. It didn't touch me. It can't be true, can it, Mother?

FATHER: There now, dear, they just want to do some more tests.

SADAKO: But how can I be sick from the bomb? It killed my grandmother, but I wasn't hurt at all.

MOTHER: *(Very gently.)* Sadako, the radiation doesn't always show up right away.

SADAKO: *(Terrified.)* I was only two when the bomb fell.

FATHER: It's just a few tests, that's all, sweetheart.

MOTHER: You'll be here a few weeks.

SADAKO: But the race . . . (MOTHER *and* FATHER *are fighting back tears.)*

MOTHER: We'll be back everyday to see you. *(Rushes off to hide tears, to music stand.)*

FATHER: Get some rest, sweetheart. *(Kisses her. Exits to music stand.)*

SADAKO: The race . . .

(ACTOR 1 *prepares to become* KENJI. *Using the instruments to punctuate her lines,* ACTOR 2 *counts.)*

ACTOR 2: Two hundred and thirty-four, two hundred and thirty-five, two hundred and thirty-six, two hundred and thirty-seven . . . *(The counting fades and* SADAKO *counts. Again, the primary numbers are spoken together by* ACTORS 1 *and* 2 *and* SADAKO.)*

SADAKO: Six, seven, eight, nine, ten . . .

(KENJI *enters the scene.)*

KENJI: What are you counting?

SADAKO: *(Sees him, delighted.)* Oh, Kenji, I'm so glad you're here! *(They embrace.)*

KENJI: What's so interesting out there?

SADAKO: I am counting how many trees I can see from my window. This morning I counted the flowers. There were fifty-two. You know, it's only been ten years since the bomb destroyed everything. But look how many trees have grown since then!

KENJI: I have a present for you.

SADAKO: You do?

KENJI: Close your eyes. *(She squinches them very tight,* KENJI *puts a piece of gold paper on the bed and some scissors.)* Now, you can look.

SADAKO: *(Looking at paper.)* What is it?

KENJI: *(Laughs.)* I've figured out a way for you to get well. Watch! *(He slowly folds paper into origami crane. Recorded music used earlier in the mimed folding is heard. He holds the crane in the palm of his hand as if it is very precious and holds it out to* SADAKO.)*

SADAKO: Kenji, it's beautiful. *(Takes crane.)* But how can this paper crane make me well?

KENJI: Don't you remember that old story about the crane? It's supposed to live for a thousand years. If a sick person folds one thousand paper cranes, the gods will grant her wish and make her healthy again. There's your first one.

SADAKO: (*Very touched.*) Oh, Kenji, it's beautiful.

KENJI: Make a wish. (*The magical sound of chimes is heard from the music stand.* SADAKO *holds it out before her, closes her eyes, and her lips move silently. She looks up to* KENJI, *very moved by his gift.*)

SADAKO: Thank you, Kenji. Thank you.

KENJI: Don't thank me. You have to fold the rest yourself.

SADAKO: I'll start today. (*Looks around.*) But I'll need paper.

KENJI: (*Putting her on.*) Now, where in the world could we get some paper? (*Pretends to think, then pulls some out of his satchel.*) Well, what do you know? Look what I have here. (*Hands it to her.*) This ought to keep you busy.

SADAKO: (*Takes the paper, smiles at his fun, becomes serious.*) Kenji?

KENJI: Yes?

SADAKO: (*Trying to be strong.*) Who won the race?

KENJI: (*Carefully.*) Oh, I don't remember her name. She wasn't very fast. She was a turtle.

SADAKO: But you always said *I* was a turtle.

KENJI: Oh, well, I was only teasing when I said that. You're more like that crane there. You run very fast, Sadako, like a bird. Like the wind.

SADAKO: (*Almost ready to cry, bolsters herself.*) So if I'm not a turtle, does that mean you're not a frog?

KENJI: What? Me? A frog. Why, that's the silliest thing I ever heard . . . Croak! Oops! There's that sound again. Croak! Uh-oh. It's starting again, Sadako. Look! Croak! I'm turning all green and warty! Croak! Croak! (*He continues to play the frog until* SADAKO *is laughing helplessly.*)

(*A percussion sound bridges the scene into transition.* ALL *count together.* ACTOR 1 *brings bough of paper cranes to* SADAKO, *moves back to music stand.* ACTORS 1 *and 2 fade away and become* MOTHER *and* FATHER. SADAKO *continues counting. She is holding a very long rope of colorful paper cranes.*)

ACTORS 1 and 2 and SADAKO: Four hundred and thirty-two, four hundred and thirty-three, four hundred and thirty-four, four hundred and thirty-five . . .

SADAKO: (*Cheerful, counting cranes.*) Four hundred and thirty-six, four hundred and thirty-seven, four hundred and thirty-eight!

(*She holds them up for* MOTHER *and* FATHER *who have just entered.*)

SADAKO: See. (MOTHER *and* FATHER *are very pleased to see her so happy and energetic.*) Kenji taught me! You shouldn't worry about me anymore. Kenji figured out a way for me to get well. Do you remember the story? If a sick person folds a thousand paper cranes, then the gods will make her well again. And look. I've already folded four hundred and thirty-eight! (*She holds them up, proud and delighted, full of new vigor.*)

MOTHER: Oh, I'm so glad. I thought you would be sad about not being able to run in the races.

SADAKO: (*Trying to hide her sudden sadness.*) Oh, that. Oh, I don't think about that old race anymore. Silly old race. What good was it? Kenji said I was better than the girl who ran. He said I run like a bird. It's like I'm flying, he said. Folding cranes is much better than any old race. (MOTHER *and* FA-

THER *glance at each other.)* It's kind of like a race anyway, don't you think? If I fold them fast enough, I won't have to die. (SADAKO *smiles radiantly at her parents. Her* MOTHER *gasps and grabs* SADAKO, *pressing her daughter's head against her breast and cries. Pause.* MOTHER *and* FATHER *move away, leaving* SADAKO *alone. She is asleep and speaks with her eyes closed.)* Mother? Mother, where are you? Father? Oh, just you wait, Father. I'll make you so proud of me! I'm going to win. I'm going to win! Oh, but Mother! Father? Where are you now? I don't like it here. It's lonely, and I don't feel well. It hurts. It HURTS!!

(ACTORS 1 *and* 2 *become* DOCTORS *and enter the scene.)*

ACTOR 1: What's the matter with Sadako?

ACTOR 2: What's the matter with Sadako?

ACTOR 1: Why did she fall?

ACTOR 2: What could be wrong?

ACTOR 1: Put her to bed.

ACTOR 2: Put her to bed.

SADAKO: No, I don't want to stay in bed!

ACTOR 1: Now, don't you worry.

ACTOR 2: You'll be just fine.

SADAKO: But it hurts! And I have such bad dreams.

ACTORS 1 and 2: Put her to bed. Put her to bed. Put her to bed. Put her to bed. *(They repeat as they move away, their voices fading to a whisper.)*

SADAKO: Grandmother? Grandmother? Can you see me? Can you hear me now?

(There is a dramatic percussion sound from ACTOR 1 *as* ACTOR 2 *dons her magnificent* GRANDMOTHER *mask and enters the scene. She makes a grand entrance with beautiful recorded music and chimes.)*

GRANDMOTHER: I hear you, Sadako.

SADAKO: *(Slowly opens her eyes, pause, sees* GRANDMOTHER.) Grandmother! You came back! You returned to earth just like they said.

GRANDMOTHER: Yes, I have returned to help you, Sadako.

SADAKO: Oh, Grandmother, I hurt so much! It's so cold and lonely here. Can I go home now?

GRANDMOTHER: *(Beckoning.)* I have come to show you something. Come.

SADAKO: Oh, I wish I could go with you, Grandmother.

GRANDMOTHER: I will take you to the mountains and rivers of our ancestors.

SADAKO: Oh, but, Grandmother, how can I go with you? They won't even let me leave my room. They say I have to stay in bed.

GRANDMOTHER: You know a way.

SADAKO: I do?

(GRANDMOTHER *stands stoically as* ACTOR 1 *brings imagined piece of paper downstage as before. He gently smoothes it on the floor before* SADAKO, *bows, and moves upstage again.)*

SADAKO: Of course. Yes, now I know.

(SADAKO *performs the mimed folding of a giant crane. This is a kind of choreographed dance that was used in the introduction. The "folding" is accompanied by specific music used in each folding sequence.* GRANDMOTHER *moves with* SADAKO *as she folds in a way that suggests she is directing* SADAKO. *When the folding is complete,* GRANDMOTHER *and* SADAKO *look at each other, then slowly move down to lift the crane together. As they stoop to pick up the crane, a dramatic music with gong sound begins. They carry the crane to bench,* SADAKO *on left side,* GRANDMOTHER *on right. They place bench/crane center stage.* GRANDMOTHER *stands on bench behind her, and* ACTOR 1 *stands on floor with back to* AUDIENCE *behind* GRANDMOTHER. *A whooshing sound is heard as* ACTORS *contract together to suggest the launching of the bird into flight.* ACTOR 1 *uses mylar streamers to "flap" elegantly as wings.* SADAKO *is thrilled.* ACTOR 1 *counts loud and dramatically, indicating the excitement of the moment. Loud, beautiful, fast-paced music accompanies their glorious flight.*)

ACTOR 1: Five hundred and sixty-three, five hundred and sixty-four, five hundred and sixty-five!

SADAKO: (*Thrilled.*) Look, Grandmother, it's just like Kenji said. I fly like the wind! I fly like the wind!

ACTOR 1: Five hundred and seventy-one! Five hundred and seventy-two! FIVE HUNDRED AND SEVENTY-THREE!!!

SADAKO: I FLY LIKE THE WIND!! (ACTOR 1 *moves before* SADAKO *and* GRANDMOTHER, *using the mylar streamers to suggest fires on the ground before them.* SADAKO *points to streamers.*) Look, Grandmother!

GRANDMOTHER: The Yaizu River.

SADAKO: But it's burning.

GRANDMOTHER: It is All Soul's Day. The day of the spirits.

SADAKO: There are hundreds of little boats with candles!

GRANDMOTHER: The spirits have visited their loved ones tonight, just as I have visited you. The candles in the river are "farewell fires." Soon the spirits will join us.

SADAKO: Join *us*? You mean I'll be able to meet the spirits?

GRANDMOTHER: Yes.

SADAKO: How wonderful! (*She is very excited, anxiously looking down for a glimpse of the* SPIRITS. *Pointing.*) There! There! Grandmother, look! (ACTOR 1 *moves around them in a circle holding red masks on poles which seem to "float" around* SADAKO *and* GRANDMOTHER.)

GRANDMOTHER: Those are spirits of a thousand, thousand years.

SADAKO: (*Delighted.*) A thousand, thousand years?

GRANDMOTHER: Yes. They were once young like you, Sadako.

SADAKO: Like me?

GRANDMOTHER: Yes.

SADAKO: (*Pointing.*) Look! He looks like an *Emperor*!

(ACTOR 1 *circles around them, holding a parasol above his head. He moves regally and spins at the sound of gongs which announce his presence. As he moves away,* GRANDMOTHER *bows to him.*)

GRANDMOTHER: Their valley is deep and their mountains hard to climb. We need not visit there. Our mountain is just ahead.

ACTOR 1: *(Using streamers as wings again.)* Five hundred and ninety-three! Five hundred and ninety-four! Five hundred and ninety-five!

GRANDMOTHER: *(Gesturing to a place before them.)* Here is where we will stop.

(ACTOR 1 slows the wings; they mime landing with a whoosh sound as before. ACTOR 1 gently flutters the streamers down to a halt. The music changes from excitement to a quiet, eerie sound of wind instruments. This music will continue through the speeches of the SPIRITS. GRANDMOTHER dismounts the crane, gestures to SADAKO to do the same. SADAKO jumps off the crane, excited with anticipation. ACTOR 1 moves bench. GRANDMOTHER offers SADAKO her arm and leads her around the stage. SADAKO is looking eagerly around. ACTOR 1 puts red mask in holder. He stands behind the waist-high mask among the pastel fans.)

GRANDMOTHER: *(Gesturing toward mask.)* This is the spirit of Mr. Araki. *(ACTOR 1 opens an oriental paper parasol. When he speaks for a SPIRIT, he will stand behind that mask with the parasol opened above his head. He does not alter his voice to suggest SPIRITS' voices.)*

ACTOR 1/MR. ARAKI: I was helping to build fire lanes for Hiroshima. The enemy may come soon they said, we must build fire lanes. I was digging with my shovel. I saw the metal grow bright before me. I watched it melt. Everything turned white. Then I was here.

(ACTOR 1 moves parasol in front of his face, closes it as he turns away, leaving the red masks. GRANDMOTHER again offers SADAKO her arm and walks her around the stage as ACTOR 1 places another red mask in its holder. SADAKO is growing confused and a little frightened.)

GRANDMOTHER: *(Gesturing.)* This is the spirit of Mrs. Watanabe.

ACTOR 1/MRS. WATANABE: *(Opens parasol.)* I had just prepared a breakfast for my baby boy. I was bending over his basket to pick him up when I felt a tremendous wind blow me across the room. My baby boy has not joined me here. *(Closes parasol as before, leaving the red mask. Again GRANDMOTHER leads SADAKO on her arm, around and up to third red mask.)*

GRANDMOTHER: *(Gesturing.)* This is the spirit of Daisuke.

ACTOR 1/DAISUKE: I was seven years old when I came here. I had studied my lessons hard for an examination. I was walking to school. I looked up to see a bird fly. Suddenly the sky was on fire. *(Closes parasol, moves to music stand, leaving three red masks placed among the pastel fans.)*

SADAKO: *(Horrified, looking at the masks.)* The bomb. They're all talking about the bomb that fell when I was two years old.

GRANDMOTHER: The bomb brought me here, Sadako. *(ACTOR 1 begins to count, continues during this conversation.)*

ACTOR 1: Six hundred and twenty-eight, six hundred and twenty-nine . . .

SADAKO: Yes, I remember.

ACTOR 1: Six hundred and thirty-one, six hundred and thirty-two . . .

GRANDMOTHER: The bomb has brought you here, Sadako. You must stay with us.

SADAKO: *(Realizing what* GRANDMOTHER *means, pleading.)* But how can that be? I'm twelve years old now. It's been ten years since the bomb fell.

GRANDMOTHER: The bomb continues to fall, Sadako. It is falling even now. (GRANDMOTHER *gestures to* ACTOR 1 *who pauses in his counting. He brings his head up slowly to look directly at* SADAKO. *Pause. He resumes his counting.)*

SADAKO: *(Panicking.)* But my cranes! I've been folding my cranes as fast as I can!

ACTOR 1: Six hundred and thirty-nine . . .

SADAKO: *(Pleading.)* I haven't folded a thousand yet!

GRANDMOTHER: *(Assuring.)* You will have a thousand. You'll see. It is better to leave them for others to finish.

SADAKO: Someone will finish them for me? But then, how can the cranes grant my wish?

GRANDMOTHER: *(Lovingly.)* What did you wish for, Sadako? (ACTOR 1 *stops counting but continues percussion rhythm during the following line.)*

SADAKO: To make you live. To make me better. I wished that there will never ever be a bomb like that again. *(Silence.* ACTOR 1 *moves dramatically from music stand carrying closed parasol before him as if it is something very precious. He ceremoniously gives it to* GRANDMOTHER, *bows, and returns to his place behind the music stand.* GRANDMOTHER *moves to* SADAKO, *holds parasol out to her, nods to encourage her.* SADAKO *takes the parasol,* GRANDMOTHER *moves away.* ACTOR 1 *begins rhythm again. They count together.)*

ACTOR 1 and GRANDMOTHER: Six hundred and forty-one, six hundred and forty-two, six hundred and forty-three . . .

SADAKO: *(Solemn.)* Six hundred and forty-four. *(There is the sound of the bomb as she opens the parasol above her head, then brings it down in front of her, like a shield, hiding her face.* GRANDMOTHER *and* ACTOR 1 *bow their heads. The bomb sound continues as* SADAKO *moves to take her place in the fans with the other red masks. Lifts parasol.)* I was two years old, and my mother held me in her arms. She sang a song to me. It was a quiet summer morning. Inside our small house my grandmother was preparing tea. Suddenly there was a tremendous flash of light that cut across the sky. *(She moves her parasol to cover her face as before.)*

(The bomb sound is quieter this time and slowly fades away. ACTOR 1 *becomes* KENJI. KENJI *enters the scene calling to* SADAKO. *He uses the bill of his hat as before to make a large mouth for his comical frog. The bill covers his eyes.)*

KENJI: *(Playful.)* Sadako! Oh, Sadako . . . How's the lazy little turtle this morning? You know, I think you're right. I'm becoming more of a frog every day. Why just this morning I found two warts on my foot. Now, what do you make of that? Croak! See, there's that sound again. *(Hopping to her bed.)* You want to see my warts? *(He puts his cap back to see her, laughing. He is stopped when he sees that she is not there.)* Sadako? *(Looks around.)* Sadako? *(He sees rope of cranes, holds it, then sits on the bench. He solemnly removes his hat and bows his head.)*

(From her place at the music stand, ACTOR 2 *narrates.)*

ACTOR 2: Sadako Sasaki died on October 25, 1955. Her friends and class-mates folded three hundred and fifty-six cranes to make a thousand. *(KENJI stands, moves upstage, mimes getting the large piece of paper as before. He gracefully places it downstage. The folding music begins, KENJI mimes folding movements of giant crane as SADAKO has done. ACTOR 2 begins recorded folding music and moves from the stand to downstage left.)* Sadako's friends began to dream of building a monument to her and all the children who were killed by the atom bomb. In 1958, the statue was unveiled in the Hiroshima Peace Park. There is Sadako standing on top of a granite mountain. She is holding a golden crane in outstretched arms.

KENJI: *(As he folds.)* Nine hundred and ninety-seven . . .

ACTOR 2: Now, every year, children from all over Japan visit her memorial . . .

KENJI: Nine hundred and ninety-eight . . .

ACTOR 2: And bring thousands of paper cranes to her monument.

KENJI: Nine hundred and ninety-nine . . .

ACTOR 2: Their wish is engraved on the base of the statue: *(KENJI begins to stand, slowly miming the lifting of the giant crane. He uses both hands as SADAKO did in the beginning. It is very light.)*
    "This is our cry,
        This is our prayer,
            Peace in the World."

KENJI: One thousand. *(He launches it in the air and blows after it as SADAKO has done before. His outstretched arms follow the path of the bird's flight, turning to a point, indicating the flight across the sky. ACTOR 2 watches the bird with KENJI. From her position upstage, SADAKO moves her parasol from its shield-like position, holding it above her head. She watches the flight of the bird with KENJI and ACTOR 2. She points up.)*

SADAKO: *(Joyous.)* Look, Grandmother! You were right! *(ALL freeze.)*

CURTAIN

THE YELLOW BOAT

by
David Saar

DAVID SAAR holds a B.A. in speech and drama from Valparaiso University, a B.S. in English and theatre education from the University of Minnesota, and an M.A. in child drama from Arizona State University. He has directed and taught for Childsplay since founding the company in 1977, in Tempe, Arizona. He has overseen and directed a number of new plays in development, including his play *The Yellow Boat* and *Hush: An Interview with America* by James Still. Prior to becoming a full-time employee at Childsplay he worked for the Mesa School District as a drama curriculum specialist. Saar served on the roster of the Arts-In-Education program for nine years and has been an adjunct faculty member of the department of theatre at Arizona State University.

Now in its twentieth season, Childsplay has performed for more than 1.5 million children and adults throughout the Southwest. In 1995, Childsplay received the Sara Spencer Award from the American Association of Theatre and Education for "sustained and exceptional achievement in the field of theatre for young audiences." Childsplay was a finalist for the 1991 National Medal of Arts Awards, presented at the White House. The same year by invitation they performed the original production of *The Masquerade of Life/La Mascarada de la Vide* by Mary Hall Surface at the John F. Kennedy Center for the Performing Arts in Washington, D.C., during the national Imagination Celebration.

Saar has received many accolades for his work as artistic director of Childsplay, including the prestigious Senator's Cultural Award by the East Valley Cultural Alliance of Arizona, which in 1988, recognized Childsplay's valuable contribution to the audiences of today and tomorrow, and the 1989 Arizona Governor's Arts Award. In 1991, he won three important honors: the national Winifred Ward "Dare to Dream" Fellowship; an invitation to participate in the Kennedy Center's New Visions/New Voices program; and a Distinguished Achievement Award from the ASU College of Fine Arts. The Phoenix Futures forum "Dream Weavers" vision awards was his in 1992.

He recently completed a six-year term on the Tempe Municipal Arts Commission of which he was vice-president in 1994. He is a board member of the United States branch of ASSITEJ, the Association du Theatre pour l'Enfance et la Jeunesse (International Association of Theatre for Children and Young People) and was Chair of the planning committee for *One Theatre World*, the first ASSITEJ/USA national conference held in Seattle in 1995. He has served as a panelist for the Theatre Program of the National Endowment for the Arts and currently serves as a site reporter for the Endowment.

———————

For me the most rewarding aspect of writing for young people is the opportunity to provide a forum for the voices of young people which affirms their validity to themselves and presents their unique perspectives to adults.

—DAVID P. SAAR

THE YELLOW BOAT

CHARACTERS:

Benjamin
Mother
Father
A chorus of 4 actors, play the following roles:
Actors #1 and #2: male
Actors #3 and #4: female.
They will play the following roles:

Chorus
School children
School teachers
Parents
School administrators
Kids
Eddy
Joy
Doctors

PLAYWRIGHT'S NOTE:

In the early drafts of the play, the chorus parts were called "T.P.'s"—shorthand for "Transformational Potential." While their names have changed, they continue to serve this purpose in the play. They play all the above roles but can also be used, for example, to "create drawing"—or anything else the director might want to use to tell the story.

Time is fluid in the play and should be approached cinematically rather than realistically. We can and will move forward, back, and across time. "*Time shift*" means just that—a cinematic shift to another moment.

The drawings that Benjamin describes in various monologues can be "drawn" in the air or on a blank piece of paper with a prop crayon.

The boat mentioned in some stage directions refers to a set piece used in the Tempe and Seattle productions, a small, movable Yellow Boat that was manipulated to become an ambulance, a bed, etc. There are many scenic solutions; this is provided as just one example.

(Soft light, sound swirl. The time is past, present, future. Lights come up on a BOY *who will become* BENJAMIN *playing with a toy boat.)*

BOY: It began . . . 10-9-8-7-6-5-4-3-2-1: Blast-off! *(Vocalized sounds of rocket launching.)* Beep, beep, beep, beep . . .

CHORUS #1–#4, MOTHER and FATHER: It began before the beginning . . .

(The BOY's *play holds stage alone for a moment, and then others, the characters who will become the parents, doctors, and community members, become part of the playing space. Their voices overlap and build.)*

#1: This is a story about . . .

#3: This story is about . . .

#4: Not an ordinary story . . .

#2: It happened . . .

#3: Did it happen?

FATHER: How could it happen?

#4: This is a story about . . .

#3: This story is about . . .

FATHER: Not an ordinary story . . .

MOTHER: It happened . . .

#2: Did it happen?

ALL: It happened.

(The BOY *looks around at this gathering for the first time.)*

BOY: This is a story about . . . me.

(From the perimeter of the playing space the other characters begin to vocalize different parental labels.)

MOTHER: Mother . . .

FATHER: Father . . .

#4: Momma . . .

#2: Pappa . . .

#3: Mommy . . .

FATHER: Daddy . . .

#1: My Old Man . . .

BOY: It began before the beginning with a sort of choosing . . .

(Choral voices continue to offer up a variety of "parental choices" from which the BOY *will make his selection.)*

MOTHER: Mommy's here.

#1: You're getting so big.

#3: What did you do in school today?

#2: Brush your teeth.

FATHER: Way to go! I'm so proud of you.

#4: Do I have to stop this car?

FATHER: That's my boy.

MOTHER: Sweet dreams.

BOY: Mom? Dad? (BOY *shifts his focus to* FATHER *and* MOTHER. *The scene "shifts" to a more realistic style.*)

FATHER: You're what!?! Are you sure?

MOTHER: I'm sure.

FATHER: Positive? You're sure? Whoooh . . . ! This is great! It *is* really great, isn't it?

MOTHER: I've never felt so happy . . .

FATHER: Can you feel him yet?

MOTHER: No, but I know he's there.

FATHER: "He." We both said, "he"!

MOTHER: I know.

FATHER: What does . . . *he* feel like?

MOTHER: He feels like himself.

BOY: (*The* BOY *points to* MOTHER *and* FATHER.) You will be my Mom. And you, my Dad. This is a story about us. And it takes . . . (*The chorus begins a vocalized list of "time choices" which overlap and build. The "choices" may be repeated if desired.*)

#4: Forty-eight years, sixty-seven years, fourteen years, three years . . .

#2: Ninety-six years, seventy-nine years, sixty-seven years, thirty-two years . . .

#3: Eleven months, five months, seven months, three months . . .

#1: Fourteen days, four days, twenty-three days, nine days . . . (*He stops the time swirl with his announcement.*)

BOY: It takes: eight years, four months, twenty-nine days. . . . That's enough!

(*This launches a "birth dance" with* MOTHER, FATHER, *and* BENJAMIN. *As* BENJAMIN *names each color, chorus members swirl colored silks into the air, transforming the playing space into a swirl of color.*)

> I see . . . red.
> I hear . . . blue.
> I feel . . . purple.
> I taste . . . green.
> I . . . choose . . . yellow.

(MOTHER *gives birth to a small yellow doll that "becomes" the baby* BENJAMIN. MOTHER *and* FATHER *use the doll as baby while the actor playing* BENJAMIN *voices and reacts for him.*)

FATHER: It's a boy!

MOTHER: A boy.

BENJAMIN: My birthday. April 19, 1979.

(*The chorus form a cradle of ribbons in which the doll* BENJAMIN *is rocked, and become various doctors, and friends.*)

#2 and #4: Congratulations!

#4: Yes, it's a boy. That I'm sure of.

#2: Yup, a boy.

#3: Ooohhhhhh! He's so little. I keep forgetting how little they always are.

#1: Now, don't wait too long to have a brother or sister for this one. . . .

#3: Is'm's Mumsy's and Dadsy's little itsy-bitsy . . . ooh, look, he's smiling at me!

FATHER: I think it's gas. . . .

(The ribbon cradle breaks away, and the parents are in another space.)

MOTHER: A beautiful boy.

FATHER: Seven pounds, six ounces.

MOTHER: His fingers are right, and his toes are on. . . . The nurse says he's the most beautiful child she's ever seen.

FATHER: She says that to everyone.

MOTHER: Still, today . . . I went down to the nursery . . .

FATHER: . . . just to check out the competition?

MOTHER and FATHER: She's right.

FATHER: So what's his name . . . ?

MOTHER: His eyelashes are the longest . . . and his little fingers, look . . .

FATHER: The nurse says they'll hold him for ransom if we don't give him a name.

MOTHER: He's small, and wise, and . . . mine.

FATHER: And mine.

(MOM gives baby to DAD, who doesn't quite know what to do with him.)

MOTHER: That's it!

FATHER: What?

MOTHER: His name. "Benjamin."

FATHER: Benjamin?

MOTHER: It works in lots of languages. Translate: Ben . . .

FATHER: "Son."

MOTHER: Ja . . .

FATHER: "Yes."

MOTHER: Min . . .

FATHER: "Mine."

(FATHER cuddles his son, and parents simultaneously translate his new name.)

MOTHER: Son. Yes, he's mine!   FATHER: Ben. Ja. Min.!

(BENJAMIN begins a fussy cry, DAD gives doll back to MOM. They move to another space. "Busen lull" underscoring begins.)

BENJAMIN: Once upon a time, there was a Mom, a Dad, and a little, teeny baby . . .

FATHER: Welcome, Benjamin.

BENJAMIN: And a song!

MOTHER: This is a story my mother used to tell to me every night before I went to sleep. It's about boats, and sails, and . . . it takes place in a harbor . . .

FATHER: far, far away . . .

(The actor BENJAMIN *"claims" the doll* BENJAMIN, *and the* MOTHER *holds both in her arms to tell the story. From this point until doll* BENJAMIN *"grows up" to actor* BENJAMIN, *the doll is manipulated by the actor.)*

MOTHER: Now, inside this harbor there were three boats. A red one. A blue one. And a yellow one. They all sailed far out to the sea, and the red one came back, and the blue one came back; but the yellow boat? The yellow boat sailed straight up to the sun.

(Singing.)

> *Busen lull, cook the kettle full,*
> *There sailed three boats from the harbor,*
> *The first was so blue,*
> *The second so red,*
> *The third was the color of the sun.*

MOTHER and FATHER: Busen lull, cook the kettle full,

> *There sailed three boats from the harbor,*
> *The blue carried hope,*
> *The red carried faith,*
> *The yellow filled itself with love.*

FATHER: I sail the blue boat

MOTHER: The red one's for me . . . *(The lullaby has almost put him to sleep.)*

BENJAMIN: I am the yellow boat. *(He falls asleep. The music resolves.* PARENTS *"pull away" from the baby to work.)*

MOTHER and FATHER: Work time!

MOTHER: I'll weave you a sail . . .

FATHER: I'll write you a world . . .

BENJAMIN: *(Sleepily.)* I'll do it myself!

*(*FATHER *and* MOTHER *separate to their individual work spaces.* MOTHER *weaves some of the colored silk ribbons,* FATHER *works on a new story. The chorus are used to help create these work environments or assist in the creation of the work itself— they are "transformational potential." Each* PARENT *works to rhythms which weave together and separate. The intention of this movement/music beat is to show the* PAR-ENTS *at work, and the baby* BENJAMIN *discovering that he has the power to interrupt that work. Use the following choral litany to underscore the scene—or figure out another way to do it!)*

#3 and #4: Shuttle, Beat. Shuttle, Beat. Shuttle, Beat. Shuttle, Beat. *(Repeat.)*

#1 and #2: Comma, Dot. Comma, Word. Comma, Dot. Comma, Word. *(Repeat.)*

(BENJAMIN *awakes, and watches the surrounding activity, perhaps joining in, or getting in the way, and then, tired of no one paying attention to him, starts to cry. Both* PARENTS *come running,* BENJAMIN *gives them his most charming smile.*)

FATHER: What's wrong?

MOTHER: Oh, you're okay.

FATHER: Now, where was I . . . ? (*They return to work, and after a short time* BEN-JAMIN *begins to cry, again.*)

MOTHER: (*Not wanting to interrupt her weaving.*) Mamma's right here. (*To* FA-THER.) Can you see what he needs?

FATHER: Yeah, sure. (*He tries to ignore the crying for a beat, so* BENJAMIN *intensifies his efforts.*)

FATHER: Okay, here's the scoop. I'll write the story, and you color it!

(FATHER *hands* BENJAMIN *a crayon, and the actor* BENJAMIN *manipulates it for the doll. Rhythm starts.* FATHER *returns to writing, and the story gets the interest of the chorus.*)
   Now, once upon a time . . .

#1, #2, #3, #4: Hmmmmm?

FATHER: Once upon a time . . .
   In a . . . land-kind-of-place,
   Where the palm trees grew . . .
   And the sky was painted . . .

BENJAMIN: (*He chooses.*) Blue!

FATHER: Blue?

BENJAMIN: Blue.

(*A bluesy kind of music is heard, the stage turns blue, and the chorus illustrates the color in movement as* BENJAMIN *colors.*)

#1, #2, #3, #4: Cool, cooler, coolest, blue. Smooth, soothing, blues . . .

FATHER: That's exactly what I mean.
   And the trees are painted . . .

BENJAMIN: (*Holding up another crayon.*) Green. (*Change in sound as he colors, the stage turns green, and the* CHORUS *explores "green" in movement.*)

#1, #2, #3, #4: It's a mean kind of green, like a scream in a dream. Like a . . .

BENJAMIN: Ghost . . . on Halloween . . . (*They all react in Bella-Lugosi style.*)

FATHER: No, that isn't what I mean. Those trees are . . .

BENJAMIN: Red. And they're dead. (*Blackout.*)

FATHER and MOTHER: Hey!

FATHER: What's going on here?

MOTHER: What happened to the lights?

FATHER: I don't know. Maybe it's . . . or the . . . ? Or maybe it's a kid?!?

(*Lights up, and* DAD *finds the chorus in shaped positions representing the wall drawings that* BENJAMIN *has created. He is in their midst, happily drawing with the crayon.* DAD *takes the crayon from him.*)

MOTHER: What?

FATHER: Well, I gave him some crayons and . . . uhhhh, he got a little carried away and scribbled across the wall and the light switch.

MOTHER: Is he alright?

FATHER: He's fine, but the wall's a goner.

(She crosses over and looks at the damage.)

MOTHER: Oh, Benjamin . . . *(Then looks more closely at the wall, assessing . . .)* Oh . . . ! (FATHER *joins her.*)

FATHER: Oh . . . ? Oh . . . ! Look at the . . .

MOTHER: And the . . .

FATHER: Not to mention the . . .

FATHER and MOTHER: *(Appreciative.)* Oh . . . Benjamin . . .

MOTHER: That's a very nice drawing . . . but it would be so much nicer on a piece of paper. . . . *(She hands him a sheet of paper. With her finger she defines the space of the paper.)* Here. Draw here. You can draw from here to here, and from here to here. (MOTHER *helps* BENJAMIN *draw a long line on the paper.*) A nice, long line that connects from here to here, and from here to here.

BENJAMIN: Line?

MOTHER: Line. (BENJAMIN *takes the crayon and draws a line.*)

BENJAMIN: Line.

MOTHER: Lovely! (MOTHER *returns to her work.* BENJAMIN *begins to explore the concept.*)

BENJAMIN: Line! Here. Line here. Here. Line here. Here. Line here. Line! (BENJAMIN *draws a long line right off the paper. Suddenly discovering another dimension, he abandons the paper and moves into the third and fourth dimension, moving through space as he explores "line." The chorus illustrates his "line exploration" with colored elastics which they manipulate to create visible lines and shapes in space.*)

BENJAMIN: Line!

#4: S-p-i-r-al.

BENJAMIN: Line!

#2: Straight!

BENJAMIN: Line.

#1: An-gle?

BENJAMIN: Line!

#3: Curving. . . .

BENJAMIN: Line!

#4: Squiggle!

BENJAMIN: Line! (BENJAMIN *is delighted by his line drawings, and his explorations grow bolder and bolder. Finally* FATHER *notices, and calls to* MOTHER.)

FATHER: Look, look what he's doing!

MOTHER: Those aren't just scribbles, those are shapes!

BENJAMIN: Shapes?

MOTHER and FATHER: Shapes! (*A music and movement section follows. As* BEN-JAMIN *draws, the* CHORUS *illustrates with the elastics and his* PARENTS *help by naming the shapes.*)

MOTHER and FATHER: Square, triangle. . . . There's a circle . . .

BENJAMIN: Circle? Wavy circle. (*The circle becomes so.*)

MOTHER: Lines and shapes for a . . .

MOTHER and FATHER: Picture!

BENJAMIN: Picture of . . . a tree!

(*#1 and #3 use yellow and orange elastics to make a tree.*)
A heart.

(*#2 and #4 use the blue and green elastics to make a heart shape that "beats."*)
A bow and arrow.

(*#1 makes the bow with yellow elastic; #3 makes the arrow with the orange elastic which is "shot" through the heart, pulling the bow and #1 with it.*)
Lines and shapes and colors make a picture . . . of a house with about a million rooms.

(*#1–4 form an abstract shape with the elastics that has lots of room shapes.*)
Roof top, mountaintop . . .

(*The house is transformed to a mountain.*)
Lines for a picture of a yellow sun,

(*The mountain is transformed into a sun.*)
Lines for a boat. Yeah! A yellow boat!

(*The elastics are formed into the shape of a small sail boat.* BENJAMIN *jumps onto the boat and beckons his* PARENTS, *all the while drawing with the crayon.*)
Come on board!

(MOM *and* DAD *come aboard.* BENJAMIN *finishes by drawing the round sun in the air above the boat.*)
Yellow Boat sailing . . . sailing . . . sailing . . . to the sun! Stop! (*The boat "disappears," and the* CHORUS *moves upstage.*) New Drawing. Benjamin's Body!

(BENJAMIN *picks up the paper he was drawing on earlier, and begins to draw again.* MOTHER *and* FATHER *are seated on the boat with the doll.* BENJAMIN *begins to draw the story as the parents live it.*)
Here's a picture of Mom, and she's singing to me. (*The* MOTHER *and the* CHORUS *begin to hum "Busen lull" softly in a minor key.*) Then she sees something funny. (BENJAMIN *"draws" a bruise.*)

MOTHER: Look at this bruise. It seems to hurt him if I touch it.

FATHER: So don't touch it.

MOTHER: What caused it?

FATHER: It's just a bruise. Stop worrying.

BENJAMIN: I cry. *(He does.)* Loud. Lots! They worry! *(He cries more.)*

MOTHER: He keeps crying, just keeps on crying . . .

FATHER: I'll change him.

MOTHER: He doesn't need changing.

FATHER: Colic?

MOTHER: Four nights straight? Something hurts! (BENJAMIN *cries more.)*

FATHER: Teeth? *(Very loud crying.* BOTH *react.)*

MOTHER: Something's wrong!

MOTHER and FATHER: Call the Doctor! *(The boat piece becomes the ambulance.* BENJAMIN *draws as he tells.)*

BENJAMIN: I'm going to the hospital in an ambulance. Just me . . . and Mom, and Dad. Big Siren! Cars scoot out of the way . . . Fast. Neat! Then . . . Doctors!

*(*DOCTORS *enter with clipboards and whisk the baby away from the parents. They are robotic, clinical; the* PARENTS *are left waiting outside, overhearing what is being said.)*

DOCTOR #1: Hematocrit every two hours.

MOTHER: What? What does that mean?

DOCTOR #3: Two pints whole blood . . .

FATHER: What's wrong?

DOCTOR #1: . . . and a CAT Scan.

FATHER: What are you testing?

DOCTOR #2: Wait here, please. Just a few more tests . . .

BENJAMIN: More checks. (DOCTORS *move to continue exam.)*

DOCTOR #1: Left pupil, three millimeters: right pupil, four millimeters. Note.

DOCTOR #3: Check.

DOCTOR #1: Charted?

DOCTOR #4: Check.

DOCTOR #1: Irregular.

DOCTOR #3: Highly irregular.

DOCTOR #1: I don't understand all this bleeding.

*(*DOCTORS #1–#3 *cross to* BENJAMIN. *He tears a piece of his drawing paper and hands it to one. Each "reads" the test result, each says "Hmmm?," and passes it to the next. The last to receive it is* DOCTOR #2.)*

BENJAMIN: Then they figure it out. (DOCTOR #2 *announces to the parents.)*

DOCTOR #1: Blood tests confirm that your son has . . . classic hemophilia, Type A.

MOTHER: What does that mean?

BENJAMIN: It means my blood isn't like everyone else's. It's missing the "Stop Bleeding Stuff." So, when I get a cut or bump inside, it doesn't stop bleeding. It just keeps dribbling and drabbling . . . like a leaky faucet.

FATHER: What do we do?

DOCTOR #1: We'll begin the infusion procedure immediately. Check the weight and order up . . . one hundred and sixty units of Factor 8.

MOTHER: What?

DOCTOR #1: Factor 8.

FATHER: What does that do?

(#1 and #3 swirl multiple red ribbons into the air, the separate blood sources that are then "mixed" to create the factor.)

BENJAMIN: It's this really great stuff that works like a bunch of plugs to stop the bleeding. It's really strong because lots of people's blood gets mixed up to make it.

MOTHER: Where does it come from?

DOCTOR #1: From thousands of blood donors. Excuse me. We have to infuse him with the factor!

(The infusion process is set up with a long length of knotted ribbons. This is the Factor 8 which is infused into the dolls body. Two chorus members control the ribbon movement in such a way that it looks like the stream of red is being infused into the doll's body. One doctor holds the doll, another holds the syringe and guides the blood line into the doll.)

BENJAMIN: *(As he draws it.)* The first time they poke me, I cry. Poke! Owww.

(The DOCTOR with the syringe "pokes" the doll, searching for a vein. Actor BEN-JAMIN "cries out" "Owww" with each attempt.)
Poke! Owwww . . .

DOCTOR #1: Once more.

BENJAMIN: Poke! Owww . . . Poke!

DOCTOR #1: Bull's-eye!

(The infusion process begins. The PARENTS speak from the waiting room.)

MOTHER: He's stopped crying.

FATHER: Is everything all right?

DOCTOR #1: Everything is under control.

FATHER: How often will he need to go through this?

DOCTOR #1: Whenever he has a bleed. Each patient is different.

MOTHER: Is it safe?

DOCTOR #1: What?

MOTHER: That . . . Factor?

DOCTOR #1: Factor Eight is completely safe. Almost finished. Done.

FATHER: Are you sure he'll be okay?

DOCTOR #1: He can do anything any other child can, with just a few precautions. Trust me. He'll have a normal life.

(The "baby" is returned to the parents. All except the family exit.)

MOTHER: A "normal life." What's that supposed to mean?

(Music may underscore this scene, which effects the time transition from baby-hood to young boyhood. The other purpose of the scene is to show the PARENTS *attempting to "protect" their young hemophiliac—and his energy and zest for living making this clearly impossible.)*

BENJAMIN: I'll show you.

(He moves to his PARENTS, *who are holding the doll, cuddling. He tries to pull the baby away from them so he can explore—*MOTHER *and* FATHER *resist, wanting him to stay "safely" with them.)*

MOTHER: You stay with Mommy.

(He tricks them into releasing the doll, and then manipulates the doll/puppet to show "himself" growing up—learning to crawl, to stand, to fall (which really worries the parents), to walk. The following lines are interspersed with this movement exploration.)

MOTHER: Look what he's doing.

FATHER: Hold his hand.

(He leaps in pure joy and runs!)

BENJAMIN: Can't catch me.

MOTHER: *(Coaxing him back onto the boat.)* Benjamin. All aboard the Yellow Boat.

*(*BENJAMIN *swims to the boat, climbs up, and shakes himself off, and fishes for a beat or two, then jumps off, swimming again.)*

FATHER: All ashore, who's goin' ashore! Set sail for destinations unknown.

*(*BENJAMIN *begins to climb a pole. Then runs to the top of the ramp.)*

BENJAMIN: Mom, Dad, look at me.

MOTHER: We see you! *(In this moment the actor* BENJAMIN *replaces the doll* BEN-JAMIN*—he is a young boy.)*

FATHER: Good going, partner.

MOTHER: You are getting so big.

BENJAMIN: Let's play . . . on the boat. *(Music begins again, they all come on board.)* Come on, Dad! Let's explore. All aboard the Yellow Boat. Bound for destinations unknown. Cargo aboard? We each get to take one favorite thing. I'll take a Happy Meal.

FATHER: I'll take a pizza . . .

FATHER and BENJAMIN: With hollandaise sauce.

MOTHER: I'll just take both of you . . . (BENJAMIN *and* FATHER *indicate that this is a lame choice.)* . . . and a bunch of white and yellow daisies.

BENJAMIN: That's where we'll go. To Flower Island! Hoist the sails!

FATHER and MOTHER: Aye, aye, Captain.

BENJAMIN: Hoist the anchor!

FATHER and MOTHER: Aye, Aye, Captain.

BENJAMIN: Set sail for Flower Island. Okay, we're there. The best flowers are always found at the top of Glacier Mountain, so that's where I'll go. *(He shimmies up a pole and falls.)*

FATHER: Are you alright?

MOTHER: I think it's swelling.

BENJAMIN: Darn. I think I need a shot! Just when Tyrannosaurus Rex was gonna attack us.

FATHER: Tell T. Rex to take a coffee break, and we'll get back to him later. Deal?

BENJAMIN: Deal.

MOTHER and FATHER: Hospital time. (*They move to the hospital, and the infusion procedure is set up.*)

BENJAMIN: It hurts, but I don't cry. Much.

(*The infusion procedure is set up by the* DOCTORS *and nurses. It takes numerous attempts before they are successful.* DOCTOR #2 *attempts a "poke."*)
Owwwww!

FATHER: Easy partner . . .

DOCTOR #2: (*To* BENJAMIN.) Now remember, watch this tube. When it fills with blood, we'll stop all this poking! (*Poke.*)

BENJAMIN: Owwwwww!

FATHER: (*Giving him crayons, as a diversion.*) Look! Crayons!

DOCTOR #2: (*To* BENJAMIN.) When you see the tube red, we . . .

BENJAMIN: I'll color it red! (*They divert him.*)

FATHER: Look, draw here on this paper . . .

MOTHER: *Use* the red crayon, color what you feel!

BENJAMIN: (*He begins to use the crayon as a vehicle for "escape."*) Red! Red . . . ? Red . . . !

DOCTOR #2: One more try. (*Poke.*)

BENJAMIN: Owwww!

MOTHER: Benjamin, *use* the red crayon; color it out.

DOCTOR #2: Hold real still . . .

BENJAMIN: Just do it! The red train is waiting for the signal.

FATHER: What's the signal, partner?

BENJAMIN: "Poke." That's the signal.

ALL: Poke, poke, poke!

DOCTOR #2: Bull's-eye!

(*With the "bulls-eye!"* BENJAMIN *pulls away from the infusion action and launches into the story, drawing it three-dimensionally in the space around the continuing infusion scene.*)

BENJAMIN: Red. Train! Color it in. Takes the factor way inside to my knee. Factor Eight! Looks like . . . *bathtub plugs!* The Red Train picks up speed, climbs all the way to my knee. Then . . . all the bathtub plugs spill out, and *that* stops the bleeding! (*He "signs" his name at the bottom of the drawing, and then moves back into the infusion scene.*) Ben . . . ja . . . min. Ta da! The End. Now that's a good drawing! (*The infusion ends.*)

DOCTOR #2: Good job, partner. You held still just the way you should.

BENJAMIN: I know. But next time *you* should do better than four pokes! *(The* DOCTOR *gives him a big sucker, and the medical staff exit.)*

BENJAMIN: Let's go back to the glacier and look for some jewels.

MOTHER: Let's go back and look for some bed.

BENJAMIN: Awwww Mom . . .

FATHER: *(Imitating . . .)* Awwww Mom. . . . Okay, three seconds of sulk time. *(They all sulk while* DAD *counts to three.)* Now, time for bed. No ifs, ands, or buts.

BENJAMIN: You said "BUTT." You're not supposed to say "BUTT," huh, Mom? You said so.

FATHER: Then how about keister? And how about bed?

ALL THREE: And brush your teeth. *(He races off.)*

MOTHER: Slow down. Take it easy on that knee.

BENJAMIN: Can I have a glass of water?

MOTHER: Time for bed.

BENJAMIN: Time . . . for a story?

FATHER: Time for bed.

BENJAMIN: I won't be able to sleep if I don't know how the story ends.

FATHER: Okay. You want to know how the rest goes, right?

BENJAMIN: Right. After we fall off the cliff and are hanging by our ankles from the bungee cords . . .

FATHER: Well. The ropes stretch and stretch, like . . .

FATHER and BENJAMIN: . . . limp spaghetti!

BENJAMIN: And we fall into a giant vat of poison!

FATHER: Nooo. We fall into a giant, soft, feather bed . . .

MOTHER: . . . and drift slowly off to sleep . . . (MOTHER *and* FATHER, *thinking they are finished, turn to exit.)*

BENJAMIN: That's against the rules!

FATHER: What rules?

BENJAMIN: The rules! If you *start* a story on the Yellow Boat, you have to *finish it* on the Yellow Boat!

MOTHER: Are you sure?

BENJAMIN: I made them up!

FATHER: I forgot, I forgot. So sue me! Okay. We roll off the feather bed . . .

BENJAMIN: Into a giant vat of acid!!!

FATHER: Rule number two. Don't interrupt! We roll off the bed, down the hill, and onto our boats. I'm blue . . .

MOTHER: I'm yellow, you're red . . .

BENJAMIN: Nuh, uh. I'm yellow.

FATHER: You sure?

BENJAMIN: I'm sure. *I'm* the Yellow Boat.

FATHER: *(Revising.)* Okay. So the blue one sails back . . .

MOTHER: And the red one sails back . . .

BENJAMIN: But the Yellow Boat sails up . . .

MOTHER and BENJAMIN: Up . . .

MOTHER and FATHER and BENJAMIN: Up . . . to the Sun!

BENJAMIN: That was awfully short!

FATHER: I know. But Union Story Time is over, and that's all you get in the off hours!

MOTHER: Good night!

BENJAMIN: Time for a hug? (As they hug together.)

MOTHER and FATHER: Love you.

BENJAMIN: Love you too. But tomorrow can I play with some kids?

MOTHER and FATHER: We'll see.

BENJAMIN: Does that mean no?

FATHER: It means we'll see.

BENJAMIN: Next day!

ALL KIDS: Tag!

KID #1: (Tagging KID #3.) You're it!

(A game of tag erupts. MOTHER hovers protectively near BENJAMIN. The game swirls around them, until everyone has been "it" except BENJAMIN. He is tagged.)

MOTHER: Oh Benjamin, be careful!

(BENJAMIN tags MOTHER and runs away to join the other KIDS. MOTHER runs after the KIDS, tags one, and the game continues until BENJAMIN is tagged again.)

BENJAMIN: Pig-Pile!!!

(A pile-up of all the kids with BENJAMIN at the bottom. The worried PARENTS make their way toward the pile and pull the other kids off of what they are sure is a smashed and bleeding child.)

MOTHER: Are you all right?

BENJAMIN: I'm fine!

MOTHER: Promise me you'll be more careful . . .

BENJAMIN: Mom. I won! (BENJAMIN returns to the group to continue playing a king of the mountain game.)

FATHER: I think it's time for school.

MOTHER: Is he ready?

FATHER: Look at him.

MOTHER: (She can't bear to watch his roughhousing.) Are we ready?

FATHER: Hang in there, Mom. We'll find the right school.

MOTHER: Where? How?

FATHER: Hey, this is America. We shop!

(The chorus quickly set up "options" for the family to choose.)

BENJAMIN: Mom, Dad? Come on over here.

(COACH #2 *enters with "students," using his whistle often, to put the* KIDS *through their paces. The first whistle, they snap to attention, at the second whistle, they begin to sprint in place.* KIDS #1 *and* #4 *are clearly the best jocks;* #3 *and* BENJAMIN *have more of a struggle to keep up.*)

COACH #1: Sports! That's what's important. Competition. Challenge. Be the best, the best!

#2 and #3: Whoof, Whoof, Whoof, Whoof.

COACH #1: (*He whistles again, they stop running. Second whistle, they start jumping jacks.*) Firm body, firm mind.

MOTHER: Our son has hemophilia so he may need to take it a little easy on some things.

(*He whistles them to a stop, then on the second whistle, they begin toe touches.*)

COACH #1: He is kind of puny, isn't he? Don't worry about a thing; few months on the field? We'll work out that "hemo" thing.

FATHER: Thanks. But no thanks.

COACH #1: Okay, one more lap . . . (*Whistle.*) . . . move it, move it, move it!

(*They all jog off, and transform into another school: the Montessori School from Hell.*)

BENJAMIN: Here!

TEACHER #3: (*The* CHILDREN *run amok.*) We have no rules. We need no rules. Children should be free. Free to explore, free to find their own limits. Our job is to gently remind them of . . . consequences. Excuse me.

(*During her speech, her shoelaces have been tied together, and Jessica* #4 *has started to pound on an imaginary Aaron. The other* KIDS *gather around the body.* TEACHER #3 *hops over to Jessica and grabs her.*)

TEACHER #3: Jessica, put down that crowbar, and why don't you think about how Aaron might be feeling right now . . .

MOTHER and FATHER: Keep looking. (*They move to another area.*)

BENJAMIN: Mom, Dad! Over here.

(TEACHER #2 *and* KIDS #1, #3, #4, *and* EDDY #1 *enter with "Me dolls" and create another school scene. The* PARENTS *meet* TEACHER #2 *and he introduces the* PARENTS *and* BENJAMIN *to the class. The* PARENTS *stay to watch the class as* BENJAMIN *joins in.*)

TEACHER: Come and join us. Class, this is Benjamin.

(*The kids immediately "react" to the newcomer, checking him out. The teacher sees this and adopts a strategy to help break the ice.*)
Today's assignment is "Me drawings."

KID #3: What's that?

TEACHER #2: Drawings of You.

EDDY #1: Of Me?

TEACHER: (*Pointing to each kid, and including* BENJAMIN.) Yes. You. And you, and you . . .

KIDS #1, #2, #4, BENJAMIN: And you and you and you! Me drawings!

KID #2: I'm brown.

KID #3: I'm pink.

BENJAMIN: I'm yellow.

EDDY: I'm green.

KID #4: Yucko.

BENJAMIN: No, that's cool.

KID #4: It is? Oh.

   (*The* KIDS *draw about themselves, using soft dolls that can "become" them in the later community rejection scene.*)

BENJAMIN: Any shape we want?

TEACHER: Any shape you are.

EDDY: Any color we like?

TEACHER: Any color you feel.

BENJAMIN: I feel purple. I see red. I hear blue. I taste green. I am . . . having a good time here. Mom, Dad? (*Shows them his drawing.*) You can go, now.

   (MOM *and* DAD *leave scene area.*)

TEACHER: Benjamin, will you share your drawing with us?

BENJAMIN: This is my blue stomach, and my checkerboard high tops, and my yellow hat, and these are my bones, and they're dancing inside my body.

KID #4: Gross.

EDDY: Cool!

BENJAMIN: And this is my knee where I had a bleed, and . . .

KID #3: I don't see any blood.

BENJAMIN: No, it's on the inside. See, it bleeds on the inside, here and here, and gets all red and hot and squishy . . .

KID #4: Gross.

EDDY: Cool!

BENJAMIN: Then I go to the doctor.

TEACHER: What happens at the doctor, Benjamin?

BENJAMIN: I get a shot of Factor 8, and the bleed stops, and then I get a sucker.

EDDY, KID #3, KID #4: (*The kids voice approval, and freeze.*) Yeah!

FATHER: (*To teacher.*) His hemophilia isn't a problem for you?

TEACHER: Problem? It's an opportunity. Welcome to our community.

   (*Adults exit. Time Shift. Playtime.*)

BENJAMIN, EDDY, KID #3, KID #4: Recess!

KID #3: So what do you want to do?

KID #4: I don't know, what do you want to do?

KID #3: I don't know.

BENJAMIN: I have an idea. We can go on the Yellow Boat. C'mon Eddy.

KID #4: Boats are boring.

BENJAMIN: This is a Yellow Boat!

EDDY: And it can fly!

KID #4: Really?

EDDY: Really.

KID #4: Cool.

BENJAMIN: Here, I'll draw it for you.

KID #4: Drawing? Drawing's boring.

BENJAMIN: Not this way. I'll draw it so you can do it! C'mon aboard. Here's the deck, and here's the mast.

(*#1 has become a* KID, *and he is hiding, waiting to be pulled up into the action of* BENJAMIN's *story. He becomes the mast.*)
Load cargo, now.

(BENJAMIN *continues drawing as the* KIDS *begin to do so.*)

KID #3: Are we going or what?

(*Music begins to support this change to fantasy storytelling.*)

BENJAMIN: Okay, hoist the sails, hoist the anchor. You're *supposed* to say: "Aye, aye, Captain."

ALL THE KIDS: Aye, aye, Captain! (*They begin to sail.*)

KID #3: Can I steer?

BENJAMIN: Nope, only the Captain gets to steer. I stand right here and draw, and steer.

KID #3: I want to be captain!

BENJAMIN: Then draw your own boat.

KID #3: I can't draw as good as you!

BENJAMIN: I know. You can be helper. She gets to steer if the Captain gets tired.

KID #3: Does that ever happen?

BENJAMIN: Nope.

(*Music changes to indicate approaching storm.*)

KID #1: Storm up ahead!

BENJAMIN: We can fly! Start special hydraulic-powered flyers.

(BENJAMIN *draws as* KIDS *become a flying Yellow Boat, complete with sound effects. They begin to fly,* KID #3 *grabs the crayon from* BENJAMIN *and draws in the air.*)

KID #3: Land ho.

BENJAMIN: How do you know?

KID #3: I just drew it!

BENJAMIN: *I'm* the captain!

EDDY: Don't be so bossy.

BENJAMIN: I'm not. Land ho!

KID #4: Where are we?

BENJAMIN: Ask her. *She's* drawing it.

(The scene shifts to a Fantasy Island.)

KID #3: Uh, it's an island. There are palm trees and monkeys. (BENJAMIN *climbs a pole as a monkey but falls.*)

EDDY: Benjamin, you all right?

BENJAMIN: I'm fine. *(They continue.)*

KID #3: And there's a cave there.

(#2 and #4 make a cave as she draws it.)

It's the home of . . . a king? A Giant King of the . . . *(Searching for a name.)*

BENJAMIN: Svengalese.

KID #3: Yeah! The Giant King of the *Svengalese.*

(When the KIDS *look up, they see that #2 and #4 have transformed themselves into the* KING, *and he is indeed, evil and vicious. A little too so!)*

BENJAMIN: No, not the Giant King. Erasers!

(They all erase it as the Giant falls apart and reforms.)

(To KID #3.) You have to be careful around here.

(He takes the crayon and continues. He whispers with EDDY, *and* EDDY's *finger becomes the midgetized king. They have played this game before, and* BENJAMIN *is clearly the director.)*

Now, we have stumbled upon the magical castle of the teeny-tiny midgetized King of the Svengalese.

*(*EDDY *slowly reveals his index finger with crown and grass skirt: The* KING.*)*

He's friendly. He speaks in Svengalese. Luckily, I know it.

EDDY/KING: *(Ten seconds of gibberish.)*

KID #3: What did he say?

BENJAMIN: Hello.

EDDY/KING: *(Gibberish.)*

BENJAMIN: "You strangers are welcome here, and have come just in time."

KING: *(Gibberish is overlapped with translation.)*

KID #4: Why just in time?

BENJAMIN: Why just in time?

*(*EDDY/KING *pantomimes a volcano erupting, and then* BENJAMIN *communicates the emergency.)*

The volcano is erupting, and you must save my people. Quick, take us on your boat, and let's get out of here!

*(*BENJAMIN *draws #1 into The Erupting Volcano as* KIDS *run around in terror.)*

EDDY: How do we save all the Svengalese?

BENJAMIN: Erase the volcano. (*They do, and the Volcano melts, turning back into* EDDY.) Draw more boats. (KIDS *sail away, saving the Svengalese.*)

BENJAMIN: Land ho!

EDDY: Safe! (*The boat vanishes as the game ends.*)

KID #4: That was fun. Let's do it again tomorrow.

EDDY: I think she likes you.

BENJAMIN: Yuck.

(*The* KIDS *exit, and* BENJAMIN *takes out a huge piece of paper to make a new drawing. The previous play has triggered a bleed, but drawing a new adventure is more important than that right now.*)

This is going to be a big one. This is a map to help the Svengalese and their friendly King *know* where to find . . . their Enemy! That Big Guy.

(MOTHER *enters.*)

MOTHER: What are you doing?

BENJAMIN: I'm drawing. His castle sits high on top of a cliff so to get there, first, you have to climb all these ladders of . . . bones. Cat bones . . . yea!

(*As he draws, he enters into the action of his picture enough so that* MOTHER *notices that he is limping slightly.*)

MOTHER: How's your knee?

BENJAMIN: Oh . . . fine. The Big Guy's hiding way up here, in this tower . . .

(*As he shows the path that will be taken on the paper, his movement betrays the knee-bleed he's trying to ignore.*)

MOTHER: Are you limping?

BENJAMIN: Mom! Now, the King has to go through these traps and mazes . . .

MOTHER: Let me see it. (*She examines his knee.*) Can you straighten it? (*It hurts.*)

BENJAMIN: Mom!

MOTHER: I'll call the hospital.

BENJAMIN: I don't have time for that; I'm working on this map . . .

MOTHER: You can take it along.

BENJAMIN: It's too big for the car! It's a whole castle!!!

MOTHER: Then just take one room.

BENJAMIN: Oh. Okay. I'll take . . . the torture room!

MOTHER: Of course.

BENJAMIN: I'll need lots of red for the blood . . .

(MOTHER *and* BENJAMIN *shift location, and the infusion procedure begins, set up as before. He draws throughout the procedure. During this infusion we see the red "blood" tinged with another colored contaminant: the HIV virus. Benjamin continues his monologue as he draws.*)

BENJAMIN: When you open this door, the skeleton is waiting with buckets of poison . . . lemonade. Drink it, you turn into . . . a ghost! So, don't drink it! But if you step here, you fall through the floor of the torture room. Ah-hhhhhhhh. . . . Splat!

MOTHER: (Returning.) They're all done. You can finish that up at home.

(They return home. Sound underscores the following. #2, #3, and #4 tear and fold the large piece of drawing paper into "newspapers," or the scene can be staged to include some other medias.)

BENJAMIN: (He begins to draw on his "Me Doll.") New drawing. Benjamin's Body. Everything looks the same. Outside.

(CHORUS [#2, #3, #4] moves and announces the following headlines. There is a sense of this information moving into, invading, the personal space of the family. The parents do not react directly to the announcements, but are affected by their sense.)

#3: Doctors alarmed by mystery illness.

#4: Disease approaching epidemic proportions.

MOTHER: I've just got this feeling . . .

FATHER: You worry too much.

(CHORUS moves and announces:)

#2: Immune deficiency linked to infant deaths.

MOTHER: Doctor says his weight is down, and he's a little anemic.

FATHER: Maybe it's a growth spurt?

BENJAMIN: Inside. Almost the same. Except my stomach.

(CHORUS moves and announces:)

#3: Transmitted by the exchange of body fluids . . .

#2: Rate of infection up among at-risk populations.

FATHER: Maybe it's the flu, everybody in his class has an upset stomach and diarrhea.

MOTHER: But he's had it over a week.

(CHORUS moves and announces:)

#3: Officials insist blood supply is 100 percent safe!

#4: Eighty-three-year-old grandmother dies of AIDS?

#2: Cause of infection unknown.

BENJAMIN: And my head turns tired. And my legs turn tired. And my fingers . . . even my drawing is tired.

FATHER: He's going to be all right!

MOTHER: How do you know that?

FATHER: I don't know that. I hope that.

(BENJAMIN begins to make "spots" on the "Me Doll," and gradually on himself. The CHORUS begins a litany of states.)

#2: Cases of AIDS reported in California.

#4: New York.

#3: Florida.

MOTHER: Something's wrong, I just know it. It's like a spark has gone out of him . . .

#2: Indiana.

MOTHER: Don't you think he should be tested?

#4: Pennsylvania.

#3: Arizona.

FATHER: Tested for what?

#4: Illinois. Michigan.

#3: Texas. Tennessee.

(DOCTOR enters.)

DOCTOR #1: We checked first with the ELISA. . . .

MOTHER: Tested for everything!

DOCTOR #1: . . . and the Western Blot Test.

MOTHER: You know . . . EVERYTHING!

DOCTOR #1: Your son . . . has tested . . . positive for the AIDS virus. I'm very sorry. We'll do *everything* that we can. *(He exits.)*

MOTHER: I just knew it. What are we going to do?

FATHER: I don't know. We'll . . . just *do,* I guess.

MOTHER: How do we tell him?

FATHER: The right words will come. *(The parents move to BENJAMIN.)*

FATHER: Uh, Benjamin, we need to talk.

BENJAMIN: About what?

MOTHER and FATHER: Well . . .

MOTHER: Well, about some things that . . . we're thinking about, and . . .

BENJAMIN: About your meeting with the doctor, yesterday?

MOTHER: Yes.

FATHER: You know he's been giving you lots of tests, to see if there's any reason why you've been more tired lately. And one of the tests . . .

MOTHER: He did a couple of special tests. And he found something in your blood that shouldn't be there.

FATHER: A bug; a kind of bug—a virus.

BENJAMIN: AIDS?

FATHER: How do you know . . . ?

BENJAMIN: TV.

MOTHER: No. Not AIDS. Not AIDS . . . But they found a little bit of the virus that can lead to the disease.

FATHER: They'll do a lot more tests; they want to make you feel better!

BENJAMIN: How did I get it?

FATHER: Some of the blood that makes the factor must have had some of the virus in it.

BENJAMIN: Does everybody who gets a shot get AIDS?

FATHER: No. And not everyone who gets a transfusion will get it.

BENJAMIN: Will I be all right?

FATHER: Yes.

MOTHER: I promise you.

FATHER: We're right here. (BENJAMIN *moves away from his parents to assimilate the news.*)

FATHER: We're going to get some answers!

(*The* PARENTS *move to where* DOCTOR #2 *has entered. The following scenes should swirl around the space as the* PARENTS *try to get some control of the situation.*)

What about this AZT?

DOCTOR #2: It looks promising.

FATHER: When can we start it?

DOCTOR #2: We can't. It's not available for children.

MOTHER: When *will* it be available?

DOCTOR #2: I don't know.

(*They move away from this* DOCTOR *over to where the* HEALER #4 *has entered.*)

MOTHER: Let's just try this.

HEALER #4: Two quarts of clover tea daily, and wear this crystal.

FATHER: Will that help?

HEALER #4: I don't know.

(*They whirl upstage to where* DOCTOR #1 *has entered.*)

FATHER: What do we call it?

DOCTOR #1: Well, it's not AIDS.

FATHER: No?

DOCTOR #1: Technically. He has the virus, but none of the diseases that the government posts as markers.

MOTHER: He has the disease? But not the disease.

DOCTOR #1: Technically.

FATHER: Which is it?

MOTHER: Yes or no?

DOCTOR #1: Yes and no.

FATHER: What do we do?

(*The* DOCTORS' *words swirl around the* PARENTS.)

DOCTOR #1: I don't know . . . appointment, next week; Wednesday, nine-thirty.

DOCTOR #2: I don't know.

HEALER #3: Appointment, Friday at one.

DOCTOR #1: I don't know.

DOCTOR #2: Appointment on Thursday, three o'clock.

HEALER #3: I don't know.

DOCTOR and HEALER: I don't know, I don't know, I don't know . . .

(This builds to their exit, leaving MOTHER *and* FATHER *totally bewildered.* BENJAMIN *jumps up.)*

BENJAMIN: Nobody knows anything, except me, and all I know is that no one knows anything!

FATHER: *(To* MOTHER.) It's going to be all right . . . but we're going to need help on this one. We've got a lot of friends.

(The community PARENTS *[#1, #2, #3, and #4] enter and gather their "children," the Me Dolls that were last seen in the recess scene. They greet* MOM *and* DAD. BENJAMIN *returns to drawing on his Me Doll.)*

FATHER: Thank you all for coming on such short notice. We need to ask for some help. Lots of help, actually.

(Community response overlaps:)

#4: Sure, anything.

#1: Anything at all.

#3: Whatever we can do to help, just ask.

#2: Hey, what are friends for?

FATHER: Benjamin has tested . . . positive . . . for the AIDS virus.

(There is a moment of total silence. Then slightly overlapping response.)

#1 and #3: Oh.

#4: Sorry.

#2: How did he . . . ?

MOTHER: *(To break the silence.)* There is so much about this that we don't know right now . . .

FATHER: We need your help!

(Community PARENTS, *without wanting to appear so, slowly begin to pull their* CHILDREN *away from the family, all the while voicing their support.)*

#3: Sure, anything. Anything at all.

#2: Whatever we can do to help.

#3: Just ask.

FATHER: The best thing we can do is just to keep things as normal as possible.

MOTHER: What he needs, what we need, is to try to have a normal life.

#1: *(Backing away.)* Hey, what are friends for?

FATHER: So, how about we take all the kids to *Ghostbusters*, Friday night?

(#1 unfurls a large sheet of plastic, which slowly forms a plastic barrier between BENJAMIN *and everyone else. His Me Doll tries to "contact" other Me Dolls through the plastic wall, but their* PARENTS *pull them away.)*

#4: Anything.

#3: Anything at all.

FATHER: Saturday afternoon?

#1: Anything at all.

FATHER: Sunday?

#1: Anything.

MOTHER: The pool is open, we could take the kids swimming?

#3: Whatever we can do . . .

#1: . . . just ask.

MOTHER: We're going camping this weekend; how about . . .

#4: Just ask.

#1: Just ask.

MOTHER: A sleep over?

#3: Just ask.

#4: Just ask.

#1: Just ask.

MOTHER: I AM asking!

(Time shift.)

BENJAMIN: Today is my birthday and I'm seven, and I'm having a party.

(EDDY enters with a box wrapped in paper with a long ribbon. He and BENJAMIN are in separate spaces, divided by the plastic wall.)

EDDY: This is so great. He'll never guess what this is till it pops out in his face.

EDDY'S MOTHER (#4): Eddy, what are you doing?

EDDY: Finishing up my present for Benjamin. *(He tries to tie the bow.)*

EDDY'S MOTHER: Finish up quickly, and I'll drop it off on my way to the grocery store.

BENJAMIN: I'm having pie instead of cake, 'cause I don't like cake, and it's MY birthday.

EDDY: You can just drop *me* off for the party . . .

EDDY'S MOTHER: I can't do that. I'm sorry Eddy, but you can't go to that party!

EDDY: But he's my best friend.

EDDY'S MOTHER: I know this is hard, but . . .

EDDY: But I have to go . . .

EDDY'S MOTHER: Don't argue with me! I'll drop the present off this afternoon. I know what's best for you.

(They exit.)

BENJAMIN: No one's coming? Not even Eddy?

(Time shift. TEACHER #1 enters.)

TEACHER #2: The board met last night. I'm afraid Benjamin won't be able to attend school here anymore.

MOTHER: What?

TEACHER: We're just not set up to handle this sort of thing.

FATHER: The doctors are positive that he's safe in school and with some simple precautions, everyone else is safe as well.

TEACHER: The board is comfortable with its decision. He'll have to leave.

MOTHER: When?

TEACHER: Immediately.

MOTHER: Can he stay to the end of the week?

TEACHER: Immediately!

MOTHER: Just another day?

TEACHER: I'll see . . . if I can help you find a tutor . . .

(He exits. Time shift.)

BENJAMIN: Why can't I go to school?

MOTHER: I don't know.

BENJAMIN: Why won't anyone come to play with me?

FATHER: We're here to play with you.

MOTHER: What would you like to play?

BENJAMIN: Nothing.

(He takes out a wide black marker, and slowly draws an outline of himself on the plastic, in silence. As he is doing this body drawing, the PARENTS are isolated in their own spaces, but try to "contact" him, and each other, with the following lines. He shuts them out.)

MOTHER: Benjamin. Would you like some juice?

FATHER: It's like he's slipped away . . .

MOTHER: How about a sandwich?

FATHER: Or a Happy Meal. You've got to eat something, so you can get better.

MOTHER: Slipped away. On his own boat . . . on his own sea.

FATHER: He doesn't speak. He doesn't eat.

MOTHER: Benjamin?

FATHER: He spends day after day curled up on the sofa . . .

MOTHER: Just picking his arm.

FATHER: Benjamin.

MOTHER: Picking. Like a little monkey.

FATHER: Benjamin.

MOTHER: Benjamin.

(BENJAMIN crosses out his image. He drops the marker. He has stopped drawing. DOCTOR #2 enters.)

DOCTOR #2: His white blood count is dangerously low. We need to admit him to the hospital immediately.

(The scene shifts to the hospital. The sound support for the hospital should be constant; hum, buzz, beep, at varying volumes for each scene. It can also be used to help

mark time shifts. By adding a sheet and pillow, the boat becomes a hospital bed. BEN-
JAMIN *is given a hospital gown and moved to the bed. The* PARENTS *move through
long hallways, answering questions.)*

DOCTOR #4: Name?

FATHER: Benjamin.

DOCTOR #4: Spell that please.

FATHER: B-E-N-J-A-M-I-N.

DOCTOR #4: Number?

FATHER: 516-43-8645

DOCTOR #2: Name?

MOTHER: Benjamin.

DOCTOR #2: Spell that please.

MOTHER: B-E-N-J-A-M-I-N.

DOCTOR #2: Number?

MOTHER: 516-43-8645.

DOCTOR #1: Name?

MOTHER and FATHER: Benjamin.

DOCTOR #1: Spell that please.

MOTHER and FATHER: B-E-N-J-A-M-I-N.

DOCTOR #1: Number?

MOTHER and FATHER: 516-43-8645.

   (As BENJAMIN *is put in the bed,* DOCTORS *repeat these requests.* MOTHER *and* FA-
THER *continue to answer, and then stop.* BENJAMIN, *in the bed, looks around, and
registers with a look that he feels completely alone. Silence for a beat.)*

   *(*JOY *[#3] enters, carrying her backpack. As soon as he hears her approach, he turns
away. She pulls a kazoo out and tootles a greeting. There is no response. She tries
again; no response. She tootles "bye, bye," and then leaves the kazoo near his feet at
the end of the bed.* JOY *exits, but watches for a moment in the doorway.* BENJAMIN
is tempted to check out what she has left, but just as he is reaching for it, three DOC-
TORS *enter.)*

DOCTOR #2: Good morning.

DOCTOR #4: . . . afternoon.

DOCTOR #1: . . . evening.

ALL DOCTORS: And how are we feeling today? Hmmmm?

   (Short pause for response.)

DOCTOR #2: Patient . . .

DOCTOR #4: Not responding.

DOCTOR #1: Check.

DOCTOR #2: Vital signs, Q-2 times 4.

DOCTOR #4: Check.

FATHER: It's like another country.

MOTHER: White walls, white floors, white sound . . .

DOCTOR #2: NPO, 48 hours.

DOCTOR #1: Charted.

DOCTOR #4: Check.

(The DOCTORS retreat; as they exit, one removes the kazoo as if it had no place here.)

FATHER: Stainless steel, hard edges . . .

MOTHER: Not a single soft thing in this whole place.

(The PARENTS move toward the room, but are intercepted by the swoop of the DOCTORS.)

DOCTOR #2: Caution! Blood Precautions!

DOCTOR #4: Oxygen in use!

DOCTOR #1: Gowns, masks, gloves suggested!

MOTHER: I'm his Mother!

(All DOCTORS snap on their gloves.)

MOTHER: I hate that sound! Benjamin . . .

(Time Shift. The PARENTS and DOCTORS move to the bed. One DOCTOR has a length of plastic tubing for a medical test.)

DOCTOR #2: We'll need samples.

DOCTOR #4: . . . specimens,

DOCTOR #1: . . . statistics!

ALL DOCTORS: Check!

MOTHER: Benjamin, these doctors need to do some tests . . .

(BENJAMIN turns away, shutting them all out.)

FATHER: Help us with this . . . they need you to swallow this little plastic tube . . .

DOCTOR #1: We need a sample . . .

FATHER: We need your help, sport . . .

DOCTOR #2: Please cough,

DOCTOR #4: Open your mouth,

DOCTOR #1: Just relax . . .

ALL DOCTORS: Breathe.

DOCTOR #2: Cough.

DOCTOR #4: Open.

DOCTOR #1: Relax.

ALL DOCTORS: Breathe.

DOCTOR #2: Cough.

DOCTOR #4: Open.

DOCTOR #1: Relax.

ALL DOCTORS: Breathe.

BENJAMIN: Leave me alone. Just *leave me alone!*

DOCTOR #2: Please, step out into the hall?

(PARENTS and DOCTOR #2 move to one side. DOCTORS #1 and #4 move away, consulting their charts.)

DOCTOR #2: We're doing our best. He's maintaining . . .

DOCTOR #4: maintaining . . .

DOCTOR #1: maintaining . . .

FATHER: Tell me what we're fighting? AIDS, depression, what?

DOCTOR #2: All of it.

DOCTORS #1 and #4: All of it.

(DOCTORS move away and continue to consult their charts and each other. MOTHER and FATHER stay to the side as JOY approaches the room a second time. She is wearing a necklace of whistles and kazoos.)

(She tootles him a "hello" on several different whistles and/or kazoos. BENJAMIN "shuts her out," both physically and with an angry sound.)

JOY: Okay, okay. I'll come back later.

(Takes three steps away, and returns. Kazoo flourish.)
It's later.

(He turns his back to her.)
Tell you what. Whenever you want me to disappear, just flick your hand, like this. *(She demonstrates with small hand flick of dismissal.)* I'm gone. History.

(BENJAMIN flicks his hand. She withdraws. Then returns.)
JOY: I'm back.

(BENJAMIN flicks his hand.)
I'm gone.

(Kazoo "good-bye." She exits.)

(Time shift. Three DOCTORS enter to bedside.)

DOCTOR #2: Good morning.

DOCTOR #3: . . . afternoon.

DOCTOR #1: . . . evening.

ALL DOCTORS: And how are we feeling today? Hmmmm?

(DOCTOR #1 goes to PARENTS. DOCTORS #2 and #3 repeat the following lines, but become increasingly more "human" in their delivery; a "time shift" that indicates a change in attitude toward this patient.)

DOCTOR #2 and #3: And how are we feeling today? Hmmmm? And how are we feeling today? Hmmmm?

MOTHER: Why is nothing working? You keep testing and poking and prodding; there's *no* change.

FATHER: He's pulling further and further away.

DOCTOR #1: We're doing everything we know. Everything we can. . . . We'll keep trying! *(He moves to join the other* DOCTORS. *To other* DOCTORS *as they exit.)* Let's take another look at those X rays.

(JOY moves to parents.)

JOY: Hi. I'm Joy, the Child Life Specialist on this wing.

MOTHER: Another doctor?

JOY: Not exactly. The doctors work with the sick parts; my specialty is the well parts.

FATHER: What?

JOY: My work is play.

FATHER: There's not much of that around here.

JOY: I'll try to change that. I'm here to work with Benjamin to try to make some sense out of this place.

FATHER: Good luck!

MOTHER: He won't eat, he won't talk. . . . He won't even draw.

JOY: Is that something he likes to do? Drawing?

MOTHER: He used to draw all the time.

FATHER: He's just not Benjamin if he's not drawing.

JOY: That's good to know. Why don't you two get a cup of coffee?

MOTHER: We should stay . . .

JOY: *(She pulls a crayon from her pack.)* Just let me have a look for a well part.

FATHER: Come on.

(They exit. JOY *approaches* BENJAMIN.)*

(She enters, heralding her arrival on a slide whistle. He flicks his hand to dismiss her. She withdraws then returns, this time with a train whistle. He flicks her away. She withdraws then returns with a duck call. BENJAMIN *almost flicks. Then changes his mind. There is a moment of "small victory" for* JOY.)*

JOY: You don't need to talk. I can just sit here with you. *(She sits, and pulls a small cloth doll and set of markers out of her backpack.)* I have some work to do. I want to make this doll for a boy here in the hospital. He hates being here, what with the shots and the medicines . . . ? But this doll needs a name. . . . Can you think of a good name?

BENJAMIN: No.

JOY: No is an excellent name! Now, No has to have a lot of tests and maybe even an operation. Can you tell him anything he needs to know?

BENJAMIN: No.

JOY: Okay. But No needs some hair, what color should it be?

(No response.)
Brown? Nah. Purple!

(This odd choice tweaks just the smallest bit of interest in BENJAMIN. *He watches as* JOY *colors the hair.)*
How about his eyes?

(She holds out some crayons between her and BENJAMIN, *and after some hesitation,* BENJAMIN *chooses an orange one.)*
Orange.

BENJAMIN: Except when he cries. His tears are red.

JOY: Red tears . . . ! And his mouth? *(She colors as he chooses.)*

BENJAMIN: Mad green.

JOY: And his eye brows are . . . ?

BENJAMIN: Yellow. Scared yellow.

JOY: So, his mouth is mad, and his eyes are scared, and his red tears are so very sad. And he feels . . . ?

BENJAMIN: Alone.

JOY: Isn't it amazing how you can have so many people in and out of here, and still feel so all alone? *(She finishes up the coloring.)* TAHDAH!! *(Or the kazoo equivalent.)*

*(*BENJAMIN *looks over at the drawing on the doll. and makes a sound of some disapproval . . .)*

BENJAMIN: EEUUuwwww!

JOY: So I'm not good at faces . . . you want to try?

BENJAMIN: No. *(He turns away again.)*

JOY: Okay. I have to go. Maybe No can come back tomorrow?

(He shrugs "Maybe . . ." She leaves the whistle necklace on his bed and exits.)

(Time shift.)

BENJAMIN: *(Remembering, and punctuating the speech with various whistles.)* And she comes back tomorrow. And the next tomorrow. And the next. She lets me talk when I want to, and she doesn't make me say "I'm fine" if I don't feel like it. She tells me about hospital things, so I know what's going on . . .

(Time shift. DOCTOR #1 *is speaking to the* PARENTS.*)*

DOCTOR #1: I've ordered up an endoscopy . . . a stomach test. We'll set it up for the morning.

*(*JOY *enters, with an armful of medical equipment: an endoscope, plastic tubing, a flashlight, an elastic string, a* NO *doll with surgical mask and cap. As part of her setup, she presents each piece to* BENJAMIN *without directly doing so. He watches, but doesn't want to be seen doing so. The* PARENTS *also enter, and* JOY *involves them in her Magical Medical Circus. She introduces the event with a kazoo fanfare.)*

JOY: Good evening ladies and gentlemen, and welcome to the Magical Medical Circus—a really big show in a really small space, hastily assembled for you today. Thank-you. Featuring No, the daredevil artiste! He's here to show you how a stomach test works. Thank-you, No. He will use this . . . *(She shows the elastic string.)* . . . and this . . . *(She pulls out a flashlight and beckons to* MOTHER. *Speaking as* NO.*)* Hey, pretty lady, come over here.

(MOTHER *comes over and* NO *hands her a flashlight.*)

(*As* NO.) Thank-you. (*As* JOY.) And he will use this.

(*She presents the endoscope. At this scary sight* BENJAMIN *turns away, but* JOY *quickly wins him back with* NO.)

Quiet please, the artiste prepares. (*She puts* NO *through traditional actor warm-up techniques, then explains the procedure in circus terms.*) He's going to fly up to a highwire stretched from here . . . (*She stretches an elastic string over* BENJAMIN.) . . . to . . . here. Could you hold this, please?

(*She offers it to* BENJAMIN, *who finally decides to take it. He holds it in the air, making a tightrope line for* NO.)

Thanks! (*As* NO.) It's time for Stomach Bungee jumping! I will descend to your stomach, fetch a sample with this . . . (*Showing him the light and tube at the end of the scope.*) . . . and then "sproing" back to my starting position, unscathed, untouched, unharmed. Watch!

(NO *is unable to jump all the way up to the elastic line with the weight of the scope, so after a few attempts, he gets an idea:*)

JOY: AAHhhh, wait. (JOY *blows up a rubber glove like a balloon and attaches it to* NO.)

(*As* NO.) Lights!

(MOM *turns on the flashlight as a follow spot.*)
(*As* NO.) Drumroll, please!

(DAD *does, at the foot of the bed.* NO *floats up to the elastic wire, walks down the wire, and prepares to descend:*)
(*As* NO.) Attach bungee! Uno, Due, Tre . . . BUNGEEE!

(NO, *with elastic end at his foot, descends to* BENJAMIN's *stomach, and bounces back up.*)
(*As* NO.) Safe! Stomach test complete!

(*Benjamin lets the line snap free, so* NO *crashes to the floor.*)
Thank-you, No!

(*The* PARENTS *clap then exit.*)

BENJAMIN: What's No going to do with it?
JOY: With what?
BENJAMIN: With that stomach stuff.
JOY: The doctors need to look at it.
BENJAMIN: Yuck.
JOY: So they can figure out the right medicines.
BENJAMIN: Will it hurt?
JOY: Just till No stops bouncing. So. Are you ready to help them?
BENJAMIN: Maybe . . .

(He holds out his hand for her to shake; when she tries to do so, he fakes her out, and quite enjoys his little victory. She exits.)

(Time shift.)

(Remembering.) Then one night, as a surprise, she sticks glow-in-the-dark stars on the ceiling over my bed, and another day, she paints a picture right on my window, so when the sun shines through it in the afternoon, it turns the white wall into colors.

(Time shift. MOTHER *enters to tuck him in, and* EDDY *enters.)*

MOTHER: Benjamin? Look who's here.

BENJAMIN: Eddy!!! *(They both silently indicate to* MOTHER *that they'd like her to leave.)*

MOTHER: I'll leave you two alone. *(She exits. There is an awkward silence.)*

BENJAMIN: Eddy . . .

EDDY: *(Indicating the bed control panel.)* So. What's all this stuff?

BENJAMIN: This is my remote control for my very own TV, and this makes my bed go up and down . . .

EDDY: Cool.

BENJAMIN: And see this tube stuck in my chest?

EDDY: Wooah!

BENJAMIN: It's for medicine, so the doctors don't have to keep giving me shots. If I had a couple of bolts, I'd look just like Frankenstein.

EDDY: I could bring you some.

BENJAMIN: Some what?

EDDY: Some Frankenstein bolts.

BENJAMIN: Could you?

EDDY: They stick right to your head.

BENJAMIN: No way!

EDDY: Way!

BENJAMIN: That'd really surprise the doctors.

EDDY: Yeah! So what's it like to be in here?

BENJAMIN: It's okay. But they never leave you alone.

EDDY: Like my Mom?

BENJAMIN: Worse than your Mom.

EDDY: Oh, no! Does it hurt?

BENJAMIN: Yeah.

EDDY: Do you cry?

BENJAMIN: No. Sometimes.

EDDY: Yeah.

BENJAMIN: Were you scared to come see me?

EDDY: No. A little.

BENJAMIN: Why? I'm just me.

EDDY: Yeah, but I never knew anyone, who . . . you know . . .

BENJAMIN: Was sick . . . ? Had AIDS?

EDDY: Yeah.

BENJAMIN: You can't catch it just by sitting next to me. It's not like cooties.

EDDY: I know that. I didn't know if you'd be mad at me.

BENJAMIN: Why didn't you come to my birthday?

EDDY: My Mom said no.

BENJAMIN: So why'd she let you come now?

EDDY: I dunno. She read a bunch of stuff, we all talked about it, and she changed her mind. You want to draw or something?

BENJAMIN: I'm a little tired . . .

EDDY: I'd better go then; they said I shouldn't stay too long.

BENJAMIN: I'm glad you came.

EDDY: Yeah.

BENJAMIN: Will you come back?

EDDY: I said I'd bring the bolts, didn't I? (*They high five,* EDDY *exits.*)

(*Time shift.* JOY *and* DOCTOR #2 *enter.* JOY *carries an X ray and backpack. The* DOCTOR *consults his chart.*)

JOY: Good morning . . .

BENJAMIN: . . . afternoon,

DOCTOR #4: Evening!

JOY: And how are we feeling today . . .

BENJAMIN, JOY, and DOCTOR #4: Hmmmmmm???

BENJAMIN: Eddy came to visit!

JOY: How did it go?

BENJAMIN: He's still my best friend. And he's bringing me . . . it's a surprise.

JOY: Did you have a good night?

BENJAMIN: No . . .

JOY: What happened?

BENJAMIN: More bleeding.

DOCTOR #4: That explains this new plan.

BENJAMIN: *More* tests?

DOCTOR #4: We're going to do an exploratory surgery, so we can take a look at what's going on in there.

BENJAMIN: I'm tired of all the looking; I'm ready for some finding.

JOY: They'll have an easier time if you'll help them.

BENJAMIN: What else are they going to do to me?

JOY: Remember when you drank that Barium stuff yesterday?

BENJAMIN: Yuck!!!

JOY: And they took an X ray of your insides? Well, here it is! (*She shows him an X-ray film.*)

BENJAMIN: (*Examining the picture.*) That's me?

JOY: Yep.

BENJAMIN: Inside?

JOY: Yep.

BENJAMIN: Well, *that's* a pretty crummy picture. It's all gray. Gray is not what it feels like.

DOCTOR #4: Then how does it feel?

BENJAMIN: Not gray.

JOY: Tell me.

BENJAMIN: This, down here . . . ? *(Indicating stomach.)* It feels . . . it feels like . . . I can't tell you . . .

JOY: Keep trying . . .

BENJAMIN: When it hurts the worst, like last night? It's like . . . like slow red spikes of hurt . . . *(Indicating on himself.)* Here and here.

JOY: *(Indicating the X ray, then his stomach.)* This part here, is a picture of that part there.

BENJAMIN: Well, it's *not* the right colors.

JOY: *(Holding out the crayons.)* You want to make it the right colors?

BENJAMIN: *(Tempted but not buying it yet.)* No. You can.

JOY: Okay, but you have to tell me how.

BENJAMIN: *(He indicates on himself. She colors the X ray.)* This is blue. It's fine, but orange is getting closer . . . burning orange. And farther down, that's where it really hurts; sharp pains like . . . pins dripping acid, purple and green. That's where it's dark, hurting, red. *Red, Red, RED!!!*

(The coloring is interrupted by the entrance of DOCTORS #1 *and* #2.)

DOCTOR #1: Good morning . . .

DOCTOR #2: . . . afternoon . . .

DOCTOR #1: . . . evening . . .

DOCTORS #1 and #2: And how are we feeling today, hmmmm?

BENJAMIN: Red.

DOCTOR #1: I beg your pardon?

JOY: He feels red.

DOCTOR #1: That's nice . . .

BENJAMIN: And here is black-and-blue, where *he* poked me yesterday.

DOCTOR #2: I needed those samples to help us prepare for exploratory surgery.

BENJAMIN: You're an explorer?

DOCTOR #2: Well, I guess so . . .

DOCTOR #4: We're exploring ways to make you feel better.

BENJAMIN: You're awfully white. Why so white?

DOCTOR #1: Doctors always wear white.

BENJAMIN: Explorers don't wear white. White's boring.

JOY: Benjamin, why don't you tell the doctors about the pain?

BENJAMIN: I can't.

DOCTOR #4: It would help us if you could.

BENJAMIN: It hurts all over.

DOCTOR #1: Where?

BENJAMIN: Some places more than others.

DOCTOR #2: When?

BENJAMIN: Sometimes, all the time, I don't know . . .

DOCTOR #1: How?

BENJAMIN: It doesn't have words, it just feels! I can't tell them!

JOY: You could show them. (*Holding out the X-ray film.*) This could be a map. Color it to help them find the hurt!

(*She holds out a crayon.* BENJAMIN *hesitates for a moment, then seizes it.*)

BENJAMIN: A map? (*He takes the X ray from her.*) I'm good at maps. New Drawing!

(*Everybody freezes in position as* BENJAMIN *takes up the crayon and holds it aloft.*)
Journey to the Center of My Guts!

(*The* DOCTORS *and* JOY *are transformed into a small band of explorers, checking supplies prior to departure on an expedition.*)

JOY: Equipment check. What do we need?

DOCTOR #2: Antibiotic.

DOCTOR #4: Hypodermic.

DOCTOR #1: Antiseptic.

BENJAMIN: Ick. Get Well Medicine. And a bazooka!

ALL DOCTORS: Bazooka?

JOY: Bazooka!

BENJAMIN: Command Central over to Field Team One. Do you read me?

JOY: Roger, Captain. How do we get in?

BENJAMIN: Through my mouth. I'll leave it open so you can see better.

(BENJAMIN *draws his mouth with big circles, as the doctors climb over the boat, starting into his body. The progress through the body should be supported with as much movement, lighting, and sound support as can be mustered.*)
First stop? My lungs. (*They enter a whoosh world.*) Air world, feels blue . . .

DOCTOR #4: This side is clear. No problems. Let's check the other lobe . . .

BENJAMIN: Here grayer, tighter . . .

DOCTOR #4: Definite congestion. I'll order up respiratory therapy.

BENJAMIN: Now find the hurt. Into the blood.

(*They are swept along through the bloodstream.*)

In one side of my heart. It's blue, 'cause I've got a strong heart—and out the other.

DOCTOR #2: Past the liver . . .

BENJAMIN: Gross. I hate liver, it's green! Be careful.

JOY: Where are we?

BENJAMIN: In my guts. That's where it hurts.

DOCTOR #1: Looks like the small intestine.

BENJAMIN: Entering danger zone. But you're not there yet, keep going . . .

DOCTOR #1: Farther?

BENJAMIN: Farther. Go farther. Feel the fire . . .

DOCTOR #2: Signs of infection ahead . . .

BENJAMIN: Dark red! Scorch arrows. Shooting fire.

(The attack begins. BENJAMIN *becomes the general of the battle.)*

JOY: What's happening?

BENJAMIN: Bad guys, attack! Guys with purple jackhammers, over there! Red-orange flamethrowers over there! Blue grenades, exploding into flaming yellow over here!

DOCTOR #1: I had no idea it was this bad.

DOCTOR #4: It's EVERYWHERE!

JOY: What do we do?

BENJAMIN: Try the bazooka!

JOY: Good idea.

DOCTOR #1: Try a little Tagamet.

DOCTOR #2: Maybe some Bactrim.

BENJAMIN: Let 'em have it! *(They fire a medical Bazooka.)* It isn't working.

DOCTOR #2: We've got to get out of here.

DOCTOR #4: We need reinforcements.

JOY: Command Central, request exit instructions.

BENJAMIN: You've got two choices: up to the lungs or down to my . . .

JOY and DOCTORS: Head for the lungs!

BENJAMIN: I'll cough you out!

(He does so, and they return to the hospital room, in exactly the same positions they held before beginning the Body Tour.)

JOY: Now, that's an excellent map!

DOCTOR #4: I'll order up respiratory therapy to start Q-4.

DOCTOR #1: I'll need some new X rays, Benjamin.

DOCTOR #2: Now, we're ready for surgery. Thanks for your help, Command Central.

*(*DOCTORS *salute and exit.)*

JOY: You look tired. You want to rest for a bit?

BENJAMIN: Yeah.

(She takes the X ray from him.)

JOY: So, that's what it feels like. You sure are good at drawing.

BENJAMIN: Yeah. But I wish we could just erase it.

JOY: Erase what?

BENJAMIN: The hurt.

JOY: Me, too. I'll see you tomorrow.

(She hands him several pieces of drawing paper to go with his crayon, which he accepts. She offers her hand to shake with him—and then fakes him out. JOY exits.)

(DOCTOR #2 brings in something to represent an IV pump and hooks it up to the bed. DOCTOR #4 brings in another.)

DOCTOR #2: Command Central? New defense weapons.

(They exit.)

BENJAMIN: After surgery, I get a little better. Everybody smiles. Dad figures out how to put plastic lizards into old IV bags, so it looks like I'm getting lizard medicine.

(FATHER does so.)

Then, I get worse. No more smiles.

(Voices of DOCTORS as they move in and out of the room, checking.)

DOCTOR #1: Colostomy complete, but he's bleeding into the abdomen now.

BENJAMIN: There are about a million machines in my room now, like robots standing guard round my bed.

DOCTOR #2: His white blood count is dropping.

BENJAMIN: I hear machines and voices all night long; whispering to me . . .

(The night takes over, with MOTHER and FATHER on either side of the bed: a vigil. The monitors and machines whir and thrum and beep softly.)

FATHER: Four A.M. Peace time.

MOTHER: Time to grab a slice of silence.

FATHER: Smooth brow, soft fingers, gentle breath. Almost normal.

MOTHER: So peaceful you can forget. Almost.

FATHER: Machines. *(Indicating medical machinery.)* Pumping food, pumping medicine, pumping blood . . . pumping hope?

MOTHER: And the sound. Like horses. Like galloping horses of hope in the night. I'm afraid of losing those horses.

FATHER: *(Trying to offer comfort and strength, for them both.)*
Busen lull, cook the kettle full,
There sailed three boats from the harbor.
The blue carried hope,
The red carried faith,
The yellow filled itself with love.

(Time shift.)

BENJAMIN: Mom! Dad! Look. Come look!

MOTHER: What is it?

FATHER: What's wrong?

BENJAMIN: Look at the moon. Just look at the moon!

MOTHER: I've never seen it so . . .

BENJAMIN: It's so big . . .

MOTHER: So close.

FATHER: So bright.

(They climb into bed with him.)

MOTHER: If I could be Queen of the World and have anything that I wanted . . .

FATHER: If I could be King of the World and have anything I wanted . . .

BENJAMIN: I've never seen it so . . .

MOTHER: It's so big . . .

FATHER: So close.

BOTH: So bright. (BENJAMIN *interrupts . . .*)

BENJAMIN: Dad, what's it like to die?

FATHER: What?

BENJAMIN: What will it feel like when I die?

FATHER: I . . . don't know.

BENJAMIN: Will it hurt?

FATHER: I don't kn—Probably. Some. *(Pause.)*

MOTHER: I don't think more than now.

BENJAMIN: Where will I go?

FATHER: I don't know.

MOTHER: But it will be a new adventure.

BENJAMIN: Will you put me in a box?

MOTHER: What?

BENJAMIN: Will you put me in a box? You know, what's left?

FATHER: What do you want us to do?

BENJAMIN: I really want to be home again.

MOTHER: Then that's what we'll do.

BENJAMIN: Love you.

MOTHER and FATHER: Love you, too.

BENJAMIN: And I'll always be your boy.

MOTHER and FATHER: Always.

(BENJAMIN *falls asleep,* MOTHER *and* FATHER *tuck him in, then exit.* DOCTORS' *voices come from outside the room.)*

DOCTOR #2: Orders?

DOCTOR #4: Eight hundred units, packed red cells.

DOCTOR #2: Have you seen the latest liver results?

DOCTOR #4: Any change?

DOCTOR #2: Not for the better.

(Time shift. EDDY enters, wakes up BENJAMIN.)

EDDY: Hey, Benjamin. I got the bolts. See? I got some for me too . . .

BENJAMIN: Wow. Thanks, Eddy. They're great.

EDDY: Don't you want to put them on?

BENJAMIN: *(He is tired, but he puts one on.)* Sure.

(They do Frankenstein impersonations, but BENJAMIN is weak and starts to cough, scaring EDDY. Silence, as he looks around the room.)

EDDY: Wow, you've got a *lot* more stuff here now.

BENJAMIN: Yeah.

EDDY: What's it all for?

BENJAMIN: So I can get better.

EDDY: Is it working?

BENJAMIN: I dunno . . .

EDDY: Really?

BENJAMIN: Really.

EDDY: Will you get better?

BENJAMIN: *(Shrugs "I don't know.")*

EDDY: Are you going to . . . *(Benjamin shrugs his shoulders, "yeah, maybe.")* I never knew anyone that was . . . well, you know . . . going to . . .

BENJAMIN: Die?

EDDY: Yeah.

BENJAMIN: Well, now you do.

EDDY: Do your folks know?

BENJAMIN: Yeah, I think so.

EDDY: What's it feel like? To know?

BENJAMIN: Better than not knowing.

EDDY: I'm glad you're still my friend.

BENJAMIN: Me, too.

EDDY: Benjamin. Can I have some of your Legos?

BENJAMIN: Sure. But not the castle.

EDDY: Deal.

(DOCTOR enters to check the machines.)

I'd better go. Will I see you later?

BENJAMIN: Sure. Sometime. Bye.

(They do a very gentle high five, EDDY exits.)

(Time shift. DOCTORS *hook up another IV pump, then exit.* BENJAMIN *begins drawing, narrating as he draws.)*

BENJAMIN: This is a yellow brick road, leading from the gangplank of my boat, all along a long, long,

*(*JOY *enters.)*

JOY and BENJAMIN: long, long . . .

BENJAMIN: . . . rock wall. I walk and I walk, and my knee doesn't hurt a bit, and when I come to a gate, I meet a gardener. That's him. He tells me that the gate is locked, but I can squeeze through the bars if I want to. Because on the other side is . . . *(He draws a rainbow shape on the paper.)*

JOY: What do you see?

BENJAMIN: See? Here. That is for Momma and Pappa. But later. You'll know.

(He continues drawing, she exits. DOCTORS *begin to move in and out of the room constantly. There is an escalating sense of crisis.)*

BENJAMIN: Then I get worse. Everybody carries worry into the room and sadness out.

DOCTOR #2: Tuberculosis present, but we don't know the strain.

BENJAMIN: The oxygen tube in my nose makes it so I can whistle, and I could never whistle before! My heart starts doing a tap dance . . .

DOCTOR #1: Heart fibrillation! Get me an EKG! *(The* DOCTORS *hook up another IV pump.)*

BENJAMIN: So they hook up a little TV with a blue squiggle and *no* commercials! And then I get worse, and everyone gets real serious. *(He quietly looks around the room.)* I sure hope heaven's not all white. 'Cause that would really be boring. It should look like this . . . *(He draws.)*

(Sounds increase.)

DOCTOR #2: Gradual enlargement of his heart muscle . . .

DOCTOR #1: Liver functions, way off . . .

DOCTOR #2: I'll up his oxygen level.

DOCTOR #4: *(Moving to the* PARENTS.*)* It's like a brush fire. You stamp out sparks in one place, it flares up in another.

BENJAMIN: They put a red light on my finger, just like E.T.

DOCTOR #2: Internal bleeding is out of control.

BENJAMIN: Phone home! Phone home!

DOCTOR #4: It's just a matter of time. I'm so sorry.

BENJAMIN: The body part just can't keep up with the rest of me. So I tell it to let go. But I'm not alone.

*(*PARENTS, JOY, *and* DOCTOR *enter and move to bed.)*
Almost time for the Yellow Boat to set sail.

FATHER: We'll all sail together . . .

MOTHER: I'll hoist the sails, Joy can do the anchor . . .

BENJAMIN: No. This time I have to go by myself.

MOTHER: Is there anything you want?

BENJAMIN: Just be here close. And a Dr. Pepper. (BENJAMIN's *breathing becomes increasingly labored.*)

FATHER: Reach up and tickle the ceiling stars . . . makes it easier to breathe.

(BENJAMIN *reaches for the sky, and then "releases" into the arms of his* PARENTS. *Time stops. After a beat, the doctors slowly unhook the IV lines and* BENJAMIN *slowly pulls away from the bed, on his way someplace else. The focus of the others in the room remains on the body left behind.* BENJAMIN *watches the scene he has just left as* JOY *steps forward and hands a drawing to the parents.*)

BENJAMIN: (*He colors the space with his words.*)

I see red.
I hear blue.
I feel purple.
I taste green.

(*Music underscores the last drawing, as the words and lights and images take us all to the "inside of a rainbow."*)

Last Drawing. The captain decides that it's time for the Yellow Boat to set sail. I sail on the path the sun makes on the water. Then, the boat shoots up, straight up to the sun. (*He signs the final picture.*) B-E-N-J-A-M-I-N.

(*He jumps onto the boat, which is slowly surrounded by the unfurling rays of the sun. He has set sail. Musical resolution. Blackout.*)

CURTAIN

SELKIE

by

Laurie Brooks Gollobin

In 1991, Laurie Brooks Gollobin's *Imaginary Friends*, adapted from a short story by her brother, fantasy author Terry Brooks, won a John Gassner Memorial Playwriting Award from the New England Theatre Conference and was featured at New Vision/New Voices, a forum for New Plays in Process at the Kennedy Center in Washington, D.C. In 1995, *Selkie* was the first play to be honored in the same year by both the Waldo M. & Grace C. Bonderman National Youth Theatre Playwriting Symposium of Indiana University–Purdue University at Indianapolis, and New Visions/New Voices at the John F. Kennedy Center.

Her plays have been produced across the United States and Ireland and have been presented at festivals in Ireland, Scotland, and Wales. Brooks Gollobin received her M.A. in Educational Theatre from New York University where *Selkie* was completed under the mentorship of children's theatre playwright Aurand Harris, and where the play received the first rehearsed reading and its official premier in 1996, under the direction of Nancy F. Swortzell. In the acting edition of the playscript Brooks Gollobin dedicates the play to "the memories of my mother who loved stories, and Aurand Harris, who loved the little girl with the webbed hands."

Although myths of the Seal People are found all over the world, Brooks Gollobin chose to set her play in the Orkney Islands north of Scotland because of their rich, dual Scots/Norse culture. She traveled to Orkney to research the mythology and traditions associated with the Selkie Folk. There she discovered the musical language of the Islands, called the Norn, that flavors the dialect in the play.

Brooks Gollobin lives in Oyster Bay, New York, and is the mother of three teenage daughters. She is currently at work on several new plays and her first novel for young people.

Storytelling is at the center of my work, stories that celebrate the courage and resilience of youth. As a child, I found comfort and inspiration in stories. They fired my imagination and gave me room to dream beyond the small town where I grew up. Most rewarding for me is the process of creating these stories: imagining new worlds, creating young protagonists, giving them plenty of trouble, then helping them discover ways to rise above their difficulties and emerge stronger from their experiences. Writing for young people offers me the opportunity to revisit the magic of childhood at a safe distance. My young characters are more courageous and determined than I was as a child. My hope is that they send a powerful message to young people about self-reliance, tenacity and hope.

—LAURIE BROOKS GOLLOBIN

SELKIE

CHARACTERS

Pa: Duncan's father, a fisherman.
Margaret: Late twenties, lovely and pale-skinned, with brown hair.
Ellen Jean: Brown-haired daughter of Duncan and Margaret, thirteen years old. Has webbed hands.
Duncan: A crofter. Early thirties.
Tam: A traveller (gypsy) lad of fourteen, with black eyes and a keen sense of mischief.
Black Hair: One of the selkie-folk women with long, black hair.
Red Hair: One of the selkie-folk women with long, red hair.

SETTING

The Orkney Islands north of the wild, rocky coast of Scotland. The stage is set to suggest the rocky seacoast. There is a large flat rock at center. Downstage of the rock, rippling lights create the sea. The upstage perimeter of the stage is dotted with rocks and grass.

A movable set piece defines the interior of a crofthouse (Orkney farmhouse). There are two small windows with shutters upstage. In the center of the crofthouse is a peat fire, which is burned down to glowing embers. There are two, low stools standing around the fire and a wooden rocking chair. There are two doors leading to other areas of the crofthouse and one leading to the outdoors.

TIME

One hundred years ago, on Midsummer's Eve (June 21) when the people of Orkney herald the coming of summer with a celebration called the Johnsmas Foy. They call this time the simmer dim, when there is daylight even at midnight.

(Fiddle music. Dim daylight. The Beach. It is Midsummer's Eve, when there is light for twenty hours a day. PA is downstage, playing his fiddle. He is scruffy and bearded, with a kind voice and warm ways.

Through the thick fog, called "the har," a large flat rock can be seen at center. Rippling lights create the sea downstage of the rock. Sounds of the wind and the sea. The sounds of the selkies singing in the distance. PA tucks his fiddle under his arm.)

PA: There was alus the sound of the sea. *(He imitates.)* and the sound of the wind *(He imitates.)* Aye, and the selkies singing. *(He imitates the selkies.)*

(DUNCAN, as a young man of about eighteen, enters, carrying a rake and a bag for gathering seaweed.)
There was also a young crofter named Duncan who lived by the sea. Through the thick fog he could see them approachin' the rocks—the selkie folk—seals that live in the water, but change into humans one magical night each year. It was that night . . . Midsummer's Eve, the night o' the grand celebration called the Johnsmas Foy.

(Three selkies, BLACK HAIR, RED HAIR, and a brown spotted selkie enter and move in the sea area toward the rock at center. DUNCAN hides himself behind upstage rocks. The selkies emerge onto the rock at center.)
He'd heard the stories told round the peat fires of the gray seals that shed their pelts and become beautiful lasses, but he niver believed them. Yet here, before his own eyes were three selkies on the shore and as he watched, they shed their skins.

(Selkie music. Joyously, the three throw off their skins and are transformed into beautiful young women; one red-haired, one black-haired, and one brown-haired.)
PA: One was a fair lass with golden-red hair, another young lass with shinin' black hair, and last . . . the fairest lass he had ever seen, with brown hair shimmerin' in the dim northern lights.

(As the music soars into the night, the selkie girls leap off the rock and do a wild dance on the beach as DUNCAN watches unseen in the shadows.)
They danced, the three selkie lasses, danced on the land, like waves on the sea. As he watched them leap wildly aboot the beach, he looked at the brown-haired selkie lass with all the eyes in his head. A strange feelin' came over him, a powerful feelin'. He knew he must take her, the brown-haired selkie lass, take her home tae be his sea-wife. Yes, and he knew he must steal her pelt, like in the stories. Withoot her pelt, she could niver go back tae the sea, but must follow him wherever he might lead her.

(DUNCAN comes out of his hiding place and approaches the women. The black-haired girl sees him and cries out a warning to the others. The selkie folk grab their pelts and enter the sea area. DUNCAN runs forward and takes up the pelt of the brown-haired girl. She reaches out her arms, imploring him to give back her pelt. DUNCAN firmly tucks the pelt underneath his arm. The girl slowly collapses on the beach, crying bitterly. DUNCAN offers his hand to the selkie girl. She hesitates. DUNCAN takes her hand, kisses it, and never taking his eyes from her face, leads her offstage.)

'Tis true. It happened. The crofter was my son, Duncan, and because she wouldna say her name, we called his sea-wife Margaret. Their only bairn, a daughter—was named Ellen Jean.

(ELLEN JEAN *enters and runs forward onto the rock at center. She gazes out to sea as if looking for something, then swiftly enters the water and exits.*)

(*Lights fade on beach and come up on the interior of the crofthouse.* MARGARET *sits on a stool, winding wool, working the yarn carefully between her fingers. She is much changed from when we saw her in the first scene. Her body is bent and she wears a shapeless homespun dress with an apron. She moves with an odd, shuffling gait, as though her limbs are too heavy for her body.*)

(PA *begins to play a lively tune on his fiddle. He enters the crofthouse, fiddling, as* ELLEN JEAN *enters and begins to dance about the room. The dancing is similar to the dancing performed by the three selkies in the first scene.* ELLEN JEAN's *long, brown hair swings about her as she dances. She wears a nondescript homespun dress tied at the waist, with unusually long sleeves which hang down, covering her hands. She shouts for punctuation as she dances.* PA *ends the tune as* ELLEN JEAN *leaps into the air and lands gracefully on the floor in a heap.*)

PA: (*Laughing.*) Well done, bonny lass! There's none can dance the music tae life as yerself.

MARGARET: Aye. She's the gift in her, our Ellen Jean.

ELLEN JEAN: Tis no' guid yet, fer all the tryin'.

PA: It'll come tae ye, in time, if ye wait.

ELLEN JEAN: Waitin' fer this, waitin' fer that. When will all the waitin' be over?

PA: When ye're stone dead, buried in the ground, and cold as the fishes.

MARGARET: Then ye're wishin' ye had the waitin' tae do.

ELLEN JEAN: Sometimes I have the strangest feelin', walkin' through the days sleepin' like. One day I'll wake up, an' everything'll be different.

PA: Different? Worse is more likely.

ELLEN JEAN: Oh, Pa, ye canno' tell the future. Mither, will ye do up me hair? It always comes all far-flunglike when I'm dancin' wild.

MARGARET: (*Smiling.*) A fine nest fer the birds ye have there.

(MARGARET *combs* ELLEN JEAN's *hair, fastening it with a clasp.*)

(Song: *Sung a cappella by* MARGARET. "Listen to the Sea." Music by Elliot Sokolov. Lyrics by Laurie Brooks Gollobin.)

> *Voices whisper with the wind*
> *Of places ye have niver been.*
> *Singin' songs of ebb and flow*
> *Of secrets ye will someday know.*
>
> *Listen tae the sea,*
> *There is a land far beneath.*

Awaken from yer sleep
Tae the mysteries doon below.

Selkies glidin' in between
Tides that play upon the sea
Callin' ye tae come along,
Beckon ye tae sing the song.

Listen tae the sea,
There is a land far beneath.
Awaken from yer sleep
Tae the mysteries doon below.

ELLEN JEAN: Thank ye, Mither, ye alus do it best.

(MARGARET *kisses* ELLEN JEAN's *forehead.*)

MARGARET: Eyes green as the sea.

PA: A brown-haired lass, there's none so fair
Neither golden nor black locks can compare.

ELLEN JEAN: Dunna be sayin' that. Ye're only feelin' sorry fer me.

PA: I like rhymin' is all.
Eetam, peetam, penny pie, Pop-a-larum, jinkam jie.
Stand thoo there til I come by.

(*Angrily,* ELLEN JEAN *starts to leave.*)

Dunna be goin' off in a huff! What's got ye so ill-bisted?

ELLEN JEAN: I canna abide rhymin' is all.

PA: I meant ye no disrespect.

ELLEN JEAN: Day after day I got tae hear the others sayin' hateful rhymes
aboot me.

PA: What a bulder o' nonsense! Dunna be payin' attention tae what the others say. It's the inside o' ye that matters.

ELLEN JEAN: No one wants to know me inside, they're too busy gawkin' at
the outside.

MARGARET: People's afraid o' what's different, fearin' what they dunna understand.

ELLEN JEAN: None o' them others wants tae be wi' me.

PA: I do.

ELLEN JEAN: I dunna care fer that.

PA: Dunna care fer yer old Grandpa?

(*He takes a stance like a puffin, and waddles about the room, making the high-
pitched "hey-al" sound of the puffin breed.* ELLEN JEAN *scowls.*)

I remember when 'at sent ye rollin' on the floor wi' laughin'.

ELLEN JEAN: When I was a bairn.

PA: How aboot this?

(He configures his body to imitate a sheep and makes ridiculous bleeting sounds.)

ELLEN JEAN: Ye've gone daft.

PA: *(Physicalizing himself into a cat. Cat voice.)* Rrrrrrrrrrrr. Meow. Skim off the cream fer me dinner, I'm a peedie bit hungry.

(PA rubs his shoulder up against her, knocking her down. ELLEN JEAN laughs.) There. I've made ye laugh.

ELLEN JEAN: Pa, ye're me family. Ye've no choice but tae be with me.

PA: Buy, buy, that's no way tae talk.

ELLEN JEAN: It's the others—I wish the others liked me.

MARGARET: The lads and lasses'll take notice when they see yer dancin' at the Foy this night.

PA: It'll be a celebration like none afore it. The torches o'heather cracklin'. The dancin' and singin' till dawn. I can see the looks on 'em. Eyes wide as saucers with the surprise.

(ELLEN JEAN hangs her head and is silent.)

(PA imitates village voices.) Look! Have ye niver seen the like o' the dancin'! More wonderous than the skelly sun hittin' the cliffs o' Hoy! Who is she, 'at bonnie lass?

ELLEN JEAN: I'll no' be dancin' at the Foy.

PA: Ye're thirteen. Yer fither expects ye tae dance. He's bragged aboot it from Kirkwall tae Stromness.

MARGARET: *(Caressing ELLEN JEAN's hair.)* Yer dancin' is a gift. Ye must no' hide what is worthy in yerself. Perhaps when the others see 'at side o' ye . . .

ELLEN JEAN: They'll hate the dancin' and think me a fool!

(ELLEN JEAN turns in anger and charges for the door. The door opens and DUNCAN enters. DUNCAN is tall and dark-haired; a lanky, awkward man who looks as though he isn't quite comfortable in his skin.)

DUNCAN: *(Stopping ELLEN JEAN at the door.)* Hover ye noo, lass. What's yer hurry?

ELLEN JEAN: No hurry, Fither.

DUNCAN: Sit ye doon then. I'd be havin' a word wi' ye.

(DUNCAN goes to MARGARET and kisses her lovingly.)

DUNCAN: Pale as the winter sky and twice as lovely.

(ELLEN JEAN tries to slip out of the room unnoticed.)

MARGARET: A lie is harder tae tell in the long haul than the hardest truth.

PA: The truth! There's a slippery fish, just when ye 've caught it up, it slides away from ye.

DUNCAN: Tae me ye're bonny as ever. Workin' each day I'm only waitin' fer evenin' tae be home with ye . . . and Jean. *(DUNCAN spots ELLEN JEAN leaving.)* Jean! Come hither, Lass. James Leslie saw ye yesterday swimmin' oot beyond the voe. Ellen Jean, I've told ye and told ye no' tae swim oot beyond the voe. Even the finest swimmer in Orkney must respect the tides. They change in a peedie minute and pull the strongest swimmer doon into the blackness.

ELLEN JEAN: I know the tides.

DUNCAN: Then why do ye swim oot beyond the voe? Is it a watery grave ye'd be after?

ELLEN JEAN: I canno' help meself. Somethin' pulls me doon tae the beach and in tae the sea.

DUNCAN: I'll no' have ye riskin' yer life when the har rolls in and ye canna see beyond yer nose. None o' the others would dare swim in these waters. I dunna understand. Why do ye no' stay on land with the others?

ELLEN JEAN: I had tae swim oot tae the skerrie.

DUNCAN: What were ye thinkin', Lass? At's near two miles oot tae sea.

MARGARET: 'Twas the selkies callin'. The red and the black.

ELLEN JEAN: They came back, Mither, just as ye said they would.

MARGARET: Aye, at Midsummer's tide.

ELLEN JEAN: One red as the sun goin' down, the other dark as peat.

MARGARET: Noses lifted straight oot o' the water, like they'us lookin' fer somethin'.

(MARGARET *looks toward the sea.*)

DUNCAN: There are hundreds o' selkies swimmin' in these waters, alike as one another.

ELLEN JEAN: I knowed 'em straight away and no mistake. I saw their eyes up closelike. Human eyes, they were. They'us cryin'.

DUNCAN: Ach, 'twas only sea water drippin'.

MARGARET: Selkies cry just as humans do. And fer the same reasons. Longin' fer what's been lost and canno' be found.

ELLEN JEAN: They'us callin' me. They wanted me tae follow 'em.

DUNCAN: I'll no' ask ye tae explain it. Just no' tae do it.

ELLEN JEAN: I try tae stay on land, Fither, but then I'm achin' fer the feel o' the water and the pull o' the waves.

(ELLEN JEAN *moves her arms to illustrate her thoughts and her long sleeves fall back to reveal her hands. The crofthouse grows silent as* ELLEN JEAN *realizes she has shown her hands to her father. She instinctively hides them behind her back.*)

DUNCAN: Sha' me yer hands.

PA: Giddy God, noo ye've done it.

MARGARET: Duncan, come have yer ale. It's waitin'.

PA: Aye. I'm thirsty as a landlocked fisherman.

MARGARET: I've fresh baked bannock. Ye must be hungry.

DUNCAN: (*To* MARGARET.) I'll no' be dissuaded. I'm waitin', Lass.

(ELLEN JEAN *slowly holds out her hands for* DUNCAN.)

Webbed, they have grown webbed again. Where's me gully knife?

(DUNCAN *pulls the knife out of the back of his belt and, using his belt, sharpens it with a stropping motion.*)

MARGARET: They'll only grow back, like alus.

PA: Leave her hands alone, won't ye? There's naught tae be done fer it.

MARGARET: Aye. Tis no guid tae cut 'em.

ELLEN JEAN: *(Bravely.)* It doesna' hurt too much, Mither.

(PA *gets up and reaches for his coat.*)

PA: 'At pony'll be wantin' tae be fed.

MARGARET: Dunna run from it, Pa. Help me.

PA: Dunna cut her, man. There's naught tae be done fer it.

MARGARET: Even if ye cut 'em clean off, she'll niver be like the others.

DUNCAN: Who will she be like, then? She's thirteen now, time tae think o' makin' a guid marriage to a crofter with land, home and hearth. She'll need more than a dowry tae fetch a husband.

MARGARET: Let the future be takin' care o' itself.

DUNCAN: Ye'd have me do nothin'! I canna bear tae hear the others laugh and make sport o' her. I wilna' stand idle, seein' her married off tae some tinker like that dirty Tam McCodrun without a sturdy tub fer washin' or a strip o' land tae keep his family fed.

MARGARET: I've heard tell o' him who took a stunder tae love a lass wi' naught but hersel' tae offer.

ELLEN JEAN: Cut them, fither. I want tae be like the others.

(ELLEN JEAN *obediently lays her hands on the table.*)

DUNCAN: 'At's a good lass. Hold yer hands steady.

(ELLEN JEAN *turns her head away.* DUNCAN *positions the knife to cut the first web.* MARGARET *rushes forward and stops Duncan.*)

MARGARET: No! Cuttin' her hands wilna keep her from the sea! Ye canno' shape her intae yer dreams o' what's tae come or cut her tae fit ye like a bit o' cloth. Look at her! Do ye no' see she's bonny as she is?

(DUNCAN *drops the knife as* MARGARET *sobs. He gathers* MARGARET *into his arms.*)

DUNCAN: There, there, darlin'. Dunna cry. I canna' bear tae hear ye cry. I'll no' cut 'em. I'll no' cut 'em.

(ELLEN JEAN *quietly picks up the knife.*)

PA: Ellen Jean, go oot tae the byre. 'At pony wants feedin'.

(ELLEN JEAN *looks toward her parents and hesitates.*)

ELLEN JEAN: Then I'll cut them meself!

(ELLEN JEAN *slashes the largest web. She cries out and drops the knife, holding her cut hand high in the air.*)

(Blackout.)

(Dim daylight. The beach. Sounds of the sea and the wind. Sounds of the selkies. ELLEN JEAN *sits on the rock at center, looking out to sea. Enter* TAM. *He wears dirty trousers, dingy white shirt, and a faded vest that might once have been colorful. His hair hangs long and stringy, falling often and annoyingly into his eyes. His face, hands and bare feet are streaked with dirt and he carries a tin pail.* TAM *begins to dig for limpets, then sees* ELLEN JEAN.)*

TAM: Look what the sea washed up on the beach. A young bit o' skirly-wheeter.

ELLEN JEAN: Go away and dunna daive me with yer gabbin'.

TAM: I warn ye once, I warn ye twice,

I warn ye oot the glowrie's eyes.

ELLEN JEAN: Stop 'at! Stop sayin' 'at hateful rhyme!

*(*ELLEN JEAN *puts her hands covered by her long sleeves over her ears to block out the sounds.)*

TAM: Hie thee Lass 'at swims in the sea,

Stay away from thee and me!

*(*ELLEN JEAN *ignores him. He laughs.)*

TAM: What're ye doin' here? Waitin' fer the King o' the Sea tae come courtin' ye?

ELLEN JEAN: If he wus, ye'd likely bash in his head with a club, skin 'im alive on the beach an' sell his pelt.

TAM: Fetch a pretty penny, too, more'n likely.

ELLEN JEAN: Ye're an evil lad, I saw ye doon on the skerrie yesterday ballin' stones at the selkies.

TAM: Aye, me and the lads. Missed 'em clean away, too. More's the pity.

ELLEN JEAN: How can ye be so cruel tae harmless creatures?

TAM: Harmless! Witches they are. Condemned fer their sins tae live in the sea.

ELLEN JEAN: That's no' true.

TAM: Eatin' up the herrin' an' starvin' honest fishin' folk.

ELLEN JEAN: The selkies have a right tae eat as much as any creature.

TAM: *(Mysteriously.)* Comin' up on the land tae steal the peedie bairns from their mithers, just like the trolls.

ELLEN JEAN: That's a lie! The selkies have done naught but kindnesses fer folk, savin' 'em from drownin' and the like.

TAM: Ye like the selkies so much, why dunna ye go live in the sea with 'em!

*(*ELLEN JEAN *is silent.)*

Cat got yer tongue, Selkie Lass? Got nuthin' tae say?

ELLEN JEAN: Nuthin' tae say tae the likes o' thee.

*(*TAM *lifts a handful of* ELLEN JEAN's *hair and flips it playfully.)*

ELLEN JEAN: *(Recoiling.)* Dunna touch me.

TAM: *(Becoming aware of his dirty hands.)* Ye'd think I had the pox, instead o' a bit o' honest dirt.

ELLEN JEAN: Honest dirt washes off. It's the dirty inside I'm thinkin' of.

TAM: Miss high and mighty. Stickin' yer nose up, keepin' away from me like I'm lower 'an sheep filth. Because yer fither's got a bit o' land and a byre doesna' make ye so grand.

ELLEN JEAN: I didna say 'at.

TAM: Ye hate me because I'm a traveller, don't ye. A wanderin' gypsy withoot a home. Ye're like all the others.

ELLEN JEAN: I'm no' like the others.

TAM: Get off this beach and leave me tae gather me limpets fer supper.

(TAM begins to forage among the rocks for limpets to fill his pail.)

ELLEN JEAN: I have a right tae be here.

TAM: Get off, I said.

ELLEN JEAN: No. I wilna be bullied aboot.

TAM: *(Threateningly.)* Get off afore I run ye off . . . or worse!

ELLEN JEAN: I'll no' give in tae the likes o' thee, Dirty Tam McCodrun!

(TAM runs to ELLEN JEAN, grabs her by her upraised wrists and shakes her.)

TAM: Dunna call me 'at! Dunna ever call me 'at!

ELLEN JEAN: Let me go! Let me go!

(In the struggle TAM loses his footing and nearly falls into the sea. ELLEN JEAN instinctively reaches out and grabs TAM to save him from falling. For a moment it looks as though they will both fall, then they regain their balance. TAM looks down at her hands. The long sleeves of her dress have fallen back to reveal her bloody fingers. ELLEN JEAN breaks free of TAM's grasp and cradles her hurt hand.)

TAM: *(Looking at his hands.)* Blood! Ye're hurt! Damn me ill-bisted temper!

ELLEN JEAN: Hie thee away from me!

TAM: I didna mean tae hurt ye, only ye called me . . . that name. No one calls me Dirty Tam tae me face.

ELLEN JEAN: Tis none o' yer doin'.

TAM: How did ye hurt yer hand then?

ELLEN JEAN: 'Tis nothin'. An accident.

TAM: A bad one, by the looks o' it.

ELLEN JEAN: A slip o' the hand is all.

(TAM pulls a crumpled cloth from his pocket.)

TAM: Here. Let me bind 'at up fer ye.

ELLEN JEAN: Tis nothin', I said.

TAM: Garn. Ye musn 't be so stubborn.

(TAM takes her hand to wrap the bandage, then stops and stares at her webbed fingers. ELLEN JEAN pulls her hand away.)

ELLEN JEAN: What are ye gleerin' at?

TAM: Yer hands, I . . . I niver saw the like o' them.

ELLEN JEAN: Then run and tell the others what ye've seen! Tell 'em ye've seen the webs. Tell 'em!

(She angrily shoves her hands in his face.)

Look! Green and slimy like seaweed, they are. They say she has horned skin on her palms. Tell 'em she goes doon tae the beach tae meet the King o' the Sea behind the rocks! Tell them! They'll think ye're a fine one fer knowin'.

(ELLEN JEAN turns to run away, but TAM catches her arm.)

TAM: Wait! I'm sorry!

ELLEN JEAN: I hate ye, Tam McCodrun, and all the others!

(ELLEN JEAN breaks away and exits, running.)

TAM: *(Calling after her.)* Wait! I'm sorry! I said I'm sorry! Devil take ye, then.

(TAM picks up his pail.)

Devil take any who call me Dirty Tam! Devil take the limpets!

(TAM throws the tin pail into the rocks with a crash.)

Devil take the selkies! *(TAM looks after ELLEN JEAN. Quietly.)* I didna mean it. I didna mean tae hurt ye.

(Lights shift.)

(Interior of the croft. DUNCAN kneels before the fire, brushing a selkie pelt with great tenderness. The sounds of the selkies can be heard in the distance. PA stands outside the crofthouse watching DUNCAN.)

PA: Ye see, Duncan couldna destroy Margaret's pelt, or she would die. But he lived alus wi' the fear 'at she would discover it and return tae the sea. So he hid Margaret's skin careful-like aboot the croft, first in one place, then another, tae keep it from her searchin' eyes, oilin' and brushin' it each year so it wouldna crack or dry up. It was as though he was carin' fer Margaret herself.

(PA enters the crofthouse and sits in the rocking chair, which squeaks noisily as he rocks back and forth. PA opens his mouth as though to say something, then stops. PA heaves a huge, audible sigh. DUNCAN looks at PA sharply.)

PA: I didna say a word.

DUNCAN: Yer gettin' ready.

(PA rocks furiously in the squeaky rocking chair.)

DUNCAN: Get on with it then.

PA: When I'm ready. When I'm ready.

DUNCAN: I'm in no rush.

(PA rocks his chair with a vengeance to the rhythm of DUNCAN's brush strokes on the pelt.)

PA: Deer, Sheer, bret and smeer,
   What shall ye have fer dinner?

(DUNCAN stops brushing and gives PA an annoyed look. He begins his rhythmic brushing again.)

   Minch meat small or none at all,
   Tae make ye fat or thinner.

DUNCAN: Ye'd best be ready soon, afore ye rock that chair intae the ground!

PA: Ye coulda had yer pick o' island lasses, fine and strong.

DUNCAN: Aye, 'ats the familiar tune.

PA: How could ye have done it, man? Ta'en one o' the selkie-folk tae wife?

DUNCAN: I didna choose it.

PA: And who forced ye?

DUNCAN: The first time I laid eyes on her sittin' on the skerrie, hair blowin' out around her like the mist, I knew I couldna rest 'til I brought her home tae wife.

PA: Now she canna rest. Walkin' doon tae the sea night after night. An' Ellen Jean, hidin' herself away on the croft, ashamed o' her hands.

DUNCAN: Things change. This year she'll be goin' doon tae the Foy with me tae dance.

PA: Ye'll be goin' alone tae the Foy this year. She's ta'en herself off tae bed.

DUNCAN: Tae bed? At this hour?

PA: She wilna dance at the Foy. She's afraid the others'll laugh. She canna find her place among the lads and lasses.

(From the sea comes the sounds of the selkies.)

DUNCAN: *(Shouting to the selkies.)* Leave off yer hoolan'. I canna think wi' the sound o' ye!

PA: The selkies're callin' tae Margaret, callin' her tae come away wi' 'em. Ye've grown careless. Best be hidin' her pelt away afore she comes back. If she finds her skin, she'll be goin' back to the sea in a twinklin'.

DUNCAN: She wouldna leave me.

PA: She couldna help herself. It's inside her, like Ellen Jean swimmin' oot beyond the voe.

DUNCAN: No! She wouldna leave us, man, after fourteen years!

PA: Then why do ye no' give back her skin?

(There is a moment of silence.)

   There's trouble in what ye've done. Ye canna run from a wrong.

DUNCAN: Are ye through?

PA: It's the bairns that pay fer the wrongs o' the ones gone afore. Ellen Jean'll be livin' wi' yer sin fer the rest o' her life. I shoulda beat ye wi' a stick 'til ye came to yer senses afore I let ye take yer wife from the sea.

DUNCAN: Ye shouldna blame yerself.

PA: I didna stop ye, noo, did I? 'At's me own wrong.

(PA *exits. The sound of the selkies calling grows louder and more plaintive. Duncan raises his fists in anger. He folds up the pelt and shoves it back into its hiding place above the aisins.*)

DUNCAN: (*Shouting out the door toward the sea.*) Be off noo! Stop yer callin'!

(DUNCAN *slams the window shutters closed as though to lock out the sound. The moaning of the selkies grows even louder.* DUNCAN *opens the door and yells into the night.*)

Go back tae the sea an' leave us alone. She belongs tae me. Do ye hear? She belongs tae me!

(DUNCAN *slams the door and exits. The sound of the selkies continues to fill the crofthouse. Within their moaning sounds can be heard the sound of the selkies calling* ELLEN JEAN's *name.* ELLEN JEAN *enters, rubbing her eyes. She is wearing a white night dress, and her hair hangs long down her back. She hugs herself and closing her eyes, sways in response to the selkie sounds. She opens the door, and the selkie sounds grow louder. Her body moves instinctively to the sounds. As though directed to do so,* ELLEN JEAN *looks in the direction of the pelt. She tries to reach it, but it is too high. She drags over a stool and stands on it.* ELLEN JEAN *lifts the pelt down from its hiding place and hugs it to her body. She closes her eyes, and swaying back and forth, imitates the selkies' moaning with her own voice. She loses her balance and falls off the stool onto the floor with a crash. The selkie sounds stop.* PA *enters.*)

PA: Ach, Jean! I thought it was the bawkie man come tae steal us away'. What're ye aboot?

ELLEN JEAN: Look. A selkie skin. I found it hidden up in the aisins.

PA: What're ye doin' searchin' up in the aisins?

ELLEN JEAN: The selkies woke me. Did ye no' hear 'em?

PA: Ye'd have to be stone deaf or dead no' tae hear their bellowin'.

ELLEN JEAN: No. No. The selkies were callin' me, callin' me name over and over.

PA: Selkies talkin'. What a bulder o' nonsense!

ELLEN JEAN: Clear as the broonie lights, they'us callin' me name. It was they made me look up in th' aisins. They wanted me tae find the pelt.

PA: Ye're dreamin', Jean. And walkin' in her sleep by the look o' ye.

ELLEN JEAN: This selkie pelt is no' a dream. Maybe it belongs tae one o' the selkie-folk . . . like in the stories.

PA: More likely stuffed up there tae keep oot the drafty air.

ELLEN JEAN: Oh, Pa, think o' the poor creature withoot its skin.

PA: Long dead noo. They canno' live withoot their skins.

ELLEN JEAN: But it feels warm. Not like somethin' dead at all. I'll be goin' doon tae the sea.

PA: I'd think atifer doin' 'at, if I were thee. It's trouble ye're askin' fer. Return the pelt tae where ye found it. It doesna belong tae ye noo, does it?

ELLEN JEAN: No.

PA: Then ye're no' tae be takin' it.

(ELLEN JEAN *lays the pelt against her cheek and breathes in the smell.*)
ELLEN JEAN: There's somethin' aboot the smell.

(ELLEN JEAN *holds out the pelt to* PA's *nose.*)
PA: (*Making a face.*) I'll no' be smellin' any old selkie skin!
ELLEN JEAN: I know the smell. It's . . . familiar.
PA: Ach, ye know the smell o' the sea, like all the Orkney folk.
ELLEN JEAN: I was meant tae find it, Pa. I know it.
PA: Ye were meant tae dance at the Johnsmas Foy, but ye're no' doin' it, then, are ye?

(ELLEN JEAN *is silent.*)

Come tae the Foy an' dance the music tae life with yer old Pa. Give the others a chance tae know who ye are inside.
ELLEN JEAN: I canno' dance fer the others. I canno'.
PA: And I canno' force ye tae dance. Sha' me the pelt, and I'll return it tae where ye found it.

(ELLEN JEAN *sighs and gives* PA *the pelt. He puts it back up in the aisins.*)
ELLEN JEAN: I'll ask Mither. She'll know what tae do about the pelt.
PA: No! Dunna be botherin' yer mither. Listen tae yer old Pa. Ferget ye ever saw the pelt.
ELLEN JEAN: But Pa, the selkies . . . they'us callin' me.
PA: (*Sharply.*) 'Twas a dream, I tell ye. Ferget it, and dunna be borrowin' trouble. Things're likely tae be lookin' different in the mornin'. (ELLEN JEAN *hesitates.*) Go on with ye, I said. (ELLEN JEAN *goes toward the door.*) Ellen Jean. (ELLEN JEAN *turns back to* PA.) Dunna be muckin' aboot with what ye dunna understand and canno' finish, do ye hear me?
ELLEN JEAN: Aye, I hear ye, Pa.
PA: Sleep well.

(*Exit* ELLEN JEAN. *The selkie sounds begin again.*)

Sleep well! That's no' likely, fer none this night.

(*Exit* PA. ELLEN JEAN *peeks around the doorway and sees* PA *has gone. She enters and takes the pelt from its hiding place. The sounds of the selkies calling fills the room.* ELLEN JEAN *hugs herself and sways as if in ecstasy. Then she tucks the pelt under her arm and exits into the night.*)

(*Lights shift. Music.*)

(*The beach. Dim light. Music fades. Sounds of the sea and the wind.* ELLEN JEAN *sits at center, looking out to sea. She wraps herself in the pelt, sways to and fro and smiles. For the first time she seems happy and at peace. Sounds of the selkies ap-*

proaching. ELLEN JEAN *tries to fit herself into the pelt. She tries to put her foot into it, while her arms, attempting several styles of drapery, cannot quite manage to decipher its mystery. Enter the two selkie sisters,* RED HAIR *and* BLACK HAIR. *The two selkies glide in the sea toward the shore.* ELLEN JEAN *sees their approach and, frustrated by her inability to wear the pelt, folds herself as small as she can, hiding herself beneath it. The selkies haul out on the beach and cautiously move nearer to* ELLEN JEAN. *Enter* TAM *from behind the rocks, carrying a club.* TAM *wears the same dirty trousers, dingy white shirt, and vest. He is barefoot. He sees* ELLEN JEAN *and the two selkies, and runs toward them, lifting the club high over his head to strike. The selkies bellow and escape into the sea.* ELLEN JEAN *jumps up and sees* TAM *about to hit her.)*

ELLEN JEAN: No! Dunna strike me!

TAM: *(Jumping up in shock and dropping the club.)* Selkie Lass!

*(*TAM *loses his footing on the slippery rocks.)*

Help me! Help!

*(*TAM *falls into the water and lies still.)*

ELLEN JEAN: *(Calling after him.)* I hope ye drown. Ye deserve tae drown. Then no more selkies will die from the likes o' Dirty Tam McCodrun!

(When there is no answer, ELLEN JEAN *looks down into the water.)*

Why dunna ye swim? Afraid they'll say ye've a bit o' the selkie in ye? I hope ye go straight doon tae . . .

(The selkies bellow and yelp again.)

ELLEN JEAN: *(Realizing.)* Giddy God! He's drownin'!

*(*ELLEN JEAN, *leaving the pelt behind on the rock, enters the water. She moves to* TAM, *floating on the surface as if dead.* ELLEN JEAN *drags* TAM *onto the beach with help from the two selkies.)*

I'm sorry. I didna mean what I said. I dinna want ye tae die!

(Selkie music. ELLEN JEAN *looks up and sees the two selkies behind her throw off their pelts. They are transformed into the two beautiful women seen with Margaret at the beginning of the play. Throughout the scene, the two selkies move in tandem as though connected.)*

Giddy God!

BLACK HAIR: Hush yer cryin'. He will no' die.

RED HAIR: Ye have saved him this night. 'Tis the way o' the selkies tae save drownin' men, even the killers.

BLACK HAIR: He'll wake soon enough with an achin' head.

RED HAIR: None the worse fer the baffin.

ELLEN JEAN: I knowed ye would come when I saw ye oot on the skerrie.

RED HAIR: Ye found the pelt.

ELLEN JEAN: I heard ye callin' me. Tellin' me tae bring it.

BLACK HAIR: Ye have the ears tae listen this night and the heart tae tell ye what tae listen fer.

RED HAIR: Aye, and look. She has her Mither's eyes.

BLACK HAIR: Green as the sea.

ELLEN JEAN: Do ye know Mither?

BLACK HAIR: Aye, as we know the flow o' the tides and the feel o' the warm sun.

RED HAIR: Ye're very like her, yer mither.

BLACK HAIR: Sha' me yer hands.

(BLACK HAIR *takes* ELLEN JEAN'*s hand and lifts back the long sleeves.* ELLEN JEAN *pulls her hands away and hides them both behind her back.*)

ELLEN JEAN: They're ugly.

(BLACK HAIR *takes* ELLEN JEAN'*s hands in her own and caresses them.*)

BLACK HAIR: They are webbed.

RED HAIR: Made fer the sea.

(RED HAIR *embraces* ELLEN JEAN.)

ELLEN JEAN: *(To* RED HAIR.*)* Dunna be afraid. I'll keep ye safe. No hunters will find ye.

BLACK HAIR: She weeps fer one ta'en by a crofter fourteen years ago an' kept from her home an' family in th' sea.

ELLEN JEAN: Like in the stories.

BLACK HAIR: 'Tis no story. 'Tis true as ye're standin' there. The pelt belongs tae yer mither, our sister.

ELLEN JEAN: Mither? But she canno be one o' the selkie folk. She's . . . old.

BLACK HAIR: Fourteen years kept from the sea has made her old.

RED HAIR: Every year at Midsummer, we return tae be wi' her. Seven children she has in the sea, a fither, mither, and we two sisters.

(ELLEN JEAN *pulls back her sleeves and looks with new eyes at her webbed hands.*)

ELLEN JEAN: I'm one o' the selkie folk.

BLACK HAIR: No, lass. Yer part o' yer mither and part o' yer fither. Sea and land. The first of a kind.

ELLEN JEAN: *(Taking up the pelt and holding it close.)* I hate the land. I'm different from the others. I want tae be in the sea.

BLACK HAIR: Yer Mither belongs in the sea, but it is no' yer home.

ELLEN JEAN: I have no home. I dunna belong anywhere!

BLACK HAIR: Belongin's no' a place, it's inside ye. Ye will find the knowin', in time.

ELLEN JEAN: More waitin', alus waitin'. I canno' wait any longer.

RED HAIR: Ye must give yer mither back her pelt.

BLACK HAIR: So she can return tae her home in th' sea.

ELLEN JEAN: Return tae the sea? But will she come back?

(TAM *begins to stir. He coughs.*)

BLACK HAIR: He's wakin'

RED HAIR: Quickly! The sea!

(BLACK HAIR *and* RED HAIR *run to grab their pelts.*)

ELLEN JEAN: Wait! If I give Mither the pelt, will she come back tae me? I need tae know!

BLACK HAIR: Give her the pelt!

RED HAIR: Give her back tae the sea!

(BLACK HAIR *and* RED HAIR *throw on their pelts, and, entering the sea, are transformed into selkies. They swim away from shore and exit.* ELLEN JEAN *stands looking out to sea, watching the selkies.* TAM *sits up, sees her and smiles, then lies back down before she sees him awake.* ELLEN JEAN *goes to* TAM, *who moans loudly.*)

ELLEN JEAN: Please. Wake up. I didna mean fer ye tae die, just no' tae hurt me.

(TAM's *arms go around her. He pulls her to him and kisses her.*)

ELLEN JEAN: (*Jumping up.*) Oh!

TAM: (*Laughing.*) A kiss from the Selkie Lass. Almost worth drownin' fer.

ELLEN JEAN: I hate ye, Tam McCodrun.

TAM: What? Fer a kiss?

ELLEN JEAN: Ye tried tae kill me. Again.

TAM: No. I was after the pelt. How was I tae know ye were darned doon in it?

ELLEN JEAN: Killin' was all ye were after. What kind o' man would club an innocent selkie?

TAM: The hungry kind.

ELLEN JEAN: The night of the Johnsmas Foy? There'll be plenty tae eat.

TAM: There's other kinds o' hunger than in the stomach.

ELLEN JEAN: What other kinds?

TAM: Did ye niver feel fairly silted tae have somethin', wantin' it so much ye can think o' naught but that?

ELLEN JEAN: Waitin' fer it tae happen, deathly afraid it niver will?

TAM: Aye, that's the feelin'.

ELLEN JEAN: What are ye silted fer?

TAM: Tae wake up every dawn in the same place. Tae have a place tae call home.

ELLEN JEAN: A place tae belong?

TAM: Aye, 'at's it. Even the feast at the Foy canno' fill up 'at yawnin' hole.

ELLEN JEAN: I know. I want tae belong, too.

TAM: Ye have a home. A fine croft wi' a byre full o' sheep and ponies, too.

ELLEN JEAN: What guid is it if none o' the others wants tae be with me?

TAM: I do.

ELLEN JEAN: Ye do?

TAM: Aye.

ELLEN JEAN: But ye're alus callin' me names and sayin' 'at hateful rhyme.

TAM: Ach, it's fer the lads. There's no meanin' in it. I'll no' be makin' sport o' ye ever again, if ye ask me.

ELLEN JEAN: Why should I believe ye?

TAM: Ye saved me miserable life, did ye no'?

ELLEN JEAN: Aye, more's the pity.

TAM: Ask me, then.

ELLEN JEAN: I'm askin' ye. Dunna be callin' me names.

TAM: Niver again.

ELLEN JEAN: Swear it tae me.

TAM: I swear I'll niver call ye names again.

ELLEN JEAN: And ye'll no' be sayin' 'at hateful rhyme?

TAM: I swear I'll no' say 'at rhyme ever again.

ELLEN JEAN: And swear tae me from this day on ye'll niver raise a hand tae hurt the selkies as long as ye live.

TAM: I've done enough swearin' fer one day.

ELLEN JEAN: Please. 'Tis all I'm askin' fer.

TAM: Do ye know the price 'ats paid oot fer a single selkie pelt?

ELLEN JEAN: There's other ways tae earn yer keep.

TAM: I'm savin' up fer somethin'.

ELLEN JEAN: What're ye savin' up fer, Tam McCodrun?

(TAM *looks at her sharply, realizing she has said his name with respect.*)

TAM: (*Eagerly.*) A bit o' land—a home. A lass tae love me as brave and true as yerself.

ELLEN JEAN: Are ye sayin' 'at because I saved yer miserable life?

TAM: Better ye let me die.

ELLEN JEAN: Niver say such a thing. It might come true. Did you mither never tell ye?

TAM: She's long dead. The day I wus born.

ELLEN JEAN: I'm sorry. I canno' imagine a life withoot Mither.

TAM: Ach, who wants all that fussin' over.

(TAM *sighs and takes up the pelt.*)

I'll content myself wi' this spotty pelt.

ELLEN JEAN: No. It belongs tae me.

TAM: I can take this pelt if I want. Ye canno' stop me. And maybe if I keep it, ye'll follow me.

ELLEN JEAN: I'll no' follow a thief. The pelt belongs tae me. Ye canno' have it.

TAM: I'll no' take yer pelt . . . if ye'll dance with me at the Foy this night.

ELLEN JEAN: Ye want tae dance wi' me? At the Foy?

TAM: Aye, that's the trade. The pelt fer a dance.

ELLEN JEAN: Dance at the Foy! Aye, I'll dance with ye! (*Suddenly shy.*) If that's what ye want.

TAM: I said it, did I no'?

ELLEN JEAN: Will ye promise no' tae harm the selkies?

TAM: It's a hard bargain yer askin' fer, Lass.

ELLEN JEAN: Aye.

TAM: Aye.

ELLEN JEAN: Done?

TAM: Done.

(TAM *hands* ELLEN JEAN *the pelt and she rolls it into a bundle.*)

ELLEN JEAN: I have somethin' important tae do. Be off with ye noo.

TAM: What's makin' ye so foreswifted tae be rid o' me?

ELLEN JEAN: I have somethin' tae do before the Foy. Get on with ye.

TAM: Ye're mighty mysterious. What're ye aboot?

ELLEN JEAN: (*Casting about for an excuse.*) Oh. Well, I canno' go tae the Foy in me nightdress, can I?

TAM: (*He looks down at his dirty hands and feet.*) Oh, I'm thinkin' I have somethin' tae do, too.

ELLEN JEAN: Dunna ferget yer promise.

TAM: I swear I'll no' hurt the selkies.

ELLEN JEAN: Ferever, no matter what comes.

TAM: I said it, did I no'?

ELLEN JEAN: (*Taking hold of his arms.*) Say it.

TAM: Ferever, no matter what comes.

ELLEN JEAN: Niver—niver forget yer promise.

(TAM *reaches out his hand and touches her.*)

TAM: I'll no' ferget.

ELLEN JEAN: Run. Dunna come back until Midnight! Until the Foy!

TAM: Until the Foy!

(*Giving a joyous shout,* TAM *turns and runs offstage.* ELLEN JEAN *looks up and down the beach, then dances around the beach whirling and high stepping with joy. As she dances,* MARGARET *enters, and quietly watches her daughter.*)

ELLEN JEAN: I'll dance—dance at the Foy! And be one o' them!

(*Panting,* ELLEN JEAN *hugs herself with pleasure.*)

MARGARET: Tis guid tae see ye smilin', Peedie Buddo.

ELLEN JEAN: Mither!

(ELLEN JEAN *runs to her mother, throws her arms around her mother's waist, and holds her.*)

ELLEN JEAN: Oh, Mither, I'm goin' tae dance at the Foy—with Tam!

MARGARET: A smart lad, that Tam. And lucky, too.

ELLEN JEAN: And . . . and look . . . I found yer pelt.

MARGARET: Ahhhh. Me pelt! Ye found me pelt!

(Laughing, MARGARET falls to her knees on the beach, caressing the pelt and breathing in the familiar smell.)

ELLEN JEAN: Mither, ye're laughin'.

MARGARET: Oh, Peedie Buddo, ye 've given me back me life.

ELLEN JEAN: Yer sisters said ye'll leave me fer the sea.

MARGARET: Leave ye? No, Peedie Buddo. I'll alus be with ye. Come.

(MARGARET holds out her hand, and ELLEN JEAN takes it in her own. MARGARET leads ELLEN JEAN down to the sea.)

MARGARET: Fourteen years I have been captive on the land. In that time I have grown old and stiff. Me skin is dry and cracked fer want o' the sea. Me bones are as brittle as driftwood lyin' on the shore. Ye have brought me what I need. It is me time tae return home.

(MARGARET folds her arms around ELLEN JEAN and holds her.)

ELLEN JEAN: Mither, please, dunna leave me!

(The sound of the wind and the sea.)

MARGARET: I will alus be with ye. Look tae the sea, and ye'll see me there. In the waves breakin' on the shore, the sun glitterin' on the sea foam. Precious shells will wash up on the beach. Fish will leap intae yer nets, and the selkies will guide ye safely through the tides in the sea.

(MARGARET kisses ELLEN JEAN on each cheek.)

ELLEN JEAN: No! Mither! Take me with ye! I want tae go with ye!

MARGARET: Are ye no' afraid?

ELLEN JEAN: Aye. Afraid o' bein' left behind among the others.

MARGARET: Listen well then, Peedie Buddo. I give ye the gift o' the wind tae travel beneath the tides. Only do as I do, and ye will have the way tae find the knowin'.

(Music. ELLEN JEAN follows her MOTHER's lead as she dances the journey beneath the sea and, in a rhythmic exchange of breath, bestows the gift of the wind upon her daughter.)

MARGARET: Me heart is turned inside oot with the pain o' leavin' ye, but it is me time tae go.

(MARGARET turns and walks into the sea with the pelt. She puts it around her body and is transformed into a selkie. She glides swiftly into the sea and, without turning back, exits. ELLEN JEAN runs onto the rock at center.)

ELLEN JEAN: Wait! Wait fer me! Dunna leave me behind!

(Music from the Foy can be heard in the background. Enter PA.)

PA: Ellen Jean. Hover thee, Lass. Ye canno' follow her. Stay and dance fer yer old Pa at the Foy.

(Sounds of the selkies calling. ELLEN JEAN looks toward the sea.)

ELLEN JEAN: Can ye no' hear 'em callin' me? I canno' stay on land.

PA: But the tides, Jean.

ELLEN JEAN: Dunna be afraid fer me, Pa. I'll find it. I'll find the knowin'.

PA: Jean, I canno' let ye go.

ELLEN JEAN: Dunna try tae stop me. If ye hold me here I'll hate ye ferever. (PA *embraces* ELLEN JEAN.)

PA: Go then and St. Magnus be wi' ye. Quickly! Duncan's comin' fer the Foy.

ELLEN JEAN: I love ye, Pa.

(*Enter* TAM. *He wears the same dirty clothes, but his face, hands, and bare feet are clean and his hair is combed and tied back neatly. He carries a bunch of heather.*)

TAM: Selkie Lass! I've come fer me dance! Listen! They're comin' up the beach fer the Foy!

(ELLEN JEAN *looks toward* TAM, *then toward the sea.*)

ELLEN JEAN: Dunna ferget yer promise, Tam McCodrun! Dunna ever ferget!

(*The sound of the wind increases.* ELLEN JEAN *runs to the water's edge and enters the sea. She swiftly follows the path her mother has taken.* TAM *runs forward onto the rock.*)

TAM: No! Wait! Ye promised me a dance!

(*Exit* ELLEN JEAN.)

TAM: Come back! Come Back! Ye'll drown!

(*Sounds of the wind as though a storm is approaching.* TAM *removes his vest, and prepares to leap into the sea to save* ELLEN JEAN.)

PA: Hover thee, Lad.

TAM: I've got tae find her!

PA: Ye canno' swim.

TAM: I canno' stand here like a fool and do nuthin'.

PA: There's naught tae be done fer it. Drownin' yerself oot there wilna bring her back. She's gone. She heard the selkies callin' her. It was her time, just as it was her mither's time tae go.

TAM: God fergive me! I made sport o' her.

PA: There, Lad, tis none o' yer doin'. It's no' yer fault.

TAM: But why did she run from me?

PA: 'Twas no' a runnin' from, Lad, but runnin' to. Ach, ye'd no' believe me if I told ye.

TAM: I want tae know.

PA: (*Struggling to find the words to explain.*) Sometimes ye have tae lose somethin' terrible dear tae gain what ye want most.

TAM: I dunna understand.

PA: Might do me some guid tae tell ye all o' it. Ye'll stay this night at the crofthouse. With a roof over yer head and a fire warmin' me bones, I'll tell ye the tale. Perhaps we need each other.

(*The music of the Foy rises in the distance. The sound of the wind howling and the sea waves crashing.*)

TAM: *(Looking toward the music.)* What will we tell the others at the Foy?

PA: We'll tell 'em a wrong was done afore ye were born. And this is the price tae be paid oot fer it.

TAM: *(Looking toward the sea.)* Will she come back?

PA: *(Crossing himself.)* Only St. Magnus knows, Lad. But if she does return, she'll have a knowin' beyond all the others.

(Lights shift. Selkie sounds. Music.)

(BLACK HAIR, RED HAIR, *and the selkie* MARGARET, *wearing their pelts, enter the sea area, doing a version of the dance seen at the beginning of the play that suggests the denser movement beneath the sea. They are celebrating* MARGARET'S *return home.)*

DUNCAN: *(Offstage voice, calling from a distance.)* Margaret!

(MARGARET *responds to the sound of* DUNCAN'S *voice then slowly returns to the dance. With each sound of* DUNCAN'S *call, she reacts less and less until she is deaf to his cries.)*
Margaret! Margaret! Come back! Margaret!

(MARGARET *and the two selkie sisters exit.* DUNCAN *enters, running.)*
Margaret! Margaret!

(DUNCAN *collapses onto the rocks.)*

(Lights shift.)

(Dim light. The beach. One year later. Midsummer's Eve, the night of the Johnsmas Foy. Sounds of the wind and the sea. At center sits TAM, *looking out to sea. He wears clean trousers, a shirt, and a new colorful vest. His hair is combed neatly. Fiddle music.* PA *enters, carrying his fiddle.)*

PA: *(To the audience.)* Listen. Can ye no' hear the music? *(He listens.)* A year has passed. It's Midsummer's Eve, the night o' the Johnsmas Foy, one year ago since our Ellen Jean was lost tae the sea. It's nearly midnight. Soon the torches'll be lit and the dancin' on the beach'll last til the cock crows. It'll be a guid harvest this year. Plenty tae eat fer everyone, rich and poor alike. But there's some hunger canno' be satisfied wi' food, no matter how rich and fine.

(The sound of the selkies singing.)

TAM: Pa, look! There's selkies swimmin' in.

PA: Aye. Like alus they come back at Midsummer's Eve.

TAM: How do they know it's Midsummer's Eve?

PA: The light. The tides. The heat in the air. It's in their blood.

TAM: Do ye think they know aboot Ellen Jean?

PA: *(Crosses himself.)* Only St. Magnus knows, Lad.

TAM: There's somethin' aboot Midsummer. It alus feels like the beginnin' o' things.

PA: 'Tis a beginnin'. Yer a fine one noo, ye are, workin' yer own bit o' land.

TAM: Thanks tae yer kindness.

PA: What a bulder o' nonsense! Ye earned the land wi' hard work. Ye're like me own family, Lad.

(Enter DUNCAN, *disheveled and dressed in rags as though he can no longer care for himself.)*

DUNCAN: There she is! 'Tis Ellen Jean comin' up the beach.

PA: No, no, Duncan, that's the others comin' fer the Foy.

DUNCAN: I see her. She's comin'. She's put on her bonnie dress, and Margaret's done up her hair with ribbons. Jean!

PA: No, Duncan. Ellen Jean's drowned followin' her mither oot tae sea. Ye know that, man.

(DUNCAN hangs his head and moans.)

DUNCAN: She'll come. She'll come tae dance.

PA: *(To Tam.)* Poor guid man. He wilna give up hopin' she'll come back.

TAM: Aye. Waitin' each day on the beach fer her.

PA: He's near lost his mind wi' the sorrow.

DUNCAN: Jean! Jean! She's comin'. She's only waitin' fer the torches tae be lit, and the music tae start. Pa! Play yer fiddle. Then Ellen Jean'll dance!

TAM: *(To Duncan.)* Sir, come wi' me tae the crofthouse. We'll pour ye some ale and sit ye by the fire.

DUNCAN: Play yer fiddle, Pa! Play and she'll come. She's only waitin' tae hear the music.

(Shaking his head, PA *takes up his fiddle and plays a tune.* DUNCAN *goes round the beach lighting the torches of heather. When the torches are lit,* PA *ends the music.)*

DUNCAN: Where is she? Where's me daughter? Where's Ellen Jean? Margaret, give her back tae me! I canna undo what I have done. Give me back me daughter!

(DUNCAN falls to his knees on the beach. Selkie music. ELLEN JEAN *rises from behind the rocks at the side of the stage, bathed in golden light. Her nightdress is changed to shimmering luminescent material the color of the sea, with sleeves short enough to reveal her hands.)*

ELLEN JEAN: Tam! Tam McCodrun. I've come fer me dance.

TAM: Giddy God! Ellen Jean!

DUNCAN: Jean! Me own darlin' daughter! Ye've come back!

(DUNCAN runs to ELLEN JEAN *and throws his arms around her.)*

I thought ye were lost, lost tae the sea ferever.

ELLEN JEAN: Lost? No, I am found. I've been tae the bottom o' the sea. Mither breathed intae me the wind tae travel beneath the tides. I have known the selkie-folk, me other family. Seven fine brothers and sisters I have below.

DUNCAN: And yer Mither?

ELLEN JEAN: She fergives ye.

DUNCAN: Will she come back tae me?

ELLEN JEAN: She will alus be with ye. Look tae the sea. If ye're hungry, the fishes will leap intae yer nets. Precious shells will wash up on the beach. Yer boat will glide safely through the tides in the ocean and the rocks on the shore. Mither will be yer guide.

DUNCAN: Jean, Jean, I knew ye'd come back.

(ELLEN JEAN goes to her GRANDPA and kisses him.)

ELLEN JEAN: The waitin' is over, Pa. I've found the knowin'.

PA: Dance, Ellen Jean! Dance the stories tae life!

(The music of the Foy swells.)

ELLEN JEAN: Have ye kept yer promise, Tam McCodrun?

TAM: Aye, I said it, did I no'? Will ye be keepin' yers?

ELLEN JEAN: I choose tae dance. I'm fairly silted tae dance wi' ye, Tam!

(ELLEN JEAN holds out her hand to TAM. TAM takes her hand. They look to PA. PA takes up his fiddle and begins to play. TAM and ELLEN JEAN do a version of the dance done by ELLEN JEAN earlier in the play, TAM following ELLEN JEAN's lead. As they dance, DUNCAN fades offstage. As the lights dim, PA ends the tune and walks downstage.)

PA: And so it was tha' the sea married the land. And in the union the island folk saw the birth o' a new kind o' folk—called the clan McCodrun. Across the islands their stories o' the sea and the land can be heard round the peat fires and the Johnsmas Foy is the merrier fer their dancin'. And on Midsummer's Eve, the seventh tide o' the seventh tide, the spirit o' Ellen Jean can still be seen sittin' on the skerrie, whisperin' softlike tae one beautiful, brown-spotted selkie with eyes green as the sea. And tae this day if ye come tae Orkney ye might see a lad or lass with the webbed hands. Dunna be surprised. They're the children o' the children o' the children o' the traveller Tam and Ellen Jean, the Selkie Lass.

(Fiddle music. Lights fade to blackout.)

CURTAIN